Content Area Reading and Literacy

Succeeding in Today's Diverse Classroom

sixth edition

Donna E. Alvermann

University of Georgia

Stephen F. Phelps

Buffalo State College

Victoria Ridgeway Gillis

Clemson University

Allyn & Bacon

Boston   New York   San Francisco
Mexico City   Montreal   Toronto   London   Madrid   Munich   Paris
Hong Kong   Singapore   Tokyo   Cape Town   Sydney

Executive Editor: Aurora Martínez Ramos
Series Editorial Assistant: Jacqueline Gillen
Executive Marketing Manager: Krista Clark
Production Editor: Mary Beth Finch
Editorial Production Service: Modern Graphics, Inc.
Composition Buyer: Linda Cox

Manufacturing Buyer: Megan Cochran
Electronic Composition: Modern Graphics, Inc.
Interior Design: Denise Hoffman, Glenview Studios
Photo Researcher: Annie Pickert
Cover Administrator: Linda Knowles

For related titles and support materials, visit our online catalog at www.pearsonhighered.com.

Between the time website information is gathered and then published, it is not unusual for some sites to
have closed. Also, the transcription of URLs can result in typographical errors. The publisher would
appreciate notification where these errors occur so that they may be corrected in subsequent editions.

Library of Congress Cataloging-in-Publication Data

Alvermann, Donna E.
    Content area reading and literacy : succeeding in today's diverse classroom / Donna E. Alvermann,
Stephen F. Phelps, Victoria Ridgeway Gillis.—6th ed.
            p. cm.
    Includes bibliographical references and index.
    ISBN-13: 978-0-13-714552-2
    ISBN-10:   0-13-714552-7
    1. Content area reading—United States. 2. Reading (Secondary)—United States. 3. Multicultural education—
United States. 4. Reading (Secondary)—Social aspects—United States. 5. Teenagers—Books and reading—
United States. I. Phelps, Stephen F. II. Gillis, Victoria Ridgeway. III. Title.
    LB1050.455.A47 2010
    428.4071′2—dc22

                                                                                              2009000183

Printed in the United States of America

10 9 8 7 6 5 4 3 2 1 [RRDV] 13   12   11   10   09

Photo Credits: pp. 1, 166, iStockphoto; p. 13, Comstock RF; p. 18, Anthony Magnacca/Merrill Education; pp. 38,
89, 124, 191, 235, 290 308, 361, Bob Daemmrich Photography; p. 64, Lawrence Manning/Corbis RF; p. 392,
iStockphoto International.

Allyn & Bacon
is an imprint of

www.pearson highered.com

ISBN-13: 978-0-13-714552-2
ISBN-10: 0-13-714552-7

For Jack—Donna
For Mira and Cristian—Steve
For Joe—Victoria

• • •

about the authors

Donna E. Alvermann is University of Georgia-appointed Distinguished Research Professor of Language and Literacy Education. Formerly a classroom teacher in Texas and New York, her research focuses on literacy instruction across the disciplines. Her co-authored/edited books include *Reconceptualizing the Literacies in Adolescents' Lives* (2nd ed.); *Bridging the Literacy Achievement Gap, Grades 4–12*; and *Adolescents and Literacies in a Digital World*. Past President of the National Reading Conference (NRC), she serves on the Adolescent Literacy Advisory Group of the Alliance for Excellent Education. She was elected to the Reading Hall of Fame in 1999, and is the recipient of NRC's Oscar Causey Award for Outstanding Contributions to Reading Research, College Reading Association's Laureate Award, and the American Reading Forum's and NRC's two service awards. In 2006, she was awarded the International Reading Association's William S. Gray Citation of Merit.

• • •

Stephen Phelps is professor emeritus of Elementary Education and Reading at Buffalo State College. In his thirty years at Buffalo State, he taught a wide range of literacy methods courses at the undergraduate and graduate level and was coordinator of the graduate literacy specialist program. His research interests include the preparation of teachers to work in urban schools and sociocultural influences on literacy acquisition and achievement.

• • •

Victoria Ridgeway Gillis graduated from North Georgia College with a BS degree in Biology and from Emory University with an MAT in Secondary Science Education. She taught science courses including life science, chemistry, physics, and physical science in Georgia, Florida, and South Carolina. In the early 1970s, she encountered the ideas and concepts in content area reading and tried them in her classroom. Her success in using content area reading strategies led her to return to graduate school after 20 years in the classroom to complete a Ph.D. degree at the University of Georgia in 1994. She currently teaches disciplinary literacy methods courses at Clemson University where she is a professor in the Teacher Education Department of the Eugene T. Moore School of Education.

contents

chapter **3**

Creating a Favorable Learning Environment   64

chapter **4**

Planning for Content Literacy 89

chapter **5**

Assessment of Students and Textbooks 124

chapter **6**

Preparing to Read   166

chapter **7**

Reading to Learn   191

chapter **8**

Increasing Vocabulary and Conceptual Growth   235

chapter **9**

Reflecting on Reading   280

chapter **10**

Writing across the Curriculum   308

chapter **11**

Studying and Study Strategies   361

preface

With each new edition of *Content Area Reading and Literacy: Succeeding in Today's Diverse Classrooms*, we welcome the opportunity to bring into sharper focus the topics and issues that you, our readers, tell us you like or wish you knew more about. How do we know these? Sometimes it's through direct contact at a conference, an inquiring late-night e-mail, or, in rare instances, a telephone call. Anonymous reviews of the previous edition also inform us, as do our own intuitions about the field of literacy education—where it is and where it might be heading.

In this sixth edition of *Content Area Reading and Literacy: Succeeding in Today's Diverse Classrooms*, we continue to operate on the assumption that, far from being an add-on, content literacy is integral to every discipline and special subject area, to the teachable moments that make less stellar ones tolerable, and, most important, to each student's motivation and capacity to learn. Our aim is to provide ideas backed by research and tested in classrooms (our own or others') that will enable you to apply what is useful in your particular area. We are also interested in sharing what is current on several fronts in anticipation of the fact that knowledge is power and that powerful teaching, like powerful learning, depends on being well informed.

Respect for diversity in language, culture, and social environment continues to drive the decisions we make about which topics to carry over from previous editions, which ones to expand on, and which to drop to make room for new information. Along these lines, here is what you will find between the covers of the sixth edition.

- Increased attention to the disciplinary literacies associated with vocabulary development and comprehension
- Attention to disciplinary ways of thinking following Hal Herber's principle of "content determines process"
- Adaptations of well-known strategies to address particular difficulties students experience in core subject areas
- New literacies for the twenty-first century, including activities for use in both traditional and online classrooms
- Sociocultural frameworks that embed both cognitive and metacognitive aspects of teaching and learning literacy
- Updated technology tips
- Updated tips for teaching readers who struggle
- A new section on assessment *of, for,* and *as* learning
- An updated treatment of portfolio assessment, including electronic portfolios

- One or more Literacy Coaches' Corner boxes in each chapter
- An expanded section on discussion strategies
- Attention to adolescents' everyday interests, including writing fan fiction and blogging
- Attention to writing as both a means of communication and a vehicle for learning
- Anticipation Guides added to each chapter to provide a venue for pre-reading discussion, either in class or online.

Chapter-by-Chapter Changes to the Sixth Edition

Chapter 1 incorporates an extensive discussion of disciplinary literacy similarities and differences, targeting the core content areas of English/language arts, mathematics, science, and social studies. An emphasis of disciplinary literacy is woven throughout the chapter's topics.

Chapter 2 outlines five issues that literacy coaches often encounter when attempting to support classroom teachers who are responsible for adapting their instruction to meet the needs of English language learners, including challenges and possible solutions to improving literacy instruction for adolescent ELLs.

Chapter 3 offers new research on bridging out-of-school literacies and content area learning. Cooperative learning techniques are found in a new, easily accessible chart. This chapter addresses the role of digital literacies in disciplinary teaching and learning, and provides information for literacy coaches on blogging as a form of professional development.

Chapter 4 incorporates the Essential Questions approach to planning instruction. It is helpful because it lends itself to a broad range of content areas. We include a discussion of how to include New Literacies as part of planning.

Chapter 5 provides coverage of several different assessments, including an explanation of results from Programme for International Student Assessment. There is newly added discussion of Strategic Content Literacy Assessment, and assessment that reflects assessment *of* learning, assessment *for* learning, and assessment *as* learning, as well as guidelines for assessing digital literacy and coverage of the Adolescent Motivation to Read Profile.

Chapter 6 provides updated research on why neuroscientists think the information processing model of reading comprehension may be a workable heuristic, but is hardly an explanation for how the human brain actually processes text. It also offers adaptations for brainstorming activities that are used with ELLs.

Chapter 7 builds on the Chapter 1 discussion of comprehension differences among disciplines, updates the discussion of using Question-Answer Relationships as a comprehension strategy, and adds a new section on comprehending on-line texts.

Chapter 8 emphasizes disciplinary differences in vocabulary in an extended discussion. The Frayer Model strategy was added to the vocabulary strategies discussed in the chapter. Words derived from Arabic were added to the figure highlighting words in English that are derived from other languages.

Chapter 9 provides an explanation for why the Four Resource Model—Code Breaker, Meaning Maker. Text User, and Text Analyst—is a useful heuristic in promoting critical literacy.

Chapter 10 has added emphasis on disciplinary writing connected to habits of thinking in each of the four core content areas. Two other additions include *found poetry* and *fan fiction* strategies.

Chapter 11 includes new strategies for note making, including structured notes, derived from research on disciplinary literacy, and chapter mapping.

Chapter 12 provides added discussion of online fan fictions, manga, and graphic novels, and addresses some problems of accurate representation in multicultural literature.

Appendixes have been updated to provide many new titles, including books for math, science and social studies and books about Islam and Muslims.

Supplements for Instructors and Students

The following supplements comprise an outstanding array of resources that facilitate learning about content area reading and literacy instruction. For more information, ask your local Allyn & Bacon Merrill Education representative or contact the Allyn & Bacon Merrill Faculty Field Support Department at 1-800-526-0485. For technology support, please contact technical support directly at 1-800-677-6337 or http://247.pearsoned .com. Many of the supplements can be downloaded from the Instructor Resource Center at www.pearsonhighered.com/irc.

Help your students get better grades and become better teachers.

Instructor's Manual and Test Bank For each chapter, the instructor's manual and test bank features chapter overviews, lecture outlines, classroom activities, discussion starters, MyEducationLab Activities, homework assignments, and multiple choice and essay test items. This supplement has been written completely by the text authors. (Available for downloading from the Instructor Resource Center at www.pearsonhighered.com/irc.)

 MyEducationLab (myeducationlab.com) is a research-based learning tool that brings teaching to life. Through authentic in-class video footage and more, MyEducationLab prepares you for your teaching career by showing what quality instruction looks like.

MyEducationLab is easy to use! In the textbook, look for the MyEducationLab logo in the margins and follow the simple link instructions to access the multimedia "Activities and Application" and "Building Teaching Skills and Dispositions" assignments in

MyEducationLab that correspond with the chapter content. "Activities and Application" exercises offer opportunities to understand content more completely and to practice applying content. "Building Teaching Skills and Dispositions" assignments help students practice and strengthen skills that are essential to quality through analyzing and responding to instructional encounters and artifacts.

MyEducationLab includes:

Video: The authentic classroom videos in MyEducationLab show how real teachers handle actual classroom situations.

Lesson & Portfolio Builders: With this effective and easy-to-use tool, you can create, update, and share standards-based lesson plans and portfolios.

Acknowledgments

As in previous editions, we would like to express our appreciation to the teachers and students who agreed to share examples of their work, thus making *Content Area Reading and Literacy: Succeeding in Today's Diverse Classrooms* both lively and practical. We thank the teachers participating in Victoria's Center for Excellence for Adolescent Literacy and Learning, who have been the source of numerous practice-based ideas.

Expressions of gratitude also go to our long-time editor and friend, Aurora Martínez, who despite her many responsibilities as Executive Editor of Literacy, ELL, and Bilingual publications, meets regularly with us at conferences and somehow manages to answer our "quick" questions in a most thorough manner. To Kara Kikel, Editorial Assistant to Aurora, we say thank you for keeping track of the many loose ends that go into publishing a text such as this one.

Finally, we acknowledge Mary Beth Finch at Allyn & Bacon and Marty Tenney at Modern Graphics, who made sure that we received answers to our questions once the final manuscript went into production.

We also thank the reviewers of the new edition: Mary E. Bowser, Shenandoah University; Lisa A. Hazlett, The University of South Dakota; Dana L. Key, The University of Alabama; Rose M. Pryor, Old Dominion University MCTP; Leah Jane Sadden, Southern Louisiana University; Cynthia E. Sharp, The Nevada Department of Education; and Janet L. Wicker, McKendree University.

chapter 1

Content Literacy and the Reading Process

Content Literacy and the Reading Process

Assumptions Underlying Content Teaching	What It Means to Be Literate	The Reading Process

Assumptions Underlying Content Teaching

- Subject Matter
- Role of the Textbook
- Active and Independent Readers
- Fluent Readers
- Fluency with Information Technology

What It Means to Be Literate

- Literate Thinking
- Content Literacy
- Disciplinary Literacy
- The New Literacy studies

The Reading Process

- A Cognitive View
- A Social Constructionist Perspective
- The Role of Motivation

Anticipation Guide

Directions: Read each of the following statements. Place a checkmark on the line in the "Before Reading" column if you agree with the statement; leave it blank if you disagree. Then predict what you think the chapter will be about, and jot down on a sticky note (or post online) any questions you have. Read the chapter; then return to the statements and respond to them as you think the authors of your text would. Place a checkmark on the line in the "Authors' Stance" column if you believe the authors would agree with the statement. If you discuss these statements with other people online, in class, or at the family dinner table, return to the statements and check any items you agree with in the right-hand column, "After Discussion." If your thinking changed, what caused that change?

Before Reading	Authors' Stance	Statements	After Discussion
_____	_____	1. Textbooks help structure curricular goals and objectives.	_____
_____	_____	2. Students use their textbooks to learn course content.	_____
_____	_____	3. Textbooks provide unbiased content.	_____
_____	_____	4. Textbooks provide accurate and up-to-date information about disciplinary knowledge.	_____
_____	_____	5. Every teacher is a teacher of reading.	_____
_____	_____	6. If students learn to read in elementary school, they should be able to read their textbooks in middle and high school.	_____

Victoria, one of the authors of this edition, remembers her first encounter with reading and science in the following vignette.

· · ·

In 1974 I had six years of teaching experience in junior high and high schools under my belt. I considered myself a good science teacher. In the fall of that year, I was asked to attend a district-level meeting on content area reading. After all my efforts to evade the meeting failed, I grudgingly went, taking papers to grade so that I could at least accomplish something while I endured what I believed would be a useless meeting. I was, after all, a science teacher—not a reading teacher. What did I need to know about reading? My students seemed to be illiterate (they did not read their assignments and rarely did their homework). I believed I could teach science without reading—I taught a hands-on activities-based course.

During that meeting, Joy Monahan presented instructional ideas that she claimed would help students learn content. I was singularly uninterested until she challenged us to try "just a few of these strategies" for two or three weeks and report the results to her. At the time, I was teaching in a school that tracked students according to academic achievement. I taught both ends of the spectrum—students designated "basic" and those designated "gifted." I decided to show this Ms. Monahan that she could teach me nothing about teaching science.

That particular year I had a student, Amy,* who had been a thorn in my side since the first day of school. She had learned to remove all the bolts securing the legs to the tops of the science tables in my room and did so with regularity. When the bolts were removed, the next student to enter the room and throw his or her books on the table had to move quickly to avoid the collapsing table. I never could catch her at this game. Amy was one of those students who by her very presence in the classroom was disruptive. I had a lot to teach Amy, and as it turned out, she had much more to teach me.

In the ensuing few weeks, I selected two of the instructional ideas presented by Ms. Monahan (they were the ideas that required the least amount of effort on my part) and tried them with my "basic" classes, teaching the "gifted" classes in my normal (and brilliant) way. I gave both groups the same test, designed for the "gifted" class. I reasoned that I could allow the "basic" students to drop one test grade, and thus my little experiment would do them little harm.

When I graded the tests for both classes, I was astounded. The "basic" group's average was higher than that of the "gifted" class. I was transformed from a cynic to a convert

*Pseudonym

in the time it took to grade those papers. My "basic" students had learned material that I previously thought too difficult for them. In fact, I had also noticed that these students were doing their assigned reading and homework and actively participating in class. Most important to me, their behavior had changed from apathetic to cooperative. This little experiment was a turning point in my life.

* * *

Imagine teaching an athlete like Venus Williams to play tennis until third or fourth grade and, because she is the best young player in the world, concluding that she needs no more instruction. Now imagine that after three or four years with little to no instruction, Venus Williams is expected to play tennis, and play well, at Wimbledon—a different context from the one in which she originally learned to play the game. There is a large crowd, the court is grass, the stakes are very high.

Although this scenario seems unimaginable, think of children in elementary schools, learning to read using narrative text. After several years with little to no instruction in reading expository text, they are expected to read high school textbooks with comprehension. There are parallels in these two scenarios that are difficult to ignore. Think about these parallels as you consider the assumptions underlying content area teaching.

Assumptions Underlying Content Teaching

Most content area teachers assume it is their responsibility to cover their subject matter in a timely, accurate, and effective manner (Alvermann & Moore, 1991; Moore, 1996). They also assume, for the most part, that textbooks are necessary for teaching and learning content (Wade & Moje, 2000). Finally, content area teachers tend to assume that by the time students enter middle school and high school, they are strategic in their approach to reading and learning (Alvermann & Nealy, 2004). These assumptions influence teachers' instructional decision making, their use of textbooks, and their perceptions of active and independent readers.

Subject Matter

The historical roots of content area reading instruction go back several decades. Prior to the twentieth century, the predominant mode of instruction in U.S. secondary schools was one of imitation and memorization. In the early part of the twentieth century, the work of humanist educators such as John Dewey and developmentalists interested in individual growth factors began to emphasize child-centered curricula over rote memorization. With the cognitive revolution in psychology in the early 1970s came the notion that reading and writing should be taught as thinking processes rather than in the mechanical manner advocated by the behaviorists, who had preceded the cognitivists. Although other writers at that time were beginning to publish books on reading at the secondary school level, Herber's (1970) text *Teaching Reading in the Content Areas* is generally regarded as the first to demonstrate how teachers can simultaneously teach content and process (reading). It is also one of the first content area methods texts to emphasize the importance of teachers' decision making.

As a content area teacher you take pride, and rightfully so, in knowing a lot about the subject matter you teach and how best to engage students in learning. You also recognize that you are responsible for monitoring students' learning and pacing their instruction accordingly. If these were the only two factors you had to take into consideration when making instructional decisions, it would be a relatively simple task to decide what to teach, when, and at what pace. Unfortunately, instructional decision making is complicated by what Newmann (1988) refers to as the "addiction" to coverage:

> We are addicted to coverage. This addiction seems endemic in high schools . . . but it affects all levels of the curriculum, from kindergarten through college. We expose students to broad surveys of the disciplines and to endless sets of skills and competencies. . . . The press for broad coverage causes many teachers to feel inadequate about leaving out so much content and apologetically mindful of the fact that much of what they teach is not fully understood by their students. (p. 346)

Addiction to coverage is dangerous because it tends to produce a false dichotomy between content knowledge and process knowledge. When *knowing what* takes precedence over *knowing how*, as it typically does when preparing students for standardized tests pressures teachers to cover a wide variety of topics in an inadequate space of time, students are deprived of the opportunity to learn how bits of knowledge fit together and generalize to other areas of the curriculum or to real life. Tovani (2000) views this milewide, inch-deep curricular approach as watering down the curriculum. In short, students are denied the kind of instruction that leads to active and independent learning.

Role of the Textbook

Textbooks and other learning materials provide a focus for several chapter sections in this book. For example, in Chapter 3, we explore how hypertext and other forms of electronic media have led to a new relationship between text and reader. In Chapter 4, we consider the decision making involved in choosing appropriate materials to use in planning content literacy lessons or longer units of instruction. Here, however, we focus on three assumptions underlying the use of textbooks.

One assumption is that textbooks will help to structure loosely coupled curricular goals and objectives. By most estimates, textbooks do indeed structure from 67 to 90 percent of all classroom instruction (Woodward & Elliott, 1990), but this varies according to the type of instructional approach—transmission or participatory—that teachers espouse (Wade & Moje, 2000).

Evidence-Based Research

A second assumption is that students will use their textbooks to learn course content. This assumption may or may not be borne out. It depends on whether students view their textbooks or their teachers as the ultimate source of knowledge. Some researchers (Hinchman & Zalewski, 1996; Smith & Feathers, 1983a, 1983b) have found that students perceive their teacher, not the textbook, as the primary source of knowledge. Students generally find their teacher easier to understand than the textbook, especially if they believe they will be tested on what the teacher says in class. Other researchers (e.g., Fournier & Graves, 2002) have found evidence that teachers put the responsibility for acquiring the information contained in the text squarely on their students' shoulders. Still other researchers (Ratekin, Simpson, Alvermann, & Dishner, 1985) have reported that in some content area classrooms, it is the custom for teachers to use the textbook as a "safety net"—something to fall back on—rather than as a vital link and a basis for class discussions. When teachers use texts as safety nets, more often than not they substitute lecturing for discussions of assigned readings.

A third assumption is that textbooks will present the content in a coherent and unbiased fashion. We know from experience that this is not always so. If you have ever attempted to read a poorly organized text, one in which the author seems to jump from one topic to another, then you know what we mean when we say coherency cannot be taken for granted. Similarly, if you have ever discovered biases in a textbook's content, then you know that textbook authors, like everyone else, have particular ways of viewing the world and reporting on it. However, given appropriate planning strategies, even the most biased of texts can lead to excellent classroom discussions in which students learn to look at both sides of an issue for sources of possible misunderstanding. We firmly believe that in today's diverse classrooms, opportunities for students to respond to biased texts should be welcomed. Taking advantage of such opportunities can contribute toward building appreciation for individual differences.

Using textbooks wisely requires teachers who know both the content and the processes needed to understand that content. In the opening vignette, Victoria recounted how she discovered that her students *could* read their textbooks; it had been her teaching methods that had resulted in her students' appearing uninterested and illiterate. As the year progressed and she implemented content area literacy strategies as a vehicle to teach science, students in her class became actively involved in their own learning.

Active and Independent Readers

Content area teachers love their subject matter. Why else would someone choose to spend five days a week immersed in science, history, mathematics, or literature? We want our students to love science or history or mathematics or literature as much as we do and to choose to read and learn about our subjects independently. What do active and independent readers look like?

ACTIVE READERS   Readers who engage in an active search for meaning use multiple strategies, including self-questioning, monitoring, organizing, and interacting with peers. In each instance, researchers believe, it is the cognitive processing that is induced in the strategic reader—not the strategy itself—that is responsible for promoting active reading (Dole, Duffy, Roehler, & Pearson, 1991; Pearson & Fielding, 1991).

Active readers *generate questions* before they read, as they read, and when they have finished reading. Before reading a chapter in a social studies book, for example, active readers ask themselves what the selection is likely to cover, whether they know anything about the topic or are interested in it, and what they intend to do with the information presented. As they read, they question the meanings of unfamiliar words or ask how a certain event is likely to trigger a reaction. After reading the chapter, active readers ask whether their prediction of what the chapter would cover was accurate, whether they learned anything new, and how they might apply what they learned to something they already know. In fact, a fairly robust finding by researchers is that teaching students to generate their own questions leads to active learning and improved comprehension of text (National Reading Panel, 2000; Wade & Moje, 2000).

Recent research on disciplinary literacy practices, discussed later in this chapter, suggests that self-questioning is qualitatively different in different content areas. When historians are presented with a primary source, they ask who wrote the document, under what circumstances, and what his or her biases are. They are also mindful of their own biases as they read (Shanahan & Shanahan, 2008). Scientists will question the procedures of a research report to be sure they understand each step of the experiment. Mathematicians will focus on every word of a proof or problem and pay attention to prepositions used as technical terms (for example, *of*).

Active readers *monitor*, or periodically check, their understanding of what they have read. Although monitoring can include self-questioning, it is used here to describe the two-part process that readers go through when they (1) become aware of a breakdown in comprehension and (2) apply fix-up strategies to regain understanding.

Active readers attempt to make sense of the large body of facts, interpretations, and principles presented in their various textbooks by *organizing* such information into meaningful units. They may do this in one of several ways: by graphically organizing the information so as to form a semantic map or structured overview, by writing summaries, by constructing outlines and taking notes, or by elaborating on the text by drawing from their background knowledge and past experiences whatever associations seem most helpful in bridging from the *known* ("in the head") to the *unknown* ("on the page").

Regardless of which organizing strategy they choose, active readers are skilled in separating important information from unimportant information. When students experience difficulty in organizing what they have read, it is quite often because they are insensitive to what is important. Sometimes this insensitivity is due to a reader's inability to identify information that an author deems important; at other times it is due to a reader's strong sense of personal relevancy. For instance, Winograd (1984) found that eighth graders who were having difficulty reading tended to identify importance on the basis of what held high personal interest for them (such as sentences containing rich visual detail), whereas good readers tended to identify important information on the basis of its superordinate or subordinate placement within the text structure. Young adolescents have difficulty organizing large bodies of information partially because they rely on personal relevance as a criterion for attributing importance.

Although we recognize that readers often reflect on what they have read and actively construct meaning from texts without the benefit of *peer interaction*, there is growing support for placing a greater emphasis on socially constructed meaning (Gee, 1996; Davis, Sumara, & Luce-Kapler, 2000; Lankshear & Knobel, 2003). Engaged readers, whether in gifted, regular, or basic-level classes, enjoy opportunities for open-forum discussions, in which a free-flowing exchange of ideas enriches and refines their understandings of what was read and heightens their motivation to read further (Alvermann, 2000). Discussions of this type, unlike lecturing and recitations, provide English language learners (ELLs) with excellent opportunities to practice English and learn content simultaneously (Met, 1994). Interactions with peers also enable students from diverse cultural groups to learn from one another.

INDEPENDENT READERS   Independent readers typically are independent learners, and vice versa. We agree with Herber and Nelson-Herber's (1987) claims that the similarities between the two are numerous and that independence can be developed by capitalizing on the following five principles:

1. *Independence comes from practice.*   Readers develop independence when they have sufficient opportunities across the curriculum to establish their own purposes for reading, to make connections between their own experiences and those they read about, to use valid criteria in making judgments about the quality and value of what they read, and to apply what they have learned in one content area to another.

2. *Independence develops by design, not chance.*   As students grow in independence, they require less and less in the way of structured learning activities. In the beginning, however, they are dependent on teacher modeling and guidance to show them how to apply the reading and reasoning processes necessary for understanding important concepts. As time goes on, responsibility is gradually released, as students assume more and more of the responsibility for applying what they have learned to new areas of study and new materials (Pearson & Gallagher, 1983).

3. *Independence is a relative state.*   This is true for all of us. As a science teacher, Victoria feels confident in reading texts related to biology and chemistry. However, even a simple mathematics text baffles her! How many of us can read an insurance document or a credit card agreement with ease? Teachers must keep in mind that in order to develop and nurture independence, the maturity level of the student must be matched with appropriate resources.

4. *Independence can be achieved in groups.*   Herber and Nelson-Herber (1987) advocate small-group learning experiences to develop students' independence in reading. We agree with their view "that students can be as much in charge of their reading and reasoning processes and their use of ideas when interacting in cooperative groups as when working individually" (p. 586). There is ample research to support this view on cooperative learning, which we discuss in Chapter 3.

5. *Independence means forever "becoming."*   No one is ever totally independent as a learner. Occasionally, we all rely on others to help us interpret, clarify, or elaborate

on what we read. Helping students become independent readers and learners will require time, skill, and patience.

Fluent Readers

What does it mean to read fluently, and what assumptions do we often make about older readers' fluency (or lack thereof)? First, a common definition of *fluency* in relation to reading in the content areas focuses on students' ability to comprehend texts of various types with speed, accuracy, and appropriate expression (National Reading Panel, 2000). Another less common definition is one that focuses on students' fluency with information technology (American Association of University Women Educational Foundation, 2000). We believe both are important in terms of their implications for content literacy teaching and learning.

Evidence-Based Research

An assumption that is often made about older students is that they have attained a satisfactory level of fluency in reading assigned content area materials. Unfortunately, this is not always the case. In fact, among readers who struggle to comprehend, difficulties with fluency are often the culprit. Why is this so? Theoretically, readers have only a limited amount of attention, and when that attention is diverted to decoding words and pausing in appropriate places, overall comprehension suffers (LaBerge & Samuels, 1974). Slow and laborious decoding at the word level also hampers students' ability to monitor their reading. When text processing at the word level is not automatic, Klenk and Kibby (2000) venture that readers will not "know how it sounds and feels to read text fluently" (p. 673).

One aspect of reading in mathematics that is often overlooked is that of fluency with symbols (Rubenstein & Thompson, 2001). Fluency in reading mathematical expressions aloud indicates understanding. Rubenstein and Thompson have identified several challenges related to fluency in reading mathematical symbols, including symbols that require the reader to verbalize phrases ($\pm$ is read "plus or minus"), expressions that may be read in a variety of ways ($x - y$ may be read as "x minus y" or as "x take away y"), and differences in directionality; that is, symbols are not always read left to right, as is text (for example, fractions). Reading in mathematics is further complicated by the fact that inappropriate translations of symbols can create confusion and misunderstanding, as happens when $-y$ is read as "minus y" rather than "negative y."

SPEED, ACCURACY, AND APPROPRIATE EXPRESSION   The underlying assumption of fluency instruction, defined in terms of a reader's speed, accuracy, and appropriate expression, is that teachers will view it as a means to comprehension and not as an end in itself. Because adequate comprehension is essential for effective studying to occur, it is clear that fluency plays a pivotal role overall. The National Reading Panel (2000), while acknowledging that fluency instruction is often neglected in day-to-day classroom instruction, found sufficient research evidence to suggest that guided oral-reading procedures have a positive impact on students' fluency and comprehension across a range of grade levels and in a variety of regular and special education classrooms. Examples of these procedures are included in Chapter 7.

Evidence-Based Research

Fluency with Information Technology

One of several new terms to make its way into the field of reading education as a result of the information explosion associated with today's computer age is *information literacy*. It refers to what is generally defined as the ability to access, evaluate, organize, and use information culled from a variety of sources. Not to be confused with *computer literacy*, which reflects a technological know-how in manipulating software packages, information literacy requires, among other things, knowing how to formulate a search strategy for zeroing in on needed information. The topic of Internet search strategies will be discussed later. For now, it is sufficient to link information literacy to fluency with information technology.

In a report focused on how to educate students in the computer age so that they become tech savvy and capable of participating fully in e-culture (American Association of University Women Educational Foundation, 2000), the argument is made that fluency with information technology is much more than static listings of how to become more proficient at word processing or e-mailing. Instead, the authors of the report note that "fluency goals must allow for change, enable adaptability, connect to personal goals, and promote lifelong learning" (p. xi).

These goals will require that all students become fluent in skills such as designing a home page, organizing a database, communicating with others whom they may never meet in person, and evaluating personal privacy concerns. A useful set of nonprint media standards for helping students achieve fluency with information technology was developed at the National Research Center on English Learning and Achievement (CELA) by Karen Swan. The nonprint media standards are divided into basic skills, critical literacies, and construction skills for each of three grade levels: elementary, middle, and high school (Swan, 2000). Examples of strategies for promoting fluency with information technology are found in Chapter 3.

In summary, content area reading instruction involves much more than covering the subject matter in a particular specialty area. It includes dealing with assumptions about the role of the textbook, promoting active and independent reading, and developing readers' fluency. Students who self-question, monitor their reading, organize information, and interact with their peers possess some of the strategies necessary for becoming fluent readers and independent learners. However, their overall sense of them-

TECHNOLOGY Tip

Media Standards
Newly revised National Educational Technology Standards (2007) focus on communication and collaboration, research and information fluency, as well as critical thinking, problem solving, and decision making. The standards are available at **www.iste.org/AM/Template .cfm?Section=NETS**.

selves as learners will depend to a large extent on how they see themselves as readers and what it means to be literate in a fast-changing world.

What It Means to Be Literate

As individuals, we tend to approach literacy with our own agendas: We are in pursuit of *something*. Depending on our ideological frameworks, our educational backgrounds, and our social, economic, and political status in life, we may hold quite different perceptions of why we are in pursuit and what it means to be literate. For many, literacy is something to value for its intrinsic worth; for others, it may be a symbol of achievement or a means for social change; and for still others, it is something to profit from. In each of these perceptions, there is the underlying assumption that being literate means having a special capacity of one kind or another.

However, as Knoblauch (1990) pointed out, this is not necessarily the case. In observing that "literacy is one of those mischievous concepts, like virtuousness and craftsmanship, that appear to denote capacities but that actually convey value judgments," Knoblauch (p. 74) reminds us that individuals who have the motivation and status to enforce literacy as a social requirement are often the same ones whose value judgments count. Failure to take note of the power relations surrounding such judgments is tantamount to buying into the idea that literacy is a neutral or innocent concept. Recognizing the political nature of what it means to be literate is important to our work as educators. It may keep us from falling into the trap of equating a student's innate worthiness with her or his competence in reading and writing. It may also prevent us from being blinded by ideological leanings that sometimes propel us to act as if our own literacy agendas were innocent or pure.

Literate Thinking

From Langer's (1989) perspective, reading and writing are "tools that enable, but do not insure, literate thinking" (p. 2). She argues vigorously against the tendency to equate literate thinking with the ability to analyze or synthesize large chunks of print, a common but uninformed notion of what it means to be literate.

Activity

Langer (1989) provides an example to highlight the distinction she draws between print literacy and literate thinking:

> When a group of American students read a social studies textbook and then discuss the contents and the implications, most people would say that the students are engaging in literate thinking (within the norms of this culture). But, what if the discussion had occurred after the students had seen a television news

(continued)

report about the same topic? I would still want to claim that the students had engaged in literate thinking even though they had neither read nor written. Now, imagine a group of students who do not know how to read or write in English or another language engaged in the very same conversation about the television news report. I would claim that they too would have engaged in literate thinking. In contrast, imagine that the students had read the same social studies text and then completed end-of-chapter questions by locating information in the text and copying the information the questions asked them to itemize. I would claim that the kinds of literacy in this activity do not reflect the kinds of school literacy that, based on the many reports and articles in both the professional and public press, are needed and valued by American society today. That activity does not involve culturally useful literate behavior, even if the students get the answers right. (p. 2)

Do you agree or disagree with Langer's argument? Why?

The 1980s and 1990s spawned a rash of reform movements, most of which had as their goal the erasing of illiteracy as a threat to the economic well-being and worldwide competitiveness of the United States. A characteristic of most of the reforms has been their emphasis on a print- or book-focused literacy. Schools in general are concerned with students' abilities to read and write—to demonstrate what is understood—regardless of grade level. The attention educators give to functional literacy, according to Greene (1991), leaves little time for asking some difficult but important questions:

[Teachers] scarcely ever ask [themselves] about the difference literacy makes in various lives. Does it overcome alienation or confirm it? Does it reduce feelings of powerlessness or intensify them? How much, after all, depends on literacy and how much on social

Source: CALVIN AND HOBBES © 1989 & 1995 Watterson. Dist. by UNIVERSAL PRESS SYNDICATE. Reprinted with permission. All Rights Reserved.

arrangements? How much on trust? On love? On glimpses of the half-moon? On wonderful ideas? On feeling, as Dickinson did, "a clearing" in the mind? (p. 130)

Similar concerns have been raised by Heath (1986b), whose research has shown that in many families and communities, being a competent reader and writer is not viewed as being a ticket to equality, a good job, or social mobility. In short, being literate has different meanings for different cultural groups, or as Langer (1989) so aptly puts it, "There is no right or wrong literacy, just the one that is, more or less, responsive to the demands of a particular culture" (p. 1).

Evidence-Based Research

Content Literacy

Generally, *content literacy* is defined as "the ability to use reading and writing for the acquisition of new content in a given discipline" (McKenna & Robinson, 1990, p. 184). To that we add the importance of oral language (e.g., small- and large-group discussions) and computer-mediated communication technologies in affecting students' ability to learn from reading and writing activities in their subject matter classes. Students' prior knowledge of a particular subject and their interest in learning more about it also mediate their ability to use their content literacy skills.

Helping
Struggling Readers

Working Generalizations

Hints for helping readers who struggle to learn the content of their subject matter classes abound. For example, Ivey (2000) has developed what she calls her "working generalizations" on teaching adolescents who struggle with reading and writing. Based on her research and experience as a classroom teacher, these so-called generalizations include the following advice:

- Provide students with access to materials that hold personal interest for them and that span a wide range of difficulty levels.

- Make room in the school day for students to have time to share their literacy experiences with others through small-group dis-

cussions, buddy reading, and choral reading activities.

- Plan activities that require students to use reading and writing to complete a task that is content related and highly motivating, such as performing hands-on science experiments or communicating through e-mail with classmates who found novel ways to complete a math assignment.

- Take into account students' desires to improve their literacy skills and help them do so through initiating the reading and writing workshop concept as a part of the regular classroom routine. (See Chapter 3 for an example of the reading and writing workshop adapted from Allen [1995] for high school use.)

CONTENT KNOWLEDGE   Content literacy is not to be confused with *content knowledge*, although the two concepts do share some common ground. For example, as McKenna and Robinson (1990) pointed out, the more knowledge students have about the content they are assigned to read in their textbooks, the more that knowledge facilitates their reading and writing—a situation that in turn sets up a cyclical pattern such that still more knowledge is acquired and applied to other tasks requiring content literacy skills.

This cyclical pattern should come as good news to content area teachers. In effect, what it says is that teachers who instruct students in a subject matter specialty are helping to improve students' abilities to read and write in that subject area by simply providing some of the necessary background information. Providing background information, however, is only half of the task. The other half involves helping students acquire content literacy, or the ability to use reading and writing strategies to learn new content. Students who have the literacy skills necessary for supplementing their knowledge of the content by reading beyond what the teacher introduces through lectures, demonstrations, and so on are well on their way to becoming independent learners.

Disciplinary Literacy

> *We shall not cease from exploration*
> *And the end of all our exploring*
> *Will be to arrive where we started*
> *And know the place for the first time.*
>
> —T. S. Eliot, "Little Gidding," from *Four Quartets*

In 1970, Hal Herber published the first content area reading text, signaling a movement to situate reading instruction in the content area classroom. Herber's mantra was "content determines process," and although more than 35 years separate this writing from his initial textbook, we are just beginning to heed his words. It seems we have been searching for ways to improve content area literacy and learning and have returned to our roots to see the original ideas anew.

Research investigating secondary teachers' resistance to content area reading has a long history (Ratekin, Simpson, Alvermann, & Dishner, 1985; Stewart & O'Brien, 1989). Over a decade ago, O'Brien, Stewart, and Moje (1995) lamented the absence of content area reading strategies from middle and secondary schools and offered three factors that work against implementation: (1) a curriculum that has been described as "a mile wide and inch deep," (2) teacher-centered pedagogies that have been entrenched, and (3) a culture that resists change. Moje, Young, Readence, and Moore (2000) differentiated the various labels that have been used in the adolescent literacy field, including *secondary reading*, with its remedial connotation and reading specialists in a clinical lab setting; *content area reading*, with a widely publicized "every teacher is a teacher of reading" slogan and focus on in-school textbook reading; and *adolescent literacy*, which casts a wider net both in terms of literacy (it includes multiple literacies of adolescents) and location (it includes out-of-school as well as in-school literacy practices). The term *adolescent literacy* focuses attention on adolescents' vast array of literacy practices rather than on texts, tasks, and domain knowledge, which are descriptors that more aptly define content area reading and disciplinary literacy.

In spite of the renewed focus on the literacy practices of older students, test scores remain nearly flat (NAEP, 2007). This lack of significant progress has prompted adolescent literacy researchers to reflect on their own practices (Conley, 2008a) and to explore differences in literacy practices across content areas (Harmon, Hedrick, & Wood, 2005; Moje, 2007; Shanahan & Shanahan, 2008). Termed *disciplinary literacy*, this line of research explores how the epistemology and linguistics of the various disciplines influence the comprehension of text in these disciplines.

One characteristic of academic writing is the frequent use of *nominalization*, which is transforming grammatical constructions such as complex phrases and verbs into nouns (Harmon et al., 2005; Moje, 2007; Shanahan & Shanahan, 2008). In science texts, nominalization is used to create technical vocabulary, resulting in a telescoping effect in which students must remember an increasing information load as they read a textbook (Shanahan & Shanahan, 2008; Unsworth, 1999). For example, in the following sentence, the first seven words are nominalized to the technical term *viruses*:

Evidence-Based Research

> *These pathogens that infected plants or animals* came to be known as viruses.

In subsequent paragraphs, when the word *virus* is used, the reader must remember the information that viruses are pathogens that infect plants or animals, thus telescoping information into one technical term. In science texts, nominalization can also be used to generalize a specific instance of a phenomenon to a more abstract or general case. In history texts, nominalization occurs with general vocabulary terms and serves to make cause–effect relationships implicit, a process Martin (1993) termed "buried reasoning." An example of this can be seen in the following sentence (Martin, 1993, p. 224):

> The enlargement of Australia's steel-making capacity, and of chemicals, rubber, metal goods and motor vehicles all owed something to the demands of war.

In this sentence, nominalization serves to bundle several events (enlargement of steel-making capacity, chemicals, rubber, etc.) and causally connect them to "the demands of war." Nominalization increases the abstract character of content area texts and serves to distance the reader from the content, making reading motivation more difficult.

Research in disciplinary literacy has focused on linguistic characteristics of disciplinary texts and on the literacy practices of disciplinary experts, disciplinary methodology professors, and content area teachers. In the sections that follow, we address salient differences in the literacy demands of the four core content areas in which students take required courses in middle and high school: English/language arts, mathematics, science, and social studies (addressed alphabetically so as not to privilege any one content area).

ENGLISH/LANGUAGE ARTS   Reading difficulties presented in English/language arts are found at the macro (discourse) level rather than the micro (word and phrase) level (Harmon et al., 2005). Current English/language arts literature requirements span several different genres, including poetry, drama, fiction, and nonfiction, and many subgenres or forms, such as mysteries, short stories, novels, and biographies, to name a few. Each of these genres and forms has a characteristic structure and organization and uses a variety of literary conventions (voice, literary devices, figurative language). Thus, a somewhat different approach is required for understanding each. Some selections, such as the plays of William Shakespeare, are simultaneously stories, plays, and poems; additionally, some are comedies, some tragedies, some histories. Not only are Shakespeare's plays multigenred, but reading them might entail silently or orally reading the text from a book, hearing it read by someone else, seeing it performed live or as a recording, or actually performing it as a readers' theater or as memorized lines, complete with movements and costumes.

As students encounter the various selections drawn from both the traditional and contemporary canon of literature, they must shift attention to accommodate differences in genres and forms. Students who have spent two weeks or more immersed in poetry may have used comprehension strategies that emphasize analyzing rhyme, meter, symbolism, and metaphor. The comprehension strategies that might be required for the next genre would perhaps focus on the literary elements of setting, characters, plot, and conflict.

In other content areas, such as science and social studies, there are a variety of text structures but only four or five standard ones (description, sequence/time–order, compare–contrast, cause–effect), which are relatively consistent across texts and content areas. (These are discussed at length in Chapter 7.) Difficulties in these content areas, as we will discuss shortly, come at the micro (word and phrase) level.

In English, in contrast to science or mathematics, students can have a surface knowledge of vocabulary without losing comprehension. Particularly in mathematics, students must have a thorough and precise knowledge of vocabulary terms. English teachers must not only teach literature but are also charged with enhancing students' vocabulary, writing, and knowledge of grammar.

In addition to the wide variety of genres and forms students must address, there is the issue of *intertextuality*. In more complex literature, comprehension often depends on knowing the works of literature referenced in the novel or short story being read. For example, Victoria often reads aloud to her content area literacy students; one passage she enjoys reading to them describes a teacher as "a Polonius-like figure" (Wigginton, 1985, p. 242). English preservice teachers understand. They have read *Hamlet* and know that Wigginton has described this teacher as a bit of a windbag. Science and math preservice teachers usually miss this information completely.

MATHEMATICS   The language of mathematics is complex and abstract (Harmon et al., 2005), is not read in conventional directions (i.e., left to right, top to bottom) (Reehm

& Long, 1996), and is the most conceptually dense of all the content area texts (Barton, Heidema, & Jordan, 2002; Harmon et al., 2005). Students are taught to look for a topic sentence near the beginning of each paragraph when reading most texts. In mathematics, however, the key information is often found at the end of a word problem in the form of a question. This requires students to reread the word problem to differentiate information that is relevant to the solution (Kenney, Hancewicz, Heuer, Metsisto, & Tuttle, 2005). Vocabulary in mathematics includes Latin and Greek roots as well as symbols, which may be concepts (Π, ∞) or abbreviations (oz., kg), involve numbers (8, 28, 838), or indicate math operations ($+$, $-$) or relationships ($>$, $\neq$).

The language of mathematics is precise, and verbalizing symbols is difficult, particularly for novices. Students cannot sound out symbols. They are the equivalent of sight words, and the meaning of each symbol must be precisely known. Having students read mathematical expressions and problems aloud is one way to identify misconceptions (Rubenstein & Thompson, 2001). In addition to symbols and numbers, general vocabulary terms take on specialized meanings in the language of mathematics. For instance, the word *of* signals an operation in mathematics, rather than a relationship between two words.

Mathematicians involved in research conducted by Shanahan and Shanahan (2008) used two primary reading strategies: close reading and rereading. Because math text is so conceptually dense, it must be read in several directions (sometimes left to right, sometimes top to bottom, sometimes diagonally), and has symbols and technical vocabulary terms that have multiple meanings and depend on context for meaning, students must attend to math texts closely. Mathematics texts depend on accuracy and precision both in writing and reading processes (Moje, 2007). One cannot skim mathematics text. In math, the devil is in the details.

SCIENCE   Science texts are the most semantically dense content area texts; that is, they have the most technical terms per sentence. Technical terms are often used to explain new concepts, which put a burden on prior knowledge (Harmon et al., 2005). Science vocabulary includes many Latin and Greek roots and affixes as well as symbols. The vocabulary in science is daunting enough, but in addition to technical vocabulary, readers must pay close attention to general phrases that indicate relationships among concepts (*similar to, considered, different from, characteristics of, the result of*) and nontechnical terms that occur frequently in science texts (*component, consist, exclude*) (Harmon et al.).

The linguistic challenges and rhetorical style also make science texts difficult to comprehend. Science is generally written in the third-person, passive voice. When Victoria began graduate work in literacy after having worked and studied in the science education field for 20 years, it was difficult for her to break the habit of writing in passive voice. (See what we mean?) Science involves prediction, observation, analysis, summarization, and presentation (Moje, 2007); these cognitive processes are also used in reading and writing science. Chemists involved in research conducted by Shanahan and Shanahan (2008) used a recursive reading process involving the interactive use of multiple representations of concepts, including text, charts, diagrams, graphs, and pictures, as well as visualization, as they sought to comprehend scientific texts.

SOCIAL STUDIES   In contrast to math and science, the language of social studies is not technical but is drawn from a wide range of related disciplines, including political science, geography, economics, sociology, and history (Harmon et al., 2005; Martin, 1993). In history, vocabulary words often name people, events, and places. Teachers who use primary sources encounter a further difficulty when the documents are rife with archaic vocabulary. In addition to considerations of vocabulary, teachers must be aware of how history is read. Historians do not read a text as truth but are mindful of the author's biases as well as their own (Shanahan & Shanahan, 2008). As historians read, they look for evidence of assertions and are attentive to how the author makes connections between and among events. Nominalization in history textbooks sometimes disguises deductions as facts (Martin, 1993; Unsworth, 1999).

Historians participating in research conducted by Shanahan and Shanahan (2008) used *sourcing* as a prereading strategy when reading primary documents, asking who wrote the document and in what context. As the historians read, they focused on subtexts and intertextual connections. They monitored their comprehension by revisiting the author's perspective and the context in which the document was written. Historians have decried the lack of voice in history textbooks because it leads to a lack of critical reading by students (Moje, 2007). For social studies students, the textbook may represent the greatest obstruction to understanding history and historical thinking. Students should have access to multiple texts, written from various stances, on the issues under study. Only then can they develop the critical-thinking skills so necessary in today's world (Moje, 2007).

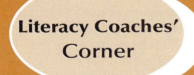

Literacy Coaches' Corner

Content Specialization

One of the things that literacy coaches must keep in mind is that content area teachers want and need to be content specialists. Content area teachers have to see that literacy strategies, carefully chosen and adapted to their disciplines, can increase students' learning. Honor-

ing the expertise of content teachers is a key step in making contact with them and developing mutual respect.

Literacy coaches can stay informed about content area trends by reading publications from professional organizations such as NSTA, NCTM, NCSS, NCTE, and IRA. You will find URLs for these professional organizations' standards and others (including information literacy, music, and foreign language) in Appendix E of this textbook.

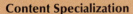

Disciplinary literacy researchers, cited in the previous sections, have focused on uncovering characteristics of discipline-specific texts and the processes that experts in these various fields use as they negotiate texts in their disciplines. Shanahan and Shanahan (2008) have had some success in developing strategies for reading and writing discipline-specific text that mirror the cognitive processes of disciplinary experts. These strategies will be discussed in later chapters.

The New Literacy Studies

In the 1980s and 1990s, an interdisciplinary group of scholars (Bloome & Green, 1992; Cazden, 1988; Cook-Gumperz, 1986; Gee, 1996; Heath, 1983; Luke, 1988; Street, 1995) began to ask questions such as "What is literacy?" "Who benefits from being literate?" and "What specific cultural meanings and practices are involved in becoming literate?" The impetus for asking these questions, all of which deal in one way or another with the differing contexts in which people read and write, was a growing mistrust in the more conventional or dominant view of literacy as a neutral or technical skill. No longer willing to think of reading as primarily a psychological phenomenon—one in which individuals who can decode and have the requisite background knowledge for drawing inferences are able to arrive at the right interpretation of a text—this interdisciplinary group of scholars began to document how the so-called right interpretation of a text rarely holds for different individuals reading in different contexts. Their work and that of others who are similarly focused on students' multiple literacies has become known as the New Literacy Studies (NLS) (Willinsky, 1990). The NLS are distinguished from the dominant view on literacy because they focus on "what literacy events and practices mean to users in different cultural and social contexts" (Street, 2003, p. 10).

In addition, related work in the areas of social cognition (Lave & Wenger, 1991; Tharp & Gallimore, 1988) and cultural studies (Lewis, 1998) has contributed to the growing sense that reading and writing are shaped by (and in turn help to shape) multiple sociocultural practices associated with becoming literate. Describing these practices as "deeply political," Gee (1999) has gone on to show how they also "fully integrate language, both oral and written, with nonlanguage 'stuff,' that is, with ways of acting, interacting, feeling, valuing, thinking, and believing, as well as with various sorts of nonverbal symbols, sites, tools, objects, and technologies" (p. 356). In summary, the NLS encompass ways of behaving, knowing, thinking, and valuing that give meaning to the uses of reading and writing that go far beyond simply mining a textbook for its literal or inferential meaning.

RETHINKING CONTENT LITERACY PRACTICES   The New Literacy Studies, which provide a different way of looking at literacy, are beginning to affect the ways in which teacher educators and classroom teachers think about content reading and writing instruction and how students learn from such instruction. This is especially the case among educators who subscribe to the so-called natural approaches to literacy instruction. Labeled typically as *process writing* and *reader response*, these approaches are being

TECHNOLOGY Tip

New Literacy Studies
For information on New Literacy Studies, check out Brian Street's online article in the May 2003 issue of *Current Issues in Comparative Education* at **www.tc.columbia.edu/CICE/ archives/contents.html**.

examined closely by individuals interested in critical literacy and critical language awareness—an awareness, that is, of why writers or speakers choose to write about certain topics, what content they include and leave out, whose interests they serve, and who is empowered (or disempowered) by the language they choose.

Some teacher educators (Kamler, 1999; Kamler & Comber, 1996), for instance, are beginning to reflect on how personal written response and other expressivist pedagogies such as reader response are teaching students to think about themselves and others in particularly naive ways—ways that rarely move them to social action and a critique of what they read or hear. Others (Lewis, 2000; Lewis, Ketter, & Fabos, 2001) are learning how to work around certain reader response approaches that emphasize personal identification at the expense of critiquing texts to look for an author's assumptions about people's identities, goals, ways of being in the world, and so on. Although there is much to admire in these natural approaches to literacy instruction, they have come under criticism of late for what they leave out.

For instance, critics (Moje, Willes, & Fassio, 2001; Patterson, Mellor, & O'Neill, 1994) say that these approaches have major flaws, but they are flaws that can be corrected so as to enable important gains realized through student-centered instruction to move forward. One of the identified flaws is that educators who teach from a reader response perspective put too much emphasis on personal experience and individual interpretation. This leads, critics say, to a naive view of the reading process, one in which it would appear that texts can somehow be neutrally produced and read. What they propose is a drawing in of the view from "without" (Green, 1991; Lemke, 1995). For example, Annette Patterson and colleagues (1994) believe it is their responsibility as literacy educators to teach students to take up a range of reading positions—some that may lead to resistant readings of what have become dominant or mainstream texts.

Helping students develop a facility and an interest in reading resistantly is an idea that has taken on increasing significance since its introduction in the late 1970s (Fetterly, 1978; Scott, 1990). Although some literacy educators might argue that *resistant reading* is just another name for *critical reading*, we disagree. A characteristic of resistant reading that we find absent in conventional descriptions of critical reading is the notion of *reading subtexts* as "a way of distancing ourselves and gaining some control over the reading experience" (Commeyras & Alvermann, 1996, p. 45).

The importance of reading the subtext is highlighted in Sam Wineburg's (1991) study, in which he compared how historians read historical texts and how high school students read the same texts. Wineburg found that the students were quite good at identifying the main ideas and answering the comprehension questions that went with the readings, but they failed to see how the authors of the texts had constructed them as social instruments "masterfully crafted to achieve a social end" (p. 502). The historians, on the other hand, read two types of subtexts. They read the texts as rhetorical artifacts, which involved reconstructing the "authors' purposes, intentions, and goals" (p. 498). They also read the texts as human artifacts, which involved identifying "elements that work at cross-purposes with the authors' intentions, bringing to the surface convictions the authors may have been unaware of or may have wished to conceal" (p. 499).

Evidence-Based Research

▶ *Some thought questions* . . .

1. Think back to a time when you taught students to read using a so-called natural language learning approach. Or perhaps you were taught to read by someone who favored one or more of those approaches. Do you agree with the criticism leveled against such approaches? Why? Why not?

2. Are you a resistant reader? When and under what conditions?

3. If you do not read resistantly yourself, do you see any reason for teaching others to read in that fashion? Why? Why not?

The Reading Process

In recent years, developments in cognitive psychology, sociolinguistics, and cultural anthropology have drawn attention to the need for explanations of the reading process that take into account a broad view of the everyday world of students and their families, teachers, schools, and communities. This section focuses on three aspects of the reading process: a cognitive view, a social constructionist perspective, and the role of motivation in the reading process.

A Cognitive View

A cognitive or psycholinguistic view of the reading process assumes "an active reader who constructs meaning through the integration of existing and new knowledge and the flexible use of strategies to foster, monitor, regulate, and maintain comprehension" (Dole et al., 1991, p. 242). Students who take a personal, adaptive view of reading understand that knowledge is constructed by them and that the experiences they bring to texts shape in large part what they will comprehend (Brown, Collins, & Duguid, 1989).

Cooper and Petrosky (1976) have made the point that "in reading, the brain supplies more information than it receives from the eye about the text" (p. 191). As you read

TECHNOLOGY Tip

ELLs and the New Literacies
Becoming knowledgeable about the social functions of written language within various linguistic and cultural communities can foster English language learners' expressive abilities. Such knowledge is vitally important for teach-ers whose linguistic and sociocultural backgrounds differ from those of their students. It is all part of rethinking one's teaching practices in light of the New Literacy Studies.

To learn how the new literacies are affecting what counts as writing in content area classrooms, visit **www.readingonline.org/electronic/ JAAL/4-01_column/**.

the next section on prior knowledge, think about this quote. If you find yourself agreeing with this assertion, then you will probably feel right at home when you read about the top-down model of text processing discussed later in this chapter. If you have doubts about this claim, you may feel more comfortable with the interactive model of reading, also discussed later in the chapter.

PRIOR KNOWLEDGE AND SCHEMA THEORY   Prior knowledge can cover a wide range of ideas, skills, and attitudes. When we use the term, we are focusing particularly on a reader's previous or existing knowledge of the subject matter of the text. What a person already knows about a topic is probably the single most influential factor with respect to what he or she will learn.

Evidence-Based Research

Cognitive psychologists use the word *schema* to describe how people organize the raw data of everyday experiences into meaningful patterns. A schema is a collection of organized and interrelated ideas or concepts. Schemata (the plural form) are fluid; they overlap and intertwine, and they are constantly modified to assimilate or accommodate new information. Schemata enable people to draw generalizations, form opinions, and understand new experiences (Anderson, 1984).

Schemata are frequently explained using the example of restaurants, probably because everyone has had some experience in going out to eat. Your schema for going to a restaurant might include the following: Someone will ask you what you would like to eat; that person or another will bring food, usually the food you asked for; you will pay for this food; you will not have to wash the dishes. Depending on actual experiences with dining out, individual restaurant schemata will vary. If your culinary adventures are mostly at fast-food outlets in your hometown on the East Coast, you will know just what to do at a Burger King in Cody, Wyoming, but you might not be sure which fork to use or which wine to order in a fancy restaurant. If your experiences were more varied, however, you would probably know about such things as making reservations, tipping, à la carte menus, and the specialties at different kinds of ethnic restaurants. You would not expect to order chicken wings at the Russian Tea Room in New York City, even if you had never been there before.

Schemata operate similarly in reading. They act as a kind of mental filing system from which the individual can retrieve relevant existing knowledge and into which new information can be filed. As you read, your schema for a topic helps you to anticipate, to infer, to decide what is or is not important, to build relationships between ideas, and to decide what information merits close attention. After reading, you use your schema as a topic to help you recall what you have read and put it into your own words.

Schemata, which are sometimes referred to as prior knowledge structures, play a large role in the reading process. They determine which of several interpretations of a text is the most probable. For example, this famous sentence, taken from the work of Bransford and McCarrell (1974), illustrates how one's culture can influence the meaning that is made of print:

The notes were sour because the seam split.

Although they may be familiar with all of the words and the syntax or ordering of those words, readers in the United States typically have difficulty constructing meaning for this sentence until they are provided with clues such as *bagpipe* or *Scottish musical instrument.*

MAKING CONNECTIONS BETWEEN THEORY AND PRACTICE Victoria likes to remind students in her content literacy classes of the importance of applying in their own classrooms what they know about prior knowledge and schema theory. She uses a series of three short passages to make her point. We include those passages here, along with several self-reflection questions aimed at helping you make connections between theory and practice.

The first passage illustrates the fact that prior knowledge must be *activated* to be of use. Note that no title is provided in order to demonstrate the difficulty in comprehending material for which prior knowledge, although available, has not been activated.

Passage 1

The procedure is actually quite simple. First you arrange items into different groups. Of course one group may be sufficient depending on how much there is to do. If you have to go somewhere else due to lack of facilities, that is the next step; otherwise, you are pretty well set. It is important not to overdo things. That is, it is better to do too few things at once than too many. In the short run this may not seem important but complications can easily arise. A mistake can be expensive as well. The manipulation of the appropriate mechanisms should be self-explanatory, and we need not dwell on it here. At first, the whole procedure will seem complicated. Soon, however, it will become just another facet of life. It is difficult to foresee any end to the necessity for this task in the immediate future, but then, one never can tell. After the procedure is completed, one arranges the materials into different groups again. Then they can be put into their appropriate places. Eventually they will be used once more and the whole cycle will then have to be repeated. However, that is part of life. (Bransford, 1979, pp. 134–135)

▶ *Self-reflection questions* . . .

1. If we had provided a title, such as "Washing Clothes," would the passage have made more sense immediately?

2. Would simply providing a title be adequate for activating your students' background knowledge about topics you regularly assign them to read? What else might you want to do to activate their knowledge more fully?

The second passage illustrates the importance of activating *appropriate* prior knowledge. Failure to do so can lead to confusion and misinterpretation of the text. For example, read the following passage twice: first, from the perspective of a *prisoner*, and then from a *wrestler's* perspective. After each of the readings, choose the best answer from the four possible ones that follow the question "How had Rocky been punished for his aggressiveness?"

Passage 2

Rocky slowly got up from the mat, planning his escape. He hesitated a moment and thought. Things were not going well. What bothered him most was being held, especially since the charge against him had been weak. He considered his present situation. The lock that held him was strong but he thought he could break it. He knew, however, that his timing would have to be perfect. Rocky was aware that it was because of his early roughness that he had been penalized so severely—much too severely from his point of view. The situation was becoming frustrating; the pressure had been grinding on him for too long. He was being ridden unmercifully. Rocky was getting angry now. He felt he was ready to make his move. He knew that his success or failure would depend on what he did in the next few seconds. (Anderson, Reynolds, Schallert, & Goetz, 1977, p. 372)

Comprehension question: How was Rocky punished for his aggressiveness?

a. He was demoted to the "B" team.

b. His opponent was given points.

c. He lost his privileges for the weekend.

d. He was arrested and imprisoned.

▶ *Self-reflection questions* . . .

1. Have you ever read something only to find out later that you had activated inappropriate background knowledge? How did it affect your comprehension? How did it make you feel?

2. As a teacher or prospective teacher, what might you do instructionally to ensure that students activate appropriate background knowledge for reading the materials required in your content area?

The third passage demonstrates why prior knowledge must be *sufficient* to be of use in comprehending text. For example, you may have had experience playing baseball—even bowling—but the batsmen and bowlers in "Today's Cricket" do not play by the rules you might expect. In short, if you grew up in the United States, it is likely you are as lost as we are when it comes to comprehending a sport played mainly in England and other parts of the Commonwealth.

Passage 3

Today's Cricket

The batsmen were merciless against the bowlers. The bowlers placed their men in slips and covers. But to no avail. The batsmen hit one four after another along with an occasional six. Not once did a ball look like it would hit their stumps or be caught. ("Wood's 100 Helps," 1978)

▶ *Self-reflection questions* . . .

1. Would knowing that *bowl* (as used in cricket) means "to put a batsman out by bowling the balls off the wicket" (*Webster's New World Dictionary*, 1991, p. 166) improve your understanding of the game? Why? Why not? What prior knowledge do you still lack?

2. If you were teaching a class in which your students were expected to read a story about cricket, how would you provide them with sufficient background knowledge?

In summary, as illustrated previously, it is one thing to develop a theoretical understanding of prior knowledge; it is quite another to apply that understanding in an actual classroom situation. However, we contend (and believe you would agree) that looking for ways to bridge theory and practice is well worth the effort.

THREE MODELS OF THE READING PROCESS   The bottom-up, top-down, and interactive models of the reading process are all concerned with a reader's schemata but to varying degrees. The *bottom-up model*, sometimes referred to as the *automaticity model*

(LaBerge & Samuels, 1976), is based on the idea that one can focus attention selectively on only one thing at a time. By this line of reasoning, until readers can decode the words of a text automatically, they will be unable to devote a sufficient amount of attention to comprehending the text and fluency will suffer, as noted earlier. As its name implies, the bottom-up model of the reading process assumes that meaning resides primarily in the text and that pieces of information are chunked incrementally to produce comprehension. Letters and their associated sounds are chunked to make words, words are chunked to make sentences, and so on.

According to the *top-down model* of the reading process, what the reader already knows is thought to determine in large part what he or she will be able to comprehend. For example, even if *triskaidekaphobia* is pronounced accurately, the reader may not be able to comprehend its meaning in text:

> Claudia's bout with triskaidekaphobia prevented her from ever staying on the thirteenth floor of a hotel.

For comprehension to occur, the reader would have to associate the meaning of the word *triskaidekaphobia* (fear of the number 13) with some previous experience or knowledge that linked the number 13 with being unlucky. Proponents of the top-down model of reading argue that meaning resides largely in one's head and that it is the reader's schemata more than the print on the page that account for what is comprehended and what is not. As its name implies, the top-down model assumes that comprehending begins when a reader accesses appropriate background experiences and knowledge to make sense of print. In other words, unlike the bottom-up model, in which the reader incrementally chunks bigger and bigger pieces of information, the top-down model proposes that the reader makes educated guesses to predict the meaning of the print.

The *interactive model* of the reading process incorporates features of both the bottom-up and top-down models. Proponents of this model argue that the degree to which a reader uses print or prior knowledge will depend largely on the familiarity of the topic being read, how interested the reader is in the topic, and the purpose for which he or she is reading. For example, if you have read about different models of reading in the past and have an interest in learning more about them or reviewing what you know, you may be reading this section of the chapter using a top-down process approach.

Alternatively, you may be reading along at a pretty good clip, making predictions about what you will find on the printed page, and slowing to examine more closely words such as *automaticity* and *triskaidekaphobia*. Perhaps you decoded a large word or looked for a familiar word part (such as *automatic*) in it. If you processed the information in this fashion, you were reading interactively. That is, you were using alternately what you knew from prior knowledge and what you were able to infer from your knowledge of the English language and the conventions of print.

Along with a majority of other literacy educators, we believe the interactive model of the reading process is a good descriptor of how students typically read their content area texts. They connect what they know about language, decoding, and vocabulary to their background experiences and prior knowledge. They also take into account the demands of the reading task or the reasons for which they are reading.

METACOGNITION *Metacognition*, simply put, means knowing about knowing. It is a term used to describe students' awareness of *what* they know, their understanding of *how* to be strategic readers, and their knowledge of *when* (i.e., under what conditions) to evaluate the adequacy of their comprehension (Paris, Lipson, & Wixson, 1983). Metacognition is an awareness of what resources (materials, skills, and knowledge) one can call up to meet the demands of a particular task (Baker & Brown, 1980).

For example, before reading a textbook chapter on the Holocaust, students might take a mental inventory of the information about the topic they have gleaned previously from books, films, and magazine accounts. They might also assess their interest in pursuing the topic further, their ability to read strategically, and/or their understanding of the purpose for the assignment. Developing such an awareness, however, does not ensure that they will succeed in comprehending the portion of text on the Holocaust. They will also need to monitor their reading.

Evidence-Based Research

Monitoring involves evaluating the trustworthiness of certain assumptions or inferences one makes while reading. It also involves applying any of a number of fix-up strategies when comprehension falters or breaks down completely. Moving backward and forward in text searches, concentrating on only the important information, making mental images, and contrasting new ideas with previous experiences are some of the most common fix-up strategies (Brown & Campione, 1994). As you might imagine, there is an important difference between knowing something is not making sense and doing something about it. Knowledge that is treated as separate and distinct from the situations in which it is learned and put to use is less helpful than knowledge that is contextually situated.

Evidence-Based Research

A LIFESPAN DEVELOPMENTAL PERSPECTIVE ON READING Reading development has traditionally been considered synonymous with early reading development. Recently, Alexander (n.d.) proposed a lifespan developmental perspective that attempts to explain how reading develops across the lifespan, "from womb to tomb" (p. 5). This view of reading holds promise for those of us engaged in educating adolescents because it helps us consider the development of literacy as students move beyond the early grades. Three stages are described in the lifespan developmental model: (a) acclimation, (b) competence, and (c) proficiency/expertise.

Alexander identifies three main factors that influence lifespan development of reading expertise across these three stages. The first factor, knowledge of language and of content topics, includes domain knowledge related to language and reading as well as knowledge about specific topics referenced in the text. The more you read, the more you learn about language and reading, and since you must read about *something*, you also acquire increased topic knowledge as you read. Across the lifespan, knowledge about language and topic knowledge increase.

Go to MyEducationLab and select the topic *The Reading Process*. Then, go to the Activities and Applications section, watch the video entitled "Academic Literacy," and respond to the accompanying prompts.

Helping Struggling Readers

Interactive-Compensatory Model

It is helpful to keep in mind Stanovich's (1980) *interactive-compensatory model* when working with readers who struggle to decode texts. According to this model, they will tend to rely more than good readers on context for word recognition and hence have less freed-up capacity for comprehension than good readers. The instructional implications of the interactive-compensatory model for content area teachers include the following:

- Provide readers who struggle to decode their assigned texts with opportunities to hear those texts read aloud, perhaps through tape-assisted instruction, and to write down what they want to remember.

- Give readers for whom word recognition is a problem supplemental materials that include visual clues to word meaning. Also consider the use of manipulatives in science and math areas.

- Allot extra time for readers who struggle to complete their assignments. Consider assigning fewer pages, perhaps concentrating on the key ideas in a passage or chapter.

- Encourage struggling readers to use the Internet. Sometimes the symbols and icons that are bothersome to good readers are the very means through which struggling readers make meaning. Writing e-mails to classmates about where to find information for a report can also be an important literacy tool for readers who struggle with content area assignments.

The second factor described by Alexander is interest. Interest can be situational (temporary interest induced by the context) or individual (representing a long-term involvement in a particular topic or field). Over time, the relative importance of these two kinds of interest shifts. In the acclimation stage, situational interest is important, whereas individual interest becomes more and more important as a reader passes through competence to proficiency.

The third factor is a reader's strategic processing, which changes as reading competence develops. In the acclimation stage, surface-processing strategies such as rereading, altering reading rate, and skipping unfamiliar words are important. Over time, deep-processing strategies that involve personalization and transformation of text develop and are more important.

As those of us who have taught in middle and high schools know, readers in the acclimation stage can be found at all grade levels. Likewise, readers can be at different developmental levels in different content areas. A student may be a competent reader in history but struggle to read in mathematics or science. If we want to help adolescents to grow to be competent readers on their way to proficiency, we must help them increase their knowledge of language in general and specific topics about which they read; offer them

Literacy Coaches' Corner

English Language Learners
Among educators in the United States, there is considerable disagreement over whether second-language learners use the same cogni-tive monitoring processes as native English speakers when reading (Garcia, 2000). There is also disagreement as to whether proficiency in one's native language and oral proficiency in the second language are prerequisites for ESL reading instruction.

interesting books, magazines, and media so they will have the desire to read; and model deep-processing strategies so that they can develop their own strategic reading skills.

A Social Constructionist Perspective

Earlier in this chapter, we discussed schema theory at length and involved you in activities that helped you see the connection between theory and practice. According to schema theory, prior knowledge is the most important factor in learning. However, this is not a universally agreed on tenet of learning (see Krasny, Sadoski, & Paivio, 2007). A number of questions have been raised related to schema theory. Perhaps the one most important to teachers is If everything is based on prior knowledge, how in the world do you get any in the first place? This is not a trivial question for a teacher planning instruction on a concept that is new to students.

McVee, Dunsmore, and Gavelek (2005) revisited schema theory in an attempt to address questions that are emerging from research about the creation of schemata and the influence of culture on learning. McVee et al. explained that knowledge, organized into schemata, grows out of transactions in which the learner is engaged in an activity or problem-solving task using tools of language, speech, and thought—all of which occur in a cultural context. This explanation seems to answer the questions about schema theory, at least for us for now. Thus, schemata can be thought of as emerging from transactions between learners and the world, and the transactions are "mediated by culturally and socially enacted practices" (McVee et al., 2005 p. 556).

The notion that learning occurs from transactions between learners and the world underlies the *social constructionist* view of learning. You will likely be able to understand this view if you have ever been in a situation in which you realized that the presence of others whom you judged to be more competent than you made you a better thinker, reader, or writer.

The term *social constructionism* is frequently used synonymously with *social constructivism*, although there are many good reasons for not conflating the two concepts (Hruby, 2001). For purposes of this chapter, we concentrate on social constructionism. Both concepts are theories of learning; they are not theories of teaching per se. To understand the differences between social constructionism and social constructivism, it is useful to first define constructivist learning theory.

CONSTRUCTIVIST LEARNING THEORY   *Constructivism* has become a catchall term for a collection of theoretical approaches to learning that rely for their explanation on the cognitive processes individuals use in making sense of their lived experiences. Literacy educators generally limit their attention to four versions of constructivism: Piagetian constructivism, radical constructivism, sociohistorical constructivism, and social constructivism (Eisenhart, Finkel, & Marion, 1996; Phillips, 2000).

Piagetian constructivism holds that conceptual development results from an individual's ability to assimilate and accommodate new information into existing knowledge structures. To count as learning, however, this newly assimilated (or accommodated) information must correspond with an authoritative body of knowledge external to the individual. Motivation for such learning rests in the individual and in the materials (content) to be learned.

Radical constructivism also situates motivation for learning in the person and the content to be learned. However, unlike Piagetian constructivism, radical constructivism assumes that evidence of new learning rests on an individual's ability to make personal sense of her or his own experiences; that is, radical constructivists have no need to apply some sort of external litmus test to determine the correctness of a student's personally constructed knowledge. Teachers who adhere to either Piagetian or radical constructivism view students as "autonomous actors who learn by building up their own understandings of their worlds in their heads" (Eisenhart, Finkel, & Marion, 1996, p. 278).

In contrast to these two perspectives are sociohistorical constructivism and social constructivism. *Sociohistorical constructivism* embraces Vygotsky's (1978) activity theory, whereas *social constructivism* is more closely associated with Bruner (1986), at least

TECHNOLOGY Tip

Understanding Constructivism
To experience what is involved in reading a passage that illustrates a constructivist perspective on learning, see "What Is Really True? A Lesson in Understanding Constructivism." This lesson was developed by Lloyd Rieber, one of Donna's colleagues at the University of Georgia, and can be accessed at **http://it.coe.uga.edu/~lrieber/constructlesson.html**.

among literacy educators. Both sociohistorical and social constructivism are concerned with how factors outside the head, such as the culture of a classroom, influence what students do in the name of learning.

SOCIAL CONSTRUCTIONIST LEARNING THEORY   The view that truth is made, not found, and the centrality of language in mediating what people come to understand about their lived experiences are features that most readily distinguish a social constructionist perspective from a constructivist perspective. Gavelek and Raphael (1996) describe how a teacher who subscribes to social constructionist learning theory would elicit students' responses:

> The teacher's role would shift from asking questions to ensure that students arrive at the "right" meaning to creating prompts that encourage students' exploratory talk. . . . Teachers would encourage talk that elicits a range of possible interpretations among individuals reading and responding at any given time. Teachers would also encourage talking about previously read texts because individuals construct different readings at different periods in life or within different contexts. . . . Textual meaning is not "out there" to be acquired: It is something that is constructed by individuals through their interactions with each other and the world. In classrooms, these interactions take the form of discussions, and the teacher helps guide and participates in them. Underlying the processes of interpretations and justifications in discussions is language. (p. 183)

In an attempt to give you a sense of how meaning is socially constructed, we have included a two-sentence short story by Richard Brautigan (1971) and an accompanying small-group activity.

Story: "It's very hard to live in a studio apartment in San Jose with a man who's learning to play the violin." That's what she told the police when she handed them the empty revolver. (p. 197)

Activity

Gather a group of three or four individuals, and respond to the following prompts after someone in the group has read aloud Brautigan's story:

- Explain what happened.
- Elaborate on why it happened.
- Defend why you know you're right.

After completing the activity, reflect on the process. As you discussed your responses to the story, did you notice the role that language played in mediating

(continued)

your own and other people's interpretations? How would you explain your choice of language in constructing your interpretation? Why is your interpretation as viable as other people's interpretations? What previous experiences have you had that might possibly account for your interpretation of the story? Reflecting on questions such as these will help you understand how individuals go about socially constructing the meanings of all sorts of texts, not just short stories.

Such reflections will also illustrate Brock and Gavelek's (1998) point that although our cultural histories do not determine how we experience or respond to texts, they do in fact channel or help to frame our responses. In fact, the very idea that reading is a socially constructed practice draws on some of the most basic assumptions from cultural anthropology and sociolinguistics (Cook-Gumperz, 1986; Gee, 1988; Heath, 1983).

One such assumption is that "students of different races, different social classes, and different genders may produce readings which challenge dominant or authoritative meanings because they have available to them different sets of values and beliefs" (Patterson, Mellor, & O'Neill, 1994, p. 66). However, it should come as no surprise that students who share cultural backgrounds and who are contemporaries may still respond to and interpret the same text very differently. This is to be expected given that each student will have had unique life experiences and different ways of using language to interpret those experiences.

Of course, nothing is as simple as it might first seem. Social constructionist learning theory will only buy us so much. Learning and teaching in a complex world involves much more than language, and it is this fact that drives home the following point:

The suggestion that all knowledge is language-based—and, hence, formulated and explicit—would imply that agents must be aware (or capable of being aware) of their knowledge. As such, statements like "My dog knows how to dig holes" or "My heart knows how to beat" are nonsensical. In other words, underpinning the claim that all knowledge is socially constructed is a presumption that "the human" is separable from the non- and sub-human. The same sort of separation is implicit in debates of nature versus nurture. (Davis, Sumara, & Luce-Kapler, 2000, p. 17)

Suffice it to say that for the purposes of this book, we will leave the discussion on socially constructed learning where we started. That is, it is a helpful construct for thinking about how the cognitive processes of reading are always "embedded in, enabled by, and constrained by the social phenomenon of language" (Davis et al., 2000, p. 67). Some researchers look at learning theories and see an evolutionary progression—one theory replacing another as we go marching on in time. We prefer to see theories more as a quilt, in which each theory is a piece that adds to the knowledge of human learning.

The Role of Motivation

Listening to the voices of students is key to understanding what motivates them to learn. Based on her review of research on student motivation, Barbara McCombs (1995) of the Mid-Continent Regional Educational Laboratory writes:

> The support is overwhelmingly on the side of learner-centered practices that honor individual learner perspectives and needs for competence, control, and belonging. The voices of the students themselves provide even more support for this perspective. . . . When students are asked what makes school a place where they want to learn, they report that they want (a) rigor and joy in their schoolwork, (b) a balance of complexity and clarity, (c) opportunities to discuss personal meanings and values, (d) learning activities that are relevant and fun, and (e) learning experiences that offer choice and require action. (p. 10)

Middle-grade students' motivations for reading, as measured by the *Motivations for Reading Questionnaire*, extend and complement this view of the importance of intrinsically appealing learner-centered instruction. Approximately 600 students in a large mid-Atlantic city school system (55 percent African American, 43 percent Caucasian, and 2 percent Asian and Hispanic) said they do not avoid difficult reading activities. Motivational dimensions related to enjoyment, curiosity, and a sense of efficacy were the best predictors of the frequency with which they read (Wigfield, Wilde, Baker, Fernandez-Fein, & Scher, 1996).

When students are positively motivated, they view themselves as competent readers who are in control of their comprehension processes; they are said to be strategic in their approach to reading. Sometimes, however, students adopt tactics that result in an avoidance of reading or of spending time on assignments. When this occurs, they are said to be using strategies in a self-serving, or negative, fashion. Both positive and negative types of motivation for reading are present among students, regardless of ability level, socioeconomic status, or racial and ethnic background. Knowledge of how both types of motivation manifest themselves in subject matter classrooms is vital to understanding the reading process and to planning for instruction.

POSITIVE STRATEGIES   Strategic readers take pride in what they are able to learn independently from text. They view reading as a means of gaining control of their academic environment. They also develop feelings of self-worth and confidence in their ability to achieve desired goals (Weiner, 1986). This sense of control can lead to increased achievement in their subject matter classes; it can also lead to better peer relations.

For example, Charley comes to mind here. Charley was 13 years old and in the eighth grade when Donna first met him. She was observing his math teacher, Ms. Wilthey, model for the class how to sort through and discard extraneous information in a word problem. The object was to choose only relevant numbers on which to perform certain mathematical operations. Charley initially showed little interest in the teacher's lesson. However, when Ms. Wilthey challenged the class to come up with different ways

Evidence-Based Research

Go to MyEducationLab and select the topic *Motivation to Read Content-Area Texts*. Then, go to the Activities and Applications section, watch the video entitled "Engagement," and respond to the accompanying prompts.

Evidence-Based Research

of solving a set of math problems for homework that night, Charley consulted "The Library of Math Forum Problems" (http://mathforum.org/library/problems/sets/funpow_all.html) and brought in numerous examples to share with the class.

As young adolescents move from the middle grades into secondary school, their perceptions of their control become stronger. According to Paris, Wasik, and Turner (1991), "[Greater] perceived control leads to greater effort in the use of particular learning strategies. Successful students persist in the face of failure and choose appropriate tactics for challenging tasks more often than students who do not understand what controls learning outcomes" (p. 626).

For students to experience a sense of control in becoming competent readers, they must believe four things. First, they must believe that they are capable of assuming responsibility for their own learning and have the ability to complete their assignments. Second, they must believe that they have a voice in setting their own objectives for reading and in determining suitable standards of excellence. Third, they must be convinced of the usefulness of certain strategies for accomplishing specific objectives. Finally, they must believe that their successes as readers are contingent on the effort and skill they invest in becoming strategic readers (Paris, Wasik et al., 1991).

AVOIDANCE STRATEGIES   Giving up on or withdrawing from situations that involve learning from text is a tactic students may use when the material they are assigned to read seems too difficult or uninteresting. This tactic may even be used by students for whom the material is neither too difficult nor uninteresting. Why? To the best of our knowledge, disengaged readers for one reason or another devalue reading; they tend to invest their time in other endeavors. Their attention is focused elsewhere, perhaps on a subject requiring less reading, a part-time job, or extracurricular activities.

David O'Brien (1998) captured this kind of student in his description of Denise, an underachieving junior at Jefferson High. When David taught her in the Jeff Literacy Lab, Denise was working 20 hours a week at a local pizza shop. He described her thusly: "Denise has been in the Literacy Lab for 3 years. She views her reading ability as a weak link in a relatively strong chain of other accomplishments. . . . She noted: 'I don't read unless I have to.' She likes the computer activities, but she does not seem to connect computers with reading and writing" (p. 38).

Another avoidance strategy students use involves shifting the blame for reading difficulties from themselves to someone or something else. For example, students may complain that their teachers dislike them, that they are distracted easily, or that other teachers load them up with homework. The least desirable avoidance strategy is the one used by students who free themselves of the responsibility for reading text to learn by copying assignments, cheating on tests, or repeatedly seeking the assistance of a friend or family member (Paris et al., 1991).

Each of these avoidance strategies shares certain attributes with the others. First, they all help to preserve students' positive self-perceptions because "passing the buck" leads to short-term success at preserving self-esteem. Second, they eventually lead to the *passive failure syndrome* (Johnston & Winograd, 1985), in which students over time fail to learn the necessary content and skills that make regular advancement in school an attainable goal. Third, students' sense of "beating the system" may lead to a false idea of what it takes to succeed in any endeavor, whether reading or something else.

SELF-MOTIVATION   The idea that teachers can cultivate within students the will, or self-motivation, to use their reading and writing skills in all areas of the curriculum is a central theme of this book. In fact, the underlying goal of most literacy instruction in middle and secondary schools is to enable students to use reading and writing as tools for learning the content of their coursework. However, teachers know that all too often adolescents do not make the effort that is necessary for this learning to take place (Bishop, 1989). Why this apathy?

Here are some answers to that question from the students' perspectives:

- Henri (a newly arrived student from outside the United States) talks about his apathy in physics class: "I know that I should work hard, do my homework, listen in class, but well, see, it's just that I don't want to stand out as being a hard worker. I know I can do the work, but I just don't want to stand out."
- Patricia (a third-year Latin student) explains how she plays down her abilities in order to strike a "just-right" balance: "See, I don't want to be called the class brain or something. . . . I do just enough to get by. That way no one knows."
- Dan (a tenth grader) never tries in history class and thus never risks the stigma of having tried and failed: "I don't know . . . Studying for a quiz in history isn't worth the effort, I guess. Look at it this way: if I tried and didn't make it then I'd say to myself, 'Dumb . . . You should have just slacked off.' "

Other answers to the apathy question come from teachers. For example, Janis Gabay, the 1990 National Teacher of the Year, argued that adolescents (especially minorities) are often labeled as "unmotivated" when actually it is a matter of their having no sense of ownership and no incentive to participate in classroom activities. To Gabay's (1991) way of thinking,

Teachers can help their students become self-motivated in a number of ways: by tapping students' prior knowledge; setting forth clear expectations and goals so students know what they are aspiring to in a specific lesson, unit, or semester; conveying to students the difficulty of the challenge but emphasizing the supports the teacher will provide to ensure their success; giving lots of genuine praise for the incremental, tentative steps students take; holding students accountable in a way that includes self-evaluation of their progress; acknowledging each student through a significant nod, a smile, or an encouraging comment (not always in front of the whole class)—especially for that student at risk of "disconnecting"; and by modeling the enthusiasm that teaching and learning engender so students can see a tangible example of self-motivation, commitment, and effort. (p. 7)

Perhaps one of the most useful things to bear in mind as we work to increase our students' self-motivation is a statement attributed to John F. Kennedy. Speaking on the importance of developing each child's potential to its fullest, Kennedy (cited in Inos & Quigley, 1995) said, "Not every child has an equal talent or an equal ability or equal motivation, but children have the equal right to develop their talent, their ability, and their motivation" (p. 1). We think this statement and its implications for classroom practice capture our sentiments exactly.

Summary

A pervasive and legitimate concern of middle and high school content area teachers is how to help students learn from texts. In the English language arts curriculum, that concern is broadened to include an emphasis on how to help readers evaluate the connotations and associations evoked by the experience of transacting with texts. In all areas of the curriculum, the goal is to support adolescents' literacy growth by providing them with access to materials they can and want to read (Moore, Bean, Birdyshaw, & Rycik, 1999). Ensuring that all students, including those who struggle with fluency in reading and who are English language learners, become active and independent learners is a primary goal of content area educators. Teachers' pedagogical subject matter knowledge and their understanding of the role that textbooks and the Internet (through its various websites) play in classroom instruction are vital links to reaching that goal.

Traditional definitions of what it means to be literate have given way to a broadened view of literacy—one that includes informational, computer, media, scientific, technological, and disciplinary literacies. These multiple literacies require skills that extend far beyond the conventional reading and writing competencies associated with print literacy. They also require that teachers attend to more than a cognitive view of the reading process. Constructivist and social constructionist perspectives on that process, as well as students' motivations for becoming literate, must be taken into account as important mediators of students' ability to learn in various content areas.

Suggested Readings

Barton, D., Hamilton, M., & Ivanic, R. (2000). *Situated literacies: Reading and writing in context.* New York: Routledge.

Brophy, J. (Ed.). (2001). *Subject-specific instructional methods and activities.* Kidlington, Oxford, UK: Elsevier Science.

Bruce, B. C. (Ed.). (2003). *Literacy in the information age.* Newark, DE: International Reading Association.

Cope, B., & Kalantzis, M. (Eds.). (2000). *Multiliteracies: Literacy learning and the design of social futures.* New York: Routledge.

Freebody, P., Luke, A., & Gilbert, P. (1991). Reading positions and practices in the classroom. *Curriculum Inquiry, 21*, 435–457.

Kenney, J. M., Hancewicz, E., Heuer, L., Metsisto, D., & Tuttle, C. L. (2005). *Literacy strategies for improving mathematics instruction.* Alexandria, VA: Association for Supervision and Curriculum Development.

Kist, W. (2005). *New literacies in action: Teaching and learning in multiple media.* New York: Teachers College Press.

Lankshear, C., & Knobel, M. (2003). *New literacies: Changing knowledge and classroom learning.* Philadelphia, PA: Open University Press.

Spivey, N. N. (1997). *The constructivist metaphor: Reading, writing, and the making of meaning.* San Diego, CA: Academic Press.

MyEducationLab is a research-based learning tool that brings teaching to life. Go to the Alvermann, Phelps, and Ridgeway Gillis 6th Edition MyEducationLab for Content Area Reading site at www.myeducationlab.com to:

- engage in multimedia exercises to help you build a deeper and more applied understanding of chapter content;

- utilize extensive resources including videos from real classrooms, Praxis and licensure preparation, a lesson plan builder, and materials to help you in your teaching career.

chapter 2

Language, Diversity, and Culture

Language, Diversity, and Culture

Language as a Vehicle for Teaching and Learning Content

- Seeing Language as a Social Practice
- Dealing with Gendered Language in the Classroom and the Text

Diversity in Language and Learning

- Second-Language Acquisition and Learning
- Dialect Differences
- Struggling or Reluctant Readers
- Gifted Learners

Teaching and Learning in Culturally Diverse Classrooms

- Today's Globalizing Influences
- Improving Literacy in Adolescent ELLs
- Integrating Language, Culture, and Content

Culturally Responsive Professional Growth

- Appreciating Diversity
- Involving Parents and Community
- Linking School and Home

Anticipation Guide

Directions: Read each of the following statements. Place a checkmark on the line in the "Before Reading" column if you agree with the statement; leave it blank if you disagree. Then predict what you think the chapter will be about, and jot down on a sticky note (or post online) any questions you have. Read the chapter; then return to the statements and respond to them as you think the authors of your text would. Place a checkmark on the line in the "Author's Stance" column if you believe the authors would agree with the statement. If you discuss these statements with other people online, in class, or at the family dinner table, return to the statements and check any items you agree with in the right-hand column, "After Discussion." If your thinking changed, what caused that change?

Before Reading	Authors' Stance	Statements	After Discussion
_____	_____	1. English language learners (ELLs) are often overlooked in gifted and talented class placements.	_____
_____	_____	2. The way we speak—the vocabulary, pronunciation, and expressions we use—identifies us as members of particular communities.	_____
_____	_____	3. Textbooks, though boring at times, offer teachers unbiased, gender-neutral sources of information they can use with confidence.	_____
_____	_____	4. Everyone in the United States speaks a dialect.	_____
_____	_____	5. Language, whether written or spoken, is not neutral, it positions readers or listeners in particular ways.	_____
_____	_____	6. English language learners and struggling adolescent readers have the same instructional needs.	_____

We open this chapter with a thumbnail sketch of Katya, one of several students who participated in a year-long study of adolescents' perceptions of classroom talk about their assigned reading materials. The sketch, compiled by Steve Phelps, a researcher in the study (Alvermann et al., 1996b), evokes images of why we believe teaching and learning in today's culturally diverse classrooms must entail more than simply attending to the assigned literacy tasks. Important as those tasks are, they cannot be isolated from the influences affecting students' everyday lives.

As you read Steve's description of Katya, which he assembled from observing her in class and interviewing her in private, think of questions that you would like to ask her or her social studies teacher, Mr. Williams. (Pseudonyms are used throughout.)

• • •

Katya had come to the United States with her mother and three siblings from the Ukraine two years before the time of the study. They were members of the local Ukrainian Pentecostal Christian community. Katya said she attended church daily. Because her English was limited, both in vocabulary and in syntax, Katya had enrolled in two classes of English as a second language (ESL) as well as an after-school English program. She said she spoke Ukrainian at home. In her high school, Katya was referred to as "one of the Russian students," seemingly because the faculty and staff did not differentiate between the Ukraine and Russia.

Katya was very reserved and shy in class. To help overcome her difficulties with the language, Mr. Williams paired her with Ahmed, an Arabian student she had known the previous year in a biology class. Although Katya rarely uttered a word in class discussions, she (along with Ahmed) was one of the more diligent and attentive students in class when it came to reading, note-taking, and following the teacher's lectures. The only instances in which Katya attempted to enter into public discourse were occasional and nearly inaudible one-word responses when the class was going over the answers to a worksheet.

Although it would be easy to attribute Katya's lack of participation to her shyness or difficulty with the English language, there were brief flashes of evidence that suggested she was willing to share interesting information. For example, when she spoke with Steve about her life in the Ukraine and when she and Ahmed paged through a magazine prior to the start of class, Katya was animated and insightful. Katya's grades were in the low 90s, and on the final state Regent's Exam, which was part multiple choice and part essay, Katya got a 76. Although she did relatively well in her other subjects as well, she was unable to graduate at the end of the year because she did not have enough physical education credits. (Phelps & Weaver, 1999)

• • •

What questions came to mind as you read this sketch? For us, one nagging question was "What might Mr. Williams have done to create spaces for Katya's private voice in the public discourse of the classroom?" However, as we ask it, we think back to other studies of student voice in which researchers have found that attempts to empower others is not something one can do *to* or *for* another person (Alvermann, 1995–1996; Orner, 1992; Perry & Delpit, 1998). In fact, some educators have begun to ask themselves "Whose interests are served when students speak?" The answers, as you might expect, are layered and complex. It is this complexity that we invite you to explore in the following pages.

The chapter is divided into four major sections, which reflect its four purposes. The purpose of the first section is to explore issues concerning language as a vehicle for teaching and learning in culturally diverse classrooms. The purpose of the second section is to describe issues regarding the various needs of English language learners (ELLs), or English learners (ELs) as they are referred to in some regions of the United States. The purpose of the third section is to examine the need for integrating language, culture, and content given today's globalizing influences. The purpose of the fourth section is to suggest ways of synchronizing professional growth opportunities so they focus on culturally responsive teaching.

Language as a Vehicle for Teaching and Learning Content

A major influence on how we currently view the teaching and learning of content literacy is the work of Lev Vygotsky, a Russian psychologist. Although Vygotsky's (1978) theory of learning took shape in the early years of the twentieth century, educators in North America did not learn of it until edited translations of his work appeared in English in the 1960s and 1970s. In a nutshell, Vygotsky believed that "mental functioning in the individual originates in social, communicative processes" (Wertsch, 1991, p. 13), which are embedded in an array of cultural, historical, and institutional contexts. In other words, a Vygotskian perspective on learning does not assume that students will learn independently but rather that they will benefit from engaging socially in groups where others more knowledgeable than them can guide their learning (Vygotsky, 1978).

This emphasis on the social, communicative processes of language as a mediator of even the most private forms of thinking has had a profound influence on how we view the reading process, as described in Chapter 1. Its influence is highlighted again here: first, in our look at language as social practice, and next, in our discussion of ways to deal with the gendered nature of classroom language and text.

Seeing Language as Social Practice

What a person says (or does) and what other people hear (or see) will vary greatly depending on the social and cultural contexts in which such communication takes place. Even though the people involved may be speaking the same language, there is room for misinterpretation.

Consider, for example, the following story told by James Gee (1996), a sociolinguist whose work informs much of what we believe about language as a mediating force in what gets said and understood in content area classrooms. In this story, Gee illustrates how language in the social context of a biker bar (or pub) reveals much more about the narrator (himself) than his proficiency in using English:

Imagine I park my motorcycle, enter my neighborhood "biker bar," and say to my leather-jacketed and tattooed drinking buddy, as I sit down: "May I have a match for my cigarette, please?" What I have said is perfectly grammatical English, but it is "wrong" nonetheless, unless I have used a heavily ironic tone of voice. It is not just *what* you say, but *how* you say it. And in this bar, I haven't said it in the "right way." I should have said something like "Gotta match?" or "Give me a light, wouldya?"

But now imagine I say the "right" thing ("Gotta match?" or "Give me a light, wouldya?"), but while saying it, I carefully wipe off the bar stool with a napkin to avoid getting my newly pressed designer jeans dirty. In this case, I've still got it all wrong. In *this* bar they just don't do that sort of thing: I have *said* the right thing, but my "saying–doing" combination is nonetheless wrong. It's not just what you say or even just how you say it, it's also who you are and what you're doing while you say it. It is not enough just to say the right "lines." (p. viii)

What you have just read is an example of a Discourse, with a capital *D*. Briefly defined, Discourses are ways of speaking, thinking, and behaving in the world. Whether in biker bars or in classrooms, Discourses operate as ways of sorting individuals and groups. When this sorting leads to different expectations for students, we need to be concerned. As Gee (1996) reminds us:

Each Discourse incorporates a usually taken for granted and tacit "theory" of what counts as a "normal" person and the "right" ways to think, feel, and behave. These theories crucially involve viewpoints on the distribution of social goods like status, worth, and material goods in society (who should and who should not have them). The biker bar "says" that "tough guys" are "real men"; the school "says" that certain children—often minority children and those from lower socioeconomic groups—are not suited for higher education and professional careers. (p. ix)

▶ *Some questions to get you thinking* . . .

1. What are some Discourses in which you claim membership (e.g., as a student, teacher, administrator, citizen, sister, mother)?

2. How would others recognize you as a member of these Discourses?

3. Do you change your ways of speaking, thinking, and behaving when you move from one Discourse to another? Why?

4. What connections can you make between the example of the Discourse of the biker bar and the Discourses you are likely to find in various school settings?

Developing an awareness of how different Discourses construct the social realities of the classrooms in which we teach is an important first step in dealing with some of these realities. Just as learning subject matter can be described as learning a kind of Discourse, so also can learning how to do school literacy. In the following section, you will learn how reading—and "doing"—gendered literacy is part of school literacy.

Dealing with Gendered Language in the Classroom and the Text

A great deal of emphasis is currently placed on student-centered literacy practices, such as personal response to texts in book clubs, literature circles, and cooperative-learning groups. However, little attention has been paid to classroom language that leads to stereotyping. In the two sections that follow on the language of classroom and text, we provide anecdotal evidence of how such stereotyping inevitably narrows students' thinking and creates a potentially unproductive learning environment.

LANGUAGE OF THE CLASSROOM

I think the girls, we're like, we dominate, we rule the class.

—Jamaica

Since we've been talking about sexism [in books], the girls got their own point of view and the boys got their own . . . [and] we're always against each other.

—David

Spoken passionately and with conviction, these statements reflected attitudes that existed in David Hinson's seventh-grade language arts class following a class reading of a play about a girls' soccer team that defeats a boys' soccer team (Alvermann et al., 1996b). The discussion of this play eventually led a student to ask, "Should boys be allowed to join an all-girls' softball team?" Although a few students said yes, most of them flatly rejected the idea.

The proverbial battle lines between the sexes were drawn when Cherie announced, "An all-girls' team talks about 'girl talk' so boys would ruin everything." The boys, sensing they were being cast as the outsiders, retorted with statements like "It just shows the stupidity of women." As the name-calling escalated, the students seemed bent on excluding each other's ideas along sexist lines rather than questioning the source of those ideas and why they might hold currency among their peers.

We believe that incidents such as this one can lead eventually to patterns of discourse that students internalize and act on in a variety of ways. When the language of the classroom centers on the meanings boys and girls attach to being male or female, as in the example just given, gender becomes something students *do*—a way of being in the world. Over time, as stereotypes form and become more firmly inscribed each time gender is socially constructed through classroom talk, students shape their identities to fit the language they hear.

LANGUAGE OF THE TEXT   Reading texts in which an author's language socially constructs gender can also inscribe stereotypes. However, gender is but one of several filters through which readers experience texts. Social class, race, ethnicity, and culture are others. Consider, for instance, the overlapping filters that are operating in the following examples from Sally Randall's eighth-grade language arts classroom:

- *Example 1:*

Rather than assign the questions at the end of an excerpt from *The Pearl* (Steinbeck, 1989) in the class anthology, Ms. Randall asked the students to consider a series of quotations from the selection. One quotation helped students consider how an author's gendered way of writing can influence the language they use in discussing the text:

> Kino had wondered often at the iron in his patient, fragile wife. She, who was obedient and respectful and cheerful and patient, she could arch her back in child pain with hardly a cry. She could stand fatigue and hunger almost better than Kino himself. In the canoe she was like a strong man. (p. 677)

After students had read this quotation aloud, Ms. Randall asked them to consider why Steinbeck wrote the description of Kino's wife in this way. The first student to respond said Juana (Kino's wife) had the physical characteristics of a man but still gave Kino the honor and respect he deserved because he was a man. Ms. Randall then underlined the word *almost* and the phrase *like a strong man*. She asked the class to think about what those words implied. A student spoke up to say that Juana may have had qualities like a man but they were also women's qualities. Exchanges such as these allow students to explore multiple perspectives.

- *Example 2:*

The Pearl became the focus of another discussion in Ms. Randall's class. This time the students were asked to consider who was the more dominant character—Kino or Juana. Most of them concluded it had to be Kino, because he was the man and he made all the decisions for his family. Ms. Randall asked, "Do you think this is pretty common in literature for the man to be the dominant one?" Heads nodded in agreement, with Paula explaining it this way: "Well, it kind of just started in the beginning. Adam was made first, and that was kind of like the man was the head of the family. And so it was just kind of in all the stories. That's just like in real life. That's just the way."

With this example, it is easy to see how the language of the classroom and the language of the text conspire to socially construct what it means to be male and, by implication, what it means to be female. Here, the weight of religion, literary history, and culture combine to leave little doubt in Paula's mind that this is just the way life is, has always been, and will always be.

INTERRUPTING THE STATUS QUO   Strategies that support students as they begin to question the source of the ideas or the values expressed in the texts they read and hear discussed in class are most effective when they call into question inequities associated with gender bias. For example, Wayne Williams, a physics teacher who collaborated in a two-year action research project with Barbara Guzzetti, a literacy teacher educator (Guzzetti & Williams, 1996), employed a simple but effective strategy for intervening in a gendered interactional style that favored boys' voices over girls' voices in his classroom. Briefly, Mr. Williams had been unaware during the first year of the study that the boys in his class generally believed that the girls' questioning style indicated an inability on their part to learn difficult concepts. In the second year of the study, Mr. Williams presented his subject matter in a way that demonstrated science involves an active questioning and exploring of ideas. In doing this, he was able to communicate that females' ways of talking should be viewed positively, rather than negatively, and that questioning is the first step in scientific inquiry.

Evidence-Based Research

Diversity in Language and Learning

We begin this section on second-language learning, dialect differences, struggling readers, and gifted learners with a cautionary note. It is easy to fall into the trap of generalizing about an individual based on one aspect of that person's group membership. How many times, for example, have you heard or taken part in conversations that narrowly define someone on the basis of his or her race, gender, age, ability, religion, and so on? Generalizing group characteristics to an individual is misleading in other ways as well. A case in point is Katya. If you were her teacher, why would it be important to identify her in more than one way?

Although Katya's nationality is Ukrainian, this is only one of her multiple group memberships. Katya, the individual, is simultaneously a woman and a member of the Pentecostal Christian community. Although she did not disclose information related to her social class or racial makeup, we do know she has at least one exceptionality—Katya is multilingual. She speaks Ukrainian, Russian, and English. Thus, if you were Katya's teacher, you would want to consider her multiple group memberships when planning for instruction, facilitating group discussions, devising assessments, and making any number of other instructional decisions. Without knowledge of the different norms, values, myths, traditions, and symbols that have meaning for different cultural groups, you will find it difficult to access or build on your students' rich and diverse backgrounds when introducing new concepts and strategies for learning from texts.

Although developing an awareness of your students' cultural backgrounds is important, it is not enough. Too often we think of other people as having a diverse set of beliefs and values and yet remain blind to our own. It is as if we simply do not see what looks and feels so normal to us. Try the following activity to gain insight into your own cultural norms.

Activity

Fold a sheet of notebook paper in half the long way. On the left side, state the values and beliefs you hold most dear. On the right side, briefly state how you practice or live out each of them. For instance, give examples of how you practice them. Then review both sides, noting as you go any statements that seem particularly narrow or finite. Inspect your more absolute ways of believing and valuing to see if you have a blind spot that may interfere in teaching a culturally diverse group of students. Think of how you might compensate for that blind spot.

Second-Language Acquisition and Learning

The distinction between second-language acquisition and second-language learning is not simply a dichotomous one; it is more like a continuum, with the two terms serving as the imaginary poles. However, the distinction is useful in drawing attention to Krashen's (1989) claim that second-language development is more a matter of acquisition than of learning through formal methods.

According to Gee (1996), "Acquisition is a process of acquiring something (usually subconsciously) by exposure to models, a process of trial and error, and practice within social groups, without formal teaching" (p. 138). For example, first-language development for native English speakers is primarily a matter of acquisition, though as most of us remember from classes in English grammar, some formal schooling was also involved. Like Gee (1996), we believe that we are better at performing what we *acquire* than what we *learn*:

> For most of us, playing a musical instrument, or dancing, or using a second language, are skills we attained by some mixture of acquisition and learning. But it is a safe bet that, over the same amount of time, people are better at (performing) these activities if acquisition predominated during that time. (p. 139)

We also believe language differences should be more than tolerated; they need to be celebrated and affirmed. As teachers, we need to help students appreciate that having two or more languages or dialects at their command gives them the prerogative to choose from among them as circumstances dictate. To literacy educator David Bloome's (1992) way of thinking,

> We need to replace the LEP (limited English proficiency) mentality with the LTEP (limited to English proficiency) mentality. Bilingualism and multilingualism need to be viewed as normal, healthy, and prevalent states of life (both for individuals and for communities). Monolingualism needs to be viewed as the aberration. (p. 7)

To appreciate the implications of Bloome's thinking for content teaching and learning, it helps to familiarize yourself with the major approaches to educating second-language learners. Advocates of sheltered English, content-based ESL, transitional bilingual, and two-way bilingual programs express strong rationales for preferring one type of instruction to another. With California's passage of Proposition 227 decreeing English-only instruction in the waning years of the past century, educators have had to rethink what it means to teach students whose primary or native language (L1) is something other than English. Because sheltered English instruction is increasingly the approach of choice in school districts throughout the United States (Echevarria, Vogt, & Short, 2000), we devote a proportionately greater amount of attention to it here. We include briefer descriptions of other approaches, however, because of their viability and presence in the research literature on bilingual education (Garcia, 2000; Ovado, 2003).

SHELTERED ENGLISH INSTRUCTION   We are living in a time when adolescents' language backgrounds are becoming increasingly diverse but those of their teachers are not. What happens to students who come to school without the proficiency in English to keep up with their peers in the various subject matter areas? How are such students expected to meet the high standards set by state and national reform movements? More and more frequently, schools are turning to sheltered English instruction as an approach that prepares ELLs to comprehend the content of their subject matter classes at the same time that they receive instruction in reading, writing, speaking, and listening in English.

Through various adaptations in their instruction, English-speaking teachers are able to adjust the language demands put on students who are not yet fluent in English but who, with supportive teaching techniques, can understand grade-level content standards and concepts (Echevarria, Vogt, & Short, 2000). These adjustments may include scaffolding their instruction (e.g., modeling teacher thinking, providing analogies, and elaborating on student responses), providing necessary background information and experiences, and organizing their lessons in ways that simplify syntactic structures (e.g., using more active than passive verbs). Teachers in sheltered classrooms may also employ strategies that emphasize visual cues and other concrete means for helping students apply what they know in their primary language to learning content in English. Students are expected to gain proficiency enough to enter mainstream classes in one year (Mora, Wink, & Wink, 2001).

The downside of sheltered English instruction is that "many ELLs receive much of their instruction from content area teachers or aides who have not had appropriate professional development to address their second-language development needs" (Echevarria, Vogt, & Short, 2000, p. 4). The demand for teachers knowledgeable in the implementation of sheltered English instruction simply exceeds the supply. The sheltered approach to teaching involves many of the same instructional methods and strategies that regular classroom teachers use with no attention given to adapting these methods and strategies that are necessary for linguistically and culturally responsive instruction. Without knowledge of the ELL's second-language development needs, a teacher is at a distinct disadvantage, as is the learner who is the recipient of such instruction. Literacy coaches can be of help here.

In schools that have initiated systemwide sheltered instruction taught by appropriately educated staff, the story is quite different. In these schools, it is highly likely that

Literacy Coaches' Corner

Supporting Classroom Teachers

Drawing from a brief distributed by the Literacy Coach Clearinghouse, Escamilla (2007) outlined five issues that literacy coaches often encounter when attempting to support classroom teachers who are responsible for adapting their instruction to meet the needs of English language learners. We agree with Escamilla's thinking and would extend it a bit by adding that these are issues that teachers would benefit from exploring with literacy coaches in their school.

■ **Issue 1: The sameness platitude, or "Good teaching is just good teaching" (p. 1).** This idea wrongly assumes that how native English speakers learn to decode and comprehend will transfer seamlessly to speakers of other languages.

■ **Issue 2: Oral language before literacy? No.** Escamilla points out that "current thinking encourages teachers to teach ELLs to learn to comprehend, speak, read, and write English simultaneously, and that it is not necessary to delay literacy instruction in English while children are learning to understand and speak English" (p. 2).

■ **Issue 3: The native language: A scaffold or a barrier?** Citing research that shows ELLs

comprehend a selection written in English better if they are allowed to discuss it in their native language, Escamilla concludes that by "allowing time and opportunities to process what [students] are learning in their first language [scaffolding] serves two purposes—that of enhancing learning and the validation that [one's] native language is welcome in a classroom" (p. 4).

■ **Issue 4: Beginning ELLs' needs are different from those of more advanced ELLs.** Escamilla concurs and states that "contrary to current practice . . . oral ESL for advanced ELLs needs to be qualitatively and quantitatively different for advanced ELLs than for beginners. ESL can and should be integrated into literacy instruction for advanced learners" (p. 5).

■ **Issue 5: Cultural schema.** According to Escamilla, cultural schema are often equated to students' background knowledge. This is unfortunate, given that teachers are typically cultural insiders and therefore often do not "recognize the cultural messages inherent in many texts that may cause confusion for ELLs; [however] it is important that teachers learn to analyze the books and stories that students are reading for cultural schema as well as background knowledge" (p. 5).

students whose first language is other than English will acquire academic literacy through instruction that shows them how to pool their emerging knowledge of English with what they know about the content and the tasks necessary for comprehending that content. The sheltered instruction observational protocol (SIOP) model (Echevarria,

Vogt, & Short, 2000) is one example of a well-researched tool for planning and implementing sheltered English instruction in subject matter classrooms. Originally designed as an observation instrument, the SIOP is also used as a source of concrete examples of the features of sheltered instruction that make it possible for ELLs to acquire a second language and academic content simultaneously. Specific suggestions and strategies that take into account sheltered English instruction can be found in Chapters 4 and 6–10.

CONTENT-BASED ESL   This instructional approach uses academic content (sometimes packaged thematically) as a vehicle for second-language learning. Unlike sheltered English instruction, in which ELLs work alongside their native-English-speaking peers, students enrolled in content-based ESL classes are all ELLs. Also, unlike sheltered instruction, in which content learning and language development are merged, the primary goal of content-based ESL instruction is to prepare ELLs for regular English-medium classrooms (Echevarria, Vogt, & Short, 2000). The two approaches, however, do share a common problem: The demand for ESL and sheltered English teachers far exceeds the supply.

ESL teachers, who typically are monolingual English speakers, often serve as "cultural brokers" by introducing learners to the mainstream culture as well as to the English language (Adamson, 1993). Critics of ESL programs charge that students are unable to keep up with their mainstream peers because they are pulled out of their content area classes and taught by teachers who emphasize English as a second language over subject matter learning.

BILINGUAL PROGRAMS   In the United States, about 80 percent of the 5 million students identified as English language learners are enrolled in programs that provide little or no support for learning in their native languages (Escamilla, 2007). This fact, coupled with research that suggests "the 'best' ways to support ELLs remain controversial" (Jacobs, 2008, p. 21), gives us pause.

Although uncommon, bilingual programs are known to contribute positively to language-minority students' long-term academic achievement, but not through any large-scale transfer of literacy skills from first- to second-language processing. Bernhardt (2003) claims that literacy researchers have for too long overgeneralized the sameness in first- and second-language (L1 and L2) reading processes. The tendency to do this, she argues, ignores the fact that "the mere existence of a *first*-language . . . renders the *second*-language reading process considerably different from the first-language reading process because of the nature of information stored in memory" (p. 112).

A National Study of School Effectiveness for Language Minority Students' Long-Term Academic Achievement, published by the Center for Research on Education, Diversity and Excellence (2003a), found that bilingual programs that were sustained for five to six years assisted ELLs in maintaining the greatest gains in both their native language and English in all content areas. Moreover, the fewest high school dropouts came from these programs. ELLs who attended only English mainstream programs were the most likely students to drop out of school. When ELLs who had been schooled in all-English-medium programs (e.g., ESL and sheltered English) first exited a language support program, they outperformed their peers in bilingual programs when tested in English. However, by the middle school years, ELLs schooled in bilingual programs reached the same achievement levels as ELLs schooled all in English, and by high school they outperformed them. Thomas and Collier (2002), the researchers who conducted the study, note:

> In order to close the average achievement gap between ELLs and native English speakers, language support programs must be well implemented, . . . sustained for 5–6 years, and demonstrate achievement gains of more than the average yearly progress of the non-ELL group each year until the gap is closed. Even the most effective language support programs can only close half of the achievement gap in 2–3 years. (pp. 3–4)

Dialect Differences

In the classroom communities in which we work, dialect is frequently the most salient feature of cultural diversity, and it is often a contentious issue. The dilemma is twofold: How does one teach the codes of power while at the same time respecting students' culture and language? How does one disentangle form and meaning in language? Dialect can be a very powerful way of expressing meaning; at the same time, it can be a powerful barrier to communication. Bidialectical speakers—that is, individuals who are facile in using both dialect and standard forms of English—recognize this dilemma, but they also know how advantageous it is to own more than one language.

Evidence-Based Research   We think Gloria Ladson-Billings (1994) presents a useful way of thinking about dialect differences in her book *The Dreamkeepers*. Ladson-Billings describes the classroom practices of eight teachers who differ in personal style and methods but who share an ability to teach in a manner that affirms and reinforces African American students' belief in themselves and their cultural identities. Patricia Hilliard, one of the eight teachers in Ladson-Billings's study, is an African American teacher who has taught in both public and private schools in a large urban area. Like Lisa Delpit (1995), Hilliard is wary of instructional approaches that fail "to make students cognizant of the power of language and the language of power" (Ladson-Billings, 1994, p. 82). In Hilliard's words (cited in Ladson-Billings, 1994),

> I get so sick and tired of people trying to tell me that my children don't need to use any language other than the one they come to school with. Then those same people turn right around and judge the children negatively because of the way they express themselves. My job is to make sure that they can use *both* languages, that they understand that their language is valid but that the demands placed upon them by others mean that they will constantly have to prove their worth. We spend a lot of time talking about language, what it means, how you can use it, and how it can be used against you. (p. 82)

One way that Patricia Hilliard affirms and reinforces her students' cultural identities while she simultaneously teaches them the value of knowing both dialect and standard forms of English is through an activity that involves what she calls the "translation" process. Placing a transparency of the lyrics of students' favorite rap on the overhead projector (double-spaced so she can write between the lines), Hilliard proceeds to engage them in a translation activity. In talking with students about the process, she compares it to what interpreters do when they translate from one language to another. Hilliard (cited in Ladson-Billings, 1994) explains her objective for doing the activity as follows:

> I want the children to see that they have some valuable knowledge to contribute. I don't want them to be ashamed of what they know but I also want them to know and be comfortable with what school and the rest of the society requires. When I put it in the context of "translation" they get excited. They see it is possible to go from one to the other. It's not that they are not familiar with Standard English. . . . They hear Standard English all the time on TV. It's certainly what I use in the classroom. But there is rarely any connection made between the way they speak and Standard English. I think that when they can see the connections and know that they can make the shifts, they become better at both. They're bilingual! (p. 84)

The point that Patricia Hilliard is making is one that linguists also make; that is, we are all speakers of one dialect or another. Whose dialect counts is often a matter of politics, however. Addressing this issue, Wayne O'Neil (1998), head of the Department of Linguistics and Philosophy at the Massachusetts Institute of Technology, wrote the following in response to the public's outrage over a school board's resolution to teach Ebonics in Oakland, California, in 1996:

> We assume . . . that there are standard versions of [all] languages, the pinnacles that each dialect speaker is supposed to aspire to, but that which normally—for reasons of class, or race, or geography—she or he is not able to reach. On this view, dialects are diminished varieties of a standard ("legitimate") language, a value judgment that has no standing in linguistics. For, on the scientific point of view, all . . . languages are rule-governed systems of equal complexity and interest—instantiations of the capacity for language that each infant enters the world with. (p. 41)

Ebonics, commonly known among linguists as Black English or African American Vernacular English (AAVE), was the term used in the Oakland school board resolution. Although members of the board never intended for Ebonics to replace Standard English, the media's distortion of the resolution led to this interpretation (Perry & Delpit, 1998). Amid much furor and heated debates through the press and TV talk shows, African Americans appeared divided on the issue. In addressing this divisiveness and the implications of Ebonics for teachers, the well-known African American educator Lisa Delpit (1998) stated,

> I have been asked often enough recently, "What do you think about Ebonics? Are you for it or against it?" My answer must be neither. . . . It exists. It is the language spoken by many of our African American children. It is the language they heard as their mothers nursed

them and changed their diapers and played peek-a-boo with them. It is the language through which they first encountered love, nurturance, and joy. (p. 17)

Delpit went on to add, however, that she, like most teachers and parents, believes that children who are not taught the power code of Standard English will not have equal access to good jobs and leadership positions. Therefore, Delpit recommends the following: Help children who speak Ebonics learn Standard English so that through acquiring an additional form of linguistic expression, they will be able to code switch when necessary and still retain pride in the language with which they grew up.

Struggling or Reluctant Readers

We are all struggling or reluctant readers at times. Reflect for a moment on the type of text you struggle with or are reluctant to put much effort into understanding. Perhaps it is the owner's manual for your new computer, the technical jargon in the latest consumer price index, or the symbolism in a much touted film that all of your friends are wild about. Whatever your struggle or reluctance, it typically consists of more than an ability to decode text, broadly defined. The same is true for adolescents who struggle with reading or are reluctant to approach a task that reminds them of past struggles and perhaps even failure.

Even with the best literacy instruction in the early grades, some adolescents will enter secondary school with numerous and debilitating reading difficulties. These difficulties may be associated with poor motivation, low self-esteem, inadequate cognitive processing strategies, underdeveloped technical vocabularies, boredom with a curriculum that seemingly has little relevance to their everyday lives, and so on. For the purposes of this book, we are less interested in the causes of reading difficulties than with the instructional strategies and activities that teachers can use in working with struggling readers.

Staying focused on what adolescents who struggle with reading bring to their coursework is an important instructional principle—one that is backed by years of research and practice (Moore, Alvermann, & Hinchman, 2000; Readence, Moore, & Rickelman, 2000). In fact, many of the teachers we know take struggling readers' prior knowledge into consideration when planning instruction, teaching content, and assessing learning. Examples of how they do this can be found in Chapters 4–6. Here, we focus on some general principles of instruction that we believe are helpful when working with adolescents who struggle with reading.

For example, we believe that scaffolding instruction through appropriate comprehension monitoring, self-questioning, and small-group discussion strategies (Palincsar, 1986; Rothenberg & Watts, 2000) provides struggling readers with the support they need to comprehend the content of their subject matter classes. We also believe that direct instruction in vocabulary (Harmon, 2000), summarizing, using text structure, and certain information-processing strategies, such as those outlined in Flood and Lapp (2000), can make a difference in struggling readers' comprehension of their assigned readings. Finally, we believe struggling adolescent readers benefit from instruction that facilitates writing across the curriculum (Andrews, 2000), provides access to a range of reading materials (Bintz, 1993; Ivey, 1999b), and encourages them to participate in their own assessment, such as engaging in portfolio conferences (Young et al., 2000). These strategies, as well as others, are highlighted in the chapters that follow, along with examples of their application in actual classroom practice and how to teach them, taking struggling readers' needs into account.

Before concluding this section, a caveat is in order. We believe, like Ivey (1999a), that "whereas terminology or categories such as problem, average, superior, or low, middle, high may provide a general sense of how much students have developed as readers, they offer limited information about the complexities of individual experiences" (p. 188). Thus, planning instruction based on how a student has been labeled as a reader (e.g., struggling, low, disabled) is a practice that lacks pedagogical soundness.

Gifted Learners

By definition, *gifted and talented students* in the United States are "children or youth who give evidence of high achievement capability in areas such as intellectual, creative, artistic, or leadership capacity, or in specific academic fields, and who need services and activities not ordinarily provided by the school in order to fully develop those capabilities" (National Association for Gifted Children, www.nagc.org/index.aspx?id=565, n.p.) Unlike the Striving Readers program (www.ed.gov/programs/strivingreaders/funding .html), which is federally funded and assists states and local education agencies in providing services to secondary students who struggle with reading, funding decisions that affect gifted and talented youth are made largely at the state level. (For an interesting state-by-state comparison of the programs and services for the gifted and talented in the United States, visit the following website: www.nagc.org/index.aspx?id=37.)

The nation's response to educating the gifted has historical underpinnings that are perhaps best captured in Richard Hofstadter's (1970) *Anti-Intellectualism in American Life.* Extending Alexis de Tocqueville's (1833/1983) characterization of American democracy in antebellum times, Hofstadter wrote,

> Again and again . . . it has been noticed that intellect in America is resented as a kind of excellence, as a claim to distinction, as a challenge to egalitarianism, as a quality which almost certainly deprives a man or woman of the common touch. (p. 51)

In short, intellect is viewed as "foreign to a society built on practicality and consensual understandings" (Resnick & Goodman, 1994, p. 110). In such a culture, gifted young people tend to stand out as special.

This label of exceptionality has brought with it a host of tensions tied to issues of social and economic inequality. For example, placements in gifted and talented classes reflect an underrepresentation of minority and poor children (Mehan, 1991). They also reflect the misguided practice of automatically assigning ELLs to basic or general-level classes, rather than gifted classes, because their proficiency in the dominant language (English) fuels the perception that they are incapable of handling a challenging curriculum.

Regardless of how restrictive or flexible one's definition of giftedness, adolescents who are highly creative and insightful will benefit from literacy instruction that offers opportunities for independent inquiry using the Internet, innovative problem solving, and expressive writing—activities that should be a part of all classrooms but especially those in which gifted and talented students live and work (Ruddell, 1997). Keeping in mind that students of high ability who come from different cultures or from backgrounds of extreme poverty have the same potential to succeed as those students from the dominant culture will ensure that they have equal access to all literacy practices, not just those of a basic nature.

Teaching and Learning in Culturally Diverse Classrooms

Go to MyEduca-tionLab and select the topic *Diversity, Culture, and Literacy*. Then, go to the Activities and Applications section, watch the video entitled "Cultural & Language Experiences," and respond to the accompanying prompts.

Although we weave suggestions for teaching culturally diverse students throughout this book, we focus here on the major challenges to improving literacy in adolescent ELLs and of integrating language, culture, and content in teaching culturally diverse students. However, first we invite you to consider the range of cultural diversity present among today's youth and the implications of this for you as a classroom teacher. Such consideration will no doubt heighten your awareness of the need to gear up to teach content reading and literacy in ways that are culturally relevant for all students, not just those who are most like you.

Today's Globalizing Influences

Each moment that teachers spend interacting with adolescents in content area classrooms is embedded in what social anthropologists Vered Amit-Talai and Helena Wulff (1995) refer to as "a range of cultural possibilities" (p. 231). They use this term to express the view that youth culture cannot be localized (and taught to) as if the classroom were a separate world of its own. Youth culture is produced at home, in school, on the streets, with friends, in malls, among siblings, through TV, music, and the Internet, and so on. To ignore this fact is to teach as if "teachers and students relate to one another undistracted by the classism, racism, and sexism that rage outside the classroom" (Brodkey, 1989, p. 139).

Although we discussed diversity issues that dealt with language, reading ability, and achievement motivation in the previous section, we barely touched the surface of the diversity present in today's youth culture. Consider, for example, the differences in working-class youth's discourse and school discourse. Patrick Finn (1999), an educator born into a working-class Irish Catholic family on the south side of Chicago, has devoted a lifetime to exploring these differences and what they mean for literacy teaching and learning. According to Finn, there are two kinds of education in the United States:

> First, there is empowering education, which leads to powerful literacy, the kind of literacy that leads to positions of power and authority. Second, there is domesticating education, which leads to functional literacy, or literacy that makes a person productive and dependable, but not troublesome. (pp. ix–x)

Arguing against the second kind, which is based in conspiracy theory, Finn places the responsibility on schools for educating all youth in ways that are empowering, not simply domesticating.

Differences also abound in how adolescents view themselves in terms of ethnic identity. For example, among Hispanics (a label given to diverse groups of people by the federal government 30 years ago), popular youth culture has proclaimed a "Latino/Latina Revolution" led by Ricky Martin, Jennifer Lopez, and Christina Aguilera (Trujillo, 2000). According to Trujillo, a poll taken by the vice president of quepasa.com revealed that of 5,000 people responding, 37 percent chose to be identified as *Latino*, 31 percent as *Hispanic*, and the remaining 32 percent as *Mexican, Cuban, Puerto Rican*, or whatever their national origin. Among Native Americans, as well as among Asian and Asian American youth, there is also the problem of being grouped together as if there were no differences among tribal groups or countries of national origin. Teachers who take the time to understand the differences between the Hopis and the Apaches or between Vietnamese and Chinese youth, for example, are on the road to achieving a more equitable and culturally responsive pedagogy (Henze & Hauser, 1999).

Finally, in matters of sexual orientation, differences also exist among heterosexual, gay, lesbian, bisexual, and transgender communities of people. Although sexual orientation is not typically a category to which authors of content area reading texts devote space, we include it here because of its place in the wider spectrum of multicultural education and because of the increasing number of publications dealing with homosexuality (Allan, 1999; Young, 2000) in professional journals focused on literacy teaching and learning. Whether coming from homes with gay or lesbian parents or embracing their own issues of sexual orientation, teenagers today need teachers who are as accepting of them and their literacy needs (e.g., appropriate reading materials and informational texts) as they are of students from various racial, ethnic, socioeconomic, linguistic, and religious backgrounds.

Improving Literacy in Adolescent ELLs

In recognition of the rising number of newcomers to the United States, other demographic trends, and changing demands brought on by a quickly globalizing economy, the Carnegie Corporation of New York commissioned a report from the Alliance for Excellent Education titled *Double the Work: Challenges and Solutions to Acquiring Language and Academic Literacy for Adolescent English Language Learners* (Short & Fitzsimmons, 2007). The authors of this report concluded the following:

Evidence-Based Research

> Although many strategies for supporting literacy in native English speakers are applicable to adolescent ELLs, there are significant differences in the way that successful literacy interventions for the latter group should be designed and implemented. These differences have serious implications for teachers, instructional leaders, curriculum designers, administrators, and policymakers at all levels of government. Moreover, because adolescent ELLs are a diverse group of learners in terms of their educational backgrounds, native language literacy, socioeconomic status, and more, some strategies will work for certain ELLs but not for others. (p. 1)

Several factors contributed to this conclusion—among them, the six challenges to improving adolescent literacy in adolescent ELLs identified in the following list. Following each challenge, we provide a brief summary of potential solutions, as described in *Double the Work*:

1. **Lack of common criteria for identifying ELLs and tracking their academic performance.** Individual states vary widely in their interpretation of the U.S. Department of Education's definition of limited English proficiency students (LEPs), which is the federal government's term for English language learners. According to that definition, ELLs are students between the ages of 3 and 21 who are "enrolled in elementary or secondary education, often born outside the United States or speaking a language other than English in their homes, and not having sufficient mastery of English to meet state standards and excel in an English-language classroom" (Short & Fitzsimmons, 2007, p. 14). Possible solutions to this challenge include the development of standards, or benchmarks, for determining correct identification and placements of these students.

2. **Lack of appropriate assessments.** Although this challenge is addressed more fully in Chapter 5 of your text, briefly, it stems from the fact that "standardized tests that aim to measure academic knowledge (e.g., math, science, literacy) are not sensitive to second language literacy development" (Short & Fitzsimmons, 2007, p. 18). Likely solutions to this challenge are the use of diagnostic assessments in the student's native language and in English, multiple measures of a student's language proficiency, and testing accommodations for ELLs.

3. **Inadequate educator capacity for improving literacy in ELLs.** Very few teachers have had initial training or professional development in teaching adolescents whose first language is something other than English. Only three states (Arizona, California, and Florida) have enacted policies that ensure that schools of teacher education will provide coursework and/or experiences that will help teacher candidates to work successfully with ELLs. Solutions to the challenge posed by inadequate educator capacity include professional development in teaching ELLs and the hiring of literacy coaches to assist teachers in adding appropriate accommodations for ELLs in daily lesson plans.

4. Lack of appropriate and flexible program options. Because most ELLs will require four to seven years of instruction in academic English to reach the average academic performance of a native English speaker, extra time must be allotted (when needed) for finishing high school. As Short and Fitzsimmons (2007) emphasize, "Finding an appropriate program that will accelerate [ELLs'] English language development and let them make progress in content-area coursework is the ultimate goal" (p. 27).

5. Inadequate use of research-based instructional practices. Although the research on effective literacy instruction for ELLs is relatively limited, there is sufficient evidence to show that "the instructional methods that secondary school teachers have typically used do *not* [emphasis in original] facilitate learning or literacy instruction for ELLs" (Short & Fitzsimmons, 2007, p. 33). Specifically, lectures and worksheets are insufficient, as are the cluttered pages of textbooks. Possible solutions include integrating reading, writing, listening, and speaking across the curriculum; explicitly teaching comprehension strategies as aids to understanding assigned texts; building background knowledge; focusing on vocabulary development; and using technology and choice as motivators. All of these practices are dealt with at length in the chapters that follow.

Evidence-Based Research

6. Lack of a strong and coherent research agenda about adolescent ELL literacy. Currently, there is a paucity of evaluation research on programs that were designed to serve ELLs. Specific needs exist in the following areas: studies of ELLs' out-of-school literacy practices to determine if such practices might be used to better engage students in classroom academic learning; longitudinal studies of ELLs' literacy development within different program models; and studies that focus on ELL assessment practices and graduation rates.

Integrating Language, Culture, and Content

Being able to adjust one's lesson in the midst of teaching is part of a teacher's repertoire of instructional decision-making skills. Fred Genesee (1994), who researches second-language immersion programs in the United States and Canada, cites studies showing that teachers make as many as 1,300 instructional decisions each day. These decisions are most effective when teachers integrate their subject matter expertise with what they have learned about their students' language and culture.

WHAT'S TO BE GAINED FROM THIS TYPE OF INSTRUCTION Sheltered English classrooms are considered by some educators as being the only viable means for reaching large numbers of second-language learners. They provide academic support in the second language (English), which is akin to Russian psychologist Lev Vygotsky's (1978) notion of the *zone of proximal development (ZPD)*. Envisioning ESL instruction as *scaffolding*—a temporary prop that helps move students from what they know (their native language) to what they need to know (English)—is a form of ZPD. Stated in more technical terms, the ZPD is the distance between a speaker's ability to handle English without guidance and his or her level of potential development under the guidance of more English-fluent adults or peers. The ZPD takes on added significance when one considers that ESL learners often experience "a pattern of insecurity or ambivalence about the value of their own cultural identity as a result of their interactions with the dominant group" (Cummins, 1994b, p. 45). Teachers who plan instruction with the ZPD in mind increase their chances of helping students learn to use elements of their own culture to understand those of the dominant culture.

Teachers who take into account students' cultural backgrounds, while being sensitive to the fact that not all young people from the same culture group think or respond in the same way, create favorable learning conditions in which students view themselves as capable and engaged learners. For example, in a news release that appeared soon after his ground-breaking book *Teaching Reading to Black Adolescent Males: Closing the Achievement Gap* (2005) was published, Alfred Tatum, who grew up in a poverty-stricken neighborhood in Chicago, offered the following advice to teachers:

- *Establish a broader definition of literacy instruction that guides the selection of text.* It must focus on skill and strategy knowledge, content knowledge, and identity development. "It is imperative that these young men have the requisite skills to read text independently. It is also imperative that they become 'smarter' as a result of their reading," he says.

- *Identify a core of "must-read" texts for African American adolescent males.* These include James Baldwin's *The Fire Next Time* and Ralph Ellison's *Invisible Man.*

- *Discuss texts in culturally responsive ways.* "Students benefit when they can extend the ideas contained in texts into their own lives," Tatum says.

- *Examine your disposition toward using texts with African American adolescent males.* Many teachers back down when they encounter resistance from their students to read beyond the required material, Tatum says. "However, no research currently shows that having students read less advances their academic and other literacy needs" (Northern Illinois University's Office of Public Affairs, 2005, n.p.).

TECHNOLOGY **Tip**

Making English Relevant
Students who immigrate to the United States often face challenges that extend beyond learning English as a second language. Viewing cultural and linguistic diversity as a valuable resource in a globalized world means "that we need to start thinking about diversity in the form of transculturation—the development of multiple modes of cultural belonging and participation that extends beyond national borders" (Lam, 2006, p. 188). When we think this way, we are open to helping newcomers make connections between the English they learn in school and the English they need to communicate globally through various electronic media, including social networking sites on the Internet.

Culturally Responsive Professional Growth

Appreciating Diversity

Allan Neilsen (1991) made the interesting observation that "while we often talk about differentiated curriculum and instruction for younger learners, we tend to act as though teachers, as learners, are 'all grown up' and all the same" (p. 67). That such is not the case is clearly the message Irvine (1990) hoped to get across when she wrote the following:

> Teacher education appears to be suspended in a serious time warp, training future educators in the pedagogy of decades past and pretending that . . . graduates will teach . . . highly motivated, achievement-oriented, . . . middle-class students from two-parent families. . . . By the Year 2010, 38 percent of all children will come from a minority group. Demographic data confirm that working mothers, poor single mothers, teenage mothers, declining fertility rates among white middle-class women, increasing fertility rates among poor minority women, the influx of immigrants, and the growing underclass will dramatically change how we will administer schools and teach students.
>
> Teacher education professionals must hastily respond to this problem of the growing, at-risk, minority student population, decreasing minority teacher pools, and increasing numbers of majority teacher education students. The profession must respond with the expectation that, at least in the near future, the majority of minority students' teachers will be white females who are unfamiliar with minority students' language, lifestyle, culture, family, and community. (p. 18)

Synchronizing professional growth opportunities so that they take into account the ever-widening gap between the number of minority students enrolled in school and the number of minority teachers available to instruct them in content literacy is a complex task. It involves educating all teachers—minority and nonminority—in a manner that

TECHNOLOGY Tip

Standards for Effective Pedagogy
To view a five-minute demonstration of a CD-ROM portraying a two-day high school multigrade lesson in ecological science, go to www.crede.ucsc.edu/products/multimedia/cdroms.html# and then click on "The Mara Mills Case: A Video Ethnography of Biological Science in a Sheltered English Classroom," by Annela Teemant, Stefinee Pinnegar, Roland Tharp, and Carl Harris (2001). Each study in the case highlights one of the five standards for effective pedagogy promoted by the Center for Research on Education, Diversity and Excellence (CREDE, 2003b). The teacher, students, a science educator, a second-language educator, and teacher educators all give their perspectives on teaching.

Note: You will need to have QuickTime installed on your computer for you to be able to see the live demonstration. A free copy of QuickTime can be installed by going to www.apple.com/quicktime/download.

helps them to understand the central role of culture in their lives and the lives of their students. Architects of such professional growth opportunities, Ladson-Billings (1994) argues, must ensure that teachers come away with more than a "foods-and-festivals" approach to understanding culture. She also maintains that it is foolhardy for any group to believe that "culture is what other people have; what we have is just *truth*."

Creating safe environments that foster classroom appreciation of diversity does not mean engaging in neutral discussions in which feelings of conflict or issues of power are submerged in teachers' and students' making-nice talk. On the contrary, according to Henze and Hauser (1999), such issues can (and should) be raised. They offer the following strategies for engaging in this kind of talk:

> In order to foster discussion about issues such as conflict or power, along with less emotionally charged topics relating to cultural values and practices, teachers need to establish an environment in which students feel comfortable expressing their views. Several strategies can be employed. For example, teachers can validate the knowledge of students at the outset through an activity where they create shared understandings of topics to be addressed, such as culture or ethnicity. Teachers can use self-disclosure as a way to humanize themselves and model the process of honest reflection. Another way in which many teachers establish safe conditions for dialogue is by setting up ground rules at the outset. For example, the class might agree that no individuals should dominate the conversation, that students have a right to pass if they do not want to share certain things about themselves, and that the opinions of others should be respected even if they disagree. (p. 3)

Involving Parents and Community

Parents are a child's first teacher. Thus, it makes sense that a focus on culturally responsive teaching strategies should include the need to develop parent and community partnerships in content literacy learning. In the past, a deficit model of home–school relations assumed inappropriately that schools needed to exert a good deal of influence on certain low-income parents' literate interactions with their children in order to make up for perceived inadequacies in the home. This manner of thinking has largely given way to one of mutual understanding in which each party (parents and teachers) develops an awareness of the other's specific cultural practices. As Cairney (2000) noted, "In this way schooling can be adjusted to meet the needs of families. Parents, in turn, can also be given the opportunity to observe and understand the definitions of literacy that schools support" (p. 59).

With this change in focus has come an increased appreciation of intergenerational literacy programs (Gadsden, 2000), which are rich with implications for culturally responsive teaching if we pay attention to what we can learn from them as teachers. There is also room in this new reciprocal way of thinking about home–school partnerships for students to see their cultures reflected in a positive light through both the school curriculum and culturally responsive teaching. In short, it is no longer necessary for students to endure what Rosalinda Barrera refers to as the "culturalectomies" that children of her generation experienced growing up under the deficit model of home–school relations (Jimenez et al., 1999, p. 217).

However, communicating with parents who are from a culture different from one's own can present challenges at times. For example, we are reminded of a research study that Lee Gunderson (2000) conducted, in which he interviewed teenagers from various immigrant groups (refugees, landed immigrants, and entrepreneurs). What he learned about these youth, their parents, and himself in the process of doing this study is worth repeating here because it illustrates what all of us—firmly established citizens and newly landed immigrants alike—need to know if we are to be culturally responsive educators. In Gunderson's words,

> I am an immigrant, a Norwegian-American-Canadian. Like millions of native English-speaking individuals in Australia, Canada, New Zealand, and the United States, my parents' first culture and language, in my case Norwegian, has withered away. . . . First- and second-generation immigrants remember their struggles learning a new language and a new culture. Most often, however, they are convinced that their losses were a consequence of their heroic or pioneer-like efforts to forge new lives for themselves and their families. They view their losses as part of the price they have paid to become members of a new society. Their willingness to sacrifice signifies in their minds their dedication to family and to the democratic ideals of their new country. They are members of the most recognizable diasporas. . . . The individuals of the third, fourth, and fifth generations are the lost ones whose first cultures like unsettled spirits haunt their angst-filled reveries. Becoming an American, an Australian, or a Canadian means the surrender of first languages and first cultures. Children and grandchildren have little sense of what has been lost.
>
> Perhaps in recognizing this loss in our own lives, we will be one step further along the path to becoming culturally responsive educators. At the very least, we will have stopped a moment to consider what it might be like to walk in the shoes of the adolescents who come to our classes each day speaking a different language, holding on to cultural practices that still make sense to them, and wishing for a teacher or two who will understand all of this. (p. 693)

Linking School and Home

In their report of a study that focused on using math literacy to link home and school, Civil, Andrade, and Gonzalez (2002) emphasize the importance of teaching in ways that respect students' construction of meaning and the connections they make outside school, in the home. This approach, the researchers argue, is important for all students but in particular for those who come from economically underprivileged homes in which English is not the first language.

Viewing parents as intellectual resources, Civil, Andrade, and Gonzalez (2002) developed a series of mathematics workshops for a core group of mothers who were Mexican immigrants and for their children's teachers. The workshops, which had as their premise that "we are all learners," were jointly negotiated by the mothers and the teachers, and the information gained from them became curriculum building blocks for teaching and learning math literacy in school. For example,

> One of the [middle school] teachers used his household visits . . . to develop a sophisticated curriculum plan around the idea of "build your dream home." Through this project, students learned many of the required mathematical skills and concepts in a familiar context—that of house construction. Furthermore, several of their family members were involved in the final projects, the making of a model for their dream home. Another teacher, knowing that her students' families were quite knowledgeable about gardening, developed a theme centered on this topic. This theme allowed her to explore in depth topics in measurement, geometry, and graphing, that while they are grade-appropriate, they are often barely touched on. (www.crede.ucsc.edu/research/md/4.2es.html, no page given)

Evidence-Based Research

English teachers, like the mathematics teachers in the preceding example, can also support second-language learners by providing prompt and helpful feedback on their written language. When editing the writing of ELLs, Carroll et al. (1996) recommend that teachers focus on the students' rich and colorful language, rather than simply correcting their grammatical errors. This attention to the positive aspects of second-language learners' written work will demonstrate "acknowledgment and respect for immigrant/ELL students, their families, their experiences and the language they use at home and in their communities" (Rubenstein-Avila, 2003, p. 133).

Summary

Envisioning language as social practice opens the door to new ways of thinking about content literacy teaching and learning in culturally diverse classrooms. With this envisioning comes an awareness of students' different ways of dialoging with the world. Listening to students' views, and especially to the views of those who come from linguistic and ethnic minority backgrounds, can provide important clues about what is valued or devalued in the curriculum and why (Nieto, 1994).

Just as the sorting practices of the school present their own special set of challenges, so too do the demographic changes in the U.S. student population. English language learners represent one of the fastest-growing groups of students in U.S. secondary schools. According to the National Clearinghouse for English Acquisition and Language Instruction Educational Programs, English language learners as a whole speak more than 460 different languages and represent multiple countries that include Mexico, Vietnam, Laos, China, Korea, Russia, Haiti, and Japan, among others (www.ncela.gwu.edu/resabout/ells/1_characteristics.htm, n.p.). According to the *2008 Conditions of Education* report, Hispanic youth alone now represent one in five public school students (http://nces.ed.gov/programs/coe/press/index.asp).

At the same time, there are far too few teachers who have expertise teaching second-language students. Because some ELLs may have unique needs that are not shared by struggling readers who are native English speakers (Harper & de Jong, 2004), it is imperative that teachers add appropriate accommodations for ELLs in their daily lesson plans.

Suggested Readings

Baker, J. (2002). Trilingualism. In L. Delpit & J. K. Dowdy (Eds.), *The skin that we speak: Thoughts on language and culture in the classroom* (pp. 49–61). New York: New Press.

Bernhardt, E. (2003). Challenges to reading research from a multilingual world. *Reading Research Quarterly, 38*(1), 112–117.

Delpit, L. (2002). No kinda sense. In L. Delpit & J. K. Dowdy (Eds.), *The skin that we speak: Thoughts on language and culture in the classroom* (pp. 31–48). New York: New Press.

Flores-Gonzalez, N. (2002). *School kids/street kids: Identity development in Latino students.* New York: Teachers College Press.

Gandara, P., Maxwell-Jolly, J., & Driscoll, A. (2005). *Listening to teachers of English language learners: A survey of California teachers' challenges, experiences, and professional development needs.* Santa Cruz, CA: Center for the Future of Teaching and Learning.

Jimenez, R. T. (2003). Literacy and Latino students in the United States: Some considerations, questions, and new directions. *Reading Research Quarterly, 38,* 122–128.

Mason, P. A., & Schumm, J. S. (Eds.). (2003). *Promising practices for urban reading instruction.* Newark, DE: International Reading Association.

Palmer, B. C., Shackelford, V. S., Miller, S. C., & Leclere, J. T. (2007). Bridging two worlds: Reading comprehension, figurative language instruction, and the English-language learner. *Journal of Adolescent and Adult Literacy, 50,* 258–267.

Rickford, J., & Rickford, A. (1995). Dialect readers revisited. *Linguistics and Education, 7,* 107–128.

MyEducationLab is a research-based learning tool that brings teaching to life. Go to the Alvermann, Phelps, and Ridgeway Gillis 6th Edition MyEducationLab for Content Area Reading site at www.myeducationlab.com to:

- engage in multimedia exercises to help you build a deeper and more applied understanding of chapter content;

- utilize extensive resources including videos from real classrooms, Praxis and licensure preparation, a lesson plan builder, and materials to help you in your teaching career.

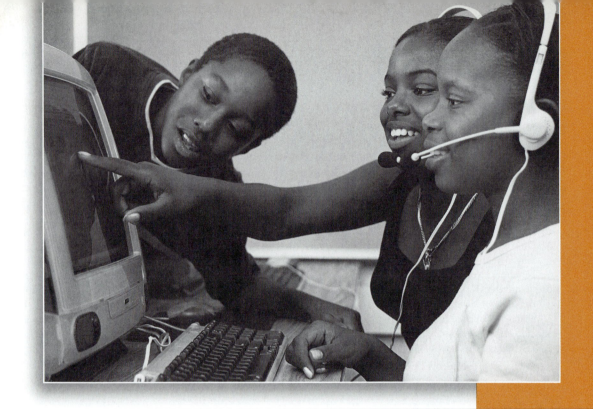

chapter **3**

Creating a
Favorable Learning
Environment

Creating a Favorable Learning Environment

Affective Characteristics

- Linking Content Literacy with Students' Lives
- Adaptive Instruction
- Providing Choices

Forms of Grouping

- Ability Grouping
- Cooperative Learning
- Cross-Age Tutoring
- Discussion Groups
- Reading and Writing Workshops

Creating Community with Technology and Multimedia

- Technology
- Multimedia
- Assistive Technology

Conflict Resolution

- What the Research Says
- Strategies for Managing Conflict

Anticipation Guide

Directions: Read each of the following statements. Place a checkmark on the line in the "Before Reading" column if you agree with the statement; leave it blank if you disagree. Then predict what you think the chapter will be about, and jot down on a sticky note (or post online) any questions you have. Read the chapter; then return to the statements and respond to them as you think the authors of your text would. Place a checkmark on the line in the "Authors' Stance" column if you believe the authors would agree with the statement. If you discuss these statements with other people online, in class, or at the family dinner table, return to the statements and check any items you agree with in the right-hand column, "After Discussion." If your thinking changed, what caused that change?

Before Reading	Authors' Stance	Statements	After Discussion
_____	_____	1. Linking the content to be learned in school to students' lives is one way to motivate students to learn.	_____
_____	_____	2. Tracking students creates inherently unequal educational experiences for both accelerated and struggling students.	_____
_____	_____	3. Students should actively set their own learning goals and evaluate their progress toward those goals.	_____
_____	_____	4. Cooperative learning helps students take responsibility for their own learning.	_____
_____	_____	5. In today's world, reading nonprint messages is as important as reading print messages.	_____

Creating a favorable learning environment involves more than just teaching to the standards. Although standards are important, Todd Goodson, a professor at Kansas State University, reminds us in his account of "Teaching in the Time of Dogs" that it is the time we spend responding to the spontaneity of students' concerns that must be our starting point. For "in the classroom there's one thing you can be sure of," writes Goodson (2004), "and that's that anything can happen."

● ● ●

Teaching in the Time of Dogs

by Todd Goodson

A number of years ago, I was a middle school teacher. One morning I was standing outside my classroom as my first-hour group assembled when one of my students approached me in tears.

"Mr. Goodson," she sobbed, "I think my neighbor skinned his dog."

As she stood there crying, and I stood there looking at her, it occurred to me at that moment that I really had no clue how to handle this situation. I knew there were interpersonal and cultural and ethical and perhaps even legal issues unfolding in front of me, but I didn't even know what they were, much less what I, as a teacher, was obligated to do. But as a crowd of curious middle-schoolers gathered around us, I knew I had to do something. I decided to start with the obvious question.

"What makes you think your neighbor skinned his dog?" I asked.

"Because it's hanging from his clothesline," she wailed.

Her answer didn't help my state of mind all that much. For a moment I wondered whether it was the neighbor's *dog's skin* or the neighbor's *skinned dog* hanging from the clothesline, but I decided it probably didn't matter. (Except, of course, to the dog.) The real problem at the moment was my student, still standing there, crying, waiting for me to resolve this matter. I decided on a bold course of action.

"Have you told your mother about this?" I asked.

She shook her head no. "I saw it on my way to school," she said.

"Why don't you go down to the office and call your mother?" I suggested, and I was more than a little grateful when she nodded and turned away, leaving me to curse those idiot education professors who didn't prepare me for this encounter.

A few minutes after she left to call her mother, she came back to my classroom. She wasn't upset anymore. In fact she bounced to her seat and started whispering and giggling with her friends. I drifted through the room and back to her seat.

"Is everything all right?" I asked, now thoroughly puzzled by her dramatic change in mood.

She seemed confused, as if she didn't know what I was talking about.

"Your neighbor's dog," I reminded her.

"Oh, yeah," she said. "It was just a coyote."

"Great," I said. And I suppose it probably was. (Except, of course, for the coyote.)

Years passed. Today I'm an "idiot education professor," trying to figure out a way to teach young people things they can only really learn from experience and writing about the curious magic of literacy and its teaching.

Note: To read more than this excerpt from "Teaching in the Time of Dogs," visit www.writingproject.org/cs/nwpp/print/nwpr/1979.

● ● ●

As you read this chapter keep Goodson's story in mind, and remember that "the art of teaching, like the art of writing, lies as much in how we respond to the irregular as in how we plan to create regularity" (Goodson, 2004, n.p.).

Affective Characteristics

A favorable learning environment supports students as they grapple with issues of affect that influence how they feel about school and their willingness to engage in academic activities. Affective characteristics of instruction that concern teachers in this kind of environment include those of linking content literacy with students' lives and providing students with choices. In advocating that classrooms become places in which the integration of heart, head, voice, and hand is the norm rather than the exception, Shelby Wolf and colleagues (Wolf, Edmiston, & Enciso, 1997) remind us of the need to teach in a manner that joins the cognitive and affective domains of knowing. As Vygotsky (1986) has written,

> Thought is not begotten by thought; it is engendered by motivation, i.e., by our desires and needs, our interests and emotions. Behind every thought there is an affective-volitional tendency, which holds the answer to the last "why" in the analysis of thinking. A true and full understanding of another's thought is possible only when we understand its affective-volitional basis. (p. 252)

We know from our own experiences as teachers the validity of Vygotsky's thinking. Time and time again, we have learned to rely on the affective currents in our classrooms as guideposts to what is possible in the cognitive domain. Working hard not to separate the cognitive from the affective is a way of life. It is an approach to teaching that we find both challenging and rewarding.

Linking Content Literacy with Students' Lives

THE LEARNING CYCLE   Creating a favorable learning environment, to our way of thinking, should involve helping students link content literacy learning to their own lives. One way of assisting them in this process is to think of learning as being "controlled as much by experiences students bring to the learning situation as it is by the way the information is presented" (Marshall, 1996, p. 81). This view of learning, which Marshall calls the *learning cycle* (see Figure 3.1), rests on the notion that students' earlier learning experiences tend to dictate in large part their attitude and willingness to engage in new learning.

Like the schema-theoretic view of the reading process described in Chapter 1, the learning cycle is heavily dependent on prior knowledge. In Marshall's (1996) words,

> To understand [the learning cycle], it is easiest to begin with *prior knowledge*. Since all new learning is based on existing knowledge, the previous experiences of the students are central to the complete cycle. Furthermore, prior knowledge helps [generate] reasons for learning or not learning. Depending on *purpose* for learning, attention is directed differently. . . . *Attention* is limited; we cannot pay attention to everything in a new situation. For learning to be efficient, therefore, attention must be directed to the most important *information*. Once the information is encountered, it needs to be *understood*. . . . Finally, to be able to use new information as the basis of subsequent learning, students must use the new understanding to *modify* existing knowledge. (p. 82)

We see the learning cycle as a useful heuristic for thinking about ways to link content literacy with students' lives. First, it suggests that teachers need to take students' prior

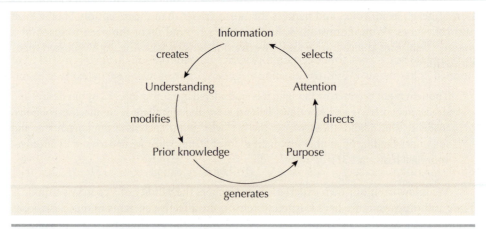

FIGURE 3.1   The Learning Cycle

Source: N. Marshall (1996). The Students: Who are they and how do I reach them? In D. Lapp, J. Flood, & N. Farnan (Eds.), *Content area reading and learning*, p. 82.) Copyright 1982 by Allyn and Bacon. Reprinted by permission.

knowledge into account when planning their instruction. Second, it implies that students will have their own purposes for engaging in (or avoiding) certain learning activities.

A closer look at the learning cycle suggests that teaching and learning are not simply mirror processes. As Wenger (1998) points out, instruction itself does not cause learning; instead, it creates the conditions and context in which learning can take place:

> Learning and teaching are not inherently linked. Much learning takes place without teaching, and indeed much teaching takes place without learning. To the extent that teaching and learning are linked in practice, the linkage is one not of cause and effect but of resources and negotiation. . . . Learning is an emergent, ongoing process, which may use teaching as one of its many structuring resources. In this regard, teachers and instructional materials become resources for learning in much more complex ways than through their pedagogical intentions. (pp. 266–267)

We like to think of teachers and instructional materials as offering opportunities for engagement in learning. Thought of in this way, teaching involves creating a favorable learning environment, one in which students become invested in their own learning. Moreover, in this kind of environment, it is often the case that the things students learn extend beyond what the teacher is hired to teach. Such learning is sometimes referred to as "stolen knowledge" (Brown & Duguid, 1996, p. 49). In other words, a literate environment contains the resources and opportunities students need to participate in a community of learners who are legitimately free to "steal" the knowledge they need to make sense of the content they are expected to acquire. As Brown and Duguid explain, the need to steal knowledge arises from the fact that "relatively little of the complex web of actual practice can be made the subject of explicit instruction" (p. 50). Much remains implicit, where it is always available to be stolen as needed.

A STRATEGY FOR LINKING CONTENT LITERACY TO STUDENTS' LIVES   Short warm-up activities can demonstrate to students the usefulness of determining what they know and do not know about a certain topic prior to reading about it. Such activities also can shed light on how willing (or unwilling) students may be to engage in learning about the topic.

For example, a strategy called Creative Thinking–Reading Activity (CT–RA) (Ruddell, 1996), which takes no more than 10 or 15 minutes to complete, offers students a chance to brainstorm solutions to the topic at hand using their everyday knowledge. This kind of activity rewards students for using ideas from their practical store of knowledge to solve textbook-related problems. The CT–RA includes the following steps (Ruddell, 1996, p. 103):

1. Develop with students the rules for brainstorming:
    a. Think of as many ideas as you can.
    b. No criticism of any ideas—even your own.
    c. Go for any freewheeling thought—the wilder the idea the better.

    d. Build on others' ideas and combine ideas when you can.

2. Give students the creative-thinking task (only one) and allow five minutes for brainstorming. For example, a task might be to estimate the amount of industrial toxins that seep into their local waterways or reservoir.

3. Share ideas in large group.

4. Announce a single criterion for students to evaluate and select an answer—for example, "Which of [the solutions to the problem] do you think is the wildest?"

5. Share these responses.

We like the CT–RA strategy because it provides spaces for English language learners (ELLs) and students who are less academically inclined to contribute their ideas— ideas that might otherwise be overlooked or dismissed. We also like it because we have observed students asking their peers for clarification in the small-group brainstorming portion of the strategy.

Evidence-Based Research

BRIDGING OUT-OF-SCHOOL LITERACIES AND CONTENT LITERACY LEARNING

Although it is not always stated, a central premise in most discussions about bridging out-of-school literacies and content area learning is that the divide between informal and formal environments is real and as such needs bridging. This is particularly significant given that the type of learning that takes place in each locale is commonly assumed to be qualitatively different. Yet Sefton-Green (2003) concluded that informal learning, while vague in terms of its pedagogic structure, "co-exists with formal learning rather than being in contradistinction to it" (p. 49). This finding was the result of a year-long study that focused on informal learning during computer gaming and chatting online among a group of boys and girls (9- to 13-year-olds) from low-income backgrounds in an out-of-school setting in the Shared Spaces Project.

School's Out! (Hull & Schultz, 2002) provides insights into the connections youth make between the literacies they use outside school and those they learn as part of the regular school curriculum. The book challenges the notion that there is a great divide between the literate practices learners use in school and out. To Hull and Schultz's way of thinking,

> Sometimes this dichotomy relegates all good things to out-of-school contexts and everything repressive to school. Sometimes it dismisses the engagement of children with nonschool learning as merely frivolous or remedial or incidental. What we want to argue . . . is that, rather than setting formal and informal education systems and contexts in opposition to each other, we might do well to look for overlap or complementarity or perhaps a respectful division of labor. (p. 3)

Policy debates over what counts as literacy (and by extension, content literacy instruction) are not only counterproductive, but they are also irrelevant if one embraces the argument made in *School's Out!* As shown repeatedly by the contributors to this book, Dewey (1899/1998) was correct in his belief that much can be learned from observing the overlap between formal education and everyday life. Without romanticizing the connections between these two worlds, *School's Out!* chronicles the tensions inherent in them and offers insights into ways of better understanding how to bridge formal and informal learning.

For example, in a chapter by Ellen Skilton-Sylvester (2002), we learn how Nan, a Cambodian girl, dealt with peer pressure and the stereotype that being interested in school writing marked her as being unpopular among her peers. In this instance, Nan's prolific out-of-school writing could have been the bridge to better in-school writing per-formance had peer pressure not intervened. As it was, much of what Nan was able to ac-complish as a writer in her home and community remained invisible to her teachers. This finding has implications for what you, as a content area teacher with students like Nan in your classroom, will need to consider as you work toward creating a favorable learning environment for all learners, including those for whom peer pressure is very much a part of their world in and out of school.

Adaptive Instruction

Teaching students how to assume responsibility for their own learning involves adapting one's instruction to fit the needs of various types of learners. Adaptive instruction is par-ticularly germane to teaching students who are members of special populations, such as English language learners, gifted students, slower learners, and students with learning disabilities. As defined by Corno and Snow (1986), adaptive teaching is student centered:

> [It] arranges environmental conditions to fit learners' individual differences. As learners gain in aptitude through experience with respect to the instructional goals at hand, such teaching adapts by becoming less intrusive. Less intrusion, less teacher or instructional mediation, increases the . . . need for more learner self-regulation. (p. 621)

Generally, adaptive instruction follows five principles (Strother, 1985):

1. Students should receive instruction based on their assessed capabilities, not their weaknesses.
2. Materials and methods should be chosen on the basis of flexibility and appeal to students' interests.
3. Students should play an active role in setting goals and evaluating their progress toward those goals.
4. Alternative activities and materials should be available for students who require additional assistance.
5. Cooperative, rather than competitive, approaches to learning should be stressed.

A point worth emphasizing here is that adapting instruction for struggling readers and English language learners should not be viewed as dumbing down the curriculum. Like Rubenstein-Avila (2003), we believe that being sensitive to the needs of youth who

Helping Struggling Readers

Writing with SPAWN Prompts

SPAWN, the acronym derived from five categories of writing options originally developed by Martin, Martin, and O'Brien (1984) and recently reintroduced by Brozo (2003), is an especially effective strategy to use with struggling readers and English language learners, who may benefit specifically from extra attention paid to their particular life experiences. The five writing options are as follows (Brozo, 2003, p. 44):

> **S**—*Special Powers.* Students are given the power to change some aspect of the text or topic. Their writing should explain *what* was changed, *why,* and the *effects* of the change.

P—*Problem Solving.* Students are asked to write possible solutions to problems posed or suggested by the books being read or material being studied.

A—*Alternative Viewpoints.* Students write about a topic or retell a story from a unique perspective.

W—*What If?* Students are asked to respond to a change the teacher has introduced in some aspect of the topic or story (an option similar to Special Powers).

N—*Next.* Students are asked to write in anticipation of what the author will discuss next, explaining the logic behind their conjecture.

struggle with reading or who are learning English as a second language "is best reflected by conveying to students that we have high expectations for all learners" (p. 129).

Adaptive instruction is common in classrooms where teachers stress the new literacies in recognition of the fact that reading and writing are always situation-specific practices yet vary within any given social context. For example, imagine a classroom where the teacher attends closely to what students actually do with texts—textbooks as well as print, digital, and visual texts that are part of the wider community in which they live, work, and play. Pahl and Rowsell (2005) suggest that when literacy is viewed as a social practice, power shifts from the teacher to include students, who share in the setting of goals and evaluating their progress toward those goals. In assessing the new literacies, especially in science and mathematics, we are able "to specify desired knowledge and skills and document their relationship to research and best practice" (Quellmalz & Haertel, 2008, p. 968).

Providing Choices

Lynn Rhodes and Nancy Shanklin (1993), two experts in literacy teaching and learning in grades K–8, say that providing students with choices in materials, activities, and time lines for finishing an assignment increases a teacher's chance of communicating genuine purposes for reading and writing. Rhodes and Shanklin also note that teachers who honor students' choices whenever possible demonstrate a willingness to listen to students.

Providing choices can extend to the kinds of questions teachers are willing to entertain. This is an area of particular interest to Donna and Steve. In our multicase study of five school sites throughout the United States, we were well aware of the questions that students and teachers considered safe or unsafe to ask (Alvermann et al., 1996b).

Self-censorship in questioning leads to what Dwight Boyd (1996) calls the " 'munch, stomp, and dress up' view of multiculturalism" (p. 612). That is, when students and teachers limit themselves to asking safe questions, they are left with a superficial approach to understanding differences—one that leads to discussing a culture's food, dance, and clothing style preferences rather than its values and beliefs. In moving away from so-called safe discussions, teachers can provide students with choices regarding what is talked about in the curriculum.

Becoming skilled in choosing topics for classroom discussion is, according to Wilber (2008), within "the purview of 'new literacies'—researching and understanding how digital technologies interact with literacy practices to create different possibilities" (pp. 61–62), such as how genre, audience, language, and intent play out differently in written, spoken, and visual texts. Teaching students how to evaluate these various kinds of texts as possible sources of information for class discussion is addressed in Chapter 11.

Forms of Grouping

Tracking is but one, though still very common, way of grouping students for instruction at the middle and high school levels. A system for deciding who should learn what and at what pace, tracking remains a controversial issue in the United States. Despite legal attempts to end or limit the amount of tracking in secondary schools, it is a system that has proven "extraordinarily resilient and resistant to change" (Welner & Oakes, 1996, p. 466). Nonetheless, in many reform-oriented school districts throughout the United States, alternative forms of grouping such as cooperative learning groups, cross-age tutoring, small-group discussions, and reading and writing workshops are gaining in popularity.

Ability Grouping

According to research reported in Akos (2007), "more than 95 percent of middle and high schools in North America employ some form of academic tracking" (n.p., para. 7). In general, schools group students for instruction in one of three ways: curriculum tracking, ability-group tracking, or within-class grouping.

Curriculum tracking involves scheduling students' courses so that they follow a particular sequence and prepare students for life after high school. This gives rise to the familiar college preparatory, general, and vocational tracks of secondary schools.

Ability-group tracking, or between-class grouping, involves assigning students to a particular class section (such as history honors or general math) based on their past performance in that subject area. Such grouping is intended to reduce the heterogeneity of an instructional group and thus make the teacher's job more manageable. At the high school level, ability-group tracking is often synonymous with curriculum tracking. A special kind of tracking, called *block scheduling*, is found in some schools and consists of grouping students for a large block of time each day.

Within-class grouping, which is more common at the elementary level than at the middle and secondary levels, consists of separating students into smaller instructional groups once they have been assigned to a particular class; for example, an English teacher might do within-class grouping to accommodate differences in students' reading or writing abilities (Glatthorn, 1991).

ARGUMENTS FOR   Traditionally, those who favor ability-group tracking do so on the grounds that it affords teachers the opportunity to adapt their instruction in a way that challenges the faster learner and supports the slower learner. Proponents say that high-ability students become bored with schooling when the pace of instruction is slowed down to accommodate less able students. According to Feldhusen (1989), "Grouping gifted and talented youth for at least part of the school day and offering a differentiated curriculum leads to higher achievement, engenders better attitudes and motivation, and does no harm to less able youth" (p. 4). More recent research, however, shows that tracking is especially detrimental to ELLs because it limits their post–high school options (Callahan, 2005).

ARGUMENTS AGAINST   Hargreaves (1967) and Oakes (1985) concluded that higher-track students feel more positively toward school than lower-track students, partly because they are exposed to more competent teachers and teachers with better attitudes. Reading practices also seem to vary according to tracks, with higher-track students receiving instruction that allows them to exercise critical-thinking skills and lower-track students being held more to factual recall.

Cooperative Learning

In cooperative-learning groups, students work together in small groups (of four or five individuals) to set goals and to learn from one another, with the incentive being a group reward for combined individual efforts. "The principal idea behind cooperative learning methods is that by rewarding groups as well as individuals for their academic achievement, peer norms will come to favor rather than oppose high achievement" (Slavin, 1984a, p. 54).

In cooperative-learning groups, students come to rely less on the teacher and more on one another. Acting as peer tutors, they learn more because they are actively engaged with the text or other instructional materials. Slavin (1984b) demonstrated the value of cooperative learning in culturally diverse classrooms and with students who have disabilities that could potentially interfere with their learning. By engaging students in cooperative learning, teachers set the stage for acceptance of diversity and valuing of individual contributions. Linguistically diverse students are known to benefit from cooperative learning because they become more actively involved and spend more time in meaningful exchanges with their peers than they otherwise would (Reyes & Molner, 1991).

One widely used cooperative-learning technique developed by Slavin and colleagues at the Johns Hopkins Center for Social Organization of Schools is Jigsaw II. Lehr (1984) describes Jigsaw II as a method of grouping students into teams of four or five members each, with each member being assigned a different topic within a common text. Team members become experts on their topics. Students from different teams with the same topic meet as a group to discuss what they have learned. Then they return to their original teams to teach their teammates what they learned in the same-topic group. In the final step of Jigsaw II, the entire class takes a quiz, for which individual and team scores are awarded.

Cooperative learning of a more informal nature than that just described is generally defined as any collaborative act that involves two or more students working together to accomplish specific pedagogical tasks (Gumperz, Cook-Gumperz, & Szymanski, 1999). This type of grouping arrangement, when used in conjunction with content literacy instruction, has been found to be a highly effective means for improving students' understanding of academic subject matter (National Reading Panel, 2000). Figure 3.2 provides an overview of different educators' views of cooperative-learning groups.

Cross-Age Tutoring

The middle grades, in particular, lend themselves to the use of cross-age tutoring because of the school-within-a-school concept that most restructured middle schools espouse. The physical setting and the emphasis on the concept of community within the middle school support older students' teaching younger students to deal with their assignments. As the authors of *Turning Points* (Carnegie Council on Adolescent Development, 1989) note,

> Cross-age tutoring could take place . . . during the part of the day reserved for activities outside the core instructional program for younger and older students. Cross-age tutoring has shown consistent positive effects on achievement outcomes for both tutors and tutees. Tutors encounter opportunities to review basic skills without embarrassment, gain experience in applying academic abilities, and develop insight into the process of teaching and learning. Tutees receive individualized instruction and work with positive role models. (p. 52)

Cross-age tutoring differs from cooperative learning on several counts. First, cross-age tutoring usually occurs in dyads as opposed to small groups of four or five members. Second, cross-age tutoring is characterized by the transfer of very specific

	Group Size	Purpose	Incentive	Essential Characteristics
Robert Slavin (1984)	Four or five individuals heterogeneously grouped	To enable students to learn from one another through peer tutoring	To reward both groups and individuals as a means of establishing peer norms that support high achievement	Individuals assigned different topics within common text; those with same topics meet in a group
Donna Alvermann (2008)	Three to five individuals homogeneously or hetero-geneously grouped	To enable students to learn from one another through peer tutoring	To reward group efforts through equitable input from each individual	Common text; each team sets its own goals and individuals tutor within the team; only team scores are recorded
Victoria Gillis (2008)	Three to five individuals homogeneously or hetero-geneously grouped, working face to face	To enable students to learn from one another through peer tutoring	To reward group interdependence but through individual accountability; to "divide and conquer" a task, making it easier to accomplish	Individual accountability; group interdependence; positive interpersonal skills
Stephen Phelps (2008)	Dyads to small groups; homogeneous or heterogeneous in structure	To quickly check facts, answer questions, solve problems, or develop a position on an issue	To engage actively in the flow of ideas in the classroom, rather than passively listen to the teacher or other students	Common task; collective accountability; results shared with a wider audience

FIGURE 3.2   Overview of Cooperative-Learning Groups

information and usually involves some form of basic skills practice, whereas coopera-tive learning tends to focus on higher-order thinking. Third, cross-age tutoring focuses on rewarding the individual, whereas cooperative learning rewards the group (although, certainly, individuals are also rewarded as members of the group) (Indrisano & Para-tore, 1991).

Guidelines from the research on cross-age tutoring offer insights on how to pair the student partners. Generally, these guidelines hold for peer tutoring as well—that is, for partners who are approximately the same age but with varying achievement levels (Rekrut, 1994):

1. The age level of the tutor and learner may vary depending on the situation. Although older, more accomplished students typically serve as the tutors, they may not always be superior achievers. For example, we know of instances in which low-achieving high school students have served as successful tutors to struggling readers at the elementary level.

2. Same-sex pairs are preferable, but if such pairings are impossible, research has shown that older girls can successfully tutor younger boys.

3. Tutors need to be taught to work with their partners without making value judgments.

4. Posttutoring debriefings should be ongoing and should give attention to both content and process skills.

5. Affective objectives, such as self-confidence and self-esteem building, are as important in cross-age tutoring as concept mastery and skill reinforcement.

A variation on cross-age tutoring is *peer scaffolding*. Mellom (2008) studied peer scaffolding in classrooms in Costa Rica, where code switching between L1 (a student's native language—in this instance, Spanish) and L2 (the new language to be learned—in this instance, English) was a common, everyday occurrence. She defined *code switching* as using both L1 and L2 in one sentence (e.g., a student might begin in English but switch to Spanish). Specifically, Mellom was interested in learning whether code switching was viewed as a problem or a resource. What she found generally was that students treat code switching as a resource. For example, the students in her study used American pop culture (movies, TV shows, comics, music, advertisements) to understand and communicate to others what a previously unknown concept in English meant to them. In one instance, a student hummed the theme song from the 1960s western movie *The Good, the Bad, and the Ugly* to express what she understood the word *homesteading* to mean during a class discussion of a social studies text.

Discussion Groups

As teachers, we continue to value classroom discussion as a means for enriching and refining students' understandings. Findings from a multicase study involving adolescents at five culturally diverse sites throughout the United States (Alvermann et al., 1996b) indicate that students perceive discussions as helping them understand what they read. They know what they like and dislike about large- and small-group discussions; they also know how various topics and tasks influence their participation. In sum, students told us that classroom discussions provide them with opportunities for testing their own ideas while learning to respect the ideas of others.

DEFINITIONS OF DISCUSSION   Multiple definitions exist for what discussion is or should be, but we prefer one developed largely from David Bridges's work with classroom teachers in Cambridge, UK:

1. Discussants should put forth multiple points of view and stand ready to change their minds about the matter under discussion.
2. Students should interact with one another as well as with the teacher.
3. Interactions should exceed the typical two- or three-word phrases common to recitation lessons (Alvermann, Dillon, & O'Brien, 1987, p. 7).

These three criteria are helpful in distinguishing between a true discussion and what sometimes passes as one—a recitation in disguise. Recitations are rarely more than fast-paced exchanges between teachers and students in which teachers elicit answers to a series of preplanned questions. Little room is left for the substantive exchange of ideas because the teacher's evaluation of a student's answer is the signal to move on to the next question.

Activity

Consider the following excerpt from a fictionalized account of an interaction between Lennie and his teacher in Betsy Byars's well-known book, *The TV Kid* (1976). Is it an example of a discussion or a recitation? Why do you think so?

"Do you think he was just talking about *one* year passing?" the teacher went on. "Or do you think, Lennie, the poet was seeing his whole life as a year, that he was seeing his whole life slipping past?"

"I'm not sure," Lennie's hand was still on his chin as if ready to stroke a long gray beard.

"Class?"

"His whole life slipping past," the class chorused together. They had had this teacher so long that they could tell, just from the way she asked a question, what they were supposed to answer. (p. 70)

PURPOSES   Small-group discussions, like whole-class discussions, should stimulate students to think for themselves rather than rely solely on their teachers or their texts for ideas. The old notion that thinking must originate within the individual before it is ready to be shared with others has given way to the belief that some of the best thinking may result from a discussion group's collective efforts (Sternberg, 1987). In fact, there is empirical evidence to suggest that "student-led small-group discussions of nonfiction are superior to both lecture and whole-class discussion in helping students recall and understand essays . . . [and] in preparing students to write analytic, opinion essays" (Sweigart, as cited in Nystrand, Gamoran, & Heck, 1992, p. 3).

Discussion groups can take many forms. Common interests, problem solving, subject mastery, and current issues are but a few of the possible foci for small-group discussion. Regardless of the focus, one thing remains constant—the need to keep in mind that as group size increases, proportionately fewer members participate. A rule of thumb is that a discussion group should consist of no more individuals than are essential for completing the task the group has taken on.

Reading and Writing Workshops

The reading and writing workshop is a form of grouping most often associated with Nancie Atwell's first edition of *In the Middle* (1987). This book is often credited with changing the way middle school language arts teachers structure their classrooms to make them more inviting as literate environments. A few high school teachers have also used the concept of reading/writing workshop to break through some of the barriers that struggling readers have constructed after experiencing years of frustration with classroom literacy activities.

For example, Janet Allen (1995), working with a group of ninth-grade "basic" students—all struggling readers—in rural Maine immersed them in a year-long encounter with all types of reading materials. Through daily read alouds, independent reading and writing time (including computer access), group sharing, journaling, conferencing, portfolios, and minilessons involving strategies and skills, by the end of the year, the 15 struggling readers in Janet's reading/writing workshop realized that it is never too late to experience the joy of reading.

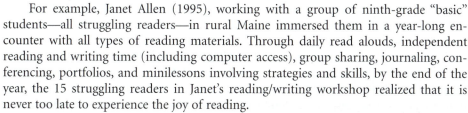

Helping Struggling Readers

Reading/Writing Workshop

Creating a safe environment for readers who struggle with school literacy tasks involves the following (Allen & Gonzalez, 1998):

- Providing sufficient time for students to complete reading and writing activities
- Building in student choice, not only in types of literacy materials and equipment available but also in types of assessments and classroom routines

- Supporting students by teaching them the strategies they will need to make connections between what they know and what they are expected to learn

- Having a variety of resources from which to choose: for example, young adult literature collections; class sets of paperbacks for whole-group shared reading; multiple copies of single titles for guided reading and literature circles; and access to computers and recorded, unabridged books

Creating Community with Technology and Multimedia

Go to MyEducationLab and select the topic *Technology*. Then, go to the Activities and Applications section, watch the video entitled "Teaching and Learning with Information Communication Technologies (ICTs)," and respond to the accompanying prompts.

Globally, a revolution is occurring in the way people exchange information. People of all ages are generating, posting, and responding to digital texts at an unprecedented rate on a scale that far surpasses what is occurring in print culture. The *digital revolution*, as it is sometimes called, is having an impact on teaching and learning in culturally diverse classrooms, or at least in classrooms with Internet access. Where this is not the case, young English language learners are finding ways to communicate among themselves in informal learning spaces on the Web. Both contexts are rich with opportunities for developing young people's digital literacies.

We use the term *digital literacies* to refer to socially mediated ways of generating and comprehending meaningful content through multiple modes of representation, such as oral, print, and nonprint language; visual imagery, including pictures, photos, and icons; sounds; and embodied performances to produce digital texts (e.g., blogs, wikis, zines, fanfiction, games, personal webpages) for dissemination in cyberspace. Digital literacies are one of many different forms of *new literacies* (Lankshear & Knobel, 2007)—a broader term that takes into account a series of events in the last decade of the twentieth century, when the notion of literacy with a big *L* and single *y* gradually gave way to the plural form, *literacies.*

Some literacy scholars, such as the late Alan Purves (1998), have theorized how the advent of *hypertext*—print and nonprint texts interlinked by the mere click of a computer mouse—has led to a new relationship between reader/writer and text. These developments strongly suggest that technology and media use in schools must be taken into account in any discussion of how to create favorable learning environments for adolescents in the twenty-first century.

Technology

Interest in using technology and multimedia to motivate students' interest in content area learning is not new, but the resources that are fast becoming available make it easier to use them in creating a favorable learning environment. In this section, we begin by focusing on a newcomer to education—the cyber school and the need to recognize students' use of new literacies.

Cyber schools, also called *online schools*, deliver the majority of their instruction to students through a website posted on the Internet instead of in a school building. Although cyber schools differ in their organizational structure, typically students work at their own pace and spend anywhere from 20 to 80 percent of their time on the Internet. Other differences between cyber schools and traditional schools include avenues for interaction and assessment. For example, teachers may spend as much as one-third of their time interacting one on one with students using the telephone or e-mail, and parents of students enrolled in cyber schools are expected to supervise their children's work. Assessments usually take the form of portfolios and a combination of online and offline tests (Long, 2004). Although research on cyber schools is spotty to date and likely does not represent accurately the number of such schools springing up across the United States, we do know from Kinzer's (2005) report on the intersection of traditional schools, communities, and technology that students' use of new literacies is reflective of the ease with which they are learning content through interactive communication software.

Given this picture, one would expect to find increasingly more state and national assessments focused on these new literacies. Such is not the case, however, as Leu and his colleagues (2005) have documented in their review of the research on the use of new information communication technologies in the United States. For example, Leu et al. note that "not a single state allows all students to use a word processor, if they wish to do so, on their state writing assessments, despite research [see Russell & Plati, 2000] suggesting that nearly 20% more students would pass their state writing assessments if they were permitted to use word processors" (p. 5). Moreover, according to Leu, Ataya, and Coiro (2002), state and national assessments do not include any of the new literacies that students need for competing successfully in a global economy.

Technology and the teaching of ELLs are related in two significant ways: (1) through instruction that makes use of computer-based programs for improving literacy skills and (2) through technology's potential to positively impact student motivation. In a study that paired multiple technologies with project-based instruction (Warschauer, Grant, Del Real, & Rousseau, 2004), adolescent literacy development in laptop classrooms improved. According to a report issued by Short and Fitzsimmons (2007),

> Projects requiring students to undertake field work, prepare a product, and present the project and its findings to a real audience by means of multiple technologies (internet research; information exchange through email, chat rooms, and bulletin boards; and production of DVDs and CD-ROMs) led to improved standardized test scores. [The projects] also provided opportunities for background reading, editing, language building, and vocabulary development. (p. 37)

Classroom teachers continue to acknowledge the role that new information communication technologies and the new literacies play in their students' lives. For example, Linda Hardin (1999) used the Internet to build a sense of community within her eighth-grade language arts classroom as part of a history project to put Greenville, South Carolina, on the Web. This interdisciplinary project involved all sections of her language arts class—80 students in all. The class, becoming what Hardin described as "tourists in their own town" (p. 7), documented parts of Greenville's history, including the controversy surrounding the Reedy River, which the Cherokees had fought to keep prior to the Revolutionary War. Initially conceiving of their project in linear fashion, the students soon learned one of the advantages of the Web. With the help of an Internet tool called WebQuest, they learned how to organize the information they were obtaining from interviews with longtime residents of Greenville, from Web surfing, from hometown library searches, and from e-mailing messages to historians across the

United States in a "hyperbranching" rather than linear manner. In effect, the students in Ms. Hardin's language arts classes were learning how to publish their history on the Internet in a way that allowed endless revisions and invited future links as newly discovered maps, photos, or updates to a story came in. As Hardin (1999) noted, "For us, it was like putting the index at the beginning of a book and allowing the reader to jump around from page to page rather than reading the entire text first" (p. 9).

Multimedia

Teachers may find it useful to take adolescents' out-of-school multimedia interests into account when planning ways to build a community of learners within their classrooms, being careful, of course, not to appropriate for school purposes the very things students find most pleasurable in their out-of-school pursuits (Luke, 2000). Teachers we know who have done this successfully have been ones who have built on their students' interests in computers, video, and the Web.

The importance of having an appreciative audience for one's writing is a major factor in adolescents' fascination with self-created online content. Rebecca Black (2007) conducted a three-year ethnography of female ELLs who affiliated around a common interest in *fanfiction*—a term for stories that fans of an original work (e.g., *Harry Potter*) write by using the settings, characters, and plot from the original to imagine and create different situations that sometimes include curious mixes across genres and media. What Black concluded from her study points to the globalizing influence of the Internet on ELLs' motivation to write in informal spaces, such as www.fanfiction.net:

> While writing [fanfiction], the adolescent ELL may be carrying on several conversations at once via instant-messaging programs, chat rooms, and/or discussion boards [with other fanfiction writers] located in her former hometown in China, her new hometown in North America, and other such diverse places. . . . She also may be drawing from her knowledge of academic forms of writing, different media genres, as well as her knowledge of English, Mandarin Chinese, and perhaps Japanese to construct the text. (p. 386)

Black's findings from her three-year ethnography of ELLs' engagement in writing fanfiction are reflected time and again in other studies of young people's digital literacies. For example, a report from the American Life Project (Lenhart, Madden, Macgill, & Smith, 2007) showed that the use of social media—blogging; working on a webpage for school or for personal use; sharing original content such as artwork, photos, stories, and videos; and remixing online content to create new texts—is central to the lives of youth growing up in a global society.

Assistive Technology

The use of assistive technological devices and equipment for youth who have disabilities is a way of enhancing the classroom learning environment and ensuring that access to high-quality content literacy instruction is an option for all students. *Assistive technology*, also known as *enabling* or *supportive technology*, provides a variety of multimodal tools (visual, auditory, kinesthetic, and tactile) that students with special needs typically require if they are to achieve greater independence and become more successful learners. For example,

> Word processing software assists children with learning disabilities in several ways. First, it reduces the frustration these children experience with awkward letter formation. Typing on a keyboard is much easier than forming letters by hand, especially since each letter appears precisely formed on the screen. Moreover, looking at letters on the keyboard may increase letter-recognition skills. Finally, word processors provide children with the opportunity to use spell checkers to improve accuracy in spelling, an area that is often difficult for children with learning disabilities. (Leu & Kinzer, 2003, p. 454)

High-speed connectivity to the Internet serves as a gateway to the World Wide Web and offers teachers resources that they can use to extend their students' knowledge of the content areas. However, often Web-based thematic units employ traditional methods and materials that are not directly pertinent to the specific learning outcomes a teacher may have in mind. This is especially problematic when some of the students in a class have learning disabilities. In such cases, experts in assistive technology recommend that the teacher impose an external structure on a collection of websites by doing the following:

1. Selecting only those sites that are directly relevant to the learning objectives
2. Informing the student of the learning activities for each site
3. Sequencing how students should access the sites (e.g., establish the order in which a student ideally views sites for the first time) (Gardner & Wissick, 2002, n.p.)

Another recommendation involves imposing a structure on Internet searches. This is what a high school science teacher in Donna's content literacy class did. He used

TECHNOLOGY Tip

According to the information on TrackStar posted at http://trackstar.4teachers.org/trackstar/; jsessionid=B00EDFF178AC9DA323834B7AFC1F1109, this website "is your starting point for online lessons and activities. Simply collect Web sites, enter them into TrackStar, add annotations for your students, and you have an interactive, online lesson called a Track. Create your own Track or use one of the hundreds of thousands already made by other educators. Search the database by subject, grade, or theme and standard for a quick and easy activity. There is a fun Track already made for each day of the year, too!"

TrackStar (http://altec.org/index.php) to organize information and activities on biomes for students in his class who were part of the school's inclusion program. TrackStar is a noncommercial site that directs students "to a single Web address, where a *track* takes over and provides structure, sequence, and annotations for Web-based learning" (Gardner & Wissick, 2002, n.p.) By using this kind of assistive technology, the teacher was able to keep students focused, attentive, and engaged in reading about biomes around the world.

Conflict Resolution

Resolving conflicts that arise among adolescents is central to the process of creating and maintaining a favorable learning environment, one in which students are free to express themselves as long as they show respect to others and take responsibility for their own actions. Often easier to write about than to do, conflict resolution is a process that requires some special skills on the part of teachers and students alike. In content literacy classrooms in which collaboration is encouraged, it is especially important that students have some understanding of this process. Best introduced by the teacher in preparation for independent group work, conflict resolution may include one or more of the following strategies: problem solving, listening to negative feedback or criticism and responding appropriately, mediating the conflicts of others, compromising, accepting the answer no, and coping with failure (Warger & Rutherford, 1997).

What the Research Says

A review of the research on understanding peer conflict (Laursen, Hartup, & Koplas, 1996) suggests that "classmates with no history of rewarding exchange and no emotional investment in one another [will] appear unconcerned about future interaction" (p. 94). This is unfortunate but all the more reason for teachers to work toward creating a learning environment in which all students have reason to feel valued for their contributions, regardless of race, ethnicity, class, gender, ability, physical size, sexual orientation, religious background, and other identity markers that set individuals apart and open them to unfair ridicule.

Having to endure the bullying behaviors of others is the consequence most often cited by those who are the target of school bias. Interestingly, *bullying*, which has been defined as "repeated oppression, physical or psychological, of a less powerful person by a more powerful person or group" (Rigby cited in Koki, 2000, p. 1), is more of a problem in the mainland United States than it is in Hawaii and other Pacific Island schools under U.S. jurisdiction. Thought to be a result of the Western ideal of rugged individualism, bullying is less evident in cultures in which peer/family/community support are traditionally valued over one's personal goals (Koki, 2000).

TECHNOLOGY Tip

Teaching Tolerance and Conflict Resolution
Teaching Tolerance, a project of the Southern Poverty Law Center, is a website that offers practical ideas that teachers can use to promote respect for differences and appreciation of diversity. At www.tolerance.org/teach/index.jsp, you will find teaching resources related to conflict resolution, opportunities for examining your role in teaching tolerance, and current events that lead to discussions of the need for tolerance.

Education World, the website of the National Education Association, offers a special theme page on bullying (www.education-world.com/a_special/bully_2000.shtml) that is current and links to many related sites on conflict resolution.

Strategies for Managing Conflict

Some of the best suggestions for managing classroom conflict that results from bullying comes from William Kreidler's book *Creative Conflict Resolution* (1984). Although written two decades ago, this book offers practical and easy-to-initiate strategies for resolving problems before they become more serious. We include two of those strategies here, adapted to fit our notion of what would work in the classrooms with which we are most familiar—our own.

NEGOTIATING A SOLUTION TO A PROBLEM   This strategy, which is easily adapted across content areas, consists of the following steps:

1. Write the words *negotiate* and *negotiating* on the board, and ask students to brainstorm meanings for them.

2. After five minutes of brainstorming, invite individuals to share their definitions with the whole class. If the idea that negotiating is a way of solving problems between people so that everyone can win does not come out in the discussion, suggest it and seek student feedback.

3. List the following procedure for negotiating a problem:

   - State what you think the problem is.
   - Say what you want.
   - Tell what the limits are (what can or cannot be changed).
   - Work out an agreement.
   - Ask if everyone is able to live with the negotiated outcome. If not, address individual concerns privately, in a small group, or as a whole class, depending on the case.

4. Walk students through the process using the following situation:

   Jill, one of the students in your TGT cooperative learning group, is not summarizing correctly the assigned readings in the social studies text. This is causing you and other students to answer test questions incorrectly during the tournament. Resentment is building.

5. After the class has negotiated a solution to the problem, ask students to describe a situation in which this type of negotiation would not work. Then ask them to explain what they would do in such a situation.

BUILDING RESPECT AND COMMUNITY   This strategy for managing classroom conflict that stems from general disrespect toward others and little sense of community is best introduced early in the school year and revisited occasionally so that students can gauge for themselves whether or not any change has occurred in their learning environment. The procedure consists of the following steps:

1. Engage students in a discussion of the actions, words, and body language that signal respect or disrespect for others. Point out that you need not like someone to behave respectfully toward him or her.

2. Ask class members to think about their learning environment and the things they would like to change (as well as those aspects of the environment they would like to keep the same).

3. Give each student an index card and pencil, and request that individuals describe what they would change (and would not change) about the class learning environment. They may choose to sign their cards or remain anonymous. Post the cards on the bulletin board.

4. After a few days (having allowed enough time for students to read and think about the cards on the bulletin board), open a class discussion focused on the following questions:

   - How would it feel to learn in the environment that you envision?
   - Is it a vision worth working toward?
   - If so, how would we begin working toward it?

In following up on any progress the class is making, you will need to ensure that discussions focus on both the positives and the negatives associated with change. For example, you might ask individuals to recall situations in which respect was shown, how it made them feel, what events tended to derail good intentions, how those derailments were addressed, and where the class currently stands in relation to its goal of creating a more favorable learning environment.

Time spent in teaching conflict resolution to adolescents is time well spent, as Van Slyck and Stern (1999) noted. According to these experts on youth-oriented conflict resolution, research has shown that "learning conflict resolution principles and techniques increases social support and decreases victimization" (p. 179)—changes that ultimately lead to higher self-esteem and less depression or anxiety among adolescents.

Literacy Coaches' Corner

Literacy Coach Blogs

Blogs are increasingly popular among professionals who must depend on getting other people's views on all sorts of topics. To find entries on how to manage conflict among coaches, principals, and teachers, check out a literacy coach blog called literacy.coach (http://literacycoaching.typepad.com) and another called Literacy Coaching Clearinghouse (www.literacycoachingonline.org/forums/forum6gainingentry.html).

Summary

A favorable learning environment supports students as they grapple with issues of affect that influence how they feel about school and their willingness to engage in the academic activities that are part of the schooling process. Although tracking by ability level is not likely to disappear in the near future, there are numerous alternatives for grouping, including cooperative learning, cross-age tutoring, discussion groups, and reading/writing workshops.

The use of technology and various media forms to create a community of learners is a literacy practice that increasingly more teachers are choosing as they strive to motivate student interest and learning in their content area classes. This practice requires that teachers be sensitive to the pleasures young people draw from the media and not appropriate them for school use in ways that will cause students to abandon their interests in reading and writing with media outside school. It also requires that teachers take time to help adolescents express their dislikes and disagreements in ways that resolve or manage conflicts before they become serious threats to classroom life and beyond. Treating conflict resolution as a necessary and natural part of creating a favorable learning environment is a first step toward ensuring that students will have opportunities to express themselves freely as they read, write, speak, and listen to others discuss the content of your classroom.

Suggested Readings

Ambrosini, M., & Morretta, T. M. (2003). *Poetry workshop for middle school.* Newark, DE: International Reading Association.

Black, R. W. (2008). *Adolescents and online fan fiction.* New York: Peter Lang.

Coloroso, B. (2003). *The bully, the bullied, and the bystander: From preschool to high school, how parents and teachers can help break the cycle of violence.* New York: HarperResource.

Delpit, L., & Dowdy, J. K. (2002). *The skin that we speak: Thoughts on language and culture in the classroom.* New York: New Press.

Frey, N., & Fisher, D. (Eds.). (2008). *Teaching visual literacy: Using comic books, graphic novels, anime, cartoons, and more to develop comprehension and thinking skills.* Thousand Oaks, CA: Corwin Press.

Tatum, A. W. (2000). Breaking down barriers that disenfranchise African American adolescent readers in low-level tracks. *Journal of Adolescent & Adult Literacy, 44,* 52–64.

MyEducationLab is a research-based learning tool that brings teaching to life. Go to the Alvermann, Phelps, and Ridgeway Gillis 6th Edition MyEducationLab for Content Area Reading site at www.myeducationlab.com to:

- engage in multimedia exercises to help you build a deeper and more applied understanding of chapter content;

- utilize extensive resources including videos from real classrooms, Praxis and licensure preparation, a lesson plan builder, and materials to help you in your teaching career.

chapter 4

Planning for Content Literacy

Instructional Decision Making	Planning and Educational Technology	Structured Frameworks for Content Literacy Lessons	Beyond the Daily Plan

- Essential Questions and Content Objectives
- Language and Literacy Objectives
- Learning Materials
- Student Capabilities and Needs
- Evaluation and Assessment

- Teaching Resources on the Web
- Planning Student Involvement with the Internet
- Planning for New Literacies

- Direct Instruction
- The Instructional Framework
- Reciprocal Teaching

- School-wide Programs
- Interdisciplinary Teaching
- Thematic Teaching
- Unit Planning

Anticipation Guide

Directions: Read each of the following statements. Place a checkmark on the line in the "Before Reading" column if you agree with the statement; leave it blank if you disagree. Then predict what you think the chapter will be about, and jot down on a sticky note (or post online) any questions you have. Read the chapter; then return to the statements and respond to them as you think the authors of your text would. Place a checkmark on the line in the "Authors' Stance" column if you believe the authors would agree with the statement. If you discuss these statements with other people online, in class, or at the family dinner table, return to the statements and check any items you agree with in the right-hand column, "After Discussion." If your thinking changed, what caused that change?

Before Reading	Authors' Stance	Statements	After Discussion
_____	_____	1. If you use a textbook, you don't need to write lesson plans.	_____
_____	_____	2. One of the most important aspects of lesson planning is deciding specifically what you want students to learn.	_____
_____	_____	3. Content area teachers cannot do much for students who are learning English until those students have developed academic competency with the language.	_____
_____	_____	4. There is no one best "recipe" for planning successful lessons.	_____
_____	_____	5. A lesson plan is meant to be a guide, not an absolute series of steps that must be followed to the letter.	_____

Victoria keeps an online journal, a blog, (http://teach2k6.blogspot.com/) and invites sudents and people like the readers of this book to comment on her entries, which offer a look into the thinking of a teacher trying to plan effective lessons. In the past, she shared entries through a listserv with her students. Student replies are often more honest than she imagined they might be, as the following exchange illustrates (Ridgeway, 1997).

• • •

At the end of one difficult day, Victoria wrote to her students about trying to teach them about planning:

> I was not greatly pleased with class today, and I'm not sure why. I didn't "cover" everything I wanted to, but that isn't the reason for the ambivalent feelings about class. I just felt "off" for some reason. I feel as though I said a little about a lot of things and in the process didn't get my message across. When planning, you must take into consideration your students, your content, your teaching style, as well your actual class activities. Maybe I shouldn't have tried to cover even more pre-teaching strategies. When will I learn??? You guys probably feel inundated already, and we've only just begun! Anyway, I think I've answered my own question. I tried to do too much—in too much detail—and ended up not really accomplishing what I had originally intended. Well, spilled milk, I guess. [The entry continues with ideas for revising the lesson and planning ahead for upcoming classes].

A student responded to this journal entry:

> I'm not sure that your "message" of determining the what, how, when and why components [of planning] is something you can teach us in a 75 minute block of instruction. You can tell us, but I think it's something that we have to learn for ourselves for it to really sink in. It'll sink in the first time I'm in front of a group of kids trying to review for a test and I say to myself, "Hey knucklehead, this isn't working. Maybe if I do this with the entire class instead of breaking up into groups. Or, this is taking too long. Maybe I shouldn't spend so much time brainstorming." It seems to me that your job here is to plant seeds of knowledge in the barren soil of our minds. They might not germinate today, or tomorrow, but hopefully they'll spring up next year or the year after when we really need them.
>
> Have you ever heard of the acronym MEGO? It stands for "My eyes glaze over." You achieved MEGO yesterday after about the third graphic organizer you showed us. By about the sixth or seventh organizer, we were somewhere else, dreaming of Pegasus, and flying ships and woodsmen made of tin.

Victoria replied to the listserv immediately with thanks for the honest response and several ideas for how she could have presented her lesson more effectively by involving students in hands-on planning experiences. This exchange illustrates several important points about planning for instruction. First of all, lessons do not always go as planned. Even experienced and effective teachers have those "off" days. Second, good teachers are always evaluating their work, looking for ways to improve. They listen to their students as part of that process. Finally, as Victoria's student acknowledges, some things have to be learned through experience.

• • •

Observing an effective and well-organized teacher can be deceptive. When a class is actively engaged in some kind of learning activity, whether it is instruction on how to graph a math equation, discussion of a poem, a chemistry experiment, or a conversation in Spanish, teacher and students can make learning seem logical, purposeful, almost effortless. Even when students become confused or ask for help, the teacher appears to know just what to do, how to ask the right question or rephrase instructions in a way that gets everybody back on track. Classroom veterans know, however, that good teaching is far from effortless. Rather, effective instruction is usually the result of thoughtful planning and careful preparation.

We too recognize that there is no one best way to plan for teaching. How a teacher prepares for the classroom will vary according to his or her particular style or preference, the subject matter, the materials available, and, of course, the students. Experience is also an influential factor in the planning process. New teachers and those who are preparing for a new curriculum or a new topic are more likely to explicitly lay out objectives and teaching strategies, whereas veterans can draw on previous lessons and classroom experience, updating and adapting as needed to maximize effectiveness.

We also acknowledge that as Robert Burns says, "The best-laid schemes o' mice an' men gang aft a-gley." Teaching can always be something of an adventure, and what actually happens in the classroom will usually be different from what one planned, as Victoria illustrates in the opening anecdote. An idea that seemed wonderful while sitting at the dining room table on Sunday afternoon may turn out to be a flop on Monday morning. Most teachers can also relate instances when they abandoned a planned lesson to pursue a "teachable moment," an idea that evolved in the classroom and became more immediate, more important, more instructive than whatever had originally been on the agenda. With experience, teachers learn to anticipate both the potential problems and the opportunities for serendipity, and they learn how to adjust instruction as they meet the needs of the moment.

Nevertheless, most good teaching and learning happen by design. What occurs in a classroom is usually the result of a complex decision-making process that begins well before the bell rings, evolves throughout the class period, and continues even after the class has ended as the teacher evaluates how students reacted and what they learned and also thinks about what to do next. Thus, we cannot emphasize enough the importance of intentionally planning for literacy learning in your content specialty. To experience effectiveness as a content area teacher, it is crucial that your students receive instruction in how to use reading, writing, listening, speaking, and visual and critical analysis to make meaning of the content they are expected to learn. In this chapter, we discuss some of the ways in which teachers design their instruction; we examine some of the decisions involved in planning for content area instruction and describe some frameworks for structuring content area literacy lessons.

Instructional Decision Making

Lesson planning, whether for a single day's activities, a two- or three-week unit, or an entire marking period, involves many complex and interrelated decisions. We have said that there is no single best way to plan, and a teacher may begin the planning process from any number of points. A chemistry teacher may begin by previewing chapter objectives in a teacher's manual. A French teacher may decide that students need more practice with translation from French to English. A geometry teacher may plan a day of review for a unit test on triangles. A language arts–social studies team may center their planning on a medieval fair, complete with costumes, games, entertainment, and food. Whatever the starting point, each of these teachers will need to consider what he or she wants students to learn, the learning materials that are available, the capabilities and prior knowledge of students, and the specific instructional strategies and evaluation options that will be most effective. This section describes some of the factors that must be considered in teacher decision making.

Essential Questions and Content Objectives

In our discussion in Chapter 1 of differences in the literacy practices of the content areas, we said that *content* determines *process*. This is especially true when it comes to planning for instruction. We believe that good planning begins with the question What do students need to learn?

On the surface, this seems like a simple question. However, if we were to examine a topic like the American Revolution, we would see that the answer is far from simple. What is important for students to know about the American Revolution? When it occurred? Who the principals were? Why it was fought? What the outcomes were? Any or all of these questions might arguably be essential. Furthermore, just knowing facts will not get a person very far in the twenty-first century. It might be more appropriate to ask, What do students need to learn, and what should they be able to do with that knowledge?

Curriculum experts at the Association for Supervision and Curriculum Development (ASCD) say that planning should start with *conceptual organizers*, or the big ideas that students should come to understand (McTighe & Brown, 2005; Wiggins & McTighe, 1998). These big ideas can be expressed as *essential questions*: open-ended, thought-provoking questions designed to guide student inquiry and give coherence to what they are learning. Essential questions will vary widely by discipline and topic. In a biology class studying plant reproduction, an essential question might be What two ways do plants reproduce, and why is the difference important? An English class's reading of Robert Cormier's novel *The Chocolate War* (1974) might be framed by the question How does a person choose between right and wrong? In a geometry class, a teacher might pose the question If we didn't have the Pythagorean theorem, what couldn't we do?

Activity

Think of a topic in your content area, and draft two essential questions that might be used to guide students' learning about that topic. Your essential questions might address any of the following:

- The big idea, or fundamental concept, of the topic

(continued)

- Why the big idea is important
- How experts effectively perform a particular task or skill
- When a person would use a particular concept or skill

Taken as a collection of facts, the American Revolution can be pretty confusing: Townsend Acts, 1776, Washington, Boston Tea Party, Jefferson, Cornwallis, "Give me liberty or give me death." This information will be easier to learn and ultimately more meaningful if the various parts can be connected to each other. It is useful to organize a topic such as this around one or two big ideas. For instance, the history teacher may decide to organize the class's study of the revolution around this theme: "The American Revolution came about because people wanted the opportunity to make their own decisions." This central idea, or *organizing concept* (Phelps, 1984), can help the teacher make decisions about what to emphasize and how. It can also form the basis of essential questions to guide students' learning, including questions such as these: What was the main issue that led to the American Revolution? Was that issue, in fact, resolved?

An organizing concept like this could also introduce a theme that would be revisited throughout the U.S. history curriculum as the class studied Jacksonian democracy, the Civil War, the rise of labor unions, or the suffrage movement. Figure 4.1 shows a planning web for the American Revolution centered on this organizing concept.

Our American Revolution example is broad and pertinent to a unit of study that may take a matter of weeks to complete. However, single class sessions may also be organized around a key idea or an essential question. For instance, a high school geometry teacher may plan a lesson around the computation of the area of a circle, centered on the mathematical expression $A = \pi r^2$. That single mathematical sentence contains all the essential components of the lesson: multiplication, area, radius, π. If students learn those components and the relations between them, they will have achieved the teacher's content objective; they will be able to compute the area of a circle. The lesson might be introduced with this essential question: When do you need to compute the area of a circle?

A teacher's primary objectives may also include content processes. That is, the teacher may want to help students to think like a writer, a mathematician, a scientist, a historian, or a linguist. Good teaching should be grounded on clearly articulated content objectives, however they may be defined or articulated. Learning will be more meaningful when teachers (and students) see the big picture and the overall point of classroom activity. Individual facts, ideas, or skills will be easier to learn when they can be related to each other and to a central concept or process. It will make it less likely that students will be involved in busywork such as filling out worksheets or copying down notes with no apparent pedagogical purpose other than to give the appearance of meaningful activity.

We want to stress that we are not talking about behavioral objectives. Nor do we believe it is necessary for teachers to laboriously write down objectives for every lesson using a particular formula or taxonomy, although this may be required in some schools

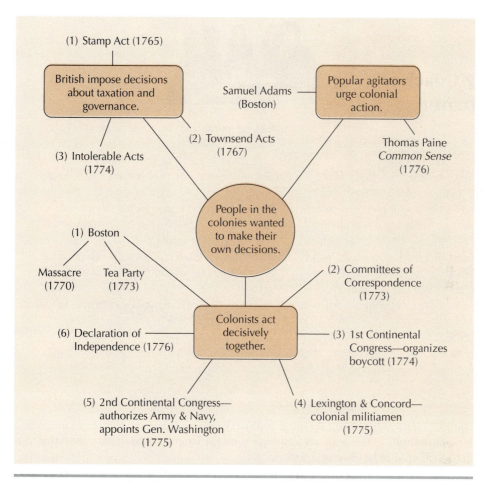

FIGURE 4.1   Planning Web for the American Revolution

and may have some utility in a methods course as a way to get teachers to think system-atically about what they are doing. Content area teaching is based on a curriculum of ideas that students are expected to learn, and it is sufficient that teachers have some part of that curriculum clearly in mind as they plan what they are going to do and what they are going to have students do in class.

Language and Literacy Objectives

In addition to the content that teachers intend students to learn, certain skills will be re-quired. For example, basic computational skills, using a calculator, and working with a protractor and compass are needed in the study of geometry. Working with laboratory

Literacy Coaches' Corner

One of the most important functions of a middle school or high school literacy coach is to help colleagues become more conscious of including literacy objectives in their planning. Whether you are working with an individual teacher or a team of teachers, you will need to approach this as an exchange of information and understand that not all your colleagues will be equally receptive to what you have to offer.

Cathy Toll (2005) classifies staff into three general categories, each of which presents challenges and requires some special handling. You may be intimidated by the Ready-to-Go group if you lack confidence, or you may be tempted to devote too much of your time to them. The Wait-and-See group may be jaded from past experiences, hesitant to make the first move, or be simply overwhelmed by all they currently have to do. Finally, the Put-on-the-Brakes group will be overtly resistant and may be quite vocal about it. With each type of staff, you need to emphasize your mutual concern for student success, acknowledge their expertise and perspectives, and indicate your willingness to listen and learn as well as your confidence in your own knowledge. Then you can begin a conversation about the role of literacy in planning and instruction.

equipment, including setup, cleanup, and safety procedures, is an important component of science study. In this text, our emphasis is on the language and literacy skills that students will need to be effective learners.

Particularly when working with students from diverse backgrounds, who may have less access to the conventions and forms of discourse commonly accepted in mainstream academic settings, teachers may need to provide frequent explicit skill instruction (Au, 1998; National Reading Panel, 2000). In the course of planning, teachers will want to think about the reading and writing activities that go along with learning and decide how their teaching will help students achieve those objectives. Reading a chemistry chapter to prepare for a quiz, reading a short story and writing a personal response, or using the Internet to search for information for a history project each requires some special skills, and these skills must be learned, usually through explicit instruction, for students to be successful.

As experts in their content specialties, teachers generally have a good deal of experience with reading and writing science, literature, social studies, mathematics, technology, and so on, but they may not be consciously aware of these abilities. The purpose of reading a text such as this one and taking a course on content area literacy is to increase teachers' sensitivity to the literacy requirements implied in a content area lesson. As teachers plan, they make decisions about what students will read and write; they analyze the literacy skills inherent in the subject and the reading material. They ask themselves, How is this reading selection organized? What is there about the selection that makes it easy to understand or that is likely to be difficult? In order to complete this written assignment, what will students need to know or understand? How can I help them with this?

Good teachers anticipate which skills may be difficult for students and plan to assist with those skills within the context of content area learning. If the biology chapter has an unusually heavy load of technical vocabulary based on Latin and Greek roots, the teacher may wish to use one or more strategies for helping students to master vocabulary. If students need some assistance with note taking and report writing, the teacher could include appropriate instruction in daily plans as students gather information and begin drafting their written products.

Other language- and literacy-related abilities that will be useful in content area classes include speaking and listening skills, working effectively with peers, preparing for tests, and abilities such as critical thinking, analysis, and prediction. (In the following chapters, we describe many teaching and learning strategies that integrate literacy learning with content learning.) Deciding what kinds of talking, listening, reading, and writing students will do and determining ways to assist students with those processes are important components of the planning process.

Learning Materials

While planning, teachers also consider what materials are at hand and what will be needed. Such things as laboratory equipment, math manipulatives, audio and video recordings, and various teacher-made materials may be used to demonstrate concepts, create interest, involve students, or provide essential background information. Regarding reading materials, teachers will think about textbooks, possible complementary readings from trade books or periodicals, worksheets and directions, exams, charts and diagrams, and reference materials.

Students of all cultural backgrounds will benefit when teachers introduce readings that authentically present diverse cultures, especially when the authors come from diverse cultural groups (Au, 1998). Writing assignments imply basic materials such as pen or pencil and paper; as well as journals, notebooks, computers and printers; and the possible formats for final written products, such as newspapers, student-made books, formal reports or essays, posters, letters, electronic transmission, and bulletin boards.

Student Capabilities and Needs

Another important aspect of planning is accommodation of student needs. Teachers will try to anticipate what students already know, what strengths or aptitudes they may have, and what difficulties they are likely to encounter. In Chapter 2 we considered some of the factors that contribute to classroom diversity. In our mobile, diverse, and rapidly evolving society, it is impossible to talk about a typical classroom. Students bring varied cultural understandings, varied language backgrounds, and a wide variety of previous experiences to school. Students will also range widely in their interests, in their aptitudes for a particular subject, and in their reading and writing abilities. In addition, many students with identified learning difficulties or disabilities are included in regular classrooms, sometimes with the support of specialists and sometimes without.

Reading difficulty is one of the most frequent signals that a student has a learning disability. Comprehension may be difficult for students with learning disabilities for one or more common reasons: (1) they are unaware of expository text structures, (2) they lack sufficient vocabulary, (3) they do not call on their background knowledge, (4) they are not fluent readers, or (5) they lack persistence in the face of difficulty (Gersten, Fuchs, Williams, & Baker, 2001). More than twenty years of research, however, shows that all students, including those with disabilities, can master content concepts and improve their performance when they are systematically taught what good readers do (Bulgren, Deshler, & Lenz, 2007). This requires an approach very much like what we recommend in this chapter: Identify critical content, analyze the difficulties students may encounter, select appropriate teaching and learning activities, and then teach strategically by explaining and modeling.

Go to MyEducationLab and select the topic *Planning Instruction*. Then, go to the Activities and Applications section, watch the video entitled "Scaffolded Instruction in Geometry," and respond to the accompanying prompts.

The growing diversity in classrooms presents both challenges and opportunities for teachers. Traditional instruction based on textbook readings, lectures, memorization, and formal academic expository writing will simply not serve the needs of all learners.

One way in which teachers are able to successfully meet the needs of diverse students is through *instructional scaffolding*. Just as a construction crew may erect a scaffold to support them as they work and then gradually dismantle the scaffold as the work is completed, so a teacher can plan a supportive framework for student learning and then gradually withdraw it as students take over more responsibility for their own learning. For example, Randi Reppen (1994/1995) describes how she taught different genres of writing to students in a fifth-grade social studies class of English language learners (ELLs). Students learned each style of writing by reading and discussing examples, with the teacher explicitly pointing out the features of the genre and comparing it with other genres. Then the teacher modeled by writing at the overhead projector for the whole class, asking students for input and describing what she was doing and why. Control over learning was gradually turned over to students, first by having them write in the particular style with peers in a small group and finally by having each student produce an individual piece of writing.

Planning to use flexible and varied patterns of in-class grouping can also help a teacher capitalize on diverse student backgrounds and meet varied student needs (Au, 1998). Alternating among whole-class instruction, various small-group activities, paired-learning tasks, and individual assignments allows students to assist each other, provides more opportunities to participate, and generally creates a learning environment based on student activity rather than passivity. Active learning environments are especially important when teaching students of diverse ability and background.

PLANNING CONTENT AREA INSTRUCTION FOR ELLS   Many of the general suggestions we have made are especially appropriate for students who are learning English, including flexible grouping, linking new content to prior knowledge, and instructional scaffolding. English language learners add a new dimension to teacher planning, however. In addition to knowledge of content and academic skills, they also need teachers who can help them develop their knowledge of the English language. Therefore, teachers who use a sheltered English approach scaffold their instruction by making adjustments both in the instructional tasks they plan and by adjusting their speech (Echevarria, Vogt, & Short, 2000). Teachers should also explicitly and clearly communicate both content and language objectives to students orally and in writing.

Sheltered English teachers adjust their speech by using simple subject–verb–object sentences, avoiding complex embedded constructions, and accompanying their spoken presentations with visual representations in the form of charts, diagrams, demonstrations, real objects, or pictures. Such visual aids are also part of adjusting instruction to meet the triple goals of expanding ELLs' vocabulary and language skill, their content knowledge, and their ability to perform increasingly complex academic tasks. Additional instructional adaptations include the following (Echevarria, Vogt, & Short, 2000):

- Preteaching vocabulary
- Reviewing previous instruction before introducing new material
- Explicitly modeling language and literacy skills
- Planning simulations, role-playing, and hands-on experiences
- Giving ELLs support in their native language through the use of L1 (first-language) reading materials, dictionaries, or bilingual peers and classroom aides
- Providing supplemental materials to support English language texts, including trade books, audiovisuals, pictures, computer-based information, audiotaped books, and specially designated textbooks with key concepts and vocabulary highlighted
- Creating graphic organizers, outlines, and study guides
- Allowing ELLs to demonstrate what they have learned through multiple channels, including hands-on activities, group projects, oral reports, and informal discussions, in addition to more formal quizzes and written assignments

A final component of sheltered English is engaging ELLs in instructional conversations that help them to improve their functional language skills. Specifically, students need opportunities to use academic language, not just social language. Peer interactions can facilitate this practice, but sheltered English teachers also directly elicit elaborated responses from ELLs. This means suppressing the instinct to compensate for students' lack of English language facility by not calling on them, speaking for them, or completing a partial response. Instead, Echevarria, Vogt, and Short (2000) recommend using prompts such as "Tell me more about that," "What do you mean by . . . ?" "What else . . . ?" and "How do you know?" It is also very important to provide the ELL sufficient wait time to formulate a response after a question is posed.

Although accommodating the needs of ELLs requires some specialized planning and instructional modifications, most of the specific teaching strategies recommended for ELLs are derived from those designed for mainstream classes. You will find these strategies and methods described in this and subsequent chapters.

Evaluation and Assessment

As teachers plan, they also think about how they will evaluate students' learning. Quizzes and exams, homework, worksheets, journals, essays, projects, in-class presentations, and observation of student performance are among the tools that teachers use to make both formal and informal judgments about what students have accomplished. Decisions about evaluation may come near the end of the planning process, after teachers have worked out the content objectives, materials, and learning activities for a lesson or a series of lessons in a unit. Other times, evaluation may actually be a primary influence in planning, as it is when teachers must prepare students for a departmentalized exam or other testing at the district, city, or state level. Evaluation and assessment will be treated in detail in Chapter 5.

All the decision-making factors that we have cited here are interrelated, and the interrelation is more weblike than linear. There is no single best sequence for lesson planning. Knowing something about students' reading ability will influence what kinds of reading materials they will be able to use successfully as well as the kinds of literacy objectives that might reasonably be achieved. Determining content objectives will help a teacher think of ways to draw on students' backgrounds and will also determine what will be emphasized in evaluation. Individual teachers will have their own preferred styles. Some will depend on external sources such as teachers' manuals, curriculum guides, or unit tests to help them formulate content objectives and teaching strategies, whereas others will draw on their own ideas of what should be emphasized. Some teachers may be student centered in their planning, whereas others may be more content oriented.

 Teachers at elementary, middle school, and high school levels will all take into account the developmental characteristics of their students as well as the relative degree to which the content areas are either distinct or integrated at each level. Specific subject matter will also make a difference; teachers in different subject areas have very different notions of what they can and cannot do in their classes, and the various subject area subcultures have a strong influence on actual instructional practices (Grossman & Stodolsky, 1995; Stodolsky, 1988).

Planning and Educational Technology

We are neither expert nor foolhardy enough to attempt detailed predictions of where technology may take us in the future. Nevertheless, it is safe to say that computer literacy, with emphasis on the Internet, will command continued importance as an integral part of students' literacy learning. Consequently, teachers will be increasingly expected to draw on computer resources in their planning and in the delivery of instruction. As they plan, teachers will also need to consider the technological skill and sophistication of their students.

The International Society for Technology in Education (ISTE), in collaboration with the U.S. Department of Education and other sponsors, has developed recommended technology standards for students at all grade levels (ISTE, 2007). Students should be able to do the following:

1. Demonstrate creative thinking, construct knowledge, and develop innovative products and processes using technology.
2. Use digital media and environments to communicate and collaborate.
3. Apply digital tools to gather, evaluate, and use information.
4. Use critical-thinking skills to plan and conduct research, manage projects, solve problems, and make informed decisions.
5. Understand human, cultural, and societal issues related to technology.
6. Demonstrate an understanding of technology concepts, systems, and operations.

Notice the explicit and implicit literacy abilities embedded in these standards. In order to use a technology resource such as the Internet, students will need basic reading and writing skills and an understanding of how they transfer to computer environments. They will also require keyboarding abilities, an understanding of computer terminology, flexible comprehension strategies, critical and analytical facilities, research skills (including Internet search strategies), and the ability to effectively combine print, audio, and visual media to communicate their ideas. Although some of this can be learned in technology classes, teachers in all content areas need to take into account the literacy ramifications as they guide students to use technological learning and communication tools.

Planning with the Internet involves two aspects. First, teachers can find lesson plans, unit plans, and many other kinds of instructional resources on the Web. Many sites welcome postings from teachers who wish to share successful ideas with colleagues. E-mail, listservs, bulletin boards, and chat rooms make it possible to communicate with other teachers or content area specialists and get specific planning suggestions. There is also a wealth of up-to-date information relative to almost any facet of any content area that one could imagine, available in an ever-expanding and ever-changing Internet environment.

The second facet of planning with the Internet is incorporating Internet activities and other technology uses into instruction. Teachers will want to plan what students will do with computers, how the Internet can complement the curriculum, and what students will need to know and do in order to have successful experiences with the Web and other technology.

Teaching Resources on the Web

There are numerous sites that give sample lesson plans and suggestions for teaching activities—many more than we can suggest here. Some good starting points include the following:

Teachers Net   http://teachers.net   Many different resources for teachers, including lesson plans, links to other useful sites, chat rooms, and message boards.

Kate Britt's Teaching Resources   www.ibritt.com/resources/   Links to content and lesson plan resources, curriculum guides, ESL resources, and more; posted by a freelance writer and editor.

Kathy Schrock's Guide for Educators   http://school.discovery.com/schrock-guide   Features links to other sites, organized into categories, including subject areas; also has a wealth of WebQuest information, including examples.

Thinkfinity   http://thinkfinity.org   Sponsored by the Verizon Foundation in collaboration with a consortium of education organizations, Thinkfinity is a mega-portal that can be searched by subject area, grade level, or purpose. Features lesson plans, materials, activities, and many other resources.

Youth Net   http://youth.net   A place where youth of all ages can meet, discuss, and participate in learning projects; many student projects, school websites, and student home pages can be accessed through this site.

In addition to lesson planning ideas, teachers will also find information on the Web to share with students. This might include useful background information, expanded coverage of a topic featured in the text, application of an important concept in some authentic context, or other information that is not included in the textbook. This is especially useful in the sciences and social studies, because the limitations of textbook technology make it impossible for texts to include the most recent developments in science, politics, or world affairs.

For instance, a biology teacher leading his or her class in a study of genetics would not find the most recent details on mapping the human genetic code in the textbook. However, the teacher could capture a series of Internet pages related to this topic, including text and graphics, using Web-capturing software such as Web Whacker (www .bluesquirrel.com/products/webwhacker). This will allow the teacher to access the sites he or she has selected even if there are no on-line links in the classroom. By using multimedia authoring software such as HyperStudio (www.hyperstudio.com) and by linking his or her computer to a large-screen display, the teacher can develop a presentation that interspersed scientific data from the Human Genome Project or other scientific agencies with Web-based news articles on the latest developments, predictions of the future benefits of genetic mapping, and perhaps some thoughtful considerations of the social and ethical issues involved in genetic science. Such a presentation could easily be a starting point and a model for hands-on student Internet projects as well.

Planning Student Involvement with the Internet

Content area teachers plan a variety of student hands-on experiences with the Internet that involve collecting, evaluating, synthesizing, organizing, creating, and presenting information. Student activities include the following:

- Collecting hot lists, a list of sites related to a particular topic
- Evaluating websites using criteria provided by the teacher or developed collaboratively in class
- Other higher-level responses to selected sites, including interpretation, relation to personal experience, or synthesis with what they are learning in the classroom
- Conducting a treasure hunt in which they find answers to specific questions tailored for specific websites
- Downloading items for a scrapbook, a collection of photos, maps, text, and audio or video clips that can be pasted into a multimedia presentation, a webpage, or other project

Helping
Struggling Readers

Internet Literacy

The Internet can be a welcome change from textbooks and a motivating environment for struggling readers, but it will also present them with some special challenges (Balajthy, 1990). The very vastness of the Web can prove frustrating for readers who are not particularly adept at finding useful information quickly and easily. The disjunctive nature of hypertext environments (where the viewer can jump from screen to screen or site to site in any order) may make it difficult for some students to keep in mind the overarching structure of a site or lose track of their purpose; they may become "lost in hyperspace" (Neilsen, 1990). Also, much of the information that students may access will be conceptually challenging, with a good deal of difficult technical vocabulary.

The following suggestions can provide support for struggling readers as they use the Internet:

- Pair struggling readers with more able peers.
- Steer them to sites that have been previewed and found to be appropriate.
- Select sites that include helpful site maps and navigation tools.
- When the site does not provide navigational aids, prepare a graphic of the site's structure and explain it to students.
- Scaffold Internet searches by providing specific questions, directions, or explicit guidance.
- Preteach potentially difficult vocabulary that may be found at a site.
- Use "talking" software, such as eReader or textHelp, that gives the user a spoken version of the text on the screen.

- Undertaking a WebQuest—a challenging task, scenario, or problem to solve in which student groups become experts on one aspect of a topic and then recombine and synthesize what they have learned with other groups either in their classroom or in other classrooms linked through the Internet
- Collaborative Internet projects (Mike & Rabinowitz, 1998), which enable students to communicate with peers in distant schools or experts in various fields, gather and synthesize information, and make their work public through electronic or other media

THE INTERNET AND ENGLISH LANGUAGE LEARNERS   The Internet can be an especially useful tool for ELLs (Leu & Leu, 1999). E-mailing back and forth between English-speaking peers or teachers, either in their own school or in remote schools, gives ELLs authentic communication contexts for reading and writing English. If students enter into an Internet project with a school in which a student's native language is spoken, that student can become a resource for translating back and forth between languages. This helps to illustrate the practical advantages of students' dual-language competency and helps to integrate ELLs socially and academically with their monolingual peers. A second-language learner can use the Internet to access sites in his or her home country and share information with peers as part of an Internet activity.

INTERNET PLANNING GUIDELINES   The sheer volume of information available on the Internet, as well as the difficulty of finding just what you want, means that the Internet can consume a lot of planning time, especially for someone just beginning to explore the possibilities of the Web. Martha Rekrut, a high school English teacher in Rhode Island, describes her own initial experiences with using the Web as well as some successful Internet applications by teachers in other disciplines. She shares some guidelines for Internet beginners (Rekrut, 1999):

- Determine instructional objectives and do some preliminary research to decide if the Internet is going to be helpful.
- Integrate the Internet into the context of ongoing instruction.
- Be aware of the literacy demands of the Web.
- Develop specific objectives for each Internet session.
- Include a written component or product to be handed in at the end of each session.
- If possible, help students disseminate their findings on the Internet via e-mail, on the school's website, or through displays and public presentations.
- Help students evaluate their Internet experiences in discussion or in writing.

To this, we add a few other general suggestions for planning Internet activities. First, be aware of varied student expertise with computers and the Internet. You may have students who are much more knowledgeable about computers and the Internet than you

are, but you may need to offer basic "how-to" instruction to others. You will also want to make sure that the more tech-savvy students do not monopolize the available workstations or dominate an activity.

Second, it is usually helpful to preselect sites for students to visit, especially if class computer time is limited and students are at the beginning or intermediate stages of Internet experience. This will save time and allow you to steer students toward sites that are reliable, reasonably well organized, and accessible at busy times of the day.

Finally, we encourage you to link *book literacy* with *computer literacy*. For instance, if students are working on a research project, you could require that they consult a certain number of book or periodical resources as well as the Internet, or you could use textbook selections as starting points for Internet exploration. Student projects should also include a student-composed written component. At the end of this chapter, we give an example of an interdisciplinary thematic unit that incorporates earth science, English, student use of the Internet and traditional print resources, student publication, and state assessments.

Planning for New Literacies

Although technology, especially the Internet, has generated many new kinds of literacy, adding technological applications to instruction does not by itself constitute new literacies in the sense used by contemporary theorists. Giving a PowerPoint presentation or researching a topic on the Internet is in many ways simply using technology to perform traditional school tasks (Kist, 2005). New literacies do involve what Lankshear and Knobel (2006) call new technological "stuff," but there is also a sociocultural dimension, what Lankshear and Knobel call a new "ethos" of literacy. As an example of old and new literacies, they cite the difference between a traditional print or online encyclopedia and Wikipedia. The first is static, authoritarian, with finite topical coverage and clear boundaries between producers and consumers. Wikipedia, on the other hand, is ever expanding and always open for new entries and editing of current entries by users themselves. The authority of Wikipedia is recognized as relative, with contested information tagged as such and with links provided so readers can explore further and make their own determinations of verity.

Integrating new literacies into a content area therefore means planning instruction that meets many of the following characteristics:

- Multimodality, or an extended definition of text to include a variety of visual, auditory, and physical representations
- Multimedia, including technological and posttypographical media
- An emphasis on learning processes as equal to or superior to learning products
- Collaborative rather than individual effort
- Critique of both explicit and implicit communication across varied media and modes
- Shared expertise and authority, rather than the authority of a text or a teacher
- Learner choices in topics, projects, modality, media, and assessment

As examples of new literacies in action, Kist (2005) details an arts seminar where one group of students collaboratively designed monuments to famous people using abstract, nonrepresentational forms; a class of eighth-graders developed multimedia advertising campaigns for products they had chosen; science students created a computerized three-dimensional simulation of the electron configuration of an element; and middle school students produced their own live news shows for broadcast over the school network.

To include some of the new technological "stuff" of new literacies, a teacher can use videos, podcasts, or Web simulations to introduce a new topic, frontload students' knowledge base, and allow them to visualize the focus of a unit or lesson. Many districts provide access to streaming video from Discovery Education (http://streaming.discoveryeducation.com), which features a searchable library of nearly 9,000 videos from sources such as PBS and Scholastic, as well as related planning resources for teachers. For instance, biology students can see a video of cells dividing, U.S. history students can see clips from World War II or the Vietnam conflict, and math students can see an explanation of the golden ratio. Youtube.com and Teachertube.com are also good sources of video, with many practical applications. A teacher who wishes to incorporate multiple modalities can find songs cataloged by subject at Songs for Teaching (www.songsforteaching.com); they can be purchased as a download or in CD format.

A new literacies ethos is promoted when planning includes opportunities for students to work cooperatively, as discussed in Chapter 3. Guiding students to read a variety of media critically is another example of new literacies ethos. This might mean appraising the stance of the author of a historical document, critiquing the way that news media or government officials report scientific evidence, or evaluating how advertising positions adolescents. (We talk more about this in Chapter 9 when we describe critical media literacy.) Providing choices for students in what and how they learn and how they are assessed also promotes the spirit of new literacies. For example, a teacher could give students a choice in how they provide evidence of their own learning by suggesting such culminating activities as producing songs, podcasts, plays, websites, interactive games, videos, comics, posters, brochures, or commercials.

Structured Frameworks for Content Literacy Lessons

The learning cycle, which we introduced in Chapter 3, is one example of a structured framework for teaching content literacy. We think it is particularly well suited for helping students make connections between the content they are expected to learn and what they already know from related experiences. As you read about other structured frameworks in this section, think about how you might use them in your own content specialty. In all probability, you will find useful ideas within each of the frameworks described. Rather than adopt any one particular framework in its entirety, you may decide to select those ideas that you feel best fit your content specialty, your students, and your own preferences.

Keep in mind as you read that the structured frameworks described here should not be confused with strategies. The latter, most of which are introduced in Chapters 6–11, can be used at various points in the learning cycle, during direct instruction, as part of Herber's (1978) instructional framework, or during reciprocal teaching (Palincsar & Brown, 1984). Strategies in and of themselves are *not* structured frameworks; rather, they may be used in any number of different frameworks (e.g., the instructional framework and reciprocal teaching both use summarizing as a strategy).

Direct Instruction

Direct instruction is useful for teaching a specific skill or process. The key steps of direct instruction include the following (Faggella & Deshler, 2008):

- State the purpose of the lesson.
- Provide instruction, including examples and modeling using a think-aloud.
- Give students guided practice with corrective feedback.
- Engage students in continuing independent practice, including generalization of the skill to new situations.

The teacher first states explicitly what is to be learned and models the skill or process. For example, a social studies teacher who wants students to learn how to write a summary might begin by explaining what a summary is, why it is useful, and how one is written. The teacher would then read a short passage from the history textbook and compose a summary on the overhead projector, explaining to the class the specific processes he or she was using.

After the process has been modeled for students, the teacher should involve them in guided practice. To continue our summary-writing example, the teacher could direct the class to read further from the text. The teacher then would compose another summary but this time base it on input from the class. As an alternative form of guided practice, the teacher could have students work cooperatively in groups of two or three to compose summaries while he or she walks around the room and offers assistance. Then the groups could compare their summaries and the teacher could help them analyze the merits of including or excluding certain information, their various choices for wording and syntax, and the accuracy with which the summaries captured the important ideas in the text.

In the direct instruction model, guided practice is followed by independent practice, in which students use the skills on their own. In the case of summary writing, the teacher could ask students to read and summarize a selection from their text as a homework assignment. The teacher would then continue having students occasionally summarize sections of their text and other reading materials, such as information they find on a historical website.

The direct instruction model is most useful when there is a single, relatively straightforward content or literacy objective that can be initially modeled and taught within a one- or two-day time frame. Direct instruction can be effectively applied to such activities as computational skills in math, map reading and interpretation in geography, paragraph structure in English class, and grammatical constructions in a modern language class. Literacy skills such as using context as a vocabulary aid or understanding question–answer relationships can also be taught by direct instruction. However, as the content or literacy objectives become more complex or abstract, direct instruction may need to be followed by extended reinforcement and guided practice, especially for struggling readers (Swanson & de la Paz, 1998).

The Instructional Framework

Harold Herber (1978) developed an instructional framework for content area literacy lessons that takes into account both the content objectives and the literacy objectives of a lesson. It incorporates some of the elements of the direct instruction model. Unlike the direct instruction model, however, the instructional framework lends itself to conceptually complex topics that may evolve over longer periods of instruction. Herber's model consists of three major components: preparation, guidance, and independence.

During the *preparation* phase of instruction, a teacher may choose one or more means to get students ready to learn:

- Employ motivational techniques to pique students' interest and encourage them to make a personal investment in learning.
- Activate students' background knowledge.
- Where prior experience is lacking, help build up background for the new concepts that are to be studied.
- Help students anticipate what they will be learning and be purposeful in their efforts.
- Give clear and careful directions about what needs to be done, especially when the assignment involves novel processes or ideas.
- Introduce technical or difficult vocabulary that otherwise might interfere with learning.

Useful strategies for working with students' prior knowledge and building antici-pation for learning are provided in Chapter 6, and Chapter 8 focuses on vocabulary development.

In the *guidance* phase of the instructional framework, teachers need to provide structured opportunities for students to develop both their learning processes, including their reading and writing abilities, and the concepts that constitute the subject area. The teacher helps students learn by structuring and guiding the interaction between reader and text or between writer and written product. According to Herber (1978), such guid-ance "must be sufficiently structured to give purpose and direction, but sufficiently open to allow personal strengths, preferences, and discoveries to emerge" (p. 220). Teachers can provide this kind of guidance through thoughtful questioning, by preparing reading or study guides, or by developing cooperative-learning activities in which students can work together on tasks with teacher assistance. A variety of guided learning strategies are described in Chapters 6–11.

Independence is the final phase of Herber's instructional framework, and student in-dependence, ideally, is the ultimate goal of instruction. As teachers, we want our students to be able to use both the learning processes and the concepts of our discipline. Math teachers want their students to apply math concepts and operations to authentic, real-life situations. The earth science teacher will hope students can apply their knowledge to local issues of environmental quality. The history teacher will hope that students will use their understanding of the past in order to more intelligently understand their positions as citizens in their communities and in the nation. Such independent applications of skills and knowledge require instruction that transcends rote memorization and per-functory coverage. Instead, teachers need to plan instruction that allows students to guide their own learning. This happens over time in classes in which teachers provide in-structional scaffolding, where guidance is highly structured and explicit at first but then gradually withdrawn as students become increasingly capable of learning on their own. Reciprocal teaching, described next, is one good example of how this works.

Reciprocal Teaching

In our discussion of accommodating diverse student capabilities, we used the term *scaffolding* to describe how teachers initially guide and support student learning and then gradually give students increasing responsibility for guiding their own learning. This is a variation of *cognitive apprenticeship* (Brown, Collins, & Duguid, 1989). Content area teachers who use cognitive apprenticeship as their approach to instruction adhere to the principle that *knowing* cannot be separated from *doing*. That is, they believe that what students are taught in school must not be different from the real-world use of such knowledge. For example, teachers who believe in this approach will argue against teach-ing students to memorize facts about U.S. history because it is not the way historians use such facts. In the real world, historians interpret so-called facts about certain events and people's actions surrounding those events; they do not simply read and neutrally record in rote fashion what they recall from their reading.

The term *apprenticeship* is used here to emphasize the central role of meaningful, authentic activity in any learning task. There is no room for activity that is not meaningful and authentic in traditional apprenticeships (in trades such as shoemaking or in professional apprenticeships such as medicine and law). However, students in middle and secondary schools are required daily to participate in activities that bear little if any resemblance to what practitioners do in the real world.

What can be done? *Reciprocal teaching* (Palincsar & Brown, 1984) is perhaps the best-known and most thoroughly researched application of cognitive apprenticeship to the teaching of reading comprehension. Reciprocal teaching involves direct instruction in comprehension strategies, most often the strategies of predicting, questioning, clarifying, and summarizing. Strategy instruction is provided with authentic classroom reading materials, either narrative or expository, instead of worksheets or other materials designed specifically for skill instruction.

An important feature of reciprocal teaching is the use of an *instructional dialogue* in which the teacher initially leads in modeling the comprehension strategies but then gradually turns the responsibility for leading the dialogue over to students. An illustration of how a teacher might initiate such a dialogue is given in Figure 4.2. We have included generic statements or questions that might prompt student participation, as well as topical statements or questions that a teacher might use to model the particular comprehension strategy. Figure 4.3 features a brief reciprocal teaching dialogue from a college class. Note how much student talk there is relative to teacher talk, and note also that students speak to each other, asking for clarification and concrete examples. Students in this example are taking charge of their own learning.

As students become more proficient with the reading strategies, the teacher gradually fades out of the dialogue and allows students to assume leadership. In a review of research on reciprocal teaching, Rosenshine and Meister (1994) concluded that the key to its effectiveness was not so much which strategies were taught but rather the importance of careful scaffolding of instruction. That is, teachers should present strategies in small steps, guide student practice, provide ongoing feedback and correction, and engage students in extensive independent practice.

Evidence-Based Research

Successful use of reciprocal teaching with varied student populations has been widely reported in professional literature. A review of 16 separate empirical studies indicated that reciprocal teaching generally yielded positive results with students ranging from fourth grade through adult (Rosenshine & Meister, 1994). This review also suggested that reciprocal teaching was effective with students who had developed some decoding skills but who were poor in reading comprehension. Reciprocal teaching has been successfully adapted for social studies instruction of seventh- and eighth-grade students with learning disabilities who were learning English as a second language (Klingner & Vaughan, 1996) and for students in Chapter I reading classes (Alfassi, 1998).

Two fundamentals of reciprocal teaching, supported by a substantial body of educational research, appear to account for its effectiveness: direct instruction and the gradual shift of responsibility for teaching from the teacher to the students (Pressley, 1998). Obviously, any implementation of reciprocal teaching requires the commitment of time

The following passage is part of the discussion of the Louisiana Purchase in *A History of the United States* (Boorstin & Kelly, 2005):

> This was perhaps the greatest test of statesmanship that Jefferson ever had to face. He was on the spot. The Constitution said nothing at all about whether or how Congress could buy land from a foreign country. Again and again, Jefferson had argued that Congress had only those powers that the Constitution had assigned in so many words. Maybe the power to buy land from foreign countries had been left out of the Constitution on purpose—to prevent the United States from playing the dangerous, old-fashioned game of empire. The people of the new United States had tried to escape from the ways of the Old World, where the rulers were in the habit of buying and selling, bartering and gambling faraway lands and unknown peoples. Now would Jefferson go against everything he had been saying for years?

Questioning

Initiating: Does anybody have a good question that we should be trying to answer for this section?

Modeling (after reading the first two sentences of the passage): What does the author mean when he says Jefferson was on the spot?

Clarifying

Initiating: Is there anything that is not clear?

Modeling: I wasn't sure what the author meant when he said the power to buy land had been left out of the Constitution *on purpose*. I had to re-read the next two sentences and think about that. Maybe it means that the writers of the Constitution left some things out because they weren't good ideas.

Summarizing

Initiating: What is the main idea of this section?

Modeling: The main point here seems to be that President Jefferson had a dilemma. He had to make a choice between changing his long-held positions or taking a step into the unknown.

Predicting

Initiating: What will Jefferson decide? What will the reaction be in Congress? What makes you think that?

Modeling: Everything we've read so far seems to indicate that Jefferson will support the purchse. The author keeps suggesting that making a bold decision would be evidence of Jefferson's leadership ability. When I look at the map on this page, I see that a huge section is colored in green and labeled "Louisiana Purchase," so Congress will probably support the decision, but with a lot of debate.

F I G U R E   4 . 2   **Initiating and Modeling Comprehension Strategies in Reciprocal Teaching**

Excerpt from a lesson on reading titles and lead paragraphs using *The Dictionary of Cultural Literacy* by Hirsch (1987)

Predicting

Teacher: Look at the chapter title, "What Every American Needs to Know." what might the author expect you to know?

Student 1: Things like the Founding Fathers, Plymouth Rock, geography, five basic food groups.

Teacher: Good predictions! Now, read paragraph one.

Questioning

Student 2: What does Hirsch mean by "cultural literacy"?

Student 3: World knowledge . . . that's what it says in paragraph one.

Clarifying

Student 2: I'm still not sure what "cultural literacy" means exactly. I need some concrete examples.

Summarizing

Student 4: "Cultural literacy" is the common background information we have stored in our minds in order to understand what we read.

Student 2: Okay, so background information means I already have ideas like the ones in the book.

Predicting

Teacher: Good. Now, look at the subheading, "The Decline of Teaching Cultural Literacy."

Student 5: I think this section will probably explain why students aren't becoming culturally literate.

FIGURE 4.3 **Strategies for Reciprocal Teaching**

and effort on the part of the teacher. To suggest a general time frame, Westera and Moore (1995) found that students with low reading comprehension scores who received 12 to 16 training sessions made significant gains on standardized tests, whereas similar students who had only 6 to 8 sessions made no gains.

Reciprocal teaching involves a high degree of social interaction and collaboration, as students gradually learn to assume the role of teacher in helping their peers construct meaning from text. In essence, reciprocal teaching is authentic activity because "learning, both outside and inside school, advances through collaborative social interaction and the social construction of knowledge" (Brown, Collins, & Duguid, 1989, p. 40).

Beyond the Daily Plan

Teachers' instructional decisions clearly transcend the question of What shall I do tomorrow? Teachers also need a long-term view of teaching and learning. Those who understand the socially constructed nature of knowledge will plan to involve students in discussion, collaboration, and problem solving related to their content area studies. Also implied in this trend is a view of the curriculum as comprising meaningfully interrelated concepts and themes, not simply as isolated bits of information to be learned by rote. All of this implies that teachers will plan activities that enable students to make connections between content areas, between the real world and the world of the classroom, and between "knowing what" (facts and concepts) and "knowing how" (using facts and concepts in authentic ways). In the following sections, we describe the planning of a schoolwide literacy program as well as two frequently recommended approaches to integrating curricula: interdisciplinary teaching and thematic teaching.

Schoolwide Programs

Reading Next (Biancarosa & Snow, 2004), a report on adolescent reading commissioned by the Carnegie Corporation, asserts that a comprehensive and coordinated literacy program is a key element in effectively meeting the needs of adolescent students, especially those who find reading and writing to be challenging. Although the efforts of individual teachers are important, they cannot have the same impact as a schoolwide program spearheaded by committed, enthusiastic leaders and implemented by knowledgeable teachers who coordinate instruction across disciplines. Because the needs of adolescents are quite diverse, the nature of coordinated schoolwide efforts will vary to meet the needs of particular communities. In some cases, the attention to literacy by content teachers may be relatively modest, while other situations may require more intensive accommodations.

In a widely cited program, a group of teachers in the San Francisco Bay area implemented a schoolwide scaffolded approach to content area instruction under the umbrella of the Strategic Literacy Initiative at WestEd Regional Educational Laboratory (Greenleaf, Schoenbach, Cziko, & Mueller, 2001; Schoenbach, Greenleaf, Cziko, & Hurwitz, 1999). They incorporated multiple research-supported elements into a literacy program for ninth graders in an ethnically and linguistically diverse San Francisco high school. As an alternative to traditional skills-based remedial reading instruction, WestEd facilitators and teachers developed a year-long course in Academic Literacy that featured what they call *reading apprenticeship*. Conceptualizing adolescent readers as inexperienced rather than deficient, expert adults inducted student apprentices into the strategies of content area literacy by systematically showing them how. Based on extensive assessment of students, teachers knew that ninth graders could decode and comprehend, but they needed to expand their fluency and experience with more diverse kinds of texts, all with direct, expert guidance on how to read more challenging material.

The primary goal of reading apprenticeship is to show adolescent readers that expert reading is a complex, problem-solving process by engaging them in "metacognitive conversations" about what they are reading and learning. These conversations involve teachers and students in talk about how they approach content area reading tasks, with teachers taking the lead by making their own reading processes visible as they pause to think aloud while reading to students. Reading apprenticeship involves four key dimensions that are necessary to support adolescent reading development (Schoenbach, Braunger, Greenleaf, & Litman, 2003):

- *Social dimension*: community building in the classroom, including recognizing the resources brought by each member and developing a safe environment for students to be open about their reading difficulties
- *Personal dimension*: developing students' identities and self-awareness as readers, as well as their purposes for reading and goals for reading improvement
- *Cognitive dimension*: developing readers' mental processes, including their problem-solving strategies
- *Knowledge-building dimension*: identifying and expanding the kinds of knowledge readers bring to a text and further develop through interaction with that text

The Academic Literacy course was divided into three units: Reading Self & Society, Reading Media, and Reading History. Throughout the year, students read, wrote, and talked about a variety of texts in various media, including literature, history texts, and print and broadcast advertising. Reciprocal teaching, direct instruction in text structures, note taking and paraphrasing, vocabulary study, regular independent reading of self-selected works, and response log writing and sharing were used as appropriate during the year.

Evidence-Based Research

The program resulted in significant gains in reading comprehension on a standardized test. In one year, students' average scores moved from the late-seventh-grade to late-ninth-grade level. Gains continued at an accelerated rate for a smaller representative sample tested in tenth grade. Students who had the most need of literacy development, such as struggling readers, English language learners, and special education students, tended to make the most gains. The Strategic Literacy Initiative has extended the Academic Literacy course to many other middle and high schools, with similarly encouraging results (Strategic Literacy Initiative, 2004a, 2004b, 2004c.) More information on the Strategic Literacy Initiative and the Academic Literacy course can be found at www.wested.org/strategicliteracy.

The results of the Academic Literacy course suggest that separate literacy classes in middle school and high school can be effective for a broad range of students if they are based on academically challenging, content-based, scaffolded instruction with a variety of texts. Reflecting on the growth of a student named Rosa as a capable and strategic reader, Greenleaf et al. (2001) contrast their Reading Apprenticeship approach with traditional skills-based remediation:

Imagine, for a moment, that Rosa had been in a reading course focused on building basic reading skills. While such a course may have strengthened her word analysis and vocabulary skills, we doubt that Rosa would have developed the kind of intellectual and ethical engagement and personal agency she demonstrates here. When we imagine such a limited outcome, we are struck with a keen sense of loss and unfulfilled potential, not only for Rosa, but for the many young people with whom we work. (p. 110)

Interdisciplinary Teaching

In the middle grades, it is common to assign students to interdisciplinary teams in order to create a school-within-a-school climate or the feeling that each student belongs to a particular school "family." Interdisciplinary teams typically include teachers from each of the core academic areas, sometimes with the addition of specialists in reading or special education. Because each team works with the same students for the whole year, teachers and students become well acquainted. Teams often have a common planning time so they can jointly plan instruction that will enable students to see how concepts learned in one discipline can apply in another. This can create an environment that is intellectually stimulating for teachers as well as students.

In high schools, however, built-in constraints such as subject matter specialization, inflexible scheduling, and large numbers of students make interdisciplinary teaming difficult. Nevertheless, special interdisciplinary programs have been successful even in very large schools. For example, the Humanitas program is an interdisciplinary, team-based approach to humanities teaching in the Los Angeles Unified School District. The Humanitas program emphasizes building understanding of issues that have relevance to urban youth, and teachers frequently bypass textbooks in favor of primary source materials, news media, and novels. Essay questions are used to develop students' abilities to think and write in a critical vein about what they have read. The following is an essay question from a unit on culture and tradition (Aschbacher, 1991):

> The cosmology of a traditional culture permeates every aspect of that culture. This is illustrated in the following three cultural groups: the Eskimos, the Southwest Indians, and the Meso-Americans. Specifically, discuss the spirit world that each group believed in, and explain how it influenced [that group's] culture and values. Include examples from your reading in art history, literature, and social studies to illustrate and substantiate your analysis. Finally, to what extent, if any, does the spirit world affect us today? (pp. 17–18)

In many schools, there may be opportunities for teachers from two or three disciplines to work together. For example, Amy Schimberg and Heidi Grant, eighth-grade science and English teachers at John Jay Middle School in Cross River, New York, found that their disciplines had many natural connections in a mystery thematic unit designed to build on students' interest in recent high-profile crimes (Schimberg & Grant, 1998). In English class, Ms. Grant's students read and discussed several types of mysteries and learned about the literary devices used by mystery writers. At the same time, a member of the local police force visited science classes to explain and demonstrate fingerprinting. Then, students were plunged into a simulated murder investigation. The crime scene was set and clues were left for the student investigators. Students analyzed chemical and physical properties in the authentic context of the "forensic lab," in which stations for analyzing fingerprints, ink, fiber evidence, a handkerchief smelling of mysterious perfume, and poisons were set up. Student teams observed the crime scene, interviewed suspects (portrayed by school staff members), conducted forensic analyses, and kept all their notes and results in investigator's notebooks and a case file. At the end of their investigations, student teams presented their conclusions to the whole class.

Individual teachers can also incorporate aspects of interdisciplinary teaching into their content areas. For instance, students who study the history of science can learn a good deal about the nature of science, the human face of science, and the links between science and society. A chemistry teacher might present students with the historical background of Mendeleev's development of the periodic table of elements and engage them in a hands-on activity that leads them through the actual thought processes that Mendeleev employed in the 1860s (McKinney & Michalovic, 2004). Exploring biographies of scientists or learning about famous scientific episodes like the development of the Salk polio vaccine helps students learn science concepts such as the tentative nature of scientific models, the use of empirical evidence, the contributions of women and people of color to science, and the fact that scientists may draw different conclusions from the same evidence (Rudge & Howe, 2004).

Thematic Teaching

The terms *interdisciplinary teaming* and *thematic teaching* are often used synonymously. For us, the major distinction is that thematic teaching can be implemented successfully within a single content area classroom (e.g., a civics class), but the success of interdisciplinary teaming often depends on special organizational school structures, such as flexible block scheduling and common teacher planning periods. We think that this distinction has practical significance since so few schools throughout the United States have implemented interdisciplinary programs of study.

The single-discipline thematic unit allows teachers to incorporate a variety of materials and instructional groupings to meet the reading interests and needs of their students. To do this, teachers must identify essential questions or organizing concepts within the subject and selectively abandon less important material that might have been emphasized if the goal were to cover a certain amount of content by the end of the year.

For example, Rodney White (1995) suggests organizing the study of world history around a thematic unit on religion. Rather than take a strictly chronological approach to history, with the topic of religion given brief attention in disparate chapters, students could undertake a comparative study of the historical evolution of the world's religions. This would allow them to understand both the commonalities and differences among people and to explore issues such as the separation of church and state in the United States, the contrast between Eastern and Western worlds, and relationships among Judaism, Christianity, and Islam. Such a unitary approach to world history would be especially appropriate in a culturally diverse classroom. White also suggests a culturally sensitive study of U.S. history that could be developed around the theme "What is an

American?" with students thinking about and discussing questions of cultural unity versus diversity.

In science as in history, there is a movement away from teaching a collection of isolated facts. Susan Offner (1992) proposes a biology unit founded on the theme of human heredity that would tie together concepts of protein structures, enzymes, DNA, genetics, and hereditary diseases. Understandings that students consolidate in this unit would carry over to the study of the various systems of the human body, evolution, and other diverse units of the biology curriculum.

Unit Planning

Whether a thematic unit integrates learning across content areas or is developed within a single discipline, careful planning and preparation are required. The steps in planning a thematic unit follow the decision-making process described at the beginning of this chapter.

The first step is to select a unifying theme or organizing concept for the unit (Goerss, 1996). The possibilities both within and across disciplines are enormous. It may help to think of three categories of themes (Fogarty, 1994): topical themes, such as dinosaurs; conceptual themes, such as systems; and problematic themes, such as "How do humans survive?"

Timothy Shanahan (1995) warns against picking topical themes that do not allow students to inquire deeply into meaningful ideas. For instance, if a unit on dinosaurs means reading *Jurassic Park* (Crichton, 1991), writing some dinosaur poems or science fiction, and printing out dinosaur graphics with the classroom computer, students might get some useful reading and writing practice, but they will not learn much about dinosaurs, about science (beyond the considerably fictionalized concepts in the novel), or about math. However, a dinosaur unit that leads students to explore concepts such as extinction, climatic change, evolution, chaos theory, DNA, geologic time, habitat, classification of species, and measurement will represent much more substantial learning.

Earlier in the chapter, when we discussed cognitive apprenticeship, we said that learning will be more meaningful if students are engaged in authentic activity—if they can discern meaningful purposes in what they are doing. Bette Bergeron and Elizabeth Rudenga (1996) propose an interrelated five-part framework for evaluating the authenticity of learning activities in a unit plan:

- **Purpose.**   Literacy activities intended primarily for practice or evaluation will be less meaningful than those designed to communicate or share ideas.
- **Choice.**   To the extent possible, students and teachers should negotiate curricular goals, activities, and materials rather than having all choices made by the teacher.
- **Audience.**   Reading and writing are less purposeful if the only audience is the teacher. Learning can be shared with peers and audiences outside the classroom.

- **Resources.**   Contrived learning materials are inherently less motivating and meaningful than real-life resources. Students benefit from using a variety of resources, print and nonprint.
- **Relevance.**   Activities should meet relevant curriculum requirements and the development of meaningful learning.

Of course, meeting each criterion for authenticity with every learning activity will not be practical. A framework such as this, however, does give you a means to focus your planning on genuine learning rather than simply covering curriculum or keeping students occupied.

Once a thematic focus or organizing concept has been selected for a unit, teachers will begin listing overall goals, related concepts and skills, available materials, possible activities and teaching strategies, and ways to evaluate students' learning, all with the particular needs and abilities of their students in mind (Goerss, 1996). This will take some time as resources are located, materials such as study guides and handouts are developed, Internet sites are located, and new ideas for the unit come from reflection, research, and conversations with students and colleagues. To keep the ideas for a unit organized, teachers often use a web or graphic organizer to map out concepts, resources, or activities. In Figure 4.1, we illustrated a completed concept planning web for a unit on the American Revolution, and Figure 4.4 shows two generic variations of planning webs.

The final stages of unit planning involve planning activities, developing assessment procedures, and constructing a time line for the unit. To enhance student interest, engagement, and learning, it is best to plan a variety of activities, including whole-class, small-group, and independent activities; some that are teacher assigned; and some that are self-selected by students. J. D. Cooper (1997) suggests the use of three chronological categories of activities. *Initiating activities* should motivate students, activate prior knowledge and build background, and help students take responsibility for their own learning. *Developing activities* involve students in reading, writing, discussing, problem solving, and hands-on experience with making something, creating, or experimenting. *Culminating activities* allow students to share their learning, reflect on the ideas in the unit, and evaluate their own efforts.

PUTTING IT ALL TOGETHER   Steve participated in a conference on using technology in education at which he heard a presentation by Gene Kulbago, an English teacher at Niagara Middle School in Niagara Falls, New York. Gene and his colleague, earth science teacher Mary Marcinkowski, have collaborated on an earth science research project that illustrates many of the ideas presented in this chapter. Niagara Middle is an urban middle school that serves a diverse population of students. It features a schoolwide technology program in which all students learn to use word processing, desktop publishing and presentation software, Internet browsers, digital cameras, and scanners. The entire three-year curriculum of the school is infused with applications of technology in virtually every content area.

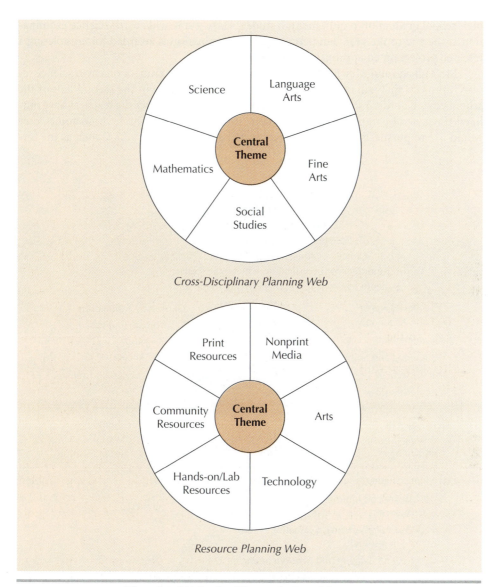

Cross-Disciplinary Planning Web

Resource Planning Web

FIGURE 4.4 **Planning Webs for Thematic Teaching**

Gene and Mary are experienced teachers, both professionally active in state and local teacher organizations. They teach approximately 50 eighth-grade students in an honors program, all of whom are taking Mary's earth science course for New York State Regents high school credit. In order to receive credit for this course (and as part of state high school graduation requirements), students take a statewide earth science examination at the end of the year. Ten percent of the examination is awarded for completing a research project on an appropriate earth science topic.

Mr. Kulbago and Mrs. Marcinkowski and their students embark on earth science research projects that will occupy much of their time, especially in the second half of the school year. Figure 4.5 shows a planning web for this project. After the teachers have outlined the general parameters of the project, students begin to think about topics they would like to pursue. Students have investigated a wide range of topics, such as the for-

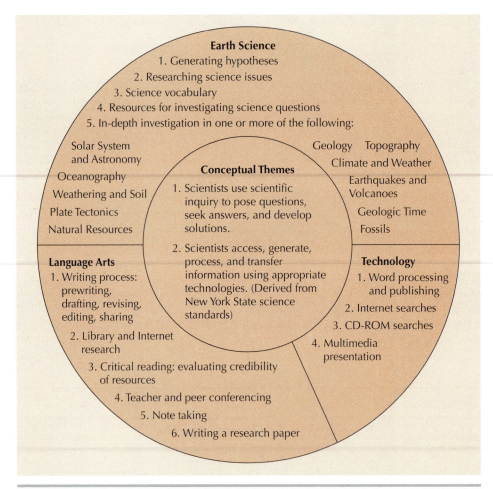

FIGURE 4.5   Planning Web for Earth Science Research Unit

Source: Gene Kulbago and Mary Marcinkowski, Niagara Middle School, Niagara Falls, New York.

mation of hurricanes or tornadoes, dinosaur extinction theories, the geology of the Niagara River gorge, New York State oil and natural gas reserves, evidence for global warming, and the causes and effects of the Buffalo blizzard of 1977.

Students are required to gather information from both electronic and traditional print resources. To get students started, the teachers have selected 18 sample Internet sites that feature reliable and useful earth science information along with links to other sites. Online, students branch out to a great variety of websites, due to the diversity of their topics. Gene says that most students would prefer to conduct their searches entirely online, but he and Mary believe that it is important that students be facile with traditional print resources as well, such as science encyclopedias, scientific journals, and science trade books. Throughout their research, students are guided to make critical judgments about the credibility of the information they are collecting, especially from the Internet, by considering the author's knowledge, purpose, and affiliations or other credentials.

By February, students are expected to begin drafting their research papers. When students have a final draft completed, Mr. Kulbago evaluates them for adherence to MLA guidelines and other standard writing conventions. Students are then expected to revise as needed, after which Mrs. Marcinkowski evaluates the papers for their scientific content. This evaluation is followed by a conference with Mrs. Marcinkowski, and then the research papers are revised and finalized during language arts class time.

As students are completing their research papers, they begin preparing a PowerPoint multimedia presentation of their findings. These presentations are designed to highlight the major findings in a creative way that will hold audience interest, along with a concluding statement of the importance of the topic. Students share the completed multimedia presentations at a special parent night.

It is important to note that for experienced teachers such as Gene Kulbago and Mary Marcinkowski, planning is usually ongoing and cumulative. They developed different aspects of the earth science research unit over the years that they have presented it. They would like to add a social studies component so that students can also consider the historical and social contexts of scientific issues. For instance, students who chose to research the Niagara River gorge might investigate the social, political, and economic issues surrounding the development of tourist attractions at Niagara Falls, the generation of hydroelectric power, or the shared border between the United States and Canada. Considering such aspects of a topic would reflect a social constructionist view as students learned that science is not just neutral facts but rather has ramifications that are socially shaped and contested.

This earth science unit exemplifies good applications of integrated language processes and interdisciplinary teaching. Teachers from two disciplines, science and English, have collaborated to integrate technology, reading, writing, speaking, and listening as fundamental tools in extending student understanding of several earth science topics. In this case, the unit theme encompasses the broad topic of scientific investigation and is specifically keyed to one of the state requirements for successful completion of the earth science course. The unit is designed to have students learn and apply skills and strategies that overlap between the two subject areas. This unit meets all the criteria for authenticity suggested by Bergeron and Rudenga (1996).

Summary

As you read about the various ways that teachers can plan lessons and units, we are sure you found some ideas attractive, felt others were impractical or incompatible with your situation, and thought of ways to modify other ideas to suit your style, your students, and your content area. We would not be so presumptive as to prescribe a particular planning approach for any teacher. However, we have tried to emphasize four points that will influence your planning. First, we encourage you to think about how students will use language and literacy in your content area. Second, you can look for ways to help students take charge of their own learning. Third, learning will be more meaningful and long lasting if your students can make connections among the concepts they learn, connections between content areas, and connections to what they know and experience outside of school. Finally, there are no short-term "fixes" for the difficulties many students encounter with their content area studies, but when teachers commit to integrating literacy learning with the learning of content over a period of time, there will be visible gains in student achievement.

Suggested Readings

Au, K. (1998). Social constructivism and the school literacy learning of students of diverse backgrounds. *Journal of Literacy Research, 30,* 297–319.

Buell, C., & Whittaker, A. (2001). Enhancing content literacy in physical education. *Journal of Physical Education, Recreation, and Dance, 72*(6), 32–37.

Bruce, B. C. (Ed.). (2003). *Literacy in the information age: Inquiries into meaning making with new technologies.* Newark, DE: International Reading Association.

Fielding, A., Schoenbach, R., & Jordan, M. (Eds.). (2003). *Building academic literacy: Lessons from Reading Apprenticeship classrooms, grades 6–12.* San Francisco: Jossey-Bass.

Frank Potter's Science Gems. (n.d.). More than 14,000 science resources sorted by category (e.g., earth science, life science, physical science), subcategory (e.g., energy, waves), and grade level. Available online at www.sciencegems.com

Kist, W. (2005). *New literacies in action: Teaching and learning in multiple media.* New York: Teachers College Press.

Leu, D., & Leu, D. (1999). *Teaching with the Internet: Lessons from the classroom.* Norwood, MA: Christopher Gordon.

Meister, D. G., & Nolan, J. (2001). Out on a limb on our own: Uncertainty and doubt, moving from subject-centered to interdisciplinary teaching. *Teachers College Record, 103,* 608–633. Also available online at www.tcrecord.org

Schoenbach, R., Greenleaf, C., Cziko, C., & Hurwitz, L. (1999). *Reading for understanding: A guide to improving reading in middle and high school classrooms.* San Francisco: Jossey-Bass.

MyEducationLab is a research-based learning tool that brings teaching to life. Go to the Alvermann, Phelps, and Ridgeway Gillis 6th Edition MyEducationLab for Content Area Reading site at www.myeducationlab.com to:

- engage in multimedia exercises to help you build a deeper and more applied understanding of chapter content;

- utilize extensive resources including videos from real classrooms, Praxis and licensure preparation, a lesson plan builder, and materials to help you in your teaching career.

chapter 5

Assessment of
Students and
Textbooks

Assessment of Students and Textbooks

Assessing Students

- Tests and Testing: a Consumer Advisory
- Types of Assessment
- Learning about Students
- Grades and Grading
- Portfolio Assessment

Assessing Textbooks

- Readability Formulas
- Consumer Judgments

Anticipation Guide

Directions: Read each of the following statements. Place a checkmark on the line in the "Before Reading" column if you agree with the statement; leave it blank if you disagree. Then predict what you think the chapter will be about, and jot down on a sticky note (or post online) any questions you have. Read the chapter; then return to the statements and respond to them as you think the authors of your text would. Place a checkmark on the line in the "Authors' Stance" column if you believe the authors would agree with the statement. If you discuss these statements with other people online, in class, or at the family dinner table, return to the statements and check any items you agree with in the right-hand column, "After Discussion." If your thinking changed, what caused that change?

Before Reading	Authors' Stance	Statements	After Discussion
_____	_____	1. Assessment is an inexact science.	_____
_____	_____	2. Standardized test scores are accurate indicators of students' abilities.	_____
_____	_____	3. Portfolios are only useful in English classes.	_____
_____	_____	4. A rubric, or scoring guide, helps to make grading students' projects easier and more uniform.	_____
_____	_____	5. Good teacher-designed tests are easy to create.	_____

As schools and teachers are increasingly pressed to be accountable for the results of instruction, students are being assessed in schools for varied and often conflicting purposes. Various constituencies look to assessment for different reasons and engage in an ongoing and sometimes rancorous debate over how student assessment should be conducted. The issues that have been raised are far from being resolved. Given the limitations inherent in educational assessment, many of them never will be resolved.

In this chapter, we address some of the issues surrounding student assessment, but because of their complexity and intractability, we do not presume to settle the many theoretical and philosophical questions that exist. Instead, we concentrate on the practical day-to-day assessment decisions that teachers make: How well can students read, write, think, and study? Can they apply what they know? How can teachers fairly and accurately reflect student knowledge through the grades they award? How difficult, interesting, and useful are available texts? This chapter explores some ways to find answers to these questions.

In the following reminiscence, Dawn Voelker, a math teacher at West Seneca (New York) Central Schools, reflects on what it was like to be on the receiving end of teacher assessment. We think it captures many of the difficulties experienced by students and teachers.

● ● ●

I can clearly remember my friend Kathy and I working on a project in high school. It involved research, reading, and an interview. We chose the same topic, so we decided to do the paper together. It started off great. We met every night possible and helped one another out. As time went on, she wasn't doing any of the reading and research. On the other hand, I was working my tail off. I got to the point where I didn't care because I knew we were getting separate grades anyway.

When the interviewing part came up, she made the whole thing up. I told her that she had better work harder, but she insisted she would do fine. I continued to do my project and put forth more effort than on any other paper. Kathy's laziness inspired me to work even harder. I wanted to do better than she did.

The projects were handed in, graded, and returned to us within a week. As the papers were being passed back, I glanced over at Kathy. I was expecting disappointment. Instead, she gleamed, held up her paper, and said, "I got an A minus." I thought to myself, "Great! This means I at least have an A."

When I got my paper back, there on the front was a huge C+. Below the grade was a note: "Misspellings, grammatical errors and run-ons." I felt like crawling under my desk. My face got red-hot as Kathy stared at me, waiting for me to announce my grade. Instead, I just stuck the project in my folder and stared straight ahead.

I couldn't understand why I had put forth all the effort and gotten an average grade. Just because I had misspellings and run-ons? That was completely unfair. Kathy put down anything and made it sound good and got an A. I didn't have the nerve to confront my teacher and tell him that I had worked so hard and deserved a better grade. I wanted to tell him that Kathy practically made hers up. I just didn't say anything because I trusted that he knew more about grading than I did.*

• • •

Most of us can commiserate with Dawn's dismay and confusion, yet we would be reluctant to criticize the teacher too harshly. After all, he saw only the product of Dawn's and Kathy's work, not the process of producing them.

There are many variables in a teacher's day, many things to consider as decisions are made about what will happen in the classroom. There are, of course, students. Middle-grade and high school teachers often see from 100 to 150 or more students in a day. Like Dawn and Kathy, each of these students has his or her own personality, aptitudes, interests, and effect on classroom dynamics. They represent at least 100 energetic bundles of human variability. Teachers must somehow plan instruction that meets their disparate needs and must make periodic judgments—in the form of grades—of how well individual students have learned a subject. Textbooks and other text and nontext materials represent another set of variables for teachers. Text materials especially will vary greatly in their levels of difficulty, interest, and utility. They may be well suited to students' needs; they may be quite inappropriate. The more you know about these variables—students and texts—the more effective you can be as a teacher.

Assessing Students

Experts on educational evaluation talk about two purposes for assessing students (Afflerbach, 2007). *Formative assessment* is intended to help form, or develop, a student. Formative assessment helps a teacher to draw conclusions about the various strengths and weaknesses of the individual, those things that might help or hinder learning. *Summative assessment* is intended to make a summarizing judgment of what a person has learned or done. Grades on tests, assignments, and report cards are examples of summative assessments.

Whatever the purposes of assessment, we believe that good assessment practices have certain characteristics:

1. *Good assessment draws on multiple sources of information.* No single test—whether it is a standardized, norm-referenced, commercially published test of student achievement or a teacher-made, ten-item multiple-choice pop quiz on last night's homework—can tell a teacher the true state of a student's knowledge.

2. *Good assessment results in information that is useful to both students and teachers.* Students need to know how they are doing, what they are doing right,

---

*Used with permission of Dawn Voelker, West Seneca Central Schools, West Seneca, NY.

and what they can do to improve. Teachers need to know about students' attitudes, interests, background knowledge, and aptitude for reading, writing, and other academic tasks.

3. *Good assessment gives students optimal conditions for showing their capabilities.* Varied assessment procedures, fairly introduced and interpreted, give students the chance to show their individual strengths.

4. *Good assessment involves students in self-assessment.* In the long run, the judgments that students make about themselves are just as important as—if not more important than—the judgments teachers make about students. Self-evaluation is an essential component of learning how to learn.

5. *Good assessment admits the potential of fallibility.* After all is said and done, teachers must acknowledge that some students will remain enigmas and that some judgments, no matter how carefully considered, may be inaccurate.

Tests and Testing: A Consumer Advisory

There are many stakeholders in the debates over student assessment, and their demands frequently conflict (Pearson, 1998). Community members have numerous concerns: Are tax dollars being well spent? Do our schools compare favorably with those in other districts or states? Are the values and culture of the community being fairly represented? Is my child learning as well as I would like? Politicians at the local, state, and national levels try to represent the many voices of their community, but they frequently view assessment as a means to further their political agendas as well. Test results may be used by politicians to promote funding for educational programs or to further attacks on public schools, teachers' unions, or particular aspects of the curriculum.

School administrators view assessment as a way to demonstrate accountability and program effectiveness, yet they must also consider how cost effective various assessment techniques may be. Teachers are looking for ways to find out how well students are progressing, both so that they can report to other stakeholders and so that they can devise effective instruction. At the same time, teachers know that their own performance will be judged by how well their students do on statewide or district testing. Of all the voices in the assessment debate, the one least often heard is that of students, yet they have perhaps the most important stake of all.

The professed purposes of testing are as varied and contradictory as the stakeholders. Reformers of all political stripes may see tests as a means to drive school reform. Some may look to state or national assessments as a way to raise student achievement, whereas others see alternative assessment procedures as a way to complement curricular reforms and increase students' participation in their learning. Some people see assessment as a means to ensure equity for students of diverse backgrounds, whereas others point out that assessment procedures often reinforce or even create an unequal playing field for children of different economic, linguistic, or cultural backgrounds. Many teachers argue that assessment should be a professional tool that they can use to evaluate and improve instruction. However, for state boards of education, college admissions officers, and employers, assessment may provide a gatekeeping function, determining whether an individual can graduate from high school, enter college, engage in certain professions, or hold a particular job.

The conflicting demands and claims surrounding educational assessment present several very real problems to classroom teachers:

- **Validity.**   How can we be sure that a particular assessment tool is really telling us what we want to know?
- **Credibility.**   How well will other stakeholders—parents, administrators, taxpayers, and so on—accept the results of assessment?
- **Time.**   Demands on a teacher's time are daunting. How can we get useful information without taking too much valuable instructional time?
- **Influences on curriculum and teaching.**   How can we deal with the pressure to "teach to the test," to alter what and how we teach in order to increase student performance on externally imposed assessments?
- **Teacher knowledge and training.**   Will we have the requisite knowledge of assessment, the curriculum, and students? Will there be opportunities for in-service training and reflection in order to design assessments and collect, analyze, and report results?
- **Equity.**   Will assessment fairly reflect the abilities of all our students, especially those from diverse linguistic, social, or cultural backgrounds? Do we promote fairness by asking all students to take the same test in the same circumstances, or do we provide students with alternatives so that each can show what he or she is capable of doing in optimal circumstances?

While reading the following discussion of tests and testing, you should keep in mind the limitations of testing. You might think of tests as being like snapshots: Some may be flattering, and some may be downright dreadful. Your friends or family might like a photo you think makes you look goofy, whereas *you* might prefer one that makes you look sleek, athletic, or intellectual, even though others say it looks nothing like you. No photo, not even a portrait by a talented photographer, is the real you. It is at best an image of you at a particular time that, by skill or accident, may communicate something of your essence.

So it is with almost any instrument or procedure designed to evaluate or assess students. A student may do well or poorly on a particular test, but the test alone cannot tell definitely why the student performed that way or whether that is typical of his or her performance. It is at best a suggestion of what was going on inside the student's head at that particular moment. However, over a period of time, after experiencing the student's oral and written output, scores on tests and assignments, and participation (or lack of it) in classroom activities, you can form a composite judgment of how well he or she is doing in your subject and of his or her general aptitude as a student. The best decisions about students will be made after carefully considering many sources of information.

CULTURAL BIAS Teachers who work with students of diverse cultural backgrounds must especially be aware of the cultural biases that can influence tests and testing (Gronna, Chin-Chance, & Abedi, 2000). Tests (and the curricula they are designed to assess) are generally devised by members of the dominant culture and may be inadequate for evaluating the knowledge, achievement, and ability of students from other cultures.

There are several sources of cultural bias in standardized tests (Garcia, 1991; Garcia & Pearson, 1994; Helms, 1992) and in more innovative forms of testing (Au, 1998). Many of these biases apply to teacher-designed tests as well:

1. *Content and conceptual bias.* Test content is most likely to reflect the knowledge and values of mainstream society. Test content may be more or less familiar to members of different cultures, who may therefore assign different meanings to the same concept. Even though some concepts may have been covered by the instructor, other concepts that are unfamiliar may appear in the wording of test questions or multiple-choice responses.

2. *Linguistic bias.* Lack of familiarity with academic English, with specific vocabulary, or with familiar synonyms (e.g., *canine* for *dog*) may influence test scores for students whose primary language or dialect is not standard English. Time limits will be especially problematic for bilingual students. It is difficult to decide whether bilingual students are better off being tested in English or in their native language, and a test in either language may not demonstrate what a student knows in both languages.

3. *Functional bias.* The mainstream conventions of testing, where adults request known answers to questions that have no apparent functional goal, may be perceived as foolish or nonsensical to members of other cultures. Some cultures may also prize answers that are imaginative or elaborative as opposed to literally true. Many tests are not flexible enough to fully assess the capabilities of English language learners (ELLs).

4. *Consequential bias.* Results of testing are often used as graduation requirements or to place students in remedial or lower-track classes. Unfortunately, students of color and low-income students are disproportionately impacted, and this is due in part to the biases inherent in test content and procedures. To compound this problem, students in remedial programs are subjected to further testing, most of which focuses on discrete skills and isolated, literal-level facts. This results in fragmented, skills-based instruction for these students.

You can minimize cultural bias in several ways (Garcia & Pearson, 1994; Helms, 1992). First, you can devise a variety of assessment forms to give all students an opportunity to demonstrate their competence. Practical, hands-on tasks may be more effective than pencil-and-paper tests. You can also include test and evaluation procedures that reflect diverse cultural content and values. Finally, you can follow up on apparent wrong answers by asking students for elaborated explanations or justifications for their responses. These may reveal more about students' actual knowledge of a concept than the test results indicate.

To be useful in addressing the literacy needs of diverse students, assessment should include more than tests of academic achievement. Tatum (2005) says that comprehensive assessment must include a variety of "close-ups." Cognitive close-ups would include a student's strengths and weaknesses with words, with comprehension, and with metacognition. Pedagogical close-ups would show what kind of instruction the student was receiving, as well as whether the student found the curricula to be relevant and challenging. Psychological close-ups would consider a student's goals, self-efficacy, and emotional disposition toward school. Finally, physiological close-ups such as specific medical conditions and vision problems might require evaluation by experts other than the classroom teacher.

Types of Assessment

The professional lexicon describes several different kinds of student assessment. Some of the terms used are relatively new, and many of them seem to be used interchangeably or in such a way that their meaning is unclear or confusing. Consequently, we will give a brief definition and description of some of the more common types of assessment used in schools.

STANDARDIZED TESTS   Standardized tests are commercially prepared tests used to assess the achievement of large numbers of students in reading, math, and other academic areas. They are designed so that their administration, scoring, and interpretation are uniform, or standard, across all settings. Many schools require that standardized tests be administered once or twice a year, and standardized test results are usually included in a student's cumulative school record.

Standardized tests are *norm referenced*. This means that an individual's score on a test is compared with a large, demographically representative cross section of American students, called a *norming population*. Comparisons are made possible by converting raw test scores to derived scores such as percentiles or stanines, which indicate the position of an individual score relative to the scores of the norming population.

Standardized tests have been the target of considerable criticism. In a review of assessment policies, Valencia and Wixson (2000) conclude that "high-stakes standardized basic skills tests led to narrowing of the curriculum; overemphasis on basic skills and test-like instructional methods; reduction in effective instructional time and an increase in time for test preparation; inflated test scores; and pressure on teachers to improve test scores" (p. 915). Critics argue, among other things, that standardized tests actually assess a narrow and artificial set of reading abilities. The test scores, on the other hand, render those abilities into global categories of "comprehension" and "vocabulary" and a composite "total reading" score, none of which really indicates much about what a student actually can or cannot do. Critics also point out that a student's performance on standardized tests is influenced by nonreading factors such as prior knowledge, test-taking skill, physical and emotional status, and cultural background.

Evidence-
Based
Research

Standardized test results are probably not particularly useful to the content area teacher. They can give a preliminary estimate, or rough sorting, of students into high-medium-, and low-ability categories, but this estimate must be tempered by the understanding that an individual student's scores are not very precise. A difference of a few raw score points is not very significant, even though it may affect the derived percentile or stanine score. Schell (1988) points out that comprehension is very often text specific: A reader may comprehend very differently in two texts at the same reading level. Therefore, a student who scores very high on a test of reading comprehension may still have considerable difficulty with a particular text or subject. Standardized tests are no substitute for informed teacher observation and judgment.

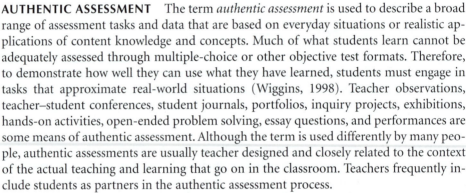

AUTHENTIC ASSESSMENT The term *authentic assessment* is used to describe a broad range of assessment tasks and data that are based on everyday situations or realistic applications of content knowledge and concepts. Much of what students learn cannot be adequately assessed through multiple-choice or other objective test formats. Therefore, to demonstrate how well they can use what they have learned, students must engage in tasks that approximate real-world situations (Wiggins, 1998). Teacher observations, teacher–student conferences, student journals, portfolios, inquiry projects, exhibitions, hands-on activities, open-ended problem solving, essay questions, and performances are some means of authentic assessment. Although the term is used differently by many people, authentic assessments are usually teacher designed and closely related to the context of the actual teaching and learning that go on in the classroom. Teachers frequently include students as partners in the authentic assessment process.

Go to MyEduca-tionLab and select the topic *Assess-ment*. Then, go to the Activities and Applications section, watch the video entitled "Authentic Assessment in Science," and respond to the accompanying prompts.

Authentic assessment tasks are complex and challenging and frequently have several possible outcomes. Grading such tasks is also complex because several variables must often be evaluated. Both teachers and students should evaluate not just the end product but also the processes that are used to complete the task. Although authentic assessments are usually more work for students and teachers, they yield a better picture of student achievement and place a premium on application, not just rote learning.

Evidence-Based Research

In addition, authentic assessments have many potential advantages over traditional kinds of testing for students of diverse cultural backgrounds, especially for bilingual students (Garcia & Pearson, 1994). Authentic assessment is more amenable to adaptations that include cultural content and values of diverse students. When students are asked to use what they have learned in more realistic settings, they are better able to relate new learning to their own cultural-specific understandings. Bilingual students have the opportunity to show what they know in both languages and how both languages interact in the learning process. Teachers have much more flexibility in collecting and interpreting information on how students are learning and developing, and students are more likely to be judged in terms of their individual progress rather than according to externally imposed criteria.

At the same time, authentic assessment poses some potential difficulties. There is a question regarding who defines *authenticity* or what counts as *real* (Alvermann & Commeyras, 1998). When teachers define authentic tasks and the parameters for analyzing performance on those tasks, there is no guarantee that the assessment has relevance to the reality of students or that the assessment will be free of cultural biases. Authentic assessment with culturally and linguistically diverse students requires a good deal of unbiased knowledge about student culture and language on the part of the teacher.

For example, an English teacher might work with students on descriptive writing. To decide what constitutes an authentic descriptive writing task for his students, the teacher would need to know not only something about their interests and experiences but also something about how writing is valued by the students, the purposes for which students use writing and language, and the linguistic and rhetorical conventions of students' vernacular. In evaluating students' written products, the teacher would also need to decide if dialect features in the writing should or could be considered separately from the persuasive power of the writing.

Both decisions—what counts as authentic writing and how dialect features can influence the effectiveness of the writing—might best be arrived at through discussion and negotiation with students. Therein lies what many consider to be the primary advantage of authentic assessments: student involvement. When assessment grows out of the everyday activities of the classroom, assessment becomes an integral component of instruction. Students can become active partners in determining what will be learned, how it will be learned, and how learning can best be demonstrated and evaluated.

We will expand on the potential advantages and disadvantages of authentic assessment later in this chapter when we discuss the use of student portfolios.

PERFORMANCE ASSESSMENT   *Performance assessment* overlaps in many ways with authentic assessment, and some educators may use the terms interchangeably. The difference is that performance assessments are graded according to externally established criteria and students usually are expected to achieve some benchmark score as an index of competency in the area being tested. Performance assessments of writing, for instance, have been commonplace for more than 20 years. In a typical writing competency test, students are given one or more actual writing tasks and their written products are then given a holistic pass/fail by trained raters.

Performance assessments are designed to simulate real-world tasks, and they require the active participation of students in the creation of an answer or product that shows application of the student's knowledge and understanding. Performance assessment and authentic assessment may be based on the same techniques, including projects, essays, problem solving, experiments, demonstrations, and portfolios. However, performance assessments involve some sort of benchmarks or criteria for judging student performance, often called *rubrics*. Although a teacher may develop a rubric for evaluating or assigning grades to authentic assessment data such as portfolios, rubrics for evaluating performance assessments are designed to allow for comparisons across classrooms or even across schools or districts. The development and dissemination of rubrics make assessment public; all stakeholders, including parents, teachers, and students, have access to the criteria for successful performance.

The use of performance assessment to judge the performance of students, teachers, or programs has some advantages over traditional standardized testing and multiple-choice exams. Performance assessments are by their very nature more closely tied to what actually happens in the classroom. When the criteria for success can be clearly stated up front, both teachers and students have a better idea of what they are doing and why, and learning may take on more relevance (Hoffman, Paris, Salas, Patterson, & Assaf, 2003). Instruction is likely to focus more on practical application and less on rote learning of isolated skills and information. Performance assessments also have many of the advantages of authentic assessment for students of diverse backgrounds. Performance assessments allow for more teacher scaffolding, more freedom to work in a variety of settings and without time constraints, and more acceptance of diverse responses than do traditional tests.

On the other hand, many questions about the utility of performance assessment remain unanswered. Technical problems of validity and reliability must be resolved (Valencia & Wixson, 2000). If teachers provide assistance with performance tasks and students work in groups, there is a question of how much an assessment can tell us about the performance of individual students (Gearhart & Herman, 1995). There is always the possibility that results will be inflated if teachers "teach to the test." As with authentic assessment, there is also the question of who decides what counts as real and what constitutes mastery. Finally, performance assessments represent a significant increase in time and cost over traditional multiple-choice assessments.

INTERNATIONAL ASSESSMENTS   The Programme for International Student Assessment (PISA) is an international assessment of reading, mathematics, and science conducted by the Organisation for Economic Cooperation and Development (OECD). It is given to 15-year-olds in participating countries every three years, with one of the three assessments areas slated as the major focus in each administration of the test. In 2000, the major focus was reading. Of 32 countries participating, the United States finished fifteenth, scoring right at the average of the OECD countries. Finland and Canada had the highest average scores.

The focus for PISA in 2003 was mathematics. Hong Kong had the highest average score, followed by Finland. The United States was twenty-fifth among the 41 countries participating. Science was the focus in 2006, when Finland and Hong Kong garnered top spots. The United States was twenty-ninth of the 57 countries participating. The U.S. math scores in 2003 and science scores in 2006 were both below the average for OECD countries.

PISA defines *reading* as "understanding, using, and reflecting on written texts, in order to achieve one's goals, to develop one's knowledge and potential and to participate in society" (OECD, 2003, p. 108). The PISA reading assessment is based on both continuous and noncontinuous (e.g., charts, tables, maps) texts. Readings on the assessment are both narrative and expository and include descriptive, argumentative, and injunctive (e.g., directions, procedures, regulations) texts. In 2000, 44 percent of the test items required an open-ended constructed response, and the rest consisted of multiple-choice and closed constructed-response items. Test items were designed to assess five reading processes:

- Retrieving information
- Forming a broad general understanding
- Developing an interpretation

- Reflecting on and evaluating the content of a text
- Reflecting on and evaluating the form of a text

In 2009, reading will again be the major focus of PISA, using a format and content similar to the 2000 assessment. In addition, PISA will assess the reading of electronic texts. As of late 2008, it appears that the United States will participate in the offline reading assessment but not the online portion. This is unfortunate, given the importance and ubiquity of online literacy and the fact that online reading comprehension is not included in any U.S. national or state assessment of reading (Leu et al., 2008).

NATIONAL ASSESSMENTS   National assessment of students has been a reality since 1971, when the U.S. Congress mandated the sampling of the reading and writing abilities of students under the National Assessment of Educational Progress (NAEP). Adolescents' reading achievement has generally remained steady, with slow but regular increases from 1971 to the present.

In the most recent NAEP *Reading Report Card* (Lee, Grigg, & Donahue, 2007), eighth graders made slight but significant increases over 2005. Seventy-four percent of eighth graders were reading at or above the basic level, which means they could demonstrate a literal understanding and make some simple interpretations. Only 31 percent of eighth graders were reading at the proficient level, or able to extend the ideas in the text by making clear inferences, drawing conclusions, making connections to their own experiences, and identifying some of the devices used by authors. Scores for low- and middle-performing students increased over the 2005 scores, but significant performance gaps persisted between white and minority students.

Writing was also assessed by NAEP in 2007 (Salahu-Din, Persky, & Miller, 2008). Writing scores for both eighth and twelfth graders improved significantly since 1998, and as with reading, low- and middle-performing students made the greatest gains. The gap between white and black eighth graders narrowed slightly, but otherwise, stubborn gaps remained between the scores of white and minority students at both the eighth- and twelfth-grade levels. Eighty-eight percent of eighth graders and 82 percent of twelfth graders scored at the basic level or better, while 33 percent of eighth graders and 24 percent of twelfth graders were proficient. There was also a large gender gap favoring girls in the assessments.

While there are some signs of improvement in the NAEP data, it is clear that too many adolescents are insufficiently prepared to meet the literacy demands of the twenty-first century.

RESPONSE TO INTERVENTION (RTI)   Special educators have recently shown an interest in an approach to teaching and assessment called *response to intervention (RTI)* (Fuchs & Fuchs, 2006). In the RTI model, students are regularly assessed to evaluate how well they are responding to a particular teaching approach, which is sometimes called an *intervention* when used with individuals who are having difficulty learning. Interventions are tiered, becoming more intensive as a student moves across the tiers.

To date, most of the research on RTI has involved students in the primary grades, with a focus on developing valid procedures for identifying individuals with disabilities. RTI also requires considerable expertise in evidence-based instruction and assessment. Consequently, the utility of RTI in content area classes has yet to be determined. However, RTI is similar in many ways to the diagnostic teaching of students with reading difficulties (Walker, 2007). Diagnostic teaching is a cyclical process of providing instruction, systematically observing students' responses, and determining the effectiveness of the teaching strategies being used.

STATE ASSESSMENTS   Many states have tried to develop more authentic types of assessments, especially of literacy. Statewide performance assessments of reading and writing "include longer and more complex reading selections from a variety of genres, higher-level comprehension questions, extended written responses, and cross-text analyses" (Valencia & Wixson, 2000, p. 917).

This movement toward establishing and assessing higher standards appears to be driven by the assumption that raising the bar for high school graduation can accomplish systemic reform of teaching and learning at the classroom level (Valencia & Wixson, 2000). However, there is reason to question whether higher standards and more rigorous assessments have the desired effects on teaching and learning (Hamilton, 2003; Hoffman et al., 2003). Standards and tests alone cannot influence what happens in the classroom unless teachers are given sufficient professional development opportunities to implement meaningful changes and sufficient time to assess students' progress. For example, John McVay, a middle school math teacher in a suburb of New York City, estimates that if he were to do a culminating performance assessment at the end of six math units during the year and spend 15 minutes on each of his 187 students' work, he would need about 35 eight-hour student-free workdays (or 18 weekends) (Focused Reporting Project, 1999).

Evidence-Based Research

High-stakes performance assessments are relatively intrusive, inefficient, costly, time consuming, and difficult to administer (Madaus & O'Dwyer, 1999) and are subject to persistent questions about their reliability and validity (French, 2003; Pearson, 1998; Valencia & Wixson, 2000). There are also serious concerns that high-stakes performance assessments may further disadvantage ELLs and other students of diverse backgrounds (Au, 1998; Short & Fitzsimmons, 2007). High-stakes tests are also likely to increase dropout rates, and this has a disproportionate effect on African American and Latino students (French, 2003).

One persistent issue in high-stakes testing is whether to "teach to the test." In many cases, school districts or individual teachers have made up parallel assessment tasks that mirror the state exams, and students have been given (sometimes extensive) practice. Practicing for the state exam is not by itself necessarily a bad thing, especially if teachers carefully deconstruct the tasks by explaining what is expected and giving guidance on how to accomplish it. However, we caution that time spent on extensive practice in test taking might be better spent by involving students in more authentic and meaningful experiences with reading and writing, mathematical problem solving, examination of pri-

Helping
Struggling Readers

State Assessments

High-stakes testing can be especially problematic for struggling readers. For them, the pressure of passing a state-mandated test can result in an excess of skill-and-drill instruction. Such was the case for Kathy Bussert-Webb (1999, 2000), who describes her experiences as the teacher of ninth-grade remedial reading in a south Texas high school in which 98 percent of the students were Mexican American, mostly native speakers of Spanish. Because the school had a poor pass rate on the Texas Achievement of Academic Skills assessment (TAAS), a high school graduation requirement, the school administration began to focus on intense, structured teaching of the skills covered on the test. For Bussert-Webb and her students, this meant a lot of reading of short passages and answering multiple-choice questions.

After becoming increasingly dissatisfied with this approach, Bussert-Webb abandoned it and did what her instincts and training led her to believe was best for her students. She focused instead on making personal connections with students, increasing their connec-

tions with reading, and having more class discussions instead of covering the curriculum. Students began reading

things they cared about, such as low-rider truck magazines, young adult novels, and stories by Latino authors. As a result, she found her students had fewer discipline problems and off-task behaviors. Most important, they did more reading—50 percent more than her previous students—and enjoyed it. Her students had the most library points of any class in the school.

What about the TAAS? Overall, the pass rate for sophomores at the school improved dramatically, from a 59 percent pass rate in 1995 to 82 percent in 1999. All but three of Bussert-Webb's struggling readers passed, a success rate of 88 percent. The three who did not pass just missed the passing score of 70 percent, with scores of 69, 67, and 65 percent, compared to a mean score of 59 percent for the other students at the school who failed. Although it would be a mistake to read too much into these data, it is clear that Bussert-Webb's student-centered, holistic curriculum did not negatively affect her students.

mary sources, laboratory activities, and research; in fact, many districts and individual teachers have used the implementation of the new standards to do just that. Rather than focus solely on devising, administering, and scoring practice tests, they have worked on ways to change curriculum and instruction to align more closely with the new standards.

Perhaps the most pertinent finding on "teaching to the test" comes from Langer's (2001) study of schools and teachers who "beat the odds" by having their students achieve relatively strong performance on high-stakes assessment. One key factor was that "beating the odds" teachers prepared students for high-stakes testing by carefully aligning curriculum and assessment. They were aware of what students would be asked to do and integrated those kinds of tasks, along with instruction on how to perform them, into ongoing instruction. On the other hand, teachers whose students achieved more typical results were more likely to allocate specific blocks of time to test preparation, usually involving practice and test-taking hints, separate from other kinds of instruction. In other words, the best "teaching to the test" was thoughtful teaching of needed knowledge and skills embedded in the curriculum throughout the year.

Learning about Students

To plan effective instruction, teachers need to learn as much as they can about students' language, reading, and writing abilities. It is also useful to know something about their interests, values, traditions, and beliefs. All these factors may affect students' performance in a content area classroom. In this section, we consider practical ways of assessing some of these variables.

STRATEGIC CONTENT LITERACY ASSESSMENT (SCLA)   The many forms of reporting student progress—including state- and districtwide assessments, final exams, and report cards—might be considered assessment *of* learning. These assessment results tell teachers something about what students have learned, but they provide little information about how students have learned, why they didn't learn, or what teachers can do to help them learn. Consequently, teachers need assessment *for* learning—that is, assessment that is based on clearly articulated curriculum targets and that provides descriptive feedback on what and how students learn. Assessment *for* learning provides information that can be used to evaluate and adjust instruction and to communicate with students, families, and colleagues about achievement (Stiggins, 2002).

When students are actively involved in the assessment process through setting goals, evaluating their own work, and communicating their evaluations, assessment becomes an integral part of learning, or assessment *as* learning (Brownlie, Feniak, & Schnellert, 2006). Later in this chapter, we describe portfolios assessment, which can be a kind of assessment *as* learning when the portfolios are co-constructed by teachers and students.

Victoria has developed a variation of an assessment-as-learning process described by Brownlie and her colleagues that she calls the *strategic content literacy assessment (SCLA)*. In SCLA, students are engaged with a common content area text and response task. Their responses are evaluated and the results are then shared with them as part of a process of identifying effective content area reading strategies.

Figure 5.1 presents an SCLA task designed by Michelle Watson, one of Victoria's students. Michelle chose a passage on magnets from a middle school science text and created open-ended questions intended to assess students' ability to make connections, find main ideas and supporting details, draw inferences, define important vocabulary, and reflect on their own reading. Students could also be asked to summarize part of the text or to make predictions about it. A math teacher might create an SCLA task that asks students to read a word problem and to identify the operations needed to solve the problem as well as the key words that indicate what needs to be done. A social studies teacher might create a task that requires students to judge an author's credibility or point of view,

Name _____ Date _____

MAGNETS

Please answer the following questions based on what you just read:

1. How does what you read about magnets connect with what you already know?

2. Choose a way to show the main ideas and details in what you read. You can write a paragraph or draw a picture or a diagram.

3. "Read between the lines" to find something that you believe to be true but that isn't actually said. Explain your reasoning. Why do you think this is true?

4. These are three challenging words from the text. Explain what you think each means:

   magnet _____

   repel _____

   North Pole _____

5. Was this easy or hard? How did you help yourself understand the text?

FIGURE 5.1 **Strategic Content Literacy Assessment (SCLA) for Science**

Source: Michelle Watson, science teacher, Honea Path Middle School, Honea, South Carolina.

to draw inferences from a map or other graphic, or to compare two different versions of a historical event.

Once the teacher has introduced the passage and previewed the response task, he or she asks students to read the text, circling unfamiliar words as they go. The teacher can create a scoring template to be used for each student. It should include the date and text used and provide a place to record evaluations of the strategies a student used, his or her comprehension of the text, and a brief analysis of his or her performance. Figure 5.2 shows such a template for Michelle Watson's science SCLA.

Once a class SCLA has been scored, the teacher can look for patterns in students' performances: Which tasks did most students perform well? What common difficulties appeared? A teacher might select one or two strategies, unfamiliar vocabulary items, or subject area concepts as goals for subsequent teaching. These goals are then shared with students. Teachers can also share information about the class's performance and samples of student responses to further engage students in the process and to show them what works well. Teachers should emphasize the positive strategies demonstrated in the sample responses. Through analysis and discussion of these student samples, the class can develop a list of effective reading strategies that can be used to guide their subsequent work over the next days and weeks.

The SCLA can be especially useful with struggling readers and English language learners. The SCLA procedures can be adapted for these students by giving them extra

Name _____ Date _____

MAGNETS

Strategies

Making Connections (Question 1)
Inferences (Question 3)
Self-Monitoring (Question 5)

Comprehension

Main Ideas & Details (Question 2)
Vocabulary (Question 4)
Words Circled:

Notes & Analysis

FIGURE 5.2   SCLA Scoring Template

time, having them read the passage aloud, or limiting the text they read to a couple of paragraphs and the response task they complete to drawing a picture or diagram. The classroom teacher or a support teacher (ESL or special education inclusion teacher) can work with a small group of students and might also invite individual students to read aloud sections of text they have practiced. Support teachers may also be able to give small groups of students more individualized feedback on vocabulary, reading strategies, and content concepts.

Literacy Coaches' Corner

Assessment *as* Learning for Teachers

Audrey Friedman (2000) describes an inquiry project she initiated as a literacy coach in a Boston middle school. Teachers from all the content areas agreed to include written answers to key questions as part of their assessment programs and rubrics for evaluating student responses. This collaborative approach was piloted by one of the social studies teachers, who gave his students the following prompt as they were studying colonial America: How did people depend on one another for survival? The teachers rated students' responses to this prompt and found that they supplied minimal basic information and engaged in little or no higher-level thinking. Together, teachers revised the prompt so that it was scaffolded and offered more guidance and more details on what was expected in the answer. Teachers then conducted a mini-quantitative study by giving the prompt to another group of students. These students' responses demonstrated more content understanding and better overall writing.

As a result of this collaborative look at assessment led by the literacy coach—actually, an assessment of assessment—the teachers in this group learned some effective strategies for helping students to better communicate what they were learning.

INTEREST AND ATTITUDE INVENTORIES   Many teachers find it helpful to find out what students think about a content area or a specific topic. Knowing that several students like science fiction will help an English teacher plan the reading selections for the whole class or decide to include science fiction as a topic for small-group book talks. On the other hand, if significant numbers claim a distaste for poetry, the teacher knows that introductory poetry selections will have to be chosen carefully and that it will be necessary to do a little sales promotion on behalf of the genre. An interest or attitude inventory can be given at the beginning of the year or at the introduction of a new unit. A sample inventory for high school English is shown in Figure 5.3.

A content area learning log or journal is another good source of information about students' attitudes and interests or their backgrounds. Teachers can ask students to jot down "What I liked best this week," "Something I'd like to know more about," or "What I thought was hardest this week." By periodically reviewing students' log entries, the teacher can get helpful feedback on what students are thinking, learning, and feeling.

Victoria recently worked with a team of researchers to develop an Adolescent Motivation to Read Profile (AMRP) (Pitcher et al., 2007). The AMRP consists of a pencil-and-paper survey and a conversational interview protocol. The survey asks questions about reading strategies and self-assessment of reading abilities, including online reading.

Inventory of Attitudes and Interests

1. Rate each item from 1 (least) to 5 (most). I like to read:

____ science fiction   ____ mysteries   ____ fantasy

____ romance   ____ sports   ____ war stories

____ adventure   ____ history   ____ current events

____ novels   ____ plays   ____ poetry

____ biographies   ____ short stories   ____ graphic novels

____ magazines   ____ newspapers   ____ comic books

____ Other

2. Rate each item from 1 (least) to 5 (most). I like to write:

____ letters to friends   ____ my opinions   ____ e-mails

____ in a diary/journal   ____ poems   ____ text messages

____ short stories   ____ nonfiction   ____ humorous stories

____ plays, scripts   ____ Other

3. Rate each item from 1 (hardest) to 5 (easiest). When I write, this is what I find hard:

____ getting started   ____ changing what I have written

____ finding ideas to write about   ____ letting someone else read my writing

____ organizing my ideas   ____ proofreading

____ putting the words on paper   ____ Other

Rate the next items using this scale:

1 = strongly disagree   2 = disagree   3 = not sure   4 = agree   5 = strongly agree

1. I am a good writer. ____ Why do you say this?

2. I am a good reader. ____ Why do you say this?

3. I have a good vocabulary. ____

4. I am good at spelling. ____

5. English is difficult for me. ____

6. English is a useful subject. ____

7. I think English is interesting. ____

F I G U R E 5 . 3   **Attitude/Interest Inventory for High School English Students**

It takes about 10 minutes to administer and provides scores for "Self-concept as a reader," "Instruction of reading," and "Value of reading." The interview includes questions about narrative and informational texts, reading at home and in school, and technology use. Sample questions include "Do you have anything at school today that you are reading?"

"In what class do you feel reading is most difficult?" and "What do you like to read when you are on the Internet?" Based on interviews of nearly 100 students in grades 6 through 11, Victoria and her colleagues found students to be involved in multiple literacies outside school, often in association with family and friends. Adolescents also spoke clearly of the importance of choice of reading materials, topics, and assignments. The AMRP can be helpful in planning instruction that is repsonsive to students' interests and abilities.

Effective teaching starts with what students already know and leads them to new understandings. Therefore, it is helpful to know not only what students feel about a topic but also what they know about it. Some of this may come out in an interest inventory or class discussion. There are also many instructional strategies that begin with what students already know or believe. You will find several such strategies discussed in later chapters, especially Chapter 6.

CLOZE PASSAGES   Cloze passages (Bormuth, 1968; Taylor, 1953) can be used to estimate how well a student will fare with a particular text. The cloze procedure is based on the idea that humans instinctively try to bring about closure to unfinished or incomplete patterns. A cloze passage is constructed by deleting words from a text passage. A reader's success with filling in the blanks suggests his or her relative potential for comprehending that reading material.

The passage should be reasonably complete and coherent on its own. The length of the passage will depend on the number of words to be deleted. Although many authorities recommend that approximately 50 words be deleted, we have found this to be frustrating for many students, especially younger students and struggling readers. Because scores are ultimately converted to percentages, we have found deletion of 25, 33, or 50 words to be most convenient, as each item is then worth either four, three, or two points. Many teachers include a practice passage with five to ten items, which they use to model the cloze procedure.

Figure 5.4 presents a short cloze passage from a middle school science text. Try filling in the blanks yourself. (The deleted words are listed below the figure. Cover them while completing the passage.)

The following are instructions for constructing, administering, scoring, and interpreting a cloze passage:

1. Construction
   a. Select a passage. Copy it on a word processor with no typographical errors.
   b. Delete a word at random from the second sentence of the passage. (The first and last sentences should be left intact to give additional context to the beginning and end of the passage.) Beginning with the first deletion, delete every fifth word until the desired number of words have been left out. To make the task somewhat easier, delete every sixth or seventh word. It is important, however, that a specific interval be selected and maintained throughout the passage. In no circumstances should words be avoided because they seem too hard or too easy.

ORES

Minerals from which metals and nonmetals can be removed in usable amounts are called ores. Metals are elements that ___(1)___ certain special properties. Metals ___(2)___ shiny surfaces and are ___(3)___ to conduct electricity and ___(4)___. Metals also have the ___(5)___ of malleability. Malleability is ___(6)___ ability of a metal ___(7)___ be hammered into thin ___(8)___ without breaking. Another property ___(9)___ metals is ductility. Ductility ___(10)___ the ability of a ___(11)___ to be pulled into ___(12)___ strands without breaking. Iron, ___(13)___, aluminum, copper, silver, and ___(14)___ are metals. Most metals ___(15)___ found combined with other substances, or impurities, in ores. After the ores are removed from the earth by mining, the metals must be removed from the ores.

Deleted Words

1. have	6. the	11. substance
2. have	7. to	12. thin
3. able	8. sheets	13. lead
4. heat	9. of	14. gold
5. property	10. is	15. are

FIGURE 5.4   Sample Cloze Passage

Source: Passage taken from Charles Coble et al., *Earth Science*, p. 159. Englewood Cliffs, NJ: Prentice Hall, 1993.

c. Leave a blank space for each deleted word. All blanks should be of equal length so as not to give any clues about word length.

2. Administration

   a. Give students a copy of the cloze passage, and instruct them to read through it before they do anything else.

   b. Instruct students to go back and fill in the blanks with words that they think make sense. They should be encouraged to make a guess at each blank. There should be no time limit for completing the passage.

3. Scoring

   a. Count only words that are exact replacements for (or intelligibly spelled facsimiles of) the deleted words.

   b. Figure the percentage of exact replacements. For instance, if you have left 25 blanks, each is worth four points. A student who gets 14 exact replacements scores 56 percent ($4 \times 14 = 56$).

4. Interpretation

   a. A score above 60 percent suggests that the text material is at a student's *independent level*. That is, the student should be able to read that material on his or her own with excellent understanding.

   b. A score between 40 and 60 percent suggests that the material is at the student's *instructional level*. The material will be challenging, but with appropriate help from the teacher it will be useful.

   c. A score below 40 percent suggests that the material is at the student's *frustration level*. It may be too difficult for that student.

Teachers who are used to encouraging good guesses and giving students the benefit of the doubt often feel it is unduly stringent not to count good synonyms when scoring a cloze passage. However, what constitutes a good synonym? Take the sentence "John got in his _____ and drove downtown," from which the word *truck* is deleted. If a student wrote *van* in the blank, a reasonable person might count that as a synonym. However, what about *car* or *Chevy* or *Trans Am*? Some teachers would accept those; they are vehicles. How about *suit*? That is not a vehicle, but it fits the sentence. The point is that teachers will vary in what they will accept as a synonym, and that variance will affect the reliability of assessments using cloze passages. If only exact replacements are counted, the task is simpler and more objective.

Instead of penalizing readers for good guesses, the suggested scoring criteria for a cloze passage account for the many synonyms that good readers are likely to use. Although a score of 65 percent would be barely passing on most exams, it is an excellent score on a cloze passage.

A teacher may avoid emphasis on right or wrong answers by letting students score their own papers. When all students have completed the passage, the teacher shows them the list of deleted words. They can write the words above their inexact guesses. This gives students immediate feedback on their efforts and allows for a discussion of why some words did or did not fit the context. The teacher should make it clear that many of the students' guesses would make sense in the passage, even though they are not the words used by the author. That is, good synonyms are not wrong.

We need to emphasize that cloze results are only estimates and must be interpreted with caution, especially for individual students. When a class or several classes of students are sampled, however, cloze passages give practical insight into the question How will these students do with this reading material?

ASSESSING DIGITAL LITERACIES   As we noted earlier in the chapter, online reading comprehension is not included in any national or state assessment of reading (Leu et al., 2008), yet these strategies are arguably among the most important literacies that adolescents need to develop. Students are increasingly using the Internet to locate, evaluate, synthesize, and communicate information related to their content area studies. As the previous sentence suggests, the efficient use of Internet technologies is far from simple.

Students can progress from basic computer skills and Web searches to more sophisticated search strategies and manipulation of information. Teachers who incorporate digital literacies into their instruction need some way to evaluate what students have learned.

Donald Leu, David Reinking, and their colleagues have been working to develop Internet comprehension strategies among adolescent students in rural and urban schools through the Teaching Internet Comprehension to Adolescents Project (TICA). TICA researchers are developing a taxonomy of Internet skills and piloting checklists that can be used to evaluate students' developing Internet comprehension skills and strategies. (More information on the TICA project, including the taxonomy and checklists, can be accessed at www.newliteracies.uconn.edu/iesproject/index.html.) The taxonomy of Internet reading comprehension skills and strategies is divided into five main categories (Leu et al., 2008):

- Identifying a question or defining a problem
- Using the Internet to locate information
- Critically evaluating the information
- Synthesizing information from multiple sources
- Using one or more Internet communication technologies to share a response

Figure 5.5 provides a sampling of the strategies being used by students in the TICA project. It is a model of the kind of assessment that a teacher might develop to determine how well students are learning to use the Internet. However, because a wide array of digital skills and strategies may be used in different settings, individual teachers should develop evaluation checklists to meet their unique circumstances.

Grades and Grading

Giving grades to students is an almost universal reality for teachers and is almost universally ignored in reading methods textbooks. This neglect may be due in part to reluctance to confront one of the primary contradictions in the teacher's role—the conflict between maintaining standards and respecting individual students. Thomas (1986) illustrates this contradiction in his discussion of the use of the grade F. He suggests that the two extremes might be stated as follows:

> Students should get an F regardless of effort if they do not meet minimum standards for the subject.
> Students should not get an F if they have made their best effort in the subject.

This dilemma applies to all of a teacher's decisions about assigning grades to students. Should the bright student who rarely cracks a book get the same grade as the average student who diligently spends hours on assignments? Should spelling and grammar count toward the grade on a history project, and if so, how much? What should end-of-

Identifying a Question

☐	Determine a clear topic and focus for questions to guide the search for information.
☐	Modify questions, when appropriate, using strategies such as the following: ■ Narrowing the focus of the question ■ Expanding the focus of the question ■ Developing a new question that is more appropriate

Locating Information

☐	Locate at least one search engine.
☐	Use key words in a search window on a browser that has this function.
☐	Read search engine results effectively to determine the most useful resource for a task.
☐	Quickly determine if a site is potentially useful and worth more careful reading.
☐	Know how to use an internal search engine to locate information at a site.

Critically Evaluating Information

☐	Recognize that all websites have an agenda, perspective, or bias; identify bias, given a website with a clear bias.
☐	Identify the author of a website whenever visiting an important new site.
☐	Investigate multiple sources to compare and contrast the reliability of information.
☐	Identify the general purpose of a website (entertainment, educational, commercial, persuasive, exchange of information, social, etc.).

Synthesizing Information

☐	Synthesize information from multiple media sources, including written prose, audio, visual, video, and/or tables and graphs.
☐	Separate relevant information from irrelevant information.
☐	Organize information effectively.

Communicating Information

☐	Use online and offline writing/editing tools.
☐	Uses a wide array of Internet-based forms of communication, such as e-mail and attachments, instant messaging, blogs, presentation software, websites, and wikis.
☐	Know how to include multiple-media sources within messages.

FIGURE 5.5   **Internet Comprehension Checklist**

Source: Adapted from Phase II Checklist, Leu et al., 2008.

term grades be based on? How much should homework count? What about class partici-pation? Should grades be used as "weapons" to discourage unwanted behavior?

The traditional system of giving letter grades has many significant drawbacks (Willis, 1993). First, a single letter grade gives no hint of what a student can actually do or not do or what an individual's strengths or weaknesses might be. When letter grades are stringently applied, only a few students do well (i.e., receive an A), and less able students are demoralized by constant negative reinforcement. On the other hand, if most students receive A's and B's, the underlying meaning of grades as indices of ability becomes even less clear. Finally, letter grades may actually undermine some teaching strategies, such as cooperative learning or writer's workshop, in which the emphases are less on product and more on process, less on individual accomplishment and more on achievement of the group, shared learning, and confidence building.

Evidence-Based Research

Despite calls for more student-centered teaching and alternative means of assessment, determining grades in high schools continues to follow largely traditional and narrow formulas. A study of the grading preferences of 91 high school science teachers determined that traditional labs, quizzes, and tests were by far the most frequently used determinants of grades (Feldman, Alibrandi, & Kropf, 1998). The teachers reported that they rarely used portfolios or journals, two forms of authentic assessment frequently recommended by reformers. Another study of high school grading practices (Stiggins, Frisbie, & Griswold, 1989) also found that grading was variable, subjective, and often at odds with the recommendations of researchers and methods textbook authors.

The dilemma of grading is especially sharp for those who work with students outside the middle-class academic mainstream. Students from diverse ethnic or cultural backgrounds, students with limited proficiency in standard English, and students with identified learning problems often find themselves in an academic game with long odds; their chances for success seem to be diminished by the very system that is supposed to bring them into the mainstream (Oakes, 1986). The national dropout rate among African American and Hispanic students is a depressing indication that too many youth give up in the face of repeated failure (Hoffman et al., 2003).

OBJECTIVITY OR TEACHER JUDGMENT?   Even though a teacher tries to design an objective grading system, it is impossible to avoid using judgment in arriving at grades. Take, for example, multiple-choice tests, which are often referred to as "objective tests" because they supposedly have clear-cut right and wrong answers and teacher judgment does not enter into the scoring—students either know the material and answer correctly or they do not. However, anyone who has ever made up a multiple-choice test knows how difficult it is to write good, unambiguous questions that reflect important content and that have answers that are clearly right. In selecting what will be tested and how test items will be worded, a teacher is making subjective decisions. Still other subjective decisions must be made if students challenge some questions because they are too hard or because more than one answer might be right. Teachers cannot escape professional subjectivity.

Schools or districts often adopt uniform grading systems (e.g., 90–100 = A and 80–89 = B) in an attempt to attain objectivity across classes and grade levels. However, individual teachers must still decide what will be evaluated, how much each such activity will be worth, and how a final grade on the 0–100 scale will be computed. It is a well-known fact that within every school that uses such a system, some teachers are known as "hard" markers and others "easy." This creates "a situation in which grades given by one teacher might mean something entirely different from grades given by another teacher" (Marzano & Kendall, 1996, p. 10).

It is no wonder, then, that students are often confused about grades. Many students do not know how grades are determined or why they got a particular grade. Low achievers especially tend to attribute poor grades to external factors, to things beyond their control (Evans & Engelberg, 1985).

Evidence-Based Research

Every teacher comes to terms with the dilemmas of grading in his or her own way; it would be foolish and presumptuous of us to suggest that any uniform approach would be possible or desirable. However, the following subsections suggest strategies that might help you avoid some of the pitfalls of assigning grades to students.

TOUGH BUT FAIR   "Old Smitty's tough but fair. She makes you work hard, but you learn a lot in her class." We have always admired teachers with reputations like that, for whom grades are not just final marks on a report card but more indicative of a process of teaching, learning, assessing, and communicating. We suggest five guidelines that will help you develop a "tough but fair" grading system:

- **Select assignments, tests, or projects that reflect and measure what you value most as a teacher.** For example, a math teacher who was interested in *how* his stu-

Source: FUNKY WINKERBEAN © Batom, Inc. NORTH AMERICAN SYNDICATE.

dents solved problems might ask students to provide a written explanation of what they did and why as well as the answers to problems.

● **Provide a variety of opportunities to earn credit.** Diverse students have diverse ways of learning and showing what they have learned. Figure 5.6 lists some possible credit-bearing activities that involve some combination of language and literacy ability. You might also consider extra-credit activities or revisions so that students can make up for less-than-optimal performances.

● **Be clear about your grading system and standards.** Begin a new year by describing clearly what must be done for credit, how different activities will be weighted, and what must be done to earn a grade of A, B, C, and so forth.

● **Be clear about how you will assess specific assignments and tests.** Many teachers develop *rubrics*, itemized lists of criteria that are distributed when an assignment is made and filled out and returned when the assignment is graded.

Evidence-Based Research

● **Collaborate with students to set and achieve goals and to deconstruct the language of both official and teacher-devised standards.** We have suggested that students should play an active part in setting goals and evaluating their progress. This is especially important when working with culturally diverse students, who may not be familiar with the nuances of school discourse and who may feel that academic tasks are arbitrarily assigned and evaluated. In a collaborative study of how portfolios could be used as part of the grading process (Sarroub et al., 1997), university researchers and eighth-grade teachers found that students were particularly interested in decoding the "secret world of assessment," recrafting the offi-

Peer conferences	Creating a display, poster, graph, etc.
Teacher conferences	Math word problems
Participation in group work	Photographs
Writing in journal or log	Audio or video recordings
Responding to another student's journal or log	Vocabulary puzzles, analogies
Attending selected out-of-school events	Self-selected vocabulary list
Reporting to class	Writing, performing, or producing a dramatic piece
Panel presentation	Sharing a book or poem with classmates
Debate	Self-evaluation
Hosting a guest speaker	Extra reading
Demonstrating an experiment or process	Book review, oral or written

FIGURE 5.6   Opportunities to Earn Course Credit

cial standards into language they could understand, and generating their own standards for assessment.

RUBRICS   Rubrics help students to know what the teacher is looking for, make grading a large number of assignments easier for the teacher, and make grading more uniform. There is no set format for developing rubrics (Wiggins, 1998). Rubrics can be generic, as when an English teacher uses the same rubric for evaluating all student writing, or they may be event specific, as in the case of a rubric designed for a single project.

Usually, rubrics feature a scale of possible points to be earned, the dimensions of the task, and the criteria that must be met. An example of a rubric for Gene Kulbago and Mary Marcinkowski's earth science research project (described in Chapter 4) is given in Figure 5.7. In this case, the dimensions of the task include organization, information, and adherence to MLA and standard language conventions. The points and criteria for each dimension are also indicated.

When Donna develops a rubric for her content reading and literacy course at the University of Georgia, she typically involves her students in creating criteria for the rubric. Working collaboratively with students to brainstorm ideas for a rubric does not preclude a teacher from putting forth her or his own criteria. In fact, some teachers whom Donna has observed at the middle and high school levels involve their students in brainstorming criteria that take into account their state's content standards (see Appendix E). In such cases, teachers will frequently ask their students to put the language of the standards in their own words and then devise criteria for a rubric that will take those standards into account. When this kind of student involvement and buy-in is achieved, the task of completing a rubric and grading student work based on it becomes much easier for the teacher.

CONTENT AREA QUIZZES AND TESTS   Probably the most frequently used means of evaluating middle-grade and secondary school students are tests made up by teachers or provided by textbook publishers. Any test—true/false, multiple choice, short answer, or essay—must be readable in order for students to be able to respond to it. This may seem a simple requirement, but it is often overlooked. The result is that some students perform

TECHNOLOGY Tip

Rubrics

To learn how to use RubiStar, a free on-line tool for creating rubrics, visit http://rubistar.4teachers .org/index.php. Here you will see rubrics in the context of a lesson, and you will be able to view, edit, and print existing rubrics as a way of customizing them for your own content area classroom.

Student _____   Name _____

Date _____

Title of Paper _____

	Concern	Possible Points	Points Earned
Organization	Paper contains an Introductory Statement which clearly defines the hypothesis.	5	
	Information is organized in such a way to make it understandable to the audience.	10	
	Paper contains a concluding statement which evaluates the hypothesis based upon information (data) discovered during research.	10	
Information	Student used a variety of informational sources, including both electronic and published (written) sources.	10	
	Student has selected appropriate sources and has evaluated them for credibility.	5	
	Student has included sufficient information in the report necessary to make a valid conclusion.	20	
MLA and Language Conventions	Paper contains a proper title page.	5	
	Paper contains a bibliography which follows the MLA style.	10	
	Paper demonstrates proper use of parenthetical documentation.	10	
	Paper demonstrates proper use of language conventions: spelling, capital letters, paragraphing, grammatical usage, etc.	10	
	Paper is reasonably neat and demonstrates effort on the part of the writer.	5	
Comments			**Final Score**

FIGURE 5.7   Rubric for Earth Science Research Report

Source: Gene Kulbago, Niagara Middle School, Niagara Falls, New York.

poorly not because they did not know the material but because they misunderstood the questions. Rakow and Gee (1987) devised a checklist for test items, which may be used to minimize student confusion (Figure 5.8).

It is difficult to write foolproof test items. In fact, the constraints of so-called objective test items frequently penalize students who are divergent thinkers or are good at inference and interpretation; they see subtleties where others see only right or wrong. Therefore, teachers sometimes use a *quiz qualifier*—simply space at the end of an objective test where students can qualify their answers. If a student feels that the answer to question number 23 could be either a or c, he or she explains why in the quiz qualifier. If the student gets the answer wrong, the teacher reads the qualification, and if it is convincing, the student gets credit for number 23.

Portfolio Assessment

Some time ago, Barney, an out-of-town friend and professional photographer, came to visit Steve and brought his portfolio. In fact, Barney brought three portfolios. One was his professional portfolio, which included photos of buildings, food, manufactured products, and people. There were color prints, transparencies, and samples of actual brochures, magazines, and books that he had illustrated. It gave an impressive overview of his best work and his capability as a commercial photographer. The second portfolio was a selection of black-and-white landscapes and portraits and a series of photographs of a model, which had evolved over several years. This was a highly personal and expressive collection that showed Barney's thoughtful and artistic side. The third portfolio was

_____ 1. Students are likely to have the experiences and prior knowledge necessary to understand what the question calls for.

_____ 2. The vocabulary is appropriate for the intended grade level.

_____ 3. The sentence complexity is appropriate for the intended grade level.

_____ 4. Definitions and examples are clear and understandable.

_____ 5. The required reasoning skills are appropriate for the students' cognitive level.

_____ 6. Relationships are made clear through precise, logical connectives.

_____ 7. Content within items is clearly organized.

_____ 8. Graphs, illustrations, and other graphic aids facilitate comprehension.

_____ 9. The questions are clearly framed.

_____ 10. The content of the items is of interest to the intended audience.

FIGURE 5.8 **Checklist for Evaluating Test Item Readability**

Source: S. Rakow & T. Gee, "Test science, not reading," *The Science Teacher, 54,* 28–31, February 1987. Used with permission from NSTA Publications, National Science Teachers Association, 1742 Connecticut Ave., NW, Washington, DC 2000.

a selection of Barney's newspaper photos, which he had assembled especially for a trip to New York City and meetings with newspaper photo editors.

Two aspects of Barney's portfolios are relevant to our discussion of assessment and grading: The work was self-selected, and a variety of items were included. The pictures in each portfolio were carefully selected for different purposes and indeed made very different impressions. Barney selected pieces that displayed a range of subjects, techniques, and moods, and he included finished work as well as work in progress.

Students can prepare similar portfolios of their work in content area courses. Kenneth Wolf and Yvonne Siu-Runyan (1996) define a *student portfolio* as "a selective collection of student work and records of progress gathered across diverse contexts over time, framed by reflection and enriched through collaboration, that has as its aim the advancement of student learning" (p. 31). They identify three portfolio models, each with a different primary purpose:

- **Ownership portfolios.**   These collections of student work emphasize student choice, reflection, and self-assessment. The main purpose of an ownership portfolio is to allow students to display and reflect on their accomplishments.

- **Feedback portfolios.**   These are co-constructed by the teacher and the student. They give an overall portrait of a student's development, strengths, and needs. The purposes of feedback portfolios are to guide student learning and to communicate with parents.

- **Accountability portfolios.**   These are portfolios that are used as performance assessments. Accountability portfolios are assembled according to structured guidelines and are often evaluated by people other than the classroom teacher with reference to an established rubric. The purpose of these portfolios is to demonstrate student achievement for accountability or program evaluation.

Evidence-Based Research

There is an especially important distinction between accountability portfolios and those designed purely for classroom use, as the two uses of portfolios are in many respects at odds (Tierney et al., 1998; Valenica & Wixson, 2000; Wiggins, 1998). Classroom-based portfolios are assembled and evaluated according to criteria established by teachers, often in collaboration with students. Their purpose is to help teachers, students, and parents understand learning, and they are often important factors in guiding teachers' instructional decisions. Interpretation of classroom-based portfolios is nuanced and sensitive to individual students and their instructional settings. Accountability portfolios, on the other hand, must meet externally imposed criteria and may form the basis for high-stakes conclusions about students, teachers, or schools. Measurement researchers have voiced serious reservations about the reliability and validity of accountability portfolios (Tierney et al., 1998; Valencia & Wixson, 2000). Although accountability portfolios certainly have the potential to influence instruction and learning, their net effect may be disruptive and counterproductive if external demands displace a teacher's professional judgment of what is best for students (Scott, 2005). In the discussion that follows, our emphasis is on classroom-based portfolios.

Sarah Drake (1998) describes a portfolio project she initiated during her second year as a history teacher at Naperville North High School in Illinois. At the beginning of the year, she told her ninth-grade ancient history and eleventh-grade U.S. history students that they would be building individual portfolios that showcased their best work and their understanding of the vital themes and narratives of history. Together, she and her students developed criteria for selecting ten items that represented their learning of history over the semester. Students included group projects, Venn diagrams, journal entries, essays, research papers, political cartoons, posters, and maps in their portfolios. They needed to write a brief explanation of why each item was chosen and a summary in which they explained the most important concept(s) they had learned.

With student input, Sarah developed a rubric for the portfolio that evaluated students on the dimensions of historical knowledge, reasoning, and communication. Students held peer-evaluation sessions three times during the semester to help them organize their portfolios and develop their selection rationalizations. At the end of the semester, each student had a 10-minute individual conference with Ms. Drake in which they discussed the portfolio. Although students were dubious at first, Sarah found most of her students were able to recognize vital themes and narratives of history and that their summaries expressed personal examinations and insightful reflections. She was especially pleased with the results of the portfolio interviews, during which she learned new information about students and built on relationships she had established.

Penelope Valdez (2001) describes a portfolio project that she implemented in her seventh-grade life science class. Each month, students were asked to choose a topic from class and submit a portfolio in which they did the following:

- Explain a science concept, a science process, or knowledge of scientific equipment in detail in their own words.
- Create a product that applies to their topic in a readily understandable way. For instance, they might take photos of someone properly using and storing a microscope.
- Evaluate an item from current media that deals with the topic. Is the science in this selection accurate?

Valdez developed a brief scoring rubric for these portfolios and awarded credit to students equivalent to a test grade. Although it took a while to evaluate the portfolios, Valdez found that the feedback she received made the effort worthwhile. Students made major improvements in their projects from month to month, and she was able to clearly see how well students knew scientific topics and could apply them.

Portfolio assessment may be adapted in many ways. In science classes, students might be asked to pick their two best lab sessions and present their procedural and observational notes along with the finished lab reports and a statement of why these labs were chosen. In social studies, students might be asked to go to their learning logs and assess their before-and-after knowledge of a subject, including examples from their work that were instrumental in changing their attitudes or understandings. In French, students might collect tape recordings of conversations from early, midway, and late in the term or the notes and drafts that led to the completed translation of a poem or piece of prose. In any course, students might include their best and worst tests, with an improved or corrected version of the poor test and a self-evaluation of the difference in performance. Other suggestions for portfolio contents are given in Figure 5.9.

Research indicates that portfolio assessment can be more effective than single, static measures of student achievement. Simmons (1990) reports that for middle-grade students, "Self-selected portfolios of their best work are significantly better than timed tests in estimating students' writing abilities" (p. 28). In another study (Garcia et al., 1990), two groups of teachers were asked to assess students with limited English proficiency. One group was given standardized test data, and the other was given portfolios of observational data with samples of student reading and writing. In all cases, the teachers who looked at the portfolios gave more complete evaluations and recommendations and more detailed requests for additional information.

Another advantage of portfolios is their potential to inform and improve instruction. In a conversation about the possibilities of portfolio assessment among researchers

Math

Story problems written for others to solve

Written report of strategies used to solve a problem

Pictures or graphs illustrating problem and solution

Examples of how math concepts are applied

Computer spreadsheets

Science

Drawings

Lab notes

Photos of projects or labs

Anecdotal stories of field work

Science reports with notes and drafts

Social Studies

Charts, graphs, and maps

Oral histories

Time lines

Written reports or essays with notes and drafts

Travel brochure for region, state, or country

Creative writing

Audio- or videotapes of debates, panels, speeches, or presentations

All Subjects

Homework assignments

Exams or tests with self-evaluations

List of self-selected vocabulary

Content area biographies: "My life as a scientist"

Semantic maps

Log or journal entries

Record of teacher and peer conferences

Brainstorming lists

Photographs

Record of outside reading related to content area

Audio- or videotapes

Movie or television reviews

FIGURE 5.9 **Suggestions for Items to Include in Content Area Portfolios**

and teachers, Tierney et al. (1998) assert that portfolios can "serve an important role in helping teachers customize teaching and learning to the students' needs, interests, background, and circumstances" (p. 478).

Afflerbach (2007) suggests that teachers consider both the demands and possible consequences of portfolio assessment:

- What are the goals, audiences, and purposes of the portfolio?
- How can I help students become familiar with using portfolios?
- What procedures will students need to learn?
- How well can I model portfolio use for students?
- How will portfolios promote assessment *as* learning and student independence?
- Given the time and resources involved, what are the practical limitations of using portfolios?

STUDENT INVOLVEMENT   An often-cited benefit of portfolio assessment is student involvement in self-evaluation and discourse about what, why, and how they are learning (Bauer & Garcia, 1997; Clark et al., 2001; Sarroub et al., 1998). To guide students' self-evaluation of their portfolio work, teachers can use questions similar to the following, adapted from Reif (1990):

What makes this your best work?

How did you go about producing it?

What problems did you encounter?

How did you solve them?

What makes your most effective work different from your least effective work?

What goals did you set for yourself?

How well did you accomplish them?

What are your goals for the next marking period?

Portfolio assessment allows students to be active participant observers of their own growth and development. When they are asked to select, polish, arrange, and analyze their own work, they have a chance to see that learning is not haphazard or incidental to any efforts of their own. They also have more direct input into what ultimately goes on their report cards. Each student can state his or her best case to the teacher.

Pat Frey-Mason, a math teacher in an urban high school, has her students keep portfolios. When students have difficulty with certain types of problems, they are asked to work similar problems and write a short reflection of what was learned in the second attempt. The problems and reflections are included in their portfolios. Excerpts from two student reflections are shown in Figure 5.10.

New technologies open up novel possibilities for constructing portfolios. That fact was demonstrated by another visit from Steve's friend Barney, who once again brought

Jennifer Z.: I feel that doing another problem similar to the first one helped me in a few ways. One, I got more practice at doing those types of problems. Two, the more I do those types of problems, the more used to them I become. Finally, by reading the corrections and trying the problems over, I have become more aware of my mistakes. Basically, I have become more conscious of each particular section of a problem situation. Though I still get a rush of adrenaline when working with math, I must admit after doing things over I do feel a bit more confident to get down and attack the problem.

Kelly R.: When first approaching the problem, I went through the directions and just graphed what

they gave me. For example, for part (a) it said to make a graph symmetric with respect to the *X* axis. The easiest way I saw of doing this part of the problem was to imagine the *X* line being folded down the middle and just flipping the image over the line. Luckily, this method worked for parts (a) and (b) but this method didn't work for parts (c) and (d). Problems occurred when I didn't follow the methods, according to the directions. When referring to "symmetric to the origin" it requires a different method. Because I did this problem so poorly, I was given a similar problem. With this problem instead of just graphing the graphs I used a sure method to graph each one, I FOLLOWED THE DIRECTIONS!

FIGURE 5.10 **Sample Self-Analyses from Student Portfolios for Precalculus Math**

Source: Patricia Frey-Mason, Chair, Math Department, Buffalo Academy for Visual and Performing Arts, Buffalo, NY.

his photo portfolios, described earlier in the chapter. Barney still travels with portfolios of his work, but as you can imagine, he now brings along a much more extensive collection of images stored on his laptop computer. And like any successful entrepreneur, Barney now has a website that also features several different portfolios of his photos.

Electronic portfolios can feature artifacts other than text, such as audio and video, visuals and graphics, and hyperlinks. Students can create individual e-portfolios using presentation or hypermedia software and save them to CD-ROM, Zip disk, or hard drive. Teachers can create Web-based classroom portfolios using Web-authoring software or open-source bulletin board technology (Fahey, Lawrence, & Paratore, 2007). These classroom portfolios allow students to post their work and to see the work of others in the classroom. If a classroom portfolio is set up as a blog or bulletin board, students and the teacher can comment on the posts of others in the class. If given access, others in the school community—students, parents, and teachers—can also see and comment on the work a class is doing.

Because the *content* of a portfolio is what is paramount, it is best to keep the complexity of an e-portfolio in line with the technological sophistication of the class. Creating an e-portfolio can require mastery of some sophisticated technology skills, so it may be necessary to teach new software or computer applications before attempting to assemble this type of portfolio.

IMPLEMENTING PORTFOLIO ASSESSMENT Using portfolios as assessment tools represents a significant shift from traditional ways of teaching and testing. If you have

TECHNOLOGY **Tip**

E-portfolios
To get more information on developing
e-portfolios, to see examples of both teacher
and student portfolios, and to find resources for
e-portfolio software, visit any of the following:

www.eduscapes.com/tap/topic82.htm

www.essentialschools.org/cs/resources/view/
ces_res/225

www.electronicportfolios.org

not used portfolios, getting started with them will take some time, patience, and trial and error.

Because much of the effectiveness of portfolio assessment is derived from students' increased awareness of their own learning, it is not surprising that students' perspectives and expectations are crucial to successful implementation of portfolios (Moje, Brozo, & Haas, 1994). Therefore, you will want to involve students from the very beginning. You will need to explain what a portfolio is, what it will include, why it is being assembled, how it is related to the curriculum, and how it will be evaluated. Although you may retain final authority over these issues, it will be helpful if you let students negotiate them with you. Students are more likely to take responsibility for their learning and to reach higher levels of achievement if they know clearly what is expected and have had a voice in determining it.

Portfolios are also likely to be more successful if you provide guidance and modeling for students as they put their portfolios together. You may wish to start with short and simple activities and group efforts before you have students undertake a complex individual portfolio project. Students will need assistance with selecting, arranging, and evaluating their portfolio contents. As students prepare their portfolios, you can use class time to demonstrate and discuss these processes. Class time can also be used to work on portfolios and get advice and assistance from peers or from you. Your feedback will be as important during portfolio preparation as it will be at the end of the process. It will also help if you negotiate incremental steps and deadlines for major portfolio projects.

Tracey Wathen describes how she implemented a two-tiered portfolio system with her middle school English as a second language (ESL) class (Smolen et al., 1995). On Mondays, she distributed index cards to the class on which they wrote their literacy goals for the week. As the students worked on various reading and writing activities, they kept their notes, drafts, reflections, and other literacy-related materials in working portfolios. On Fridays, students used the blank side of their goals cards to reflect on how well they had achieved their weekly goals, and they selected pieces from their working portfolios to include in showcase ownership portfolios that displayed their growth in literacy and English language proficiency. Because students initially tended to write relatively simplistic goals ("I will read four books this week"), Tracey led the class in brainstorming reading and writing strategies and classifying them. She modeled various strategies, such as predicting and visualizing story settings, and emphasized them with poster charts. As a result, students began to set more complex goals, and their achievement of these goals was reflected in their portfolios.

PORTFOLIO PROS AND CONS   As with other forms of assessment, portfolios have both advantages and drawbacks. On the plus side, we have repeatedly emphasized the value of portfolios in increasing students' awareness and involvement in their own learning. Portfolios can also provide detailed, authentic representations of what students have learned and what has taken place in a classroom, which can be shared with parents, colleagues, and administrators. Finally, portfolios can give us an opportunity to reflect on our practice as teachers. More than numeric scores on a test, portfolios allow us to take stock of what has worked, what has been learned, and what is important to learn.

By now, it is probably apparent to you that portfolios also require considerable time to introduce, create, and evaluate. That is indeed a potential drawback. Portfolio assessment takes much more teacher time and effort than simply giving a multiple-choice unit test from the teacher's manual. However, because portfolios intimately integrate assessment and instruction, many teachers believe that the time and effort are well spent (Valdez, 2001).

Evidence-Based Research

Although portfolios can help to inform teachers' instructional decisions, that potential may not always be realized. Eurydice Bauer (1999) reviewed 19 classroom studies of alternative literacy assessments, 13 of which featured portfolios. She found that some teachers had difficulty moving from assessment to instruction. She also reported few indications that alternative assessments led to more equitable instruction for struggling readers. Portfolio assessment is probably more prevalent in elementary grades and English classes; teachers in other disciplines may be more resistant to any departure from traditional assessments. Indeed, teacher training, knowledge, and beliefs are all essential determinants of whether portfolios will be used, how they will be implemented, and what ultimate effects they may have on teaching and learning (Sarroub et al., 1997; Valencia & Wixson, 2000).

There is a final negative potential in portfolios that should be considered—the possible infringement of students' personal privacy (Hargreaves, 1989). If we were to substitute the term *dossier* for *portfolio*, very different images might be conveyed—images of aberrant behavior, surveillance, and control. When we ask students to engage in self-evaluation, to open up their thought processes and personal reflections for scrutiny, or to include their social relationships as part of an assessment of group projects, we are collecting very sensitive information. The information in a portfolio may be stored for future reference, subjected to interpretation according to standards imposed by a teacher or external authority, and used to make high-stakes decisions about students, all of which create a potential "threat to individual liberty, personal privacy, and human diversity" (Hargreaves, 1989, p. 138). When accountability portfolios are used in a performance assessment, teachers are subject to similar threats.

We do not mean to suggest that portfolios should not be used. We believe that the potential benefits of portfolio assessment far outweigh any potential harm. Rather, we return to a point we made when discussing the potential biases that are inherent in assessment: Assessment involves responsibility. Because we are in the position of making important judgments about students, we must take special care of how judgments are made and the possible consequences.

Assessing Textbooks

Although less than perfect, no doubt, textbooks are still a fact of life in most content area classrooms. Teachers often have little choice of texts; a single text is available for each subject. Sometimes a department chooses more than one text for a subject, assigning different books to different tracks. Many times teachers participate with school administrators in deciding which of several competing texts should be adopted. What teachers need in any of these situations are ways to look at textbooks, to see their strengths and weaknesses and their suitability for students.

Earlier, we discussed the cloze procedure, which was originally developed to assess the difficulty of text (Taylor, 1953). It applies a kind of Goldilocks test, which suggests whether students will find the book "too hard," "too easy," or "just right."

There are two other general approaches to judging textbooks' suitability: readability formulas and consumer judgments. Readability formulas are quantitative yardsticks for estimating differences in difficulty among texts. They can be tedious to apply, but they are relatively objective and useful if a large number of texts must be formally compared. Teachers and students make consumer judgments when they look through a text, sample a few passages, and identify features they feel make the book easy or hard, interesting or dull. If teachers collaborate with one another and with students to develop a checklist of predetermined criteria, group judgments of a textbook can be quite reliable and closely correlated to the scores of readability formulas (Klare, 1984).

Evidence-
Based
Research

Readability Formulas

Most readability formulas rely on two assumptions. The first is that longer sentences on the average are more difficult to read than shorter ones. Theoretically, sentence length gives an estimate of syntactic complexity. The longer the sentence, the more likely it is to have imbedded clauses, passive constructions, and other features that can cause difficulty for readers. The second assumption is that unfamiliar words make text harder to read. These assumptions and the way they are applied in the use of readability formulas are not without controversy.

Fry (1977) takes the second assumption a step further and asserts that on average, long words are more likely to be unfamiliar or difficult to understand than short words. The Fry readability formula is one of the most popular methods for estimating text readability. It is useful for our purposes because it provides estimates over a wide range, from primary to college level. The procedures for using the Fry formula are given in Figure 5.11.

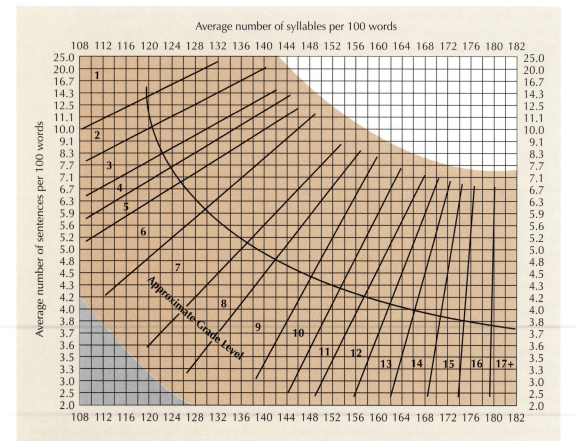

Average number of syllables per 100 words

Average number of sentences per 100 words

Approximate Grade Level

Directions for Computing Readability

1. Randomly select three 100-word samples from the text. A word is any group of symbols with a space on each side. A number such as 1776 counts as a word; so does an initialization such as USA.

2. Count the number of sentences within each 100-word sample. If a 100-word sample ends in the middle of a sentence, figure the decimal fraction of the sentence that is included.

3. Count the number of syllables in each 100-word sample. A syllable is defined as a phonetic syllable. In numerals and initializations, each symbol counts as a

syllable. For example, 1776 counts as four syllables, and USA as three. Hint: A 100-word sample has at least 100 syllables. Make a light tic mark above each additional syllable, count the total number of tic marks and add to 100.

4. Compute the average number of sentences and the average number of syllables per 100 words.

5. Plot these two averages on the graph. They should intersect either above or below the curved line within one of the numbered segments. The number in the segment is the approximate grade level of the text. A few books may fall in the shaded gray areas; they grade-level scores are invalid.

FIGURE 5.11 Fry Readability Graph

Source: Edward Fry, Rutgers University Reading Center, New Brunswick, NJ 08904.

The use of readability formulas has caused considerable debate. First, formulas perpetuate a common but erroneous impression that educators can mechanically and precisely match student reading levels to text difficulty levels. The whole concept of reading level is subject to question, whether it is applied to people or to texts (Cadenhead, 1987; International Reading Association, 1982). Reading level is at best a metaphor for certain observable facts: Some people read better than others, and some books are harder to read than others. Two books identified as being at the tenth-grade level may vary considerably in the difficulties they present to readers; two readers at the tenth-grade level will vary widely in their aptitude for reading different kinds of texts. Reading level is hardly a precise metric.

Critics such as Cullinan and Fitzgerald (1985) and Sewall (1988) charge that formulas consider only a very narrow range of text characteristics and completely ignore student variables such as interest and prior knowledge. Short sentences can be hard to read, especially if important connecting words are omitted. Many short words are unfamiliar to most students, and many multisyllabic words are commonly understood. When authors and publishers try to make textbooks fit readability formulas, the resulting prose is frequently lifeless and hard to read.

Fry (1989) defends the simple two-variable formula. He acknowledges some limitations but points to the utility of readability formulas for those in schools, publishing firms, libraries, and businesses who must have some yardstick for estimating the difficulty of books. He contends that even though sentence length and word length are not absolute indicators of difficulty, they are valid when considered in the average. He also argues that formulas are not intended to be writers' guides and that the mindless application of formulas in producing text is in fact blatant misuse.

We take a pragmatic stance on readability formulas. They can be useful adjuncts to teacher judgments, especially when teachers must survey a large number of books. However, the formulas also have obvious limitations. We doubt that many experienced teachers would place unreserved trust in results based solely on formulas. Common sense suggests that teachers consider many factors when deciding which books to use.

Consumer Judgments (or Don't Judge a Book by Its Cover)

In practice, most teachers assess textbooks by using them. They preview the text while planning, they observe students interacting with the text, and they see how students react to reading assignments. From these practical observations, they form judgments about how good the text is and how they should use it.

If a group of teachers are working on textbook adoption and need to screen several texts, they can decide among themselves what is important and possibly devise their own checklist. Science teachers are interested in what sort of laboratory activities are included in a textbook and how they are explained and illustrated. Writing style is important in a social studies text, but it would be impossible to judge style in an English anthology

Content

Does the content complement the curriculum?

Is the content current?

Is there balance between depth and breadth of coverage?

How many new or difficult vocabulary terms are included and how are they introduced and defined?

How dense are the new concepts in the text?

Is the content generally appropriate to students' prior knowledge?

Format

Are there good graphic aids and illustrations? Are they distracting or irrelevant to the content?

How are chapters set up? Are there introductions, summaries, heads and subheads, and marginal notes?

Are layout and print attractive and easy to read? How useful are the index, glossary, etc.?

Utility

How good are the activities at the end of the chapters?

Do text questions call for interpretation, evaluation, and application as well as literal recall?

Is there a teacher's manual? Would it be helpful?

Are quizzes or test questions provided? How good are they?

Does the text or manual suggest additional readings or related trade books?

Style

Is the writing lively and interesting to read?

Is the syntax at a suitable level of complexity?

Is the writing coherent and clear?

FIGURE 5.12   Framework for Assessing Texts

containing the work of many authors. Math teachers want to know what kinds of problems are featured in a text and how many problems focus on each kind of math concept. When we consider the unique content and instructional problems of foreign languages, health, industrial arts, and computer science, we must conclude that no single checklist can cover all of them.

Whatever the content area, there are some general factors to consider when judging a text. Instead of a checklist, we offer a framework that you can use to develop your own checklist for assessing text materials (Figure 5.12).

Summary

There are many variables in a teacher's day—variables that require countless decisions about students, teaching methods, materials, and assessment. The more information a teacher has, the better the quality of those decisions will be. This chapter offered many suggestions for collecting and interpreting information on students' reading and writing abilities and for utilizing that information when planning instruction and assigning grades. It also looked at ways of deciding how difficult or useful textbooks might be. All of these decisions are ultimately professional judgments. As a profession, teaching is more art than science. The teaching art has many legitimate forms of expression, and good teachers, like good artists, are constantly evolving.

There is no right way to assign grades, no best test of reading ability, no perfect text for any subject, but good teachers keep looking and experimenting.

Suggested Readings

Afflerbach, P. (2007). *Understanding and using reading assessment, K–12.* Newark, DE: International Reading Association.

Hall, K. (2003). *Listening to Stephen read: Multiple perspectives on literacy.* Philadelphia: Open University Press.

Purcell-Gates, V. (2002). The irrelevancy—and danger—of the "simple view" of reading to meaningful standards. In R. Fisher, G. Brooks, & M. Lewis (Eds.), *Raising standards in literacy* (pp. 105–116). London, UK: Routledge.

Strickland, K., & Strickland, J. (1998). *Reflections on assessment: Its purposes, methods, and effects on learning.* Portsmouth, NH: Boynton/Cook.

Van Kraayenoord, C. E. (2003). Toward self-assessment of literacy learning. In H. Fehring (Ed.), *Literacy assessment* (pp. 44–54). Newark, DE: International Reading Association.

Walker, B. (2007). *Diagnostic teaching of reading: Techniques for instruction and assessment* (6th ed.). Upper Saddle River, NJ: Merrill.

MyEducationLab is a research-based learning tool that brings teaching to life. Go to the Alvermann, Phelps, and Ridgeway Gillis 6th Edition MyEducationLab for Content Area Reading site at www.myeducationlab.com to:

- engage in multimedia exercises to help you build a deeper and more applied understanding of chapter content;

- utilize extensive resources including videos from real classrooms, Praxis and licensure preparation, a lesson plan builder, and materials to help you in your teaching career.

chapter **6**

Preparing to Read

The Role of Prior Knowledge	Assessing and Building Prior Knowledge	Activating Prior Knowledge with Prereading Strategies
• Barriers to New Learning	• The List-Group-Label Strategy	• Anticipation Guides
• The Teacher's Task	• Graphic Organizers	• Problem-Solving Activities
	• Reading and Listening	• K-W-L
	• Writing	

Anticipation Guide

Directions: Read each of the following statements. Place a checkmark on the line in the "Before Reading" column if you agree with the statement; leave it blank if you disagree. Then predict what you think the chapter will be about, and jot down on a sticky note (or post online) any questions you have. Read the chapter; then return to the statements and respond to them as you think the authors of your text would. Place a checkmark on the line in the "Authors' Stance" column if you believe the authors would agree with the statement. If you discuss these statements with other people online, in class, or at the family dinner table, return to the statements and check any items you agree with in the right-hand column, "After Discussion." If your thinking changed, what caused that change?

Before Reading	Authors' Stance	Statements	After Discussion
_____	_____	1. A reader's prior knowledge is more important to comprehension than what is on the page.	_____
_____	_____	2. A teacher's task is to activate students' prior knowledge after they have read the assigned text.	_____
_____	_____	3. Culture can strongly influence conceptual change when a reader's existing knowledge conflicts with ideas presented in the text.	_____
_____	_____	4. Students should read the textbook to prepare for a lecture on the information.	_____
_____	_____	5. What teachers do before reading to prepare students can be more effective in promoting learning than what they do after reading.	_____

In previous chapters, we discussed the importance of helping students make connections between their own knowledge, values, and concerns and the ideas in their texts and coursework. In this chapter, we elaborate on these suggestions by describing ways to activate and build prior knowledge, create interest and motivation for reading, and focus students on their reading and learning activities.

The following scenario illustrates what can happen when students are *not* focused on a reading assignment. It is based on events that have been reported to us by teachers and students and that we have observed ourselves in many classrooms. As you read it, ask yourself how the teacher might have helped students connect with the reading assignment.

● ● ●

The tenth-grade class had finished a short film on the geography of Japan with 20 minutes left in the period. Mr. Gregory told them to use the time to begin reading "Traditional Japan," the second chapter in the new unit. He wrote on the board: "Read Chapter 16, pages 252–257. Answer question 1, p. 255 and questions 1 and 3, p. 257 for tomorrow."

As Felicia began to read, her mind was on the track meet. In a little less than two hours, she would be running the mile relay for the first time. A series of incomprehensible dates and unpronounceable names swam before her eyes as she read. She plodded through a long passage on government written by some Japanese prince in the seventh century. Finally she came to question 1, "What principle did the Shotoku constitution stress?" Her eyes wandered back to the heading "Shotoku's Constitution." In the first paragraph, she found what she needed. She put her name and the page and question number on a clean sheet of paper and began to copy from the text: "Confucian values of orderly society and obedience to authority were especially stressed." Wasn't there something about Confucius in the unit test on China? Maybe he was an emperor or something. Oh, well. Mr. Gregory would explain it tomorrow, and she had done the first part of the assignment. If she could finish this in class, she could go get pizza with some of the girls after the track meet. She ought to do well on her leg of the relay; her quarter-mile times had been improving. Felicia thought of all their drill on the exchange of the baton. She rehearsed it in her mind . . . be sure to get a firm grip on the baton before starting to sprint . . . Her eyes moved across more names and dates.

● ● ●

Felicia's difficulty was not that she *cannot* read but that she was not *ready* to read. Before a person begins to read, whether for work, for pleasure, or for school, several interrelated factors influence how and what he or she will understand and remember:

1. *Interest.* If students want to know more about a topic, curiosity will help to guide their reading. Students are more likely to recall something of interest to them.
2. *Motivation.* Reading done for pleasure is different from reading done for work or school. Reading will be less labored in a class that students enjoy, and it will be more purposeful and serious when they are trying to get a good grade.

3. *Purpose.*   Purpose can be either long term or short term. One purpose may be to do well on a test or in a class discussion. A student may also have a more immediate purpose, such as the need to answer a question, solve a problem, or find a particular piece of information. If the student's main purpose is simply to get through the reading, his or her efforts will be less fruitful.

4. *Attention.*   If a student's mind is on the reading, without distractions from the immediate surroundings or competing thoughts, he or she will probably comprehend more.

5. *Strategy.*   Having an effective plan or strategy increases the likelihood of success, and the anticipation of success also increases motivation. Anyone may conduct reading methodically, whether it is a particular order for reading the Sunday paper or a plan for studying a difficult chemistry chapter.

6. *Prior knowledge.*   In some ways, this factor is a composite of all of the above. Students' knowledge of language, of reading and study, of the world, and particularly of the topic at hand will influence how they proceed through a text. Prior knowledge helps students set purposes, direct their attention, fill in gaps, make connections or inferences, monitor their progress, and recall what they have read.

Students vary widely in the knowledge, skill, and enthusiasm they bring to a reading assignment. Like Felicia in the previous scenario, they may frequently read without interest, motivation, or attention; without adequate purpose or strategy; and without full awareness of their pertinent prior knowledge. Good teachers recognize this and realize that preparing students well will go a long way toward making their reading successful. Most of the teaching strategies in this chapter not only help to prepare students for reading but also carry over into the reading itself. Furthermore, most of them are designed for cooperative learning or small-group interaction or can be so adapted.

The Role of Prior Knowledge

Prior knowledge can cover a wide range of skills, ideas, and attitudes. When we use the term, we are focusing particularly on a reader's background knowledge of the subject matter of the text. What a person already knows about a topic is probably the single most influential factor in what he or she will learn. In a recent review of effective classroom literacy instruction in the middle and high school grades, teachers who used prior knowledge activation strategies were equally effective in teaching high-, average-, and low-achieving readers. Students in these teachers' classrooms outperformed their control-group peers on a variety of comprehension measures (Alvermann, Fitzgerald, & Simpson, 2006).

Evidence-Based Research

Studies in the neurosciences may have the potential to explain, at least partially, how the human brain processes text and by extension makes use of the prereading strategies that we include in this chapter. Yet a review of the neuroscience literature suggests exercising precaution when considering the role of prior knowledge in students' process-ing of textual information.

For example, in a review of this literature, Hruby (in press) is careful to point out that much of what literacy educators would attribute to an information-processing model of comprehension is in fact challenged by neuroscience research. Citing the work of Gernsbacher and Kaschak (2003), Hruby explains that nature may not have designed the human brain in accord with the information-processing view of comprehension that undergirds the strategies in this chapter. Research in neuroscience does not prove the information-processing view as a literal explanation of learning and literacy in brains, even when such research relies on models drawn from it, and many neuroscientists are doubtful that the brain is best understood in this way. Thus, employing prior knowledge as an aid to comprehension might better be thought of as a figurative account based on the metaphor of the mind as an information-processing system. It may facilitate better instruction without being an accurate account of how the brain actually incorporates and makes use of prior experiences.

Barriers to New Learning

In Chapter 1, we discussed how people use schemata to organize and collect their thoughts and synthesize their experiences. Many research studies have demonstrated how inappropriate or missing schemata can influence learning from reading (Anderson, 1984). Distortions or misinterpretations may result when readers attempt to make sense of unfamiliar ideas by drawing on their cultural schemata.

For example, Steffensen, Joag-Dev, and Anderson (1979) asked Americans and natives of India to read two letters, one about an American wedding and the other about an Indian wedding. Both the Americans and the Indians needed less time to read the letter that had culturally familiar content and recalled more information from the familiar material. Each group interpreted the same information differently, depending on their cultural perspec-tive. For instance, some American readers thought that the dowry described in the Indian passage referred to an exchange of gifts between the families or favors given to the atten-dants by the bride and groom. Because the American bride was wearing her grandmother's wedding gown, one Indian reader inferred that the dress was badly out of fashion.

Problems also arise when a reader has no relevant schema or an insufficient schema, if relevant schemata are not recalled, or if an existing schema is inconsistent with infor-mation in the text. A reader will often ignore ideas in a text or discussion that conflict with conventional wisdom or supposed real-world knowledge (Alvermann, Smith, & Readence, 1985; Guzzetti & Hynd, 1998; Hynd et al., 1995). Students with reading diffi-culties appear to have particular trouble using their prior knowledge to modify miscon-ceptions or to learn new information from reading. Often, a reader who is struggling to understand a difficult text will fasten on isolated details in the text, call on an inappro-priate schema to fill in the gaps, and consequently make unwarranted inferences.

We should not underestimate the tenacity with which students will hold on to their beliefs, even in the face of conflicting evidence. Watson and Konicek (1990) discuss a class of students in Massachusetts who were studying heat transfer. All of them knew from experience that hats, sweaters, and blankets made them warm in winter. They conducted a series of experiments in which they wrapped thermometers in various articles of warm clothing and waited for the temperature to rise. Even when this failed to happen, they maintained their belief that the clothing made them warm.

According to Watson and Konicek, several barriers make it difficult for students to change previously developed concepts. The first is stubbornness, or "the refusal to admit one's theory may be wrong" (p. 682). Second, language itself gets in the way of changing old beliefs: Sweaters are "warm clothes." Third, perceptions can reinforce beliefs: When you put on a sweater, you feel warmer.

Factors such as cognitive, social, and moral development also influence the ease with which students can accommodate new ideas that conflict with everyday experience and conventional wisdom. Anyone who has ever tried teaching the difference between fact and opinion to middle-grade students will sympathize with this because the typical middle schooler will tell you, "If I agree with it, it's a fact!" Students are much too canny to accept an idea simply because a textbook or teacher says they should.

A factor that has strong potential to affect conceptual change is culture. The misinterpretations of American and Indian readers in the study by Steffensen, Joag-Dev, and Anderson (1979) resulted from cultural differences. In another study, black and white teenagers were asked to read a passage that described "sounding," a kind of verbal duel common in African American communities (Reynolds et al., 1982). The white readers tended to interpret the episode as dangerous, even violent; the black readers were more likely to see it as a nonthreatening contest of wits. Although cultural schemata determine in part how students perceive what they read, making culturally based assumptions about what students will or will not understand holds the danger of devolving to stereotypes, which may themselves create barriers to learning.

The effects of culture are much more subtle than is indicated by common stereotypes such as "Italians/Irish/Hispanics are emotional," "Students from single-parent households lack discipline," and "Yuppie children are achievement motivated." Shirley Brice Heath (1983) details the complex and subtle interplay of family, neighborhood, economic circumstances, and religion that influences what children learn about language and literacy. She describes how children from two small working-class communities came to school with quite different ideas about what language, reading, and writing are; how they should be used; and what should be thought about them. The culture of the school reflected yet another set of ideas—the mainstream values and attitudes of the town. What often resulted was a conflict of expectations between school and student—to the detriment of the student.

The Teacher's Task

We draw three broad implications from our understanding of how schemata affect the reading process:

1. What the reader brings to the page in the way of prior knowledge is more important to comprehension than what is actually on the page.

2. What teachers do before reading to prepare students can be more effective in promoting comprehension than what they do after reading.

3. Before reading, teachers should try to activate students' prior knowledge, assess the sufficiency and accuracy of that knowledge, and build appropriate background knowledge when necessary.

Drawing implications from research, no matter how good the research is, raises several questions for both teachers and literacy coaches. Research has shown that what is considered a best practice in one subject matter area does not necessarily transfer easily to a different discipline. Research on best practices may also draw literacy coaches into the discussion, as suggested in the following Literacy Coaches' Corner box.

Good teachers have long understood the necessity of preparing students, and this is reflected in the teaching practices commonly used in content areas. New material is often introduced by a review of what has already been covered, by presenting essential background information via a lecture or media such as films and pictures, and by brainstorming and class discussion. Vocabulary instruction, which is another way to prepare students for reading or studying new topics, is discussed at length in Chapter 8.

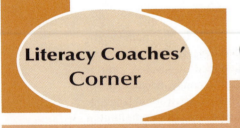

Literacy Coaches' Corner

Knowing Your Limits

Rozycki (2005) reminds us that it is sometimes difficult to say "I don't know" or "I'm not sure," especially when one's reputation is on the line. We agree and suggest that when a teacher's expectations increase to the point that a literacy coach feels overwhelmed by questions—in terms of either the volume or level of specificity—it is time to say "I don't know" or "I'm not sure." Just as a teacher is not an endless source of knowledge, neither is a literacy coach an inexhaustible source of solutions.

Knowing when to involve the teacher in finding answers to questions or when to provide answers as a matter of expedience is part of the nuanced job of being an effective literacy coach. Joint problem solving can also provide opportunities for the coach to acknowledge respect for the teacher's expertise in his or her subject area.

Assessing and Building Prior Knowledge

This section presents some teaching strategies that help students build a schema before reading a selection. Each strategy is designed to "bridge the gap between what the reader already knows and what the reader needs to know before he or she can meaningfully learn the task at hand" (Ausubel, 1968, p. 148). Each of these techniques is relatively easy to plan and introduce in the classroom. As you read about these strategies, keep in mind how students' different sociocultural backgrounds and the varying knowledge they bring to a task will need to be taken into account.

The List-Group-Label Strategy

The strategy called List-Group-Label (Taba, 1967) is a variation on brainstorming that can be done with a whole class, in small groups, or by individual students. Students first list all the words they can think of that are associated with a new topic; then they group the words they have listed by looking for words that have something in common. Several variant groupings are usually possible, and a particular word often fits into more than one group. Once groups of words are established, students decide on a label for each group. An important part of List-Group-Label is the discussion of why words belong in a certain group.

If students' background is fairly extensive, a List-Group-Label session should be sufficient to help them activate and organize what they already know. Students will learn from one another; only where significant gaps or misconceptions exist will the teacher need to fill in additional background. List-Group-Label is also effective as a review activity after students have read about a topic.

Brainstorming activities such as the List-Group-Label strategy often assume students have a common set of experiences that derive from their shared cultural and linguistic knowledge. But what happens when that assumption is challenged? For example, imagine a history class in which students' native countries and languages represent the Pacific Rim, the Middle East, Europe, and North America. If the List-Group-Label strategy were introduced in that classroom and if the topic for brainstorming happened to be *tragedy*, one might expect words associated with Australia's indigenous communities, the destruction of Iraq's museums, Europe's World War II, the United States' 9/11, or the clash between police and students ten days before the 1968 Summer Olympics opened in Mexico. The same topic (*tragedy*) introduced into a brainstorming activity in an English literature class or a biology class would likely evoke quite different responses by the same group of students.

In some instances, a wide variation in brainstormed responses would likely be welcomed and useful. In other instances, too great a variation might distract from the topic that the teacher is hoping to introduce. In the latter case, activities for building rather than merely activating students' prior knowledge would be preferable (e.g., those involving multimedia, teacher read-alouds, or graphic organizers).

Graphic Organizers

When a teacher and students diagram their labeled groups of ideas, they are in effect creating what Barron (1969) called a *graphic organizer*, or structured overview. Barron suggested that important vocabulary terms can be arranged in a diagram that illustrates the relationships between ideas. A typical graphic organizer, with coordinate and subordinate ideas arranged in a branching pattern, is shown in Figure 6.1. Other formats for graphic organizers are presented in Chapter 7. Like the List-Group-Label strategy, graphic organizers can also be used to review information at the end of a unit or chapter. (You probably noticed that graphic organizers present chapter content throughout this text.)

A teacher may prepare a graphic organizer ahead of time and explain it to the students while displaying it on the chalkboard or with a projector. However, a graphic organizer is more effective when students participate in its development. The example in Figure 6.1 was designed to introduce a unit on the novel as a literary form. If the teacher prepared this organizer ahead of time, he or she might have included only the title and top three labels. The teacher could have introduced the new topic by asking students to discuss what they know about novels—characteristics, authors, novels they have read, and so on. The teacher could then have displayed his or her partial graphic organizer and begun to fill in some of the ideas that students generated. Where students did not volunteer essential information, the teacher could have filled in the blanks.

Reading, Viewing, and Listening

For mature readers, much of the background for reading a particular selection comes from previous reading experiences. They have prepared for reading by reading (Alexander & Jetton, 2000). Similarly, a relatively simple method for building students' background for a reading selection is to have them first read another selection on the same topic. In a study with eleventh graders, Crafton (1983) found that reading two articles on the same topic improved students' comprehension of the second article. Specifically, those students generated more inferences, used more outside information and personal

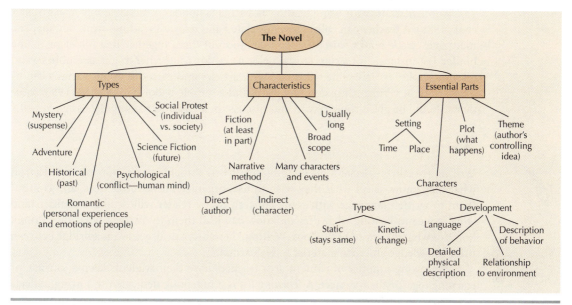

FIGURE 6.1 **A Graphic Organizer with a Branching Format for a High School English Class on the Novel**

involvement, and focused more on higher-level information than did students who read two unrelated articles.

Viewing a streamed video or reading a pertinent selection from a different textbook, a trade book, or a magazine should help to activate and build background for subsequent reading of a targeted selection in a content area text. For instance, a biology teacher introducing a unit on biomes might give the class an excerpt on rain forests from *Scientific American*. A social studies teacher who plans to introduce a unit on intergenerational family relationships might begin by reading a short essay titled "My Name," by Sandra Cisneros (1989). If time is a factor, the teacher might choose to concentrate on a particular section of the essay, such as the part in which Esperanza, a young girl growing up in a Chicano barrio and the narrator of the essay, recalls how she was named after her great-grandmother:

> A wild horse of a woman, so wild she wouldn't marry. Until my great-grandfather threw a sack over her head and carried her off. Just like that, as if she were a fancy chandelier. That's the way he did it. And the story goes she never forgave him. She looked out the window her whole life, the way so many women sit their sadness on their elbow. Esperanza, I have inherited her name, but I don't want to inherit her place by the window. (p. 11)

As students listen, the teacher might ask them to pick out what Courtney Cazden (2000) calls their "strong lines"—especially memorable phrases or sentences—and be prepared to share them at the end.

Another strategy for using reading as a schema builder is called *Skinny Books* (Gilles et al., 1988). A teacher can collect several related and relevant readings from newspapers, magazines, trade books, and other sources and put them together in a folder or theme binder. For instance, for a class studying local elections, a teacher might assemble several "skinny books" or an online wikispace with articles and cartoons about various candidates, rules of voting, campaign literature, and a sample ballot (Gilles et al., 1988). Students should be given time to read and discuss these prior to reading the assigned text.

Writing

Writing is really a special kind of thinking. When students write, they must reflect on what they know, select what they wish to use, organize the selected ideas, and commit them to written language with some concern that a reader will be able to understand what is meant. Writing what they *do* know can lead them to discover what they do *not* know or what they need to find out. Writing, therefore, can also serve as a bridge between prior knowledge and new material to be learned.

A growing number of content area teachers have their students keep a journal, or learning log, for their subject. A *learning log* is a notebook dedicated to jotting, reflecting, drafting, and sometimes doodling. (We discuss learning logs in depth in Chapter 10.) Students are regularly given five to ten minutes during a period to write in their logs, and the teacher periodically collects and reads the logs. If the teacher responds to a particular entry by writing a short note in a student's log, it becomes a kind of private dialogue between teacher and student. Students can use their learning logs for listing, speculating, or predicting before reading.

After a brainstorming session or some other preliminary organizing activity, a teacher might give students five minutes for *free-writing* on a topic ("Write whatever comes to mind on the topic of insects"). For free-writing, the only requirement is that students continue writing for the time period specified (Elbow, 1973). If students protest that they do not know what to write, the teacher can spend a few minutes brainstorming and jotting ideas on the board to help focus the writing activity. Free-writing products are often rough and disjointed, but the object of free-writing is not polished prose. Free-writing promotes written fluency and helps writers to begin collecting and organizing their thoughts.

A teacher might also precede a reading assignment using a strategy of previewing and predicting. A three-step process, *preview, and predict,* incorporates a writing component as the second step. First, students preview the assignment by reading the title and looking at the illustrations to get a sense of the content presented or, in the absence of illustrations, by reading the title and the first few paragraphs of the text. Second, students predict in writing what they think they will learn (if reading an informational text) or what they think will happen (if reading a narrative). Third, they read the selection to verify their predictions. The teacher must be sure to point out that good readers monitor their own comprehension—that it is important for the students to think about their predictions as they read and to change them if warranted.

Research dating back to the early 1980s (e.g., Graves, Cooke, & LaBerge, 1983) supports the practice of building on students' prior knowledge and motivating interest in reading through writing, previewing, and predicting. Throughout the rest of this chapter, you will find other activities that involve writing, some used before reading and some used after. For instance, as you read the following sections, you will see many possibilities for writing activities. Some of the strategies will stimulate learning log entries or even evolve into more formal written products.

Activating Prior Knowledge with Prereading Strategies

Like Felicia at the beginning of this chapter, most middle school and high school students have a lot more on their agendas than schoolwork. After all, in addition to their academic development, they are hard at work on social, physical, and personal growth. It should not come as a surprise that many are not particularly interested in using trigonometric ratios, reading *Julius Caesar*, conjugating Spanish verbs, or learning how the valence-shell electron-pair repulsion model helps in predicting the shapes of molecules. We like to take a realistic view of this by paraphrasing Abraham Lincoln: You can interest some of your students all of the time, you can interest all of your students some of the time, but you will never get all of them excited about the valence-shell electron-pair repulsion model at the same time.

Interest is an important factor in learning, as we said at the beginning of this chapter. Many of you can probably remember teachers who, through their enthusiasm and commitment, brought to life subjects that you ordinarily dreaded. Student interest is relative, though; you might not expect great enthusiasm ("Golly, Ms. Trimble, I now realize that John Milton is the greatest writer who ever lived!"), but you would like to see some curiosity, commitment, and engagement on the part of students during the few minutes they are with you each day.

Martha Ruddell (1996) suggests three principles that can serve as a basis for planning interest-generating instruction:

1. Learning occurs most rapidly and efficiently when new concepts and information build on what is already known.
2. The easiest way to gain and hold students' interest and attention is by engaging them in intellectually rich activities that require problem solving, critical thinking, and active participation.
3. Personal identification with and investment in an activity increases and sustains a learner's persistence and productivity.

A major purpose of prereading strategies is to engage students' interest by focusing a lesson on their ideas and beliefs. Although activating prior knowledge effectively takes into account students' background knowledge and thus may increase their motivation for engaging in content learning, it is also a strategy that can lead to unwanted results. As teachers in our content area literacy classes frequently point out, prior knowledge activation can lead to misunderstandings that might undermine future learning if left unaddressed and uncorrected. Thus, it is important to leave sufficient time for clarifying and redirecting discussions that follow prior knowledge activation.

Anticipation Guides

An *anticipation guide* (called a *prediction guide* by Harold Herber [1978]) is a series of statements that are relevant both to what students already know and to the materials they are going to be studying. As part of a well-planned lesson, such a guide serves as a catalyst for activating relevant schemata and leads students into reading with some personal investment in finding out what is in the text.

Helping
Struggling Readers

Using Anticipation Guides

Anticipation guides are especially helpful when working with students who struggle with their textbook assignments. We recommend using these guides in conjunction with various media formats and the Internet:

- Tape-record relevant sections of a text to assist readers who struggle with decoding and need extra help in completing the guides. Signal on the tape where the information is to be used on the guide.

- Provide a list of websites for students to explore who do not have the requisite background knowledge to complete an anticipation guide. Ask students to add to that list as they search the Internet for related sites.

- Encourage struggling readers to use the classroom or school media center collec-

tion of videotapes and CD-ROMs on topics that you assign for reading. Make sure that the directions and activities on the anticipation guides are stated in such a way that students can use what they learn from the media to complete the guides.

- Make use of struggling readers' everyday knowledge—knowledge that comes from out-of-school experiences—to scaffold school literacy tasks on the anticipation guide. For example, let adolescents use their interest in music CDs to scaffold text-based learning. This might involve letting them rap their answers to the guide material.

- Use sheltered English techniques that rely on visuals and manipulatives when designing anticipation guides for students who speak a language other than English as their first language.

Anticipation guides are useful tools for effecting conceptual change. Dufflemeyer, Baum, and Merkley (1987) explain this function: "By virtue of [their] potential for provoking disagreement and bringing to the surface notions which represent a challenge to students' existing beliefs, anticipation guides serve not only as prior knowledge activators but also as springboards for modifying strongly held misconceptions about the topic" (p. 147). When students' prior knowledge is inaccurate, as is often the case, especially in math and science, confronting their misconceptions directly can be helpful in bringing about new understanding (Guzzetti et al., 1993).

Paul Mance, a teacher at a middle school in Angola, New York, a predominantly rural school district bordering on a Seneca Nation reservation, used an anticipation guide in his ninth-grade English class. The class was going to read *The Rising of the Moon*, a play by Lady Augusta Gregory about a rebel in the Irish Revolution. Paul began by writing on the board "Thou shalt not kill except . . . " and asking "Is it ever right to take another person's life?" The students had many ideas. They discussed euthanasia (a word volunteered by a member of the class), self-defense, and war. He listed these topics on the board. Then he distributed the anticipation guide (Figure 6.2). After a minute or two, students began to compare responses within their small groups. The Native American students in the class had particularly telling insights on some of the issues in the guide.

ANTICIPATION GUIDE: *THE RISING OF THE MOON*

We are going to read a play called *The Rising of the Moon*. It is about a rebel on the run during the Irish Revolution. He tried his best to outsmart the police and avoid being captured. The play deals with many issues of basic human rights for all people.

A	B	
(You)	(Author)	
_____	_____	1. It is always wrong to kill.
_____	_____	2. A person should be willing to die for his or her country.
_____	_____	3. People who live in the same country usually think alike.
_____	_____	4. All men are brothers.
_____	_____	5. Police are cold and unsympathetic.

Once we have discussed these items in class, read the play. If you think the author would agree with you, make a check in column B. You must be able to cite evidence from the play to support your choices in column B.

FIGURE 6.2 **An Anticipation Guide for a Ninth-Grade English Class**

Source: Paul Mance, Lake Shore Middle School, Angola, New York.

When the groups had considered each of the items in the guide, the class weighed the pros and cons of each issue, bringing up many experiences and current events in support of their opinions. Then Paul asked the class, "Based on what you've discussed and the little bit you know about this play, do you think the author would agree with you?" Again the students had a number of ideas. Several students wanted to know if the playwright was Irish, and if so, which side she was on. The teacher suggested this would be a good thing to try to figure out when they read the play for homework.

The next day, students sat again with their working groups. They got out their anticipation guides and literature anthologies and began to go back through each of the issues in the guide. Students frequently turned to a particular section of the play and pointed out information that supported their interpretation. Once again, Paul called the class together to review and summarize. Although there was a high degree of consensus on what the author intended, a few students remained unpersuaded on particular points. Each student had a chance to explain his or her point of view, however. Finally, Paul asked students to pick one statement from the anticipation guide and write in their learning logs why they thought the author agreed or disagreed with them on that particular issue. This log entry became the basis of an essay that each student polished and submitted for a grade.

DEVELOPING ANTICIPATION GUIDES   The use of anticipation guides requires some planning on the part of the teacher. We suggest the following steps in preparing and using an anticipation guide:

1. Analyze the reading assignment to identify key ideas and information.
2. Think of points of congruence between text ideas and students' prior knowledge. To do this, you may need to look beyond the facts and literal information in the text. Try to find the ideas underlying the facts.
3. Anticipate ideas that may be counterintuitive or controversial, especially any misconceptions that students might have about the material.
4. Devise written statements that address students' existing schemata. Although the number of statements will vary, five to eight is recommended for most one- or two-day lessons.
5. Write a brief background or introduction to the reading assignment.
6. Write directions for students. Be sure to provide a bridge between the reader and the author. Direct students to read the text with reference to their own ideas. (Note that the guide in Figure 6.2 says, "If you think the author would agree with you . . . ")
7. Have students work on the guide after a brief introduction to the topic. (Refer to the section on building prior knowledge for some good introductory techniques.)
8. Small-group discussion of the guide, both before and after reading, is an effective means for generating student involvement.

There is one mistake that teachers sometimes make in developing an anticipation guide. When a statement on a guide is too passage dependent—that is, when it is too far removed from students' personal knowledge and experience—they can only make wild guesses about whether or not it is true. This discourages student investment and curiosity and instead reinforces the impression that the textbook is much "smarter" than the reader and is therefore unapproachable.

For example, to prepare eighth-grade students for a science chapter on physical properties, a teacher might draft a guide that included the following definition from the text: "A physical property is a characteristic of matter that may be observed without changing the chemical composition of the substance." If this were the only introduction the students had to the topic, they might have difficulty activating schemata for the following statements:

> You can change a physical property of an object by applying heat to the object.
> Water has a lower boiling point than alcohol.
> We use physical properties to identify and describe objects.

The definition of a physical property is too abstract, and the statements contain potentially unfamiliar technical terms from the text, such as *boiling point*. The following statements should be more accessible because they appeal more directly to students' experiences:

> Heat can change objects.
> Water and alcohol are different.
> We use our senses to identify and describe objects.

Other factors that contribute to the effectiveness of anticipation guides (Dufflemeyer, 1994) include these:

- Statements should reflect important ideas in the text.
- Statements that reflect common knowledge are less likely to stimulate thinking and discussion.
- Statements should be general rather than specific.
- Statements that challenge student beliefs will highlight discrepancies between what they believe and what is in the text.

An important element of the anticipation guide is the bridge between students' prior knowledge and ideas in the text. (Note that the guide in Figure 6.2 directs students to read the text and decide whether or not the author would agree with them. They must also be ready to support their decisions.) In what they call an *extended anticipation guide*, Frederick Dufflemeyer and colleagues (Dufflemeyer, Baum, & Merkley, 1987; Dufflemeyer & Baum, 1992) take this element a step further by asking students to paraphrase what they found in the text. In the example of an extended anticipation guide in Figure 6.3, students

---

ANTICIPATION GUIDE: POPULATION CHANGES

Isle Royale National Park is a large island in Lake Superior. In 1900, a few moose found their way to the island. By 1920, more than 2,000 moose lived there. Between 1920 and 1970, the number of moose on the island went up and down several times.

Directions: Below are several things that influenced the moose herd. Decide whether each one would increase (+) or decresase (–) the number of moose in the herd. Be ready to explain your choices.

+/–

_____ 1. There are approximately four moose for every square kilometer on the island.

_____ 2. A forest fire burns over a quaarter of the island. This land is then grown over with moss, lichen, and new trees (moose food).

_____ 3. The birth rate of the herd goes up. The death rate goes down.

_____ 4. A pack of wolves comes to the island.

Directions: Now read pages 453–455 in your text. If what you read supports your choices, place a check in the Yes column. If the text does not support your prediction, place a check in the No column. For each item, write in your own words what actually happened.

Support?

Yes	No		In Your Own Words
_____	_____	1.	_____
_____	_____	2.	_____
_____	_____	3.	_____
_____	_____	4.	_____

FIGURE 6.3   An Extended Anticipation Guide for a Seventh-Grade Science Lesson

Source: Based on W. Ramsey et al., *Holt Life Science.* New York: Holt, Rinehart & Winston, 1986.

are asked to decide whether the text information is compatible with what they discussed before reading. Finally, students write their own paraphrase of what the text says.

APPLICATIONS OF THE ANTICIPATION GUIDE   Anticipation guides can be created for a variety of subjects. The guide in Figure 6.4 was developed for a first-year French class by their teacher, Beth Anne Connors. The students were going to be reading a dialogue in which a hotel clerk and a guest discussed hotel amenities, room rates, and reservations. Most of the new vocabulary in the selection was specific to travel and hotels. Several differences between hotels in France and in the United States were implied in the passage.

Beth Anne began by asking the class, "Combien parmi vous est jamais resté dans un hôtel pendant un voyage?" ("How many of you have ever stayed in a hotel during a

ANTICIPATION GUIDE: À L'HÔTEL

Part I: We are going to read a story about a man who is trying to make hotel reservations in France. Think about the types of things that people usually expect when staying in a hotel. Read each of the following statements and then mark the appropriate column stating whether you agree or disagree with each expectation. You must be able to explain your choices.

Agree	Disagree	
_____	_____	1. Unless it is vacation season, you will have no trouble getting a room.
_____	_____	2. There will be a phone and a TV in the room.
_____	_____	3. There will be a bathroom in the room.
_____	_____	4. The hotel will have a pool and/or other recreational facilities.
_____	_____	5. The hotel will be reasonably priced.

Part II: In column A, list 5 words in English that will most likely appear in the text. Then read "À l'hôtel." If you find any of the words you listed, write the French word in column B. Write any other new words or phrases from the selection that you think are important at the bottom of the page.

A. Anglais   **B. Français**

1. _____   _____

2. _____   _____

3. _____   _____

4. _____   _____

5. _____   _____

Autres mots ou phrases importantes:

FIGURE 6.4   An Anticipation Guide for a First-Year French Class

Source: Beth Anne Connors, Royalton-Hartland Junior-Senior High School, Middleport, New York.

trip?") She distributed the anticipation guide and asked the students to respond to Part I in groups. In Part II of the guide, they listed in English any words they thought would be used in the passage. As they read the text silently, the students jotted down the French equivalents of the words they had anticipated. Additional French words were written in the bottom section. They compared their postreading lists and discussed the terms, with assistance from the teacher. The students then reread the dialogue orally in pairs. Finally, they used their vocabulary lists to write a summary of the story, in which they described one similarity and one difference between hotels in the United States and France.

The teacher found that the anticipation guide made students less dependent on her for help with new vocabulary. Because they had anticipated many of the ideas and words that were found in the text, they were able to attend more to the overall meaning of the passage and were less concerned with understanding every single word.

Jennifer Ostrach was presenting a new concept to her sixth-grade math class: "When integers with unlike signs are added, the sum will be the difference between the integers and will have the sign of the greater integer." To help her students understand this concept on their own terms, she prepared the anticipation guide in Figure 6.5, which featured everyday situations she knew her students would be familiar with. She began class with a preview of the previous lesson on adding integers with like signs. Then she placed the following problem sentence on the board and asked the class to brainstorm possible solutions: $+4 + -6$.

After they had talked about the problem, Jennifer distributed the anticipation guide and had students work on it in groups of three or four. Students talked about their responses, read the pertinent selection in the math book, and then reexamined their responses. Then Jennifer assisted them as they wrote their own problem sentences using the integers in the statements. As a concluding activity, each student designed a problem like those in the anticipation guide and gave it to the other students in the group to solve.

ANTICIPATION GUIDE: ADDING INTEGERS WITH UNLIKE SIGNS

Directions: Read each statement below and decide whether you agree with it or not. Write A (Agree) or D (Disagree) in the blank before each. Compare responses with others in your group. Be ready to explain your choices.

A or D

_____ 1. If a team wins 6 home games and loses 4 away games, they have won more games than they have lost.

_____ 2. If a football team gains 17 yards on one play and loses 9 yards on the next play; they have gained yardage.

_____ 3. If you spend $15 at the mall and find a $20 bill on the way home, you are ahead.

_____ 4. If you get a bill for $53 and a paycheck for $35, you have enough money to pay the bill.

_____ 5. If you have $8 and buy a movie ticket for $6, you will have enough to buy a supersize bucket of popcorn for $3.

_____ 6. You can add two numbers and still have less than zero.

Directions: Now read p. 408 in your math book. Note the rule for adding positive and negative integers and the examples. Go back to the statements above and see if you have changed your mind. In the space following statements 1 through 5, write an addition sentence using integers and solve the problem. After statement 6, design your own word problem like those in the guide, and give it to others in your group to solve.

FIGURE 6.5   Anticipation Guide for Adding Integers with Unlike Signs

Source: Jennifer Ostrach, Maryvale Middle School, Cheektowaga, New York.

ANTICIPATION GUIDE: THE ORDER OF OPERATIONS

Directions: We have already studied the four basic number operations. Now, we are going to examine expressions that involve two or more operations. Before reading about the order of operations agreement, think about the mathematical expressions and their simplified values listed below. Based on the expression and its simplified value, predict a rule for the order in which mathematical operations are computed. Be able to explain your decisions.

Expression	Simplified Value	Predict Rule
1. $4+8\div2$	8	
2. $18\div2+7$	16	
3. $4*3+4*4$	28	
4. $10-3*5$	-5	
5. $5(3+2)$	25	
6. $36\div2*3$	54	
7. $(5-2)^2$	9	
8. $2+7^2$	51	
9. $(4+8)\div2$	6	
10. $(10-3)5$	35	
11. $8+[13-5(6-4)]$	11	
12. $[2(5*5)-7][6-(12\div3)]$	86	

F I G U R E   6 . 6   An Anticipation Guide for the Order of Operations

The anticipation guide in Figure 6.6 was created by Victoria's math students in her content area reading class several years ago. It is designed to be used in a middle school pre-algebra class just before students study the order of operations agreement. In mathematics, when several operations are necessary to simplify an expression, the order in which those operations are completed really matters. In pairs or small groups, students complete the anticipation guide in Figure 6.6 and predict the rule used to produce the simplified value of the expressions in the first column. This activity enables students to generate their own order of operations rules before reading about the International Agreement on order of operations. It also prepares students to read their mathematics text with better comprehension than if they had read it without any preparation.

Problem-Solving Activities

Another way of activating students' prior knowledge is to engage them in problem-solving activities such as those generated in a problem-based approach to learning and in designing WebQuests. Both approaches are viewed as constructivist teaching methods and thus espouse the assumption that developmentally appropriate, teacher-supported learning should be initiated and directed by the student.

PROBLEM-BASED LEARNING   In a problem-based learning approach, "students are presented with an ill-structured problem and instructed to work in small groups to arrive at some resolution to the problem" (Lambros, 2004, p. ix). For example, the following problem-solving activity could be aligned with the science curriculum in most high schools today:

Activity

Lost Without a Cell Phone

You are the member of a camera crew for an award-winning film company. You are doing a documentary on the human body and have been miniaturized and injected into a human body to film. However, you quickly find yourself trapped inside the nucleus of a pancreas cell when your micro-vehicle malfunctions. You have no way of communicating with anyone on the outside to tell them where you are or to get help. Without a propulsion system, you need to find your way out of the cell safely.

- What do you know from the problem statement?
- What additional information would you like to have?
- How will you proceed? (Lambros, 2004, p. 99)

The acquisition and structuring of knowledge in problem-based learning is thought to work as a result of engaging students in the following cognitive processes (Schmidt, 1993):

- Initial analysis of the problem and activation of prior knowledge through small-group discussion
- Elaboration on prior knowledge and active processing of new information
- Restructuring of prior knowledge
- Stimulation of curiosity related to real-world problem solving

Cognitive development is but one of the positive features associated with a problem-based learning approach. According to Lambros (2004), experienced teachers have reported that this approach can actually eliminate some of the behavioral problems that occur when students are bored or disinterested in content learning. Further, it is important to bear in mind that adolescents are at a stage in their development when career options become increasingly important. Thus, opportunities to engage with real-world problem solving take on additional relevance.

TECHNOLOGY Tip

Problem-Based Learning
Do-it-yourself (DIY) projects are increasingly popular among secondary teachers who see value in connecting hands-on skills to subject matter learning. Some projects are particularly well suited for problem-based learning. For example, at Edutopia's website, www.edutopia .org/maker-faire-DIY-projects, teachers can find directions for carrying out DIY projects in biology, the life sciences, physics, and physiology.

DESIGNING WEBQUESTS   A WebQuest, as defined by Wikipedia, a free online encyclopedia, is "an inquiry-oriented activity in which some or all of the information that learners interact with comes from resources on the Internet" (http://en.wikipedia.org/wiki/WebQuest). Developed by Bernie Dodge in 1995, a WebQuest is usually divided into the following sections: introduction, task, process, evaluation, conclusion, and teacher page. Students typically complete WebQuests in groups, often with individuals being assigned role-playing personas (e.g., a critic, a historian, a researcher, and so on).

Rubric for Evaluating a WebQuest

"A WebQuest about WebQuests" available at http://edweb.sdsu.edu/WebQuest/webquestwebquest-hs.html

Information

❐ Describe a specific topic or lesson with which you might use a WebQuest of your choice. (1 point)
❐ State specifically the value (or lack of value) of a WebQuest for the topic or lesson named. (1 point)

Personal Reaction

❐ State the difficulties (significant or relatively insignificant ones) that you experienced while attempting to complete this assignment "A WebQuest about WebQuests" (2 points)
❐ Self-assess what you learned from the assignment that could conceivably help you make the very same assignment more meaningful to *your* students. (2 points)

Discussion

❐ Participate in a whole-group (videotaped) discussion of the points you made in your paper. (2 points)
❐ Reflect on the videotaped discussion at a later time. (2 points)

FIGURE 6.7   **Rubric for Evaluating a WebQuest**

An effective way to learn about WebQuests is to evaluate an existing one. For example, use the rubric in Figure 6.7 to evaluate "A WebQuest about WebQuests" (http://edweb/sdsu.edu/webquest/webquestwebquest-hs.html. Then locate WebQuests that are related to your subject area and apply the same rubric to them.

K-W-L

Go to MyEducationLab and select the topic *Activating Prior Knowledge and Interest.* Then, go to the Activities and Applications section, watch the video entitled "Using K-W-L in 8th-Grade Math," and respond to the accompanying prompts.

K-W-L is a prereading strategy suggested by Donna Ogle (1986). Students first identify what they *know* about a topic, then decide what they *want* to find out about it, and finally discuss what they have *learned*. (Some teachers, when their students profess that there is nothing they *want* to find out about the topic, use the term *need* to find out instead—K-N-L).

In the first phase of a K-W-L lesson, students brainstorm and discuss the ideas they have on a topic they will be reading about in their text. They can jot down their own ideas on worksheets or in their learning logs. With teacher guidance and modeling, they categorize the information they have discussed and anticipate other categories of information that they may find as they read.

Figure 6.8 shows a K-W-L worksheet developed by a high school self-contained special education class during a lesson on the U.S. Constitution. The students in this class ranged from 13 to 16 years old, and formal testing suggested their academic functioning levels ranged from second to sixth grade. The teacher, Michelle Beishline, began by reviewing the previous chapter; she asked the class to recall why the Colonists were unhappy with Great Britain. Then she asked who had heard of the Constitution and distributed a blank K-W-L worksheet. She told students to write down everything they could think under the K (*Know*) column, first individually and then in small groups. Then she called on students to share what they had written. As students volunteered, Michelle wrote their responses on a large chart on the board and interspersed some general questions: What is the Constitution? Why is it important? When do you think it was written? Who wrote it? She filled in more information under the K column as students elaborated on their answers.

Michelle then asked students what they would want to find out about the Constitution, and she asked them to list their questions under the W (*Want to Know*) column, first individually and then again in their groups. Once more, she called on students and filled in their responses on the chart on the board. Before students read the text, Michelle asked them what the most important categories of information were going to be, and the students responded with the categories in the lower-left-hand corner of the chart: What was it all about? Why was it written? When? Who?

The text selection on writing the Constitution was assigned as homework, and students were told to fill in the final column of the worksheet, L (*Learned*). Later in the day, a teacher aide read the text aloud for a few of the students with severe reading difficulties and helped them fill out the L column. The following day, students first compared what they had written in their small groups, and then the class completed the master chart with the help of the teacher.

K (Know)	W (Want to Know)	L (Learned)
—It was an important paper. —It had to do with freedom. —A lot of people involved (John Hancock, George Washington, Ben Franklin) —It happened a long time ago. —Secret —Had to do with Boston Tea Party. —Was written with feather pen.	—How many people wrote it? —Who wrote it? —Why was it written? —How long did it take to write? —When was it written? —Were there any women in on it? —How long was it? —Why was it kept a secret? —What was it all about?	—55 men wrote it—farmers, merchants, and lawyers. They were called Framers. —Written in Philadelphia, summer 1787. —Kept secret so Framers could speak freely. —Where was it written? —Nation needed a better government. —6 ideas:
Categories: What was it all about? When? Who? How?		1. protect rights of people 2. powers controlled by law 3. power is from people—voting 4. power of government divided into three branches 5. checks & balances 6. federalism—a central gov't that shares power with the states —Problems solved through compromise

FIGURE 6.8   **K-W-L Worksheet for "Writing the Constitution"**

Source: Michelle Beishline, Stanley G. Falk School, Buffalo, New York.

K-W-L lends itself to several variations. Students who have had several experiences with K-W-L could devise their own K-W-L lists in small groups, in pairs, or individually. Teachers can add columns to the basic K-W-L format. For example, a "How" column could be added after the "Want to Know" column, and students could predict ways of finding answers to their initial questions.

Summary

Prior knowledge is a powerful determinant of reading success. Reading about something interesting and familiar seems effortless; the reader is not really conscious of reading at all. Plowing through difficult and unfamiliar reading material, however, can be a frustrating and fruitless task. A person may read and reread with little comprehension or retention of the ideas encountered.

This chapter described many strategies for activating and building students' prior knowledge before they read. These strategies can promote motivation, purpose, and confidence in readers. Students are more likely to be successful with challenging reading material when they can discuss what they know or believe, when they get a preview of what they will be reading, and when the teacher has stimulated a need to know—an itch of curiosity that can be scratched by reading.

Suggested Readings

Godina, H. (1999). High school students of Mexican background in the Midwest: Cultural differences as a constraint to effective literacy instruction. In T. Shanahan & F. V. Rodriguez-Brown (Eds.), *National Reading Conference Yearbook 48* (pp. 266–279). Chicago: National Reading Conference.

Nesbit, J., & Adesope, O. (2006). Learning with concept and knowledge maps: A meta-analysis. *Review of Educational Research, 76,* 413–448.

Readence, J. E., Moore, D. W., & Rickelman, R. J. (2000). *Prereading activities for content area reading and learning* (3rd ed.). Newark, DE: International Reading Association.

Rubinstein-Avila, E. (2006). Connecting with Latino learners. *Educational Leadership, 63*(5), 38–43.

PEARSON
myeducationlab
The Power of Classroom Practice
www.myeducationlab.com

MyEducationLab is a research-based learning tool that brings teaching to life. Go to the Alvermann, Phelps, and Ridgeway Gillis 6th Edition MyEducationLab for Content Area Reading site at www.myeducationlab.com to:

- engage in multimedia exercises to help you build a deeper and more applied understanding of chapter content;

- utilize extensive resources including videos from real classrooms, Praxis and licensure preparation, a lesson plan builder, and materials to help you in your teaching career.

chapter 7

Reading to Learn

Reading to Learn

Constructing Meaning with Text	Helping Students Comprehend	Questions and Questioning	Comprehension Guides	Sensing and Responding to Text Structure	Online Comprehension
• Teaching Students to be Strategic • Making Text Comprehensible • The Role of Fluency in Comprehension	• When to Ask • What to Ask • How to Ask		• Three-Level Guides • Selective Reading Guides • Interactive Reading Guides	• Common Text Structures • Teaching about Text Structures	

Anticipation Guide

Directions: Read each of the following statements. Place a checkmark on the line in the "Before Reading" column if you agree with the statement; leave it blank if you disagree. Then predict what you think the chapter will be about, and jot down on a sticky note (or post online) any questions you have. Read the chapter; then return to the statements and respond to them as you think the authors of your text would. Place a checkmark on the line in the "Authors' Stance" column if you believe the authors would agree with the statement. If you discuss these statements with other people online, in class, or at the family dinner table, return to the statements and check any items you agree with in the right-hand column, "After Discussion." If your thinking changed, what caused that change?

Before Reading	Authors' Stance	Statements	After Discussion
_____	_____	1. Every text has a range of possible meanings.	_____
_____	_____	2. Asking questions should help students learn, not just assess what they have learned.	_____
_____	_____	3. Asking higher-order questions produces more learning than asking fact-level questions.	_____
_____	_____	4. Students have few opportunities to ask their own questions in today's middle and high school classrooms.	_____
_____	_____	5. Different reading strategies are needed to comprehend texts in different disciplines.	_____

The following poem was written by Christine Woyshner, formerly a teacher in Lackawanna, New York, who was thinking back on her own days as a student. It raises some questions that are central to this chapter: What happens when a student sits down to read a content area text assignment? What strategies might the student use, and how effective are they?

• • •

'Twas the night before English and to my dismay
I had not finished the reading due the next day.
My pencils were sharpened and laid on my desk.
As far as I was concerned, I'd do my best.

We were asked to read *Hamlet*. "No problem," I thought.
I cracked open my copy the school district just bought.
"Thee, though, thou" the words they did say.
Just what the heck does that mean, anyway?

Let's see . . . that Hamlet, he seems pretty wild.
I think I'll go see what's on TV for a while.
Now *E.R.* is over, I'll return to my book,
But first I'll open the fridge for a look.

Okay, this is great. I'm up to page ten.
I still can't figure out who did what and when.
It's too bad it's so late, or I'd go to the mall.
I'd better go give my friend Pat a call.

It's getting so late, there's so much more to read.
Pat mentioned a book she thought I might need.
It's by someone named "Cliff" or something like that.
Now I can be an A student, like Pat.

Reading *Cliff's Notes* is the way to go
If you're ever stuck reading "thee, thou, and though."
Now that *Hamlet*'s behind me, I really am glad,
And reading Cliff's *Iliad* won't be so bad.*

• • •

Christine's strategies included sharpening pencils, taking TV and food breaks, and getting expert help. Some of these strategies worked, and some didn't. In the end

---

*Reprinted with permission of Christine A. Woyshner, Temple University.

Christine was able to look back and reflect on the confidence she had gained from the experience.

The focus of this chapter is reading to learn, or what happens when a student opens a book and reads. Ideally, what happens is that the reader learns something about algebra, chemistry, history, or whatever the subject might be. However, as Christine's poem illustrates, text content does not transfer directly and intact into the mind of the reader; it is not like loading a text file from a flash drive into your computer. Although this chapter may seem to emphasize the text, we have not forgotten the importance of the reader or the fact that reading is socially situated. What is learned from reading depends, among other things, on the reader's prior knowledge, attitudes, intention, and learning strategies (Alexander, 2005–2006) as well as the social context in which reading and learning occur (Gee, 1996). Learning implies more than just rote mastery of facts, formulas, and "who did what and when"; it also means thinking about and using that information. Rather than see a particular text as having a single meaning that all successful readers must apprehend, it is more accurate to think of text as representing a range of potential meanings.

Students generally view their textbooks as sources of important information, necessary for success on tests and assignments. However, they are often unsure of their own ability to understand and think about text materials. Some good students develop effective strategies for learning from their texts, but many others find the increased demands of learning from their texts overwhelming. Even though they may want to learn and try to learn, the complexity and abstraction of something like Shakespearean language or the laws of physics may pose seemingly insurmountable problems.

Although the content of their studies becomes more complex, the actual strategies that middle-grade and secondary students have for learning often remain relatively primitive. For content area teachers, experts in their subject matter, the difficulties of their novice students can be frustrating and perplexing. How can students learn when they seem to lack the necessary background and skills? There is no easy or quick solution, but there are several things a teacher can do that will help students read to learn.

Constructing Meaning with Text

Learning from text involves constructing meaning from the author's message. We do not mean to diminish the role of the reader; rather, we emphasize that for text to be a useful learning tool, a reader needs to be able to construct a mental representation of what is conveyed by it. In Chapter 1, we outlined a cognitive view of the reading process that emphasizes the mental operations of the reader in comprehension and a contrasting social constructionist view that recognizes the influences of language and social factors on a reader's understanding of text. From a cognitive standpoint (Goldman & Rakestraw, 2000), comprehension of text involves building coherent mental representations of information. It means processing the meaning of individual words and phrases in the text as well as how these individual words and phrases relate to one another, both within the text and within a larger, preexisting knowledge base. To accomplish this, readers rely on both text-driven and knowledge-driven processes. (p. 311)

A social constructionist would view the question of comprehension quite differently (Gergen, 1999):

Constructionists take meaning to be continuously negotiable; no arrangement of words is self-sustaining in the sense of possessing a single meaning. The meanings of "I love you," for example, border on the infinite. Such reasoning suggests that all bodies of thought are spongy or porous. Whatever is said can mean many different things; meaning can be changed as conversations develop. . . . Vocabulary is also porous, and every concept is subject to multiple renderings depending on the context. (p. 236)

Each of these two viewpoints has its merits, and they are continuously debated among researchers and theorists. (We have exchanged several faxes and e-mails regarding this passage, trying to reach a mutually satisfactory version.) There appears to be some common ground between the two. Comprehension requires transaction between the text and the reader's prior knowledge. If we include a reader's socially constructed ways of speaking, thinking, and behaving (Gee, 1996) as part of prior knowledge, then these two views of the reading process become more complementary than contradictory.

A hypothetical example may help to illustrate the complementary roles of author, reader, and social context. Steve lives in a northern city with a more than 30-year history as a hockey town; he is an ardent, season-ticket-holding hockey fan. Donna lives in the South near a major city that has only recently reacquired a major league hockey team; she is mildly interested in the sport, mostly out of courtesy to her friend Steve. Imagine that we both read a news article on the decline of fighting as a part of the sport. Donna, reading from her position as a pacifist and a relative hockey outsider, might see that decline as a good thing. Steve, although he shares many of Donna's understandings of the world, nevertheless might find fighting to be an acceptable facet of the sport. The two could talk endlessly about their interpretations of the article, and their discussion would be grounded partly on what the author of the article actually said, partly on their prior experience and beliefs about such things as sports and violence in our society, and partly on their long-standing friendship and discussions of many varied topics and ideas. In other words, their different understandings of the article would be textually, personally, and socially constructed.

Sometimes, constructing meaning with text is easy, especially when the reading material is interesting and well written and the topic is familiar. However, even the most experienced and effective reader will encounter text that must be closely read, reread, and pondered before an approximation of the author's intended message can be teased out and an interpretation of that message formed.

Disciplinary Differences in Constructing Meaning

Constructing meaning from text also varies in each content area. In Chapter 1, we discussed differences in the literacy demands across the four core content areas. Those disciplinary differences may be seen as social practices, or conventional ways of talking, reading, thinking, and acting that experts employ within each discipline (Heller & Greenleaf, 2007). Over time, initiates learn these literacy practices in their interactions with others (teachers, peers) as they read, write, and talk about the discipline.

Reading a novel is fundamentally different from reading about history or math or chemistry (Shanahan & Shanahan, 2008). Reading a novel requires the ability to follow plot, understand characters and their motivations, appreciate literary devices, and have some understanding of particular fictional genres. Reading about history demands attention to the author or source and reading the text not as truth but as an interpretation of events. In math, close reading and rereading are two important strategies readers use to gain precise understanding of the interrelation of formal operations, terms, letters, and symbols. Reading about chemistry requires transforming information from prose to visualization, charts, formulas, or graphs, along with paying close attention to precise descriptions of experimental procedures and results.

Go to MyEducationLab and select the topic *Comprehension Strategies*. Then, go to the Activities and Applications section, watch the video entitled "Dimensions of Comprehension," and respond to the accompanying prompts.

What it means to *comprehend* literature, history, math, or science is also complicated by the social practices of educators. Each content area has different pedagogical positions that influence what should be taught and how (Conley, 2008b). Within each discipline, these theoretical orientations generally range from a traditional emphasis on content to a more constructivist emphasis on process, with accompanying differences on whether the function of education is to perpetuate sociocultural practices or to critique and transform them. Consequently, the term *comprehension* will mean one thing in an English class studying canonical literature from a traditional critical perspective and quite another in a class reading contemporary young adult fiction with an emphasis on students' own experiences and constructed responses.

Discipline-Specific Literacy Strategies

Students in middle and high school need to learn the diverse social practices of each discipline and of specific teachers, which is quite a challenge. It is also a challenge to recommend how teachers should teach such varied kinds of comprehension. Generic strategies such as activating prior knowledge, creating graphic organizers, and using questioning techniques need to be adapted to the distinct needs of a content area and a particular topic, as well as to the individual goals of the teacher.

For example, Moje (1996) has shown how a high school chemistry teacher taught literacy strategies such as note taking and summarizing as a consequence of her philosophy of science, her understanding of chemistry as concepts to be learned and organized, and her student-centered beliefs about teaching. In turn, students used these strategies largely because of their relationship with the teacher. The research of Deshler and his colleagues (Bulgren, Deshler, & Lenz, 2007; Deshler et al., 2001) demonstrates that strategies such as activating prior knowledge, using graphic organizers, and teaching about text structure are effective in improving comprehension for students in content classes. However, teacher implementation of these strategies is variable and not always optimal, often because strategy instruction is not part of teachers' social practice or because it displaces critical curricular requirements.

A good example of what can happen when generic strategies are *not* adapted to disciplinary social practices can be seen in a seventh-grade science class that was implementing a new project-based science curriculum (Moje, Collazo, Carrillo, & Marx, 2001). Over the course of a year, the researchers found that assignments often asked students to respond in a narrative or fictional mode, with the result that their writing often had very little science content. The researchers also found that the teacher and students often used the same language but meant different things, as when the teacher used the word *quality* in the narrow scientific sense of air or water quality, while students had the concept of general excellence or superiority.

As we have said in earlier chapters, the *content* needs to determine the *process*—both the literacy processes that students will need to employ and the teaching processes that teachers will use. The research on discipline-specific literacy strategies is still preliminary and inconclusive (Conley, 2008b; Shanahan & Shanahan, 2008), so we will not attempt in this chapter to treat each content area separately. Instead, we will illustrate the various strategies with examples that show how teachers can adapt a strategy to a particular topic. As a reader, you will need to think about how you might tailor these strategies to your own particular conceptualization of what it means to comprehend your subject area.

Helping Students Comprehend

Comprehension is influenced by several interrelated factors, including the text itself, a reader's prior knowledge, the strategies a reader can use, and the goals and interests of the reader (Alexander & Jetton, 2000). One other important influence on comprehension is *instruction*, or what a teacher does to help students comprehend.

Evidence-Based Research

It is important to make a distinction here between two kinds of comprehension instruction: student-centered and content-centered (Brown, 2002). *Student-centered comprehension instruction* involves teaching students how to use specific comprehension strategies independently. This can be done in the context of content area teaching, so that students are learning comprehension strategies and content at the same time, but in the initial stages at least, it requires a good deal of explicit emphasis on reading and thinking.

With *content-centered comprehension instruction*, teachers use materials such as graphic organizers and reading guides to help make text more comprehensible. This chapter, for instance, describes several kinds of reading guides that teachers may design to help students understand content area text. In this approach to comprehension, the primary objective is understanding new content area information.

Clearly, these two approaches are not mutually exclusive. Rather, it is more a matter of where emphasis is placed: on content learning or on comprehension strategy learning.

Teaching Students to Be Strategic

No scripted program, instructional package, or workbook can teach students how to be strategic comprehenders (Duffy, 2002). To teach comprehension strategies effectively, a teacher must be knowledgeable, flexible, and methodical. A knowledgeable teacher must understand the unique literacy demands of the subject area, which strategies fluent readers use, and how to teach those strategies. Comprehension is complex, and our understanding of how comprehension works is still developing. A single comprehension term such as *inference, main idea,* or *critical thinking* may take on varied meanings in the context of different theoretical approaches. It is therefore not surprising that a review of reading methods texts and journal articles yields a confusing array of strategies and teaching suggestions.

The U.S. Congress authorized the National Reading Panel (NRP) expressly to bring clarity to the often bewildering and contradictory recommendations of educational authorities and to determine which reading strategies and instructional approaches had strong research support. The NRP's research itself was not without its critics, who charged that its definition of *scientific research* was too narrow and unscientific (Cummins, 2002); that it did not review qualitative and correlational studies; that its methodology and some of the results of its research reviews were questionable (Allington, 2002; Alvermann, 2002; Yatvin, 2002); and, of particular concern, that it excluded studies of second-language readers. Nevertheless, the NRP subgroup report on comprehension yielded a handful of recommendations for instruction that most informed readers of educational research would include on their top-10 lists. (Every one of the NRP's recommendations for comprehension instruction has been prominently featured in each edition of this textbook.)

 Evidence-Based Research

The NRP report (National Reading Panel, 2000) lists seven categories of comprehension instruction that met the panel's criteria for strong research support:

- Comprehension monitoring
- Cooperative learning
- Use of graphic and semantic organizers
- Question answering
- Question generation
- Story or text structure
- Summarization

The report also notes the essential role that vocabulary development and instruction play in comprehension.

Notable omissions from the panel's findings include teaching readers to use their prior knowledge and to actively make predictions as they read, which has strong evidence-based support, and the integration of reading and writing, which can also be a powerful aid to comprehension. In addition, Alvermann (2002) notes that much of the NRP's research on comprehension instruction has been conducted on students in grades 3–8 and that teachers must therefore be cautious about applying those findings to older students.

Despite the limitations of the NRP's investigations, its findings are of practical value. Of the panel's seven recommended comprehension strategies this chapter will give special attention to three: question answering, question generation, and story or text structure.

DIRECT INSTRUCTION OF COMPREHENSION STRATEGIES   Effective comprehension strategy instruction follows the direct instruction model outlined in Chapter 4. To help students learn to use a comprehension strategy independently, a teacher should introduce the strategy, model the strategy for students, guide them as they practice the strategy with easy-to-read text, and then provide continued independent practice in a variety of reading situations with frequent feedback (Baumann, 1984; Faggella-Luby & Deshler, 2008; Pressley, 2002). Direct instruction is facilitated when both strategies and content are the subject of collaborative discourse between student and teacher and among students themselves (Langer, 2000; National Reading Panel, 2000).

There are clear costs and benefits to direct instruction in comprehension. Bringing students to the point where they can use a comprehension strategy independently rarely happens quickly and easily. Comprehension instruction is most effective when a few well-validated and pertinent strategies are taught, when they are discussed and practiced repeatedly over time, and when students are reading interesting content area text that requires application of the strategies they have been taught (El Dinary, 2002; Guthrie & Ozgungor, 2002; Ogle & Blachowicz, 2002).

For teachers in the middle and secondary grades, meeting the optimal conditions of time and context for direct instruction may be impractical in the face of intense curricular pressures and high-stakes testing (Faggella-Luby & Deshler, 2008; Scanlon, Deshler, & Schumaker, 1996). However, when students are explicitly and systematically taught strategies for comprehending, teachers find noticeable improvement in achievement, critical thinking, self-confidence, and student-to-student interaction (El Dinary, 2002; Faggella-Luby & Deshler, 2008; Fritschmann, Deshler, & Schumaker, 2007; Langer, 2001; Mastropieri et al., 2003).

Making Text Comprehensible

Although intensive student-centered comprehension instruction may be impractical, teachers can still help students read, discuss, and comprehend their assignments by using teaching strategies that place content objectives in the forefront (Bulgren et al., 2007; Faggella-Luby & Deshler, 2008; Mastropieri et al., 2003). Making connections between

Helping Struggling Readers

Comprehension Help

Students who get to middle or high school with reading difficulties are likely to have many years of frustration, remediation, avoidance, and failure behind them and very little time left in school to address their predicament. These students' difficulties are often severe, complex, and seemingly intractable. At the same time, these students are expected to process increasingly difficult expository texts with higher levels of comprehension, even though they tend to read expository text with less fluency and comprehension than they do narrative text (Sáenz & Fuchs, 2002).

Based on more than twenty years of research with struggling adolescent readers at the University of Kansas, Donald Deshler and his colleagues recommend a five-tiered approach to intervention for struggling secondary students. Each successive tier requires more intensive and focused instruction (Faggella-Luby & Deshler, 2008):

1. Teachers improve the delivery of content instruction.
2. Teachers include content-specific literacy strategies as part of their instruction.
3. Students receive intensive literacy strategy instruction from trained specialists.
4. Students receive intensive basic literacy skill instruction from trained specialists.
5. Students are given therapeutic intervention for significant language deficits.

While many struggling students can and do make significant improvement in reading when given focused instruction by a knowledgeable specialist, it is unfair and impractical to expect content area teachers to correct all problems (Greenleaf, Jiménez, & Roller, 2002). Effective strategy instruction for students with severe reading disabilities requires intensive efforts in small group or one-on-one settings provided by a teacher who views that instruction as a major responsibility (Beers, 2003; Fisher, Schumaker, & Deshler, 2002; Mastropieri, Scruggs, & Graetz, 2003).

So, what can classroom teachers do? Teachers can mediate comprehension for these students by employing content-centered teaching strategies like those discussed in the section "Making Text Comprehensible," in this chapter.

students' prior knowledge and new concepts using prereading strategies will facilitate students' understanding as they read.

A lesson structure such as K-W-L can guide student comprehension by drawing on well-researched principles of learning, even though students may not be explicitly aware that they are being strategic. Graphic organizers, introduced in various formats before or after reading, can also help students comprehend. Questioning strategies, including self-questioning by students, and knowledge of expository text structures can improve comprehension as well. Careful teaching of content-specific vocabulary is another way to help make text comprehensible for students. Finally, comprehension increases when reading and discussion are included in cooperative-learning activities that promote engagement with new concepts and thinking aloud by students.

In the remainder of this chapter, you will see how the judicious use of questions, teacher-created reading guides, and guidance with text structures can help students understand their content area reading. Further content-centered strategies for enabling student comprehension are featured in the following chapters on vocabulary (Chapter 8), reading (9), writing (10), and study skills (11).

The Role of Fluency in Comprehension

The ability to read fluently is an important precondition of comprehension (Rasinski et al., 2005). Fluent readers, according to the National Reading Panel (2000), are able to comprehend texts of various types with speed, accuracy, and appropriate expression. Nonfluent readers, on the other hand, expend much of their attention and effort on decoding and are distracted by frequent and often nonsensical miscues. Nonfluent reading leaves precious few cognitive resources for comprehension. It is impossible to decode, figure out unfamiliar vocabulary, keep a reading strategy in mind, and comprehend important content all at once (Sinatra, Brown, & Reynolds, 2002).

Evidence-Based Research

The NRP, while acknowledging that fluency instruction is often neglected in day-to-day classroom instruction, found sufficient research evidence to suggest that guided oral-reading procedures have a positive impact on students' fluency and comprehension across a range of grade levels and in a variety of regular and special education classrooms. However, the panel did not find sufficient evidence to recommend independent silent reading as an effective way to improve reading achievement, in part because there were only ten studies that met the panel's research criteria. In criticizing this conclusion, Krashen (2002) argues that the NRP omitted a large number of relevant studies and misinterpreted the studies it did review.

Admittedly, setting aside significant blocks of time for independent reading is probably impractical for most content area teachers, although it is an important component of reading-skills courses in middle school and high school. Because of its long-standing usage and the strong correlational evidence of its effectiveness, independent silent reading remains a part of this text's discussion of fluency.

GUIDED ORAL-READING PROCEDURES   Repeated reading, shared reading, paired reading, and other similar procedures make up what are generally referred to as *guided oral-reading procedures*. These procedures share several key characteristics. They typically involve students in rereading the same text over and over again until a specified level of proficiency is reached. They also tend to rely on one-to-one instruction through tutoring (including peer tutoring and cross-age tutoring), audiotapes, or some other means of guided oral-reading practice. Unlike whole-class, round-robin oral reading, in which individuals read aloud for only a brief period of time, the guided oral-reading procedures just named maximize the amount of time any one student spends practicing fluency.

Readers need to attain a level of fluency such that difficulties with word recognition and slow, choppy reading do not interfere with comprehension and studying. However, it is an especially important goal for students who are English language learners (ELLs). Although the National Reading Panel (2000) did not address issues relevant to second-language learning, a growing body of research on guided oral-reading procedures used with Latino students tends to support the panel's findings that such procedures do indeed improve reading.

For example, Robert Jiménez and Arturo Gámez (2000) were successful in their efforts to build reading fluency and improved attitudes toward reading among a group of middle school Latino students who, without such instruction and opportunities for guided oral rereading, might have been viewed simply as at risk for school failure. Similar results were found for a fluency procedure called *cooperative repeated readings* used with a group of African American eighth graders who struggled with reading and who were considered at risk of school failure (Tatum, 2000). As Jiménez and Gámez noted, too often the at-risk label is applied to students who "may possess untapped potential for success in literacy" (p. 81) if given appropriate instruction.

INDEPENDENT SILENT READING   The assumption here is that by encouraging students to read on their own, teachers influence the amount of time they spend practicing their literacy skills. Although procedures such as sustained silent reading, drop everything and read, and a number of incentive programs (e.g., Million Minutes and Pizza Hut's Book It) are thought to motivate students to read more, the relationship between increased voluntary reading time and reading achievement is still murky.

As the National Reading Panel (2000) took pains to point out in their report, the data connecting time spent reading and reading achievement are correlational rather than causative in nature. Thus, it could be the case that reading more makes an individ-

Helping
Struggling Readers

Rereading for Comprehension

When experienced readers encounter difficult text, they will reread sentences, paragraphs, or even chapters, asking questions, seeking clarification, and reflecting in order to construct meaning. This simple but effective comprehension strategy is so automatic for many of us that we hardly realize we are doing it. Less experienced readers and those who have difficulty with reading often think that rereading difficult material is futile or somehow "cheating," because they don't see their more accomplished peers rereading. Besides, the assignment only said to *read* the chapter, not reread it or understand it.

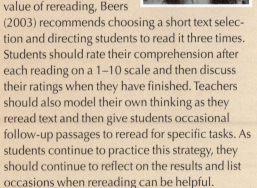

To demonstrate the value of rereading, Beers (2003) recommends choosing a short text selection and directing students to read it three times. Students should rate their comprehension after each reading on a 1–10 scale and then discuss their ratings when they have finished. Teachers should also model their own thinking as they reread text and then give students occasional follow-up passages to reread for specific tasks. As students continue to practice this strategy, they should continue to reflect on the results and list occasions when rereading can be helpful.

ual a better reader, or it could be simply the fact that better readers opt to read more. The lack of conclusive evidence in support of independent silent reading does not mean that teachers should cease to encourage it. On the contrary, as Saunders and Goldenberg (1999), researchers with the Center for Research on Education, Diversity and Excellence, are quick to note, pleasure reading and teacher readalouds are designed "to expose students to the language of expert writers and the fluency of an expert reader" (p. 5).

Questions and Questioning

Using questions to help students learn is at least as old as Socrates. Asking questions about texts is "perhaps the most common kind of academic work in comprehension instruction" (Dole et al., 1991). Good questions can guide students' search for information, lead them to consider difficult ideas, and prompt new insights.

Long tradition and widespread use do not mean that questioning is always effective, however. Too often, questions test what students have learned rather than help them to learn. A high proportion of teachers' questions tend to be literal, "what's it say in the book" questions, asked after students have read (Durkin, 1978/1979). In Chapter 3, we considered the differences between discussion (which prompts thinking and learning) and recitation (which prompts memorization). In a traditional classroom recitation, the teacher dispenses questions and is at once the repository and arbiter of correct answers. Students are frequently given little time to formulate a reply before the teacher either calls on someone else or asks a new question. Although such recitations probably have their place in helping students to review and remember the vast curricular content they are expected to cover, they do little to help students learn as they read.

Questioning is among the most common classroom activities, but all students may not be equally prepared for question–answer situations. Responses to a teacher's questions may vary depending on a student's cultural background. Mainstream middle-class families prepare young children for school by rewarding the kinds of language behavior that are also rewarded by schools (Heath, 1991; Gee, 1996). This behavior includes answering questions that focus on labels, on information known to the questioner, and on recounts of previously learned information. Such adult–child questioning situations usually require children to give a straightforward expository response.

The same kinds of language behavior are not necessarily prized in other cultural groups, in which labels and language may be learned cooperatively in functional settings, often from siblings rather than adults. In some communities, question–answer exchanges between adults and children take on a different form from what is routinely done in schools. Shirley Brice Heath (1991) found that in home settings, young African American children in one community were frequently asked playful or teasing questions and questions that encouraged their interpretive or analytical powers. Students from diverse cultural backgrounds may also possess extraordinary language powers that can be utilized in school settings. Lisa Delpit (1995) notes that Native American children come from communities in which storytelling, featuring a wealth of meaning with an economy of words, is highly sophisticated. Delpit also notes the "verbal adroitness, the cogent and quick wit, the brilliant use of metaphorical language, the facility in rhythm and rhyme" (p. 57) that are developed and celebrated in the African American community.

These cultural differences in language use imply a need to modify the traditional recitation session with its emphasis on single correct, literal answers. Some students may need support and guidance in formulating answers to conventional classroom questions; they may perform better when responses are formulated in small discussion groups rather than in whole-class recitations. Equally important, the kinds of questions that are asked and the answers that are rewarded should reflect the verbal strengths of students. Higher-level questions and active give-and-take in discussion facilitate learning by culturally diverse students (Hill, 1989).

Research on questioning has suggested many ways in which teachers can make their questioning more effective. To use questions well, teachers need to know when to ask, what to ask, and how to ask.

When to Ask: The Right Time and the Right Place

Questions appear to have different effects, depending on when they are asked (Just & Carpenter, 1987). Generally, questions asked before reading tend to help readers focus on the targeted information. Prereading questions in effect tell the readers what to look for and, by implication, what to ignore. On the other hand, questions that follow reading tend to improve understanding not only of the targeted information but also of information that is not covered by the questions. Furthermore, questions seem to be more effective the closer they are to the information in the reading material. Interspersing questions within text is sometimes called "slicing the task" because it reduces the amount of text that students must read and comprehend at a given time (Wood, 1986).

These findings have some practical implications for teachers. When students are especially in need of guidance—for example, when they must digest relatively long and difficult text assignments—prereading questions help them separate the important from the unimportant by alerting them to essential ideas and information. Conversely, when selections are more manageable or when the teacher is aiming for a broader general understanding of a selection, postreading questions might be the best approach. In practice, many teachers use a mix of prereading questions to guide students' reading and postreading questions to assess their understanding and stimulate them to reflect.

The physical proximity of questions to text is more difficult to accomplish. Obviously, a teacher cannot insert questions in students' textbooks or be there in person to ask the right questions just as a student finishes a particular passage. One solution is to give students a question guide that is keyed to particular sections of the text, with instructions to complete the answers as they go. Anytime a teacher gives students a list of questions beforehand, though, there is the probability that some students will resort to simply reading the questions and skimming the text to match words in the questions to words in the text.

What to Ask: The Relation between Questions and Answers

There are many different types of questions. At one extreme is the factual question with a single correct answer: Who is buried in Grant's tomb? When was the War of 1812? Responding to some questions, however, requires a good deal of thought: How do the presidencies of Grant and Nixon compare? What were the causes and the immediate and long-term consequences of the War of 1812?

Factual questions can be useful, but they are overused in too many classrooms. According to Just and Carpenter (1987), "Questions that require high-level abstraction (such as the application of a principle) produce more learning than factual questions. High-level questions probably encourage deeper processing and more thorough organization" (pp. 421–422).

Different questions may prompt answers from different sources, and so it is useful to think of *question–answer relationships (QARs)* (Pearson & Johnson, 1978). The answer to some questions may be *textually explicit*, or literally stated in the text. A reader might paraphrase the text, point to the exact words, or read them aloud to answer the questions. Other questions may call for a response that is *textually implicit*, not directly stated but suggested or implied by the text. To formulate an answer, a reader has to think about what the author has said and perhaps integrate information from several places in the text. Sometimes the answer to a question does not come from the text at all. The reader must call on prior knowledge or beliefs to answer the question. Pearson and Johnson call this prior knowledge a reader's "script" and say that such an answer would be *scriptally implicit*.

In a series of studies, Taffy Raphael further developed the concept of QARs and demonstrated their potential for helping students to comprehend their reading (Raphael, 1982, 1984, 1986; Raphael & Pearson, 1982). Raphael suggested that younger students, those in second grade or below, could most easily distinguish two main sources of information—the text itself and their own background knowledge. She coined the phrase *In the Book* to describe answers that were either textually explicit or textually implicit, and she used the phrase *In My Head* for answers that were scriptally implicit.

 Evidence-Based Research

As readers become more conceptually mature, they are able to make finer discriminations between the kinds of answers they produce, and it is possible for them to think of four different QARs. Older readers are able to see that some answers are textually explicit, which Raphael (1986) labeled *Right There*. They are also able to understand that some answers are not directly stated but rather require inferences drawn from different parts of the text. These textually implicit answers are derived by the reader *Putting It Together*.

By the middle grades, students can identify two different types of questions that call on their background knowledge. Some scriptally implicit questions require the reader to combine prior knowledge with information from the text to derive a response; hence, these are *Author and You* answers. Finally, some questions can be answered solely from the reader's knowledge base; they may even be answered without reading the text. As a reader, you are *On Your Own*.

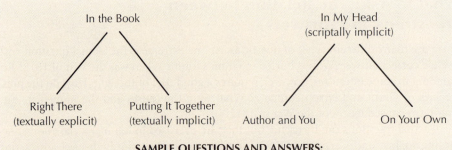

SAMPLE QUESTIONS AND ANSWERS:
"GOLDILOCKS AND THE THREE BEARS"

1. **Right There:** What were the Three Bears eating for breakfast?
   Answer: They were eating porridge.

2. **Putting It Together:** Why was Baby Bear so upset when he came home?
   Answer: Because his breakfast was gone, his chair was broken, and there was a stranger sleeping in his bed.

3. **Author and You:** what kind of a person was Goldilocks?
   Answer: She was not very nice. She was bold. She was hungry and tired, and maybe she was lost or homeless.

4. **On Your Own:** Why is it a bad idea to go into a stranger's house when no one is home?
   Answer: It is against the law; it is trespassing. The people would not like it. They might be mean people and do something bad to you.

FIGURE 7.1   **Question–Answer Relationships**

Figure 7.1 gives a graphic representation of the various QARs, with sample questions and answers based on the story of "Goldilocks and the Three Bears." To give you a further idea of how the four QARs might work with textbook material, we invite you to try the following activity.

Activity

Here is a short passage titled "Why the British Lost" from a high school American history text (Boorstin & Kelley, 2005). Following it are eight questions. The first four are answered for you and labeled *Right There, Putting It Together, Author and You*, and *On Your Own*. A brief rationale is given for each relationship. See whether you can answer the last four questions and decide what the QAR is for each of them. (The answers are at the bottom of the box on page 208.)

The British were separated from their headquarters by a vast ocean. Their lines of communication were long. The British government was badly informed. They thought the Americans were much weaker than they really were. And they expected help from uprisings of thousands of Loyalists. But these uprisings never happened.

The most important explanation was that the British had set themselves an impossible task. Though they had an army that was large for that day, how could it ever be large enough to occupy and subjugate a continent? The British knew so little of America that they thought their capture of New York City would end the war. After the Battle of Long Island in August 1776, General Howe actually asked the Americans to send him a peace commission, and cheerfully expected to receive the American surrender. But he was badly disappointed. For the colonists had no single capital that the British could capture to win the war.

American success was largely due to perseverance in keeping an army in the field throughout the long, hard years. George Washington was a man of great courage and good judgment. And Americans had the strengths of a New World—with a new kind of army fighting in new ways. Still, it is doubtful the Americans could have won without the aid of France.

Although many Americans opposed the Revolution, and some were lukewarm, it was a people's war. As many as half of all men of military age were in the army at one time or another. Each had the special power and special courage that came from fighting for himself, for his family, and for his home. (p. 100)

1. *Question*: What did the British expect from the Loyalists?

   Answer: They expected uprisings from thousands of Loyalists.

   QAR: Right There—The answer is almost a direct quote from the text.

2. *Question*: What evidence is there that the British were responsible for defeating themselves?

   Answer: The were badly informed. They were overly confident and made many poor judgments. They tried to fight a war that was too far away from their headquarters.

   QAR: Putting It Together—The reader must select information from several places in the text and make inferences about this information.

3. *Question*: What could Britain have done to win the war?

   Answers: They could have gotten better information. They could have had better generals who would have adapted to a new kind of warfare. They could have captured General Washington. They could have negotiated a treaty with France.

   QAR: Author and You—The reader must know many of the issues and events from the text, but the question also calls for the reader to use prior knowledge and reasoning to think of possible answers.

(continued)

4. *Question*: What qualities are important in a leader during a time of crisis?

   Answers: During a crisis, a leader should have courage, good judgment, ability to inspire loyalty, and confidence, intelligence, coolheadedness.

   QAR: On Your Own—The reader can rely entirely on prior knowledge; no knowledge of the text or the events of the American Revolution is required.

5. *Question*: In what way was the American Revolution a people's war?

6. *Question*: If the United States were invaded by a foreign army, what might people in your community do?

7. *Question*: What did the British think would happen when they captured New York City?

8. *Question*: What lessons might we learn today from Britain's experience in the American Revolution?

5. *Answer*: Half of all the men served in the army. People were fighting for their own families and homes. America won because people were willing to sacrifice and keep fighting even though they met some early defeats. *QAR*: Putting It Together—The answer is not directly stated. The reader must infer the answer from what the authors say. 6. *Answer*: People in our community might fight back. They would join the army or go underground and fight a guerrilla war. Some people might become collaborators, though, depending on what they thought of the invaders. *QAR*: On Your Own—The question can be answered with background knowledge and the readers' suppositions; no knowledge of the text is necessary. 7. *Answer*: The British thought the war would end once they captured New York City. *QAR*: Right There—The answer is stated explicitly in the text. 8. *Answer*: We should know what we are doing before we become involved in something. We shouldn't try to take on impossible tasks. It is imprudent to enter into a war in a faraway country when the people of that country are mostly against you. Be sure you have the means and the will to follow through whatever you start. *QAR*: Author and You—A number of answers are possible, depending on readers' background knowledge and opinions, but a person must also have knowledge of the factors that are discussed in the text.

In her work with middle-grade students, Raphael demonstrated that students can be taught about QARs and that this knowledge of where answers come from can actually improve students' ability to answer questions (Raphael, 1982, 1984, 1986; Raphael & Pearson, 1982). There is also evidence that students maintain their use of QAR strategies over time and that QAR training with narrative text transfers when students read expository text (Ezell et al., 1996).

A content area teacher might teach students about QARs using a procedure similar to that suggested by Raphael and Au (2005). They propose a developmental sequence beginning with two QARs: *In the Book* and *In My Head*. Once students show they understand these relationships, they can be introduced to the two kinds of *In the Book* QARs: *Right There* and *Putting It Together*. Finally, once those distinctions have been learned, the teacher can introduce the two kinds of *In My Head* QARs: *Author and You* and *On Your Own*. Depending on students' ages and reading abilities, this sequence might take anywhere from a class period to several weeks.

Whatever the duration of QAR instruction, each phase should be scaffolded as follows:

1. Explain each QAR, and demonstrate it with a relatively simple example or two.

2. Once students seem to grasp the relationships, give them questions based on simple or familiar text and labeled with the QARs, and have them develop answers. Lead students to discuss their results.

3. As students become competent with labeled questions, begin posing unlabeled questions and instruct students to develop answers and decide which QAR applies. Again, engage them in discussion of their decisions.

Throughout this instructional sequence, discussion of questions, text, and answers is essential to help illustrate and reinforce the relationships. The emphasis should be on comprehension. What is important are the answers that students supply and the sources of those answers. QAR instruction should not become a task of simply labeling questions as *Right There*, *Putting It Together*, and so on.

Instruction in QARs readily complements the kind of question–answer reading assignments and discussions often used by content teachers. All of the examples can be based on students' actual textbook reading assignments, and discussion of QARs requires minimal additional classroom time.

TECHNOLOGY Tip

QARs and Questioning the Author

ReadingQuest.org, a website designed for social studies teachers who wish to more effectively engage their students with the content in their classes, has a discussion of how teachers can use Question–Answer Relationships and Questioning the Author, each with examples.

For more suggestions on classroom questioning strategies, visit the University of Delaware's Center for Teaching Effectiveness website. As part of the university's handbook for teaching assistants, you will find a list of specific strategies for encouraging students to ask and answer questions at http://cte.udel.edu/TAbook/question/html.

Lesson ideas for teaching QARs, as well as other comprehension strategies, for middle and high school can also be found at ReadWrite-Think, a joint venture of the International Reading Association and the National Council of Teachers of English (www.readwritethink.org/lessons/index.asp).

The QAR taxonomy is simple and intuitively easy to comprehend. In practice, however, teachers have found a few difficulties inherent in this very simplicity. Comprehension (in this case, the answers to questions) is too complex to be tidily classified by four relationships. The QAR taxonomy also implies a linear process that simply does not exist. Readers do not begin by comprehending information that is right there, then move on to putting ideas together, and end up being on their own. In fact, these kinds of comprehension occur simultaneously and interdependently.

In addition, the definitions of the four relationships are not precise. For instance, if a student answers a question with the exact words from two different paragraphs in the text, is the QAR *Right There* because the exact words were used or *Putting It Together* because the answer integrated information from different parts of the text? Often, a reader will answer a question using an *Author and You* or *Putting It Together* QAR when the information is actually *Right There*. The answer is not necessarily wrong just because it came from a source other than one the teacher had intended.

Despite these limitations, we believe that QARs provide a useful framework for teachers and students. First, there is a good argument for teaching students about QARs. When students are consciously aware of the different sources of information available to answer questions, they become more strategic in their reading and thinking and their comprehension is improved (Raphael, 1984). Second, we have found that the four QARs are helpful in teacher planning. Classroom questioning is more effective when questions are planned in advance, and thinking in terms of QARs will help teachers strike a balance between literal questions and more thought-provoking questions.

Planning questions should begin with one or more *essential questions* that focus on the "big ideas" and guide students' inquiry into the topic. (Essential questions were discussed in Chapter 4.) From there, teachers can think about related questions across the four QAR categories. Raphael and Au (2005) recommend using *On My Own* and *Author and You* questions before reading to activate students' prior knowledge and focus them on the topic, title, or illustrations in the text. During reading, teachers will likely use more *Right There* and *Think and Search* questions to establish important information, along with some *Author and You* questions to help students make predictions and evaluate the text. After reading, *Author and You* questions should predominate, along with *Think and Search* questions to help students find evidence to support their conclusions. Questions beyond the literal, or *Right There*, level help students see relationships, make connections, and associate new ideas with their own prior knowledge. Such questions frequently have more than a single good answer, which stimulates students to think for themselves rather than passively wait to be told the *right* answer.

Another benefit of QAR instruction is that it provides a shared language for teachers and students to talk about comprehension processes, which otherwise are largely invisible and unexamined (Raphael & Au, 2005). For instance, if students are assiduously scanning the text for an answer to a question, the teacher can help by pointing out that the answer calls for their own input (i.e., it's *Author and You*). Having a shared language for talking about comprehension is also helpful when preparing students to take high-

Literacy Coaches' Corner

Asking Questions

A successful coaching relationship must be built on mutual respect between the teacher and coach. Cathy Toll, in *The Literacy Coach's Survival Guide* (2005), suggests that asking good questions about a teacher's goals is more effective than trying to contrive ways to make the teacher achieve the coach's goals. Perhaps the most effective question a coach can ask a teacher is "What do you think?" Such an open-ended question encourages a teacher to provide information, to reflect, and to take ownership.

A good question is especially valuable when the literacy coach gets that uneasy feeling that he or she is being put on the spot. Asking questions buys time and helps the coach understand where the teacher is coming from. At the same time, a coach wants to be careful not to put others in an uncomfortable or defensive position. If a teacher says a particular idea won't work with his or her students or in his or her subject area, asking "Why not?" invites an argumentative response. An alternative question might be something like "Can you tell me about your experiences?"

stakes tests. It gives teachers and students a tool for analyzing questions on practice tests and planning effective answers.

How to Ask: Questioning Strategies

Teachers frequently devise prereading questions, assign end-of-chapter questions, or use questions to guide reading and class recitations and discussions. This section offers some alternative questioning strategies that can help students become more actively involved in formulating and answering questions. In conjunction with instruction on QARs, these techniques can facilitate students' development of independent strategies for reading to learn.

QUESTION GUIDES   Questions can be devised to guide students as they read the text and to promote discussion after reading. The QAR guide in Figure 7.2 was designed by Ed Beard, a math education student in one of Steve's classes, for a middle-grade math lesson on variable equations. The reading for this lesson was typical of math texts in that it began with a practical demonstration, followed by precise mathematical definitions and examples, and finally a series of exercises. Ed knew this lesson would require close reading of the text, with special attention to the definitions and operations (Shanahan &

QUESTION GUIDE: VARIABLE EXPRESSIONS

Right There: Read p. 92 and answer the following three questions.

1. What is a variable?
2. What is a variable expression?
3. How do you evaluate a variable expression?

Think & Search: Read p. 93 and the example on p. 94. Then answer the following questions. Be ready to explain your answers.

4. If $Z = 6$, what does $6Z$ equal?
5. What are three ways you can write a word phrase for $y + 7$?
6. Can a variable expression be equal to more than one number?

Author & You: As you work the assigned exercises on pp. 94–96, think about the following questions. When you have finished with the exercises, write out answers to these questions.

7. What are some examples of variable expressions in sports?
8. Suppose you wanted to buy two DVDs and a $10 CD. Find the total cost of your purchase if the DVDs cost $14.95 each. Write out the variable expression you used to calculate the total cost.
9. For what types of data are variable expressions useful?

On Your Own: We thought about these two questions at the beginning of the lesson. Use what you have learned about variable equations to answer them now.

10. Suppose you are putting up posters for your friend's band. How would you determine the total cost of posters if the cost of each poster is $2?
11. At a grocery store, what does a cash register do?

FIGURE 7.2   QAR Guide: Variable Expressions

Source: Edward Beard, Buffalo State College, New York.

Shanahan, 2008). He wanted to be sure students understood the examples provided and that they would be able to apply the new math concepts to real-world situations.

Ed introduced the lesson and the reading by asking for student responses to two *On Your Own* questions:

- Suppose you are putting up posters for your friend's band. How will you determine the total cost of the posters if the cost of each poster is $2?
- At a grocery store, what does a cash register do?

Once students had formed and compared responses, Ed explained that they were going to be reading to find out how to use variable expressions to manage data in much the same way that a cash register does, or as they would need to do in order to figure out the total cost of band posters.

The chapter in the math text began with a hands-on demonstration that involved students in measuring their heart rates for 15 seconds in small groups and then figuring out how many times each person's heart would beat in five minutes, a day, and a week. After discussing how students' arrived at their answers, Ed handed out the question guide (Figure 7.2) and read over the questions with the class. He read the next half-page with the group and led them to answer the *Right There* questions, rereading the sections of text that provided definitions to key math concepts. He then asked students to read the next page-and-a-half, paying special attention to the two real-world examples given, and to write down answers to the *Think and Search* questions.

When most of the class had finished reading, students volunteered their answers to the assigned questions. Ed gave them feedback on their answers and then led them as they solved three sample problems presented in the text. As homework, he assigned selected problems from the exercises featured in the next three pages of the text and told students to write out answers to the *Author and You* questions when they were finished. The next day, the class discussed the solutions to the homework problems and the answers to the questions. Ed then revisited the original *On Your Own* questions and asked students to apply what they had learned about variable expressions to the questions.

QAR guides for other math lessons and other subject areas might look a little different. As we said at the beginning of this chapter, teachers will need to adapt a strategy like this to fit their particular topic and their understanding of their discipline. A history QAR guide might emphasize cause-and-effect connections or *Author and You* questions that will lead readers to think about an author's point of view or credibility. A science teacher might fashion a QAR guide that concentrates on a *Right There* understanding of technical terms and *Think and Search* relationships among concepts. When teaching a novel, an English teacher might want to emphasize *Author and You* connections that readers might make with other things they have read or with their own experiences.

Again, we reiterate that *content* will determine *process*. If you begin with the essential questions—the "big ideas" of a topic that you feel are important—the subsequent questions should complement them and guide students' inquiry and reflection.

QUESTIONING THE AUTHOR   Developing readers often accept uncritically the authority of the textbook without stopping to consider that texts are written by authors who have made decisions about what to include and how to present information. Questioning the Author (QtA) is an approach that helps students see that a "book's content is simply someone's ideas written down, and that this person may not have always expressed things in the clearest or easiest way for readers to understand" (Beck et al., 1997, p. 18). The researchers who developed QtA use the term *queries* to differentiate their questioning strategy from the usual teacher-dominated classroom routine of recitation in which the teacher asks questions and evaluates students' responses.

Material from content area textbooks can be classified as *expository text*, or writing that explains something. This is in contrast to *narrative text*, which tells a story, such as in novels, plays, and short stories. There are two types of QtA queries that can be used with either narrative or expository text (Beck et al., 1997). *Initiating queries* are used to begin consideration of important ideas in the text. The following are generic examples of initiating queries:

- What is the author trying to say?
- What is the author's message?

Follow-up queries are designed to guide students in evaluating and connecting ideas and constructing meaning. The following are sample follow-up queries:

- Does the author explain this clearly?
- Does the author tell us why?
- How does this connect to what the author told us before?

Whereas initiating and follow-up queries can be applied to expository or narrative text, *narrative queries* specifically help students to think about what an author is doing with character and plot:

- How do things look for this character now?
- What do you think this character is up to now, given what the author has told us?
- How has the author let you know that something has changed?
- How has the author settled this for us?

QtA strategies require thoughtful planning and implementation. The teacher must analyze the reading assignment carefully to determine key ideas (both explicit and implicit), anticipate concepts or connections that may cause comprehension difficulties for students, plan queries, and segment the text into meaningful sections to determine stopping points for discussion. QtA can be used selectively to introduce new selections that students will be completing as homework or to support students' reading of especially difficult segments.

When introducing QtA for the first time, it is a good idea to explain the purposes of this approach. Students should be told explicitly that comprehension difficulties are often as much the fault of the author as they are of the reader, and that part of the work of reading well is to question whether authors are making their ideas clear. When Doug Buehl, a high school teacher in Madison, Wisconsin, introduces QtA, he helps his students to identify the authors of their text by name and speculate on any biographical information that might be available (Buehl, 2001).

After explaining the nature of QtA, students should read a selection from the text, and then respond to teacher queries to initiate discussion. In addition to posing queries, the teacher's role during discussion is to help students construct meaning by highlighting key points, returning students' attention to the text, and refining and interpreting student comments. Teachers also model their own thinking, fill in gaps left by the author, and guide students in summarizing and moving on through the text.

QtA obviously requires a good deal of teacher knowledge, preparation, and in-class practice. However, Beck and associates (1997) have found that QtA has resulted in more student talk, more student-initiated questions, and more emphasis on meaning and integration of ideas than in traditional question–answer sessions, in which the focus is on evaluating student comprehension and recall of literal-level information from the text.

Wineburg (1991) found that high school students and actual historians read history very differently. Historians would often look first to see who the author was and then noted the author's point of view and the various subtexts that were implied. High school students who had taken four years of history courses and who had achieved high SAT scores and grade-point averages seldom considered the authors of their texts. They did not question whether the author was trying to promote a particular point of view, whether information was selectively included or excluded, or whether the textbook was a trustworthy source of information. They tended to see history as a collection of facts and truths, not as something that could be interpreted either by authors or by readers; they "failed to see text as a social instrument masterfully crafted to achieve a social end" (Wineburg, 1991, p. 502). Therefore, their reading was primarily a search for information. A strategy like Questioning the Author could be used to help students develop a more critical eye, so that they might read more like historians. You will find more suggestions for this kind of critical reading in Chapter 9.

REQUEST   Reciprocal questioning, or *ReQuest* (Manzo, Manzo, & Estes, 2001), is a relatively simple variation on classroom routine. Instead of the teacher asking questions, the students are given the opportunity to ask questions of the teacher. The ReQuest procedure works as follows:

1. Identify a text selection that has several obvious stopping points for discussion and prediction. Prepare a few higher-level questions for each section of the text.

2. Prepare students for the reading selection by previewing it, by discussing background information or selected vocabulary, or by instigating some other appropriate activity.

3. Tell students that they will be reversing roles with you. As they read the first part of the selection, they are to think of questions that they will ask you.

4. Let students read to a predetermined point. Then allow the students to ask you as many questions as they can think of. Respond without looking at the text.

5. After students have asked their questions, have them close their books and direct questions to them. At this point, you should model higher-level questioning.

6. Repeat the reading–questioning procedure through successive segments of the text until a logical point is reached at which to make predictions about the rest of the material. Lead students to turn their predictions into one or more purpose-setting questions. Once they have completed the reading, continue the discussion by asking them for answers to their purpose-setting questions.

In our experience, students are very eager to take on the role of teacher. The questions they initially ask are often factual, but with teacher modeling, they quickly begin asking more complex and thoughtful questions. The ReQuest procedure combines very neatly with direct instruction in questioning and other comprehension strategies (Ciardiello, 1998). If the class has previously learned about QARs, the teacher can think aloud about the sources of information used to formulate answers: "I know that information isn't right there in the book, but my previous experience would lead me to say that . . . "

The amount of text covered between questioning episodes can be varied to meet the reading ability of the students and the difficulty of the material. Also, ReQuest can be a cooperative-learning activity if students are allowed to formulate their questions with a partner or in small groups.

Evidence-Based Research

SELF-QUESTIONING   One attribute of active readers is that they generate questions before, during, and after reading. Teaching students to ask questions about their reading improves their comprehension (National Reading Panel, 2000; Rosenshine, Meister, & Chapman, 1996). Self-questioning has a high level of success in improving comprehension, probably because it leads to more active reading and thinking.

Instruction in self-questioning can be adapted to the requirements of different content areas. Students of poetry can be guided to ask their own questions about rhyme, meter, or imagery. Social studies teachers can show their students how to ask questions about causes and effects or comparisons and contrasts. When students encounter math problems, they can be shown how to ask their own questions about what is given and what is to be found. Students familiar with the QARs can formulate their own *Right There, Putting It Together, Author and You,* and *On Your Own* questions (Helfeldt & Henk, 1990). As homework, students can be asked to make up a certain number of self-questions and answers for the next day, and their questions can become the departure point for class discussion.

You could adapt a quadrant activity similar to one that Roni Draper used in her middle school math class (McIntosh & Draper, 1995). Over several class periods, she gave her students explicit instruction in QARs and demonstrated how they applied to their mathematics text. Once students had a good working knowledge of QARs, she gave them a sheet of paper divided into four quadrants labeled *Question, Answer, Relationship,* and *Explanation.* Working alone, in pairs, or in small groups, according to their preferences, students wrote their own question in the appropriately labeled quadrant. They made a note in their math logs as to which type of QAR they thought this question was and then traded papers with someone else. In the remaining three quadrants, they answered each other's questions, wrote down what type of QAR it was, and noted the explanation for this choice. They exchanged papers again and compared their responses. Where there was disagreement between those who wrote the questions and those who answered them, discussion continued until students agreed. Draper found that this procedure facilitated mathematical communication among her students, who were thus able to clarify and consolidate their understanding of mathematical concepts.

QUESTIONING STRATEGIES FOR ENGLISH LANGUAGE LEARNERS Self-questioning is also an effective strategy for students who are learning English (Jiménez & Gámez, 2000). Formulating questions and answers helps them to express their thoughts in English, often by borrowing and manipulating the language of the text. Self-questioning also allows bilingual students to actively monitor their own comprehension rather than passively respond to questions posed by the teacher.

Evidence-Based Research

Answering questions in class can be especially daunting for students who are not academically proficient with English. In order to maintain the flow of a question-and-answer session, it is easy to overlook English language learners or to simply settle for a yes/no response. It is also tempting to speak for ELLs or finish their responses.

Wait time, or the time between when a question is asked and when someone responds, is especially important for ELLs. Three or four seconds of silence can seem like an eternity, but it will take that long or longer for many students to formulate an answer, especially an elaborated response to a higher-level question. Be sure that students, especially ELLs, are given sufficient time to think over and complete their responses.

Teachers can draw out more extended responses by asking follow-up questions such as "Tell me more about . . . ," "What do you mean by . . . ?" and "What does that remind you of?" Another technique helpful to ELLs is to restate their responses in standard English, with a prompt such as "In other words [response restated]. Is that accurate?"

Helping
Struggling Readers

Self-Questioning

In a review of research on QARs, Raphael and Gavelek (1984) note that "classroom training in QARs appeared to make average- and low-ability students look much like high-ability students in their ability to answer questions" (p. 241). It is noteworthy that self-questioning seems to be especially beneficial to poor readers (Brozo, 2000; Gillespie, 1990).

Nolan (1991) used a combination of prediction and self-questioning to boost the reading comprehension of middle-grade students, and he found that those with the most severe reading difficulties made the most gains. André and Anderson (1978/1979) also found

self-questioning to be particularly effective with students having low verbal ability. They hypothesized that self-questioning gave these readers a strategy much more effective than their usual "plow through the words" approach and that students with high verbal ability may already have the component skills of selecting and organizing information.

When teaching questioning strategies to struggling readers, teachers should begin with simple materials and provide ample practice, support, and feedback to help students gain confidence in using the strategies correctly across a variety of reading assignments (Swanson & de la Paz, 1998).

(Echevarria, Vogt, & Short, 2000). Also, cooperative-learning settings will allow ELLs more opportunities to respond to questions with less anxiety about speaking in front of a large group. When students work on activities such as self-questioning in pairs or cooperative groups, it gives them an opportunity to practice their language skills while talking about the content they are learning, all in a less formal and less threatening atmosphere than whole-class recitation (Nelson, 1996).

Comprehension Guides

Many variations of the reading or study guide exist, but all share a common purpose: to help students comprehend key ideas in their reading. This section describes three kinds of comprehension guides. The first is a three-level guide that features a list of statements instead of questions. The other two variations, the selective reading guide and the interactive reading guide, combine questions with specific directions for where and how to read the text. Like the QAR guide, these three guides are intended as general models to be adapted by teachers to fit their particular circumstances.

Three-Level Guides

Harold Herber (1978) suggests that students in content areas can benefit from being walked through a comprehension process similar to that used by expert readers. To accomplish this, Herber proposes that teachers devise a comprehension guide designed to support students in constructing meaning at three different levels. The *literal level* consists of specific facts and concepts that are explicitly stated. The *interpretive level* requires "reading between the lines," or drawing inferences about ideas that the author implies. The *applied level* represents comprehension that extends beyond the text to form new ideas or use ideas from the text in different contexts. Like QARs, these three levels of comprehension are neither discrete nor linear. That is, there will be a good deal of overlap among levels, and readers will move back and forth among these kinds of comprehension as they work their way through a text.

A three-level comprehension guide presents students with a list of declarative statements at each level before they read. This alerts readers to potentially important ideas and supports their search for meaning. As they read, students look for the ideas featured in the guide. After reading, the guide can be used as a departure point for discussion in small groups, as students compare their reactions to the guide and look back through the text to support their decisions.

A three-level comprehension guide designed by Amy Sanders for her class of seven 13- to 15-year-old special education students is shown in Figure 7.3. Previously, Amy had introduced the three levels of comprehension to her students and illustrated each level with a reading guide based on a short, familiar passage. Now she and her class were going to be spending three days learning about the sense of taste. The key ideas for this lesson

READING GUIDE: THE SENSE OF TASTE

I. Literal. Place a checkmark next to the statements you think say the same thing the author says. (The words may be slightly different from the text.) Be prepared to show where you found this in the text.

_____ 1. Your sense organ for taste is your tongue.

_____ 2. Taste buds send messages to your tongue.

_____ 3. You don't taste food when it is dry.

_____ 4. Your tongue is sensitive to four tastes: sweet, sour, bitter, and salty.

II. Interpretive. Check the statements you think the author implies. Some thinking is required! Be ready to support your answers.

_____ 1. The front sides of your tongue taste the salt from a potato chip better than the back of your tongue.

_____ 2. Different parts of your tongue are sensitive to salt, bitter, sweet, and sour.

_____ 3. You can see your taste buds on your tongue.

_____ 4. Smell and taste work together.

III. Applied. Check the statements that you agree with, based on your experiences and what you learned from the passage. Choose *one* statement and write why you did or didn't check it.

_____ 1. If something doesn't smell good, you probably shouldn't eat it.

_____ 2. Two can do better than one.

FIGURE 7.3   Three-Level Comprehension Guide: The Sense of Taste

Source: Amy Sanders, Baker Victory Day Treatment Center, Lackawanna, New York.

were presented in five pages of their science text, which included two experiments to be carried out in class along with exposition on how people perceive taste.

To begin the lesson, Ms. Sanders passed out the reading guide and read through the instructions and statements with students. Note that in the guide in Figure 7.3, literal level statement 2 is intended as a distractor. It is literally *not* true according to the text. Similarly, teachers may include ideas in the interpretive or applied levels that have more than one legitimate response. These distractors are intended to generate thought and discussion and to keep readers from simply checking all the items on the guide without doing the reading.

Ms. Sanders asked them to speculate what the reading passage might be about and what ideas they might be learning. Because most of her students had difficulty reading the science text on their own, she paired six of them to read the text and complete the guide together, while the seventh student worked on his own. After they had finished reading, she brought the class together to share their responses to the guide. Together, the group listed key facts and ideas from the passage and then used their list to complete a graphic organizer. They then performed the first of the two experiments, which involved finding the parts of their tongues that were more sensitive to a piece of candy and a lemon slice. They reconfirmed their reading guide responses based on their findings.

On the second day, the class went to the computer lab, in which they accessed Neuroscience Resources for Kids (http://faculty.washington.edu/chudler/tasty.html). This site was used to reinforce and extend concepts that had been encountered in the text. Although some of the material here was a good deal more challenging and technical than what had been described in the text, Amy asked her students to review their reading guides and see if the website supported their responses or added any new insights. She also asked each pair of students at their computer to find at least two new technical vocabulary terms related to taste, and to be prepared to explain them to the rest of the class.

On the third day, the class reviewed the reading guide and graphic organizer and then performed the second experiment described in the text. As a culminating activity, the students were given a quiz that consisted of filling in a blank version of the graphic organizer and writing a short essay that explained the relationship between taste and smell.

By combining reading, writing, the Internet, and experimentation in this lesson, Ms. Sanders was enabling her students to develop several of the concepts and abilities specified in the national content standards for science (National Research Council, 1996). These include the following:

- Conducting a scientific investigation
- Using tools and scientific techniques to gather, analyze, and interpret data
- Developing scientific explanations that incorporate existing scientific knowledge and new evidence from observations and experiments into internally consistent, logical statements
- Communicating experimental procedures and results
- Understanding the structure and function of living systems

Selective Reading Guides

Another way to support students' learning is to create a selective reading guide that points students to important information in the text. This is similar to the kinds of end-of-chapter review questions that are found in many textbooks. However, teachers may prefer to make their own decisions regarding which facts, ideas, and terminology are most important and devise a guide that directs students to specific sections of the text. When such a guide is given to students before they read, it makes their reading more purposeful and efficient. The expectation here is that students will not necessarily need to read *all* the text but only those sections that contain essential information.

An example of a selective reading guide designed by Kim Miller, a high school health teacher, is shown in Figure 7.4. Kim introduced the guide to her class along with a brief introduction to the topic of cardiovascular disease. She explained that this is the number-one killer in the United States and asked how many students knew someone who had been affected by cardiovascular disease. Then she read through the reading guide with students, explaining the directions. She was careful to point out that some of the information

CARDIOVASCULAR DISEASE

Directions: Read pages 569-578 in your text, looking for answers to the following questions.

1. (p. 569) Define "hypertension." Can hypertension cause death? How?

2. (p. 570) Describe the difference between "atherosclerosis" and "arteriosclerosis." Which is more deadly? Why?

3. (pp. 571–572) Explain how you could tell if someone were having a heart attack. List three ways to prevent a heart attack.

4. (p. 573) Explain how "cardiac arrest" is different from a heart attack.

5. (pp. 573–574) Define "thrombus" and "embolus." Tell why these are dangerous.

6. (pp. 569–574 and p. 578) Compare the *causes* of cardiovascular disease with ways of *preventing* it. The first one has been done for you.

Causes	Prevention
a. Eating foods high in fat.	a. Follow a low-fat diet
b.	b.
c.	c.
d.	d.
e.	e.

7. Based on your comparison chart, make an overall conclusion about the relationship between the causes and prevention of cardiovascular disease.

FIGURE 7.4   **Selective Reading Guide: Cardiovascular Disease**

Source: Kim Miller, Kenmore West High School, Kenmore, New York.

asked for in the guide was explicitly stated in the text but that there were also ideas that were implicit or that required them to use some of their prior knowledge. She suggested that students read the text through once and then go back and reread specific pages as needed to complete the guide. Students were asked to complete the reading and the guide for homework. The next day, students were put into groups of three or four to check over each other's responses, and then Mrs. Miller reassembled the whole class to compare responses, clarify any confusion, and provide additional explanations as necessary.

Interactive Reading Guides

As the name implies, an *interactive reading guide* (Buehl, 2001; Wood, 1988) is designed to guide the in-class reading of students as they interact in cooperative groups or pairs. Preparation of the guide begins with previewing the text selection, deciding on the main points that students need to understand, and identifying potential spots where students may have difficulty. The teacher should think about which sections of the text might be read orally or silently, which might be skimmed, or as with the selective reading guide, which passages may be skipped entirely. The guide will present specific tasks and questions that help students identify key ideas, make connections, and read critically.

The interactive reading guide in Figure 7.5 was designed for a section of a chapter in a U.S. history text on the Great Depression. Students could be given a class period to

---

READING GUIDE: "THE BIG CRASH"

Directions: With your partner, follow the instructions below. You will share your results during the whole-class discussion of this section.

1. **Student A:** Read paragraph 1 on p. 601 aloud. **Group:** Listen and briefly predict some things you will be learning in the rest of this section.

2. **Student B:** Read the section on "Black Thursday" aloud. **Group:** Listen and summarize:
   - What happened to the stock market on Black Thursday?
   - What did the leading bankers decide to do?

3. **Group:** Skim the section on "The Big Crash" and read the *New York Times* page reprinted on p. 602. Together, draft a two-sentence summary:
   - Sentence 1: Explain what happened in the Big Crash.
   - Sentence 2: Give at least one statistic that illustrates what happened.

4. **Group:** Read the sections on "Unequal Distribution of Wealth" and "Other Flaws in the Economy," silently. Answer the following:
   - Give three reasons that factories were laying off workers and shutting down.
   - Consider what you have read since the beginning of this chapter. Why do the authors call the stock market a "gambling arena"?

5. **Group:** Read the next two sections, "Hoover Takes Action" and "Aid for Farmers and Business," silently. Answer the following:
   - List four things that the government did to try to help ease the effects of the crash.
   - Why did imports and exports drop after the Hawley-Smoot Tariff Act?

6. **Student B:** Read aloud the third and fourth paragraphs of the section on "The Run on Banks." **Group:** Listen and answer the following questions:
   - Give two reasons why banks were failing.
   - What did bank failures mean to the people who had money deposited?

7. **Group:** Read the next two sections, "Beginning of the Great Depression" and "Unemployed Strike Back," silently. Write a short summary of the effects that the Great Depression had on Americans.

8. **Group:** Read the rest of "The Big Crash" silently. President Hoover tried to help businesses, the unemployed, farmers, and homeowners through loans and construction projects, but he was against giving money directly to people. Answer the following and be ready to support your conclusions!
   - Why did he take this approach?
   - Do you agree or disagree with this?

FIGURE 7.5   Interactive Reading Guide: "The Big Crash"

work on the reading guide, followed by another class session in which they would report on their results with guidance and feedback from the teacher. If one class period were not enough time to complete the whole reading, different segments could be assigned to each group, who would then present their findings to the whole class, as in the Jigsaw strategy described in Chapter 3.

Sensing and Responding to Text Structure

A chapter in a history textbook, a poem, or a short story is not just a random collection of words, facts, and ideas. Within each type of text are structures that tie ideas together. Texts "have both a content and a structure, with the knowledge of both entering into the comprehension process" (Just & Carpenter, 1987, p. 241). Teachers can aid student comprehension both by teaching students about text structure and by using the structures inherent in texts to help students organize the information that is presented (Goldman & Rakestraw, 2000).

Evidence-Based Research

Common Text Structures

Eight kinds of structures, or organizational patterns, are commonly found in textbooks:

1. *Simple listing:* A collection of related facts or ideas, sometimes presented in order of importance. An example is the presentation of different types of bacteria in a biology text.

2. *Description:* An explication of traits, functions, or properties. A chemistry text would describe the physical properties of metals, and a U.S. history text might describe the functions of the three branches of the federal government.

3. *Explanation of concepts:* A new concept is introduced and elucidated. For instance, in a chapter on probability, the concept of random sampling would be presented with an explanation of populations and sampling, the requirements for true randomness, and the theoretical importance of random sampling to statistical inferences.

4. *Definition/example:* Similar to explanation of a concept. Terms are introduced and examples are provided. In an earth science discussion of ecosystems, the terms *biotic* and *abiotic* might be defined as living and nonliving things, and common examples would be identified in nature.

5. *Sequence or time order:* A series of events that occur in a particular order. An example is a discussion of early African societies, from ancient Egypt to Timbuktu in the 1500s, in a global studies text.

6. *Compare and contrast:* A description of similarities and/or differences among two or more things. An example is the explanation of mean, median, and mode in a mathematics text.

7. *Cause and effect:*   A description of events and their causes or consequences. Often, a single cause will have more than one effect, and a single event may have more than one cause. An example is a discussion of how temperature, pressure, concentration, and catalysts affect chemical reactions.

8. *Problem–solution:*   Similar to cause and effect, except that outcomes are a result or solution of a perceived need or problem. An example is an explanation in a history text of how New Deal legislation was passed during the first 100 days of Roosevelt's presidency in response to the Great Depression.

Authors rarely use one of these patterns exclusively. Instead, they use multiple patterns. Within a section of text, however, the essential content is often presented via a single pattern. A chapter on color in a physics text, for example, *lists* the complementary colors and the colors of the spectrum and *compares* color by reflection with color by transmission. However, most of the chapter is concerned with how humans perceive color, and this is explained in terms of *causes and effects*, such as what happens when colored pigments are mixed, why the sky is blue, and why sunsets are red.

We will not emphasize simple listing, description, explanation, or definition in this discussion of text structures, because they do not present as much difficulty for readers as the other structures. Working with more complex text structures—such as compare and contrast, cause and effect, and problem–solution—appears to promote deeper levels of processing for students, including those with learning disabilities (Gersten, Fuchs, Williams, & Baker, 2001). Teaching strategies from the earlier section "Questions and Questioning" can easily be adapted to address the simpler text structures.

Although these eight organizational patterns are commonly used throughout expository text, they are also found in narrative text and poetry. The plot of most fiction is driven by characters in search of a solution to a problem, as when Ahab seeks to destroy the white whale or Huck Finn tries to escape from his father. These problems set off chains of cause-and-effect events. Literature also makes frequent use of comparison and contrast, such as the comparisons of two lovers found in several of Shakespeare's sonnets.

Literature presents additional structural complexities, however. Although it is beyond the scope of this text to consider in detail the varied structures of poetry, drama, and fiction, it is worth noting that narrative text generally follows a structure sometimes referred to as *story grammar*. Like the grammar or syntax of a sentence, a story is made up of certain components that fit together in a predictable sequence.

The first common element in story structure is a *setting*, which establishes the time and place of the events. Authors also establish *characters* early in the story. An *initiating event* sets the plot in motion by establishing a problem or a *conflict* that one or more characters must try to resolve. What follows then are one or more episodes or *attempts* to resolve the problem, each with an *outcome*. The culmination of the plot is the *resolution* of the problem.

The elements of story grammar are usually arranged in a predictable manner, although authors often manipulate story structures for literary effect. For instance, time and place may be purposely vague, the origins of a problem or conflict may only be implied, or an author might end a story without a definite resolution. Complex novels may feature numerous intertwined subplots with several characters, conflicts, attempts, and outcomes.

Teaching about Text Structures

There is evidence that text structure affects the reading comprehension of middle-grade and secondary students (Goldman & Rakestraw, 2000). In a study with fourth, sixth, and eleventh graders, Hare, Rabinowitz, and Schieble (1989) found "that both comparison/contrast and cause/effect texts (but not sequence texts) did pose greater difficulty for [students] than listing texts" (p. 86). Furthermore, awareness of text structures seems to have a positive effect on comprehension.

Evidence-Based Research

Richgels et al. (1987) found that sixth graders had a high awareness of comparison/contrast structure and a low awareness of causation and that structure-aware students were likely to use their awareness strategically as they read. Thus, the researchers believed that these students were "promising candidates for instruction in how to apply a structure strategy" while reading (p. 192).

After studying fifth- and seventh-grade students' knowledge of text structure, Garner and Gillingham (1987) concluded that students benefit from direct instruction in the use of text structure. There is also evidence that students who are taught about text structures will use their knowledge to improve the structural coherence of their writing as well as to enhance their reading comprehension (Goldman & Rakestraw, 2000; Gordon, 1990; Miller & George, 1992).

TEACHER MODELING WITH THINK-ALONGS   To introduce students to text structures, the teacher should identify and describe a specific structure, drawing simple examples from the textbook. The teacher could read aloud short passages, pointing out words that signal a particular text pattern and modeling the thinking processes that those words trigger. (A list of words commonly used to signal text patterns is given in Figure 7.6.) This modeling of thinking processes is called a *think-along* (Ehlinger & Pritchard, 1994).

For example, a biology teacher might demonstrate the pattern of comparison and contrast with the following passage, which serves as a transition between two major sections of a chapter (Schraer & Stoltze, 1993):

> The problems of life in aquatic biomes are different from the problems in terrestrial biomes. For one thing, in aquatic biomes, water is always present. However, in fresh water, organisms must excrete less water, and in salt water, excess salt may be excreted by organisms. Temperature changes in the course of a year are much less in aquatic environments than they are on land. Temperatures in the oceans show the least change, while those in lakes and ponds show more change. Other physical factors that affect living things in aquatic biomes are the amounts of oxygen and carbon dioxide dissolved in the water, the availability of organic and inorganic nutrients, and light intensity. (p. 854)

Sequence/Time Order	Compare and Contrast	Cause and Effect Problem–Solution
first, second, third, etc.	on the other hand	because
next	however	since
initially	less than, least	therefore
later	more than, most	if . . . then
following that	other	due to
finally	differently, difference	hence
before	similarly, similarity	thus
after	dissimilar	as a result
when	but	consequently
now	not only . . . but also	subsequently
in the past	either . . . or, neither . . . nor	accordingly
previously	while	eventually
presently	yet	initiated
	likewise	precipitated
	also	the outcome
	in comparison	the aftermath
	in contrast	
	conversely	

FIGURE 7.6 **Signal Words for Text Structures**

As the teacher reads this passage with the class, he or she could point out the use of the signal words *different from*, *however*, *less than*, *least*, and *while*. The teacher might also show how the comparisons and contrasts are layered, with contrasts drawn between aquatic and terrestrial biomes, fresh water and salt water, and oceans and lakes. The passage helps to bridge the information in the two sections of the chapter, and the teacher can show how this passage helps to anticipate some of the new material. Students could be involved in a discussion of why the authors use comparison and contrast and how knowledge of that structure might help them comprehend the text. Calling on students to volunteer examples from earlier lessons or their previous experience is also helpful.

Once attention has been drawn to a specific structure, one of the following teaching strategies can be used to help students work with further text passages in which that structure is predominant.

 GRAPHIC REPRESENTATIONS The use of graphic and semantic organizers is one of the comprehension strategies recommended by the National Reading Panel (2000). Semantic maps are also useful for giving readers a graphic representation of the structural relationships between ideas in a passage. According to Jones, Pierce, and Hunter

(1988/1989), students can be taught how to construct their own graphic representations of text ideas through a five-step teaching process:

1. Students survey the reading passage to see which organizational pattern, if any, the author appears to use.

2. Students construct a predicted outline of the passage. At first, they will need guidance to do this, perhaps with the teacher modeling on the chalkboard or overhead projector. Over time, students will become increasingly able to construct their own outlines.

3. Students read the passage.

4. The outlines are revised and completed, again, with help from the teacher if needed.

5. Students use their completed outlines to formulate a written or oral summary of the passage. This can be done independently or as a cooperative-learning activity.

Jones, Pierce, and Hunter (1988/1989) suggest a general graphic form for each of several text structures (Figure 7.7). Each graphic form has associated *key frame questions* that can be used to guide students as they read the passage.

GUIDES TO ORGANIZATIONAL PATTERNS   Just as a motorist uses a road map to plot a route, students can use a reading guide to help them navigate through a complicated text. The guide allows them to find the right intersections, avoid detours, recognize landmarks, and arrive at their destination with minimal delay. Teachers may design guides that can help students read assignments that feature potentially difficult organizational patterns or text structures. According to Herber (1978), an *organizational pattern guide* allows a student to "focus on the predominant pattern, using it as an aid to understanding relationships within the material and as an aid for recall after the reading has been completed" (p. 79).

TECHNOLOGY Tip

Several software programs, such as Timeliner and Inspiration, can be used by teachers or students to prepare and print out graphic representations of ideas. Timeliner can be used to prepare time lines of historical events. It is available in a version that can switch back and forth between English and Spanish. Inspiration can create webs, diagrams, maps, or outlines with information provided by the user.

Timeliner 5.0
Tom Snyder Productions
Watertown, MA
www.tomsnyder.com

Inspiration 8.0
Inspiration Software
Portland, OR
http://inspiration.com

(a) Series of Events Chain

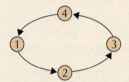

Key Frame Questions:
What is the object, procedure, or initiating event?
What are the stages or steps?
How do they lead to one another?
What is the final outcome?

(b) Cycle (This form could be used for either sequence or cause/effect structures).

Key Frame Questions:
What are the critical events in the cycle?
How are they related?
In what ways are they self-reinforcing?

(c) Compare/Contrast Matrix

	Name 1	Name 2
Attribute 1		
Attribute 2		
Attribute 3		

Key Frame Questions:
What things are being compared?
How are they similar?
How are they different?

(d) Cause/Effect Fishbone Map (A single cause that has multiple effects can be represented by reversing the cause and effect labels.)

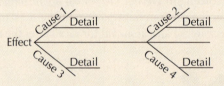

Key Frame Questions:
What are the factors that cause X?
How do they interrelate?
Are the factors that cause X the same as those that cause X to persist?

(e) Problem-Solution Outline

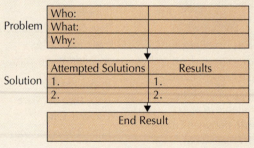

Key Frame Questions:
What was the problem?
Who had the problem?
Why was it a problem?
What attempts were made to solve the problem?
Did those attempts succeed?

FIGURE 7.7 **Graphic Forms for Representing Text Structures**

Source: From B. F. Jones, J. Pierce, & B. Hunter, "Teaching students to construct graphic representations," *Educational Leadership, 46,* 20–25, 1988/1989, December/January.

For example, a sixth-grade science teacher is planning to spend a week working with a chapter on diseases. She knows from past experience that her students will have difficulty understanding the cause-and-effect relationships involved in the chapter. To help them, she devises a reading guide (Figure 7.8). On Monday, she reviews

---

READING GUIDE

I. Directions: Read the list of possible causes and effects below. As you read Chapter 6, match the causes to the effects. Note: some letters (causes) will be used more than once, and there may be more than one cause for a single effect. Be ready to back up your answers with information from the text.

Causes

a. skin stops microorganisms
b. white blood cells "remember" how to make antibodies
c. viruses
d. microorganisms in water or air
e. disinfectants kill germs
f. malnutrition, heredity, chemicals in air or water
g. bacteria
h. white blood cells destroy germs and damaged tissues
i. direct contact
j. mucus traps germs
k. vaccine causes the body to produce antibodies that kill bacteria
l. animal carriers
m. fungi

Effects

_____ 1. infectious diseases
_____ 2. strep throat
_____ 3. disease is stopped or prevented
_____ 4. a person becomes immune
_____ 5. polio
_____ 6. infection stops and healing takes place
_____ 7. noninfectious diseases
_____ 8. infectious diseases spread from one host to another
_____ 9. diseases in plants

II. Directions: Below you will find some ideas about catching or preventing diseases. Check the ones you agree with, based on your own experience and what we have read and talked about. You must be able to explain why you did or didn't check each one.

_____ 1. People get sick from many different causes.
_____ 2. What you can't see won't hurt you.
_____ 3. Even though the human body has many natural defenses against disease, it still can use some help.
_____ 4. A good offense is the best defense.

FIGURE 7.8   A Reading Guide that Reveals the Cause-and-Effect Structure of a Chapter on Diseases

recent class discussions of cause-and-effect patterns in the text, introduces the topic of the chapter, and leads the class as they brainstorm about diseases and their causes and cures.

The teacher then distributes copies of the guide and goes over the instructions for Part I, emphasizing that there will be several possible ways to match the causes and effects. She assigns the first half of the chapter as homework. During the next three days, the teacher refers to Part I of the guide as students work their way through the chapter and carry out a lab experiment on the effect of disinfectants in preventing bacterial growth. When students have read the whole chapter, the teacher has them complete Part II of the guide and compare responses for both parts with their lab partners. The class reviews the guide, lab work, and important vocabulary terms on Thursday. On Friday, students take a two-part chapter test. The first part consists of multiple-choice questions. For the second part of the test, students must pick one of the four statements from Part II of the reading guide and explain in writing why they agree or disagree with it.

You have probably noticed that Part I of the guide leads students to work with ideas within the predominant organizational pattern—cause and effect. Part II is what Herber (1978) calls the "So what?" part of the guide. That is, it challenges readers to draw conclusions, refer to their own experience and in effect answer the question "So what does this all add up to?" The science teacher could have omitted this part of the guide if she felt such tasks could be addressed in other ways. She could also have given students only the items in the effects column, with directions to find the causes. This activity would be more difficult but might be effective with students who have the ability to determine causes on their own.

To develop an organizational pattern guide, first determine whether essential information and ideas are conveyed through one of the common text structures and whether this is likely to cause difficulty for students. Sequence, for instance, is inherent in most fiction and historical writing, but it may not be problematical for students unless the sequence in the text is different from the actual chronological sequence, as when an author uses flashbacks or otherwise presents events in a nonlinear fashion. The example in Figure 7.9 shows a format for comparison/contrast guides. The teacher lists comparisons, some literal and some inferred, from a passage on feudalism. Students have to decide whether or not the author actually makes those comparisons. As they explain their decisions, they will discuss the similarities and differences between serfs and free peasants, the Middle Ages and the Renaissance, and so on.

STORY MAPS   Research on story grammar suggests that children as young as five or six have a well-developed sense of the elements in story structure (Mandler & Johnson, 1979; Stein & Glenn, 1979). Extensive teaching of story structure beyond early elementary grades, therefore, is probably not warranted. However, as literary offerings become more sophisticated or complex, some readers may have difficulty tracking a story's development (Goldman & Rakestraw, 2000). To help readers navigate through a complex or unusual narrative, teachers may employ a variation of a story map. When working

COMPARE AND CONTRAST: THE MIDDLE AGES

Directions: Read the list of comparisons below and then read pages 152–158 in your text. When you have finished reading, check those comparisons you believe are made either directly or indirectly by the author.

_____ 1. hopeless/hopeful

_____ 2. military service by knights/taxes

_____ 3. serfs/free peasants

_____ 4. work for the lord/pay rent

_____ 5. feudalism/national governments

_____ 6. fields of crops/raising sheep

_____ 7. Middle Ages/Renaissance

_____ 8. knights in armor/guns and cannons

_____ 9. vassal of a lord/number in a nation

Directions: Once you have finished the first part of this guide, check those statements below that you feel can be supported by what you read or your own experiences. Compare your responses with those of other members of the class. Be sure you can support your choices.

_____ 1. You get what you pay for.

_____ 2. Advances in technology often bring about the need for social and political changes.

_____ 3. Necessity is the mother of invention.

_____ 4. Guilds of the Middle Ages were much like the unions of today.

_____ 5. It takes a woman to get the job done right.

FIGURE 7.9   Comparison/Contrast Guide for a Sixth-Grade Social Studies Lesson

Source: Marilynne Crawford, Maya School, Guatemala City, Guatemala.

with story maps, teachers should expect varied student opinions regarding the initiating event, main problem, and what constitutes important events.

Figure 7.10 illustrates a story map for *Romeo and Juliet*. Note that this story map does very little to involve readers in thinking about the theme of the play, Shakespeare's poetry, or the main characters and their dilemma. Outlining the structure of a story may help readers to follow the plot, but it is not sufficient engagement with a good literary work. A story map should be used as a foundation for other, more thoughtful consideration of the story.

ROMEO AND JULIET

Time & Place:
Middle Ages
Verona, Italy

Characters:
Romeo—a Montague
Juliet—a Capulet
(Montagues & Capulets are bitter enemies)

The Event That Starts the Main Plot:
Romeo sneaks into a Capulet costume party and meets Juliet.

Characters' Response and Main Problem:
Romeo and Juliet fall in love, but they can't do anything about it because their families hate each other.

Major Events:
1. Romeo goes to Juliet's at night; they pledge their love to each other.
2. Romeo and Juliet secretly get married.
3. In a street fight, Romeo kills Juliet's cousin. He has to leave town to avoid arrest.
4. Juliet's father tells her she has to marry Paris, a young nobleman.
5. Juliet arranges to fake her death so she can escape with Romeo.

Resolution:
Romeo doesn't know the plan, sees Juliet "dead," kills himself.
Juliet wakes up, sees Romeo dead, kills herself.
The Capulets and Montagues see the result of their hatred for each other.

FIGURE 7.10   Story Map for *Romeo and Juliet*

Comprehending Online Texts

The skills and strategies used to comprehend traditional print texts are also used in comprehending online texts. However, online texts are part of a complex, open-ended ocean of information that is vastly different from the world of expository content area textbooks. Navigating that ocean presents additional challenges and requires some sophisticated strategies.

In a study of Internet-savvy sixth graders, Coiro and Dobler (2007) asked students to explore a multilayered science website and to think aloud while searching for answers to literal and inferential comprehension questions. Students were also asked to think aloud while they used a search engine to find answers to questions derived from their science curriculum.

Coiro and Dobler (2007) found many similarities between the comprehension processes used with printed expository text and online text. Students drew on prior knowledge, used inferential reasoning, monitored their comprehension, and thoughtfully planned and evaluated their reading. However, the researchers found many additional complexities associated with online comprehension. Skilled online readers called on their prior knowledge of website structure and search engines and made a large number of predictions—for instance, when they encountered one or more hyperlinks onscreen. They also extended traditional print inferences with an understanding that the information they needed might be concealed within several layers of a website. Online readers' cognitive reading strategies were augmented by physical reading actions, such as typing, scrolling, clicking, and dragging. Finally, online reading called on a very rapid process of reading and evaluating search engine results, as readers swiftly predicted, planned, monitored, and evaluated what they read in repeated cycles.

Coiro and Dobler (2007) suggest that online reading is in many ways a process of *text construction*. As readers navigate an enormous number of choices and possible distractions, they construct their own paths between and within linked texts and thereby create a unique understanding of the information available.

Not every student in middle or high school has the same amount of Internet experience or expertise as the advanced users studied by Coiro and Dobler (2007). Thus, it is not reasonable to expect that students will be able to successfully conduct self-directed Internet inquiry without some explicit instruction.

Donald Leu and David Reinking and their colleagues (Leu et al., 2008) at the Teaching Internet Comprehension to Adolescents (TICA) project (www.newliteracies .uconn.edu/iesproject) have found that before they can begin to teach actual online comprehension, they need to ensure that students have basic skills in using a computer, searching the Web, navigating between windows, and sending and receiving e-mail. In the TICA project, researchers have used a process they call *Internet reciprocal teaching (IRT)* with seventh graders in urban and rural schools who displayed a diverse range of technological abilities (Leu et al., 2008). Internet reciprocal teaching emphasizes questioning, locating, critically evaluating, synthesizing, and communicating information with the Internet. In the course of IRT, teachers model online comprehension strategies, but this is in conjunction with student modeling of their own often novel and powerful strategies.

In the first phase of IRT, whole-class instruction time is used to establish basic skills and strategies. In phase 2, students engage in group work and the reciprocal exchange of strategies with their peers. For example, they may be directed to find the answer to a question using at least two Internet sources and then asked to determine which is more accurate and why. Phase 3 involves individual inquiry into questions that students develop themselves, sometimes involving collaboration with others online, and the continued sharing of strategies. Through their work with IRT, Leu and his colleagues (2008) emphasize the progressive development of sophisticated Internet comprehension strategies, as well as the importance of scaffolding instruction and the continued sharing and discussion of student Internet work.

Summary

Using textbooks as tools for learning can be a challenge for many students. Through instruction and support, teachers can help students develop useful strategies for learning from reading. Thoughtful questioning can guide students' learning, especially if they are shown how to ask their own questions as they read.

Readers of textbooks also need to learn how to work with different text structures and how to interpret an author's message. When teachers model these strategies and lead students through meaningful practice with content area text materials, students become more effective learners.

Suggested Readings

Allington, R. (2001). *What really matters for struggling readers: Designing research-based programs.* Portsmouth, NH: Heinemann.

Beck, I., McKeown, M., Hamilton, R., & Kucan, L. (1997). *Questioning the author: An approach for enhancing student engagement with text.* Newark, DE: International Reading Association.

Beers, K. (2003). *When kids can't read: What teachers can do. A guide for teachers 6–12.* Portsmouth, NH: Heinemann.

Block, C., & Pressley, M. (2002). *Comprehension instruction: Research-based best practice.* New York: Guilford.

Raphael, T., & Au, K. (2005). QAR: Enhancing comprehension and test taking across grades and content areas. *The Reading Teacher, 59,* 206–221.

Wood, K., Lapp, D., & Flood, J. (1992). *Guiding readers through text: A review of study guides.* Newark, DE: International Reading Association.

MyEducationLab is a research-based learning tool that brings teaching to life. Go to the Alvermann, Phelps, and Ridgeway Gillis 6th Edition MyEducationLab for Content Area Reading site at www.myeducationlab.com to:

- engage in multimedia exercises to help you build a deeper and more applied understanding of chapter content;

- utilize extensive resources including videos from real classrooms, Praxis and licensure preparation, a lesson plan builder, and materials to help you in your teaching career.

chapter **8**

Increasing Vocabulary and Conceptual Growth

Increasing Vocabulary and Conceptual Growth

Learning Words and Concepts	How Students Learn Vocabulary	Teaching Vocabulary	Developing Students' Independence	Reinforcing Vocabulary
• Word-Learning Tasks • Levels of Word Knowledge • Types of Vocabulary • Discipline-Specific Vocabulary Characteristics • Readers' Resources for Learning New Words	• Criteria for Selecting Vocabulary • Guidelines for Vocabulary Instruction • Strategies for Introducing and Teaching Vocabulary	• Using Context Clues • Using Familiar Word Parts • Using Dictionaries • Vocabulary Self-Collection • Intensive Approaches for Struggling Readers and English Language Learners	• Matching Activities, Puzzles, and Games • Categorizing Activities • Analogies • Concept Circles	

Anticipation Guide

Directions: Read each of the following statements. Place a checkmark on the line in the "Before Reading" column if you agree with the statement; leave it blank if you disagree. Then predict what you think the chapter will be about, and jot down on a sticky note (or post online) any questions you have. Read the chapter; then return to the statements and respond to them as you think the authors of your text would. Place a checkmark on the line in the "Authors' Stance" column if you believe the authors would agree with the statement. If you discuss these statements with other people online, in class, or at the family dinner table, return to the statements and check any items you agree with in the right-hand column, "After Discussion." If your thinking changed, what caused that change?

Before Reading	Authors' Stance	Statements	After Discussion
_____	_____	1. Teaching vocabulary is the responsibility of English teachers.	_____
_____	_____	2. In math, words like *of* have very specific meanings, which makes reading math problems difficult.	_____
_____	_____	3. When you teach vocabulary, you teach content.	_____

		4. Prefixes, suffixes, and root words are important in science vocabulary.	_____
_____	_____	5. Teachers should teach all the words students don't know in order to ensure comprehension.	_____
_____	_____	6. Learning vocabulary in the content areas means learning the relationships between words and concepts.	_____

Polonius: What do you read, my lord?

Hamlet: Words, words, words.

If Hamlet is right and reading is just "words, words, words," then common sense suggests that a person who does not know the words is not going to have much success. In fact, it has long been recognized that vocabulary knowledge strongly influences reading comprehension (Nagy & Scott, 2000). Students need to learn the meanings of many new words, and to the extent that they can do this, they will be able to read and understand. Learning vocabulary is much more than memorizing words and definitions, however. In content areas, words are labels for important concepts and can only be mastered through repeated experience within meaningful context. The following anecdote from Lori Eframson, a rehabilitation counselor in Buffalo, New York, dramatically illustrates this point.

• • •

On a September day in 1973, when I was ten years old, I dove into what I thought was a pile of hay in a barn. It turned out to be only a floor-covering of hay, and I broke three vertebrae in the cervical region of my neck. This left me paralyzed from my shoulders down. My dive into the hay had changed my life forever. It also forced me to learn a whole new language—the technical language of medicine.

I spent six months in traction in a teaching hospital in Syracuse, New York. When the doctor would come to see me on his daily rounds, he would bring ten or twelve students with him and talk about me and my body as if I weren't there. I listened intently to every word he said, but understood almost none of it. None of this technical jargon was explained to me, either. Being a very curious kid, I wanted to know what they were saying about me. This was information that was very important to me, and I absorbed it all. I began to put pieces of the puzzle together. After a month or so, I found it easier to follow what the doctor was talking about. He said almost the same thing every day!

One day, he came in with his group of curious students. Before he could open his mouth, I spewed out his usual phrases. He and his students stood with their mouths hanging open as I told them about my central nervous system, the compression of the cervical, thoracic, and lumbar regions of my spine, the contraction and spasms of my muscles, the loss of sensation, and the conditions of paraplegia and quadraplegia. From this point on, the doctor would come in and say, "This is Lori. I'm going to let her tell you what's going on with her." It was kind of a joke, but I began to understand and accept my condition as I spoke about it.*

● ● ●

In this chapter, we first consider how readers learn vocabulary, paying particular attention to disciplinary differences related to vocabulary. Then we discuss several techniques for guiding and reinforcing students' vocabulary and conceptual growth addressing differences across the content areas. Finally, we emphasize ways to develop readers' strategies for learning vocabulary on their own.

Learning Words and Concepts

A close look at vocabulary development reveals several knotty questions: What exactly is a *word*? How many words are there that need to be learned? How are they learned? What do we mean when we say a person has *learned* a word?

On a simple typographic level, a *word* is a group of letters surrounded by white space. Such a definition hardly accounts for the richness of meaning that a word can represent, however. The word *fidelity*, for instance, represents a whole range of philosophical, psychological, and practical concepts in contexts ranging from ethics to matrimony to electronic sound reproduction.

For our purposes, it may help to think of *word families*, or groups of words with clear relationships (Nagy & Herman, 1987). For instance, the words *specify*, *specifies*, *specific*, and *specification* are all members of the same family. Knowing the meaning of one of these words increases the chances of being able to infer the meanings of the others.

Nagy and Herman (1987) estimate that there are about 88,500 distinct word families in the printed English used in grades 3–9 and that the average schoolchild learns approximately 3,000 new words each year through twelfth grade. That is approximately eight new words each day! It is important to remember that these are rough averages. Students from different backgrounds vary considerably in their learning of vocabulary (White, Graves, & Slater, 1990), and students who are having reading difficulties have more trouble learning new words (Shefelbine, 1990).

It is not likely that students are absorbing eight new meanings a day from direct instruction by their teachers or by old-fashioned rote memorization. Although direct instruction is effective in teaching new word meanings, students also learn new meanings from wide reading, from conversation, and from the rich language environment of school, family, community, and mass media.

*Used with the permission of Lori Eframson.

What is meant by saying a person *knows* a word is not simple. Students might understand the word *order* as something one does in a restaurant and as a general term having to do with arranging things. However, they would find new and different meanings for this word in content areas. Within social studies, they would find many meanings: a military order, a religious order, the Order of the Garter, law and order, and a new world order. Would they know the word if they did not understand all these? In biology, *order* has a specific meaning in the classification of organisms. Would it be enough to know that an *order* is a way to classify living things, or would students also need to know that *order* comes between *class* and *family*, two other words that everybody knows?

The point is that in content areas, words are more than marks on a page, more even than dictionary definitions. Content area vocabulary represents concepts, and learning the vocabulary means understanding the concepts well enough to apply them in a meaningful way. Although *declarative knowledge* (being able to define a term) may be sufficient for some technical vocabulary, much of the vocabulary learned in content areas requires *procedural knowledge*, or being able to do things with a concept, to apply it in combination with other ideas (Nagy & Scott, 2000).

In addition, a number of terms (particularly in science and mathematics) require *conditional knowledge*. Words (and symbols) that have multiple meanings within a discipline require students to acquire not only declarative and procedural knowledge but also conditional knowledge—that is, the ability to distinguish which of several meanings a particular word or symbol takes on, depending on the context in which it appears. For example, in science, the word *equilibrium* is used in chemistry, physics, and biology. The word is also found in the general vocabulary, meaning "mental or emotional balance." In chemistry, the term *equilibrium* indicates a balance in the forward and reverse reactions in a chemical reaction so that the concentrations of all reactants is stable. In physics, the term applies to bodies in motion that are at rest or not accelerating so that the resultant of forces acting on it is zero and the sum of all torques about any axis is zero. In biology, *equilibrium* is associated with the ear, the organ for hearing and equilibrium.

Clearly, vocabulary is a complex topic that requires specific attention if teachers want their students to learn targeted content. We will return to the topic of vocabulary in specific disciplines later in this chapter.

How Students Learn Vocabulary

Every content area has a large collection of specialized or technical terms that denote important concepts. Sometimes these words and concepts are already familiar to students—for example, when high school seniors study *political parties*. Other words with commonly known meanings have specialized (and often different) meanings in a content area, as exemplified by the word order and by mathematical terms such as *proof*, *point*, *line*, and *root*. There are also technical terms that are specific to a particular content area, such as *abscissa*, *metaphor*, *photosynthesis*, and *archipelago*.

Word-Learning Tasks

When we talk of learning vocabulary, we are really talking of four different relationships between words and schemata or concepts (Graves & Slater, 1996; Herber, 1978). These four relationships, or word-learning tasks, are (1) known word/known concept, (2) new word/known concept, (3) known word/new concept, and (4) new word/new concept. These relationships are illustrated in Figure 8.1.

In the first, a common or known word represents a concept that students understand. When seventh graders begin a unit on *weather*, they are using a familiar word to label familiar phenomena. This is more than review, however. In their study of weather, they will enlarge and refine their concept.

The second kind of word-learning task is to apply new words to familiar concepts. The teacher may introduce the terms *meteorology* and *precipitation*. Students will be familiar with rain or snow, but some may not know the generic term for "wet stuff that falls from the sky." Most have seen weather forecasts on television and heard the word *meteorologist*, but they may not know the meaning of *meteorology*.

The third word-learning task requires students to learn a new concept but use a familiar word. For example, students will have several ideas about what pressure means, but the concepts of air pressure (or barometric pressure) and how changes in pressure affect weather may be new. All students know the words *watch* and *warning*, but these terms have specific technical meanings when the National Weather Service issues a *storm watch* or *storm warning*.

This word-learning task may present some special difficulties when students have to unlearn or at least suspend a known meaning for a word in order to learn a new concept. A good example is the word *work*. In everyday usage, this refers to a variety of things that people do: go to work, work out an agreement, work up a sweat, and work on a problem. In physics, however, *work* has a very precise meaning: It is the amount of force applied to an object multiplied by the distance the object moves. By this definition, studying for a chapter test or doing 30 math problems is no work at all! This seeming paradox can be very frustrating, especially for middle-grade students. However, every content area has many examples of this kind of word.

The final word-learning task is probably the most difficult. In this case, students must learn both a new concept and a new word to describe it. Although seventh-grade students may have heard the term *humidity* used in weather reports, the concept of mois-

Words	Concept	Examples from a Science Unit
1. Known word	Known concept	*weather*
2. New word	Known concept	*meteorology, precipitation*
3. Known word	New concept	*pressure, storm watch, storm warning*
4. New word	New concept	*humidity, hygrometer*

F I G U R E 8 . 1   **The Four Word-Learning Tasks**

ture in the air will be new for many. The term *hygrometer* and the way in which this instrument measures humidity will almost certainly be novel. These students will be developing new concepts and vocabulary within the overall schema of weather.

Levels of Word Knowledge

We have questioned what it means to *know* or *learn* a word. There is no easy answer. Words have many uses and meanings. Like people, they may be complete strangers or intimate friends, with many intervening gradations of acquaintanceship, from "Weren't we in an English class together once?" to "Hey, it's great to see you again!"

A word may be in a student's *receptive vocabulary* (recognized when seen or heard) yet may rarely or never be part of that person's *expressive vocabulary* (used in speech or in writing). Some words (and associated concepts) are learned so well in school that people never forget them. Other words are learned superficially, and all but a vague residue seems to evaporate from memory as soon as the student has taken a test or moved on to another subject.

Teachers require different levels of word and concept knowledge. To match a word and definition in a multiple-choice test, a student must recognize the word and associate it with the information given. For example, the following question could be answered even if the student had never seen a hygrometer:

A _____ is used to measure humidity.

a. thermometer   b. barometer
c. hygrometer   d. hydrometer

If the student were supposed to actually use a hygrometer to measure humidity and to explain how the hygrometer works, the task might seem much more difficult. Certainly, the knowledge required would be deeper and more complex. However, if the student had practiced using a hygrometer and had been carefully taught how it works, the task might be easier than the rote memory retrieval required for the multiple-choice test.

The question of what it means to learn a word is relative. The answer depends on how the word is to be used, when it will be encountered again, how the word is taught, and how a person's knowledge is to be assessed.

Types of Vocabulary

There are a number of differences in disciplinary vocabulary, and each discipline poses unique challenges for student learning. In our experience, secondary teachers in mathematics, science, and social studies tend to think that vocabulary is taught in English class and absolve themselves of any responsibility for this topic. Victoria, who was a science teacher prior to her encounter with content area reading, certainly felt that way.

Teachers who assume vocabulary is taught in English class are usually thinking of *general vocabulary*—the everyday words that are in general use among people. General vocabulary terms include function words, verbs, adjectives, adverbs, and nouns. Function words, such as *the*, *at*, and *from*, and verbs are more difficult to define than concrete nouns (Nagy & Scott, 2000). As we will see shortly, in mathematics, function words can be particularly problematic. General vocabulary words enable us to communicate our thoughts and feelings clearly. When President George H. W. Bush said he "loathed broccoli," he was being clear! "Loathing broccoli" conveys much more emotion than merely "disliking broccoli."

Having a rich and deep general vocabulary is the result of multiple exposures to a wide variety of words. Although English teachers focus on enlarging students' general vocabulary, all teachers should do so. Victoria remembers learning the word *behoove* the hard way: A science teacher mentioned in class that "It would behoove you to read your assignment tonight." The pop quiz she failed the next day helped her remember the word *behoove*.

Some general vocabulary terms have multiple meanings and as such are known as *polysemous* (or *polysemantic*) *terms* (Mason, Kniseley, & Kendall, 1979). For example, a military *base* in social studies is a place where military personnel and equipment are kept. In science, a *base* is a type of solution that turns litmus paper from pink to blue. In mathematics, a *base* may be part of a triangle and is found in the mathematical formula for the area of triangles. It may also be used to describe a number system, such as *base 10* or *base 2*, or it may be applied to references related to exponents. However, to many students, the word *base* is clearly associated with the game of baseball. It is a white, flat, square, and you run to it when you hit the ball or are walked by the pitcher.

When studying concepts that include polysemous terms, teachers must be sure that students are operating with the appropriate meanings of the words. Victoria remembers that one of the most difficult concepts to teach her physics students was that of *work*. To a physicist, *work* is accomplished only when an object has been moved through a distance. Students' general concept of the word *work* as meaning "effort of labor" interfered with their learning of the technical meaning of the term used by physicists.

General terms that are technical terms in science and mathematics pose particular problems for students. Polysemous terms are perhaps the most difficult vocabulary words because students are sometimes unsure of the appropriate meanings to use in specific instances. As we will see shortly, polysemous terms can be particularly problematic in mathematics.

Technical terms are those that are specific to a particular discipline. *Theorem*, *metaphor*, *polyatomic*, and *legislature* are examples of technical terms found in the disciplines of mathematics, English, chemistry, and social studies, respectively. Curiously, these words may be easier to learn initially because they have specific meanings, and those meanings are not confused with general meanings.

Discipline-Specific Vocabulary Characteristics

ENGLISH/LANGUAGE ARTS   In English, teaching vocabulary carries a double load: English teachers must teach vocabulary terms essential to understanding the literature students read along with the technical vocabulary terms of the discipline. Vocabulary words are easier to learn when taught in relation to other vocabulary (Harmon, Hedrick,

& Wood, 2005). When focusing on vocabulary terms drawn from the literature under study, the difficulty is that the terms are not usually conceptually related. Words such as *blandishment, contemptuously, inconsequential,* and *imprecations* may be drawn from a novel being studied but are not conceptually related and therefore can be difficult to learn. In addition, depending on the literature included in the curriculum, students may have to contend with archaic words. This is particularly so in a number of classic pieces of literature. Fortunately, in literature study, it is not always necessary for students to know each word intimately; for a number of words that students encounter in literature, being acquainted with them is sufficient (Harmon et al., 2005).

Technical terms in English can be learned in conceptually related groups, but even then some confusion can exist. (Victoria still has a hard time with *metaphor* and *simile.*) Terms such as *metaphor, simile, oxymoron, irony,* and *hyperbole* are kinds of figures of speech. They can be compared and contrasted, helping students to refine their knowledge of the words themselves as well as the general topic of figurative language.

MATHEMATICS   Of the technical terms in mathematics, those with invariant meanings are perhaps the easiest to learn (Harmon et al., 2005). General terms such as *of, negative,* and *difference* that take on specific technical meanings in mathematics can be problematic if students do not read them closely with a focus on the mathematical meanings.

Harmon and her colleagues (2005) describe two additional categories of vocabulary for mathematics, and we think they apply to science as well. *Subtechnical terms* are polysemous terms that have multiple meanings across the content areas. Words like *base* (discussed earlier), *degree,* and *volume* are difficult because their meanings change according to the content area and according to the conceptual domain within the same content area, as in the case with *base.* (In math, there are 360 *degrees* in a circle; in science, temperature is measured in *degrees* Celsius.) *Symbolic vocabulary* can be abbreviations (oz., ft.), numbers (2, 25, 236, and 5^2 all contain the number 2, but the 2 has a different meaning in each case), or symbols (Π, ∞). Symbols can be used to name a concept (24, x, or -4); to state a relationship ($2 > 1$ or $2 \neq 5$); to indicate an operation or function ($-(6)$, 3^2, $n!$); or to indicate a grouping ($2(x - y)^2 + (x + y)$) (Rubenstein & Thompson, 2001). Symbols create further difficulty because they can be polysemous. A small dash ($-$) may indicate an operation (subtraction) or name a concept (negative 4). Mathematics vocabulary is also difficult because (1) subtechnical terms that receive little attention in general reading must be read closely; (2) polysemous terms require conditional knowledge of the term within the discipline of mathematics, so that students must be aware of context clues in the text; and (3) symbols are widely used for a variety of purposes and can be polysemous as well.

SCIENCE   General terms used in specific ways as technical, subtechnical, and symbolic vocabulary also occur in science. In science, technical terms are often used to explain new concepts, putting a burden on prior knowledge. Many technical terms in science (and math) are based on Latin and Greek roots. A positive aspect of this is that focusing on words and word parts helps students learn vocabulary and enables them to independently learn new terms with the same roots and bases. As in math, some science vocabulary terms are subtechnical. A *cell* in biology is the basic unit of life, but in physical science, students might be reading about a chemical cell that produces electricity.

An added complication in science is that some words and phrases that are not science vocabulary per se must be understood because they indicate logical links among technical, subtechnical, and symbolic vocabulary. Phrases such as *similar to*, *characteristics of*, *the result of*, and *different from* signal relationships that are at the heart of science. Nontechnical words that appear frequently in science texts and must be understood include *component*, *consistent*, *exclude*, and *interpret*.

In both science and mathematics, it is important that students understand the conceptual relationships that exist among vocabulary terms, whether they are technical, subtechnical, or symbolic.

SOCIAL STUDIES   There are fewer technical terms in history, but vocabulary can be difficult because the words are often borrowed from other fields, such as political science, economics, sociology, and psychology. Vocabulary difficulties in social studies arise because vocabulary terms represent abstract concepts and can be archaic or metaphorical. Vocabulary words in social studies, particularly history, often identify people, events, or places (Harmon et al., 2005).

See Figure 8.2 for a graphic organizer that visually represents the complexity inherent in vocabulary across the curriculum. As you read the remaining sections of the chapter, think about the characteristics of vocabulary from your area of specialization, and consider how strategies might be adapted to enable your students to own, rather than rent, disciplinary vocabulary.

Readers' Resources for Learning New Words

When a reader comes across an unfamiliar word, there are four ways he or she might approximate the meaning: context clues, morphemic analysis, expert advice, and the dictionary (Nagy & Scott, 2000).

CONTEXT CLUES   Written and spoken contexts are the richest resources for learning new words (Nagy & Herman, 1987). What other possible explanation is there for the rapid growth in vocabulary in children and the fact that adults are constantly learning new words and new meanings for old words?

Evidence-
Based
Research

When proficient readers encounter an unfamiliar word, they usually read on, content to ignore that word or derive a partial understanding as long as their overall comprehension of the passage is satisfactory. Although initial exposure to an unfamiliar word in context may have limited usefulness, seeing or hearing the word again in different contexts may build a more complete meaning, until eventually the word becomes well understood (Nagy & Scott, 2000).

Context is not always helpful, however. Unfamiliar words often appear in contexts that offer few, if any, hints to the word's meaning (Schatz & Baldwin, 1986). In fact, the context may be misleading or confusing. To demonstrate just how little help context can

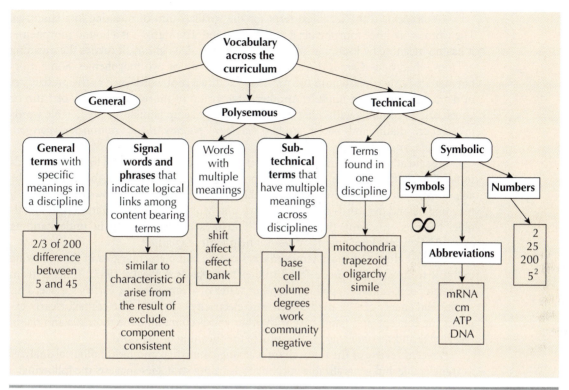

FIGURE 8.2 Vocabulary Across the Curriculum

Source: Victoria R. Gillis, IRA Convention, Pre-Convention Institute, Adolescent Literacy: Policy and Practices, May 4, 2008.

be, read the following passage from *A House for Mr. Biswas*, by Nobel laureate V. S. Naipaul (1984), and try to figure out what the italicized word means:

> His tailless shirt flapped loose, unbuttoned all the way down, the short sleeves rolled up almost to his arm-pits. It was as though, unable to hide his *prognathous* face, he wished to display the rest of himself as well. (p. 244)

If you did not previously know the meaning of *prognathous*, you may have guessed something like "ugly" or "homely" because of the implication that the man's face should be hidden. However, nothing in the context suggests the actual meaning of the word, which is "having a protruding jaw."

MORPHEMIC ANALYSIS Familiar word parts—roots and affixes—are another aid in wrestling with unfamiliar words. Using these parts to approximate meaning is sometimes called *morphemic analysis.*

A *morpheme* is the technical term for the smallest unit of meaning in a language. The word *car* is a free morpheme; it can stand alone. The suffix *-s* is a bound morpheme; it has no meaning by itself, but when added to a word, as in *cars*, it carries the meaning of "more than one." *Cars* is therefore a word made up of two morphemes. Some morphemes are fairly consistent in the way they modify a root word, such as the prefixes *re-* in *reproduce* and *un-* in *unlikely*. Another large group of morphemes, many of Latin or Greek origin, combine with other morphemes to make up familiar or predictable words in science, math, and social studies (*biology*, *photosynthesis*, *centimeter*, *polygon*, *automation*, and *monopoly*).

We said at the beginning of the chapter that it is really more useful to think of words in families than as discrete entities. When a person learns one word, she or he may be able to generalize to other variations of the word. A person who knows the word *exist* may understand the words *existence* and *existent*. Morphemic generalization is not infallible, however. Knowing the variations of *exist* is not much help in understanding *existentialism*, and knowing *sign* does not help with *resignation*.

Context clues and morphemic analysis can be complementary, as in the following example from a middle-grade social studies text (Rawls & Weeks, 1985): "Energy from the earth's core can be tapped through hot water or steam near the earth's surface. This *geothermal* energy can be used to generate electricity" (p. 727). The context clearly explains the concept, and familiarity with other words containing the roots *geo* and *therm* (*geography* and *thermometer*) will reinforce the meaning of the word.

A recent review of the research on teaching contextual and morphological analyses as transferable and generalizable vocabulary learning strategies suggests the following:

1. Use of context clues is a relatively ineffective means for inferring the meanings of specific words; rather, semantic relatedness procedures and mnemonic methods are preferred approaches for teaching the meanings of specific words.

2. When definitional information is combined with contextual cues, students are more apt to learn specific new vocabulary than when contextual analysis is used in isolation.

3. Teaching contextual analysis does facilitate students' ability to infer word meanings from surrounding context, although the relative efficacy of instruction in specific context clues versus simple practice in inferring meanings from context remains in question.

4. There is some indication that students can be taught specific morphemes (e.g., prefixes) that may enable them to unlock the meanings of unknown words containing these elements; also, there is some evidence that teaching students the meanings of unfamiliar words enables them to infer the meanings of morphologically related words. However, additional research is required in this area (Baumann, Kame'enui, & Ash, 2003, p. 774).

EXPERT ADVICE   A reader who is stumped by a word can ask for expert advice. The "expert" can be a teacher, a parent or sibling, or the student at the next desk. Often, ask-

TECHNOLOGY Tip

**Bidialectical Dictionaries
for Dialect Speakers**
In an article titled "Ebonics and Culturally Responsive Instruction" in *Rethinking Schools Online* (www.rethinkingschools.org/archive/12_01/ ebdelpit.shtml), Lisa Delpit (1997) describes the importance of having students create bilingual dictionaries of their own language form and standard English. According to Delpit, "Both the

students and the teacher become engaged in identifying terms and deciding upon the best translations. This can be done as generational dictionaries, too, given the proliferation of 'youth culture' terms growing out of the Ebonics-influenced tendency for the continual regeneration of vocabulary" (Delpit, 1997, n.p.).

To stay current with similar issues related to culturally responsive instruction, visit the regularly updated *Rethinking Schools Online* website at www.rethinkingschools.org/archive.

ing someone is the simplest and most satisfying solution. By asking and receiving a good answer, the reader gets the needed information while the motivation to learn is strong and with minimal disruption of the reading process.

DICTIONARIES   When context or roots and affixes fail to help with the meaning of a word, a reader can consult a dictionary or glossary. In fact, when students ask for help with a word, many well-meaning teachers tell them "Look it up in the dictionary."

Although the dictionary is a valuable tool, it is not always effective for learning vocabulary. Students may turn to the dictionary, read a definition, and come away no better informed than when they started. For instance, if you look up the term *radioisotope* in the dictionary, you will find the definition "radioactive isotope," which is not very useful unless you happen to know those words. Looking up *microtubule* in the glossary of a high school biology textbook yields "long, cylindrical organelles found in cilia and flagella." (Help!)

It is not that dictionaries, glossaries, and thesauruses are not useful tools or that students should never be told to look a word up. The point is that students must be shown how to use various resources for learning words. The following section on teaching strategies presents several ways to enhance students' use of context clues, morphemic analysis, and dictionaries.

Teaching Vocabulary

A teacher must decide how much attention to give to vocabulary, which words should be taught, and when and how they should be taught. There is an important cost–benefit ratio to consider (Graves, 1986; Graves & Prenn, 1986). Simply put, the harder the task

Evidence-Based Research

Go to MyEducationLab and select the topic *Developing Vocabulary, Concepts, and Fluency.* Then, go to the Activities and Applications section, watch the video entitled "Vocabulary and Content Area Learning," and respond to the accompanying prompts.

and the deeper the knowledge expected of students, the more time that must be put into instruction, as illustrated by the earlier example about the word *hygrometer*. Given the necessity of meeting many curriculum objectives in too little time, teachers must try to keep the costs of instruction low and the benefits high.

Because school reading materials present so many potentially unfamiliar words, this is quite a challenge. Nonetheless, content area teachers should be mindful that the content they are teaching is embodied in the vocabulary of their discipline. When you teach vocabulary, you teach your content.

To illustrate this problem, we examined two very different samples of content area text: a chapter from a sixth-grade science textbook and a short story from a ninth-grade literature anthology. We listed words from each selection that might be unfamiliar to a significant portion of students in the respective grade levels (Figures 8.3 and 8.4). Although each word is a candidate for special attention, no science or English teacher would be able to take time to teach all of the words on either list.

Examination of the two lists yields some important insights into content area vocabulary. First, it becomes easier to understand how students might encounter an average of eight unfamiliar words each day. There are some similarities between the lists. Both have common words used in uncommon ways (*eye, runner, daughter, egg, rise, game, lots*). Each list includes terms made up of two or more words (*third-person narration, preparatory school, asexual reproduction, daughter cells*).

The two lists are also indicative of some of the differences between expository and narrative text. Roughly two-thirds of the terms in the science chapter (Figure 8.3) are written in boldface, explained in context, and defined in the margins of the textbook. Most of them are repeated throughout the chapter as concept builds on concept. Clearly, the science passage is dense in new words and concepts, and to understand the chapter,

trait*	oyster	pistil*
reproduction*	cell division*	stigma*
heredity*	daughter cells*	ovary*
inherited*	regeneration*	stamen*
asexual reproduction*	organisms	anther*
sexual reproduction*	salamander	pollen*
unique	potato eyes	budding*
cell*	strawberry runners	sea anemones
amoeba	fertilization*	hydra
nucleus*	egg*	
clone*	sperm*	

*Printed in boldface and defined in the margin

FIGURE 8.3   Potentially Unfamiliar Terms from a Chapter (about 3,800 words long) on Reproduction in a Sixth-Grade Science Textbook

5. Include discussion as one of the vocabulary activities. When students know they may have to explain new terms in their own words, they tend to process the meanings of the terms more thoroughly.

6. Make your classroom a word-rich environment in which students are immersed in rich disciplinary language and appreciation for the power of words.

The teaching strategies presented throughout the rest of this chapter were selected to meet these guidelines.

Strategies for Introducing and Teaching Vocabulary

This section discusses several strategies for introducing and teaching content area vocabulary. Depending on the number and difficulty of the vocabulary terms in a lesson, teachers may choose to use any of these strategies before students read, while they read and discuss the text in class, or after they have read an assignment as homework.

HANDS-ON EXPERIENCE Whenever possible, teachers should provide students with an experience that will help them develop the concept before introducing the technical vocabulary that names it. This is particularly applicable in mathematics and science. For example, when teaching the term *congruent* in math, providing students experiences with drawing and cutting out triangles and other geometric figures that are congruent, as well as playing with Tangrams (Chinese puzzles), will be more effective than simply telling students the definition or having them read it in their textbook. In science, providing time for students to experiment with water drops on waxpaper, toothpicks, and soap prepares them to learn about cohesion. The combination of experience with the concept, discussion about the term, and finally reading about the concept and terms makes for more powerful teaching.

IN-CLASS PRESENTATION Perhaps the least costly strategy in terms of time is simply presenting students with a list of important vocabulary and briefly discussing each term. For instance, a teacher in an eleventh-grade history class might quickly refer to the following six terms written on the blackboard: *free enterprise, monopoly, trust, holding company, Social Darwinism,* and *laissez-faire.* The teacher asks the students if they know any of these terms, then briefly defines each, and finally tells them to pay careful attention to the terms as they read the section titled "The Age of Industry" for tomorrow's class. A simple presentation such as this may be all that is required if there are relatively few terms, if they are clearly explained in the text, and if students have sufficient ability.

SEMANTIC MAPPING One strategy has attracted more attention than any other as a means of introducing new vocabulary, perhaps because it is so versatile and because two decades of research have shown it to be effective with learners of diverse reading abilities, ages, and ethnicities (Baumann et al., 2003). The basic idea is to place key terms into a

Go to MyEducationLab and select the topic *Developing Vocabulary, Concepts, and Fluency.* Then, go to the Activities and Applications section, watch the video entitled "Intentional Vocabulary Instruction," and respond to the accompanying prompts.

Evidence-Based Research

diagram, sometimes called a *semantic map* or *semantic web* (Johnson & Pearson, 1984). Key words are arranged in clusters that represent how semantic information is organized in one's memory. The main topic is at the center, with related concepts radiating outward from it (Figure 8.5).

A semantic map is most effective when it is developed with students' input and discussion. The example in Figure 8.5 was constructed for a tenth-grade general biology class. The teacher told students they would be studying the nervous system next and wrote that topic on the blackboard. She then asked students what they knew about the nervous system—what its function was, what the various parts were, and how they were related. As students came up with terms like *brain* and *nerves*, she added them to the growing semantic map on the board, along with terms that she added and defined herself, such as *neurons*. Through questioning, students were able to give examples of *voluntary* and *involuntary actions* and *reflexes*. Finally, the teacher added the terms for the various parts of the brain and explained each one briefly. Students copied the resulting map into their notebooks and referred to it frequently as they worked through the chapter. Another version of the semantic map, called the *graphic organizer* (Barron, 1969), was introduced in Chapter 6.

CONCEPT OF DEFINITION MAP   Readers often have trouble giving their own definitions for words because they do not have a fully developed concept of what a *definition*

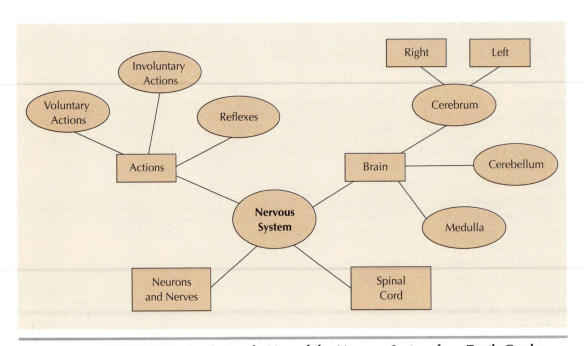

FIGURE 8.5   Semantic Map of the Nervous System for a Tenth-Grade Biology Unit

is. Word maps have been used to teach students about three types of information that together make up the concept of a definition (Schwartz & Raphael, 1985; Schwartz, 1988). As students discuss a particular term, they are asked to consider the *category* into which it falls ("What is it?"), its *properties* ("What is it like?"), and *illustrations* of the term ("What are some examples?").

A completed *concept of definition map* is shown in Figure 8.6. Using such a map, students should be able to write a full definition of the term. Once students are familiar with the concept of a definition map, they can develop definitions for one or two words in small groups and report their work to the whole class.

Semantic maps and graphic organizers have been successfully adopted by many teachers, who see several advantages to them. When students are involved in discussing and developing a semantic map or graphic organizer, they are able to combine their prior knowledge with new information. The map or diagram also allows them to see the interrelation of the concepts they are studying—how one idea fits with another. These techniques have a solid research base. As noted earlier, semantic organizers have been shown to be particularly effective with students of diverse reading abilities, ages, and ethnic backgrounds (Baumann et al., 2003) because they allow students to use their background knowledge and experience in learning new vocabulary.

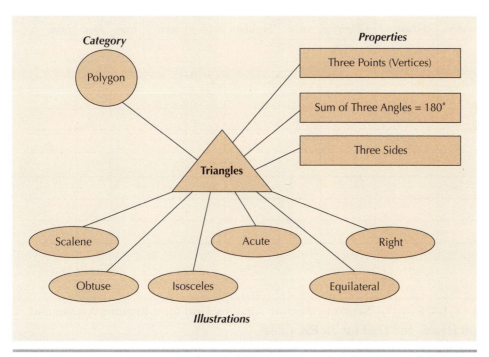

FIGURE 8.6   A Concept of Definition Map on Triangles for an Eighth-Grade Math Class

Evidence-
Based
Research

SEMANTIC FEATURE ANALYSIS   Another strategy for teaching vocabulary that has been effective with diverse student groups is *semantic feature analysis* (Anders & Bos, 1986; Baumann et al., 2003; Johnson & Pearson, 1984). Semantic feature analysis helps students see relationships among key concepts and vocabulary, particularly the many dimensions of meaning that may be associated with a particular term.

The example given in Figure 8.7 was developed by Lavon Smith, a teacher of English language learners (ELLs) in Athens, Georgia, for a reading assignment on health and diet. In the far left column of the grid, Lavon listed various foods and included spaces for students to fill in other favorites. Across the top of the grid, he listed several characteristics of foods that students were going to be reading about and discussing. He gave each student a copy of the grid and also displayed a copy on the overhead projector.

First, the class went down the left-hand column and discussed each kind of food listed, practicing pronunciation and making sure that all students understood the terms. Then Lavon reviewed the words written across the top of the grid, briefly defining the terms *protein, cholesterol, ethnic,* and *gourmet.* The discussion of ethnic food elicited a lot

Food	Has animal protein	Has cholesterol	Fattening	Has added sugar	Very healthful	Often eaten raw	Ethnic food	Fast food	Junk food	Gourmet food
Beef										
Mars Bar										
Egg										
Carrot										
Salmon										
Apple										
Egg roll										
Hamburger										
Whole milk										
Whole wheat bread										

F I G U R E   8 . 7   Semantic Feature Analysis Grid for a Reading Assignment on Health and Diet for an ESL Class

Source: Lavon Smith, Athens, Georgia.

of enthusiastic participation from this ethnically diverse group, and Lavon pointed out how many ethnic foods had become staples in the American diet. As they talked, the group marked each box on the grid. A plus (+) signified a positive relationship between two terms (e.g., beef has animal protein). A minus (−) meant a negative relationship (e.g., egg roll is not eaten raw). A question mark (?) indicated that the class was unsure of the relationship. Lavon left these decisions up to the class. For some columns, such as "Fast food" and "Junk food," there were diverse opinions.

After the students had completed discussion of the feature analysis grid, they were assigned a four-page reading in their ESL reader. As they read, the students verified or re-vised their responses on the feature analysis grid. The next day, they discussed the grid again as a whole class, paying special attention to the previously unknown relationships.

Semantic feature analysis is particularly effective in math and science (Barton, Hei-dema, & Jordan, 2002). Bear in mind that for mathematics, the vocabulary listed in the first column do not have to be words but can be mathematical expressions (Gay & Keith, 2002)—for example $y = x$; $y = 3x + 2$; or $y = 7 - x$. In this case, the characteristics writ-ten across the top of the grid would include "Has a positive slope," "Has a negative slope," "Has a slope of zero," and so forth.

POSSIBLE SENTENCES   *Possible sentences* (Moore & Moore, 1992; Stahl & Kapinus, 1991) is a technique that requires relatively little preparation time but is quite effective for getting students actively involved in discussing, writing, and reading, all focused on key vocabulary terms. It works as follows:

1. Identify five to eight key vocabulary words and list them on the board. Pro-nounce each word for the students. For instance, as a math teacher, you might select the words *random*, *outcome*, *event*, *sample space*, and *equally likely* from a unit on probability.

2. Also list a few key words that are likely to be known by students. In this case, you might use *chance* and *possible*, two words that are important in the unit.

3. Ask students to make up sentences using at least two words from the list. This can be done in small groups or individually. Record the student sentences on the board until all the words on the list have been used at least once. It does not mat-ter if some words are used incorrectly. The following are possible sentences using the examples listed previously:

   Each *outcome* has the same *chance* of occurring.
   Probability is the *chance* that an *event* will happen.

4. Ask students to speculate what the unit might be about. Then have students read the text, looking for the targeted vocabulary terms. They should verify whether or not their sentences are possible. That is, are the words used in the same sense in which they are used in the text?

5. Have students participate in either small-group or whole-class discussion to reach a consensus on whether their sentences are possible. If the sentences are not, they should be amended or refined as needed. A dictionary may be used if the context of the selection does not yield a satisfactory meaning.

6. As a final step, ask for new sentences using at least two of the words. This reinforces the meanings of the words and gives students yet another exposure to them.

VISUAL ASSOCIATIONS It is often easier to remember a new word and its meaning if one can connect it with a strong visual image. Verbal–visual associations are often recommended as particularly useful word-learning strategies for ELLs (Echevarria, Vogt, & Short, 2000).

Gary Hopkins (Hopkins & Bean, 2000) used a strategy he called *vocabulary squares* to teach roots and prefixes to junior and senior high school students at Lame Deer High School on the Northern Cheyenne Reservation in Montana. He drew a square and subdivided it into four panels. (An example of a vocabulary square is shown in Figure 8.8.) In the first panel, Gary wrote a root or prefix that he wanted students to learn. In the second panel, he wrote the dictionary definition. The third panel featured an example of how the root or prefix was used in a word. Then Gary drew a picture to illustrate the example in the fourth panel.

Instead of roots and prefixes, vocabulary squares could be modified to teach content area vocabulary terms. The first panel would contain the target word, the second

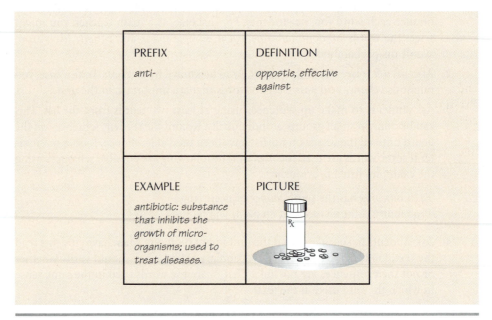

F I G U R E 8 . 8 **Vocabulary Square**

Source: © Tribune Media Services, Inc. All Rights Reserved. Reprinted with permission.

square the dictionary definition, and the third square could feature a sentence using the word. An illustration would again go in the remaining space. Content area teachers working with Victoria have had great success with this strategy, also known as Four Square, using a variety of adaptations, such as having students write the definition in their own words, writing antonyms or synonyms in one of the squares, including personal connections, or offering clues to help students remember the meaning of the term.

FRAYER MODEL   Like semantic feature analysis, discussed earlier, the *Frayer model* (Frayer, Frederick, & Klausmeier, 1969) focuses on discriminating features of words. As with the vocabulary square, there are four quadrants, and the featured word is written in the middle (see Figure 8.9). Typically, the four quadrants are labeled Essential Characteristics, Nonessential Characteristics, Examples, and Nonexamples. Sometimes, knowing what a word is *not* helps clarify what it means.

The Frayer model is particularly helpful in mathematics (Harmon et al., 2005) to help students refine their knowledge of vocabulary. Kenney, Hancewicz, Heuer, Metsisto, and Tuttle (2005) suggest adapting the Frayer model quadrant labels to Definition, Facts, Examples, and Nonexamples. Figure 8.10 provides an example of a slightly different adaptation of this strategy.

SELLING WORDS   Teachers can be "wordmongers," or sellers of words. Learning vocabulary is not just a matter of strategies and instruction, costs and benefits. There is an affective dimension, too. Students need to have fun with words, to become "word aware" and "word curious." As good role models, teachers can nurture appreciation of words. Teachers can "sell" words by discussing connotations and ingenious usages, exploring word histories and derivations, and sharing new additions to their personal lexicon.

Appendix A presents a list of books that deal with vocabulary in various content areas. Teachers might include some of these books in their classroom libraries and refer to them during class discussions. Looking up word histories, acronyms, and interesting or amusing words is a good activity for odd and idle minutes when the teacher is taking attendance or when a student has finished a test or seatwork assignment before the rest of the class. Teachers can also generate interest and appreciation for language by playing

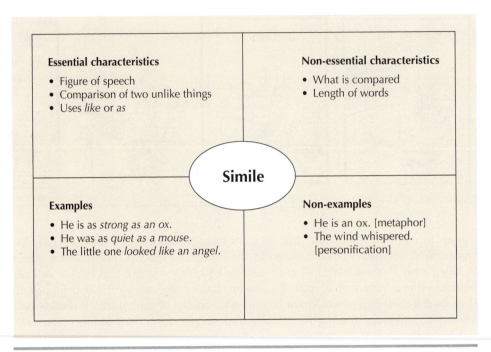

FIGURE 8.9   **The Frayer Model**

with words in riddles, puns, and language games. Several of the books in Appendix A illustrate the humor of language use and misuse. Other examples of the interest, power, and humor of words can come from newspaper clippings and cartoons.

Activity

- Select a concept or unit of study in your discipline. Generate a list of vocabulary terms for that concept or unit. Share your list with a colleague in your discipline. Together, categorize the list into those words that are crucial, those that would be nice to know, and those that students need only to be aware of.
- Choose one or more of the following to complete with a colleague in your discipline:
  1. Decide how you might introduce each of the crucial terms.
  2. Create a semantic feature analysis activity with your terms.
  3. Create a model concept of definition map for one or more of the vocabulary terms on your "crucial" list.

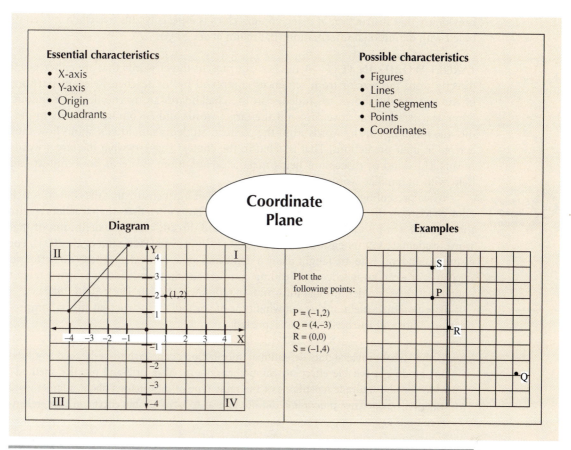

FIGURE 8.10   The Frayer Model

Created by Kristen Bodiford. Used with permission.

Developing Students' Independence

Teachers should try to teach more than the terms needed on the next test; they should also emphasize strategies that readers can use to deal with unfamiliar words in other contexts. This section examines some vocabulary-teaching techniques that also reinforce word-learning strategies that readers can use independently.

Using Context Clues

When we discussed how readers learn vocabulary, we said that context clues are useful but sometimes misleading. Despite the potential difficulties in relying on context, there is evidence that instruction in using context clues is especially effective when it is combined with definitional information (Baumann et al., 2003).

TARGET WORDS IN TEXT   A teacher can present target words that are either taken directly from the text or from sentences composed by the teacher. Relevant portions of the text can be shown to students on the chalkboard, an overhead, or a handout. Some teachers initially cover or omit the target words and encourage students to predict the meanings of the words from the context. Students should talk about how they arrived at their predictions. That is, what in the context suggests what the target words mean? This kind of discussion helps make students more aware of how context can help with unfamiliar words.

Evidence-
Based
Research

When presenting target words in text, the teacher must ensure that the context is rich enough to imply the meaning of the word. Research has shown that when teachers ensure that a target word is embedded in rich context and directly teach the definition of that word, students' comprehension of text passages is improved (Baumann et al., 2003). For example, students who are taught using a definition-plus-context approach do better on measures of word knowledge and reading comprehension than students who are taught contextual clues and definitional information separately (Kolich, 1991; Stahl, 1983).

Based on their meta-analysis of what type of vocabulary instruction affects comprehension, Stahl and Fairbanks (1986) reported:

> Methods that provided only definitional information about each to-be-learned word did not produce a reliable effect on comprehension. . . . Also, drill-and-practice methods, which involve multiple repetitions of the same type of information about a target word using only associative processing, did not appear to have reliable effects on comprehension. (p. 101)

Citing this evidence and other research on teaching definitions, Baumann et al. (2003) concluded that "definitional instruction alone is not likely to promote comprehension of passages that contain taught words. Additional instructional dimensions—contextual information or semantic relatedness, for example—must support or extend definition instruction" (p. 765).

KNOWLEDGE RATING   To introduce a list of potentially unfamiliar words, teachers can use a strategy called *knowledge rating* (Blachowicz, 1986). Figure 8.11 presents a knowledge-rating chart developed by Gretchen Bourdeau, a sixth-grade science teacher, as an introduction to a chapter on astronomy. Students who thought they could define a word checked the first column, "Know it well." Students who had heard or seen a word but were unsure what it meant checked the second column, "Heard of it." If the word was completely unfamiliar, students checked the "Clueless" column. Students were told to jot down the meanings of "Know it well" terms on the backs of their papers. They were especially motivated by this activity because it was all right not to know an answer.

RATE YOUR SPACE KNOWLEDGE

	Know it well	Heard of it	Clueless
aurora			
galaxy			
quasar			
big bang theory			
black hole			
pulsar			
neutron star			
supernova			
corona			
sunspot			
fusion			
prominence			
Milky Way			
telescope			
red giant			
nebula			
solar flare			

FIGURE 8.11   A Knowledge-Rating Chart for a Sixth-Grade Science Lesson

Source: Gretchen Bourdeau, Oglethorpe County Middle School, Georgia.

After students had worked on their own for about 15 minutes, Ms. Bourdeau led the class as they developed a list of the terms they knew and discussed what these words meant. Of the 17 terms, there were only 3 for which all the students were "clueless": *quasar, big bang theory,* and *prominence.* Ms. Bourdeau defined these for the class and noted that they would need special attention as they continued their study of astronomy. At the end of the class period, students left the class with an awareness of how much they already knew about this new topic, a firm understanding of most of the vocabulary, and a significant investment of interest and attention. In the following days, as they read and discussed the chapter, the class confirmed, altered, or expanded on their understanding of these terms.

WIDE READING   Regular independent reading is frequently suggested as an effective vocabulary-building strategy (Nagy, Herman, & Anderson, 1985). Many content area teachers encourage students to read beyond their textbooks by assigning projects that require outside reading and by frequently sharing content-related books and articles with students. In fact, using literature in content areas is the subject of Chapter 12.

Nonetheless, despite a large body of anecdotal evidence supporting the use of wide reading to develop young people's vocabulary knowledge, the fact remains that very few well-designed research studies have been conducted on this topic to date (Baumann et al., 2003; National Reading Panel, 2000).

Using Familiar Word Parts

Students can learn many words by morphemic generalization, especially when they use it in conjunction with context clues (Blachowicz & Zabroske, 1990; Wysocki & Jenkins, 1987). Through the intermediate grades and into high school, the number of words in content areas that are built with common roots and affixes increases dramatically. Therefore, it makes sense to help students by teaching them the strategy of morphemic analysis and by teaching them directly many of the important building blocks of the English language.

TEACHING MORPHEMIC ANALYSIS   When a new term is made up of familiar or easily analyzable parts, students should be led to infer the meaning. Good examples are *reproduction* and *regeneration* from the list in Figure 8.3. Once attention has been drawn to the prefix *re-*, students can be asked for other *re-* words they know. A general meaning for the prefix can then be derived from words such as *rebuild* and *repay*. The next step is to ask what other familiar parts they see in the two new words, leading to a discussion of *produce* and *generate*. Finally, the class can derive possible meanings for the two words.

Not all words are made up of familiar parts, however. Teachers can still help students by directly teaching the meanings of selected morphemes, as Gary Hopkins did in the vocabulary squares activity discussed previously. If students learn that the root *gen* in *regeneration* refers to "birth" or "species," they will have a clue to the relationship among the various meanings of *generation* and related words such as *gene*, *genetics*, and *generic*.

ETYMOLOGY   When a teacher and students talk about the meanings of roots and affixes, they are essentially discussing the origin and history of words. This is called *etymology* (from the Greek word *etumen*, which means "the real or true sense of a word").

There is much more to etymology than the study of roots and affixes, however. It is especially interesting to consider the contributions to American English that have been made by various nationalities and ethnic groups (see Figure 8.12) and to see how the language is constantly being enriched by borrowing from many vital language communities. For example, as English-speaking immigrants first encountered the Americas, they borrowed Native American words for the many places and things they were seeing for the

BORROWED WORDS

Spanish	African	Arabic	Native American
fiesta	banjo	algebra	racoon
macho	jazz	amber	kayak
mesa	tote	check	tomato
canyon	okra	chess	moccasin
alligator	yam	coffee	squash
patio	phony	hazard	hickory
ranch	zombie	magazine	potato
hammock		mattress	chocolate
		orange	
		soda	
		sugar	
		tariff	

FIGURE 8.12 Origins of a Few English Words

first time. As a result, American English has more than 300 loan words from Native American languages, primarily those of the Algonquian language family (Carver, 1991).

Regional variations in language are another source of interest. In New England, for instance, a fresh water stream is called a *brook*. In the North or Northwest, it is called a *creek* (which may rhyme with "leek" or "trick," depending on regional preferences). In New York State, along the Hudson River, it may be called a *kill*, a Dutch derivation. In Kentucky, it is called a *branch*. In Louisiana, it would be called a *bayou*, a word the French borrowed from the Choctaw natives. In Arizona, it would be an *arroyo*, a Spanish word.

Using Dictionaries

"Look these words up in the dictionary and write a sentence for each one." How many times do you think that assignment has been given in U.S. schools? In many content area classes, it is the only vocabulary-teaching strategy ever employed. In desperation, students often respond to the "look 'em up and write" assignment by finding something familiar in the dictionary definition, inventing a sentence that includes the familiar term, and substituting in the word they are supposed to be learning. Here are some typical results (Miller & Gildea, 1987):

I was *meticulous* about falling off the cliff. (*meticulous*: careful)
Our family *erodes* a lot. (*erode*: to eat out, to eat away)
Mrs. Morrow *stimulated* the soup. (*stimulate*: to stir up)

We believe that the teachers who made those assignments got pretty much what they deserved.

The best use of the dictionary is in conjunction with other strategies that encourage students to anticipate or predict word meanings. Strategies such as context clues, morphemic analysis, knowledge rating, and vocabulary self-collection are discussed in various sections of this chapter.

Given that most middle-grade and high school students have mastered the basic skill of finding a word in the dictionary, we suggest that content teachers enhance "look 'em up" assignments by modeling and giving students occasional guided practice in the following dictionary skills:

1. *One solution:* For example, *unrepentant* (Figure 8.4) is not a main entry in the *American Heritage Dictionary.* You must look up the word *repentant* and the prefix *un-* and infer the meaning of the word from both definitions.

2. *Matching the dictionary definition with the context:* A character in the short story *The Lie* discusses a situation "with growing incredulity." If *incredulous* means "disbelieving or skeptical," what does this phrase mean? Why might the character be incredulous?

3. *Deciding which definition fits:* In one dictionary, the word *game* has 13 definitions. Which one fits the phrase "a game, ambitious woman"?

4. *Using the information and abbreviations in an entry:* In addition to definitions, a dictionary entry may also give the part of speech of a word, variant spellings, derivation, pronunciation, and synonyms or antonyms.

When students know *how* and *when* to use a dictionary, it becomes a natural adjunct to learning new words. Keep in mind that looking up a word in the dictionary is disruptive and time consuming. Few adult readers run to the dictionary for every unfamiliar word, and it is unrealistic to expect students to do so. When students ask for help with a word, telling them to "look it up" is probably less effective than simply providing a quick definition.

Vocabulary Self-Collection

Martha Haggard (1982, 1986) describes a simple but effective method for getting students to become more "word aware." As they read, students identify words they think the class should learn, perhaps using sticky notes to mark them. After reading, students are organized into teams to compare and discuss the terms they identified. The steps for *vocabulary self-collection* are as follows:

1. Each student team identifies a word that is important for learning content information. The teacher also identifies one word.

2. The teacher writes the words on the chalkboard as teams give definitions from context.

3. Class members add any information they can to each definition.

4. The teacher and students consult references for definitions that are incomplete or unclear. Final definitions are derived.

TECHNOLOGY Tip

Vocabulary on the Internet

The Internet provides many vocabulary resources. References, word origins, and word games suitable for all grade levels and content areas can be found at the sites listed here.

Thinkfinity

www.thinkfinity.org

Thinkfinity is a *megaportal* that provides many vocabulary resources, if you search on that term. Specify the content area and grade-level band, and you will find many resources.

Web English Teacher

www.webenglishteacher.com/vocab.html

The vocabulary page of this English-teaching website has interactive games, lesson plans, and other vocabulary ideas for English/language arts. There are also links to the subjects Shakespeare, mythology, poetry, and journalism.

Visual Thesaurus

www.visualthesaurus.com

This website creates a web of synonyms for any word you input. Links radiate from the central word to its synonyms. When you click on different words in the synonym web, it rearranges itself so that the central word changes. This website also has a Word of the Day and featured word lists.

OneLook Dictionary

www.onelook.com/index.html

OneLook Dictionary uses more than 6 million words from more than 959 dictionaries; it includes entries from dictionaries in English, French, German, Italian, and Spanish.

World Wide Words

www.worldwidewords.org

World Wide Words is devoted to the English language—its history, quirks, curiosities, and evolution; new words, weird words, questions and answers, and many articles on the English language.

Take Our Word for It, the Bi-Weekly Word-Origin Webzine

www.takeourword.com

This site contains a feature called "Words to the Wise," which answers all your etymological queries.

Common Errors in English

www.wsu.edu/~brians/errors/errors.html

This site includes a lengthy list of commonly misspelled words and misquoted phrases; it is a great quick reference guide for young writers.

ESL Idiom Page

www.eslcafe.com/idioms/id-mngs.html

Phrases such as "hit the hay" and "easy as pie" are illustrated in sentences that are fairly obvious and helpful in determining meanings for these nonliteral expressions.

Vocabulary University

www.vocabulary.com

This site is a great place for games and puzzles that promote word power. It includes thematic word puzzles on a range of topics set up by grade level.

Dictionary of Affixes

www.affixes.org/

This site is based on Michael Quinion's book *Ologies and Isms*, which is out of print; it offers information about types of affixes, as well as over 1,200 entries of affixes, meanings, and examples. This site is an excellent resource for all content areas.

5. Students and the teacher narrow the list to arrive at the final class list.
6. Students record the class list and agreed-upon definitions in their journals.
7. Students record any additional personal vocabulary in their journals.
8. Words from the class list are used in follow-up study activities.
9. Words are tested as they apply to content information.

These steps are suggested for small teams of students involved in reading content area textbooks, but they can be modified in several ways. Different teams may take responsibility for finding and teaching vocabulary on different days or in different sections of the text. Once students are familiar with the procedure, they may collect vocabulary terms individually in their content area notebooks or learning logs. The teacher can expand vocabulary self-collection outside the classroom and textbook by asking students to bring in and share content-related words collected from other sources.

Teachers should scaffold vocabulary self-selection by modeling their own strategies for selecting vocabulary as well as how they use context, morphemic analysis, or the dictionary to help determine word meanings (Blachowicz & Fisher, 2000). Teachers can point out words that they have selected and explain to students how they decided the relative importance of each word. They can also demonstrate how to use textbook vocabulary aids such as boldfaced type, contextual or side-bar definitions, pronunciation keys, chapter vocabulary lists, and glossaries.

Self-collection shifts the responsibility for identifying and teaching vocabulary from the teacher to the students. This has several significant benefits. First, students are likely to identify different words from those the teacher might pick, ones they identify as unfamiliar yet important. Second, compared with teacher-compiled vocabulary lists, word study through self-collection is more directly related to students' prior knowledge and more actively involves students in their learning. Third, by selecting and discussing vocabulary on their own, students increase their sensitivity to words and develop new strategies for word learning.

Intensive Approaches for Struggling Readers and English Language Learners

The teaching strategies presented so far have been fairly economical in terms of preparation and presentation time. For some students, especially those who have reading difficulties or limited proficiency in English, a more elaborate approach may be appropriate. Students with reading difficulties tend to be dramatically less "wordwise" than capable readers and less adept with printed language in general (Blachowicz & Fisher, 2000). They often know fewer words and have a less complete understanding of the words they do know (Shefelbine, 1990).

In an intensive year-long program developed for middle-grade struggling readers, teachers and students compiled a list of the types of context clues that helped them with

Helping
Struggling Readers

Vocabulary Self-Collection

Students who typically struggle to comprehend their content area texts can become avid word learners when they participate in the Vocabulary Self-Collection Strategy (VSS) (Ruddell & Shearer, 2002). The VSS is also recommended as a means of expanding English language learners' vocabulary knowledge because it provides opportunities for building on concepts that are meaningful to them in their first language and offers them choices in word learning.

word meanings. Students were shown how to use this four-step process (Blachowicz & Zabroske, 1990):

1. *Look* before, at, and after the word.
2. *Reason* about what is already known and what is in the text.
3. *Predict* a possible meaning.
4. *Resolve* by trying again or consulting a person or a dictionary.

The students worked with context clues throughout the school year. Activities included direct teacher modeling, class discussion, frequent practice, and writing. Although using context was the major focus of instruction, these students were actually involved in an intensive program of heightened word awareness. Words, word meanings, and ways of learning words were emphasized throughout the year. In addition to context, students also considered roots and affixes, dictionary definitions, and word histories.

By the third month, student teams began to lead weekly vocabulary lessons, identifying words and leading their peers to use the strategies they had developed. They also invented a contest called "Mystery Word." A photocopy from a book, magazine, or newspaper on which a word was highlighted was posted. Students wrote down what they thought the word meant and what clues they used to figure it out. At the end of the day, the student team who had posted the word reviewed all the guesses with the class and consulted a dictionary if necessary to resolve uncertainty about the meaning.

ENGLISH LANGUAGE LEARNERS   Vocabulary will present special challenges to students who are learning English as a second language. Students in ESL or bilingual education classes often have a difficult time making the transition to mainstream content area classes. Even when students appear to have developed English fluency in social situations, they may need more time to develop academic proficiency with the language. Some authorities estimate that it may take as long as five or more years for students to develop academic proficiency (Cummins, 1994a). Students may nevertheless be expected

Helping Struggling Readers

"Small Puppies," "Big Dogs"

Alfred Tatum (2000) describes a multifaceted approach to teaching a class of eighth-grade struggling readers in a Chicago school. These African American adolescents, assigned to the class because of low reading test scores, were reluctant to read, seldom finished assignments, refused to respond, and equated reading with worksheets, assessment questions, and chronic inadequacy. This was Tatum's dilemma: Subjecting students like these to isolated skill instruction only serves to deepen their sense of failure and alienation, but trying to engage them in meaningful reading experiences is frustrating because of their lack of skills.

Tatum identified three major barriers to student success: fear of embarrassment, lack of word attack ability, and limited vocabularies. To reduce the potential of embarrassment, he set about building a supportive classroom community in which the difficulty of reading could openly be acknowledged, miscues were considered part of learning, and students could be actively involved in teaching each other and assessing their own progress.

Within this supportive community, Tatum offered a balanced instructional program that featured skill and strategy instruction along with reading of fiction, nonfiction, and poetry relevant to the African American experience, materials that challenged students to think and talk about their social and cultural traditions. Students read and discussed each selection with a partner three times before whole-class discussions and written follow-up. Tatum guided class discussion and modeled comprehension strategies such as self-questioning and constructing graphic organizers.

Because the students had great difficulty decoding words, their attention was too often diverted from comprehension. To help with this, Tatum began an intensive study of syllables and phonogram patterns, what the students called "attacking the small puppies (syllables) to get to the big dogs (multisyllabic words)." Each day, he selected several multisyllabic words from their readings and taught students how to break them down into syllables and then blend them together into their correct pronunciations. Students were given varied activities to practice decoding and encoding these words.

Pronunciation and spelling were not the only goals, however. The meanings of the words were discussed, their use in the literature selections was highlighted, and students were encouraged to use them in writing and class discussion. The class thought up excerpts from songs to help them remember the meanings of some words. (For example, *reciprocate* was associated with "It's the big payback" from a song by James Brown.) The words on the "word wall" were continuously reviewed, and vocabulary tests were given every other week. More than 450 multisyllabic words ended up on the "word wall," and all but a handful of the students could recognize and spell words such as *ambitious*, *cognizant*, *mediocre*, and *indefatigable*.

The combination of intensive word study and culturally relevant literature brought about a dramatic shift in both students' attitude and competence. At the end of the year, 25 of 29 students, all of whom started the year several years behind grade level in reading, were promoted to high school by meeting the requirement of a grade-equivalent score of 7.0 on the Iowa Test of Basic Skills.

to pass district or state examinations in content areas, with little or no accommodation made for their language status. Vocabulary has a particularly adverse affect on ELLs' performance on such testing (Fitzgerald, 1995; Garcia & Pearson, 1994).

ELLs are likely to have more difficulty than native speakers with deriving meaning from context (Lebauer, 1985). They will need a substantial core vocabulary to facilitate contextual learning (Blachowicz & Fisher, 2000). Although English or bilingual dictionaries can be very helpful for ELLs, they may prove frustrating for some students who cannot find inflected forms of words or who find inadequate or confusing definitions (Gonzalez, 1999). Figurative or idiomatic usages and unknown connotations will be especially problematic. Marie Vande Steeg (1991) relates the problems her high school ELLs had with life science vocabulary such as *tissue* and *organ*; some thought *tissues* were for blowing noses and *organs* were played in church. A partial or incorrect understanding of a word may interfere with understanding an entire passage.

On the other hand, students who are learning English have many strengths on which they can draw. Their basic reading processes are substantially similar to those of native speakers, although they may use certain strategies less effectively and more slowly. Among the strategies that bilingual students use in reading are the transfer of reading skills and background knowledge across languages, monitoring of comprehension, looking for cognate words, using context, and making inferences to determine word meanings (Fitzgerald, 1995; Jiménez, Garcia, & Pearson, 1996).

Teaching ELLs requires some general considerations in regard to vocabulary. Among these are patience and anticipation that there will be many unknown or confusing words, help with recognizing cognate vocabulary, and careful development of students' prior knowledge. To help students with limited proficiency in English succeed, many schools have established *sheltered English classrooms*, in which content is taught with the help of gestures, visual aids, and hands-on experiences. A sheltered English classroom operates on the following principles (Pierce, 1988):

1. The focus is on meaning rather than form. Students' language miscues are not overtly corrected.
2. Simplified sentences and controlled vocabulary are used.
3. Content area concepts are presented using a variety of clue-rich contexts, such as demonstrations, visual aids, maps, and experiments.
4. Students are involved in content-related conversational interaction.
5. New students are allowed a silent period; they do not have to speak until they are ready.

Vocabulary activities are particularly well suited to sheltered English classes. Teachers can model correct usage of vocabulary terms and paraphrase difficult text passages. They can also tailor the selection of vocabulary to the needs of ELLs by focusing on a few key terms, rather than a long list of words, and by having students keep individual word-study books.

In her life science class, in which nine different languages were represented, Marie Vande Steeg (1991) had her students use their senses to help them learn. When studying cells, they made gelatin cells using fruits and vegetables as organelles. As they ate their gelatin cells, they drew them on the board and explained them. The teacher had a lab assistant make popcorn in the back of the room to illustrate the concept of diffusion. When students smelled the popcorn, the principle of diffusion became easier to understand.

For a review of important concepts, Vande Steeg printed scientific sentences on cards with one word to each card. She gave packets of these sentence strips to students, who arranged them to make scientifically (and grammatically) correct sentences. She also printed scientific vocabulary on index cards and gave them to cooperative-learning groups to discuss. After a designated amount of time, groups took turns sharing their words with the whole class.

Mary Blake and Patricia Majors (1995) found that ELLs of intermediate proficiency can benefit most from holistic instruction that reinforces new vocabulary through reading, writing, listening, and speaking. They suggest a five-stage instructional process:

1. *Prereading activities:* The teacher presents selected vocabulary, leads students to practice pronunciation, and gives students definitions. Other activities such as knowledge rating, semantic mapping, semantic feature analysis, or contextual analysis could be used as well.

2. *Oral reading and responses:* Students and teacher take turns reading aloud with periodic stops for comprehension. Targeted vocabulary is given special attention. Students may write about the selection in their learning logs.

3. *Focused word study:* Students work with individual study cards that include the target word, a meaningful sentence, a definition, and perhaps the word written in the students' first language. Students play word games. They could also use any of the various vocabulary-reinforcing activities that are described in the next section.

4. *Evaluating word knowledge:* Students are quizzed on their understanding through crossword puzzles, cloze passages with definitions provided, and other formats.

5. *Writing workshop:* The teacher models a written summary or short composition that uses as many of the target terms as possible. The final step of the process is for students to brainstorm, draft, and revise their own written pieces featuring the new vocabulary.

In a study focused on closing the gap between ELLs and English-only (EO) native speakers, Carlo and her colleagues (2004) chose to focus on vocabulary-learning strategies such as word analysis, use of context, morphology, and cognate knowledge and introduce fewer vocabulary words. The focus on word-learning strategies resulted in a significant improvement in reading comprehension.

In content area classes with a large proportion of nonnative English speakers or students reading significantly below grade level, intensive focus on vocabulary is beneficial. Motivating such students to think about and acquire new words may be one of the best strategies for helping them overcome reading difficulties, especially if the program also provides ample opportunities to practice reading independently.

Reinforcing Vocabulary

Whether vocabulary terms are briefly presented, discussed after reading, or form the focus of one of the more elaborate teaching strategies we have described, it is often desirable to give students additional independent practice to reinforce the words they are learning. This may be done through discussion, games, writing, pencil-and-paper exercises, or computer activities. This section describes several different kinds of vocabulary reinforcers.

Matching Activities, Puzzles, and Games

The simplest type of reinforcing activity requires students to match words with their definitions. Teachers often use matching exercises after vocabulary has been introduced, either before or after students read a text selection. Presenting matching activities in the format of a crossword puzzle or other type of self-correcting activity adds a motivational dimension. There are many computer programs that can generate word puzzles for duplication or completion at the computer (e.g., visit www.vocabulary.com/VUhowtouse.html).

Matching activities, in whatever format, are limited in that they only require students to associate a word with a definition. Although this may be useful, it does not by itself guarantee that students will master the concepts associated with the words, the possible variations in meanings, or the association between terms. Thus, it is important to provide some practice in using words in context.

Categorizing Activities

In some vocabulary reinforcers, students are asked to consider the relationships among various terms by deciding how they might be categorized. In order to decide what words do or do not go together, students must know more than definitions. Categorizing activities

Helping Struggling Readers

Morphology Practice

Flip-a-Chip (Mountain, 2002) is a word-game strategy for building students' vocabulary and comprehension that is particularly good to use with English language learners and readers who struggle. Played with a partner, Flip-a-Chip provides students practice in working with inflectional endings (e.g., *-ing* and *-ed*), comparative and superlative suffixes (e.g., *-er* and *-est*), prefixes and roots, plurals and possessives, and more advanced morphology (e.g., a suffix like *-en* can turn adjectives into verbs, as in *dark/darken*).

A cautionary note is in order here. Words should always be introduced and practiced within the context of meaningful subject matter. Simply memorizing parts and meanings of words is both ineffective and inefficient.

develop relational knowledge and provide an opportunity for students to talk about connections among terms under study. When students know more than mere definitions, they begin to "own" (rather than "rent") words.

In a particularly difficult chapter on geometry in an eighth-grade math text, more than 60 technical terms are introduced. The chapter is typical of much math material because the vocabulary is cumulative. Terms that are introduced at the beginning (*line*, *angle*, *point*, and *vertex*) must be thoroughly understood because they are used throughout the chapter. A math teacher could help students review for a chapter test by giving them the vocabulary reinforcer in Figure 8.13.

Sorting words is a very simple but effective categorizing activity that encourages active student involvement. In pairs or small groups, students are given a list of words to

---

VOCABULARY REINFORCER

Directions: In each group of words, there is one word that does not belong with the others. Cross it out. Then pick a word from the "Labels" list to describe each group of words. You must be able to tell how the words are related.

1. _____

   acute
   right
   line
   obtuse
   vertex

2. _____

   sphere
   pyramid
   polyhedron
   cube
   parallelogram

3. _____

   prism
   arc
   chord
   radius
   diameter

4. _____

   triangle
   trapezoid
   rhombus
   circle
   pentagon

5. _____

   scalene
   diameter
   isosceles
   equilateral
   congruent sides

6. _____

   complementary
   perpendicular
   90°
   supplementary
   right triangle

Labels

RIGHT ANGLE
LINES
ANGLES
TRIANGLES
POLYGONS
CIRCLES
CONGRUENT
3-DIMENSIONAL FIGURES

FIGURE 8.13   **Categorizing Vocabulary Reinforcer for an Eighth-Grade Geometry Lesson**

sort into meaningful categories. Using selected geometry terms from Figure 8.13, for instance, the teacher might tell students to sort words into the categories "Angles," "Polygons," "Triangles," and "Circles." For a more challenging activity, which would result in a greater variety of responses, students could simply be given words to sort without predetermined categories. Each group would then have to explain their arrangements. This kind of sorting activity is also known as List-Group-Label.

Analogies

Using analogies is another powerful tool for helping students see relationships among vocabulary terms. The traditional form of the analogy sets up a parallel relationship between four terms: A is to B as X is to Y. Several types of analogous relationships, with examples, are presented in Figure 8.14.

The key to these analogies is the various relating factors. The relationship on one side of an analogy must parallel the relationship on the other side. In order to be logically correct, term A must bear the same relationship to term B that term X has to term Y. Thus, the relating factor of "Places" in Figure 8.14 is that Sacramento and Springfield are the capital cities of their respective states. The relating factor between "Action" and "Object" is that the stomach digests food, while the lungs breathe air. Analogies can be fairly difficult for teachers to devise and students to complete, but they are quite effective for reinforcing thinking skills and conceptual understandings.

Figure 8.15 provides an example of the use of analogies to reinforce vocabulary for a high school biology assignment. After reading and discussing the chapter, students worked in small groups to complete the analogies. Then the class went over the reinforcer, with groups taking turns explaining the reasons behind their responses and the relationships among the four terms.

Part to Whole
noun : subject :: verb : predicate

Synonym/Antonym
obscure : vague :: potent : strong
affluence : poverty :: safety : peril

People
Gandhi : India :: Martin Luther King : America
Samuel Clemens : Mark Twain :: Theodore Giesl : Dr. Seuss

Places
Sacramento : California :: Springfield : Illinois
Fredericksburg : Confederacy :: Gettysburg : Union

Dates
1776 : United States :: 1917 : Russia

Degree
hot : searing :: cold : frigid

Cause and Effect
virus : measles :: bacteria : food poisoning
drought : starvation :: flood : devastation

Characteristic
credit card : finance charge :: loan : interest

Action/Object
digest : stomach :: breathe : lungs

Function
legislature : make laws :: judiciary : interpret laws
keyboard : enter data :: disk drive : store data

FIGURE 8.14   **Types and Examples of Analogies**

VOCABULARY REINFORCER

Directions: Fill in each blank with the word from the list below that best completes the analogy. Be able to explain your answer.

Example: beagle : dog :: robin : bird
Read the line as follows: Beagle is to dog as robin is to bird.

1. circulation : blood :: streaming : _____

2. capillaries : earthworm :: _____ : grasshopper

3. open circulatory system : grasshopper :: closed circulatory system : _____

4. protists : cyclosis :: hydra : _____

5. grasshopper blood : colorless :: earthworm blood : _____

6. single-celled : amoeba :: multicellular : _____

7. grasshopper : heart :: earthworm : _____

8. transport across cell membranes : _____ :: transport within a cell or organism : circulation

9. slow : fast :: open circulatory system : _____

10. earthworm : circulation :: protist : _____

Word List

earthworm	hemoglobin (red)	hydra
cyclosis	closed circulatory system	absorption
sinuses	aortic arches	cytoplasm
diffusion		

FIGURE 8.15   A Vocabulary Reinforcer Using Analogies for a High School Biology Unit

Source: Ruth Major, School 81, Buffalo, New York.

Before students are asked to work independently with analogies, we suggest that teachers discuss analogies with them and give them several simple examples so that they become familiar with the format and relating factors. It would also be helpful to work through the first item or two on an analogy reinforcer.

Concept Circles

Concept circles (Wandersee, 1987), a type of graphic organizer, visually represent hierarchical and nested conceptual relationships among vocabulary words. Concept circles use circles to represent concepts, and the position of the circles relative to each other visually represent the relationships that exist among the ideas in the conceptual scheme.

The concept circle in Figure 8.16 is used in physics to help students understand the relationships among terms studied in mechanics. The fundamental units are at the

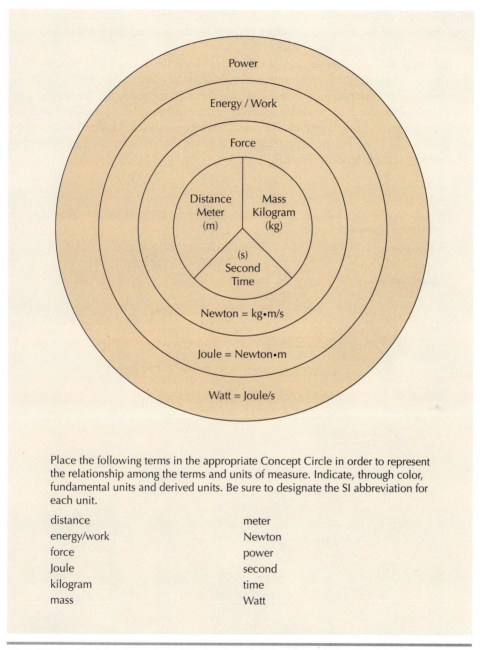

Place the following terms in the appropriate Concept Circle in order to represent the relationship among the terms and units of measure. Indicate, through color, fundamental units and derived units. Be sure to designate the SI abbreviation for each unit.

distance	meter
energy/work	Newton
force	power
Joule	second
kilogram	time
mass	Watt

FIGURE 8.16   Concept Circles (completed) for a Physics Unit on Mechanics

center because all other units are derived from them. This visual representation makes it clear that units of work are derived from or built on the units of force and that units of power are derived from units of work.

In Figure 8.17, another version of concept circles is illustrated using mathematical concepts. As students discuss placement of the vocabulary terms, they clarify their understanding of the relationships existing among them. In this example, the teacher provided some of the words for students, scaffolding their learning. When students need less scaffolding, a teacher might provide the same diagram unlabeled. This particular example of a concept circle exercise also illustrates how vocabulary activities can be used to differentially scaffold student learning.

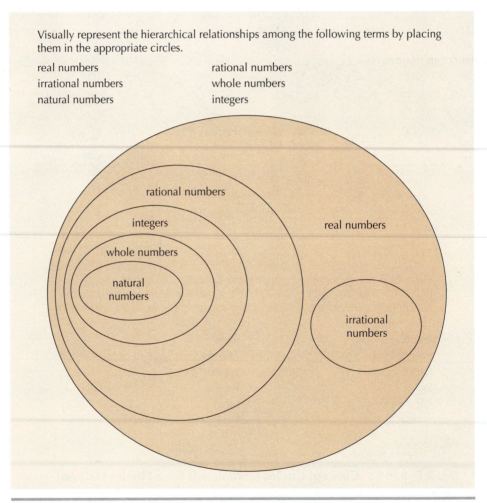

FIGURE 8.17   Concept Circles (completed) for a Review of Real Numbers

Activity

Create a reinforcement activity that emphasizes relational knowledge of vocabulary (category, analogy, concept circle) with the vocabulary list generated in the activity earlier in the chapter. If you choose to generate a categorizing activity similar to that in Figure 8.13, you will find it easier if you first generate a graphic organizer that illustrates the relationships among the terms in the vocabulary list and then use that graphic organizer to select words for your categorizing activity.

USING VOCABULARY IN WRITING   Several of the vocabulary teaching strategies we have described involve writing. Using a new word in writing helps to reinforce its meaning and also gives students a greater feeling of confidence in their understanding. Students can use new terms in their learning log jottings, in written summaries, in writing paragraphs based on category exercises or graphic organizers such as concept circles, or in other kinds of writing assignments devised by the teacher. Cindy Borowski, a math teacher, has her students use new math vocabulary to write their own word problems. An example from one of Cindy's students is given in Figure 8.18.

Developing Word Problems

Directions: Use at least three vocabulary words from the list below to write a word problem. Please make it legible. After you have written the problem, solve the problem showing all your work.

Bob makes a salary of $400 a week, plus straight commission of 4% on all sales. He made his sales quota of $5,000 for the week. What were his gross earnings for the week?

$5,000 × 4% = $200

$200 + $400 = $600

Vocabulary

salary	wages	rate of commission
sales	gross earnings	quota
straight commission	graduated commission	overtime

FIGURE 8.18   Using Vocabulary in Writing

Source: Cindy Borowski, Frontier Central Schools, Hamburg, New York.

Literacy Coaches' Corner

Modeling Vocabulary Strategies

Modeling vocabulary strategies for teachers is an excellent activity for faculty meetings. Victoria remembers telling a principal that his "classroom" was the faculty meeting. Just as students should leave every class with useful and important information, teachers should leave each faculty meeting with useful and important information.

Victoria's principal gave her 15 to 20 minutes at each faculty meeting to model a strategy for fellow teachers. She chose strategies that took little teacher preparation time but resulted in increased student engagement. Teachers left the faculty meeting having experienced a strategy they could implement the next day, if they wished. A short one-page handout summarizing the procedures for the strategy, together with perhaps one example, was enough instruction for teachers. Strategies such as List-Group-Label, categories, the vocabulary or Four Square, the Frayer model, and the concept of definition map are good choices because they take little teacher preparation time.

A good source of strategies is the Center of Excellence for Adolescent Literacy and Learning website, www.clemson.edu/ceall (click on Resources). Among other strategies and materials, there is a blackline master for semantic feature analysis already formatted and ready to complete.

S u m m a r y

Content area texts introduce many new and difficult concepts, which are usually represented either by unfamiliar words or by familiar words used in new ways. The conceptual load of a single chapter or even a single page can be quite heavy, and the effect is cumulative. Mastering a term introduced on one page may be a prerequisite for grasping other terms presented on the next page. The demands of content area vocabulary can be especially daunting for students who are not very good readers or lack proficiency in English.

Given the pressures of extensive curricula, limited time, and a wide range of student abilities, teachers need vocabulary strategies that can yield the greatest benefit in student learning with the least cost in planning and instructional time. Many effective strategies for introducing and reinforcing vocabulary meanings have been presented in this chapter. Students learn best when they encounter new words in various contexts, when they can relate new words to their previous experiences, and when they have varied opportunities to use new words in discussion, in writing, and in practice.

Suggested Readings

Blachowicz, C., & Fisher, P. (1996). *Teaching vocabulary in all classrooms*. Columbus, OH: Merrill.

Blachowicz, C., & Fisher, P. (2000). Vocabulary instruction. In M. Kamil, P. Mosenthal, P. D. Pearson, & R. Barr (Eds.), *Handbook of Reading Research*, Volume 3 (pp. 503–523). Mahwah, NJ: Erlbaum.

Fisher, D., & Frey, N. (2008). *Word wise and content rich: Five essential steps to teaching academic vocabulary, grades 7–12*. Portsmouth, NH: Heinemann.

Nilsen, A. P., & Nilsen, D. L. F. (2002). Lessons in the teaching of vocabulary from September 11 and Harry Potter. *Journal of Adolescent & Adult Literacy, 46*, 254–260.

Pittleman, S., Heimlich, S., Berglund, R., & French, M. (1991). *Semantic feature analysis: Classroom applications*. Newark, DE: International Reading Association.

Rosenbaum, C. (2001). A word map for middle school: A tool for reflective vocabulary instruction. *Journal of Adolescent & Adult Literacy, 45*, 44–49.

MyEducationLab is a research-based learning tool that brings teaching to life. Go to the Alvermann, Phelps, and Ridgeway Gillis 6th Edition MyEducationLab for Content Area Reading site at www.myeducationlab.com to:

- engage in multimedia exercises to help you build a deeper and more applied understanding of chapter content;

- utilize extensive resources including videos from real classrooms, Praxis and licensure preparation, a lesson plan builder, and materials to help you in your teaching career.

chapter **9**

Reflecting
on Reading

Reflecting on Reading

Engaging Students through Discussion	Guiding Student Reflection	Promoting Critical Literacy

Engaging Students through Discussion

- Small-Group Discussions
- Peer-Led Literature Circles

Guiding Student Reflection

- Reaction Guides
- Reading for Different Purposes
- Discussion Webs
- Intra-Act Procedure
- General Discussion Techniques

Promoting Critical Literacy

- Teaching Literacy for Critical Awareness
- Incorporating Critical Media Literacy into the Curriculum

Anticipation Guide

Directions: Read each of the following statements. Place a checkmark on the line in the "Before Reading" column if you agree with the statement; leave it blank if you disagree. Then predict what you think the chapter will be about, and jot down on a sticky note (or post online) any questions you have. Read the chapter; then return to the statements and respond to them as you think the authors of your text would. Place a checkmark on the line in the "Authors' Stance" column if you believe the authors would agree with the statement. If you discuss these statements with other people online, in class, or at the family dinner table, return to the statements and check any items you agree with in the right-hand column, "After Discussion." If your thinking changed, what caused that change?

Before Reading	Authors' Stance	Statements	After Discussion
_____	_____	**1.** Discussion does not work as well in math as it does in other content areas.	_____
_____	_____	**2.** Discussions can easily get out of hand and off track, so they should be used infrequently.	_____
_____	_____	**3.** Discussion promotes a deeper understanding of content and provides an opportunity for students to construct their own knowledge.	_____
_____	_____	**4.** Teaching for critical literacy can help students understand how texts represent, or position, different readers differently.	_____
_____	_____	**5.** Remixed texts show few signs of creativity.	_____

Most of you can probably remember a teacher whose class you looked forward to because you knew you were going to have a chance to think, to talk, and to come up with new and sometimes surprising ideas. Maybe it was a history teacher who helped you see the relevance behind the dry dates and names of people and places. Perhaps it was a math teacher who helped you think like a mathematician for an hour or so each week. It might have been a science teacher who gave you a little shiver when you realized how complex, how systematic, and yet how mysterious our world really is.

Whatever the subject, the memorable teacher was probably one who had high expectations and for whom you worked hard. That teacher may be the very one you keep in mind as you seek a model for your own efforts in the classroom. Perhaps it was someone like José Gonzalez, a teacher in an urban high school in which nearly 40 percent of the students come from Hispanic/Latino backgrounds.

● ● ●

Mr. Gonzalez is leading a discussion of four stories that the class has read. The stories are quite different, written from the 1930s to the 1990s by authors from Argentina, Spain, Mexico, and Puerto Rico. Most of the 15 students are of Puerto Rican background, about half of them born in the United States. A few are recent immigrants from Central America. They have varying degrees of English proficiency, but in this class there are no language barriers to discussion, for the class is conducted entirely in Spanish. Mr. Gonzalez is particularly interested in preparing these students for success in college. As he tells a visitor, "I want them to think; I want to treat them like adults."

Mr. Gonzalez begins by asking questions about "El Cuento," the story most recently read. At first only two or three students respond as they talk about the basics of plot and character. But then they come to the most dramatic moment of the story—the death of a child—and more students become animated. Students begin talking to each other, and Mr. Gonzalez talks less, interjecting occasionally to arbitrate disputes, include other students in the discussion, or pose an alternative point of view. He asks students to reflect on similarities and differences in the social and political views of the several authors. The discussion also touches on contemporary social issues, especially those he knows are relevant to his students' lives.

During the 45 minutes of the class, the discussion ebbs and flows. At any one time, only a few students seem to be actively participating, but the individual discussants change as students engage in the conversation, argue their point of view for a while, and then drop out to reflect and listen. The atmosphere in the class is relaxed and informal, but the discussion is thoughtful, the participants animated, the listeners attentive. Nearly every student there has something to offer during the class, and it is obvious the students enjoy being treated like adults who have important thoughts to share.

● ● ●

Mr. Gonzalez leads his students to make connections, draw conclusions, and extend their thinking in many directions. Although he shares many of his own ideas, the emphasis in this class is on what students think. According to many critics of education, too little of this sort of teaching is done in U.S. schools. Reading and writing assignments, class activities, and examinations too often require an accumulation of facts and largely ignore higher levels of thinking.

By placing an emphasis on what his students think as they discuss what they have read, Mr. Gonzalez is scaffolding their understandings of the four texts. Through discussion, he is helping them make connections between literature and their everyday lives. Many teachers find it difficult to let go of the traditional classroom response pattern in which they initiate a question, a student responds, and they in turn evaluate that response (the IRE pattern). Judith Langer tells teachers with whom she works that learning new response patterns, such as the one Mr. Gonzalez uses, is like "getting new bones" (Langer, cited in Allington & McGill-Franzen, 2000).

Evidence-Based Research

Difficult as it may be, we believe that the effort spent doing so will pay dividends in the end. In fact, there is research to suggest that students at the middle and high school levels view discussions that invite a wide range of responses as helping them comprehend what they read (Alvermann et al., 1996b; Duff, 2004). This finding holds for English language learners (ELLs) and bilingual learners as well as for students typically served through inclusion programs (Floriani, 1993; Goatley, Brock, & Raphael, 1995).

In this chapter, we consider some ways that teachers can encourage students to think beyond the facts in the text, to reflect on what they have read. A reflective reader can talk or write about what he or she has read and, in the process, come up with new meanings and new ideas, often quite different or even opposed to those intended by the author.

The ability to read and think reflectively—to build one's identity as a competent reader—does not develop naturally. As with other learning, students must be given models, support, and continued practice (Marsh & Stolle, 2006). The strategies included in this chapter are designed to integrate reading, thinking, and oral language. Although a fair amount of writing is also involved, we have saved for Chapter 10 those strategies that focus primarily on writing as a means of reflecting.

In this chapter, we first suggest some ideas for grouping that you might consider when engaging students in discussions of various types of texts. Then we offer several classroom-tested strategies for guiding students' reflections. Finally, we discuss ways of promoting critical literacy as a special form of reflection using multiple forms of media.

Engaging Students through Discussion

Important as they are to student engagement in general, cognitive and motivational factors alone cannot fully account for students' willingness to participate in academic tasks that require reflecting on what they have read. The culture of the classroom also clearly plays a significant role in how readily students are willing to engage in reflection.

Small-group discussions and peer-led literature circles are two vehicles for engaging students in reflecting on reading and learning with texts. Because small-group discussions require interpersonal skills and a sense of responsibility for contributing to the group's learning , it is essential that students be made aware of classroom expectations for staying on task without direct teacher supervision (Palumbo & Sanacore, 2007).

Small-Group Discussions

In a whole-class discussion, only a few students can participate at any one time. In such a situation, it is difficult to avoid domination of the discussion by the teacher and a handful of articulate students. In Chapter 3, we discussed various ways to group students. Although both small-group discussion and cooperative learning require that group members collaborate on a common task, the latter is more highly structured and typically demands greater individual accountability in relation to team effort.

Small-group discussion, as its name implies, places more emphasis on members' ability to communicate orally than does cooperative learning, allowing them to voice their ideas on a topic in greater detail and to express a greater diversity of views and beliefs. Small-group discussion also reduces the competition between individual students and promotes group interdependence and a sense of community. It gives ELLs more opportunity to practice their language skills, to learn technical vocabulary, and to benefit from peer teaching. Moreover, a review of the research on adolescent literacy instruction in classrooms with large numbers of students with reading disabilities showed that students' participation level rose when their teachers encouraged small-group class discussion (Alvermann, Fitzgerald, & Simpson, 2006).

Finally, small-group discussion activities allow students to assume and practice a variety of important roles. They may be proponents, devil's advocates, mediators, researchers, summarizers, task-minders, monitors, or spokespersons. Sometimes these roles may be assigned, but more often than not, they emerge as part of the natural processes of the group.

Evidence-Based Research

Roles, although important, are not the first things that students mention when they are asked what makes a good discussion. Based on our interviews from a multicase study of classroom discussions in middle and high school classrooms throughout the United States (Alvermann et al., 1996b), we know that students are well aware of the conditions they believe are conducive to effective discussions. First is the importance of small-group discussion. The students we interviewed said that small-group, unlike whole-group, discussions provide them with greater opportunities to voice their opinions:

> *John:* I kind of like those [small groups] because you don't have to fight over, you don't have to wait and wait and wait before you have a chance to talk. You only have like five people in the group and everybody is close enough to hear you, so you just kind of say your thing when you feel like it.

> *Alice:* The small group is kind of nicer [*sic*] because it is more personal and people kind of listen to you more and get interested in it.

Christy: It seems like it takes forever for [the teacher] to call on me, and by that time we have gone on to another subject, by the time I get to say anything [in whole-class discussions].

Melanie: It [whole-group] gets me nervous to talk in front of a whole lot of people about, like, opinions and stuff. But then, small group, it's like me and my friends, so it is easier. (p. 254)

Classroom cultures that support students' perceptions of a good discussion have a second characteristic in common. According to the adolescents whom we interviewed, students should have a say in how small discussion groups are formed and the rules for participating in them. Students prefer to choose their own working groups and to make rules that will guard against off-track discussions due to members not having read their assignments in advance.

Although characterizing effective small-group discussions in this way is hardly news, it is noteworthy that in the classrooms we observed, peer-group pressure was an important factor in how the groups used talk to mediate their comprehension of assigned materials. Overall, students were adamant in their belief that they had a better understanding of what they read when they listened to their peers discuss a selection.

A particular form of small-group discussion that bears special mention here is the *instructional conversation (IC)*, which offers teachers a way to engage students in the academic language of the various content areas (Tharp & Gallimore, 1988). Advantages of the IC include the opportunity to structure discussions so that student talk occurs more often than teacher talk and focuses on the concepts and vocabulary of particular subject matter. The IC is especially beneficial to ELLs, who may have achieved considerable proficiency in everyday English usage but need more time and instruction to gain competency in academic language. Teachers who are adept at using the IC are guided by what Dalton (1998, p. 30) describes as the "three checks":

- *Clarification:* Teachers ensure students' understanding (e.g., Are we clear?).
- *Validation:* Teachers provide opportunities for students to explain their reasoning (e.g., How do you know?).
- *Confirmation:* Teachers encourage students to negotiate with each other about what meaning to construct from the text (e.g., Do we agree?).

IMPLEMENTING SMALL-GROUP DISCUSSIONS   Some teachers worry about implementing discussion activities designed to limit their talk while increasing the number of opportunities for student talk. Generally, they are concerned that their classrooms will become noisy and unfocused and that students will spend too much time off task, socializing instead of working.

This need not be the case. However, the alternative—a virtual lack of student talk—is just as worrisome. Effective small-group discussions are in fact the product of thorough

Helping Struggling Readers

Immersing Readers in a "Sea of Talk"

In my 20 years of teaching I had found that students in lower tracks were often relegated to classrooms that had virtually eliminated talk. I certainly understood teachers' hesitancy about involving students in discussions. I have many memories of trying to build and sustain conversation in remedial classes—experiences that haunt my dreams to this day. In seconds one comment can spark another's anger, and fists

compensate for an inability to disagree with words. I also knew that if I continued a practice based on silence and worksheets, I was denying students access to a system based on one's ability to use language. Whatever it took to help students become able to carry on conversations, whether about books or life, I was willing to try. . . . Jan Duncan, a New Zealand educator, says that in our classrooms, "Reading and writing should float on a sea of talk" (Allen, 1995, p. 112).

preparation and on-the-spot facilitation by the teacher. Here are several experience-based recommendations:

1. *Assign clear and manageable tasks.* Before they begin work, group members must have a clear idea of their purpose: to accomplish a specific task through reflection.

2. *Prepare and guide students for the task.* Be sure students have enough background information. It may be necessary to model, or walk them through, a similar activity before they try the task on their own.

3. *Set limits.* Tell students how long they have to complete their task and how much they are expected to produce. For instance, say, "You have ten minutes to come up with two different solutions to this problem." If a task has several steps, remind students occasionally how much time has elapsed and where they should be in the process.

4. *Monitor and assist group work.* As students talk, move around the room to observe, question, encourage, and, when necessary, keep groups focused on reflecting. Draw out reticent group members and make sure that more talkative participants give others a chance to speak. It is especially important for the teacher to avoid actively participating in group reflection.

5. *Moderate a whole-class follow-up.* Let the various groups share and compare their conclusions and reasoning.

6. *Be a model.* During both small- and large-group discussions, model reflective thought processes, good listening, tolerance, and ways to handle conflict.

Peer-Led Literature Circles

A *literature circle* occurs when a group of youngsters come together to reflect on and discuss a book they have read in common (Daniels, 1994). The discussion, which is peer led, typically is conducted by a discussion *director*, whose job it is to prepare a list of questions for the group to answer. Others in the group assume roles such as the *connector* (responsible for connecting the text to everyday life experiences or to other texts), the *word* or *phrase finder* (responsible for locating language in the text that is colorful, unusual, funny, etc.), the *literary luminator* (responsible for identifying sections of the text the group might find interesting to read aloud), and the *illustrator* (responsible for visually representing his or her favorite part of the story, sharing it with other members of the group, and receiving their feedback). Students alternate in these roles so that everyone has responsibility for guiding the discussions in different ways.

An underlying assumption of peer-led literature circles is that young people can reflect on what they have read and take responsibility for their own discussions when they are given choices and sufficient structure in which to apply them. The teacher's role is one of facilitator or guide in getting the groups to function on their own, which includes deciding how much reading will be done prior to the next group discussion and the roles each member will play in it.

Although literature circles and book clubs (McMahon & Raphael, 1997) are similar in their goals and the procedures for realizing them, the two are distinct. The book club program, for example, is particularly useful in integrating content knowledge and the language arts, whereas literature circles are more focused on getting students to reflect on what they have read.

Recently, literature circles have been used to stimulate students' interests in reading in their second language. For example, Claudia Peralta-Nash and Julie Dutch (2000) initiated cycles of literature circles over an entire school year to engage Julie's bilingual classroom in reading and discussing books in both Spanish and English. What they discovered was that Spanish-dominant youngsters were more apt to take risks and join groups reading an English novel when they had the support of their group (self-chosen) to do so. Likewise, English-dominant students were more apt to choose books written in Spanish when they participated in discussions in which both Spanish and English were used to discuss a book.

Although peer-led literature circles may be slightly stilted at first, the creativity they may unleash is considerable after students have had sufficient practice in making choices and assuming responsibility for organizing and carrying out discussions on their own (Burns, 1998; Peralta-Nash & Dutch, 2000). For example, students can be encouraged to analyze a book's storyline for underlying assumptions, to imaginatively create alternative solutions to a protagonist's problems, and to make text-to-life connections by exploring a literary theme in relation to their own lives.

Indeed, this type of activity illustrates the triarchic theory of intelligence (Sternberg & Grigorenko, 2000), which maintains that an individual's intellectual and creative abilities are not fixed but instead can be developed just like any other form of expertise.

Moreover, Denig (2004), in his comparison of theories of multiple intelligences and learning styles, suggests that "teachers who use a combination of both theories may be able to improve student learning over the range of intelligences" (n.p.).

Guiding Student Reflection

In our experience, students usually appreciate genuine opportunities to flex their thinking muscles. The results are not always predictable; adolescents can be quirky and extravagant in developing their opinions. The concept of *cognitive apprenticeship* is especially pertinent here. The teacher can be a model of reflective thinking, guiding and supporting students as they think about and beyond the text. With persistence and a measure of tolerance from the teacher, students can develop their independent reflective powers.

Evidence-Based Research

Content teachers have found a number of activities that promote reflective thinking, student interaction, and the application and extension of ideas. The strategies presented here are adaptable to various content areas and age levels. Each one encourages students to think and talk about what they have read, and each one has the potential to lead to thoughtful writing as well. Reflective thinking is not just for gifted and talented students or those who are academically proficient; ample research evidence suggests that students of all intellectual ability levels can benefit from instruction in higher levels of thinking (Haney & Thistlethwaite, 1991; Kennedy, Fisher, & Ennis, 1991; Sternberg et al., 2000).

Reaction Guides

Go to MyEducationLab and select the topic *Reflecting on Learning.* Then, go to the Activities and Applications section, watch the video entitled "Engaging Students Through Discussion," and respond to the accompanying prompts.

When class members have completed a reading assignment, watched a video or movie, or attended a dramatic performance, how does the teacher get them to reflect on and talk about their reactions, with special attention to one or two issues, in small groups? To help focus the groups on such a task, the teacher could prepare a *reaction guide* similar to the reading guides discussed in previous chapters.

A reaction guide can be tailored to facilitate students' thinking along various paths. The teacher might want students to engage in an intensive analysis of the text or performance, or the goal could be to stimulate a deeper reflection. In the guide shown in Figure 9.1, the teacher wanted students to reflect on some of the specific incidents in the movie *Conrac.* He also wanted them to relate the ideas from the movie to the ongoing unit theme of prejudice, which they had been reading and talking about for the past two weeks.

To create a reaction guide, first identify a few key ideas or possible lines of thought you would like students to pursue. It is probably best to avoid crowding too much into the guide so that students can have time to fully reflect on their reading. Directions to students should make it clear that they must be able to support their responses. The actual format of the guide is flexible; it may feature questions, statements, or a checklist. Another possibility is to ask readers to reflect on polar opposites along a semantic differential scale (Bean & Bishop, 1992). For instance, to guide students' reflection on the use-

REACTION GUIDE: *CONRAC*

I. Directions: Identify the character in the movie who made each statement. We have talked about prejudice based on age, sex, social class or group, race or ethnicity, and religion. If you think the statement shows prejudice, write in the kind of prejudice you think is involved.

1. "Colored children need the whip."
   Character?_____
   Prejudice?_____

2. "We [teachers] are overseers, and things are tough on overseers."
   Character?_____
   Prejudice?_____

3. "You got that thin white skin. I don't have that advantage. So I just try to please the man."
   Character?_____
   Prejudice?_____

4. "Kids don't need trips; they need drill."
   Character?_____
   Prejudice?_____

5. "I'm white and I'm proud."
   Character?_____
   Prejudice?_____

II. Directions: Reflect on what you saw and heard in the movie and on your own experiences. Which of the following statements do you agree with? Be able to give examples to support your choices.

_____ 1. Anybody can learn if he or she is given the chance.

_____ 2. Prejudice is usually too strong for a single person to overcome.

_____ 3. Teachers can learn as much from students as students can learn from teachers.

_____ 4. Things like poetry and classical music are only for the upper classes.

FIGURE 9.1   Reaction Guide for a Movie for an Eighth-Grade English Class

fulness of worms in medicine, you might ask them to respond on a five-point scale to statements such as the following:

Leeches are _____.

unwelcome bloodsuckers   anti-inflammatory agents

     1   2   3   4   5

Maggots are _____.

causes of infection   used for treating wounds

 1   2   3   4   5

James Middleton (1991) describes a strategy he uses to promote problem solving and creative thinking among his biology students. He identifies a problem in biology, asks students to think of an analogous everyday problem, and then encourages them to find solutions to both the everyday and the biological problems. The following is an example of this analogical problem solving (p. 45):

Biological Problem: How can we get rid of trapped heat from the greenhouse effect?

Everyday Problem: How can we get rid of heat in a greenhouse?

Everyday Solutions: Punch holes in the greenhouse. Turn on fans.

Biological Solutions: Punch holes in the CO_2 cloud. Create storms in the upper atmosphere.

Reading for Different Purposes

To encourage students to move beyond surface-level understanding in their reflections and to challenge them to extend and elaborate on the ideas of others, you might ask members of a class to read the same material for different purposes or from different perspectives (Dolan et al., 1979). The procedure works as follows:

1. Assign all students the same material to read. (News stories, editorials, and magazine articles on current issues are particularly well suited to this activity.)

2. After students have read the material, break the class into groups and give each group a different task, such as the following:

   a. Name an obvious and a less obvious, or hidden, purpose the author may have had.

   b. Determine one relevant and one irrelevant sentence in the text.

   c. Look for evidence of biased reporting or emotive language in the text.

   d. List three fact statements and three opinion statements, and ask students to determine which is which.

   e. Present an alternative argument to one in the text, and ask students to choose the stronger of the two.

   f. Test the author's assertions by referring to other sources.

   g. Devise a set of questions that can be answered only by consulting additional sources.

3. When groups have completed their discussions, a spokesperson for each group pre-sents its findings to the class for discussion. For instance, the first group might ask the class to decide which of the two purposes, obvious or hidden, seems more probable and why.

4. As a follow-up, students can write a summary of their group's issue or perhaps rewrite the text leaving out the irrelevant material or substituting different words for the emotive language.

Activity

Try reading for different purposes. If you are part of a group, have each person read the following abstract from a journal article for one of the purposes listed; then compare responses. If you are working alone, read the abstract for at least two of these purposes:

1. Read from the point of view of a nutrition expert. How would you critique the abstract?

2. Read from the point of view of an athlete in training for the Olympics. How would you critique the article?

3. Name an obvious and a less obvious, or hidden, purpose the author may have had in writing the article.

4. Find one statement of fact and one opinion.

5. Devise an alternative reason for why determination of the effectiveness of supplements has been hampered.

Active persons ingest protein supplements primarily to promote muscle strength, function, and possibly size. Currently, it is not possible to form a consensus position regarding the benefit of protein or amino acid supplements in exercise training. Determination of whether supplements are beneficial has been hampered by the failure to select appropriate endpoints for evaluation of a positive effect. Furthermore, studies focused at a more basic level have failed to agree on the response of protein metabolism to exercise. An additional complication of dietary studies that is not often taken into account is amount of energy intake. (Wolfe, 2000, p. 551)

This procedure can be adapted or modified to fit different types of reading assignments. For example, in literature class, students can reflect on the points of view of different characters in a short story. In social studies, groups can take different slants on social issues; they might be asked, for example, to assess the Chicago Haymarket Riot of 1886 from the points of view of the workers, the strikebreakers, the police, the anarchists, the politicians, and the general public. Students can also look at events from different cultural perspectives. For instance, how might Native Americans, Hispanic Americans, and African Americans view the arrival of Columbus or the Emancipation Proclamation? A chemistry class might reflect on a chapter on air pollution from the standpoint of an environmentalist, a Los Angeles automobile commuter, and an employee and an officer of a major manufacturing firm (Frager & Thompson, 1985).

Discussion Webs

Consideration of more than one point of view gives students the opportunity to reflect on and expand their understanding of what they have read. However, when whole-class discussions are monopolized by a few highly verbal students, those who are less verbal may be unwilling or unable to think through and voice their opinions. Students who are learning English may have difficulty using their newly acquired language skills in academic settings. Female students especially may be at a disadvantage in classrooms in which male voices and male conversational styles are privileged (Alvermann, 1995/1996; Guzzetti & Williams, 1996).

 Evidence-Based Research

A discussion web (Alvermann, 1992) can help to structure discussions in such a way that more students have an opportunity to contribute. Discussion webs make it easier to keep a discussion focused and to ensure that discussants support their assertions with relevant information rather than generalizations, emotional arguments, or conversational intimidation. A discussion web is a graphic aid that presents a central issue or question along with spaces in which readers can fill in evidence supporting opposing points of view. The example shown in Figure 9.2 has the central question "Was Athens a true democracy?" On either side of the web, there are spaces for students to list reasons for answering no or yes to the central question.

The discussion web is used to encourage discussion and reflection as part of a five-step procedure (Alvermann, 1992):

1. Prepare students for reading using any of the strategies suggested in Chapter 6.

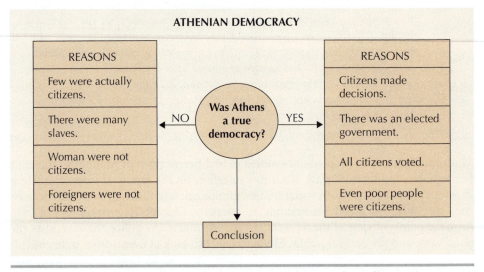

F I G U R E   9 . 2   Discussion Web for Sixth-Grade Social Studies Unit on Athenian Democracy

2. After students have read the assignment, introduce the central question and the discussion web. Have them discuss in pairs the points of view defined by the web and take turns jotting down reasons in the two support columns. To ensure that students consider both sides of the issue, instruct them to give an equal number of reasons in each column.

3. After students have jotted down a few of their reasons, pair one set of partners with another. To give all members of the new groups a chance to participate, ask each member to present at least one reason to the rest of the group. Have each group compare its discussion webs and ask the members to reach a group conclusion. If all members cannot agree, tell them to develop a dissenting opinion, or minority report, as well. In the unlikely event of an evenly split opinion, the group is considered deadlocked.

4. When the groups of four have reached their conclusions, give each group three minutes to present its conclusion, its strongest reason (or two strongest, in the case of a deadlock), and any dissenting opinion. (If each group gives a single reason, it reduces the likelihood that the last few groups will have little or nothing to say.) Finally, open the discussion up to the whole class.

5. As a follow-up activity, have students use their webs and the ideas they have heard presented to write individual answers to the central question.

Many variations on the basic discussion web can be created by changing the labels on the basic structure. The web may be used to stimulate a prereading discussion of students' predictions by using a central "What do you think . . . ?" question and labeling the columns "Prediction 1" and "Prediction 2." In science, students who are preparing to conduct an experiment might generate hypotheses about the outcome and list their reasons in columns labeled "Hypothesis 1" and "Hypothesis 2." In social studies or literature, readers can compare two people or characters. For example, they might compare the positions of Lincoln and Douglas on slavery or think about who was the dominant character in the trip down the Mississippi—Huck or Jim. A discussion web can even help students decide what information is relevant in math word problems. The web shown in Figure 9.3 was designed so that pairs of students could decide which information is needed to solve three problems. Then the pairs were combined into groups of four to compare their decisions and work together to solve the problems.

Intra-Act Procedure

Easily adapted to guide reflection in most content areas, the Intra-Act procedure (Hoffman, 1979) spurs verbal interaction around a group problem-solving task. It derives its name from the inferred *intra*personal dialogue that takes place among individuals who are engaged in an exercise of self-*act*ualization leading to concept formation. The Intra-Act procedure was developed during a time in education history when values

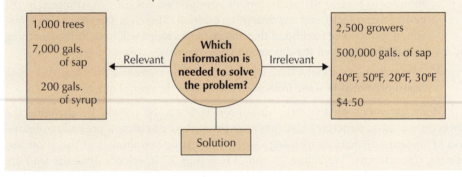

A SAPPY STORY

Vermont is one of the country's major producers of maple syrup. There are close to 2,500 maple growers in Vermont, each of whom taps an average of 1,000 trees. About 500,000 gallons of maple syrup are produced each year.

When the sap is running, growers collect it from their trees daily and boil it down to make the syrup. Traditionally, the season for "sugaring," as this process is called, begins on the first Tuesday in March. In reality, though, the sap runs only when temperatures rise to 40°F–50°F during the day and fall to 20°F–30°F at night.

A grower can tap 7,000 gallons of sap from 1,000 trees per season, yielding 200 gallons of syrup, which is then sold at $4.50 per half-pint.

1. On average, how many trees are there per grower?
2. How many gallons of sap are tapped per tree?
3. What is the ratio of the gallons of sap a grower taps to the gallons of syrup made from it, in simplest form?

1,000 trees

7,000 gals. of sap

200 gals. of syrup

← Relevant

Which information is needed to solve the problem?

Irrelevant →

2,500 growers

500,000 gals. of sap

40°F, 50°F, 20°F, 30°F

$4.50

Solution

FIGURE 9.3 **Discussion Web for Eighth-Grade Math**

Source: Problem from S. Chapin, M. Illingworth, M. Landau, J. Masingila, & L. McCracken, *Middle grade mathematics: Course 3.* Needham, MA: Prentice Hall, 1995.

clarification was at the forefront. Today, we see it being useful as a way to encourage students to reflect on what they read by predicting how the meaning that they construct of a particular text is likely to be the same as, different from, or some combination of how others in their peer group construct the same message.

In the following example of an Intra-Act supplied by Victoria, groups of students (no more than five students in a group) would read an article on bionic trees by Hillary Rosner, which was published by the *New York Times* on April 3, 2004, and is available for downloading at www.speechfriendly.org/cgi-bin/nyt.cgi/http://www.nytimes.com/learning/teachers/featured_articles/20040803tuesday.html?pagewanted=print). In her article titled "Turning Genetically Engineered Trees Into Toxic Avengers," Rosner describes a research project directed by Dr. Richard Meagher, a professor of genetics at the University of Georgia. Briefly, Dr. Meagher has genetically engineered trees to extract mercury from the soil, store it without being harmed, convert it to a less toxic form of mercury, and release it into the air.

After reading the article on bionic trees, a student leader starts the discussion by summarizing the selection as he or she understood it, and then others join in with their reactions. Because newspaper articles do not have the overt structure of textbooks, with lots of headings and subheadings, Victoria recommends giving students a list of topics such as the following to guide their discussion of the important points of the article:

- Heavy metals (like mercury) in the soil
- Logging of old-stand forests that could possibly result in the loss of wild forests
- Greenhouse gas in the atmosphere, resulting in global warming
- Loss of trees (like the American chestnut) due to disease

At the end of the discussion period, students work individually on their copies of Intra-Act Figure 9.4), recording whether they agree (A) or disagree (D) with each statement. They also predict (by circling A or D under the names of the other group members) how their peers will respond to the various statements, based on how they remember the discussion in which they were all involved.

In the final phase of the activity, students share their responses to each of the statements and reflect on whether or not their predictions square with their peers' actual responses. It is particularly important for teachers to stress that agreement (or lack of agreement) with a statement has nothing to do with that statement's validity as such. It is also important to give students time in this final step to reflect on why they responded as they did and to encourage discussion of their reflections.

General Discussion Techniques

The following discussion techniques (adapted from Harste, Short, & Burke, 1988) are easy to implement and require little if any advance preparation. Although none has specific support in the research literature (at least not to our knowledge), there is evidence that discussion in general fosters a deeper understanding of content, particularly in mathematics and science (Harmon, Hedrick, & Wood, 2005).

SAVE THE LAST WORD FOR ME   As students read a book, peruse a website, or view a video, they watch for passages or quotes that catch their attention because the language is interesting, powerful, wrong, confusing, or contradictory. Students record what caught their attention on the front of a 3″ × 5″ index card. On the back, they write a response as to why they found the passage or quote noteworthy. Alternatively, students can mark the passage or quote with a Post-It. Then, in small groups, one person begins by sharing one of the passages or quotes that he or she selected but without telling why. Other members of the groups discuss their responses to the same

	Student 1	Student 2	Student 3	Student 4	Student 5
It is okay to change a plant's genetic make-up if it is going to benefit human beings	A D ____	A D ____	A D ____	A D ____	A D ____
Just because human beings have the capability to alter the genetic code of an organism doesn't mean we should do so.	A D ____	A D ____	A D ____	A D ____	A D ____
Dangers posed by genetically modified organisms to the environment and to human health outweigh the possible uses of such organisms.	A D ____	A D ____	A D ____	A D ____	A D ____
Global warming is a danger to the continued way of life we enjoy in the United States.	A D ____	A D ____	A D ____	A D ____	A D ____
A genetically modified tree can replace a natural tree without causing any harm to the ecosystem.	A D ____	A D ____	A D ____	A D ____	A D ____
Genetically modified organisms are dangerous to human health.	A D ____	A D ____	A D ____	A D ____	A D ____
I would feel comfortable eating a fruit or vegetable from a plant or tree that was genetically modified.	A D ____	A D ____	A D ____	A D ____	A D ____

FIGURE 9.4 A Sample Intra-Act

material. When the discussion wanes, the person who shared the passage or quote tells why he or she chose it. That person has the last word, and then the group moves on to another person who shares a passage or quote.

ANOMALIES—HAVE I GOT A QUESTION FOR YOU As students read, they write down any questions they have or things that surprised them about the text. Once they have finished reading, they reread their questions to identify those they still wonder about. Even if they now have an answer to a question, they may want to keep the question because they are interested in what others think about it. In small discussion groups, students discuss the questions and generate new questions or anomalies.

MAKING A CONNECTION   As students work, they jot down other stories or experiences that a book, video, or website reminds them of. In small discussion groups, students share their connections with each other and talk about how the connections relate to the book, video, or website.

CLONING THE AUTHOR   As students read, they write 10 points from the text that they believe are important on individual index cards. After reading, each student discards three cards/points that no longer seem as important. Each student then chooses one card/point from those left that seems to be the central idea of the text. Each student then arranges her or his cards in terms of how each idea relates to another. In pairs, students share their cards and organization with each other, talking through their reasoning. Students then mix up their cards and hand them to another student, who then tries to organize the cards in a way that makes sense to him or her.

LOOKING AT DIFFERENCES   This is a strategy that Wineburg (1991) found historians used frequently in his study of how experts and novices differ in the way they read history texts. The historians read to see who the author of a text was; for example, they noted the author's point of view and they took into account the various subtexts that view implied.

With few exceptions (e.g., see Katz, Boran, Braun, Massie, & Kuby, 2003), students at the middle and high school levels are seldom encouraged to take a reflective, critical stance as readers. Teaching students how to analyze both online and offline texts to develop an awareness of how, why, and in whose interests particular texts might work is part of teaching from a critical literacies perspective.

Promoting Critical Literacy

Developing adolescents' critical awareness through literacy practices that engage them in interpreting and evaluating all forms of text (print, nonprint, image-based, and verbal) is an important aspect of guiding students in their response to reading. When we use the word *critical* to modify literacy, as in the title of this section, we do so with the notion of critical theory in mind.

If critical theory is a relatively new concept for you, or even if you know a great deal about it and its premises, we think you will find Hinchey's (1998) retelling of the following Zen parable and her analysis of it quite helpful.

> In a Zen parable, a young fish asks an elder fish to define the nature of the sea. The young one complains that although everyone talks constantly about the sea, he can't see it and he can't really get a clear understanding of what it is. The wise elder notes that the sea is all

around the young one; it is where he was born and where he will die; it is a sort of enve-
lope, and he can't see it because he is part of it.

Such is the difficulty of coming to understand our own cultural beliefs and how they
influence our actions. Like the fish who has trouble understanding the very sea surrounding him, we have trouble identifying the influence of our culture because we are immersed
in it and are part of it; we have been since birth and we will be until death—or until an experience with a different culture shows us that things might be other than the way we've
always known them to be.

It is in overcoming this difficulty that critical theory is especially valuable. It offers
us a new perspective to use in analyzing our experiences, as the fish would get an entirely new perspective on the sea if he were able to consider it from a beach. The lens
of critical theory refocuses our vision of the place we've lived all our lives. As is true of
all theory, the usefulness of critical theory is that it helps open our minds to possibilities we once found unimaginable. (Maybe standardized tests aren't reliable. Maybe tracking promotes inequality rather than equality.) Once such heresies are imagined, we can
explore them. And maybe in our explorations, we can change the face of the way things
are, forever. (p. 15)

Indeed, it must be quite obvious by now that when we refer to *critical literacy*, we
mean a form of reading that goes well beyond responding to words on a page. Among
other things, "critical literacy makes possible a more adequate and accurate 'reading' of
the world" (Lankshear & McLaren, 1993, p. xviii). That is, it gives readers a way of reflecting on an author's point of view and how that view affects who we are and how we interpret the author's message.

As Temple (2005) notes, critical literacy is usually traced to Paolo Freire, a Brazilian
lawyer turned educator who popularized the notion that before one can learn to read the
word, one must learn to read the world. Freire taught illiterate peasants in Brazil the importance of orally naming their socioeconomic problems before anchoring such insights
in the written word.

A pedagogical framework for building this kind of awareness is the *four resources
model*, which engages students in four tasks or rules (Luke, Freebody, & Land, 2000):

- *Code breaker* refers to decoding
- *Meaning maker* to composing and comprehending a written, visual, or spoken
  text's message
- *Text user* to understanding and acting on the functions of text structure, tone, and
  sequencing of information
- *Text analyst* to unpacking social, economic, and political assumptions of a text's
  message in order to redesign the message

Although the ability to decode and comprehend what is learned from and with
texts is commonly expected in most content area classrooms, the capacity to analyze

how different texts position different readers in different ways is not. This is unfortunate, given that the increasing number of newcomers in U.S. schools today would seem to point to the necessity of considering how individuals from different cultural backgrounds see themselves represented (or not represented) in the textbooks they are required to read.

Teaching Literacy for Critical Awareness

At the center of much of this teaching is the perceived need to assist students in their critical awareness of how all texts (both print and nonprint) position them as readers and viewers within different social, cultural, and historical contexts. The implications of all this for facilitating students' thoughtful reflections on what they read were described in Chapter 1 in our discussion of rethinking content literacy practices, multiliteracies (New London Group, 1997), and the New Literacy Studies (Willinsky, 1990). Briefly, and by way of review, when we teach critical literacy awareness, it is generally for one or more of the following reasons:

- To motivate students to explore the assumptions authors seem to have been operating under when constructing their messages
- To facilitate students' thinking about the decisions authors make (and why) with regard to word choice, content (included as well as excluded), and interests served
- To encourage multiple readings of the same text from different perspectives

Here, we expand this list by considering how readers respond to hypertext and the impact of this medium on critical literacy awareness. An expert in hypertext literacy, Jay Bolter (1992) has observed that "above all, hypertext challenges our sense that each [text] is a complete, separate, and unique expression of its author" (p. 22). This observation, coupled with the potential for readers to reconstruct an author's text while at the same time leaving "tracks" for subsequent readers to follow or revise, suggests that teaching

TECHNOLOGY Tip

Building Critical Literacy Awareness
If you are concerned that your students lack know-how in critically evaluating websites, check out ways to develop this skill at www .anovember.com/articles.zack.html.

For information specific to educating girls to be tech savvy in today's computing culture, visit www.aauw.org or e-mail the American Association of University Women (foundation@aauw .org) for a copy of *Tech-Savvy: Educating Girls in the New Computer Age.*

critical literacy awareness with hypertext will need to take into account the following questions:

- In manipulating the text to meet our own desire for information (or entertainment), what do we come to know about ourselves that we would not otherwise know?
- Are hypertext readings of authors' messages privileged in ways that linear readings are not? If so, what might be the consequences of this privileging?
- How does linking materials in hypertext influence readers' thinking about issues of race, class, gender, ethnicity, sexual orientation, ability, age, wellness, and other identity markers?

Finally, this section would not be complete without drawing an explicit connection between engaging students through discussion and teaching for critical awareness. Listening to the moment-by-moment exchanges between teachers and students or among students themselves, as they work collaboratively in small-group settings, can reveal a great deal about how discussion is working or not working and for which students (Fradd & Lee, 1999).

For example, Duff (2007) found that introducing popular culture texts into academic discussions in a Canadian high school served to engage English-proficient students; however, those same texts tended to marginalize immigrants whose native language was not English and who did not possess the appropriate culture-specific knowledge for interpreting the texts. This need for a sense of belonging was also a factor in a study conducted in a high school in Texas, where Lesley (2008) found that students' ability and willingness to connect with the curriculum through discussion depended on the opportunity to read texts in which they recognized aspects of their own voices and lives. Until that condition was met, the students in Lesley's research project were unwilling to assume a critical stance toward texts.

Incorporating Critical Media Literacy into the Curriculum

Just as the word *literacy* is used differently in various contexts, so too is the term *critical media literacy*. Depending on one's perspective or theoretical frame, the latter may be characterized as the ability to do the following:

- Reflect on the pleasures derived from popular media (e.g., TV, radio, video games, movies, music CDs, the Internet, and cyberpunk culture).
- Analyze how popular media texts shape and are shaped by youth culture.

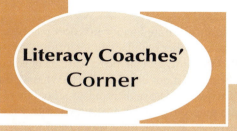

Literacy Coaches' Corner

Critical Media Literacy

Victoria recalls that in Orange County, Florida, where she was a Reading in the Content Areas project teacher trainer and science teacher in the 1970s, literacy coaches were expected to run an in-service activity each period of the day to which teachers could come if they wished. (Literacy coaches were called *reading resource specialists* at the time.) The coaches would demonstrate literacy strategies, using some of the same ones featured in this text. For example, they might show the usefulness of strategies that tap into or build on students' critical thinking about a particular topic in their assigned texts.

If Victoria were a coach today, she is certain that she would attempt to enrich teachers' thinking about ways to instruct students in critical media literacy by pointing out various websites that are filled with resources for content area teaching. In particular, she would be sure to include Kathy Schrock's home page (http://kathyschrock.net) and the *New York Times* Learning Network (www.nytimes.com/learning).

- Map the ways in which individuals assimilate popular culture texts differently.
- Uncover the codes and practices that privilege some messages and silence others.
- Problematize the relationship between audience and mode of media production (Alvermann & Hagood, 2000).

It is important to note that in offering a range of defining characteristics for the term *critical media literacy*, we deliberately refrain from referring to it as simply visual literacy or critical viewing literacy because the emphasis on viewing implies that audiences are passive in relation to the media's messages. In guiding students' critical reflections on the media, teachers would do well to point out that audiences (such as the students themselves) are typically neither passive nor predictable.

In fact, as cultural studies scholars Hall and Whannel (1998) emphasized in their analysis of the entertainment media, "The use intended by the [media] provider and the use actually made by the audience never wholly coincide, and frequently conflict" (pp. 61–62). It is this potential for conflict—the oppositional reading of a media text—that makes it possible for some audiences to perceive Madonna as nothing more than a "boy toy," whereas others observe in her the personification of resistance to patriarchy's definition of what a woman should be, do, and say.

The extent to which school curricula can incorporate literacy practices related to TV, video and computer games, music, comics, and other popular culture forms is yet to be determined (Alvermann & Hagood, 2000). Obviously, not all media texts are of equal value, and concerns about the pleasure they bring must not override all else. What we do know, however, is that when students are not required to leave their out-of-school literacies at the classroom door, they are eager responders to popular media texts, with a few offering critiques on their own that have surprised even the most seasoned of teachers (Lewis, 1998). Although some educators endorse this blurring of in-school and out-of-school literacies (Alvermann, Moon, & Hagood, 1999; Buckingham & Sefton-Green, 1994), others, although not opposed to the idea, offer a variety of caveats worth considering (Duncan, 1996).

For example, Australian educator Carmen Luke (1997), in discussing the problems of incorporating critical media literacy into the school curriculum, noted the following:

> [Asking students to critique the media texts they find pleasurable] is likely to cue a critical response which can often be an outright lie . . . [for while] students are quick to talk a good anti-sexist, anti-racist, pro-equity game . . . what they write in the essay or what they tell us in classroom discussion is no measure of what goes on in their heads. (p. 43)

In similar fashion, David Buckingham (1993) cautioned about the danger of asking young people to critique the very pleasures they derive from popular media texts. He suggests that teachers take time to engage with different media for which they have little or no background experience (such as computer games) to get a sense of what their students find so enjoyable. Doing so need not end up in some naive celebration of popular culture, nor does it necessarily lead to an appropriation of students' outside interests in the service of schooling. Rather, it serves as an introduction to what students value and find motivational. Sometimes the findings are totally unexpected.

For instance, when literacy teacher educators Alleen and Don Nilsen (2000) took it upon themselves to investigate the controversial Gameboy version of Pokémon and the trading cards associated with the game, they found that children were using many school-related literacy skills to improve their game playing. Banned in many schools throughout the United States for distracting kids of all ages from serious learning, the 150 Pokémon, all with their own names and descriptors for how they evolve (e.g., Bulbasaur evolves into Ivysaur, which in turn evolves into Venusaur), in fact provided much morphemic analysis and spelling practice on the side. The Nilsens also found evidence of literary allusions in the game cards (e.g., Geodude evolves into Graveller, who evolves into Golem, the creature in J. R. R. Tolkien's *The Lord of the Rings*).

Although literacy researchers have begun to study the effects of teaching students to read between the lines of text in order to uncover hidden messages in magazine advertisements (e.g., Linder & Falk-Ross, 2004), there are still very few studies that explore how teachers incorporate critical media literacy into their schools' curricula. The research on critical literacy in general has been done in out-of-school settings, with a few notable exceptions. One of those exceptions is a study by Hagood (2002) in which she traced how Timony (pseudonym), a middle school youth, was produced and objectified by those who identified him as troubled (and troubling) while he attempted to push back by positioning himself differently. As Hagood noted, "A broadened application of critical literacy that acknowledges the working of both identity and subjectivity [is needed]" (p. 247).

APPROACHES TO TEACHING CRITICAL MEDIA LITERACY Before incorporating critical media literacy into an already full curriculum, teachers will want to examine various approaches to determine what best suits their classroom. Figure 9.5 provides a rough sketch of three possibilities, each with a different focus: consumerism and the media, mindless consumption versus critical analysis of popular media, or a balanced consideration of the pros and cons of media texts. The "Application" column should help in deciding which approach is most applicable and relevant, depending on the desired focus, the topic or topics under discussion, and the classroom style. Each approach serves effectively to promote students' powers of reflection and critical awareness.

Commenting on a report released in December 2007 by researchers in the PEW Internet and American Life Project (Lenhart, Madden, Macgill, & Smith, 2007), Donna asked if it might be useful to tap into what motivates young people to create online content in their out-of-school hours in ever-increasing amounts (Alvermann, 2008). According to the PEW report, the use of social media—blogging; working on a webpage for school or personal use; sharing original content such as artwork, photos, stories, and videos; and remixing online content to create new texts—is central to the lives of many young people living in the continental United States. Of the 935 adolescents between the ages of 12 and 17 who were interviewed by phone in the PEW survey (a nationally representative sample), 93 percent treated the Internet as a venue for social interaction. Of those young people who were identified as having online access, 64 percent reported creating online content on a regular basis.

The drive to create online content is in large part inspired by adolescents' penchant for remixing texts (e.g., writing fanfiction, blogging, maintaining a presence on MySpace or Facebook)—activities that some (perhaps most) educators frown on because such authorship is neither a solitary nor completely original enterprise. Yet as Black (2008) has pointed out, youth who create derivative texts are "far from being 'mindless consumers' and reproducers of existing media, as they actively engage with, rework, and appropriate the ideological messages and materials of the original text" (p. xiii). In fact, it could be argued that young people's engagement with these kinds of ideological messages and materials is central to their developing a critical awareness of how texts position themselves and others.

Approach	Perspective	Application
Viewers as Consumers	When students learn the detrimental effects of most popular media, they become wiser consumers.	"Turn off the TV" week-long initiative calls attention to and sparks discussion about the amount of TV—and commercials—young people watch.
Teacher as Liberating Guide	Students seek to become "the ideal viewer" in learning to avoid the thoughtless consumption of popular media texts.	Critiques of media texts downplay the pleasures students might derive from them. Teaching becomes a process of demystification.
Pleasures without Parameters	All media texts are equally good. Views and voices from everywhere become views and voices from nowhere; the slippery slope of relativism prevails.	Concerns for students' pleasures override all else; teachers are careful not to require students to analyze and critique that which they like (or don't like).
Media as Source of Both Pleasure and Learning	Critical media literacy is not merely a cognitive experience, nor is it solely a pleasure-seeking experience without challenges. In maximizing its educational value, it is important to acknowledge (1) the expertise students bring to the learning environment, (2) the pleasures they derive from popular media texts, and (3) the multiple readings students produce from these texts.	Teachers provide opportunities for students to explore how popular media texts position them socially, culturally, materially, and otherwise; the goal is not to spoil students' pleasure but to extend their understanding.

F I G U R E 9 . 5   Approaches to Teaching Critical Media Literacy

Source: Adapted from D. E. Alvermann, J. S. Moon, & M. C. Hagood, *Popular Culture in the Classroom: Teaching and Researching Critical Media Literacy*, pp. 23–28. Newark, DE: International Reading Association and the National Reading Conference, 1999.

Activity

Take either a "pro" or "con" side in the argument just stated: that young people's engagement with online ideological messages and materials is central to their developing a critical awareness of how texts position themselves and others. Use Toulmin's elements of an argument (Felton, 2005, p. 8), outlined below, as a basis for your written claim and rebuttal (if you are meeting in an onsite class or have e-mail access to others in an online class).

Toulmin's Elements of an Argument

Claim: a statement that you want others to accept. Inferences and interpretations, conclusions, opinions, and proposals can all be examples of claims.

Data: the evidence used to substantiate a claim. This evidence may or may not be indisputable; therefore, part of critical dialogue may center on challenging the truth or interpretation of the data used to support a claim.

Warrant: links data to a claim. A warrant is an explanation of how the data cited in an argument support the claim. Because that link is often self-evident, the warrant is often left unstated in an argument. However, in critical dialogue, someone might accept your evidence as true but challenge the relevance of that evidence to your claim. You would then need to supply an acceptable warrant.

Backing: the justification used to validate the warrant. It is an explanation of the grounds or authority on which a warrant is based.

Qualifier: establishes the strength of a claim or the conditions under which a claim is valid. Qualifiers often emerge in critical dialogue as you discover the limits of your position.

Rebuttal: a response to a counterargument leveled against your claim. All informal arguments are open to counterargument, since by definition, they are inconclusive. Again, rebuttals often emerge in critical dialogue as you answer opponents' challenges to your claims.

TECHNOLOGY Tip

Online Safety

At the 2008 National Educational Computing Conference in San Antonio, a panel of Internet safety experts (including Amanda Lenhart, author of several PEW Internet Reports) agreed that "education is the best tool to keep kids safe online." For a list of suggestions that educators can use in promoting students' online safety, view a short video at www.eschoolnews.com/conferenceinfo/necc/highlights/?i=54386;_hbguid=64297a3a-cd5f-49d6-be8534d2eccd3422&d=necc.

Helping Struggling Readers

Multimedia Inquiry

In his online article "Juxtaposing Traditional and Intermedial Literacies to Redefine the Competence of Struggling Adolescents" (www .readingonline.org/newliteracies/obrien2/), David O'Brien critiques the notion of struggling readers being at risk in light of the New Liter-

acy Studies framework. O'Brien focuses on a four-year collaborative project that he co-designed with his colleagues in a public high school in Indiana. The outcomes of the project demonstrated that low-achieving readers' interest in and mastery of multimedia inquiry served to redefine their literacy competencies.

Summary

Teachers at the middle and high school levels are under intense pressure to cover their curricula. It seems that each year, local or state authorities add new requirements regarding what should be included in a content area course. It is hardly surprising that some teachers, struggling to cover all the required topics by June, are skeptical when they are told they should also be teaching students how to apply thoughtful and critical strategies as they reflect on what they read.

Yet thinking critically, or the ability to go beyond the text or lecture and use information in productive ways, is arguably more important than much of the information itself. State and national assessments are increasingly focusing on the sort of thinking processes discussed in this chapter. Content coverage and higher-level critical thinking are not mutually exclusive in classrooms where students are involved in talking about and reflecting on what they are reading.

Suggested Readings

Alvermann, D. E., & Hagood, M. C. (2000). Fandom and critical media literacy. *Journal of Adolescent & Adult Literacy, 43*, 436–446.

Boyd, F. (2003). Literature circles and national standards for social studies teachers: A plan for reading and discussing children's literature. *The California Reader, 36*(4), 16–21.

Connolly, B., & Smith, M. W. (2002). Teachers and students talk about talk: Class discussion and the way it should be. *Journal of Adolescent & Adult Literacy, 46*, 16–26.

Cowan, J. (2008). Diary of a blog: Listening to kids in an elementary school library. *Teacher Librarian, 35*(5), 20–26.

Hobbs, R., & Frost, R. (2003). Measuring the acquisition of media-literacy skills. *Reading Research Quarterly, 38*, 330–355.

Johnson, H., & Freedman, L. (2005). *Developing critical awareness at the middle level.* Newark, DE: International Reading Association.

Pescatore, C. (2007/2008). Current events as empowering literacy: For English and social studies teachers. *Journal of Adolescent & Adult Literacy, 51,* 326–339.

Tanner, M. L., & Casados, L. (1998). Promoting and studying discussions in math classes. *Journal of Adolescent & Adult Literacy, 41,* 342–350.

Thornburg, D. (1991). Strategy instruction for academically at-risk students: An exploratory study of teaching "higher-order" reading and writing in the social studies. *Reading, Writing, and Learning Disabilities, 7,* 377–406.

MyEducationLab is a research-based learning tool that brings teaching to life. Go to the Alvermann, Phelps, and Ridgeway Gillis 6th Edition MyEducationLab for Content Area Reading site at www.myeducationlab.com to:

- engage in multimedia exercises to help you build a deeper and more applied understanding of chapter content;

- utilize extensive resources including videos from real classrooms, Praxis and licensure preparation, a lesson plan builder, and materials to help you in your teaching career.

chapter **10**

Writing across the Curriculum

What Content Teachers Need to Know about Writing

- Writing and Reading
- The Writing Process
- Social Construction of Writing
- Writing and the Computer

Writing Activities for Content Areas

- Writing Assignments
- Learning Logs and Journals
- Other Informal Writing Activities
- Reviewing and Summarizing
- Guiding Student Writing

Writing to Inquire

- Preparing for Student Inquiry
- Collecting and Organizing Information
- Writing a Report
- Alternatives to the Traditional Research Report

Responding to Student Writing

- Peer Responses
- Teacher Conferences
- Formal Evaluation

Anticipation Guide

Directions: Read each of the following statements. Place a checkmark on the line in the "Before Reading" column if you agree with the statement; leave it blank if you disagree. Then predict what you think the chapter will be about, and jot down on a sticky note (or post online) any questions you have. Read the chapter; then return to the statements and respond to them as you think the authors of your text would. Place a checkmark on the line in the "Authors' Stance" column if you believe the authors would agree with the statement. If you discuss these statements with other people online, in class, or at the family dinner table, return to the statements and check any items you agree with in the right-hand column, "After Discussion." If your thinking changed, what caused that change?

Before Reading	Authors' Stance	Statements	After Discussion
_____	_____	1. Teaching students to write is English teachers' responsibility.	_____
_____	_____	2. Reading and writing should be treated as separate processes.	_____
_____	_____	3. To be effective tools of writing instruction, learning logs and journals should be regularly corrected and graded.	_____
_____	_____	4. Not all student writing is intended for publication.	_____
_____	_____	5. Creative writing is only appropriate in English classes.	_____
_____	_____	6. Writing is thinking that has been written down.	_____

Victoria tells this story to her content reading students as an introduction to writing to learn:

• • •

Years ago, as a junior high teacher with two young daughters, going out to a movie was a special treat, one I looked forward to. One evening my husband and I went to see *The Last of the Mohicans*. As the movie began, my husband leaned over and whispered, "That guide is a traitor." Sure enough, he was. Later, he leaned over and whispered, "These troops are going to be ambushed." Sure enough, they were. This continued throughout the movie, with my husband leaning over to whisper his predictions about every 20 minutes. When the movie was over, I asked him (not very nicely, I admit) why he had taken me to a movie he had already seen.

"I've never seen that movie before," he said.

"Well, how did you know everything that was going to happen?" I asked.

"Let me ask you something," he said. "What do you do when you go to the movies?"

"I sit quietly and let the movie wash over me like some warm ocean wave, and I keep my mouth shut!" I replied.

"Well, that explains it," he said.

"Explains what?" I asked in an irritated tone, and then added, "Okay, mister smart guy, what is it that *you* do when you go to the movies?"

"I make predictions and ask questions . . . I *think* my way through the movie," he said.

And with that, he had me. I believe students often experience school like I experience movies—like some warm, comforting ocean wave—passively letting the teacher's voice wash over them. And teachers know when this happens. We can tell when a student is present in body but absent in spirit and mind. Students sort of slump down in their seats; their breathing slows down; their eyes go a bit unfocused. When we look out over a classroom and see these disengaged students, we suddenly think, "I have to jazz this lesson up! I have to do something creative!" And we frantically buy activity books and invent games to entertain students.

Let me tell you something right now: teachers are NOT entertainers. If you doubt that, take a look at the average teacher's salary. We don't make anything near what Tom Cruise makes! Our job is not to entertain. Our job is to *engage students' minds.*"

• • •

One way to engage students' minds is through writing, both writing to communicate and writing to learn. Lucy Calkins (who recounts a similar situation in her book *The Art of Teaching Writing* [1994]) puts it this way: "Learning isn't something we can do for (or to) our students" (p. 484). Calkins reminds us that *learning* is an active verb: We can create conditions conducive to learning, but the students must make the choice to learn.

Teachers are charged with preparing students for a world they cannot imagine and will never experience. How can they possibly accomplish this task? Part of the answer to this question is to help students learn to think in disciplined ways. When students commit ideas and knowledge to writing, they must be more thoughtful, organized, and precise than when speaking. Writers make choices, make changes, and make meaning. Writing is thinking written down (Zinsser, 1988). Donald Murry describes it this way: "Writing, in fact, is the most disciplined form of thinking" (1984, pp. 3).

What Content Teachers Need to Know about Writing

For English language arts teachers, much of this chapter may be "preaching to the choir." After all, teaching writing is a significant part of your job. Usually, secondary teachers leave writing and writing instruction to the English teachers. As a former science teacher, Victoria readily admits, "I didn't have a clue about grammar or punctuation and what's more I didn't really care! Based on my own schooling experience, I assumed that writing was about punctuation, grammar, and spelling. Writing was for English class—*doing science* was for science class."

One problem with this sort of thinking is that writing in English class is vastly different from writing in science. Victoria learned this when she returned to graduate school in literacy education, twenty years after earning a master's degree in science education. She had learned to write in third-person, passive voice (Victoria says, "I hadn't a clue as to what that was—I could only do it, not name it") with lots of prepositions thrown in for good measure. Her professors in the Reading department at UGA (Donna was one!) went through dozens of red ink pens trying to break her of these habits.

Another problem with leaving writing instruction to English teachers is that writing is more than grammar and punctuation. Grammar and punctuation help us write with clarity so that our message is understood by others, but all writing is not for public consumption. Certainly, none of us want to publish our personal journals, grocery or To-Do lists, or notes to ourselves jotted on sticky notes and pasted all over our computer screens. Because writing is thinking written down, it is a powerful tool that helps students learn how mathematicians, scientists, and historians think (De La Paz, 2005; Fernsten, 2007; Keys, Hand, Prain, & Collins, 1999). This, it seems to us, is a main purpose of math, science, and history in the curriculum.

Writing and Reading

Research suggests that there is an especially beneficial effect to combining writing with reading activities (Graham & Perin, 2007). Tierney et al. (1989) noted that "reading and writing in combination have the potential to contribute in powerful ways to thinking" (p. 166).

Evidence-Based Research

When Judith Langer (1986) compared the ways in which high school juniors completed short-answer questions, took notes, and wrote essay answers, she found that writing essays not only contributed the most to their topic knowledge but also seemed to improve their thinking about the content: "When writing essays, students seem to step back from the text after reading it—they reconceptualize the content in ways that cut across ideas, focusing on larger issues or topics. In doing this, they integrate information and engage in more complex thought" (p. 406).

In another study using social studies material with high school juniors, Martin and Konopak (1987) employed a relatively simple combination of brainstorming, writing, and reading. In a three-day trial, they found this procedure helped students synthesize information from several sources and integrate new information with their prior knowledge. The researchers got similar results when they tried the same procedure with sixth-grade students (Konopak, Martin, & Martin, 1990).

Writing, then, is a potent tool for learning and reflecting across the school curriculum. Many teachers have found that writing means much more than an in-class five-paragraph essay or a one-shot term paper. As you read the following examples, consider the kinds of thinking required as students read, talk, and write:

- *Example 1:* At the end of the year, a sixth-grade teacher involves her class in a review of all they have studied in science, including the scientific method and famous scientists, the environment, electricity, the plant and animal kingdoms, astronomy, and meteorology. After reading *The Magic School Bus Inside the Earth* and *The Magic School Bus Inside the Human Body*, by Joanna Cole, groups of students write and illustrate their own adventure stories about field trips to the labs of famous scientists, a forest ranger station, a nuclear power plant, and other places related to their studies. For three weeks, students converge on the media center with three-by-five index cards and buzz together in composing and editorial conferences. When their books are written, illustrated, laminated, and bound, they proudly show them off to visiting fifth graders who are getting a preview of their next year in school.

- *Example 2:* An eighth-grade history class is considering the relative effectiveness of violence and nonviolence in conflict resolution. On the first day, each cooperative learning group receives two case studies to read. Following the instructions given in Figure 10.1, they collectively write brief comparisons of the two cases. On the second day, the groups report their interpretations to the class. Through questioning, the teacher helps the class focus on the long- and short-term effects, both personal and social, of conflicts between aboriginals and colonials in New Zealand and North America, between blacks and whites during the American civil rights movement of the 1960s, and between muggers and victims on city streets. The teacher lists these cases on the blackboard, and students add other historical and current events to the list. The teacher makes an assignment: Pick one event, research it, and write a position paper advocating violence or nonvio-

REFLECTIVE WRITING: VIOLENCE VERSUS NONVIOLENCE

Directions: Read the case studies given to your group. Each one includes acts of violence and nonviolence. Complete the chart below with information you find in the case studies.

	Case Study 1	Case Study 2
A. 1. Identify act(s) of violence.		
2. What was the intended goal/objective?		
3. Was the goal/objective achieved?		
B. 1. Identify act(s) of nonviolence.		
2. What was the intended goal/objective?		
3. Was the goal/objective achieved?		

C. Decide: How are these acts similar? How do they differ? Are they more alike than different, or vice versa? Why?

D. Write: As a group, draft a brief written comparison of your two cases, including essential information from A, B, and C above. You will be presenting this in class tomorrow.

FIGURE 10.1   A Reflective Writing Activity for a Tenth-Grade History Class

Source: Reprinted by permission of Margaret Boykin, Buffalo Public Schools, #18, Buffalo, New York.

lence. In the following two weeks, the teacher devotes part or all of several classes to media center visits, drafting, and conferencing. When students have completed their inquiries and writing, the cooperative learning groups present their individual papers in the format of an academic roundtable. As a finale, students write individually about what they have learned from their study of conflict resolution and how this relates to their personal experience.

Activity

Working in small groups (perhaps by disciplinary area), locate the number of times writing is referred to in the content standards of your professional organization. For a list of websites for those standards, see Appendix E. Prepare a short list of the different ways that writing is a tool for learning in your specific content area, and share that information in whole-class discussion or with a partner from a different discipline.

The Writing Process

The use of writing in schools has changed as teachers have broadened their understanding of how writers work. All writers, from beginners to professional authors, go through similar steps to produce a piece of writing:

1. *Prewriting:*   This involves deciding on a topic, collecting one's thoughts, gathering data, organizing ideas mentally or on paper, and perhaps rehearsing in one's mind or in writing some of the things that will be said.

2. *Drafting:*   This is actually putting words, sentences, and paragraphs down on paper. The word *drafting* necessarily implies something unfinished or unpolished, for a piece of writing may go through many drafts before it reaches its final form. During drafting, the emphasis is on fluency and getting ideas onto paper.

3. *Revising:*   Revision literally means "to see again." As a writer reads what has been written with the eyes of a reader, he or she can look for meaning and clarity. The writer may add, delete, or rearrange information at this point. During revision, it may also be helpful to have another person read the work and share his or her impressions.

4. *Editing:*   The distinction between revising and editing is important. When revising, the focus is on content or meaning. When editing, the focus is on form, on things such as spelling, punctuation, grammatical conventions, and finding just the right word.

TECHNOLOGY Tip

Tutorials

For help understanding how blogs, wikis, wordles, and podcasts work, we have found the following YouTube videos and website very helpful:

- **Blogs:**   Essentially online journals, blogs are explained by the YouTube video *Blogs in Plain English* at www.youtube.com/watch?v=NN2I1pWXjXI. (It may be easier to go to www.youtube.com and type in the title of the video, rather than use the URL provided here.)

- **Wikis:**   These are spaces on the Internet where groups of authors can edit and save text; wikis are explained by the YouTube

video *Wikis in Plain English* at www.youtube.com/watch?v=-dnL00TdmLY. (Again, it may be easier to go to the YouTube site and type in the name of the video.)

- **Wordles:**   These works of word art (technically called "word clouds"), created from text you input into the website, are explained on the Wordle site at http://wordle.net.

- **Podcasts:**   These are audio recordings that can be saved, posted on the web, or e-mailed. They are explained by the YouTube video *Podcasts in Plain English* at www.youtube.com/watch?v=y-MSL42NV3c. (Access the video from the YouTube site, as desired.)

5. *Postwriting:* Sometimes this is called *publishing*, in the sense that when a piece of writing is finished, it is often made public. For most student writing, this means handing it in to the teacher. However, there are other audiences and venues for student writing—classmates, parents, students in other classes and grades, and school publications. Students often find opportunities to share their writing outside the school community as well. They may write letters to authors, politicians, newspapers, or students in another school. Local businesses, professionals, civic organizations, and community agencies may agree to sponsor student writing projects and respond to the final products.

With the increasing accessibility to the Internet, opportunities to make writing public can be found in blogs, wikis, and websites. Victoria has kept a professional journal for years and recently converted it to a professional blog, which her students (and you) can access, read, and respond to (http://teach2k6.blogspot.com/). Wikis enable group editing, which is much easier than collaborating via e-mail. We used a wiki to revise the text for this edition, although none of us was familiar with wikis before we began. Wordle is a new 2.0 Web tool that enables you to input any text and have the website create a *wordle*—word art that uses the words from a given text and varies the size of each word based on how many times it appears in the text. If you are not familiar with these new technologies, see the Technology Tip box for websites with tutorials.

Activity

Look at the wordle below, which was created from the words in the Declaration of Independence. Free write for five minutes on the impact of the graphic. Be prepared to share your thoughts.

Although we have described the steps of the writing process in numerical order, we must emphasize that this process is *not* strictly linear; a writer does not march through the process as if it were so many steps in a recipe for apple pie. Writing is recursive. At any stage in the development of a piece of writing, the author may go back or forward in the process. While writing this text, for instance, we frequently (more often than we like to think about) revised our outline, changed our focus, gathered more information, and rewrote. As part of this process, we shared parts of the book with each other, with colleagues, and with friends. Even as we sat at our word processors, we found ourselves continuously rereading, revising, and editing.

Another important point about the writing process, especially in the context of content area teaching, is that writing activities do not always have to culminate in finished products to be useful. A lot of writing is informal and never shared with a wide audience or intended for the evaluative eye of a teacher. This informal, unfinished writing is valuable because it promotes reflective thinking. It also gives the writer (and others) an opportunity to look back and trace changes and development in learning and thinking. For this reason, many content area teachers have adopted learning logs and other informal writing activities.

When teachers are familiar with the writing process, they find that it affects their expectations and their teaching in at least five important ways. First, they realize that there will be a great deal of variability in students' writing. Within a single classroom, there will be writers who are fluent and confident as well as some for whom it will be a struggle to put a few words or sentences on the page. There will also be great variability in writing styles and approaches. Although the basic writing process is similar for all writers, each individual develops his or her own preferences and strategies for writing.

Second, process-oriented teachers know that developing writers need regular and frequent practice. Competence comes with experience. When students write regularly in a variety of modes, including unfinished writing, both their ability and their confidence increase.

Third, these teachers emphasize the writing process, especially prewriting and revising, in their assignments and instruction. Rather than overwhelm students with a multipage handout titled something like "Requirements for the History 11 Term Paper," teachers provide students with incremental modeling, guidance, and practice in the different phases of the writing process. These teachers also confer with students regularly as they work on their writing and provide structured opportunities for students to confer with each other.

Fourth, the more teachers know about writing processes, the more they understand that *writing well is hard work*, whether you are a student or a published professional writer. Teachers who are themselves writers are in an especially good position to communicate this important message to their students, as Anne Shealy (2000), a middle school teacher, learned in a graduate writers' workshop: "I discovered that writing was almost always a difficult process, but the exertion is a natural, acceptable step in becoming a better writer. My continued development as a writer informs my teaching of writing" (p. 11).

Finally, these teachers are likely to emphasize the content of students' writing over the form. They recognize that developing writers are not perfect. Even professional authors must rely on copyeditors. It does not seem sensible to hold learners to a higher standard than that applied to experts. Rather, process-oriented teachers respond primarily to the meaning in students' writing and view the mechanics as a secondary, but important, consideration.

In 2007, the year of the most recent National Assessment of Educational Progress (NAEP) writing assessment, average writing scores for both eighth and twelfth graders were higher than in previous assessments, and there were increases in the percentages of students performing at or above the basic level but not at or above the proficient level. In addition, there was evidence that gaps between majority and minority students were narrowing (NCES, 2007). Findings also indicated that students at both grade levels used at least some parts of the writing process during the assessment. (Seventy-four percent of eighth graders and 70 percent of twelfth graders used a prewriting activity.) However, just over half of the students in each group indicated that their teachers sometimes require more than one draft of a paper. Ten percent of each group responded that their teachers never require more than one draft of a paper (www.nationsreportcard.gov/writing_2007/w0022.asp). While we can applaud the increased NAEP scores, we must be mindful that in a world as saturated with writing as ours—where e-mail, instant messaging, blogs, and wikis are a part of everyday life and many jobs, writing proficiency is essential.

In a recent report, the National Commission on Writing (2008) reiterated the importance of writing in today's world but pointed out that although today's adolescents spend a lot of time communicating electronically, they do not consider their e-communication as *real* writing. This report included several findings pertinent to our discussion of writing in schools. Adolescents are motivated when given or allowed to chose relevant topics, when writing to an interesting audience, when allowed to write creatively, and when presented with teachers' high expectations. Writing for school was pervasive during adolescents' schooling, but most assignments were short, a paragraph to a page in length. Adolescents who had access to cell phones, computers, and other gadgets did not write any more or less than adolescents who did not have ready access to technology, according to the report. However, teen bloggers wrote more online and offline. As you read this chapter, consider your own writing process, both personal and professional.

Social Construction of Writing

Our description of the writing process has largely emphasized the individual cognitive aspects of writing, at least up to the point at which writing is shared with others. However, there are also important social dimensions to both the long-term development of writing abilities and the actual composition of a particular piece of writing. As with other facets of literacy, writing is socially constructed, and therefore involves

> the historical, cultural, and social identities the individual brings to writing, the social world in which the writing occurs, the peer and teacher interactions that surround the writing, and the classroom organization, including the curriculum and pedagogical decisions made by the teacher and the school. (Schultz & Fecho, 2000, p. 54)

Writing is more than a set of technical skills that can be taught and learned in a normative progression; rather, it is a complex interplay of writer, audience, language, and social context.

LANGUAGE, CULTURE, AND WRITING   Written words, as language made tangible and subject to public scrutiny, reveal the interrelationships of language, culture, and education. In a fundamental way, to be educated in U.S. society means to be literate. Facility with writing, especially in the direct exposition of thesis and elaboration most often associated with school writing tasks, is a significant marker of an individual's mastery of schooled literacy. Some features of written language, such as spelling, dialect, and code switching miscues by ELLs, are especially apparent. However, the relation between culture and language is much deeper and more complex than what is revealed in these surface features (Gee, 1996; Heath, 1983; Delpit, 1995).

Pragmatics is a term used by linguists to describe how people use language socially "for demonstrating intelligence, apologizing, asking for a favor, telling someone what to do, claiming allegiance with others, displaying status, getting one's point across, even telling a story" (Meier, 1998b, p. 122). People from different cultural and linguistic communities have varied strategies for negotiating these situations, and pragmatics may often be a significant source of misunderstanding both within and across cultural groups.

For example, Chinese cultural traditions place more emphasis on collectivism and fitting in than U.S. traditions, which are more likely to prize individualism. Native Chinese who are learning to write English tend to favor a style that emphasizes contingency, avoids strong assertions, features the collective "we" rather than the individual "I," and relies on rhetorical devices such as proverbs and analog. This is in contrast to native English-speaking U.S. writers, who are more direct, quicker to assert and defend polarized positions, and more likely to employ personal anecdotes (Wu & Rubin, 2000).

African American oral and written traditions also feature many unique patterns of style and pragmatics that are absent or not so richly developed in other North American language communities. These include

> characteristic intonational patterns; metaphorical language; concrete examples and analogies to make a point; rhyme, rhythm, alliteration, and other forms of repetition, including word play; use of proverbs, aphorisms, biblical quotations, and learned allusions; colorful and unusual vocabulary; arguing *to* a main point (rather than *from* a main point); making a point through indirection. (Meier, 1998a, p. 99)

These are highly prized and effective conventions in many contexts, although they may not be awarded points in the five-paragraph persuasive essay or the history term paper if standard rhetorical conventions are expected.

Social class is another factor that may denote writing styles. Hemphill (1999) found that working-class adolescents produced responses to poetry that prominently featured their own role as readers and elaborated on the characters' thoughts and actions in the narrative, whereas middle-class students were more likely to concentrate on abstracted meaning or "big ideas" and suppress explicit self-references.

Although diverse language communities all have their individual styles and strengths, it is nevertheless important that students gain facility with standard academic English. The question is not whether students should learn Standard English spelling, grammar, and rhetoric but how (Delpit, 1995). First, teachers of linguistically diverse students need to understand and appreciate language differences. When asked what advice she would give white teachers of Ebonics-speaking students, high school English teacher Hafeesah Dalji replied:

> Respect the language of the students. Let them know that no language is inferior or superior. Give them examples. And of course you have to feel that way, too, because if you don't there is no sense in trying to teach what you don't feel, because students will see it. You also have to be knowledgeable about Ebonics before you are able to work with students in transferring their language to Standard English. . . . A European teacher has to recognize that there is a rhythm to the language, they have to recognize the cadence of the language, they have to recognize the rich metaphors, so they can draw upon this when they are trying to tell their students, "Now let's say this in another way, in Standard English." (Dalji & Miner, 1998, pp. 114–115)

While acknowledging and appreciating language differences is an essential first step in teaching Standard English, it is not always a comfortable position for monolingual teachers, who may be unfamiliar with other language forms. Teaching Standard English also has ideological and social implications that may cause discomfort for some teachers and students. To be blunt, "It is difficult to talk about black language/Ebonics in a meaningful way without simultaneously talking about racism" (Meier, 1998b, p. 120).

English teacher Bob Fecho found this out when he read a poem by Nikki Giovanni with his African American students, who were initially offended that this writer, whom they assumed to be white, was making fun of their language (Fecho, 1998, 2000). Understanding that Giovanni was in fact an African American led Fecho and his students into a year-long study of language usage, during which students investigated and debated language differences both within and across cultures.

Teaching Standard English forms to linguistically diverse students can best be accomplished by comparing and analyzing different uses of language and by explicitly modeling and teaching standard conventions. Authors such as Alice Walker, Amy Tan, and Judith Ortiz Cofer, who effectively meld or switch between linguistic and rhetorical styles, help to illustrate language differences at the same time that they validate the multicultural power of language. It is much easier to explicitly compare language forms and make students aware of standard styles and conventions in an atmosphere in which language variation is celebrated rather than suppressed. Exercises in which students translate from one style to another, write in different voices or from different points of view and for different audiences, practice specific language forms or features, and read aloud from a variety of published and student-written texts all help to increase students' metacognitive awareness of language and expand their language power.

WRITING AND ENGLISH LANGUAGE LEARNERS Learning Standard English written forms is especially challenging for students who are still learning to hear and speak the language. However, ELLs are able to begin writing even as they are learning spoken English. Sarah Hudelson (1999) lists several widely accepted principles of second-language writing:

- Students need to be able to take risks and make mistakes.
- They need support through all phases of the writing process, including multiple drafts, revisions, and opportunities to share their writing with others.
- ELLs need practice writing for different purposes, including reflections on content learning, responses to literature, and inquiry writing.
- Reading different kinds of text, especially good expository writing, will have a positive influence on students' writing.
- Learning logs (described later) provide an excellent medium for ELLs to write informally about their content subjects.
- ELLs who have learned to write in their native language can transfer much of what they know about writing to English contexts. Writing development in both languages can be simultaneous and complementary.

Emphasizing the role that writing plays in second-language acquisition, Harklau (2002) has called for more research on this topic.

Writing and the Computer

The personal computer gets our vote as the most useful tool for the writer since the invention of papyrus. Because computers are now commonplace in schools at all levels and in many homes, increasingly more students are discovering new writing fluency and power as they become liberated from the physical constraints of paper and pencil. Part of this new writing fluency can be attributed to the fact that youth today are quite at ease when communicating in writing on the Internet. Teachers who recognize this fact are finding new ways to teach writing genres that are particularly relevant to their content areas.

Take for example the case of Glenn Beaumont, a teacher of 12-year-olds who believed that his students' unfamiliarity with written argumentation was at the root of the difficulty they were experiencing in learning to write persuasively. Working with Wendy Morgan, a researcher from a nearby university, Beaumont arranged for a series of chatroom sessions in which students engaged in online dialogue to converse about issues that were of importance to them (e.g., the school district's plan to set up a gender-segregated middle school). The school in which the students were enrolled was in a working-class neighborhood, and each classroom had six computers with Internet access. In the first few sessions, Beaumont's goal was to get the students to recognize the need to back up their assertions with facts, to listen to another person's point of view, and to evaluate the various arguments being made for their appropriateness and effectiveness. Later, he in-

TECHNOLOGY Tip

Writing Links
The following websites are maintained by Capital Community College, Hartford, CT:

Guide to grammar and writing
http://grammar.ccc.commnet.edu/grammar

Guide to writing research papers
www.ccc.commnet.edu/mla/

Guide to avoiding plagiarism
www.ccc.commnet.edu/mla/plagiarism.shtml

Purdue University's Online Writing Lab (OWL) for ELLs
http://owl.english.purdue.edu/handouts/esl/eslstudent.html#purdue

troduced other computer-mediated learning strategies to support the students' growing competency in justifying their arguments.

Although the outcomes were mixed, generally students demonstrated improvement in their persuasive writing from the first term to the second. From this online project, Morgan and Beaumont (2003) developed the following guidelines for other teachers interested in pursuing similar activities involving the computer and writing:

- First, become comfortable with the workings of chat-room environments yourself.
- Find "hot" topics with diverse justifiable positions.
- Model and encourage courteous acknowledgment of the views of others, requests for clarification of words and meanings, and so on.
- Trace and reward instances where students make concessions or change their point of view thoughtfully as a result of arguments made in the course of the dialogue.
- Be explicit in reminding students about the dialogic nature of argument and show them how to accommodate other points of view and incorporate the voices of others in their own subsequent writing.
- Find reasons for students to reframe and re-present their case. (p. 155)

Writing Activities for Content Areas

Writing in content areas may range from informal notes and jottings to lengthy formal research reports, complete with footnotes and bibliography. In the following sections, we describe some of the useful writing activities that content teachers use.

Go to MyEducationLab and select the topic *Writing*. Then, go to the Activities and Applications section, watch the video entitled "Writing in Science," and respond to the accompanying prompts.

Writing Assignments

A student's successful writing experience begins with a good writing assignment. When an assignment is precise and specific and offers the writer appropriate guidance, he or she is more likely to produce a satisfactory product. Five elements of an assignment can be crafted to heighten student involvement and interest and to avoid frustration and confusion:

1. *Choosing a topic.* Writing is hard work, and enthusiasm can be especially hard to maintain when the topic is of little or no interest to the writer. The more discretion a student has in selecting what to write about, the more care and effort he or she is likely to invest in writing. In content area classes, it is usually necessary for the teacher to specify a general topic related to the area of study. However, there are still many ways to allow student choice. In the examples presented earlier, the sixth-grade scientists chose the topics for their adventure stories, and the writers in the high school history class chose the event and point of view they presented at the round table.

2. *Specifying an audience and purpose for writing.* Writers need experience with writing for a variety of realistic purposes and for audiences other than the teacher (Graham & Perin (2007). The sixth graders were writing to explain one area of science to a general, uninitiated audience and specifically to younger students who would be in sixth grade the next year. The high school students were writing as advocates of a particular point of view to an audience of their peers. If writers have a purpose and audience in mind, they can decide what information is needed, what voice or stance to take, and what will best meet the needs of their readers.

3. *Writing in varied modes.* There are many forms that content area writing can take. Students gain competence and avoid boredom when they have opportunities to write in different formats. (See Figure 10.2 for some possibilities.)

4. *Accommodating the writing process.* Students will need help and guidance with the various phases of the writing process. This means supporting students' prewriting decisions and data collection, allowing sufficient time for drafting and revising, and providing opportunities for teacher and peer conferences to aid revision. Supplying the necessary guidance implies that some in-class time will be used for working on the assignment.

5. *Guiding students' writing.* Students can be overwhelmed and dismayed by all the work and potential for frustration and failure built into a writing assignment that comes with a lengthy list of specifications and requirements. Instead of springing all this detail on them at once, the teacher can introduce a writing project in increments while offering guidance at each stage. Discussion, brainstorming, and semantic webbing facilitate student engagement and planning during the introduction of an assignment. Data collection, drafting, conferencing, and editing can be supported by the teacher-designed guides discussed in this chapter.

Graham and Perin (2007) make a number of recommendations for effective writing instruction:

- Teach students strategies for planning, revising, and editing their writing.

Journals or diaries	Memos
Fiction:	Poems
Fantasy	Scripts:
Historical	Plays
Adventure	Radio
Science fiction	Television
Choose-your-own-adventure	Prophecies, preditions, visions
Children's books	Newspaper writing:
Picture books	Articles
Dictionaries	Editorials
Fact books	Features
How-to books	Advertisements
Biographies	Proposals
Letters to real or imaginary people	Social programs
Dialogues and conversations	Grants
Thumbnail sketches of:	Research
People	Construction
Places	Position papers and responses
Important concepts	Reviews of:
Historical events	Books
Requests	Movies and TV shows
Job descriptions	Recordings
Applications and resumés	Performances
Acceptance or rejection letters	Math:
Research reports	Word problems
Science:	Problem solutions
Observations	Practical applications
Notebook	Cartoons
Lab reports	Debates
Hypotheses	Songs and raps
Interviews (real and imaginary)	Games and puzzles
Photos and captions	Posters, displays, collages
Recipes	Instructions or directories
Catalogs	Travelogues
Obituaries, epitaphs, eulogies	Quick writes

FIGURE 10.2   Possible Modes for Content Area Writing

Source: Adapted from S. Tschudi & J. Yates, *Teaching writing in the content areas: Senior high school.*
Washington, DC: National Education Association, 1983.

- Teach students how to summarize text. This is particularly effective in content areas such as social studies and science, where text tends to be abstract and conceptually dense.

- Involve students in collaborative writing activities, in which they plan, draft, revise, and edit compositions in small groups.

- Have students create specific products, and provide clearly delineated goals for these products.

- Use computers and word processors in the writing process. Doing so makes multiple revisions and editing less painful and more efficient.
- Teach students to produce more complex sentences through the use of sentence combining.
- Engage students in prewriting activities to help them generate and/or organize ideas for writing.
- Use inquiry activities to present particularly rich opportunities for authentic writing.
- Take a process approach to writing, even in mathematics (Fernsten, 2007). Doing so provides extended opportunities for students to develop writing skills as well as content knowledge.
- Study models of good writing, which can be found in all the content areas. Having students explore the characteristics of good models of writing in a variety of disciplines can help them develop habits in writing for specific disciplines.
- Use writing as a tool for learning content.

As you read about and try the various strategies for writing across the curriculum described in this chapter, keep these elements of good writing instruction in mind.

Helping
Struggling Readers

Scaffolding Writing Instruction

Writing instruction for struggling adolescent readers has become a focal point as a result of new accountability systems on writing and evidence of achievement gains when students refine their writing in the course of several drafts.

Working from this information and a gradual-release model of instruction, Doug Fisher, a university-based instructor, accepted an invitation to co-teach a ninth-grade section on genre studies at an urban high school in San Diego (Fisher & Frey, 2003). The students in the class were all reading significantly below grade level and had to pass the genre

studies class to become eligible to enroll in an English class. Using an idea popularized in the movie *Finding Forrester* (Wolf, King, & Van Sant, 2000), Fisher asked his class of struggling readers to use a piece of writing from a well-known author's previously published work as a scaffold for creating their own original writing. This scaffold, which is consistent with a gradual-release model of instruction in that it provided support as students took on more responsibility for their own writing, resulted in increased writing and reading achievement for the class. Moreover, 19 of the 24 students made enough progress to transfer into an English I class by midyear.

RAFT ASSIGNMENTS   The acronym *RAFT* can help a teacher plan successful writing assignments by varying some of the elements discussed previously (Santa, Havens, & Harrison, 1996). The letters stand for *Role, Audience, Format,* and *Topic.* A writer might take many roles: reporter, scientist, famous historical figure, a character from a story, an animal, or even an inanimate object. In a given role, the writer may address a variety of real or imaginary audiences. The format may be a poem, a letter, or any of the other modes listed in Figure 10.2.

We have recently adapted RAFT to RAFT[2]—Role, Audience, Format, Topic, Task. The assignment should include a task in the form of a strong verb such as *persuade, compare, describe,* or *explain,* which will help the writer understand the tone and purpose of the writing. When studying fractions, for example, math students might write a want ad for an improper fraction or a letter from the numerator to the denominator explaining why it is the most important part of the fraction.

A word of caution is necessary concerning RAFT[2] assignments. The purpose of using a planning device such as RAFT[2] is to increase student motivation and interest in a writing assignment and to devise writing assignments that vary from the traditional student essay written for the teacher. As we have said, good writing, especially good academic writing, requires hard work. Writers are likely to invest the most effort and motivation in topics that hold strong personal interest (Graves, 1983). A role or topic that may seem creative to one person may hold little attraction to another. Not every student will be eager to write from the point of view of a rain forest animal, Captain Ahab's second mate, the unknown variable in a two-step equation, or a red blood cell traveling through the circulatory system. One possibility is to develop assignments that allow students to choose from more than one possible role, audience, format, or topic. Another is to let students assist in determining possible roles, audiences, and so on.

Evidence-
Based
Research

An example of a RAFT[2] assignment is seen in Figure 10.3. This RAFT[2] asked students to choose a role as one of the vocabulary terms being studied (mode, mean,

---

Dear Outlier:

I was just wondering why you feel that you're different—you are so standoffish! You stake out a place so far away from everyone else that is messes up our fun. We do appreciate, however, the fact that you show up. Your friend, mode, never shows up unless he brings his twin brothers along, even when they aren't invited. As for mean, we've heard so much about her that we'd really love to meet her. We're beginning to think she doesn't really exist. She only shows up after we all come and go.

We're having a big party here in the middle next week. Ask your girlfriend if she'll let you off the leash to join "sum" of your colleagues for "sum" fun.

Sincerely,

Median

FIGURE 10.3   Sample RAFT[2] Written by English Majors in a Content Reading Class in Response to a Math Lesson

median, outlier), and write a friendly letter to an audience of another of the vocabulary terms on the topic of measures of central tendency. The task was to show that they understood each of the three types of measures of central tendency and how they were related to each other. This example was written by English majors in Victoria's content area reading class in response to a lesson on measures of central tendency in mathematics.

Figure 10.4 illustrates another adaptation of RAFT[2]. Alan Crawford, who invented this RAFT version, calls it Reciprocal RAFT (personal communication, January 26, 2004), one in which two groups write to each other. The example provided was written by Guatemalan teachers who were participants in the Guatemalan Reading and Writing for Critical Thinking project. In the first communication, the role assumed by the writers was indigenous Guatemalans writing to an audience of Spain to protest that country's treatment of them (topic and task). The answer from Spain (the reciprocal part) chastises the Guatemalans for being ungrateful for all the wonderful things Spain has done for them, a tongue-in-cheek reply.

Learning Logs and Journals

Evidence-Based Research

Learning logs, or content area journals, have been enthusiastically and effectively adopted by many content area teachers in both middle and secondary schools. For instance, eleven- to thirteen-year-old math students who wrote in their math journals for seven to ten minutes three times a week over twelve weeks showed improvement in their conceptual understanding, procedural knowledge, and math communication compared to a similar group that did practice problems instead of journal writing (Jurdak & Abu Zein, 1998). Such journaling is among the most frequently recommended strategies for helping students learn English as a second language (Ardizzone, 1992; Arthur, 1991; Dolly, 1990).

As mentioned in Chapter 6, learning logs are notebooks that are dedicated to informal writing, note taking, and musing on content area subjects. Regular log entries give students opportunities for risk-free reflection. The log is a place for students to try out ideas, to put their thoughts down on paper so they can see what is there, and to develop writing fluency that can transfer to other written assignments. Learning logs are also good platforms for prewriting and drafting. Some of what students write in their logs may eventually find its way into their more formal writing. They can be excellent resources when reviewing for a quiz or test, and students might even be allowed to consult their learning logs as "lifeline" resources during an examination. Learning logs also constitute a valuable record of student growth and learning over a marking period, a semester, or a year.

What students actually write in their logs varies widely. Entry topics can be specified by the teacher or left entirely to the student. Almost certainly, teachers will need to suggest topics or questions at first. Figure 10.5 lists some generic prompts that you could tailor to your subject area. *Process entries* generally ask students to reflect on *how* they have learned; *reaction entries* focus more on *what* they have learned. We think both kinds of prompts are useful, even though the distinction between the two may get blurred in students' writing.

Initial letter of protest from indigenous Guatemalans:

Pergamino de Protesta

Guatemala hacia España:

Haz dejado mis arcas vacias.

Haz sometido a mi raza a tus viles deseos.

Haz derramado la sangre bendita de mis hijos.

Haz alterado la paz de mi suelo.

Haz cambiado sus ideales religiosos.

Y hoy, hoy España, nuestra Patria lamenta tu traicióal haber mancillado nuestra libertad.

Miriam de Serech

Edna Portales de Núñez

Letter of reply from Spain:

Derecho de Respuesta al Pergamino de Protesta de aEspaña aGuatemala.

¡Que poco reconocimiento al esfuerzo conjunto, tenza y audaz de mi gente!

¿Acaso fue fácil ingresar a un inhóspita lugar, para llevar civilización?

¡Deciis que cambiamos vuestros ideales y libertad! ¡y de qué libertad hablais? Si ni siquiera pensamiento critico teniais.

¡Deciaiis que vaciamos vuestras arcas! Pero si quereis saber, fueron ustedes quienes nos las entregaron a manos llenas, con una sonrisa de oreja a oreja, después qye nosotros les dimos los espejito!

¿De qué paz hablais?, si cuando llegamos a estas tierras matándose ustedes estaban entre si.

¡Traición! ¡De qué traición hablais? Más dijera yo, ¡Agradecidos deberiais estar por los animales, alimentos, idioma y muchos ostros beneficios más que hemos traido, de los que hoy disfrutais.

¡Que Dios les perdone por tanto odio que guardais en vuestros corazones! ¿Sabeis una cosa? El odio es un sentimiento muy malo que hace mucho daño a vuestro organismo y a nada bueno os conduce, más bien enfermedades vais a tener.

Chichicastenago 4-2-2,002

Miriam de León

Olga de Motta

Maria Luisa Salazar

FIGURE 10.4 **Example of a Reciprocal RAFT Written by Participants in the Reading and Writing for Critical Thinking Project in Guatemala**

Dirnberger, McCullagh, and Howick (2005) suggest using a *naturalist's journal*, much like that of Meriwether Lewis during the Corps of Discovery exploration of the Louisiana Purchase, in which students record observations, sketches, diagrams, maps, and other representations of data. Journals and learning logs have been suggested in

Process Entries	Reaction Entries
What did I understand about the work we did in class today?	If I were the teacher, what questions would I ask about this assignment, chapter, etc.?
What didn't I understand? What was confusing?	Explain a theory, concept, vocabulary term, etc., to another person.
What problems did I have with a text assignment?	Free-writing: simply write for 5–10 minutes about a specific topic, whatever comes into the writer's mind.
How did I solve a problem with understanding, vocabulary, text, etc.?	
At what point did I get confused?	Summarize, analyze, synthesize, compare and contrast, evaluate an idea, topic, event, person, etc.
What did I like or dislike today?	
What questions do I have about what we did today?	Connection with prior knowledge or experience.
Notes, lists, or jottings relevant to my upcoming assignments.	"Unsent letters" to people, living or dead, historical or mythical, about topic of study.
My reflections on cooperative-learning group processes—what did or didn't work and why, my role, the roles of other participants.	Doodles; words and pictures that reflect feelings or thoughts on a topic.
My predictions and expectations about a new topic.	Response to higher-order questions posed by the teacher.
What was the most difficult homework problem? What made it so difficult?	Reread a log entry from last week. Write a reaction to what was written.

FIGURE 10.5 **Sample Prompts for Students' Learning Log Entries**

mathematics as a way to support the NCTM communication standard and to help students acquire mathematical habits of mind (McIntosh & Draper, 2001; Williams & Wynne, 2000). Williams and Wynne (2000) conducted a year-long inquiry into the use of journals in their respective high school classrooms. They suggest allowing 10 minutes of writing time when students are provided a prompt and expected to complete the journal entry outside class.

Some students may need more support than a prompt. Forms for a number of types of learning logs may be found online at the Strategic Literacy Initiative website (www .wested.org/cs/sli/print/docs/842). One kind of learning log we particularly like is the metacognitive reading log, which is intended for outside reading in science but can easily be adapted for other disciplines. The Strategic Literacy Initiative provides resources for reading and writing in science, mathematics, and social studies on its website (www .wested.org/cs/sli/print/docs/685).

The *double-entry journal* is another variation on content area learning logs (Bromley, 1993; Fretzin, 1992). In a double-entry journal, the writer either draws a line down the middle of the page or uses two facing pages. The left-hand side is used to jot down a stimulus for thought. This could be a personal experience, a quotation from a book, something said in class, a new vocabulary term, or an important issue or concept. On the right side, the writer can enter his or her reactions, thoughts, and feelings. At first, teachers can provide prompts for the left side of the journal. When students become familiar with the double-entry format, they can be asked to find their own prompts.

The double-entry journal format can be used across all content areas. Math students could write out a particularly difficult problem on the left side and explain their solutions on the right. Physics students could state one of the laws of thermodynamics on the left side and describe one way in which it has practical application in their lives on the right. In literature study, readers could choose characters, plot events, figurative language, or specific quotations to include on the left side and record their personal interpretations or reactions on the right. The double-entry format could also be used to have students juxtapose pros and cons on an issue, causes and effects, or comparisons and contrasts, which would work well in social studies classes.

Pamela Carroll (2000) suggests a *triple-entry format* for journal writing. Writers make three columns or divide the page into thirds horizontally. The first space is used to note specific parts of the text that intrigued or amused them—words, phrases, or sentences, along with page numbers. The second space is used to note reactions to, questions about, or elaborations on the passages they have cited. The final space is reserved for a peer who reads the first two entries and then writes a response. This is most effective when students are given a few minutes following writing to converse in reader–responder pairs.

Many students may initially resist the idea of writing in a learning log, especially in science or math classes, in which writing is not traditionally required on a regular basis (Berenson & Carter, 1995). It may help to begin learning log writing with feeling-type prompts that have no right or wrong answers and to move on to more conceptually oriented prompts after students have become used to the routine of learning log writing. Learning log entries will be longer and more thoughtful if you talk with the class about what they might write, specify your expectations for their learning log writing, and model entries that have been written by other students. Finally, it will help to set a timer or to have a specific time period each day or week dedicated to learning log writing.

A learning log is an excellent repository for all sorts of miscellanea. Students may use their logs to take lecture notes, to keep procedural and observational notes during labs, and to jot down new or essential vocabulary. If they are assigned reading beyond their textbooks, reactions can be noted in their logs. They may jot down quotations from their reading, their classmates, or the teacher. They can copy discussion webs or other graphic representations from the board, or they can create their own webs in the log.

Teachers have worked out different strategies for keeping track of students' learning log entries. When one or two class sections are writing in logs, it is easy to review entries on a weekly or biweekly basis. Multiple sections can turn in their logs on a staggered schedule. If teachers regularly review student logs, they get a sense of what is or is not working, both for individual students and for a whole class, and students see that the logs are important to the teacher.

Reading student logs does not have to be a Herculean task. Because learning logs contain unfinished writing, the teacher should not be assigning a qualitative grade or marking mechanics. Log entries can be a messy mixture of trash and treasure, so a quick, impressionistic reading is usually sufficient to ferret out the important parts and ensure that the writer is making the expected effort. Gradebook credit can be given on a pass/fail basis for making regular entries.

Another approach to evaluating learning logs promotes students' reflections on their own learning. At the end of the grading period, teachers can have students reread their entries, select one or more that exemplify their best thinking, and put a title to only these entries. Having students flag these entries with sticky notes will help teachers quickly locate them. Whether students select one or several entries for the teacher to read is his or her choice. Students should number pages, create a table of contents, and write an introduction in which they explain how they have used the journal/learning log and why they chose specific entries for the teacher to read. The grade can come primarily from "bean counting"—giving points for having numbered pages, created a table of contents, and so on.

When Victoria taught physical science in junior high, she graded students' learning logs each quarter. She would take a week, and each day she would evaluate the learning logs from one class, making brief responses to the entries students had selected to be read.

Responding to log entries is a matter of choice. A checkmark or a word or two in the margin may be enough. A teacher who prefers not to write directly in the students' logs can use sticky notes. Occasional elaborated responses to questions or observations will motivate students and make the learning log a more meaningful tool. Teachers sometimes use logs to conduct ongoing dialogues with students, and they find that this promotes a type of teacher–student communication that otherwise would not occur in daily classroom exchanges (Atwell, 1998). Mason and McFeetors (2002) suggest *interactive writing* in mathematics, a dialogue journal between the students and teacher, to help students develop mathematical knowledge, solve problems, and allow the teacher to see where misunderstandings occur.

Martha Dolly (1990) points out that when teacher and students carry on a dialogue in this manner, the learning log becomes a reading activity as well as a writing one for students. She says that this intertwining of reading and writing is especially beneficial for ELLs, since it makes literacy both active and functional. Students who struggle with formal reading and writing assignments find the exchange of questions, answers, and observations stimulating.

Other Informal Writing Activities

Students can engage in informal, unfinished writing activities even if they do not keep learning logs. A teacher could use the first five minutes of class for a writing warm-up, based on one of the prompts listed in Figure 10.5. A teacher can assign brief "Entrance visas" to be written outside class and handed in at the beginning of the next class period. "Exit visas" can be written in class and collected from students at the end of the period.

Another simple writing-to-reflect activity, often called *think-writes* in science, mathematics, and social studies (Mayher, Lester, & Pradl, 1983) and termed *free writes* in English, can be used at the beginning, middle, or end of a lesson or a unit. Students can compare their free-writing products in groups or free-write for five minutes as a follow-up to group work.

What students do after writing is an essential element in the success of an informal writing activity (Tierney, Readence, & Dishner, 2000). They need an opportunity to share their written responses so that they can see how others have interpreted the reading. This reinforces the understanding that a variety of responses are possible. When teachers write and share their responses with students, they add their experience to the discussion and serve as good reflective models.

Another informal writing activity called *writing roulette* (Bean, 1992) can be used to reinforce content area vocabulary. The teacher provides a simple story structure consisting of three elements: a setting and a character, a problem or goal for the character, and a resolution. Students are told they must use and underline at least one word from their content unit in each section of the story. Students begin writing about the setting and character and continue for a specified time, perhaps five minutes. When the time is up, papers are exchanged within a small group, and a new time limit is set. Each student reads the paper he or she received and writes the problem section of the story. Papers are exchanged a final time so that a third student writes the resolution. The finished stories are then returned to the original authors, who share them with the small group.

RESPONSE HEURISTIC   Response Heuristic (Bleich, cited in Tierney & Readence, 2000) is a strategy that guides student response to learning. It is particularly well suited to poetry and to literature rich with figurative language. When using Response Heuristic, students are guided to make three levels of response using a three-column grid:

1. *Text perceptions:*   The reader records important information. Sometimes you may want students to record direct quotes, as in the example below. "As you read, jot down any words or phrases that you find interesting or that you think are particularly important." This is essentially a literal-level response.

2. *Reactions:*   The reader tells what she or he thinks or feels about the text or what the author is trying to say. "What does this mean? How does it make you feel?" This is an interpretive-level response.

3. *Associations:*   The reader makes connections between the text and personal knowledge, prior knowledge, and beliefs. "What else does this selection call to mind? Does this remind you of anything you have experienced?" This is an application-level response.

Victoria remembers one English class studying Zora Neale Hurston's *Their Eyes Were Watching God*. The student teacher she was observing used Response Heuristic to guide her students' interpretation of the novel. She asked students to read a selection from the text and record a quote from the book that struck them as interesting, amused them, or was for some reason noticed by them. One of the concepts she was emphasizing was figurative language, and this strategy was particularly effective in teaching students how to understand figurative language. An example of Victoria's response is illustrated below:

Quote from text	Author's meaning	Your associations
"Women are the mules of the world"	I think Hurston means that women do most of the work in the world but don't get credit for it. I think she also intends to illustrate that men think women are dumb and stubborn, as mules are usually portrayed.	It makes me think of myself, working full time both at home (cleaning, cooking, buying groceries, etc.) and teaching school when my husband was in graduate school. He went to class (on occasion) and did a lot of hunting and fishing on weekends, while I took care of laundry!

What students do *after* writing is an essential element in this strategy. Students need an opportunity to share their responses so that they can see the variety of responses to the text. When teachers write and share their responses with students, they provide a valuable model for students. Response Heuristic can be adapted to suit other content areas as well. For example, in a history class, you could emphasize the residual effects of events in history by using the following column headings: Event—Immediate Effect/Result—Residual Result.

Reviewing and Summarizing

Go to MyEducationLab and select the topic *Writing*. Then, go to the Activities and Applications section, watch the video entitled "Summarizing," and respond to the accompanying prompts.

Evidence-Based Research

Many students believe that if they have read each page, they have conscientiously fulfilled an assignment to "read Chapter 12." If there are no questions to answer, no reading guide to complete, they are content to let the teacher tell them in class what it all meant, or at least what was important. Consequently, their efforts at reading and learning are passive and less effective than if they had actively sought to consolidate what they had learned. They have omitted the final, integrative step in reading to learn—taking the time to review the text and summarize what was learned. Summarizing reinforces and consolidates the many processes involved in learning from text, such as determining important information, perceiving text structure, and drawing inferences.

Numerous studies have shown that students of varying ages benefit from learning how to produce written summaries of what they have read (Armbruster, Anderson, & Ostertag, 1987; Taylor & Beach, 1984). Hare and Borchardt (1984) found that summary writing was effective with urban African American and Hispanic high school students. In order to write a summary, a reader must know how to perform three basic processes (Hidi & Anderson, 1986):

1. Select and delete information.

2. Condense information by combining or by substituting a general term for a group of specific terms (e.g., *farm animals* instead of *horses, goats, pigs, and sheep*).

3. Transform the information into writing.

Although basic, these processes are hardly simple. As with other reading processes, students need to be shown how to summarize and need continual, long-term practice in order to effectively add summarizing to their repertoire of reading strategies.

STRATEGIES FOR TEACHING STUDENTS TO SUMMARIZE Hierarchical summaries, REAP, and GIST are three formal procedures for teaching summarization. Each has several useful features.

Hierarchical summaries are structured around the headings and subheadings found in most content area texts (Taylor & Beach, 1984). The procedure is as follows:

1. Students preview the reading selection with emphasis on headings, highlighted vocabulary, and other typographical cues.

2. Based on the preview, teacher and students together develop a skeleton outline that the teacher writes on the chalkboard, overhead projector, or projected computer screen.

3. Students read the text using the outline as a reading guide.

4. After reading, students compose main idea statements for main points in the outline and add essential supporting details, again with teacher guidance.

5. Finally, students develop a key idea or summarizing statement for the entire passage, which becomes the first sentence of the summary.

The hierarchical summary is a strategy that students can learn to use independently. The strategy depends, however, on the heading/subheading format of textbooks, and it would not be appropriate for narrative or other material that does not have clear graphic signals for important information and text organization.

REAP is an acronym for four stages in reading and understanding: *R*ead the text; *E*ncode into your own language; *A*nnotate by writing the message down; *P*onder, or think about, the message on your own and with others. Skilled readers make many different kinds of annotations. Sometimes they jot down a critical comment, a question, a note on the author's intentions, or a personal reaction. The simplest kind, though, is a summary annotation.

Eanet and Manzo (1976) suggest that students be introduced to summary annotations of paragraphs through a four-step sequence:

1. Show students a sample paragraph and a summary annotation. Explain what an annotation is and why readers might use annotations to help them understand and remember what they have read.

2. Show students another paragraph, this time with three annotations. One is a good summary, and the other two are flawed. Lead students to select the best summary and discover the problems with the other two.

3. Show students how to summarize by modeling the process for them with a third paragraph.

4. Have individual students develop their own summary annotations, and then in groups, analyze their summaries and combine ideas to come up with a concise and complete summary.

Evidence-Based Research

GIST stands for *Generating Interactions between Schemata and Text* (Cunningham, 1982). Using the GIST procedure, students produce progressively more condensed summaries of a text selection. To begin the GIST procedure, you need a short, coherent expository paragraph. You then proceed as follows:

1. Show students the first sentence of the paragraph, and ask them to retell it in 15 words or less. Write their summary on the chalkboard or overhead as they dictate and edit it as a group.

2. Show students the second sentence of the paragraph. Erase their first summary statement, and ask students to summarize both sentences in 15 words or less.

3. Continue this procedure, one sentence at a time, until the group has summarized the entire paragraph in 15 words or less.

4. Repeat this procedure as many times as necessary until students become adept. Then lead them to summarize an entire paragraph at one time, rather than sentence by sentence.

5. Finally, when the group has built some proficiency with the GIST procedure, have students produce summary statements individually.

All students need guided practice in summarizing before they can be expected to produce summaries independently. Initial efforts can be carried out in cooperative-learning settings to maximize student participation. Intermediate and middle-grade students and secondary students with lower reading ability will need several guided practice sessions, but they can take more responsibility for generating the outlines and summaries each time.

Teachers should not expect that students' independent efforts will be flawless, however. Summary writing is a difficult skill that requires plenty of practice. Implicit information and text passages that are long and complex will be especially problematic, even for relatively advanced students. Honors students and students with learning disabilities alike will struggle in learning how to summarize, as the writing examples in Figure 10.6 demonstrate.

Narrative text is generally easier to summarize than expository text, so it might be advisable to start inexperienced students with a short story in an English anthology or a chapter in a novel. If that is not practical, students will have the most initial success with relatively short passages of expository text, perhaps five or six paragraphs at most. Self-contained passages with explicitly stated main ideas and a clear structure will be the easiest to work with. For typical science, math, or social studies text material, this might

ADAM'S SUMMARY
(Adam is classified as learning disabled.)

(2) The souets our go Canee communiom
The presedent changed out
The cleabrated that they were
fire

JONATHON'S SUMMARY
(Jonathon is in an honors class.)

GOOD - BYE COMMUNISM

COMMUNISM IS WHEN THE GOVERNMENT CONTROLS EVERYTHING. THE

SOVIET UNION JUST GOT RID OF COMMUNISM. DURING THAT TIME

WHEN COMMUNISM RULED MANY REPUBLICANS TREATENS TO LEAVE

AND BECOME INDEPEND COUNTRES. THE GOVERNMENT CONTROLED WHAT

YOU WOULD GROW WHAT JOB YOU GOT WHAT TO BUY AND SO ON,

PEOPLE WANTED TO BE FREE, THEY WANTED TO BE ABLE TO DO WHAT

THEY WANTED TO. NOW THAT COMMUNISM IS OVER THEY ARE FACING

PROBLEMS. THEY NEED MORE FOOD FOR THE PEOPLE OTHER

COUNTRIES ARE GIVING SUPPORT SUCH AS FOOD SUPPLIES AND SO ON

**FIGURE 10.6   Sample Summaries of a Social Studies Reading by
Two Seventh Graders**

mean working with a single important subsection of a chapter, perhaps a page or two in length. Able high school readers can be expected to work with longer selections of text.

The main ideas may seem obvious to us as expert readers and summarizers, but students learning how to summarize may pick out ideas that are personally important or interesting to them instead of trying to find the main ideas in the text. Therefore, it is helpful to point out that a summary should try to capture the ideas that would probably be important to the author (Anderson & Hidi, 1988/1989). Students who are learning

Evidence-
Based
Research

Helping Struggling Readers

Summarizing

There are important developmental differences in the way students summarize (Anderson & Hidi, 1988/1989; Hill, 1991; Paris, Wasik, & Turner, 1991). The variability of summarizing skill within a single grade level is illustrated by the contrasting examples from two seventh graders in Figure 10.6. The students read an article, "Good-bye Communism," in a current events newspaper. The teacher placed the following list of key words on the board: *communism, independence, coup,* and *economic crisis.* Students copied these words in their notebooks to guide them in writing a short summary of important events in the article. Both summaries capture the key idea, but Adam's is short and features only two additional details, with no connections among the information in the summary. Jonathon, on the other hand, includes several key ideas with direct support and provides definitions of key terms.

Like Adam, younger or less able readers have difficulty combining ideas, rearranging information, and translating ideas into their own words. Although most students know that a summary should include important information from a passage, struggling readers are less adept than good readers at identifying what is important and are less likely to include important information in their summaries (Winograd, 1984).

For Adam, including the main idea of the article in his summary is a good beginning. For his next summary, his teacher might give him a shorter selection of text to work with and model for him how to elaborate on his main point, perhaps by asking himself "who," "what," and "why" questions. She could also pair Adam with a more able student or enlist the help of a resource teacher who could give Adam more practice and support in summarizing. Even though his skill level is quite different from Jonathon's, Adam should be able to improve his reading ability through summarizing.

how to summarize should also be allowed to work with a copy of the text to refer to. Summarizing requires careful consideration of the text, including rereading and checking for information. It is not an exercise in memorization.

Guiding Student Writing

Some content area teachers say that they are reluctant to assign writing because students' written products are often not very good. When students are asked to write on a topic from a reading assignment, many simply do not have enough experience to know how to proceed. They end up churning out a vague paragraph or two that can be as hard to read as it was to write. Of course, if students do not write much, they will not get any better, and a vicious circle becomes established. If teachers can give some support and structure to students' writing, the writing will be easier and the products should improve.

GUIDED WRITING PROCEDURE   The *guided writing procedure* (Smith & Bean, 1980; Konopak, Martin, & Martin, 1987) has six steps that can be implemented over two or three days:

1. Students brainstorm on their prior knowledge of a new topic.
2. As a class or in groups, students label their ideas and organize them into a semantic web or other graphic format.
3. Each student writes on the topic.
4. Students read the assigned text selection.
5. Based on their reading, students revise their original writing.
6. A brief quiz is given on the material.

As we mentioned earlier, this writing procedure has been successfully implemented with both middle-grade and high school students. Writers in both age groups produced fewer text-explicit details and more higher-level ideas than their peers who did not write before reading (Konopak, et al., 1990; Martin & Konopak, 1987).

The guided writing procedure is also effective with students who are developing proficiency in English (Reyes & Molner, 1991). The combination of oral language, reading, and writing helps linguistically diverse students synthesize their thinking and go beyond the highly structured grammar exercises that are characteristic of many ESL writing programs. Reyes and Molner (1991) recommend modifying this procedure to include cooperative-learning formats in which second-language learners can achieve greater success. They also caution that teachers should not overemphasize form and mechanics when reading ELLs' drafts.

Evidence-Based Research

WRITING GUIDES   When students write after studying a textbook chapter or unit or after reading a novel, they are able to pull many ideas together, see meaningful relationships, and consolidate what they have learned. When discussing writing assignments earlier, we said that a teacher can help students understand what and how to write by manipulating certain elements of the task. *Writing guides* constitute a good illustration of how this can be done.

In the writing guide shown in Figure 10.7, the teacher uses the format of a grant proposal to get students to write about what they have learned in their study of genetics. This format gives writers a clear purpose (to obtain a research grant) and a voice (formal and scientific) for their writing. The hints give students guidance about what should be included in their proposals. The teacher acknowledges the importance of revising and editing by asking each student to trade papers with a fellow scientist to make sure the proposal includes the important information and is free of errors in spelling or grammar.

SAME FACTS, DIFFERENT AUDIENCE   Lawrence Baines (2000) describes an activity that can be adapted to most content areas. To begin with, students are given a fact sheet related to a controversial or debatable topic in current events or their content area

WRITING GUIDE: GENETICS

Imagine you are Gregor Mendel's lab assistant. Pretend that you are writing an explanation of your findings so that you can receive a grant to further your research. Write a well-developed explanation of your findings from your experiments with pea plants. You should have a clear explanation of Mendel's research and a description of a Punnet square.

Hint: Remember that you are writing a scientific paper. Be sure to include and explain the following terms:

heredity	genetics	dominant
pure	hybrid	recessive
genotype	generation	genes
	phenotype	

Hint: Scientists are thorough people. Don't forget to explain the outcomes of each of the pairs below.

1. Two dominant genes

2. Two recessive genes

3. One dominant and one recessive gene

Give an example of the genotype and phenotype that result from each of the above combination.

Hint: Make sure you do not lose the grant because of silly grammatical errors or spelling mistakes. Trade papers with a friend. Ask him/her to be sure that you have clearly covered the necessary information.

FIGURE 10.7   Writing Guide for an Eighth-Grade Science Unit

Source: Reprinted by permission of Judith L. Stenroos, Buffalo Public Schools, #31, Buffalo, New York.

curriculum. After a class discussion of the fact sheet, students can be divided into groups of three or four and given a worksheet that lists different audiences and possible writing topics for each. Figure 10.8 gives an example for facts related to the sinking of the *Titanic* and subsequent discovery of the wreck. Each group should select three projects they would like to work on and make a plan for dividing up the labor.

After a day or two of in-class writing time, groups present their projects to the rest of the class, which gives them feedback on the effectiveness of the writing. This should be followed by a whole-class analysis of the different kinds of appeals that were used in the writing. The number of audiences and writing projects can be varied, and this could also be an individual writing activity instead of a cooperative group task.

SAME FACTS, DIFFERENT AUDIENCE

Directions: Select one project for each of the audiences.

1. Audience 1: Royal Maritime Commission appointed in 1912 to study the sinking.

   a. Write an investigative report that attempts to assign blame for the disaster.

   b. Write a series of recommendations for avoiding such accidents in the future.

2. Audience 2: Family members of victims.

   a. Write a letter from the steamship company expressing condolences.

   b. As an attorney, write a proposal for a lawsuit against one or more parties to the accident.

3. Audience 3; Contemporary *Titanic* fanatics.

   a. Write an advertising brochure for submersible trips to the wreck.

   b Write a proposal to ban further exploitation of the *Titanic* wreckage.

FIGURE 10.8 Same Facts, Different Audience Guide: The Wreck of the *Titanic*

CREATIVE WRITING You may believe that so-called creative writing is the exclusive province of the English or language arts teacher, but there are many forms of creative writing that lend themselves to other content areas. In fact, several kinds of fiction, such as science fiction and historical fiction, have been developed around concepts that come from those disciplines. You could use RAFT[2] to develop fiction-based writing assignments around ideas in your content areas.

Jokes, riddles, cartoons, songs and raps, and advertisements are other examples of creative writing that can be adapted to various content areas. Several poetry formats lend themselves to content areas, too. An *acrostic poem* spells out a key word or phrase with the first letter of each line, as in the following example written for a geography class studying Africa:

Shifting sand dunes
Across a vast area.
Harsh landscape with
Ancient highways.
Rain is scarce
And temperatures are high.

The *cinquain* is another poetry format that lends itself to writing in content areas. It is a five-line poem with a set number of syllables in each successive line. The syllable pattern is two-four-six-eight-two. The following is an example that incorporates concepts from a middle school earth science lesson:

> The moon (2)
> Reflects the sun, (4)
> Revolving 'round the earth, (6)
> Waxing and waning and pulling (8)
> The tides. (2)

The *biopoem* is frequently used as a beginning-of-the-year exercise to fire up the writing synapses and help students get acquainted with new classmates. The basic format can be adapted to include many facts and concepts focused on particular people, things, places, or events from various content areas. Figure 10.9 illustrates how an autobiographical biopoem and a biopoem based on a historical personage takes shape.

With a bit of revision to the prompts for the lines, biopoems can also be used in science, math, and other subjects. Figure 10.10 is an example of a biopoem Victoria created as a model for her physical science students when they were studying the periodic chart of the elements.

Another form of poetry that is well suited to social studies, specifically history, is the *found poem* (Harvey & Povletich, 1999), which is created from an existing text. In an English class, found poetry might be used to bridge from more familiar prose to poetry. Students could choose a personal journal entry or a descriptive or emotionally charged literature selection. In social studies, found poetry provides opportunities for students to process historical information, or "do history," as well as to develop creativity and writing skills. The procedure is made easier because primary source documents, such as letters and diaries, are available online at a number of sites. (See, for example, the Library of Congress's American Memory site at http://memory.loc.gov/ammem/index.html.)

Autobiographical Biopoem	Historical Personage Biopoem
Line 1: Your first name	Line 1: First name of subject
Line 2: Four adjectives that describe you	Line 2: Four adjectives that describe subject
Line 3: Resident of . . .	Line 3: Resident of . . .
Line 4: Son or daughter of . . .	Line 4: Lover of . . . (3 people, places, things)
Line 5: Brother or sister of . . .	Line 5: Who believed . . . (1 or more ideas)
Line 6: Lover of . . . (3 items)	Line 6: Who used . . . (3 methods or things)
Line 7: Who likes to . . . (3 things)	Line 7: Who wanted . . . (3 things)
Line 8: Who hates to . . . (2 things)	Line 8: Who said "_____" (Give a quote)
Line 9: Who would like to . . . (3 things)	Line 9: Who gave . . . (3 things)
Line 10: Your last name	Line 10: Last name of subject.

FIGURE 10.9 Biopoem Formats

Sodium

A reactive, soft solid metal, gray in color, an oxidizer

Sibling to Li and K

Lover of all halogens, especially Cl

Who feels explosive in the presence of water, producing a base as the result of the reaction

Who needs to get rid of one electron in order to have a complete outer electron shell

With an electron distributionof 2-8-1, you fear your own instability

Who gives one electron to its halogen compounds, forming ionic bonds

Provided with a willing recipient, you would love to get rid of that single outer electron

Resident of Group IA on the Periodic Chart of the Elements

Na

FIGURE 10.10 **Model of a Biopoem Written by Victoria for Physical Science Students**

Here are the steps for creating a found poem:

1. Select a historical document. Documents that are emotionally moving are the best sources for found poetry.

2. Provide copies for all students so they can underline words and phrases as you read the selection aloud to the class. Tell students to select the words and phrases that seem to be the most important ideas from the passage.

3. Provide students with sentence strips (three to five strips per students on average), on which students will record their words and phrases.

4. In small groups (two to four students), have students organize their sentence strips and create a poem. All the sentence strips can be used, regardless of repetition.

5. Have each group confer, revise, practice, and perform the poem it creates.

6. Revision techniques to consider include the following:

   - Consider line breaks and the overall structure of the poem. Create line breaks where the reader's voice naturally pauses, and add words if a line seems too choppy.

   - Make the first and last lines especially powerful.

   - Use space to create an effective visual presentation.

   - Use repetition to create emphasis and rhythm.

   - Add details to images to create vivid word pictures.

   - Consider the use of metaphors, similes, and other figures of speech.

Original Text . . .

"Law, I reckon I was born to work in a mill. I started when I was ten year old and I aim to keep right on jest as long as I'm able. I'd a-heap rather do it than housework. . . . Yessir, when I started down here to plant No. 1, I was so little I had to stand on a box to reach my work. I was a spinner at first, then I learned to spool. When they put in them new winding machines, I asked them to learn me how to work 'em and they did. If I'd a-been a man no telling how far I'd-a gone."

Found Poem

I was born to work in a mill.
I started when I was ten year old.
I was so little I had to stand on a box to reach my work.
I was a spinner at first,
then I learned to spool.
When they put in them new winding machines,
I asked them to learn me how to work 'em
And they did.
I was born to work in a mill.
I'd a-heap rather do it than housework.
If I'd a-been a man no telling how far I'd-a gone.

FIGURE 10.11 **Found Poem**

Source: The text of the recording is available at http://memory.loc.gov/ammem/wpaintro/alice.html.

Victoria models a found poem for her content area reading students before she asks them to create one. Figure 10.11 is an example of a found poem she created based on an audio recording available on the American Memory website. You may wish to go to the URL identified in the source note of the figure to hear the recording as you read the poem.

A variation on found poems is *found photographs*, which can be used as the basis for a poem, letter, newspaper article, or other appropriate writing in response to the picture. Photographs are particularly useful in writing for social studies and English. Photographs, maps, music, and audio recordings related to U.S. history, literature, the environment, architecture, and other topics can also be found at the American Memory website.

FANFICTION Reading trade books, comics, or graphic novels can provide the impulse for writing fanfiction. Writers of fanfiction (*fanfic* for short) take characters and situations from television, movies, manga and anime, video games, and books and create new stories.

Thousands of fanfic writers are sharing their stories on the Internet. One site, www.fanfiction.net, provides an extensive collection of fanfics organized into varied categories. Fanfiction.net also hosts forums for writers and readers to discuss the stories, and the site provides access to so-called beta readers, people who preview stories before they are posted for the general public and offer guidance and support to the writers. Specialized fanfic sites, such as http://fanfic.theforce.net, are dedicated to fanfics based on certain movies and books, such as *Star Wars*.

Fanfiction shares many of the characteristics of a new ethos that differentiates new literacies from traditional print literacies, especially school literacy (Lankshear & Knoble, 2006). Fanfic is interactive. Writers post drafts and stories online, where they are open to comments from readers. Because fanfic writers and readers are bound up in mutual appreciation and celebration, there is a communal aspect to this medium. Members of fanfic communities help and encourage each other. Fanfiction websites abound in guides and tips for writers and special help for "newbies," or writers just getting started. Some sites post "plot bunnies," ideas for stories that other writers are invited to try out. Finally, fanfiction is a platform for building and exploring identity—not just the development of fanfic characters but also the development of the individual as a participant in an online community (Chandler-Olcott & Mahar, 2003.)

How might the fanfic medium be used in school settings? Fanfic writing requires a sophisticated understanding of character, motivation, and plot, similar to that needed for sustained critical analysis of fiction or drama. However, fanfic is clearly different from more formal writing, in which collaboration is often frowned on and there is rarely time for the extended and intensive work that goes into much fanfic writing. Internet fanfic authors are also ardently enthusiastic about particular genres, stories, and characters. (*Fan* is, after all, a shortened version of *fanatic*.) That kind of passion cannot be assigned.

Lankshear and Knobel (2006) recommend that teachers spend some time browsing or even participating in fanfiction websites to get a feeling for how they work and then think about how aspects of this phenomenon might be integrated into school literacy. On a very simple level, fanfic might be a motivating alternative to the traditional book report. If teachers could also incorporate the aspects of interactivity, community, and identity building into the activity, they would be going a long way toward importing new literacies into the curriculum.

THE LIGHTER SIDE   Not all content-related writing need be serious. Playing with language is another useful creative outlet that can lighten the classroom atmosphere and promote language development. Jokes, puns, and satires have always been used to critique leaders, highlight social issues, and score points in public discourse.

Humorous writing, then, can serve a more serious purpose of engaging students in critical thinking about a topic. Students can write short pieces that feature humorous repetition, exaggeration, or unexpected associations (Weber, 2000). A class can brainstorm content-related top-ten lists or variations on Ten Things to Do with a Dead Cat. (Our apologies to cat lovers for this example; we are decidedly dog people.) Students might create wacky advertisements or want ads based on content area facts or concepts. Many other humorous variations are possible among the modes of content area writing listed in Figure 10.2.

Sydeana Martin (2000) suggests a tabloid exposé format that can be used to write about literature, history, scientific developments, or current events. This would start by sharing some humorous headlines with the class, either real or teacher created, typical of tabloids such as the *National Inquirer*. The teacher then introduces the topic, and

Helping
Struggling Readers

Too often, instruction for students with writing disabilities focuses heavily on drill with spelling and mechanics. This narrow concentration, added to the difficulties that struggling writers have with handwriting, organization, and sustaining fluency, means that they often do very little actual writing.

Bernice Wong and associates (Wong, 1997; Wong et al., 1997) have shown that a three-phase instructional process can lead to significant improvement in the writing of adolescents with learning disabilities. The three phases are as follow:

1. Teacher modeling of specific expository genres combined with collaborative planning

2. Drafting at a word processor, which helps to attenuate handwriting, spelling, and fluency problems

3. Revising with peer and teacher conferences

In an instructional study, Wong et al. (1997) gave explicit instruction in writing compare-and-contrast essays to 21 struggling adolescent writers. After writing six compare-and-contrast essays, these students demonstrated significantly improved clarity and organization and utilization of facts and details to support comparisons and contrasts. Wong and associates credited this success to their explicit focus on a single genre, to the intensity of the instruction, and to the interactive dialogues among teachers and peers.

students brainstorm tabloid headlines. Finally, students take the role of tabloid reporter and write up the topic in tabloid style.

In chemistry, Ron DeLorenzo (1999) uses tongue-in-cheek mystery titles to engage student interest, build communication skills, and illustrate important science concepts. For example, he gives a detailed analysis of the temperature of hell (slightly above 246°F based on biblical reference and scientific fact, according to DeLorenzo). Other mystery topics include the following: Why do humans kiss? How can sand predict earthquakes? Why do ice cream and car batteries explode? Why is electricity free in the winter? Given some hints and guidance, students can write their own solutions to these mysteries. They can also create their own science mysteries.

Julia Barnes (1999) uses creative writing in trigonometry as she poses humorous problems for students to solve and then write about in a variety of forms. One problem involves linear velocity, the ability to convert units, and critical thinking about a character named Jethro driving a pickup truck that crashes into a telephone pole. Evidence involved in the crash includes a helicopter traffic cop who times the accident and Billy Bob's video, which is intended for *America's Funniest Home Videos*. Students are asked to investigate the case, determine whether Jethro was speeding, and then decide whether to be the prosecuting or defending attorney. After choosing which side of the case they will support, students write a case for the court, in which they explain the evidence and build an argument using mathematics. Another problem involves snoring pigs and a napping farmer. Although humorous, the problems involve students in solving complex problems and presenting their solutions in unique formats.

Writing to Inquire

We are living in what is sometimes called the Information Age and are witnessing the rapid expansion of knowledge across many disparate fields. What is taught in science, social studies, and mathematics will almost certainly change dramatically over the next decade. In an age of rapidly changing and expanding knowledge, a well-educated person must have the ability to inquire into a topic—to investigate it, read about it, think about it, and communicate about it.

All too often we find that when students in our teacher education courses reflect on their own experiences in writing a report when they were youngsters, they recall a scenario not unlike that told by Amy Haysman. As you read this excerpt from Amy's reflections, think about the problems she encountered and what specialized skills she needed to write her report:

> The one research report that really impacted my life was due on January 30, 1984. I don't think I will ever forget that date or the term paper assignment I turned into Mrs. Hudson on that cold, dreary morning. When my ninth-grade teacher had first presented this assignment in class, I was excited. I was all grown up now! I was in high school and had finally been told to do the famous, dreaded task of writing a term paper. . . . I was given a slip of paper that said, "The characterization of Lady Macbeth in *Macbeth*." "Was I supposed to know what this means?" I thought to myself. Suddenly, this coming-of-age assignment wasn't too appealing. Luckily, my teacher anticipated my panic attack and told everybody not to worry because she planned to teach us how to do the research step by step. Writing the paper was then up to us.
>
> For the next few weeks, Mrs. Hudson led the class, page by grueling page, through a 38-page folder entitled "The Term Paper: A Guide to Research, Documentation, and Format." We were then set loose in the school library. . . . After countless hours in several libraries, I had compiled a stack of note cards too big to fit in even a jumbo-size rubber band. I decided it was time to stop researching and start writing. As I read my note cards, I realized two problems. One, I didn't really understand what was written on these cards from the 13 books I had quoted, and two, I really had no idea how to write this paper. I had not learned anything about the characterization of Lady Macbeth in my frenzy to take notes and write bibliography cards in the correct form.*

Chances are, this scenario brought back vivid memories of the term paper, one of the most dreaded of all school projects for students and teachers alike. One obvious

---

*Reprinted by permission of Amy P. Haysman.

problem for Amy was her assigned topic. Perhaps if her teacher had considered aspects of an assignment represented by the RAFT[2] acronym, she might have had a better idea of why she was writing, what she was writing about, and for whom she was writing. When students are sent forth to "do research" for little more reason than it is ninth grade and the term paper is part of the ninth-grade curriculum, the results are too often exactly as Amy describes them.

Evidence-Based Research

One way to make writing to inquire more authentic and engaging is to consider how professionals in various content areas use writing. In a study of the writing of five research scientists, Debby Deal (1999) found that they used a progressive combination of expressive writing (personal, tentative, and meant primarily for themselves) and transactional writing (more formal, structured, and intended to communicate ideas to others) as they moved from the early stages of designing an experiment, through data collection and analysis, to the final preparation of a report to a funding agency or an article for a professional journal.

Carolyn Keys (1999) argues that science students need to be engaged in authentic scientific writing, which she says should involve the production of new knowledge. Traditional scientific genres that promote scientific thinking include the following:

1. Writing about experiments that are student designed or that may yield more than one data set
2. Writing explanations of scientific phenomena and processes
3. Writing reports based on secondhand sources
4. Biographies of one or a group of scientists
5. Persuasive expository writing on a controversial topic, such as whether dinosaurs are warm or cold blooded

Authentic historical inquiry should help students understand that history is not just a dry, noncontroversial recitation of facts, dates, and names but rather a frequently contentious interpretation of diverse perspectives and experiences with direct relevance to our contemporary lives. Therefore, students of history need to be guided to ask authentic questions, select and examine a variety of evidence, appreciate the context of historical events, evaluate divergent perspectives, and reach logical (albeit tentative) conclusions (Foster & Padgett, 1999).

Catherine Miller (2000) involves her math students in an inquiry into problem solving. Students are provided six problems to use in their research. They select participants (neighbors, parents, and siblings, if not too young) and then record their observations of how each participant solves a chosen problem. Students share and make sense of their data in class and then generate lists of problem-solving strategies and positive and negative behaviors exhibited by the participants as they solved the problem. Students then create posters for the classroom, which serve as reminders of effective strategies for students during the year and can be added to as students discover new problem-solving strategies.

Preparing for Student Inquiry

Asking students to embark on an extended inquiry project requires thoughtful planning and guidance. We suggest some general planning parameters here and describe more specific strategies in following sections.

Preparation should begin well before the assignment is explained and topics are selected. First, teachers need to decide on a conceptual framework within which students will select topics. By narrowing the scope of possible topic selection, teachers can do more advance preparation. They can alert media center colleagues and begin to identify resources. By placing some limits on the range of topics, teachers will be in a better position to provide resources and assistance as students pursue their research.

Establishing an overall theme for inquiry also makes it possible to build appropriate background through lecture, audiovisuals, read-aloud selections from literary works or nonfiction, primary sources, and guest speakers. For example, Cena and Mitchell (1998) describe how they began a research unit on the Middle Ages by showing a PBS video based on David Macaulay's book *Cathedral* (1973). After seeing the video and reading the book, students were able to suggest several major themes related to life in the Middle Ages, including technology of building construction, social class distinctions, the arts, and the roles of religion, politics, and economics.

Once students understand the general issues related to their research theme, they can begin to brainstorm specific questions to investigate. Teachers should encourage reflection on the suitability of these topics—whether they are too narrow or too broad, whether the question is open or closed, and whether there are likely to be sufficient resources available for their inquiry.

As students embark on their inquiries, teachers may need to provide varied kinds of assistance. Directing students to appropriate resources, including people to interview, print sources, CD-ROMs, and websites, is a given. Students may also need guidance on how to evaluate their resources. Minilessons might cover any of a number of research skills that will facilitate inquiry.

- Note taking
- Using indexes and tables of contents to pinpoint needed information
- Generating search terms for online indexes and the Internet
- Interpreting a "results" page from an Internet search
- Organizing gathered information and putting it into readable form
- Applying appropriate citation techniques
- Understanding stylistic requirements for final reports

Throughout the inquiry process, from brainstorming topics to preparation of a final draft, teachers should encourage students to share their work with each other. This kind of peer collaboration and feedback was an important part of the inquiry process of the scientists interviewed by Deal (1999).

A final consideration in planning for student inquiry is time. Not only should teachers allow sufficient time for research and writing, but they should also establish reasonable deadlines for various stages of the inquiry process, such as topic selection, identifying resources, developing an outline, beginning a draft, and completing a draft. Teachers can monitor student progress with a checklist or by periodically looking at student research logs. Meaningful inquiry takes a good deal of time for professionals, so it would be difficult to expect much less from apprentices.

Although much of the inquiry process can be done outside class, it is reasonable to expect that concentrated periods of class time will be devoted to students' research. For instance, the early stages of inquiry might require a few days to get everybody started. Then, a specified day each week might be devoted to student projects, with two or three days reserved for the final stages of preparation and presentation.

Collecting and Organizing Information

The following two techniques for collecting and organizing information, when introduced to your students over a reasonable period of time, will keep them from experiencing some of the same frustrations Amy felt when it came time to write her paper.

RESEARCH OR THREE-SEARCH?   Term papers can be as vexing to the teacher who has to read them as they are to the students who have to write them. For example, consider Terry Phelps's (1992) recollections:

> After years of grading research papers, I began to question their value. To begin with, I hated reading the wretched things. They were usually boring strings of quotes with none of the students' own thoughts. Most students fitted the papers to the quotes rather than vice versa. True synthesis was rare, and evidence that any learning had taken place was scant. (p. 76)

Phelps's dislike of grading term papers prompted him to look for alternatives to the traditional method of report writing. First, he wanted to develop a process that would enable students to rely more on their own ideas and interpretations and less on meaningless strings of quotations. To do this, he developed what he calls a *three-search paper* (Phelps, 1992). Named after the three search processes students must go through to produce a final written paper—reflecting, interviewing, and reading—the three-search paper discourages students from building their reports around quotations. It does this by engaging them in more personally and socially active kinds of research before sending them off to the library to find printed sources that support, expand, or explain what they have learned from personal reflection and interviews.

The three-search process for report writing begins with several reflective, or introspective, activities. Students examine sample papers that were written by former students to give them an idea of what their final papers may look like. Names are removed from the papers to preserve anonymity, and examples of both good and not-so-good papers are provided. Students also engage in a free-writing activity that encourages them to jot down whatever experiences they have had in relation to the topic on which they will write. Then, working in groups of three, students give each other feedback by focusing on what can be eliminated and what must be added to each person's list.

At the interview step, students examine the sample papers once more, this time for the purpose of noting how good writers incorporate specific examples and ask open-ended questions rather than questions that can be answered with yes or no. Then, each student interviews at least two people, including a peer and an authority on the topic he or she has chosen to research. For example, a student living outside Charlottesville, Virginia, who is planning to do a three-search paper on Thomas Jefferson, might interview a representative of the Jefferson Memorial Foundation at Monticello as well as an African American peer. The interviews might focus on these persons' views about Jefferson, author of the Declaration of Independence and owner of more than 170 slaves. (For more information, see *Confronting Thomas Jefferson, Slave Owner*, by James Blackman [1992].)

The final step—reading periodicals, books, pamphlets, and so forth—is usually the first step in the traditional approach to report writing. However, in the three-search process, printed sources are consulted only after students have had opportunities to reflect on previous experiences with the research topic and after they have interviewed at least two individuals. As Phelps (1992) discovered, "By this time, students are fairly well immersed in their subjects; hence, a trip to the library for the third area of research is more focused and less odious" (p. 77).

I-CHARTS An inquiry chart, or *I-chart* (Hoffman, 1992), capitalizes on what students already know about a particular research topic prior to reading. I-charts can be the basis for whole-class, small-group, or individual inquiry.

A sample I-chart is illustrated in Figure 10.12. Students list their topic and an inquiry question about the topic, along with any information they already know on the topic. Then they consult various resources, noting bibliographic information and important ideas from each. Figure 10.12 has spaces for three resources, but I-charts can be expanded to include more. It is useful, however, to limit the amount of note-taking space to discourage wholesale copying of resource text. The I-chart has a place to list key words that students will want to use in their written reports, and it also provides space for the student to jot down any new questions that arise once their inquiry is under way.

Sally Randall (2000), a teacher at Oconee County Middle School in Watkinsville, Georgia, adapted the I-chart to make it fit her eighth graders' needs. She wanted to help her students build on prior knowledge and develop critical-thinking skills as they collected and organized information for writing a research report. The I-chart provided a structure that suited her instructional goals.

First, Sally prepared her students for the eighth-grade interdisciplinary unit on the wilderness by teaching specific language arts skills that they would need in researching the topic. These skills included letter writing, paraphrasing, interviewing, and reference skills for use in looking up information in source materials and in constructing a

I-CHART

Name: *Dan*   Topic: *Rainforest canopy*

Subtopic:

What are the different layers in a rainforest canopy?

What I Already Know:

A rainforest has special kinds of plants and animals

Resource:	Important Ideas:
1	*If there are a few high trees, others will grow higher to compete for light.*
2	*Most seedlings start on forest floors.*
3	*Rain helps leaf molds grow.*

Interesting Related Facts:

Animals knock fruit down from the highest trees. This fruit is food for animals that can't climb trees.

Key Words:

ecology, habitats

New Questions to Research:

What are the names of some of the giant rainforest trees?

FIGURE 10.12   I-Chart

bibliography of those materials. She relied on her colleague in science to prepare the class for topics related to the wilderness unit.

After students had chosen a topic that suited their interests, they wrote proposals, listing what they already knew about the topic, what they wanted to learn, and where they would look for the information. This step in the process helped the students to narrow their topics.

Next, students brainstormed questions they had about their topics—questions that could not be answered by a simple yes or no. Following this brainstorming activity, they set up their individual I-charts. They turned their subtopics into questions. As they wrote their different subtopics/questions at the top of each of their I-charts, the students also recorded what they already knew about a particular subtopic.

Then, turning to their source materials, they began to read for information that would help them answer their questions. They also wrote letters to people in the community who they thought would be knowledgeable on their topics of interest. This appeal to outside sources opened opportunities for meeting and talking with people who represented a diversity of interests and backgrounds.

Recording the information involved students in using what they had learned about note taking and paraphrasing. It also introduced them to an efficient way of recording bibliographic information. Briefly, they drew a line on the I-chart after they had finished writing down what they had learned from a particular source. Then, on a separate sheet of paper labeled "References," they wrote the complete bibliographical information about that source, assigning a number (1, 2, 3) to each source and recording the number on the I-chart. From that point on, they only needed to refer to a source by its number when they wished to add information to the I-chart.

The I-chart is similar to, but not to be confused with, Macrorie's three-step *I-Search* (cited in Anders & Guzzetti, 1996). In the first step of this inquiry process, a student describes something he or she already knows about the topic under investigation and states a goal for learning new topic-related information. The second step entails a written description of the process used in learning the new information (i.e., the search), and the third step is an interpretation of what was found. The student then writes a conclusion and reflects on the value of what was learned and how the new information will be used.

Writing a Report

Report writing calls for some specialized skills if students are to succeed in researching and writing about what they find. One of these skills is outlining, and another is paraphrasing.

OUTLINING   After Sally Randall's eighth graders had completed their I-charts, they were ready to begin the writing process. Each student had accumulated information on eight to ten subtopics (e.g., "What animals live in the rain forest?"), and they had organized their answers to the subtopic questions on their I-charts. By attaching a Roman numeral to each subtopic in their respective I-charts, the students had the beginnings of a formal outline. They added the details and interesting related facts found within their

Helping
Struggling Readers

Conducting Inquiry
Martha Rekrut (1997) recommends a collaborative approach to helping low achievers conduct inquiry. Inquiry topics should be of high interest to students and should be derived from questions that arise during the course of instruction. She recommends placing students in heterogeneous research groups of two, three, or four. She also says it is important to carefully teach and practice summarization or paraphrasing skills before students begin their research.

I-charts to complete the rest of their outline. As Randall (2000) noted in her discussion of the eighth graders' work, some used their outlines to create a visual display:

> The final product was a visual display for a wilderness convention much like the typical science fair. Students used the information they had learned to create a display of maps, charts, listings of facts, pictures, graphs, and timelines. They [also] created . . . a pamphlet informing the public of their expertise. These were showcased at an evening program to which we invited parents, experts who had been interviewed, and county librarians who had provided research assistance. (p. 540)

PARAPHRASING   Too often teachers assume students are able to paraphrase and find later, much to their dismay, that entire sections of a text have been copied verbatim with or without the use of quotation marks. Singer and Donlan's (1989) steps in teaching students how to paraphrase are easy to follow and demonstrate both *syntactic paraphrasing* (changing the order of the words) and *semantic paraphrasing* (substituting synonyms for the original words):

1. Present a passage from a text along with a paraphrased version. Lead students to discuss how the two differ.
2. Lead students to practice paraphrasing short passages from a text. Help them by identifying phrases to reword, using a dictionary to find synonyms, and modeling how long passages can be rewritten in shorter form.
3. Gradually introduce longer passages and eliminate or reduce your support.

Alternatives to the Traditional Research Report

In earlier chapters, we featured several student inquiry projects that involved computer or media technology both in the research process and in the presentation of the results. It is clear from these examples that the days are long gone when research meant little more than time spent with the *Readers' Guide* and stacks of index cards. New technologies have dramatically changed the ways in which inquiry can be conducted and reported. In the following sections, we take a closer look at some alternatives to the term paper.

MULTIGENRE REPORTS   Inquiry results can be reported in genres and media other than the traditional expository research paper (Moulton, 1999). Students who have learned about the Curie family of scientists, for instance, might create birth, marriage, and death certificates to convey important details of their lives, along with newspaper accounts of the Nobel prizes won by members of the family in 1903, 1911, and 1935. Another possibility would be to create "laboratory notes" explaining one or more of the Curie discoveries. Students investigating Elizabethan theater might create posters and playbills for Shakespeare's plays.

Inquiry results can also be incorporated into poems, skits or plays, and songs. Students might bring in short music clips that relate to some aspect of their research, along

TECHNOLOGY Tip

Evaluating Web Sources

The Internet is largely unregulated, rapidly expanding, and continuously changing. Anybody with minimal technology skills can post a website and say whatever they wish. Therefore, one important Internet inquiry strategy is the ability to evaluate the reliability of what is found there.

The following guidelines are adapted from suggestions made by Gardner, Benham, and Newell (1999) and Foster and Padgett (1999). Most of them can be applied to other inquiry resources as well:

1. Explain extension domains. Common extensions include the following:

.com	commercial entity
.edu	educational institution
.gov	government agency
.mil	military
.net	network resource
.org	other type of organization, usually not-for-profit
.web	Web-related organizations

2. Is an author's name listed? Who is the author? What are his or her credentials? What is his or her affiliation and relation to the sponsors of the website? Is there an e-mail address, phone number, or other way to contact the author?

3. How accurate is the information? Are there references, links, or other ways to verify it? Is there any conflicting or supporting evidence?

4. How objective is the site? Why was this written? Do the language, graphics, or imagery reveal the author's perspective?

5. When was this written? Is there a date when the site was created and/or revised? Is the information current?

6. Does this site adequately cover the topic? How well does the information compare to other published resources? What is missing, hidden, or confusing? What additional information would be useful to know about this?

For more on evaluating Web sources, see Kathy Schrock's *Guide for Educators* at http://school.discoveryeducation.com/schrockguide.

with a written explanation of the significance of their musical selection to their topic. Photos with captions, original artwork, and audio and video recordings are other media that can be used to present inquiry findings. These various genres and media can be motivating and provide a creative outlet for student learning but still be based on significant data collection, synthesis, and evaluation.

An example of the impact of creating multigenre lab reports in science was reported by Gunel, Hand, and Gunduz (2006). They compared the understanding of quantum physics that resulted when students generated a multimodal presentation versus a summary report. Students who created the multimodal presentation had significantly higher scores on the posttest than those using the unimodal summary report format. Gunel et al. hypothesized that enhanced learning of students who created multimodal presentations resulted from students' translations of multiple representations of the target concepts.

HYPERMEDIA   Hypermedia software allows users to create computer-based files that may include text, sound, and visual images. The contents of a hypermedia file may be original creations of the person who is making the file, or they may be imported to the file from another computer file, a scanner, CD-ROM, the Internet, videodisk, or audio CD.

The information within a hypermedia file is connected by hyperlinks, much like the Internet, so that anyone who accesses the file may move from link to link in whatever order may be of interest. For example, if a student were to create a hypermedia file on the jazz trumpeter Miles Davis, he or she might include photos of Davis, pictures of his album covers, a discography, reviews of his recordings, a biography, sound clips from his recordings or interviews, and pictures of a trumpet with a written description of the instrument and how it is played.

With many hypermedia programs, it is possible to include links to Internet sites. The student could use this file to make a presentation of his or her research, or it could be accessed on the computer by other interested people. If done as an HTML file, it could be posted to the Internet for an unlimited audience.

Teachers and students have found many uses for hypermedia. Nancy Patterson (1999) describes how her eighth-grade students began their research with Native American poems. Students highlighted words and phrases they were curious about in the poems and began searching for more information on the Internet. For example, a poem about the Spanish conquistadors led some students to learn more about the Spanish Conquest, which then led to Spanish galleons and Spanish weaponry of the sixteenth century. At the same time, students were also following leads to information on the Anasazi, the Navajo, and other Native Americans of the Southwest.

Typically, Patterson's students read dozens of online articles as well as other information they found in library reference materials. When they accumulated sufficient information on one of their subtopics, they created a "page" file which became part of a web of links from one topic to another. Their final hypermedia products opened with their selected poem. By clicking on highlighted words in the poem, a reader could move to another page, which in turn would have links to other pages. Each student created an average of 20 pages for his or her final product. In contrast to the traditional research paper, Patterson found this project to be much more motivating. It also gave her students an expanded sense of what text is and how it can be manipulated. It allowed them to make choices about what to investigate, how to present information, and what organizational logic might link their varied findings.

COLLABORATIVE INTERNET PROJECTS   The Internet makes it possible for collaborative inquiry to extend beyond a single classroom to different schools, states, and countries. E-mail communications, collaboration with experts in various fields, so-called virtual gatherings (in which on-line presentations introduce people from different countries), electronic publishing, and shared data collection projects are a few of the collaborative Internet projects described by Mike and Rabinowitz (1998). One example is the We Are One project, which involves students from throughout the world in acting on an issue relevant in their area and sharing their work with others (www.weareoneday.com). Teachers can find other projects or register a project of their own, along with an invitation to others to join, at the Global Schoolhouse Projects Registry (www.gsn.org/GSH/pr/index.cfm).

There are many more applications of technology for inquiry than we could possibly catalog here, and teachers and students are continuously finding new ways to use technological tools for conducting inquiry and disseminating the results. To learn more, you might consult some of the references we have cited here as well as the Suggested Readings at the end of Chapter 4.

Responding to Student Writing

We recently met a friend, who is an English teacher, for dinner at a sidewalk café. When we had told him we might be a little late, he said that would be no problem. He was planning to spend a couple of hours there anyway, enjoying the pleasant spring weather and doing what English teachers do in the evening—read student papers.

Although English teachers may accept that as part of their turf, teachers in other disciplines usually do not. As you have been reading our recommendations for encouraging students to write, you might well have been wondering how you would read and correct all that writing. For high school teachers who have 100 or more students writing on a regular basis, that is something to consider. Fortunately, responding to student writing does not have to be an overwhelming chore for a teacher.

First, responding to writing need not be left entirely to the end of the writing process, when papers are handed in and it is too late to do anything about problems of content, clarity, or form. Second, responding does not have to be the sole responsibility of the teacher. Much of what students write can be read and responded to while it is still in process, and students can be very effective reviewers of one another's work.

Peer Responses

Throughout this chapter, we have made many suggestions for peer collaboration on writing. Group brainstorming and composing, exchanges of drafts, and conferences for revision and editing all help students get feedback on their work, see that others have similar questions or problems, and enhance the quality of their final written products. Collaboration among student writers does not occur spontaneously, however. Teachers need to take a little time to model good responses and to set some ground rules.

The key to responding to a writer's work is what Donald Graves (1983) calls *receiving*. By this he means responding to what the writer is saying or letting the writer

Go to MyEducationLab and select the topic *Writing*. Then, go to the Activities and Applications section, watch the video entitled "Peer Editing," and respond to the accompanying prompts.

know that his or her message has come across. Teachers can show students how to receive each other's writing by modeling the process with an anonymous piece of student writing that can be duplicated or displayed on the overhead projector. (To protect the feelings of the writer, we recommend that you not use writing from any member of the class.) The teacher can begin by rephrasing the main points of the piece and commenting on its strengths and then move on to one or two questions for the writer or suggestions for possible revision. Observations and questions from the class should be invited.

Once class members have discussed what would and would not be helpful comments for the writer, they might collectively establish some ground rules for peer responses. We suggest some variation of three basic rules:

1. *Be positive.*   Respond to what the writer is trying to say and what the writer does well. Tearing down another person's work will only result in discouragement and hurt feelings.

2. *Be helpful.*   Do your best to make comments that will be useful to the writer.

3. *Be specific.*   Talk about specific words, phrases, or paragraphs.

To facilitate peer conferences, you might prepare a checklist or a *peer review guide* similar to the one in Figure 10.13. Such a form gives you a way to monitor peer confer-

---

PEER REVIEW

Writer: _____

Reviewer: _____

Topic/Title: _____

1. Read your partner's draft.

2. Which words or phrases struck you most? (Write them here.)

3. What do you feel the author was trying to say? Summarize it here in one sentence.

4. What are the main strengths of the draft?

5. What questions do you have for the author?

6. What one suggestion would you make to the author?

F I G U R E   1 0 . 1 3   **A Peer Review Guide**

ences, and it could be included in a portfolio as part of the record of how a writing project developed.

Successful peer conferences depend on successful peer relations, which of course are not always conducive to helpful cooperation. Timothy Lensmire (1994) has described how social relations among students play themselves out in writing workshop activities, sometimes to the detriment of students with low social status. He concludes that teachers should recognize peer culture and social relations and take positive steps to sustain what he calls an "engaged, pluralistic classroom community," in which the voices of all students are valued and students learn to be considerate of their peers. It is unrealistic to expect that a teacher can heal all peer conflicts and maintain perfect harmony for a 45-minute period, despite whatever exchanges may be occurring in the hallways, on the street, or over the Internet or telephone. However, thoughtful modeling, guidance, and assignment of working groups can help to nourish civil and productive academic relationships.

Teacher Conferences

Teachers can respond to work in progress. In a short conference lasting two to five minutes, a teacher can read or listen to what a student is working on, ask a question or two, and respond to the writer's concerns. The goal of this kind of conference is to be helpful without being prescriptive. Teachers should confer without a pen or pencil in hand; marking a student author's draft voids the author's ownership and responsibility for the piece. Specific suggestions for adding, deleting, or altering the content of a draft may also diminish the writer's control and what Murray (1984) calls "the satisfaction of the writer's own learning, the joy and surprise of finding what [one has] to say" (p. 4).

Instead, the teacher should try to adapt generic questions such as the following to each piece of writing:

What do you think you will do next with this?

What do you like best about this piece so far?

What problem or difficulty are you having?

Could you tell me more about *X*?

What is the connection between *X* and *Y*?

Questions such as these generate talk that can help writers work out problems and make their own discoveries.

There are several benefits to in-process teacher conferences. First, conferences can help students develop their general writing skills. Teacher guidance and feedback can improve the actual written products. Conferencing also pays off when the time comes for teachers to make a formal evaluation of students' writing. The better the writing is, the easier it will be to read. Also, reading and responding will go faster when the teacher has been involved in the development of a piece of writing.

Formal Evaluation

All writing by students need not be subjected to formal evaluation. Learning logs, informal written reflections, and other unfinished writing can be read quickly and given a simple checkmark to indicate completion of the assignment, with a brief written acknowledgment or response if appropriate. Assigning formal grades to such writing defeats the purpose of informal writing-to-learn activities, in which the process of writing (and thinking) is more important than the product.

In those pieces that are polished and handed in for grading, teachers should respond first to the content. When a teacher uses the red pencil to mark each and every mechanical or stylistic miscue, it sends two unfortunate messages to the writer. First, it signals that form is more important than content. Second, it implies that there is little hope of mastering a skill so technical and arcane. Receiving a paper covered with red marks is discouraging to a writer. Where could one possibly begin to improve such a mess?

If students are writing to show what they have learned, grades and written comments should be based primarily on content. There is no question that spelling and other mechanics are important or that numerous mechanical errors detract severely from the effectiveness of writing. However, if students are writing to show what they have learned, the information presented and the quality of the reflection and thinking should merit more weight than spelling and other mechanical aspects. If necessary, a teacher might point out one or two mechanical problems that are repeated or are especially troublesome for a reader, and it is reasonable to expect that students learn how to spell the technical vocabulary of a subject area.

Mechanics should account for a portion of a grade, and we have no quarrel with rigorous academic expectations. However, "three wrong and it's a C" requirements seem too stringent for developing writers, at least for content area assignments in which the emphasis is on mastery of ideas, not mastery of conventions.

Dialect features in writing represent a particularly sensitive, complex, and controversial aspect of evaluating student writing. As we said in our earlier discussion of dialect, there is no question that all students need to be fluent with Standard English writing conventions. However, standard conventions need to be modeled and taught in a context that recognizes the legitimacy and power of diverse language forms and the importance of an individual's voice. This implies that in some situations, nonstandard stylistic features may be appropriate. In writing for which Standard English is expected, the marking of dialect miscues should be done with consideration of the age of the writer, the instruction in standard forms that he or she may have received, and the importance of content versus form in the writing task.

For assignments such as inquiry projects whose development is complex and time consuming, you might consider some variation on portfolio assessment, as suggested in Chapter 5. Along with the finished product, students may hand in notes, outlines, early drafts, journal entries, and conference records. Self-evaluation should also be part of the portfolio. In fact, self-evaluation can be factored into the final grade on any formal written assignment.

Literacy Coaches' Corner

Trying New Strategies

Literacy coaches sometimes have a difficult time getting teachers to cooperate with them. To build mutual respect, literacy coaches should respect teachers' content knowledge, focus on the teachers' goals (rather than their own), and perform their job as one of service to the teachers. Even then, literacy coaches' job is complicated by the culture of secondary schools, which is discipline-focused and organized by departments rather than grade levels as is elementary school. High school teachers want to teach their content, and they see literacy as something extra that they must teach in addition to their content, rather than as a vehicle that can enhance their content instruction.

One strategy to begin building a relationship with a teacher is to "borrow a class" so you can try a strategy you are interested in. Ask the teacher for input on the appropriateness of the strategy to make sure it is congruent with the content he or she wants students to learn. Collaboratively plan the lesson, and ask the teacher to observe you and provide feedback on both student engagement and the success of the strategy. When teachers see you are focused on students' learning, rather than on "fixing" their teaching, your job will get easier.

Summary

Writing is a rigorous kind of thinking; it can be hard work even for the most adept. Teachers who understand writing processes know that students need guidance, reassurance, and plenty of practice.

When teachers thoughtfully assign, guide, and respond to student writing in content areas, students benefit in many ways. They gain increased content knowledge and understanding. When students write, they learn. Whether it is a short note reflecting on a new concept or a term paper involving several weeks of effort, writing helps them to connect and clarify their thinking.

Regular informal writing activities prepare students for the more formal demands of writing papers and examinations. However, perhaps more important, writing empowers. In a world of expanding information and technology, the ability to express oneself clearly in writing is likely to become more, not less, of a social, professional, and economic determinant.

Suggested Readings

Atwell, N. (1990). *Coming to know: Writing to learn in the intermediate grades.* Portsmouth, NH: Heinemann.

Atwell, N. (1991). *Side by side: Essays on teaching to learn.* Portsmouth, NH: Heinemann.

Baines, L., & Kunkel, A. (Eds.). (2000). *Going Bohemian: Activities that engage adolescents in the art of writing well.* Newark, DE: International Reading Association.

Bright, R. (1995). *Writing instruction in the intermediate grades: What is said, what is done, what is understood.* Newark, DE: International Reading Association.

Burns, M. (1995). *Writing in math class.* Sausalito, CA: Math Solutions.

Countryman, J. (1992). *Writing to learn mathematics.* Portsmouth, NH: Heinemann.

Daisey, P. (2003). The value of writing a "how-to" book to reduce the writing apprehension of secondary preservice science and mathematics teachers. *Reading Research and Instruction, 42*(3), 75–111.

Dyson, A. H., & Freedman, S. W. (2003). Writing. In J. Flood, D. Lapp, J. Squire, & J. Jensen (Eds.), *Handbook of research on teaching the English language arts* (2nd ed., pp. 967–992). Mahwah, NJ: Erlbaum.

Freedman, R. (1999). *Science and writing connections.* White Plains, NY: Seymour.

Fulwiler, T. (1987). *The journal book.* Portsmouth, NH: Boynton/Cook.

Hammann, L. A., & Stevens, R. J. (2003). Instructional approaches to improving students' writing of compare-contrast essays: An experimental study. *Journal of Literacy Research, 35,* 731–756.

McIntosh, M. E., & Draper, R. J. (1997). *Write starts: 101 writing prompts for math.* Palo Alto, CA: Dale Seymour.

Perry, T., & Delpit, L. (Eds.) (1998). *The real Ebonics debate: Power, language, and the education of African-American children.* Boston: Beacon.

MyEducationLab is a research-based learning tool that brings teaching to life. Go to the Alvermann, Phelps, and Ridgeway Gillis 6th Edition MyEducationLab for Content Area Reading site at www.myeducationlab.com to:

- engage in multimedia exercises to help you build a deeper and more applied understanding of chapter content;

- utilize extensive resources including videos from real classrooms, Praxis and licensure preparation, a lesson plan builder, and materials to help you in your teaching career.

Studying and Study Strategies

Studying and Study Strategies			
Prerequisites for Effective Studying	**Accessing Information**	**Preparing for Tests**	**Using Study Strategies**
• Motivation • Teachers' Expectations • Knowledge of the Criterion Task • Domain Knowledge	• Information Literacy and Library Skills • Web Site Evaluation	• Objective Tests • Subjective Tests • Role of Homework	• Task Awareness with SQ3R • Strategy Awareness • Performance Awareness • Note-Making Strategies • Compare/Contrast Study Matrix • Internet Search Strategies

Anticipation Guide

Directions: Read each of the following statements. Place a checkmark on the line in the "Before Reading" column if you agree with the statement; leave it blank if you disagree. Then predict what you think the chapter will be about, and jot down on a sticky note (or post online) any questions you have. Read the chapter; then return to the statements and respond to them as you think the authors of your text would. Place a checkmark on the line in the "Authors' Stance" column if you believe the authors would agree with the statement. If you discuss these statements with other people online, in class, or at the family dinner table, return to the statements and check any items you agree with in the right-hand column, "After Discussion." If your thinking changed, what caused that change?

Before Reading	Authors' Stance	Statements	After Discussion
_____	_____	1. Studying is hard work.	_____
_____	_____	2. Teaching students to take notes is English teachers' responsibility.	_____
_____	_____	3. Teachers who give notes on an overhead deprive their students of the opportunity to become independent learners.	_____
_____	_____	4. Information literacy is knowing how to read library books and other expository texts.	_____
_____	_____	5. The more homework students complete, the better they will do on tests of academic achievement.	_____
_____	_____	6. Engaging students in self-assessment promotes their metacognitive thinking.	_____

Victoria recalls the shock to her system when she first entered college. Her story may seem familiar to you.

• • •

I had been a very good high school student—which is to say, I had learned to play the game of school well. Although I didn't make all A's, as a senior I garnered a small scholarship from the local education association. When I went off to college, it was great—no one took up homework, there were only one or two exams for each class back then—fabulous! I played bridge and drank coffee in the canteen all quarter long . . . but when I sat my first exam, it occurred to me that perhaps I had missed something. The first test was English, but it might as well have been Greek. I didn't have a clue about gerunds or adjective clauses. I was physically ill. I knew something had to change and change fast.

During the next quarter, I studied as though my life depended on it, as indeed it did. I took notes in lecture and made notes from reading, I drew detailed diagrams, color coded and labeled. I learned some effective, if not efficient, study strategies. And my grades did improve, but it took real work—that was the first time I understood that studying *was* work. It was years before I learned about study strategies that could be effective and efficient.

Most of my students, both graduates and undergraduates, say they were never really taught how to study, and based on that experience they don't really think about that in relation to their students until we discuss study strategies in content area reading. Frequently undergraduates will say that learning note-taking strategies helps them do better in the classes they are taking that semester; they complain that if just one teacher had taught them about taking notes and studying, they would have higher GPAs. They lament all the hours they've wasted because they didn't have a strategic study plan, and it makes them consider the importance of doing for their own students what wasn't done for them.

• • •

Paulo Freire and Donaldo Macedo (1987) are two literacy educators who want their students to read the *world* as well as the *word*. To Freire and Macedo's way of thinking, "To study is not easy, because to study is to create and recreate and not to repeat what others say" (p. 77). We think this definition of what makes studying difficult aptly summarizes the intent of this chapter on studying and study strategies. We view studying as an active process—one born of creative and critical thinking, not of passive acceptance and mindless regurgitation.

In this chapter, we describe several prerequisites for effective studying and accessing of information. We also provide some tips on preparing students to take tests. Finally, we present several study strategies that are designed to help students develop the metacognitive and self-regulatory processes necessary for effective studying. We hope you will think about your own history as a student as you read this chapter.

Prerequisites for Effective Studying

To be effective in their studying, students need to develop a certain metacognitive awareness of the task and of themselves as readers; that is, they need to check their comprehension periodically for loss of meaning, apply appropriate fix-up strategies, monitor the effectiveness of those strategies, and evaluate their efforts to learn from studying (Baker & Brown, 1984). They also need to pay attention to what motivates them to learn. Beyond that, they can benefit from knowing their teachers' expectations of them as learners, understanding the nature of the criterion task, and possessing adequate domain knowledge.

Motivation

Students generally find studying a worthwhile activity only when they see real and meaningful purposes for doing it (Brozo, 2003) or when the reward structure is sufficient for the goals they hold as learners (e.g., studying to make good grades so they can go on to college, so they can play high school sports, be a member of the marching band, and so on).

Motivating students to study in a way that makes clear what is in it for them is of primary importance. Although it is fairly easy to teach students new study strategies, it is something else to get them to apply those strategies on their own if they find no reason to do so. The strategies we introduce in this chapter will be most effective if taught at a time when students can use them to complete an assignment in one of their content area classes.

Teachers' Expectations

Teachers expect students to study the content of various subject matter specialties and to pass their courses. Because studying is mostly a self-directed activity (Thomas & Rohwer, 1986), teachers are aware of the need to teach students how to be effective studiers. Just knowing that their teachers expect them to master the content is sometimes motivation enough for students to value the study strategies they are taught (Nolen & Haladyna, 1989).

However, when this is not the case, it may be useful to let them experience the difference a good study strategy can make. For example, students might find that by previewing a chapter they are able to reduce the time it actually takes them to read it. Even better, as Richardson and Morgan (2000) point out, teacher-guided previewing can help students reduce uncertainty about a reading assignment, especially when they discover that they do know something (however little) about the material. Reassuring students in this way can create a sense of shared responsibility in that they become aware of what they know and do not know (and thus need to study) at the same time that their teacher senses the difficulties a particular assignment will entail. When a teacher's expectations for effective studying are made explicit and easy-to-use strategies are demonstrated, as in the previewing example just given, a more relaxed and productive learning environment becomes possible.

Knowledge of the Criterion Task

Test-taking skills depend on a great deal more than students' ability to comprehend textual material. For example, there is considerable evidence that instruction in study skills is effective when students' knowledge of the criterion task enables them to study in a manner that ensures a match between the study technique and the items on a test (Alvermann & Moore, 1991; Anderson & Armbruster, 1984).

This being the case, why don't more teachers tell students about the criterion task so that they can study more effectively? As Otto (1990) so aptly puts it, "Teachers, themselves, often don't have a clear notion of the criterion task or its importance for studying, so they can't or don't make it clear to students" (p. 369). Faced with a lack of evaluation data on which study strategies work best for which types of learners and tasks, teachers often find themselves left with but one choice: to teach a variety of such strategies in the hope that at least one of them will be applied by their students.

This hit-or-miss approach to strategy instruction is complicated further by the fact that even with a clearly set criterion task, there is no guarantee that students will use an appropriate study strategy. The mismatch between task and strategy is made worse when students do not possess adequate content area, or domain, knowledge.

Domain Knowledge

Many students lack the prerequisite content knowledge to study effectively. Excessive absences and inattentiveness in class contribute to this knowledge deficit and make studying particularly difficult. Students who know little about a topic will find that their strategic knowledge cannot compensate for their lack of domain knowledge.

Evidence-Based Research

To complicate matters further, Young, Arbreton, and Midgley (1992) observed that "all content areas may not be created equal" (p. 1). That is, students' ability to acquire knowledge in a specific domain (e.g., social studies, science, mathematics, or English) may rest partially on their motivational orientation to learning. According to Young et al., the middle-grade students they studied were more likely to enjoy learning for its own sake in mathematics and science than in English and social studies.

In classrooms of the twenty-first century, being literate in a particular domain is not limited by what students are able to access from printed texts using conventional study strategies. Instead, it is becoming increasingly common for readers who struggle with their content area textbooks to turn to electronic study aids to help them organize their thinking around a set of domain-specific tasks. Consider, for example, the case of Andrew Sheehan (Sheehan & Sheehan, 2000), a ninth grader whose writing disability and attention-deficit disorder have been partially compensated for by the use of assistive technology such as a voice-to-text computer software program, an electronic pocket organizer, and a portable keyboard. In the following "Helping Struggling Readers" box are Andrew's own words and some ideas that teachers may find useful in helping other students like him acquire crucial domain knowledge through special study aids.

Helping Struggling Readers

Assistive Technology

Electronic Organizers

If memory is the library of the mind . . . I've lost my card catalog! I use an electronic pocket organizer for day-to-day survival. I type in my homework, notes, reminders, phone numbers, et cetera. . . . I can jot something down before I forget it, and all my important messages stay in one place. Handwriting is not necessary, nor is organization on a page. . . . This is far superior to having notes to myself scattered all across the globe. (Sheehan & Sheehan, 2000, p. 27)

Portable Keyboards

For daily notetaking I use a product called Alpha Smart (made by Intelligent Peripheral

Devices, Inc., 20380 Town Center Lane, Suite 270, Cupertino, CA 95014; alphasmart. com). The Alpha Smart is like an overgrown organizer. This device is nearly a full-sized keyboard with an LCD screen and eight files. Each file can be used for a different school subject. Even though keyboarding is necessary, I can get down enough information in classes to serve as notes. Then I can send this information to a word processor on a Macintosh or PC and edit and print the notes. The new Alpha Smart 2000 model has a built-in spell checker, which is a big help. This device runs on three AA batteries and fits in my backpack. (Sheehan & Sheehan, 2000, p. 28)

Accessing Information

Online resources abound for students interested in using the World Wide Web as a learning environment—one in which accessing information efficiently plays an important role in effective studying. How well students do in this digital environment will depend to a great extent on how well teachers prepare them to become independent learners capable of applying information literacy and library skills in critical and creative ways. Part and parcel of what it means to be information literate is the ability to evaluate websites and their various resources. Without critical evaluation, these resources are hardly worth accessing.

Information Literacy and Library Skills

As noted in Chapter 1, one of several new terms to make its way into the field of literacy education as a result of the information explosion on the Web is *information literacy*. It refers to what is generally defined as the ability to access, evaluate, organize, and use information culled from a variety of sources. It involves knowing how to formulate a search strategy for zeroing in on needed information.

This is not easy, especially for learners who are barely acquainted with efficient search strategies in traditional print texts. For example, Gavin Brown's (2003) research into young adolescents' use of text characteristics to locate main ideas and details in informational texts showed that students easily located answers that required using only a single, verbatim search term cued through typographic and signaling markers. However, they experienced considerably more difficulty locating answers that required complex, multiword search terms. From Brown's research (reported in full at http://readingonline.org/articles/art_index.asp?HREF=/articles/brown), he concluded the following:

> The real challenge in searching for main ideas and details, whether within paper-based documents or digital environments, is not the location of verbatim terms, but lies rather in the incorporation of implicit terms that need to be inferred across passages of text. The results of this research suggest that if teachers draw attention to and assist students in learning various navigation tools . . . [e.g., headings, titles, organizational structure, typographic features, page layout], then student ability to locate information should improve. Naturally, the goal in students' learning to search for main ideas and details by utilizing a variety of text and task characteristics is not simply rapid location of materials. . . . Rather, these skills are used to solve informational problems. Unless presented, developed, and exercised in such a context, they will remain rather pointless.

The library skills necessary for accessing information in printed texts or on the Internet when studying or completing a homework assignment are very similar to those needed in any problem-solving activity. One first defines the task and then determines which available search strategies will most likely yield the best results in terms of locating and accessing the desired information. Many resources on the Internet can help teachers and students learn Internet search strategies. Two sites we have found useful are Twenty-First Century Information Fluency, maintained by the Illinois Mathematics and Science Academy (http://21cif.imsa.edu), and The Big 6, maintained by Mike Eisenberg and Bob Kerkowitz (www.big6.com).

TECHNOLOGY Tip

Standards for Integrating Technology

A useful set of nonprint media standards for helping students access and evaluate information is available through the National Research Center on English Learning and Achievement (CELA). Developed at CELA by Karen Swan, the nonprint media standards are divided into basic skills, critical literacies, and construction skills for each of three grade levels: elementary, middle, and high school. A pdf file of the standards is located at www.albany.edu/cela/reports.html#S.

The Twenty-First Century Information Fluency website identifies five things today's students do not do well: (1) create a query at the beginning of a search, (2) choose an appropriate database, (3) recognize relevant information, (4) improve keywords as they search, and (5) verify the credibility of information located. This site also has resources to help teachers create powerful lessons, either as units focused on information literacy or as activities integrated into ongoing instruction. The resource kits offer articles, podcasts, learning games, curricula, and assessment tools and are linked to the International Society for Technology in Education (ISTE) National Educational Technology student (NET-S) standards.

The Information Literacy Standards (see Appendix E) form the backbone of Mike Eisenberg and Bob Berkowitz's problem-solving curriculum. Basically, The Big 6 curriculum is a six-stage approach to teaching information literacy in the Information Age. Visit the Eisenberg and Berkowitz website (see above) to learn more about their approach and to view strategies and lesson plans for helping students conduct more efficient Web searches as part of their studying routine.

Website Evaluation

Teaching students how to access resources on the Internet in a timely and effective manner is a necessary but insufficient step toward achieving digital literacy. Students also need to know that information that is biased or inaccurate is best left alone.

Kathy Schrock, who maintains an excellent website for teachers (http://school .discoveryeducation.com/schrockguide/index.html), points out in her article "The ABCs of Web Site Evaluation" (2002) that with more than 350 million documents available on the Web alone, students may feel like they are drinking from a fire hose when they search the Internet. Students must be aware that there is no editor regulating information posted on the Web, and they should be taught how to evaluate what they find. Students

Helping Struggling Readers

Information Literacy Standards and the K-W-L Strategy

As spelled out in the Information Literacy Standards of the American Association of School Libraries (see Appendix E), the nine standards are subdivided into three categories: information literacy, independent learning, and social responsibility. To better understand how these standards relate to reading and studying in content area classrooms, visit http://www .big6.com/2002/09/02/activate-a-big 6%e2%84%a2-tool-to-improve-learning-grades-7-12. There you will see how the K-W-L strategy described in Chapter 6 can be adapted and made into a chart for planning and gathering information.

need to know how to evaluate websites and be able to practice as they learn how to evaluate websites located in their own searches.

Victoria has used a Web-based activity generated and maintained by Susan Beck on a website titled The Good, the Bad, and the Ugly (http://lib.nmsu.edu/instruction/eval .html). This website has a page of evaluation criteria that include authority, accuracy, objectivity, currency, and coverage as well as a page of example websites organized into four topics with three websites each. The topics are controversial and include smoking and tobacco; AIDS; immigration; and drugs, hormones, and human tissue. Students can be divided into small groups in which each member evaluates the websites on one topic for one or more of the criteria.

Joyce Valenza has created a WebQuest (www.sdst.org/shs/library/evalwebstu.html) in which students take on the role of a content specialist, authority/credibility specialist, bias/purpose specialist, or usability/design specialist and evaluate a designated website from that perspective. After all the students have evaluated the website, they compare notes and discuss their rankings. The following chart summarizes possible questions each specialist might ask:

Role: Specialist in	Questions
Content	• Does the information seem accurate based on what you know about the topic?
	• Is it important to know when the material was last revised? Why?
Authority/Credibility	• Who is responsible for this site? (Hint: Inspect the URL.)
	• Who else links to the site? Are they credible sources?
Bias/Purpose	• Is the site trying to persuade you or change your opinion?
	• Can you distinguish facts from opinion?
Usability/Design	• Is the site easy to navigate?
	• Do the links on the site work?

Preparing for Tests

By relieving some students' natural anxiety about taking tests, teachers may help them improve their performance. Providing students with information about the criterion task, such as the number of questions about each major topic being tested, and involving students in activities that help them prepare for the test are examples of how teachers reduce the demands of testing. This type of help lessens students' need to second-guess what the teacher thinks is important and unimportant.

Students are also less anxious about taking tests when they know in advance that the tests will consist of objective items (multiple-choice, true/false, fill-in-the-blank) or subjective items (short answer and opinion essay). Because objective and subjective exams place different demands on students, teachers usually find it helpful to provide a separate set of test-taking tips for each type of exam.

Objective Tests

Objective tests evaluate students' recall or recognition of information. Fill-in-the-blank items require students to recall information, and multiple-choice, true/false, and matching items require them to choose from among two or more options. Although students typically find it easier to recognize a correct answer than to recall one, there are exceptions. For example, the student for whom English is a second language generally finds recognition tasks difficult because each option presents the possibility that vocabulary meaning will be distorted. Consequently, foils (incorrect answers) are double jeopardy for such a student.

Tips on helping students prepare for objective tests include teaching them to use mnemonic devices. For example, the first letter of each word in the sentence "George Everett's old grandfather rode a pig home yesterday" will help them recall and spell the word *geography*. Similarly, HOMES is a mnemonic for the names of the Great Lakes and ROY G BIV for the colors in the visible spectrum. In addition, imagery (such as visualizing where the Ohio River joins the Mississippi River) may help students recognize the meaning of a word such as *confluence* in a matching test.

List-Group-Label, a strategy introduced in Chapter 6 to assess and build on prior knowledge, is also useful in helping students review for major tests over large amounts of information. It is helpful to have students brainstorm important words and concepts and record them without looking at notes or the text. Next, students might compare their lists with each other and consult their notes, learning logs, or textbooks to add additional terms in another color ink. Using different colors of ink helps students see those words and concepts they remembered less well and therefore need to study more carefully. Alternatively, you might provide students with a list of important terms, particularly if time is an issue.

Victoria has used this technique with sticky notes, which works well for the next step, in which students sort the terms into conceptually related groups. Once students have the terms sorted, they can label each group. Or if students need scaffolding, you can provide them with a range of the number of groups to use in the sorting, or provide the labels for them. Using sticky notes and multiple sorts, students can be guided to create their own graphic organizers, which can then be used to study independently.

Sometimes words such as *always* and *never* are included in a list of foils; when students see them, they can be almost certain that these are not the correct answers. Exceptions, of course, are instances in which the inclusive term describes a generally accepted fact, as in "All carrots are vegetables."

Objective test items may have more than one correct answer. When this occurs, it is possible that a mistake has been made, and students should check with the teacher. If the items are correctly written and students believe that more than one answer is correct, they may bring the matter up with the teacher after the test has been marked, or teachers may give students the option of justifying their answers to objective test items as part of the examination process (see Chapter 5). Doing this, of course, greatly increases the amount of time required to grade the exam.

Subjective Tests

Subjective tests, such as short-answer tests and opinion essays, evaluate students' abilities to organize, analyze, synthesize, and integrate ideas. They are easier to construct than objective tests, but they take longer to grade and are open to more dispute regarding the correctness of answers.

Both holistic and analytic scoring methods have been used successfully with essays. As its name implies, *holistic scoring* is based on the overall impression a teacher has of an essay after reading it for the general meaning of its message. Unlike holistic scoring, *analytic scoring* enables a teacher to grade separate components of an essay (its content, form, argument, grammar, and so on). The analytic scoring method is time consuming, but it gives students a clear idea of how teachers arrive at a grade.

Tips on helping students prepare for subjective tests include providing them with information on what should be included in an essay and what the point distribution will be if analytic scoring is to be used. Letting students know whether grammar, spelling, and punctuation will be taken into consideration is also helpful. (See Chapter 5 for a discussion of rubrics.)

Using the List-Group-Label procedure as the basis for paragraph-writing exercises helps students prepare for short-answer and essay tests. Students take the label for a category and turn it into a topic sentence; then they write the paragraph using the remaining terms, being sure to explain what the terms mean and how they are related to each other conceptually.

Scaffolded instruction, or instruction that begins with the teacher modeling a particular process and gradually turning the responsibility for the task over to students, can be used to teach students how to write essays. Based on the ideas of Wood, Bruner, and Ross (1976), "the metaphor of a scaffold has been proposed to describe this process since a scaffold is erected at the outset of construction and gradually withdrawn as a building becomes self-supporting" (Pressley, El-Dinary, & Brown, 1992, p. 106). To provide scaffolded instruction in writing essays, teachers can show students model essays that have prompts written in the margins to indicate the types of information that should be included. A model also provides students with an idea of the form a finished product should take.

Role of Homework

Historically, opinions about the value of homework have fluctuated widely. There was a renewed interest in homework in the late 1950s after the Soviets launched *Sputnik*, and recently, there has been a resurgent interest in the topic in response to increasing accountability measures, particularly in the early grades (Gill & Schlossman, 2004).

Evidence-Based Research

Current research on homework has examined issues related to home school interaction, the effect of media on homework performance, and the impact of different types of homework. Van Voorhis (2003) found that middle school science students who were assigned interactive homework turned in more accurate assignments and had significantly higher science grades than those who were assigned conventional homework. Interactive homework requires students to involve family members in the assignment. For example, students might interview family members about clothing styles, music, or television shows that were popular when they were the student's age. Assignments that have students interviewing residents of a retirement center about life during the Great Depression, interviewing a local pharmacist about drug interactions, or collecting data by recording the ingredients for selected products at the grocery store for a discussion in chemistry are all examples of interactive homework assignments. Interactive homework helps make connections between the curriculum and students' lives outside school.

Overall, the research literature on assigning homework supports the view that the amount of time spent doing homework is associated with students' academic achievement. Intuitively, of course, it would seem that the more conscientious a student is in completing her or his homework, the better that student will do academically. For example, in a booklet distributed by the U.S. Department of Education (Paulu, 1995), we learn that

> in the *early elementary grades*, homework can help children develop . . . [good] habits and attitudes. . . . From *fourth through sixth grades*, small amounts of homework, gradually increased each year, may support improved academic achievement. In *seventh grade and beyond*, students who complete more homework score better on standardized tests and earn better grades, on the average, than students who do less homework. The difference in test scores and grades between students who do more homework and those who do less increases as children move up through the grades. (p. 5)

The nature of homework varies according to the purpose for giving the assignment. Generally, there are three types of assignments: practice, preparation, and extension (LaConte, 1981). Each of these types of assignments can be interactive or conventional.

When homework is given for the purpose of reinforcing new learning, it is thought of as a *practice assignment*. Research on expert and novice teachers indicates that the experts assign homework only after they have monitored and guided students' practice in

Helping Struggling Readers

Power Writing for Students Who Struggle with Essay Exams: A Fluency Activity

Sometimes students experience difficulty writing essay exams because they are not fluent writers. When this is the case, try power writing (Fisher & Frey, 2003), a fluency activity that requires students to write (in one minute) everything they can on a topic the teacher gives them. They can chart  the number of words they write at the end of each one-minute timed activity and then note the progress they make over several days or weeks.

TECHNOLOGY Tip

Homework Websites
The Internet Public Library at www.ipl.org offers general homework help and a listing of numerous links to useful websites. For example,

BJ Pinchbeck's Homework Helper at http://school.discoveryeducation.com/homeworkhelp/homework_help_home.html provides a large number of links organized by subject, with brief annotations, and offers up-to-date lesson plans by teachers for teachers in all content areas.

class, but the novices are likely to assign material that they were unable to find time to teach in class (Leinhardt, 1983).

As the name implies, *preparation assignments* are meant to provide students with the background information they will need in order to understand new information when it is introduced in their textbook or in class discussion. The assumption is that students will acquire "hooks" on which to hang new information if they have the appropriate background knowledge.

Unlike practice and preparation assignments, *extension assignments* are given to encourage students to move beyond their textbooks in acquiring, synthesizing, and using the information they find. Increasingly, with greater access to the World Wide Web, extension assignments are becoming popular with both teachers and students. Although this development has its upside, there is a downside as well. Unfortunately, too often students are left to flounder when it comes to completing an extension assignment for which they must develop their own search strategies, a topic we address later in this chapter.

Using Study Strategies

Reading to learn specific information for the purpose of performing some criterion task is what defines studying and sets it apart from merely comprehending the information (Anderson & Armbruster, 1984). This type of reading, or *studying*, requires students to think about and control their own learning processes (Zimmerman, 1994). However, before students can become metacognitively aware of what these learning processes are, they must know the following (Wade & Reynolds, 1989, p. 6):

Evidence-Based Research

1. What to study in a particular learning situation, or *task awareness*
2. How best to learn it, or *strategy awareness*
3. Whether and to what extent they have learned it, or *performance awareness*

Thus, before students can actively monitor their own studying, they need to learn about and develop task, strategy, and performance awareness. Sufficient research exists on the subject of metacognitive awareness to merit basing instruction on its findings.

The instructional activities for developing these three areas of awareness discussed in this section are derived from the research literature on metacognition. They have also been field-tested by Wade and Reynolds (1989).

Task Awareness with SQ3R

Helping students locate information that is important according to external criteria (although not necessarily interesting to them) is the first step in developing their task awareness. Ways of doing this include having students brainstorm about the important ideas in a short selection they have read. After recording their responses on the chalkboard, ask them to give reasons why the ideas are important, based on external criteria. *External criteria* imply that information is relevant if it is one of the main ideas put forth by the author of a selection. This does not mean that *internal criteria*, such as students' interests, are unimportant. However, for the purpose of developing task awareness, external rather than internal criteria are employed.

To point out the importance of task awareness in answering an essay question, show students what information they would need to answer a sample question satisfactorily. As a follow-up to this activity, show students how to arrange the needed information in a hierarchical manner. Selectively focusing attention on relevant material also teaches students to self-question. For example, students might ask themselves why they placed a particular piece of information in a position subordinate to another piece of information.

Evidence-Based Research

Deciding what to study in a particular reading assignment is at the core of task awareness. An effective way to focus students' attention on important information is to introduce them to SQ3R—an acronym that stands for *Survey, Question, Read, Recite,* and *Review* (Robinson, 1961). This study system has been in use for several decades and for good reason. It works if introduced and practiced under teacher guidance, though not perfectly for every student in every study setting (Devine & Kania, 2003). As a systematic way of previewing, questioning, and reviewing information that is read, SQ3R offers students a chance to be proactive in developing task awareness as they study expository text. When combined with a note-making strategy, discussed later in this chapter, SQ3R becomes more powerful, a strategy Victoria calls Active SQ3R.

In Figure 11.1, we describe the five steps in SQ3R, and then we show how these steps relate to locating and remembering information that is considered important in a selection.

Strategy Awareness

After students have analyzed the task to determine while information is relevant or irrelevant, the next step is to develop an awareness of the type of strategy needed to comprehend and remember the relevant information. For example, if an assessment or criterion task consists of taking a true/false test, a different kind of strategy is needed than would be the case if the task consists of writing an essay.

One way of teaching students how to develop an awareness of the type of strategy needed to meet a particular task is to model the process yourself. Choose a passage from

Step	Description of Step	Relation to Task Awareness
1. Survey	Preview a selection by reading titles, headings, subheadings, captions accompanying illustrations, and a summary if one is available.	Enables a reader to locate information that the author of a selection thought important enough to highlight structurally or to illustrate through examples.
2. Question	Turn each title, heading, and caption into a question.	Makes clear to a reader what he or she already knows (or doesn't know) about the assigned informational text.
3. Read	Actively read to answer questions posed in step 2.	Focuses attention on what the author believes is important and worth remembering.
4. Recite	Close the text and orally summarize what you just read; then make notes using your own words.	Improves memory and aids attention span after initial reading of the selection.
5. Review	Study your notes periodically, and refresh your memory of the text by using its main headings to cue your recall of the subheadings.	Keeps relevant information foremost in mind, and reinforces relationships between important ideas and the evidence that supports them.

F I G U R E   1 1 . 1   The SQ3R Study System

your class text that is particularly dense or laced with difficult vocabulary. As you read the passage aloud, describe which strategies you use to help you remember what you are reading. List those strategies on the chalkboard under one of the two categories ("Observable" or "In-the-Head" study methods) shown in Figure 11.2.

Next, ask students to construct a similar list using a different passage from the class text. After they have exhausted their list of strategies, ask them to compare their list with the list in Figure 11.2. A discussion might follow in which students give their reasons for sometimes, always, or never using a particular study strategy. At this point, it is important to remind student that not every strategy meets everyone's needs, nor should students feel compelled to adopt a particular strategy. Research has demonstrated that students who are effective studiers use the strategies that work for them (Swafford, 1988).

Performance Awareness

According to Wade and Reynolds (1989), "A strategy can be considered effective only when it has a strong, positive effect on learning" (p. 11). Developing students' performance awareness enables them to monitor whether or not they have understood the task and used the appropriate study strategy. If they have done both, their performance on the

Helping Struggling Readers

The MURDER Study System

A study system that is especially helpful to struggling readers is one known by the acronym *MURDER*. Adapted from John Hayes's (1989) work in problem solving, the acronym is explained this way:

- **M**ood: Set a positive mood for yourself to study in.

- **U**nderstand: Mark any information you don't understand.

- **R**ecall: After studying, stop and put what you have learned into your own words.

- **D**igest: Go back to what you did not understand and reconsider the information.

- **E**xpand: In this step, ask three kinds of questions concerning the studied material:

  1. If I could speak to the author, what questions would I ask or what criticism would I offer?

  2. How could I apply this material to what I am interested in?

  3. How could I make this information interesting and understandable to other students?

- **R**eview: Go over the material you've covered.

Source: From a study guide developed by Joe Landsberger; see statement that permission is granted to freely copy, adapt, print, transmit, and distribute at www.studygs.net/murder.htm.

criterion task should reflect it. Research has shown that metacognitively aware readers know when their learning breaks down and how to adjust the strategies they are using (or adopt new ones) to remedy the problem (Ghatala, 1986).

A good way to develop performance awareness among students is to have them determine whether the strategies they use to study a selection are effective. Ask students to read a short selection, and then have them record the strategies they used on a separate sheet of paper. Next, ask them to respond to ten objective questions on the selection they have just read without looking back at the text. Finally, grade answers to the questions as a class activity, and encourage students to discuss why they think the strategies they used were or were not appropriate for the task.

Note-Making Strategies

In the following discussion, we discuss note making as a study strategy. We use the term *note making* because it conveys a more active task than the usual term *note taking*, which seems passive. The key to effective note making is writing the information in one's own words, which requires active thinking about the text. Any of the note-making strategies can be coupled with SQ3R (Active SQ3R) and taught to students so they become independent users of the study strategy.

Study Strategies	Think aloud—Why you use the strategy
Observable	
• Select important information: highlight or underline	Highlighting or underlining helps to direct your attention to ideas in the text. Don't highlight or underline everything. A good rule is not to highlight or underline unless you are going to make a note summarizing the information in your own words.
• Make notes	Translating text information into your own words helps to hold your thinking. Always *make* notes—paraphrase information. Copying information verbatim provides practice in handwriting but is not as effective as representing the information in your own words.
• Organize meaningfully	Two good ways to organize information meaningfully are outlining and drawing a diagram or graphic organizer. Either method visually organizes information so that you can immediately see how the ideas are related.
In-The-Head	
• Preview	Survey or preview the reading. This helps to familiarize you with the organization of the information. You can preview the graphics, headings, subheadings, first an/or last sentences. If there is a good summary, read the summary first.
• Vary reading rate	Familiar text can be read more quickly than unfamiliar text. Text about new concepts or dense text (with many new ideas introduced in a few paragraphs) should be read slowly. Read as you might drive—quickly when the road is familiar and straight but slowly when the road twists and turns or is unfamiliar.
• Visualize	Make a picture in your head—see what you are reading. This helps you make sense of the reading.
• Predict	Think ahead. What might the author describe next? Use text structure and the author's organizational clues to think your way through the text. This helps you pay close attention.
• Make connections	Associate what you are reading with what you already know, have experienced, or have read about in other texts. This aids understanding.
• Summarize	Periodically summarize what you are reading. This helps to check your understanding and keep you focused on the task.
• Ask questions	Ask questions when you are confused, and try to answer them. Alternatively, ask questions you think a teacher might ask and try to answer them. Self-questioning keeps you alert and on task.
• Reread	When you are confused, don't understand what you are reading, or feel lost, stop! Reread the last sentence, paragraph, or section you understood.

F I G U R E   1 1 . 2   Study Strategy Awareness: Helpful Study Strategies and Reasons to Use Them

Evidence-Based Research

Both research (Devine & Kania, 2003) and practical experience emphasize the importance of direct instruction in teaching students how to make notes. Such instruction should explain the purpose of note making, and it should take place over a reasonable period of time. Brozo and Simpson (1995, p. 284) provide the following criteria for helping students develop expertise in using study strategies:

1. Strategy explanations and rationales (e.g., steps, tactics, advantages)
2. Strategy modeling and talk-throughs by the teacher
3. Examples from real texts and tasks that students will encounter
4. Guided practice with real texts, followed by specific, qualitative feedback
5. Debriefing sessions that deal with questions, student doubts, and fix-up strategies
6. Frequent independent practice opportunities across appropriate texts
7. Guidelines on how to evaluate a strategy's success or failure.

Go to MyEducationLab and select the topic *Study Strategies*. Then, go to the Activities and Applications section, watch the video entitled "Cornell Notes," and respond to the accompanying prompts.

TWO-COLUMN NOTES   Palmatier's (1973) split-page method of note making, which is different from the double-entry journal (see Chapter 10), gives students a systematic approach to organizing and studying their class notes. Using the split-page method, teachers instruct students to do the following:

1. Use only one side of an 8½-by-11-inch sheet of paper that has been divided lengthwise by folding it into two parts. The left column should be about one-third of the paper; the right column, about two-thirds of the paper.
2. Record the lecture notes in the right column, using both subordination of ideas and spacing to indicate the importance of information.
3. Review and organize the notes by first reading over the information in the right column to obtain a sense of the major concept and then placing that concept in the left column opposite the related information in the right column.
4. If the notes are unclear or sketchy, refer to the textbook or the source that was the basis for the lecture. Additional information may be added to the back of the paper if no space remains on the front.
5. Study the notes by folding the paper so that only the left column is visible. The labels in that column serve as a focal point for recalling information found in the right column.

Spires and Stone (1989) suggest a way to use videotapes to provide instruction in the split-page method of note making. Teachers' lectures can be taped and played back as students view the tapes and practice applying the split-page method. Initially, the

Literacy Coaches' Corner

Teaching Note Making

Victoria was a science teacher in Orange County, Florida, in the 1970s. Her involvement as a teacher trainer with the Reading in the Content Areas project there put her in contact with colleagues who were *reading resource specialists* (RRSs). (Today, these professionals are called literacy coaches.)

Victoria remembers one RRS who worked in a rural high school of about 3,000 students. One of the things Sharon (a pseudonym) did annually was to teach every ninth-grade student how to make notes. She would tap into the required biology or U.S. history course and teach students how to make notes using content the teacher was covering at the time. Sharon also worked with the teachers to help them gradually release the responsibility for making notes to the students.

By the middle to the end of the second quarter, students were using their favorite note-making strategies independently. Teachers were able to spend less time introducing a reading assignment, collaboratively pointing out headings and subheadings for students to use as guidelines for their notes as they read the text. Teachers no longer had to make up study guides on a regular basis; they only did that for very difficult texts, when students needed extended support to comprehend the reading.

practice sessions should be no longer than 15 minutes. As students' comfort level with the method increases, so too should the time allotted to practice sessions.

Two-column notes, or Palmatier's split-page note-making method, is ideally suited to social studies and science texts. For mathematics, adapting the method is easily accomplished by using two evenly spaced columns, with math on one side and an explanation and/or rationale for the math on the other. Having students work just one or two problems using the split-page method promotes their mathematical thinking and provides a window into their understanding.

INSERT Interactive Notating System for Effective Reading and Thinking (INSERT) (Vaughn & Estes, 1986) helps readers maintain sustained engagement with text and promotes metacognitive activity in the reader. The method is quite simple and consists of recording symbols and notes as you read, either in the margin or on sticky notes to avoid writing in the text. The sticky notes may be transferred to split-page notes after class discussion.

Helping Struggling Readers

Read-Aloud/Note-Taking Method

To prepare her self-contained eighth-grade reading class for the New York State English Language Arts exam, Rebecca Meyers engaged in an action research project to determine if her students would improve their listening and note-taking skills as a result of participating in an eight-week direct-instruction approach to the split-page method of note taking. All participants were enrolled in the school's special education program and attended inclusion classes for their core academic courses.

Ms. Meyers began the project by interviewing students about note taking. Then, after obtaining a baseline measure of their note-taking skills, she read aloud a short expository passage while the students listened for important information but did not take notes. Before reading aloud the same passage for a second time, Rebecca taught her students how to set up their papers for the split-page method of note taking. On the second read-aloud, students jotted down facts in the right-hand column of their papers. The class worked as a group to classify the facts (details) they had identified into main idea topics, which were listed in the left-hand column of their papers. In the weeks that followed, Ms. Meyers taught her students how to abbreviate words or draw stick figures that would convey their understanding of the important information they heard as she read aloud from a variety of expository and informational texts.

By scaffolding her explicit instruction of the split-page method of note taking, Rebecca was able to assist the class in moving from almost total dependence on her for structuring their notes to independence in note taking. She was also able to shorten the time that she paused between paragraphs as she read aloud from the passages. After only six sessions of explicit instruction in this method, Rebecca noted an increase in the number of facts they wrote down. She also learned from poststudy interview data that all students felt comfortable taking notes using the split-page method, although not all were comfortable using abbreviations. One girl said she could not always remember what her abbreviations stood for when she reviewed her notes.

Source: Used with permission of Rebecca Meyers, Wilson Middle School, Wilson, New York.

The procedure for the INSERT strategy is as follows: As you read, place one of four different marks in the margin of the text or on sticky notes to note your own knowledge or understanding. Record annotations in your own words on each sticky note as you read. You may devise any symbols you wish, but the following are commonly used:

✓ → Put a ✓ (check mark) in the margin if you read text that confirms something you already knew.

−   ⇢   Put a − (minus sign) in the margin if you read information that contradicts what you think you know.

+   ⇢   Put a + (plus sign) in the margin if you encounter new information.

?   ⇢   Put a ? (question mark) in the margin if you encounter information that is confusing or if you want to know more about something in the text.

The number of symbols and annotations you record will vary. It is not necessary to annotate each line or idea. In very dense text, you might annotate every idea, or several per paragraph. In text about familiar information, you may not need to annotate every paragraph.

After you complete your reading, construct a chart like the one below and categorize information from the reading:

✓	−	+	?
Record information and ideas that confirmed what you knew as you read the text	Record information that contradicts what you thought you knew as you read the text	Record information that was new to you	Record questions you have or ideas that were confusing to you

After all students have read, recorded symbols and annotated the text, and created their own INSERT summary charts, have them compare their charts with those of one or two peers. Discussion based on these charts will help to clarify information for students.

INSERT is particularly powerful for struggling readers who need to develop metacognitive habits of mind. This strategy is most powerful when students create conceptually based maps from their INSERT charts. INSERT can also be adapted easily for a narrative text. Some English teachers have adapted the method using different-colored sticky notes for each character in a story and had students jot down their thoughts about the characters' actions. Another adaptation focuses on literary devices used by the author, such as symbolism and figurative language.

CHAPTER MAPPING   *Chapter mapping* (Bragstad, 1983) is a form of graphic representation that provides scaffolding for readers of expository text. Teachers can also apply the chapter-mapping strategy to narrative text, in which case it is called *story mapping*.

Chapter mapping depends on a well-structured text—one with clear headings and subheadings. The use of chapter mapping requires thinking about and transforming ideas. Note-making efficiency is increased because the reader stays focused during reading and has a set structure/procedure for making notes.

Here are the steps for chapter mapping:

1. Use a regular 8.5-by-11-inch sheet of paper. Unlined paper is preferable, but lined is acceptable.
2. Find the chapter title. Illustrate it with a diagram or drawing or by simply writing the title in the center of the page and drawing a box around it.
3. Identify the subheadings. (Chapter subtitles may help here.) Limit the number of major concepts to seven or fewer, if possible.
4. For each subheading, draw a line out from the chapter title (see Figure 11.3). Alternatively, you can divide the sheet of paper into equal-sized sections, one for each subheading (see Figure 11.4).
5. Print the subheadings in capital letters along the lines connected to the chapter title or in each section of a divided sheet.
6. Determine supporting details by carefully reading the text under each major subheading. Connect these details to each subheading. Make the connections in any way that makes sense. Be sure to record the information in your own words.

When students are finished, they have notes for all of one chapter or one section of a chapter on one side of a single sheet of paper. This provides a very portable study aid.

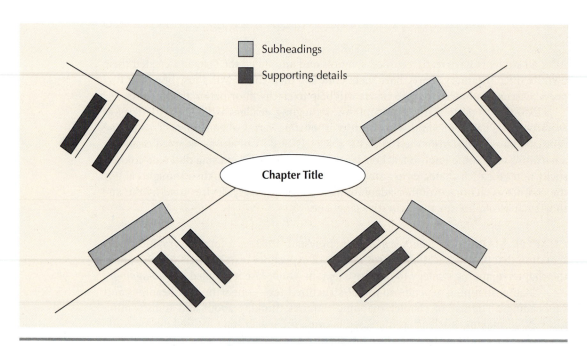

Subheadings

Supporting details

Chapter Title

FIGURE 11.3   Chapter Mapping Using a Spider Map Arrangement

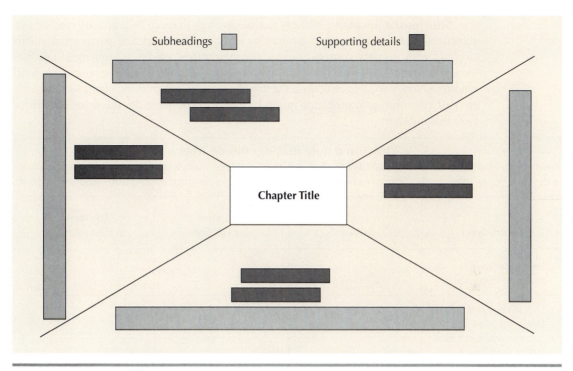

FIGURE 11.4   Chapter Map Using on Alternative Arrangement

STRUCTURED NOTE MAKING   *Structured note making* was created by Shanahan and Shanahan (2008) in response to input from the experts involved in their study of disciplinary reading. This form of note making requires students to use a chart structure based on essential ideas in a particular discipline. Teachers create the structured note making chart based on appropriate headings for a particular text about a concept, process, or event. Students are directed to record relevant details in their own words in the chart, using the teacher-specified headings to guide their reading. In structured note making, content and instructional focus determine the relevant headings. As students gain experience with the method, teachers can gradually release responsibility for creating the chart headings to students. In chemistry, for example, column headings might include (a) Substances, (b) Properties, (c) Processes, (d) Interactions, and (e) Atomic expression. In mathematics, the column headings might include (a) Concept, (b) Explanation, (c) Example, (d) Formula, (e) Illustration, and (f) Precise Mathematical Definition. In history, the column headings might include (a) Who, (b) What, (c) Where, (d) When, (e) How, and (f) Why. Students are then asked to make connections among historical events summarized from the reading, showing how they interact. In addition, students consider how the text positions them as a reader; that is, who stands to gain and who stands to lose from the view of the events presented in the text.

Evidence-Based Research

Structured note making is a very flexible strategy that can be used with readings assigned from textbooks, primary sources, as well as journal and newspaper articles. Particularly with primary sources, journal and newspaper articles column headings may vary in order to focus student attention on relevant information. For example, students reading a *New York Times* article on the use of genetically engineered plants to solve a variety of environmental problems might be asked to complete the following structured note making chart:

Structured note making: Bionic Trees

Directions: As you read the article *Turning Genetically Engineered Trees into Toxic Avengers,* record the ideas you find in the chart below. [downloaded from www.nytimes.com/learning/teachers/featured_articles/20040803tuesday.html].

Problem	Solution	Argument for solution	Argument against solution
Heavy metals (like mercury) in the soil			
Logging of old stand forests that could possibly result in the loss of wild forests			
Greenhouse gas in the atmosphere, resulting in global warming			
Loss of trees (like the American chestnut) due to disease			

Likewise, students reading a short article about Columbus' "discovery" of the New World might be asked to focus attention on the items that were exchanged when that contact was made, including plants that were taken to the Old World from the New and disease that came to the New World from the Old. In this case, students might be required to identify the important items exchanged, the immediate effects [50 > 100 years] and the long term effects [> 100 years]. the Structured Note Making chart would look something like this:

Items Exchanged	Immediate effects [50 > 100 years]	Long terms effects [> 100 years]

To extend students' thinking, they might be asked to identify the one most important item exchanged, and provide a line of reasoning for that choice. As you can see in these two examples, this strategy is very flexible and may be used with a variety of texts. Structured note making helps students acquire a sense of how scientists, historians, and mathematicians read text and provides support for identifying important information in a text.

The note-making strategies discussed here have unique characteristics and emphasize different cognitive processes. Students who are taught all of the note-making methods can choose the most appropriate one for a particular task. Figure 11.5 summarizes the targeted note-making methods and may be useful in decision making about which method is appropriate for a particular text or task.

Teachers should also help students recognize the value of good note making. One way to do so is to allow students to use their notes on a quiz but only to answer the questions for which they have information in their notes. Another way to help students see the

Note-Making Method	Emphasis	Unique Characteristics	Adaptations
Palmatier's two-column notes	Main idea—details	Can be used to make notes from reading or during a lecture.	Adapted for math, two-column notes become a Thinking Chart: math on one side, explanation or rationale for the math on the other.
INSERT	Metacognitive skills	Excellent for struggling readers who need to develop metacognitive abilities. Useful with both narrative and expository texts.	Can be used with narrative text to note predictions of upcoming events or to note changes in characters' thinking.
Chapter mapping	Text structure	Requires a well-structured text. Notes are on one side of one sheet of paper, which is handy for studying.	For conceptually dense text, can be modified to focus on a section of text.
Structured notes	Disciplinary structure	Mirrors thinking in specific content areas.	Can adapt the chart structure with different column headings for each discipline.

FIGURE 11.5   **Note-Making Strategy Comparison**

Literacy Coaches' Corner

Note-Making Strategies

Literacy coaches' knowledge of note-making strategies, coupled with teachers' knowledge of content, can enable fruitful collaborations that help students become more independent learners. Modeling note-making strategies enables a literacy coach to model a strategy while teaching content. Working with content area teachers to provide instruction in note-making strategies and then gradually releasing responsibility to students provides an opportunity to

model how to use students' notes, completed as homework, when they return to class. Students can compare their notes with their peers' notes and then revise them.

A powerful way to help students learn the content is to have them transform their notes into another format. If students have taken notes using the split-page method, for instance, have them create a graphic organizer. If students have created a chapter map, have them transform their notes into structured notes, write a summary, or draw a diagram. Figure 11.5 may be helpful in making a strategic choice of note-making method.

value of note making is to have them compare their notes with those of other students; then allow students time to revise their notes to include additional information or eliminate unimportant details.

Compare/Contrast Study Matrix

This study strategy assists students in organizing information as they read their content area assignments. It simultaneously involves them in summarizing that information in a compare/contrast pattern (Santa, 1988). Developing a sense of a text's organizational structure enables students to recall information more fully and efficiently.

Thus, the compare/contrast study matrix illustrated in Figure 11.6, is a natural tool for students to use with reading assignments that present information that differs along various attributes. For example, in Figure 11.6 Victoria uses six attributes, stated in the form of questions, to demonstrate to the students in her content literacy course how seven different types of government differ. She also asks them to include an example of each type of government (e.g., The United States is an example of a democracy).

When using the compare/contrast study matrix the first few times with your classes, we recommend that you model the procedure. This might consist of partially filling in each column and row while referring to the text. Also, you might want students to pre-

	Anarchy	Monarchy	Democracy	Dictatorship	Oligarchy	Fascism	Theocracy
Who governs?							
How do you get power?							
How is power maintained?							
How is power transferred?							
How are laws made?							
Essential elements?							
Example:							

FIGURE 11.6   Compare/Contrast Matrix: Social Studies—Forms of Government

Source: From V. Ridgeway's adaptation of C. M. Santa, *Content reading including study systems*, pp. 75–83, Dubuque, IA: Kendall/Hunt, 1988.

dict what they think they will find in their reading, using their predictions to fill in some of the columns and rows. Then, after reading the material, they can check the accuracy of their predictions. After students become more familiar with this study matrix, they may begin to construct similar matrices on their own.

If you are using the compare/contrast study matrix for the first time with students who find reading a struggle, it is advisable to have them listen for signal words such as *however*, *but*, *different from*, and *while* as you read aloud a passage from their textbook and model how you would fill in the matrix. As noted by at least one middle school teacher of considerable classroom experience, readers who have difficulty comprehending will find it frustrating if they have to divide their attention between learning a new study strategy and perceiving the organizational structure of the text (Marlene Willis, personal communication, April 11, 2000). See Chapter 7 for a compare/contrast guide for teaching about text structure.

Compare/contrast matrices also help students organize information from several sources. Pertinent questions can be listed in the first column, while information from different sources can be entered in each column thereafter. This helps students organize information and see patterns that exist across several sources.

Internet Search Strategies

Surfing the Web for information requires strategies that differ considerably from those used in locating information in printed texts. In a growing number of school districts, curriculum standards mandate that teachers help students become efficient and effective at searching on the Internet for information that can be used in completing homework assignments and studying. Among the guidelines that now exist for how teachers might accomplish this task, those developed in Australia by Sutherland-Smith (2002) in collaboration with students from two sixth-grade classes are the most helpful and explicit in their recommendations. Figure 11.7 offers a number of the strategies that worked in Sutherland-Smith's study, which spanned a ten-week term and involved students from multilingual backgrounds.

We conclude with a brief section on the importance of teaching students strategies for searching for information that will supplement their textbooks when they are studying or attempting to complete an assignment. Based on several months of firsthand observations of middle and high school students in a public library as they searched for websites for which they had no specific URLs (website addresses), we concluded that their lack of a search strategy often led to their giving up or becoming distracted by irrelevant website information (Alvermann et al., 2000a).

In helping these students develop independent search strategies, we began with an introduction to Ask Jeeves Kids! at www.ajkids.com. This user-friendly website does not teach a strategy per se, but through using it, students learn to narrow their questions, which is the first step in helping them become more efficient in their searches. For example, if one types in the question "Where can I learn about ants?" on the website's home page, the reply is "Jeeves knows these answers":

Where can I learn about the insect or arachnid ant?

What if I get bit by a fire ant?

Where can I find a concise encyclopedia article on ants?

Where can I learn about ant interactions in a tropical rain forest?

If none of these answers proves satisfactory, students are given the option to check out links from the website's metasearch partners or to ask a new question.

After the students we were observing in the public library became fairly comfortable with the Ask Jeeves Kids! format, we introduced them to subject matter websites, such as the History Channel (www.historychannel.com/home/index.html). Here, they were able to further hone their search strategies by deciding what types of information would satisfy their needs. At this website, students have the option of searching a particular topic by century (and then decade). They can also participate in a quick poll, find out what happened in history on the day they were born, and so on. One drawback to this website is the overabundance of options, most of which are unrelated to the topic the student types in to begin the search. Even so, we took advantage of this potentially distracting

- *Use the "snatch-and-grab" reading technique.* The objective is to read Web pages superficially—that is, skim to identify a key word or phrase, surf the relevant links, bookmark sites, and compile a grab-bag of references. It is important to remind students, however, that once they have gathered a sufficient number of potentially helpful references, they will need to read the accompanying texts in a much more careful manner.

- *Focus on refining keyword searches.* Once students have identified a keyword or phrase (e.g., printing press), teach them how to narrow the scope of their search by refining the original keyword or phrase. For example, if they are interested in the history of the printing press, they might search under *history of* or *invention of the printing press*.

- *Provide clear search guidelines.* Providing students with clear statements of the purpose for a search, giving them an approximation of how many sites they should search, and offering tips on how to use the toolbar for efficient searches are a few of the ways you can prevent panic from setting in when you require them to do an online research assignment.

- *Use the "chunking" technique.* This involves teaching students who have poor organizational skills to break a complex topic into smaller, more manageable bits of information. For example, if they are searching on the topic of *September 11,* they might brainstorm keywords and phrases re-

lated to that event, such as *terrorists, rescue workers, location of buildings,* and *clean-up.* By focusing on one chunk at a time, students are less likely to feel overwhelmed or waste time getting lost in cyberspace.

- *Develop teaching meachanisms to overcome frustration with technology.* Students can become frustrated when the topic they are researching involves a good deal of moving back and forth between links. One mechanism for alleviating some of their frustration is to model how to ignore certain links but click on others. Talking through your reasons for doing so and letting students predict which ones will be useful are ways of handling this problem.

- *Provide short-cut lists to sites or search engines.* Give students in advance a list of bookmarks to reliable sites (e.g., those least likely to have broken links). Or prepare a simple step-by-step handout that explains how to use search engines and then model the process one step at a time.

- *Evaluate nontextual features (images, graphics).* Visual elements can distract some readers, whereas others may think the visuals are merely illustrations of something in the written text. Teaching them to become what Leu (1997) describes as "healthy skeptics" of website information and modeling for them how you know certain kinds of drawings, photographs, and graphs can manipulate what you see are helpful evaluation techniques.

FIGURE 11.7   Internet Search Strategies

Source: Based on Sutherland-Smith, 2002, pp. 665–667.

website to discuss with them the importance of staying focused (a skill we ourselves often find difficult to master).

For those students who were ready for more advanced Internet search strategies, we introduced them to some of the more popular search engines and subject directories. Yahoo! quickly became their favorite, so much so in fact that we noticed students teaching other students some strategies for searching Yahoo! that they had figured out on their own (mostly in relation to music websites). However, these self-taught strategies seemed to transfer well across topics and domains.

Finally, we showed students how to avoid getting too many listings when searching on a topic of their choice. For example, we took the advice of experts on teaching with the Internet (Leu & Leu, 1999) and cautioned against using words such as *the*, *of*, or *a* as part of the search question. We also paired less proficient navigators of the Web with more proficient ones, being careful of course to avoid pairings that might aggravate a problem rather than solve it.

Summary

Being personally motivated to learn, valuing study strategies, knowing something about the criterion task, and possessing adequate domain knowledge are all factors that help students become effective studiers. Like learning to study, acquiring proficiency in Internet searches takes time, effort, and specialized knowledge.

So does studying for an exam. Preparing for exams is made easier when teachers take individual differences into account and reduce the de-

mands associated with taking tests. Test taking is also made easier for students when they become knowledgeable about the differences in objective and subjective tests.

Finally, learning how to study is facilitated by developing an awareness of the task, choosing potentially useful strategies, and identifying performance criteria needed to complete the task successfully.

Suggested Readings

Caverly, D., Mandeville, T., & Nicholson, S. A. (1995). PLAN: A study-reading strategy for informational text. *Journal of Adolescent & Adult Literacy, 39,* 190–199.

Hayasaki, E. (2003). 2Rs left in high school: Out of choice or fatigue, many teachers have abandoned the term paper, leaving a hole in college-bound students' education. *Los Angeles Times,* May 19, n.p. Available online at http://www.readfirst.net/2rs.html

Manzo, A. V. (1985). Expansion modules for the ReQuest, CAT, GRP, and REAP reading/study procedures. *Journal of Reading, 28,* 498–502.

Rekrut, M. D. (2000). Peer and cross-age tutoring: The lessons of research. In D. W. Moore, D. E. Alvermann, & K. A. Hinchman (Eds.), *Struggling adolescent readers: A collection of teaching strategies*

(pp. 290–295). Newark, DE: International Reading Association.

Riemberg, R. (1996). Reading to write: Self-regulated learning strategies when writing essays from sources. *Reading Research and Instruction, 35,* 365–383.

Sakta, C. G. (1999). SQRC: A strategy for guiding reading and higher level thinking. *Journal of Adolescent & Adult Literacy, 42,* 265–269.

Santeusanio, R. P. (1983). *A practical approach to content area reading.* Reading, MA: Addison-Wesley Publishing company.

Taylor, B. M. (1986). Teaching middle grade students to summarize content textbook material. In J. F. Baumann (Ed.), *Teaching main idea comprehension* (pp. 195–209). Newark, DE: International Reading Association.

MyEducationLab is a research-based learning tool that brings teaching to life. Go to the Alvermann, Phelps, and Ridgeway Gillis 6th Edition MyEducationLab for Content Area Reading site at www.myeducationlab.com to:

- engage in multimedia exercises to help you build a deeper and more applied understanding of chapter content;

- utilize extensive resources including videos from real classrooms, Praxis and licensure preparation, a lesson plan builder, and materials to help you in your teaching career.

chapter 12

Developing
Lifetime Readers:
Literature in
Content Area
Classes

Developing Lifetime Readers: Literature in Content Area Classes

Reading among Adolescents

Using Literature in Content Areas

- Benefits of Using Literature
- Encouraging Responses to Literature

Integrating Literature into Content Areas

- Uses of Literature in Content Areas
- Fiction and Nonfiction for Content Areas

Developing Awareness of Diversity through Literature

- Advantages of Using Multicultural Literature
- Resistance to Multicultural Literature
- Choosing and Using Multicultural Literature

Anticipation Guide

Directions: Read each of the following statements. Place a checkmark on the line in the "Before Reading" column if you agree with the statement; leave it blank if you disagree. Then predict what you think the chapter will be about, and jot down on a sticky note (or post online) any questions you have. Read the chapter; then return to the statements and respond to them as you think the authors of your text would. Place a checkmark on the line in the "Authors' Stance" column if you believe the authors would agree with the statement. If you discuss these statements with other people online, in class, or at the family dinner table, return to the statements and check any items you agree with in the right-hand column, "After Discussion." If your thinking changed, what caused that change?

Before Reading	Authors' Stance	Statements	After Discussion
_____	_____	1. The books available in schools generally reflect the range of adolescent reading interests.	_____
_____	_____	2. Picture books and graphic novels are appropriate for use in middle and secondary schools.	_____
_____	_____	3. Reading multicultural literature is beneficial for mainstream as well as minority students.	_____
_____	_____	4. Reading widely increases students' vocabulary and therefore helps them learn content.	_____

So far in this book, we have talked almost exclusively about school reading, or reading for academic purposes. In this chapter, we will take a look at the bigger picture and consider what people do with reading beyond school. At work or at leisure, each day millions of people in the United States turn to a book, a magazine, a newspaper, or the Internet and read for information, for personal gain, or for pleasure.

In the following anecdote, Marie Saladino, a high school history teacher, reflects on her life as a reader.* As you share her thoughts, consider your own uses of reading and how you have evolved as a lifetime reader.

• • •

I love to read. I can remember being four years old and demanding that my mother read to me and let me try to read parts of stories. I am certain that since reading was encouraged and worked on in my home, I had an easier time of learning in school.

I often wonder what has changed since my early days of reading. Up until eighth grade I used to read at least three books per week just for my own enjoyment. Once I entered high school, and then later in college, I never had enough time to read for personal satisfaction. In high school there was just too much going on, and in college there was so much subject matter reading.

I remember that reading was never really stressed when I was starting high school. We never read any literature except in English class, and I really did not care for the novels we had to read. I always wanted to read books related to my social studies classes. The only book we ever read in four years of social studies, besides textbooks, was *The Jungle* by Upton Sinclair. I learned that I really enjoyed reading books that were fictional yet based on real-life historical events.

Now that I am teaching I have even less time to read for pleasure than I did in college. I do try to read books that deal with the subject matter I teach. Presently the most reading I get to do is a few novels or books per year, some magazines, Sunday newspapers, and a ton of African, Asian, and American government books.

Please do not think that I never read for enjoyment. I like fictional books that deal with controversy in society. They get me thinking and then criticizing the direction society seems to be going. I guess the major benefit I get from reading is my thinking power. While reading I am always learning new things, analyzing what I am reading, and forming my own opinions about new topics. There is always so much to learn in the world.

• • •

This anecdote touches on several themes that will be developed in this chapter. First, it illustrates how an appreciation for reading develops over a lifetime, as the contexts, sub-

---

*Used with permission of Marie Saladino.

jects, and various externally and internally imposed imperatives change. Marie mentions how the pressures of adolescence and early adulthood militated against reading for enjoyment and how she wished she had been given more opportunities to read (and enjoy reading) literature related to her content area studies. The anecdote also gives a fairly common picture of the reading activities of a professional adult, who must read extensively for work, bemoans the lack of time to read for pleasure, yet finds great satisfaction and significance in the reading that does occur.

Finally, there is social significance in what Marie reveals when she tells us her reading gets her "thinking and then criticizing the direction society seems to be going." The founders of this country guaranteed freedom of the press in order that citizens might have free access to the information they need to govern themselves. There was no more passionate believer in the necessity of an informed public than Thomas Jefferson, who said, "If a nation expects to be ignorant and free, in a state of civilization, it expects what never was and never will be." All the advances in telecommunications and mass media have not usurped the role of reading as a means for in-depth learning, reflection, and decision making.

Reading among Adolescents

Of course, not all adults become readers like Marie Saladino. A study by the National Endowment for the Arts (2007) reports that nearly half of young adults, ages 18 to 24, read no books for pleasure and that family spending on books is at a twenty-year low. Moreover, the percentage of college graduates who read literature has declined from 82 percent in 1982 to 67 percent in 2002. Still, bookstores, libraries, and publishers continue to flourish. The Internet has also become a major source of information, entertainment, communication, and commerce. Casual observation reveals people from all walks of life reading at home, at bus stops, on lunch or coffee breaks, at the beach—wherever they have a few minutes to themselves.

With adolescents, reading outside school must compete for attention with television, video games, sports, and social activities. However, research contradicts the popular conception that most adolescents would never be caught reading a book. In a recent study of the leisure time preferences of 200 students in the sixth and ninth grades (Nippold, Duthie, & Larsen, 2005), adolescents reported listening to music, watching television or videos, playing sports, and playing video or computer games among their top activities. However, reading was reported as a moderately popular activity. Forty-three percent of the surveyed students reported reading between 20 and 60 minutes a day on average, with ninth graders reading slightly less than the younger students. A study of 584 urban minority middle school students yielded similar results (Hughes-Hassell & Rodge, 2007). Twenty-two percent of those students said they read constantly, and 50 percent said they read when they got a chance. Sixty-nine percent reported that they read more than two books a month outside school.

Two separate surveys of sixth graders also showed that early adolescents are engaged readers. Worthy, Moorman, and Turner (1999) queried more than 400 students about their reading preferences. Almost every one was able to cite a favorite title, type of reading, or author, evidence that their attitudes toward reading were not as negative as is often suggested. Ivey and Broaddus (2001) elicited reading preferences from 1,700 sixth graders. Highly rated materials in both studies included scary stories, humor, popular magazines, sports, and nonfiction about varied topics.

The authors of both surveys were especially impressed by the wide range of materials that students enjoyed reading. However, in both studies, students' stated reading preferences did not match what they found in school. Although students reported a variety of reading interests outside school to Ivey and Broaddus, they reported a much narrower selection of in-school titles, mostly award-winning fiction read by a whole class at the same time. Similarly, Worthy, Moorman, and Turner (1999) found that the most popular reading materials were not readily available in school, especially the preferred reading of boys and struggling readers. Teachers and librarians cited lack of money, inappropriate or objectionable content, lack of academic merit, and the fact that popular materials were either always checked out or tended to "walk away" or become lost. In both studies, students were more likely to obtain their preferred reading materials outside school.

Given time and appropriate materials, adolescents are surprisingly complex and multidimensional readers who are willing to read when it satisfies their personal needs (Ivey, 1999). Like many adults, they especially enjoy light reading on topics that are pleasing and important to them. Indeed, it is likely that students do not lose interest in reading as they progress through school; they just lose interest in school reading (Bintz, 1993). Adolescents' experiences with reading in school may very well influence what they read, their reasons for reading, and how often they read outside school. If you believe that it is important for students to continue their development as readers after their school years, you will find many suggestions in this chapter that can help you expand their experiences with literature in school.

As we worked on this edition of our book, we considered whether to broaden our scope in this chapter to include new technologies and literacies. A good deal of what has traditionally been thought of as literature is now available for reading online, and the Internet is spawning a multitude of new and exciting literary genres. Much of adolescents' reading both for study and for pleasure is done online. Conceptualizing literature and literacy more globally like this raises questions like "What is text?" and opens up a whole world of possibilities—more than we could adequately address in a single chapter.

We also recognize that traditional literacies and technologies continue to have a place in the contemporary world and will probably continue in the future, although the form, function, and interrelation of old and new literacies will clearly continue to evolve. Familiarity with traditional print-based reading will continue to be an important attribute of a well-educated person. Therefore, we use the word *literature* in this chapter in a broad sense to mean reading materials other than textbooks but most especially fiction and nonfiction books and periodicals that students might read as part of their content area studies.

Using Literature in the Content Areas

Benefits of Using Literature

If students have positive reading experiences beyond their textbooks, their chances for becoming lifetime readers increase. There are more immediate benefits, too. Reading from fiction and nonfiction sources can enhance content area knowledge as well as readers' overall reading and thinking abilities.

There are many reasons for using literature, both fiction and nonfiction, in content areas:

1. Reading increases vocabulary, including content-specific terms. (The role of wide reading in vocabulary development was cited in Chapter 8.) Through content-related literature, students increase their exposure to the language of a discipline. The examples are as diverse as the literature available. Readers of *The Hunt for Red October* (Clancy, 1984) will find many words specific to the technology of nuclear energy. David Macaulay's books, such as *Mosque* (2003) and *City: A Story of Roman Planning and Construction* (1974), illustrate many terms specific to architecture and civic planning as well as vocabulary that describes the people and social institutions of the respective eras.

2. Literature is often more up to date than textbooks. A textbook may be several years in development; one with a 2005 copyright may only reflect information available in the early years of the century. Timely written accounts of developments in science and social studies may be available only in recent periodicals and books.

3. Although textbooks tend to pile up facts, dates, and concepts in a didactic avalanche, trade books can present much of the same information in a more appealing context (Beck & McKeown, 1991). (The term *trade books* is used for books, both fiction and nonfiction, written for the general public, as distinguished from textbooks, which are designed for classroom use.) Readers incidentally learn and store away countless facts as they enjoy trade books.

4. Literature goes beyond the facts. Readers get a sharper understanding of the issues and of the various stands they might adopt by sharing the experiences of fictional characters or reading nonfiction reportage and analysis. Through literature, students can begin to understand some of the uses and abuses of science, statistics, and political power. The social and emotional implications of topics as far ranging as racism, immigration, war, nuclear energy, genetic engineering, climate change, and computer technology can be explored in works of fiction and nonfiction.

5. Literature allows readers to experience other times, other places, other people, and other cultures with empathy. For example, Spears-Bunton (1991) describes the reaction of Courtney, a white high school student in an Ohio River town in Kentucky, to the events in Harriet Jacobs's (1987) account of her life as a slave girl. When asked what she would have done in Harriet's place when the elderly

Evidence-Based Research

slave owner made his sexual desires clear, Courtney "turned her blue eyes toward the river and replied, 'I would have run, and I would have taken my children' " (pp. 12–13).

6. Trade books can be a powerful catalyst for thoughtful analysis (Alsup, 2003; Bean, Kile, & Readence, 1996). When students read about controversial topics, they learn to exercise critical thinking. As they compare two or more views, they will find discrepancies, contradictions, and differences of interpretation; they must decide which source is most compelling, complete, or accurate. *Johnny Tremaine* (Forbes, 1945), *My Brother Sam Is Dead* (Collier & Collier, 1974), *Sarah Bishop* (O'Dell, 1980), and *Bloody Country* (Collier & Collier, 1985), for instance, present events in the Revolutionary War from the points of view of characters of different genders, ages, races, and social standings.

7. Good experiences with reading breed motivation to seek other reading experiences. This is particularly important for reluctant readers or students who have difficulty with reading. When a teacher can help a troubled reader make a connection with an interesting and readable piece of literature, that reader gains the practice and confidence necessary to read further. Many adolescents who find reading boring surprise themselves when they find the right material.

Activity

The following is an excerpt from *Catherine, Called Birdy* (Cushman, 1994),* a young adult novel told from the point of view of a 12-year-old girl living in thirteenth-century England. As you read it, look for vocabulary, facts, and concepts about the Middle Ages, and see what you can tell about Birdy, the narrator:

> Just three days to the feast of Saint Edward, my brother Edward's saint day. When Edward was still at home, we celebrated this day each year with feasting and dancing and mock battles in the yard. Now our celebrations include my father's face turning purple, my mother tightening her eyes and her mouth, and the cook swinging his ladle and swearing in Saxon. The cause of all the excitement is this: On this day each year, since Edward went to be a monk, my mother takes wagons full of gifts to his abbey in his honor. My father shouts that we may as well pour his precious stores in the cesspit (one day his angry liver will set him afire and I will toast bread on him). My mother calls him Pinch-Fist and Miser. The cook boils and snarls as his bacon and flour and Renish wine leave home. But each year my mother stands firm and the wagons go. This year we send:
>
> 460 salted white herring
> 3 wheels of cheese, a barrel of apples

4 chickens, 3 ducks, and 87 pigeons

4 barrels of flour, honey from our bees

100 gallons of ale (for no one drinks more ale than monks, my father says)

4 iron pots, wooden spoons, and a rat trap for the kitchen

goose fat for the making of everyday candles and soap (lots of candles and little soap, I wager, seeing that they are monks)

40 pounds of beeswax candles for the church

a chest of blankets, linens, and napkins

horn combs, for those who have hair

goose quills, down, and a bolt of woven cloth (black) (pp. 23–24)

A check of three randomly selected samples of this book with the Fry readability formula (see Chapter 5) estimates that it is at the seventh-grade reading level, and the cover of the book recommends it for ages 12 and up. Do you think this book might be easier to read than a typical textbook intended for the sixth or seventh grade? Why might it be more motivating to learn about the Middle Ages by reading a book like this than by reading a typical middle-grade history textbook?

Throughout this chapter, we will suggest ways to complement a full curriculum with literature, from short read-alouds to the use of novels and other full-length books. Consider carefully the potential understanding and appreciation that can come from literature; it is well worth including in a busy schedule.

Encouraging Responses to Literature

Some people are troubled by the idea of using trade books, especially fiction, to enhance students' understanding of content area concepts. They recall all too clearly how teachers ruined perfectly good novels by assigning questions and papers and by wringing out, chapter by chapter, every last bit of significance and interpretation, demolishing any possibility of enjoying a book purely for the personal and emotional responses it evokes. But surely, you are thinking, there are less heavy-handed ways to use literature as a basis for understanding content area information.

How should students respond to literature? How much should students' response be influenced by a teacher? The literary theory of Louise Rosenblatt (1978) suggests some possible answers. She describes reading as a complex transaction between reader and text. How a reader responds and what meaning a reader constructs from a text are influenced by the stance or purpose that the reader chooses. Rosenblatt (1985) defines two possible stances, the *efferent* and the *aesthetic*:

The difference between the two kinds of reading lies in the reader's "selective attention" to what is being stirred up in the experiential reservoir. The predominantly efferent reader focuses attention on public meaning, abstracting what is to be retained after reading—to be recalled, paraphrased, acted on, analyzed. In aesthetic reading, the reader's selective attention is focused primarily on what is being personally lived through, cognitively and affectively, *during* the reading event. The range of ideas, feelings, associations activated in the reservoir of symbolizations is drawn upon. . . . Any text . . . can be read either way. (pp. 101–102)

Rosenblatt (1982) makes it clear that neither teachers nor readers have to make an all-or-nothing choice between efferent and aesthetic purposes for reading. She maintains that any reading act falls somewhere on a continuum between efferent and aesthetic, with most reading somewhere in the middle. She also recognizes the need for both kinds of reading and the need to teach students to read for both efferent and aesthetic purposes, although she cautions that greater emphasis needs to be placed on aesthetic reading.

 Evidence-Based Research

Cynthia Lewis (2000) argues that the aesthetic stance is too often limited strictly to personal identification and interpretation. She suggests that aesthetic reading also encompasses a social or critical dimension, especially when readers are reading about cultures or experiences that are quite different from their own. She cites as an example *The Watsons Go to Birmingham—1963* (Curtis, 1995), a novel about an African American family at the time of the civil rights movement. The interactions of this close-knit family will have a personal aesthetic appeal to all readers, who can identify with the humor, warmth, and varied personalities. However, in the details of the Watsons' experiences with and resistance to white racism, European American readers are clearly positioned as outsiders. In this instance, the aesthetic experience is not one of close personal identification but rather understanding how the characters' lives are different from one's own.

How does a teacher translate theory into practice? That is, how can you teach a novel and leave room for students to experience it aesthetically? First, teachers need to be receptive to students' stances. That means that teachers should listen carefully for students' reactions—whether efferent or aesthetic, positive or negative. Students need the freedom to determine their own purposes for reading and their own reactions to reading.

Obviously, the very fact that a book is assigned for reading limits student choice and suggests an efferent purpose. Therefore, teachers must be careful how assignments and questions are posed if they wish to retain the possibility of aesthetic response. Rosenblatt (1982) warns that requests for verbal responses from students are especially liable to get in the way of aesthetic reading. In their questions, adults often telegraph what the correct response should be or steer students toward what the adult finds pertinent or interesting.

To encourage aesthetic reading and response, teachers can begin discussion of literature by asking for the readers' responses first. Rosenblatt (1982) suggests questions such as "Did anything especially interest . . . annoy . . . puzzle . . . frighten [or] please [you or] seem familiar [or] weird?" (p. 276). Knowledge of students, their interests and their outlooks, helps a teacher choose questions that allow them to connect with other texts, other ideas, and other experiences. It is also useful to let students connect with each other, to let them see the similarities and differences in their points of view, perhaps by using some of the ideas presented in Chapter 9 and Chapter 10 or one of the strategies discussed later in this chapter.

Integrating Literature into Content Areas

This section describes several uses of literature in content areas and suggests some resources that should facilitate your search for pertinent books.

Uses of Literature in Content Areas

Evidence-Based Research

Literature can complement any content area. For English teachers, of course, literature study represents a sizeable segment of the curriculum. Literature complements the study of history and contemporary social issues by dramatizing and personalizing issues and events. There is also support in the research literature for integrating literature into content areas. For example, Wineburg (1991), a highly respected scholar in the field of history education, draws from his research on novice and expert readers when he recommends that young people should be given more than just history textbooks to read as part of the school curriculum. Although literature is less likely to be associated with content areas such as science and math, numerous nontextbook resources provide an added dimension to these subjects as well.

READ-ALOUDS AND BOOK TALKS   By talking about books and reading aloud from books in class, teachers demonstrate that experts in a content area enjoy reading and actively pursue reading related to their field. Furthermore, such teacher modeling can be contagious. Teachers who actively promote reading and share what they read create interest on the part of students and illustrate the range of reading materials available. Equally important, hearing a teacher read high-quality sources can enhance the receptive language and broaden the conceptual scope of students from diverse linguistic and cultural backgrounds.

Reading aloud to students is one of the best ways to share a love of books. Read-alouds can be anywhere from 5 to 20 minutes or more in length and might be a daily or weekly occurrence in most any content area classroom. Short read-alouds can be used to develop interest and motivation, to introduce a new topic, to illustrate practical applications of content area concepts, and to inject a measure of humor into the classroom.

CONSIDER THIS EXAMPLE   In *Life on the Mississippi* (1961), Mark Twain writes about his experiences living and working on the great river in a book that is part travelogue, part natural history, and part tall tale. In one short passage, he describes how the river often cuts through a narrow neck of land, thereby shortening the course of the river by many miles. Using statistics creatively (but accurately), he calculates that in exactly 742 years, the Lower Mississippi will be only a mile and three-quarters long. He ends the passage with a typical Twain epigram: "One gets such wholesale returns of conjecture out of such a trifling investment of fact" (p. 120).

Mark Forget describes how he uses this passage in his algebra class, first reading it aloud and then plugging Twain's numbers into an algebraic formula, calculating the slope of the line, and plotting it on a graph (Richardson, 2000). Forget also points out that this passage would be an ideal read-aloud for a geography class, with its accurate descriptions of how the river works its will and the many citations of places readily found on different kinds of maps.

The following are some dos and don'ts for reading aloud (Trelease, 2006; Richardson, 2000; Sanacore, 2000):

1. Choose a selection that you enjoy and that you think students will like as well. It should be something that will encourage discussion and further inquiry. Your listeners will appreciate humor, strong emotion, action, or the unusual.

2. Preview the material. Look for parts you might want to shorten, eliminate, or discuss.

3. Reader and audience should get comfortable. Sit or stand where your audience can see you easily, with your head above the heads of your listeners so your voice can carry; make frequent eye contact with your audience.

4. Practice. Be expressive with your reading and do not rush; vary your intonation to heighten the action or indicate different characters.

5. Encourage predictions, questions, and discussion during reading, but do not impose your own point of view or lecture as you read. Inferential and critical-thinking questions can be used to follow up a read-aloud session.

6. Once you start a book or story, follow through unless it turns out to be universally unpopular. Students may not seem to be enjoying a book but will howl in protest if you decide not to finish it.

Appendix B is a list of books that contain short read-aloud selections pertinent to a variety of topics, historical events, and dates. A teacher could begin a class by reading about the physics of a curveball, what happened 100 years ago on a given day, or how dirty tricks were used in early presidential campaigns. A book-loving colleague especially recommends collections of weird and curious facts, for which he uses the delightful word *gallimaufry* (which originally referred to a kind of hash made up of leftovers). In this type of book, you can learn how crickets chirp, how Beethoven was able to compose even though he was deaf, and how the *Mariner I* space probe was lost because a minus sign was omitted from instructions fed into a computer. Such tidbits augment textbook information and add appeal to content area studies. Students also enjoy browsing through these books, even reluctant readers who would never consider the idea of reading a whole book cover to cover.

Judith Richardson (2000) illustrates suggested read-aloud selections for a wide range of content areas, including English as a second language. For English language learners (ELLs), read-alouds provide exposure to intonational and syntactic patterns, vocabulary, idioms, and important cultural and conceptual information. Among the read-aloud selections that Richardson recommends is *Grab Hands and Run* (Temple, 1993), the story of a Salvadoran family waiting for Canadian citizenship. This book treats issues of politics, immigration, assimilation, language differences, and language learning, many of which are pertinent to the experiences of ELLs.

Book talks are another medium through which a teacher can promote content-related literature. When a teacher does a five-minute "show-and-tell" with a book, whether it is an old favorite or a current page-turner, students see a reader who takes pleasure from books. Book talks can also create interest for a particular author or title. A teacher may even recommend titles for specific students, just like a recommendation between friends. It is a powerful incentive to a student to have a teacher hand him or her a book and say something like "I know something about you, and I think you'll enjoy this—try it!"

FREE-READING TIME   Some teachers have successfully instituted a regular time when everybody in the class simply reads. This activity, called *SSR* (sustained silent reading) or *DEAR* (Drop Everything and Read) time, has only two simple requirements. First, everybody reads, including the teacher. Second, students must read something other than their textbooks (and the teacher is not supposed to grade papers). This second requirement might be modified in content area classes by restricting students to reading material related to the subject area. That is, students in science class should be reading something relevant to science, other than the class text.

In secondary-level content area classrooms, time is probably the biggest obstacle to implementing free-reading time. Even if it is impractical to schedule free reading throughout the year, teachers can institute SSR when students are working on outside reading projects, especially at the beginning, when they need to make a selection and get a good head start on reading it.

In-school free reading requires that students have access to reading materials. Some students will bring their own books to read, especially if they know independent reading will take place at a regular time. Those who do not have their own books will need to select something from the classroom library. Content area teachers can stock their classroom libraries with materials that represent a variety of reading levels, lengths, and formats. Many of the titles listed in Appendix B make excellent SSR resources, along with paperbacks, periodicals, newspapers, and graphic novels.

The purpose of SSR is to give students an opportunity to practice lifetime reading skills, to read for their own purposes and pleasure. Independent reading is not a for-credit activity. Students are not graded, nor are they expected to produce anything as a result of their reading. It might be helpful to use a part of free reading time for book talks by the teacher or by student volunteers, but otherwise it is devoted simply to reading for the sake of reading.

Independent reading is an essential component in the language development of ELLs. Reading interesting, ability-appropriate materials provides ELLs with *comprehensible input* (Krashen, 1985). Opportunities to read without academic pressure can help ELLs make a transition from easier to more difficult materials. Furthermore, reading exposes ELLs to a wider range of topics, concepts, syntactic patterns, and vocabulary than they are likely to encounter in their oral-language interactions.

Janice Pilgreen (2000) describes a successful SSR program established for high school ELLs. She lists eight factors that will influence the success of such a program:

1. *Access:*   Students will need a wide variety of reading materials at suitable levels.
2. *Appeal:*   Magazines, comic books, and series books will be especially popular.
3. *Conducive environment:*   Posters, artwork, and comfortable places to sit make it pleasant to read. Silent-reading time should also be free of interruptions and distractions.
4. *Encouragement:*   Teachers can model their own enjoyment of reading during free-reading time and explain the benefits of reading for students' language development.
5. *Distributed time to read:*   Students need regularly scheduled times for free reading throughout the week. Daily practice is optimal.
6. *Nonaccountability:*   Free reading should involve no book reports, journal entries, or comprehension assessments.
7. *Follow-up activities:*   Students should have opportunities to share information with each other about their reading on a voluntary basis.
8. *Staff training:*   Teachers need to understand the substantial benefits of free-reading time as well as how to implement a formal free-reading program.

High school ELL students were asked to comment on the free-reading program. The following samples indicate their enthusiasm (Pilgreen, 2000):

"My vocabulary is better, and I have noticed that my understanding of English has improved."

"When I began reading, I didn't want to stop, even for a minute. Now I want to read the harder books."

"Sometimes when I read I get excited, and I don't want to stop reading so I take the book home."

"I like a lot when you allowed us to read newspapers and magazines because I could get information about modern things."

"The books are getting harder and longer now than before because I used to read short easy books." (pp. 82–85)

We have heard from some teachers that their schools have discontinued SSR time because the National Reading Panel (NRP, 2000) found that in-school independent reading was ineffective. In fact, the NRP subgroup report on fluency found only fourteen studies that met their stringent criteria for experimental research. The subgroup concluded that the results were mixed and that there was insufficient evidence to recommend in-school independent reading.

However, Stephen Krashen (2002) points out that the NRP misinterpreted some of the studies included in their analysis and overlooked other studies that did meet their criteria. When Krashen added studies that involved college-age students and ELLs and recalculated the results, he found that SSR students did as well as or better than comparison students in 50 out of 53 comparisons. In fact, SSR students were superior in 8 out of 10 studies that lasted for more than a year. Krashen points out that SSR appears to have the greatest effect for students who have the greatest need—that is, struggling readers and ELLs. It is also noteworthy that in the subsection on vocabulary, the NRP recommends independent reading as an effective means for building students' word knowledge.

Implementation of SSR has shown consistently strong correlation with reading improvement. For example, Douglas Fisher (2004) reports on an urban high school where 75 percent of the students were ELLs and 99 percent of the student body qualified for free lunch. (Qualifying for free lunch is often used as an indicator of students' low-income status.) Although the school had an SSR program, observations revealed that it was not being uniformly implemented. Many students had no opportunity for independent reading in school, and teachers knew from surveying students that many did not have opportunities for free reading at home either. A review of the school's previous standardized reading tests scores showed that students in classrooms where SSR was regularly practiced had higher reading scores by 0.6 of a year over classes where SSR was not done. Based on this information, the faculty decided to implement a new standard at the school—the Opportunity to Read standard, which resulted in more effective schoolwide implementation of SSR.

This suggests that decisions about using SSR in a school or a specific classroom should be made locally and based on the particular needs of the students in that setting. Such decisions should be made after considering multiple criteria, including data from testing, student surveys, characteristics of the student body, the availability of sufficient and suitable reading materials, administrative support, and the willingness of faculty to buy in to the program.

COMPLEMENTARY READINGS   Literature can be used in a variety of ways to complement textbooks. Some teachers may have a whole class reading a single book or story during a thematic unit. For instance, a social studies class might read *Roll of Thunder, Hear My Cry* (Taylor, 1976) as part of a unit on the Great Depression. Many of the prereading, comprehension, writing, and vocabulary strategies presented in earlier chapters are appropriate when the whole class is reading the same book. To maximize students' involvement and self-direction, we especially recommend anticipation guides and K-W-L (Chapter 6), ReQuest and self-questioning (Chapter 7), vocabulary self-selection (Chapter 8), discussion webs (Chapter 9), and learning logs (Chapter 10).

Whole-class study of a single book requires enough copies of the book for every student to have one, which can stretch a tight school budget. There is also the problem that some students may find a particular text uninteresting or too challenging. An alternative strategy is to select several titles, all related to a single topic or theme. (You will find books related to specific themes suggested in Appendixes B, C, andD.) When several different books are available, students have a choice of what to read.

Multiple titles also present the possibility of offering different cooperative-learning arrangements. If students are grouped with others reading the same book, they may work cooperatively on developing a book talk, a poster or visual display, a read-aloud, or a multimedia presentation based on the book. Students in a group all reading different books may do book talks within their group, or the group may develop some cooperative project such as a website devoted to student inquiry and writing.

Complementary reading does not need to be focused on a particular topic or theme. Content teachers often assign outside reading projects, for which students are allowed to choose their own books. Social studies teacher Edwin Biloff (1996) incorporated complementary trade book reading with his eleventh-grade American history class. During their study of the Civil War, he assigned *The Killer Angels* (Shaara, 1974), a novel about the Battle of Gettysburg. Over a period of seven weeks, students read the novel, chose one of three major characters from the novel, conducted outside research in nonfiction resources on this person, and then wrote an essay that analyzed the person's character and leadership. In the essay, they were to compare the novelized treatment of their subject with the information found in the nonfiction sources.

Sprague and Cotturone (2003) describe the frustration of a high school physics teacher when she discovered that only about 10 percent of her students could readily answer questions based on short passages from their physics text. To motivate her students to read about physics, the teacher obtained a class set of *The Science of Star Wars* (Cavelos, 2000) and showed the first *Star Wars* film. Drawing on the movie and selected readings in the *Star Wars* book, she posed a series of physics problems for students to solve, resulting in a spirited exchange of ideas and information. The teacher offered extra credit for students who did additional reading in the book.

Based on the success of this initial trade book reading, the teacher divided students into small groups and gave them short selections from two other trade books, *The Einstein Paradox* (Bruce, 1997) and *Mr. Tompkins in Paperback* (Gamow, 1993). Each selection dealt with topics featured in the state physics standards. Over two 90-minute class periods, students discussed prereading questions, read the selections, and then prepared presentations for the rest of the class. Students selected presentation options in a variety of media, including PowerPoint, videos, storybooks, models, and role-playing. The presentations revealed a thorough and accurate understanding of the physics concepts involved, and students were surprised to find how much science they could learn from reading.

TECHNOLOGY **Tip**

Linking Science and Literature
Visit www.tc.columbia.edu/centers/sci_lit/ teacherresources.html to learn how interdisciplinary inquiry linking science and literature through a teacher-developed Web site created opportunities for middle school students "to investigate and document their environment, and figure out ways to incorporate into the website what they saw, wondered about, and learned" (Howes, Hamilton, & Zaskoda, 2003, p. 494).

Teachers at an urban high school with a large number of English language learners wanted to help students read and enjoy science (Creech & Hale, 2006). They instituted four nontextbook reading projects in the ninth-grade science curriculum. The first was a monthly Science in the News activity, in which they guided students to find science-related news stories and summarize the procedures, results, and "big ideas" of the articles. The second project involved reading a nonfiction science book and creating a children's science book based on what was learned. For the last two projects, students read the biography of a scientist and read a fiction book with solid science content. The last project, the fiction reading, was done in a book club format, where students met twice a week to plan their reading schedules and discuss their books. As the teachers implemented these projects, they found that they needed to augment the school library's science collection to provide ample books of varied genre and reading level. (A list of the books they added, along with additional information on the various assignments and activities, can be found at www.wested.org/cs/sli/print/docs/842.) After three years of inquiry on these efforts, Creech and Hale (2006) found that their students were becoming more capable and more willing science readers.

Fiction and Nonfiction for Content Areas

One major difference between lifetime readers and school readers is the matter of choice. Young people and adults who enjoy reading as a regular pastime choose their reading materials from among many genres, authors, and subjects; in school, readers are limited for the most part to what they are assigned or what is available in the school library. However, these school reading materials are not reflective of the wide range of adolescent reading preferences (Ivey & Broaddus, 2001; Worthy, Moorman, & Turner, 1999).

Lack of choice in school reading is one reason frequently cited by secondary students who are willing readers outside school but resist assigned reading (Bintz, 1993). *Aliterate* students, those who can read but choose not to, cited "choosing their own books" as the number-one thing that would motivate them to read more (Beers, 1996). The choices teachers can offer students are constrained by time, curriculum, and resources. However, teachers recognize the importance of selecting books and readings that will appeal to readers (Palmer & Stewart, 1997).

Evidence-Based Research

It is difficult to assess what adolescent readers are likely to enjoy because their tastes are as varied as those of adult readers. In a study of Illinois high school students, Moffit and Wartella (1992) found a preference for romance among females and for fantasy, science fiction, and sports among males. When Bank (1986) surveyed students in grades 6 through 12 in the New York metropolitan area, their interests ranged across a total of 58 different topics. The top 10 topics were young people, mystery, humor, adventure, love, sex, movies, famous people, romances, and horror, but preferences varied widely by grade level, ethnicity, native language, and other student characteristics. Urban adolescents' preferences are similarly diverse, with the most popular topics being celebrities, sports figures, musicians, and people with whom adolescents can personally identify (Hughes-Hassell & Rodge, 2007).

Boys generally lag behind girls in reading achievement and tend to spend less time reading, especially in adolescence (Brozo, 2002; Smith & Wilhelm, 2002). Teachers and librarians can make a difference, however, if they provide male readers with materials that they find motivating and accessible. For instance, boys are more inclined to read informational texts, graphic novels, and comic books. They like to read about sports, hobbies, and other active pursuits. Jon Scieszka, author and illustrator of books designed to appeal to boys, recommends a variety of titles for boys on his website, www.guysread.com.

The annual survey of young adult choices in literature conducted by the International Reading Association and published in the *Journal of Adolescent & Adult Literacy* confirms this interest in a wide range of topics, authors, and genres. It is important to remember, too, that nonfiction may account for as much as half of adolescents' leisure reading (Abrahamson & Carter, 1991).

With so many interests and so many available titles, it is difficult to pick a winner every time. Knowing your students and the available literature increases the possibility that you will make good choices, however. Appendixes C and D suggest some books that have been recommended to us by colleagues and teachers. These selections are far from exhaustive. To give you an idea of the range of options, we have tried to pick books that are of general interest as well as some that pertain to specific topics. In cases in which the title alone does not suggest the subject matter, we offer brief annotations. We also designate books written for young adults with a *YA*. This is tricky because so-called young adult books vary considerably in their format and content. Many are quite suitable for secondary school readers, but others are likely to be rejected as too immature. Ultimately, the teacher's judgment and a bit of trial and error will be necessary to match books and students.

Those who are looking for a trade book to complement a particular unit of study might find guidelines suggested by Biloff (1996) useful:

1. The reading should match students' reading levels, be interesting, represent content area concepts accurately, and complement curricular goals.

2. If choosing a novel, look for action, crisp dialogue, and empathic characters.

3. Select material for which you have special interest or expertise.

4. Consider piloting the material with a representative student sample.

5. Readings that can be coordinated with audiovisuals are especially useful.

6. Look for material that could be used in varied and interesting ways from year to year.

PICTURE BOOKS, MANGA, AND GRAPHIC NOVELS FOR CONTENT AREAS
Picture books and so-called graphic novels tell stories and illustrate concepts from literature, science, social studies, and mathematics (Miller, 1998; Schwarz, 2002, 2004.) While traditional picture books are familiar to most people, manga and graphic novels are relatively new genres.

Manga are printed comics with stylized drawings and common themes that originated in Japan and have become enormously popular with American young people. The animated versions are called *anime* and can be seen on U.S. television. To learn more about manga and anime, visit www.koyagi.com, a site dedicated to fans of these genres. There are many links to examples and resources, as well as guides for teachers, librarians, and parents.

Graphic novels (some done in manga style) are essentially extended comic books, and along with contemporary picture books, they treat a wide range of subjects, including the environment, families, ethnic heritage, relationships, war, love, social problems, and historical events. Many picture books and graphic novels feature exceptional artistic and literary accomplishment. For instance, Art Spiegelman's graphic novel about the Holocaust, *Maus* (1986), won a Pulitzer Prize.

You may think of picture books and comics as being unsuitable for serious use in middle and high school, but they can serve multiple purposes. They can be used to introduce abstract topics, develop technical vocabulary, provide information for inquiry projects, prompt writing, and provide both visual and conceptual experiences with people from diverse cultures.

The themes of many picture books and graphic novels have appeal that transcends age levels, and they are often written at fairly advanced conceptual and maturity levels. For example, Neal and Moore (1991–1992) cite *Rose Blanche* (Innocenti, 1985), a disturbing story of the Holocaust, and *The Wall* (Bunting, 1990), which tells the story of the Vietnam Veterans Memorial, as two picture books that address worldly and emotional topics in a realistic fashion.

Schwarz (2004) points out that many graphic novels also give nuanced treatment to a wide range of worthy topics and lend themselves to teaching multiple literacies, including print literacy, visual literacy, and media literacy. Graphic novels also address a wide range of issues and cultural diversity. First Second, a publisher of high-quality graphic novels, offers lesson plans for some its works related to history and current events on its website, www.firstsecondbooks.com.

Go to MyEducationLab and select the topic *Multimodal Texts*. Then, go to the Activities and Applications section, watch the video entitled "Using Picture Books in 8th-Grade Language Arts," and respond to the accompanying prompts.

Helping
Struggling Readers

Picture Books

The availability of picture books for both independent and content-specific reading helps to establish them as acceptable for *all* students (Miller, 1998). This is especially helpful for struggling readers, who can get pleasure and useful content from picture books but who might be embarrassed if they felt they were being targeted to read "kids' books." High-quality picture books with challenging ideas and interesting content can provide struggling readers with much-needed practice and confidence.

The short format of picture books makes them especially well suited to complement the short class periods in most middle and high schools. A picture book can be read in its entirety during the period, with time left for discussion or other activities. Graphic novels are also relatively short, and their often colorful formats provide a welcome and motivating change from textbooks.

Picture books can help make visual and verbal connections for students who are learning English. Nancy Hadaway and Jane Mundy (2000) outline a unit on weather that they developed for high school ELLs. They decided to emphasize the seasons, weather phenomena, and weather disasters. Students used informational picture books, newspaper weather reports, national weather maps, and books with weather experiments as their texts. During the course of the unit, students wrote poetry that featured weather vocabulary, created their own graphic organizers of weather concepts, wrote about their weather experiments and observations in weather journals, and made a weather collage of words and pictures. To culminate the unit, students researched weather-related disasters such as floods, tornadoes, and hurricanes. Their inquiry was scaffolded with picture books before they moved to the school library to consult standard reference materials.

Like picture books, graphic novels also provide productive literacy experiences for struggling readers and English language learners. Frey and Fisher (2004) used graphic novels as writing prompts for a ninth-grade class of struggling readers in a San Diego high school, three-quarters of whom were ELLs. The class participated in shared reading of the graphic novels, beginning with *New York: The Big City* (Eisner, 1986), which features short independent chapters. The class brainstormed descriptive vocabulary, and then students wrote out their own versions of the story. Graphic novels continued to be used for several weeks as prompts for writing and for consideration of word choice, sentence structure, and varied ways to develop ideas. As a culminating activity, students used photographs, original manga art, and images taken from graphic novels and the Internet to illustrate their own extended fictional stories about urban life, interactive Internet games, and other popular culture themes. The authors found that the graphic novels afforded a visual vocabulary for talking about writing techniques and that this popular culture artform was an effective bridge to school literacy.

INTEGRATING POPULAR CULTURE   Earlier in this book, we raised the question of how popular culture and the new literacies might be incorporated into school curricula. An expanded conception of adolescent literacies must take into account both the pleasure and the utility that adolescents find in such popular media as movies, television, music CDs, phones and pagers, magazines, graphic novels, electronic games, and the Internet. Whether we bid them to or not, adolescents bring these literacies into school.

Lorri Neilsen (1998) tells the story of her son David, a high school junior who downloaded parts of the filmscript to the movie *Pulp Fiction* from the Internet. David and his friends memorized long passages of the movie dialogue and produced their own videotaped versions of favorite scenes. David also directed scenes from the movie for a school drama project. Neilsen explains that a movie such as *Pulp Fiction* can become a "touchstone text" for adolescents, a text that helps adolescents to "make and shape meaning in their lives through literacy" (p. 4). She goes on to consider the implications of these texts for teachers and teaching. She says that adolescents like her son remind her

> that their ongoing curriculum is the lives they lead; that they teach one another and can teach their teachers; and that they will explore learning, grow in their literacy, and dream their dreams in settings often much more influential than school settings. What important paths to learning are we blocking off at the school door? How can we learn to listen to that learning and bring it into school settings and curricula? (p. 22)

In an intergenerational conversation, Tom Bean and his adolescent daughters explored the many functions of text and media for the two girls, both in school and out (Bean, Bean, & Bean, 1999). Both girls had teachers who encouraged them to make connections between home, school, and peer cultures. Sixteen-year-old Shannon's social studies teacher allowed students to express their understanding of historical periods through artwork, models, and rap songs. For a science project on animals, twelve-year-old Kristen used her home computer to write about dogs, specifically the cocker spaniel that she has trained and shown. In both cases, the girls were able to use their multiple literacies and interests in the service of school-based learning. If we expand our conceptions of literacy and text to incorporate popular media and culture, we will find many ways to help make such connections.

Literacy Coaches' Corner

Because content area teachers may not have a lot of time to locate resources for the kinds of trade book projects discussed in this chapter, so the literacy coach can help locate and organize these materials. If you have a colleague who would like to have students read beyond the textbook, you can offer to help him or her locate suitable materials at varied levels. This chapter and Appendices B, C, and D can give you some guidance. Also contact the library media specialist at your school, who just might be your best resource in this endeavor.

As a literacy coach, you may also find colleagues who are interested in forming a book club or study group, either across disciplines or specific to a particular content area. Some states and school districts give teachers in-service credit for participation in a study group. A group might read professional literature related to their subject area or pedagogy, or they may be more interested in reading fiction or nonfiction trade books. If so, you can again be a resource for locating suggested reading, scheduling, and facilitating meetings.

CENSORSHIP A discussion of using literature in content areas would not be complete without considering the problem of censorship. When community groups or parents exert pressure to remove reading materials from the school library or classroom, school boards and administrators often acquiesce, with the result that an entire class or school may be denied the right to read a particular text (Bucher & Manning, 2007). The potential threat of external protests as well as personal objection to certain works of literature may also lead teachers to self-censorship.

For example, the *Harry Potter* series has prompted numerous protests by people who object to the alleged promotion of witchcraft and magic in the books. Other books that are regularly the object of censorship attempts include *The Catcher in the Rye*, *Huckleberry Finn*, *The Diary of Anne Frank*, and *I Know Why the Caged Bird Sings*. Much contemporary young adult fiction addresses issues such as sexuality, violence, and drug use that may make teachers, parents, or administrators uncomfortable. Nevertheless, many teachers feel an ethical as well as intellectual duty to help students read critically about topics that, while potentially controversial, are relevant to important social issues and to students' lives outside school (Alsup, 2003).

Evidence-Based Research

In interviews with five experienced high school English teachers, Jane Agee (1999) found that all wanted to include diverse, rich, contemporary literature in their curriculum, but all had found themselves, at one time or another, in risky territory because of their book choices. In very real terms, teachers who want their students to read a wide range of texts may be putting their careers in jeopardy. When schools have formal policies and procedures for handling book challenges, active book screening committees, collegial discussions of potential texts, and supportive administrators and colleagues, they are less likely to succumb to the pressures of censors. Even in the best of circumstances, however, books are banned and teachers learn to be cautious about what they bring into the classroom.

The teachers that Agee (1999) interviewed detailed many strategies for introducing potentially controversial texts into their curricula, and they also practiced some form of self-censorship. One defense is to carefully weigh the maturity and family backgrounds of students and decide how much of a fight a particular book is worth. Another is to communicate carefully with parents about what students will be reading and why. For instance, at the beginning of the year one teacher sent home a list of 30 films she *might* show during the year, although in practice she only used five or so a semester. Students and parents could review the list, and if there were potential problems, students could drop the class. Sometimes teachers offer to provide alternative readings if there is isolated objection to a proposed assignment.

Another proactive strategy is to include censorship issues as part of the curriculum, thus engaging students directly in the debate over their right to read. For example, to prepare for the reading of *Huckleberry Finn*, teachers often discuss the history of censorship attempts on the book. This prepares both European American and African American students to critically consider the racial issues prompted by Twain's portrayal of Huck and Jim and his use of the vernaculars of the place and time in which the story is set. Although such preparation does not settle all the controversies, it helps to diffuse them and set the stage for critical but civil discussion, in which students of different backgrounds and beliefs are better prepared to understand diverse points of view.

Developing Awareness of Diversity through Literature

In many large urban centers, linguistically or culturally diverse children often comprise half or more of the school population, a fact that challenges the very notion of a mainstream or majority culture. African American and Hispanic/Latino students represent the largest cultural minorities in schools, but they are by no means the only representatives of culturally diverse groups.

To cite one example, Grover Cleveland High School in Buffalo, New York, has approximately 1,000 students, of whom approximately 38 percent are Hispanic, 24 percent are African American, 18 percent are Asian, and 20 percent are of European origin. However, that does not tell the whole story, because nearly half of these students are classified as having limited English proficiency, and their numbers encompass students from 19 different language groups, including Spanish, Vietnamese, Cambodian, Russian, Ukrainian, and Arabic. Labels such as "Hispanic" and "Asian" obscure the true diversity of these students, who include native-born Americans as well as immigrants from Puerto Rico, El Salvador, Mexico, Venezuela, Honduras, Ethiopia, Somalia, China, Japan, Korea, Vietnam, Thailand, Cambodia, and Laos. The specific demographics and ethnic mixes will differ, but most large cities have selected schools with similar diversity.

This diversity poses both challenges and opportunities. For the students, there are the challenges and dilemmas of alienation, assimilation, and acculturation. For schools whose expectations, curricula, and methods are based on mainstream culture, there are the challenges of reaching out to an increasingly diverse student population and of fostering tolerance and understanding among all students. There is also the opportunity to celebrate this diversity, to use the varied talents of people from many cultures, and to break down the barriers between "us" and "them," while adding to the rich texture of the United States' cultural tapestry.

Advantages of Using Multicultural Literature

Literature provides a vehicle for both meeting these challenges and realizing the potential of cultural diversity. First, several positive effects occur when students read about their own culture. Culturally relevant literature validates students' cultural identity and projects a positive image of them and their culture. In a review of African American children's literature, for instance, Bishop (1990) notes five important positive themes:

1. Warm and loving human relations, especially in the family
2. A sense of community among African Americans
3. African American history, heritage, and culture
4. A sense of continuity
5. Physical and psychological survival in the face of overwhelming odds

When such personal validation comes from books read at school, students' positive identification with the school itself is strengthened, and school becomes a place where students can explore issues that are culturally and personally relevant. In a study of African American girls in a high school honors English class, Sutherland (2005) documented their responses as they read *The Bluest Eye*, by Toni Morrison (1994.) The girls were particularly focused on the Eurocentric concept of beauty as it related to them, as well as beliefs about who they were expected to be and how they were expected to behave. Although these social issues were far from resolved in the girls' discussions, the opportunity afforded by the book to talk about them was empowering.

Culturally relevant literature can also be an important tool for developing students' motivation to read. The personal appeal of reading about culturally familiar subjects can be especially effective with students who are otherwise disinterested in books.

The value of reading stories by and about people of various cultures extends to all students, however, regardless of ethnic or cultural affiliation (Spears-Bunton, 1998). From a strictly curricular standpoint, reading culturally diverse literature can increase students' knowledge of history and geography and expand their understanding of literary technique (Norton, 1990). More important, readers can gain a greater understanding and appreciation of cultures other than their own when they identify with the characters in a novel. The literature of different cultures helps to break down some of the myths and stereotypes people hold.

Resistance to Multicultural Literature

Unfortunately, there is evidence of resistance to the use of multicultural literature on the part of some students, teachers, administrators, community members, and politicians (McCarthy, 1998; Stallworth, Gibbons, & Fauber, 2006). Some object on the grounds that schools should focus on traditionally recognized and accepted great works that transmit values and ideas common to the mainstream culture (Bloom, 1994; Hirsch, 1987). Administrators may feel that using multicultural literature will not be accepted by parents, will interfere with a more skills-based approach to literacy, or will unfairly focus attention on particular ethnic or cultural groups (Godina, 1996).

Glazier and Seo (2005) describe discussions of *The Way to Rainy Mountain* (Momaday, 1996), a book about the Kiowa nation, in a culturally diverse ninth-grade classroom. They found that in conversations about the book, non–European American students frequently gave voice to ideas and feelings that had not been previously expressed, often in the form of personal narratives about their own cultural backgrounds and understandings. European American students, on the other hand, did not make the same text-to-self connections. When asked about his cultural background, Mark, a European American, replied, "I don't know . . . it's American. That's all I have—that's all the culture I know . . . I don't know what my culture is" (p. 696). Students like Mark did not see themselves reflected positively in the text, and the culture of the mainstream remained covert, unvoiced and unexamined.

Teachers' concerns fall into two general categories (Jordan & Purves, 1993). First, they see institutional constraints: whether literature should be used to foster cultural identity or to develop critical understanding, whether multicultural literature should bump the so-called classics from the curriculum, and whether a teacher from one cultural background can effectively teach multicultural literature to students of another culture. Second, teachers may feel constrained by the reactions and attitudes of their students. A teacher in an affluent suburb said, "Our students can feel superior to the literature of others as long as it deals with the suffering of others, but when it presents a point of view that they can't feel sorry for, then it is not welcome" (p. 10). In contrast, another teacher felt that her students could not relate to multicultural literature "because nothing we read at school makes them feel important. The school's lower-middle-class whites get nothing from multicultural literature" (p. 100).

The apparent resistance of some students to multicultural literature is confirmed by Richard Beach (1997), who suggests that some of the high school readers he interviewed resisted a stance that acknowledged institutional racial or gender bias and instead adopted a stance of individual prejudice. That is, they rejected the notion that they might be prejudiced and instead attributed bias to other individuals rather than to the society as a whole. Thus, mainstream readers may deny ethnic or gender differences, profess a lack of relevant cultural knowledge, resist feelings of guilt or complicity, and contest challenges to their privileged status in society. At the same time, Beach found other readers who adopted alternative stances that allowed them to empathize with people of other cultures and to reflect on their own status in society.

These are complex issues that do not have easy answers. It is our feeling that the very resistance to multicultural literature is an argument for its inclusion in the curriculum. The United States is a pluralistic society, and the more its people understand about each other, the better off they will be. There is much in multicultural literature that reinforces basic beliefs and aspirations that are common across U.S. society, while still pointing out important differences in the way people can think, act, live, and feel. It is important that Americans understand where their similarities and differences lie, even if their differences cannot always be easily reconciled.

Insistence that student readers must be limited to a narrow corpus of great works simply does not make good sense. First, it assumes the impossible, which is that people could ever agree on what should be included in such a body of work. It ignores the fact that greatness is a fluid concept that changes with time, location, and those who define it. Insisting that there are certain works that students must read in school is to assume that they would or could never read anything else, that their reading will be limited exclusively to what they get in school (Hughes, 1993). Finally, there is a high degree of artistic and intellectual merit in the best of multicultural fiction and nonfiction so that inclusion of such works does not displace an emphasis on reading works of quality.

There are ways that a teacher can help to reduce students' resistance to reading about other cultures. It is important, first of all, to understand why some students may be uncomfortable with what they perceive as challenges to their position or to the beliefs

TECHNOLOGY Tip

Culturally Appropriate Materials and Lesson Plans on the Internet

Young people's resistance to academic reading practices can sometimes prompt teachers to look for alternative kinds of material in an attempt to help students make connections between their everyday lives and content area learning. Sometimes these well-intentioned attempts can backfire, especially when middle-class teachers make assumptions about lower-level socioeconomic communities that are incongruent with the culture of those communities (e.g., see Hicks & Dolan, 2003).

A website for choosing appropriate multicultural books, along with criteria for guiding your choices, is one titled How to Choose the Best Multicultural Books, available at http://teacher .scholastic.com/products/instructor/ multicultural.htm. For choices in other kinds of material, check out The CyberHunt Library at http://teacher.scholastic.com/products/ instructor/cyberhunt_kids.htm. This site offers opportunities for surfing the Web in search of fascinating facts that can be used to answer puzzles and other challenges in social studies, science, sports, and the language arts. Another site you will want to explore is one maintained by the Young Adult Library Services Association (www .ala.org/yalsa), which offers information on Teen Read Week and links to electronic discussion lists.

For examples of teacher and media guides to accompany young adult multicultural books, visit Cynthia Leitich Smith's Web page at www .cynthialeitichsmith.com/; it has been named one of the top-ten writer sites on the Internet by *Writer's Digest*. Finally, for lesson plans that are aligned with the IRA/NCTE *Standards for the English Language Arts*, visit www.readwritethink .org.

---

of their peers and family members. As models and facilitators, teachers can set a tone of tolerance and nonconfrontational dialogue.

Before introducing a multicultural text in class, a teacher should prepare by learning some biographical details of the author, reviewing the historical setting of the story and the period when the author wrote, and making "cultural footnotes" on things that may be unfamiliar to students (Willis & Palmer, 1998). This will allow teachers to share factual background information, clarify potential cultural misunderstandings, and prepare students to react to the story, characters, and action, not just to the culture (Jordan & Purves, 1993). To that end, many of the prereading activities in Chapter 6 could be employed.

Finally, it is important to bring mainstream students into the conversation, to give them a chance to tell their own stories, to consider their own culture, and to recognize that culture is a multifaceted concept (Glazier & Seo, 2005). Mainstream students need to see that one can have pride and confidence in one's heritage without necessarily being oppressive to others. To that end, Beach (1997) suggests that we give students examples of people who have transcended bias in their lives. Such people can be found in most communities, and their stories are recorded in the popular media and in biographies and autobiographies. Best of all, we can strive to be such models ourselves.

Choosing and Using Multicultural Literature

Locating suitable multicultural literature, planning for its instruction, and actually teaching it requires a considerable investment of time (Willis & Palmer, 1998). Nevertheless, the results are worth the investment.

Athanases (1998) reported on a year-long study of two urban tenth-grade classrooms in which teachers committed themselves to an exploration of diverse texts. During the year, the classes read short stories, poems, autobiographical pieces, plays, and novels by a diverse group of authors, including Amy Tan, Maya Angelou, Maxine Hong Kingston, Shakespeare, Sophocles, Langston Hughes, and Albert Camus. Both teachers encouraged students to develop their own literary responses and exploratory thinking through collaborative projects and presentations, journal writing, and open-ended questioning by both teachers and students that emphasized analysis, synthesis, and speculation over literal recall. Most important, both teachers encouraged students to explore racial and ethnic issues openly and to use their personal and community knowledge to help them interpret what they were reading.

The students represented diverse academic levels, ethnic backgrounds, and language communities. African American, Chinese American, Filipino, European American, Puerto Rican, Mexican, and Central American heritages were all represented in significant numbers. Half of each class spoke a language other than English at home, and one-fourth of the students had been formally identified as at risk for school failure. During the course of the year, Athanases (1998) documented responses over a wide range of categories:

- Family and adolescent concerns
- Pride of culture and place
- Developing cultural identities
- Developing gender and sexual identities
- Learning from new experiences and ideas about cultures
- Rethinking stereotypes

Of course, there was also resistance to challenging ideas and portrayals in the literature as well as occasional tensions and conflicts during discussions. Nevertheless, the varied texts and the exploratory talk in these classes helped students make connections and discoveries that many of them recalled vividly two years afterward. In his summary of the study, Athanases (1998) notes that simply introducing diversified texts into the classroom is not enough. He says we need to "move beyond debates on *what* should be taught, to analyses of *how*—an essential step, because changing course materials alone has not historically yielded humanistic benefits" (p. 293).

For the teacher, however, deciding what should be taught is the first step. Teachers who are not familiar with or are a little overwhelmed by the growing body of multicultural literature might start by reading works that fit their particular interests or curricular needs and teaching what they are learning (Spears-Bunton, 1998). It is important to make a distinction between *world literature* (e.g., stories about people in

Africa or Latin America) and *ethnic American literature* (stories about African Americans or Latino Americans). Selecting literature that is representative of diverse cultural backgrounds also requires sensitivity to potential cultural and gender bias.

One issue is whether the author is writing from the perspective of an insider or an outsider (Harris, 1991). Some earlier works by outsider authors tended to be paternalistic or patronizing in their portrayals of culturally diverse groups. Although many authors write with sensitivity about cultures other than their own, being an insider may give an author more license to interpret a particular ethnic group's experience. There is also a need to avoid lumping different cultures together into "cultural conglomerates" (Reimer, 1992). As we pointed out earlier, *Hispanic* does not mean just Mexican or Puerto Rican, and a term such as *Asian* or *European* encompasses many different cultures. Also, teachers should not make the mistake of assuming that all members of a particular cultural group will enjoy the same books. To do so can lead to stereotyping and damaging overgeneralization.

Problems of representation occur when a handful of books are used to exemplify complex and diverse communities (Harris, 1997). This is illustrated by what might be called the "*Shabanu* syndrome" (Phelps, 2007). *Shabanu: Daughter of the Wind* (Staples, 1989) is an award-winning book that tells the story of a young girl in a nomadic tribe in the desert area of western Pakistan. It is perhaps the best-known example of young adult fiction about Muslims and continues to be widely read in U.S. schools. Although it is a well-written book with an interesting plot and a particularly compelling heroine, it has been criticized for perpetuating stereotypes of Muslims with its desert setting, camels, patriarchal nomadic society, and arranged marriages (Crocco, 2005). While the setting and plot of *Shabanu* are not necessarily inaccurate, the book does not reflect the circumstances of millions of cosmopolitan and educated Muslims living in countries from the United States to Indonesia. When reading a book like *Shabanu* is the only exposure that students have to a complex and diverse culture, it promotes a banal concept of *culture* that tends to essentialize people and gloss over diversity, differing perspectives, inequalities, and histories of colonialism and intervention (Abu El-Haj, 2002.) (For a representative list of alternative resources about Muslims, see Appendix D.)

The following guidelines, adapted from Hansen-Krening and Mizokawa (2000) and Pang et al. (1992), can help teachers to avoid stereotypes and choose books that accurately portray people of varying cultural identities. Good multicultural literature should have these qualities:

- *An authoritative author:*   If the author is not a member of the portrayed ethnic group, he or she must have some knowledge or experience that allows for credibility.
- *A culturally pluralistic theme:*   Cultural diversity should be valued and issues of cultural assimilation should be treated sensitively. Also, the work should transcend the "food, festival, and folktale" approach to multicultural literature.

- *A good plot and characterization:* An interesting plot and compelling characters are what make a book enjoyable. However, plot and characters may not necessarily adhere to traditional European American literary traditions.

- *Positive and accurate portrayals:* Characters from diverse cultures should be seen as empowered people and not be stereotyped. Ethnic Americans should be accurately portrayed, but it must be clear that they are at the same time American, not foreign. Many Asian Americans and Hispanic Americans are native born and may actually represent families whose history in the United States precedes that of many immigrants from the British Isles and Europe.

- *Accurate illustrations:* If there are pictures, they should not stereotype people's physical features, dress, and mannerisms.

- *Historical accuracy:* Books should be carefully researched by their authors.

For teachers who wish to broaden the cultural scope of their students' reading, there is both good news and bad news. The good news is that there are many diverse authors from diverse backgrounds turning out excellent works. The bad news is that many ethnic groups, most notably Hispanics/Latinos, who are the fastest-growing ethnic group in the United States, are not proportionately represented in literature (Barry, 1998). Also, in the competitive literary marketplace, many titles quickly go out of print and may be difficult to find.

With this caution in mind, we offer in Appendix D a list of titles that reflect some of the diverse cultures in today's schools. We intend this list to be representative, not exhaustive. Several of the authors presented have published numerous outstanding books besides those given, and many other authors we might have included but could not because of space limitations.

In addition, many of the articles and reviews cited in this chapter and in the Suggested Readings include excellent lists of culturally diverse literature. We especially recommend *Teaching and Using Multicultural Literature in Grades 9–12*, edited by Arlette Willis (1998), which has chapters on the literature of the African American, Puerto Rican, Asian/Pacific American, Native American, Mexican American, and Caribbean American communities.

S u m m a r y

A local video outlet advertises with the slogan "So many movies, so little time." That is how we feel about books. For a lifetime reader, there is both joy and frustration in the great wealth of reading material available. In this chapter, we have shown how literature can accomplish two important purposes. First, good literature can present content area facts, concepts, and issues in a form that is often more palatable and memorable than textbooks. Second, and perhaps more important, exposure to good literature can cultivate in students a passion for lifetime reading.

Suggested Readings

American Library Association. *Best books for young adults, High-low books for young adults, and Booklist: Young adult editors' choices.* Available online at www.ala.org/ala/yalsa/yalsa.cfm

Carr, C. (2001). Not just for primary grades: A bibliography of picture books for secondary content teachers. *Journal of Adolescent & Adult Literacy, 45,* 146–153.

Copeland, M., & Goering, C. (2003). Blues you can use: Teaching the Faust theme through music, literature, and film. *Journal of Adolescent & Adult Literacy, 46,* 436–441.

Harris, V. (Ed.). (1997). *Using multicultural literature in the K–8 classroom.* Norwood, MA: Christopher Gordon.

International Reading Association. Young adults' choices. Annotated bibliography of newly published books appears each fall in the *Journal of Adolescent and Adult Literacy.*

National Council for the Social Studies/Children's Book Council. Notable children's trade books in the field of social studies. Appears each spring in *Social Education.*

National Science Teachers Association/Children's Book Council. Outstanding science trade books for children. Appears each spring in *Science and Children.*

Pilgreen, J. (2000). *The SSR handbook: How to organize and manage a sustained silent reading program.* Portsmouth, NH: Heinemann.

Rand, D., & Parker, T. (2001). *Black books galore! Guide to more great African American children's books.* San Francisco: Jossey-Bass.

Reeves, A. R. (2004). *Adolescents talk about reading: Exploring resistance to and engagement with text.* Newark, DE: International Reading Association.

Richardson, J. (2000). *Read it aloud! Using literature in the secondary content classroom.* Newark, DE: International Reading Association.

Schon, I. (2002). From *Dias de pinta* to *Las Christmas*: Noteworthy books in Spanish for adolescents. *Journal of Adolescent & Adult Literacy, 45,* 410–414.

Smith, M., & Wilhelm, J. (2002). *"Reading don't fix no Chevys": Literacy in the lives of young men.* Portsmouth, NH: Heinemann.

Sprague, M., & Keeling, K. (2000). A library for Ophelia. *Journal of Adolescent & Adult Literacy, 43,* 640–647. (Novels that examine critical issues faced by girls)

Willis, A. (Ed.). (1998). *Teaching and using multicultural literature in grades 9–12: Moving beyond the canon.* Norwood, MA: Christopher Gordon.

MyEducationLab is a research-based learning tool that brings teaching to life. Go to the Alvermann, Phelps, and Ridgeway Gillis 6th Edition MyEducationLab for Content Area Reading site at www.myeducationlab.com to:

- engage in multimedia exercises to help you build a deeper and more applied understanding of chapter content;

- utilize extensive resources including videos from real classrooms, Praxis and licensure preparation, a lesson plan builder, and materials to help you in your teaching career.

Word Lover's Booklist

American Heritage Dictionaries. (2002). *The American heritage dictionary for learners of English.* Boston: Houghton-Mifflin.

Ammer, Christine (1989). *Fighting words: From war, rebellion, and other combative capers.* New York: Dell.

Amner, Christine (1997). *The American heritage dictionary of idioms.* Boston: Houghton Mifflin.

Blumenfeld, Warren (1989). *Pretty ugly: More oxymorons and other illogical expressions that make absolute sense.* New York: Putnam.

Bryson, B. (2002). *Bryson's dictionary of troublesome words: A writer's guide to getting it right.* New York: Broadway Books.

Burchfield, Robert, & Fowler, H. W. (2000). *The new Fowler's modern English usage,* 3rd ed. New York: Oxford University Press.

Carver, C. (1991). *A history of English in its own words.* New York: Harper-Collins.

Clark, Audrey (2003). *The Penguin dictionary of geography.* New York: Penguin.

Cole, Chris (1999). *Wordplay: A curious dictionary of language oddities.* New York: Sterling.

Cutler, C. (1994). *O brave new words: Native American loan words in current English.* Norman: University of Oklahoma Press.

Dunkling, Leslie (1990). *A dictionary of epithets and terms of address.* New York: Routledge.

Freeman, M. (1993). *Hue and cry and humble pie: The stories behind the words.* New York: Plume.

Garrison, W. (2000). *What's in a word? Fascinating stories of more than 300 everyday words and phrases.* Nashville, TN: Rutledge Hill.

Hendrickson, R. (1994). *Grand slams, hat tricks, and alley-oops: A sports fan's book of words.* New York: Prentice Hall.

Lederer, Richard (1989). *Anguished English.* New York: Pocket Books.

Liberman, A. (2005). *Word origins—and how we know them.* New York: Oxford. (Explains how etymology is actually done.)

McKean, E. (2006). *Totally weird and wonderful words.* New York: Oxford University Press.

McKean, E. (2007). *That's amore: The language of love for lovers of language.* New York: Walker & Company.

Mills, J. (1993). *Womanwords: A dictionary of words about women.* New York: Henry Holt.

Neaman, Judith, & Silver, Carole (1990). *Kind words: A thesaurus of euphemisms.* New York: Avon.

Randall, Bernice (1991). *When is a pig, a hog? A guide to confoundingly related English words.* Englewood Cliffs, NJ: Prentice Hall.

Rawson, Hugh (1989). *Wicked words: A treasury of curses, insults, put-downs, and other formerly unprintable terms from Anglo-Saxon times to the present.* New York: Crown.

Rovin, J. (1994). *What's the difference? A compendium of commonly confused and misused words.* New York: Ballantine.

Sheehan, Michael (2000). *Word parts dictionary: Standard and reverse listings of prefixes, suffixes, and combining forms.* Jefferson, NC: McFarland.

Smitherman-Donaldson, G. (2000). *Black talk: Words and phrases from the hood to the amen corner.* Boston: Mariner Books.

Spears, Richard (2001). *Contemporary American slang: An up-to-date guide to the slang of American English.* New York: McGraw-Hill.

Urdang, Laurence, LaRoche, Nancy, & Hunsinger, Walter (Eds.) (1998) *Picturesque expressions: A thematic dictionary.* New Lyme, CT: Verbatim Books.

Wasserman, P., & Hausrath, D. (2006). *Weasel words: The dictionary of American doublespeak.* Sterling, VA: Capital Books.

Westbrook, Alonzo (2002). *Hip hoptionary: The dictionary of hip hop terminology.* New York: Harlem Moon.

Read-Aloud Books for Content Areas

History and Social Studies

Beyer, Rick (2003). *The greatest stories never told: 100 tales from history to astonish, bewilder, and stupefy.* New York: HarperResource.

Boardman, Barrington (1988). *Flappers, bootleggers, "Typhoid Mary" and the bomb: An anecdotal history of the United States from 1923–1945.* New York: Harper and Row.

Davis, Kenneth (2001). *Don't know much about the presidents.* New York: HarperCollins.

Farquhar, M. (2003). *A treasury of great American scandals: Tantalizing true tales of historic misbehavior by the founding fathers and others who let freedom swing.* New York: Penguin Books.

Felton, Bruce (2003). *What were they thinking? Really bad ideas throughout history.* Guilford, CT: Globe Pequot Press.

Hay, Peter (1988). *All the presidents' ladies: Anecdotes of the women behind the men in the White House.* New York: Viking.

Hoose, Phillip (1993). *It's our world, too! Stories of young people who are making a difference.* Boston: Little, Brown. (Young social activists, including those from the Revolutionary War, abolitionists, labor, and civil rights)

Kane, Joseph, Anzovin, Steven, & Podell, Janet (1997). *Famous first facts: A record of first happenings, discoveries and inventions in American history* (5th ed.). New York: Wilson.

O'Brien, C. (2004). *Secret lives of the U.S. presidents.* Philadelphia: Quirk Books.

Rossi, Melissa (2003). *What every American should know about the rest of the world: Your guide to today's hot spots, hot shots, and incendiary issues.* New York: Plume.

Spinrad, Leonard, Spinrad, Thelma, Miller, Anistatia, & Brown, Jared (1999). *On this day in history.* Paramus, NJ: Prentice Hall.

Wagman, John (1990). *On this day in America: An illustrated almanac of history, sports, science, and culture.* New York: Gallery Books.

Science and Mathematics

Adair, Robert (1990). *The physics of baseball.* New York: Harper & Row.

Aschenbach, Joel (1996). *Why things are & why things aren't.* New York: Ballantine.

Berry, A. (1993). *The book of scientific anecdotes.* Buffalo, NY: Prometheus.

Bryson, Bill (2003). *A short history of nearly everything.* New York: Broadway Books.

Flaste, Richard (Ed.). (1991). *The New York Times book of science literacy: What everyone needs to know from Newton to the knuckleball.* New York: HarperCollins.

Flatow, Ira (1992). *They all laughed: From the lightbulb to the laser.* New York: HarperCollins.

Gardner, Martin (2001). *The colossal book of mathematics: Classic puzzles, paradoxes, and problems.* New York: Norton.

Goldberg, Philip (1990). *The Babinski reflex and 70 other useful and amusing metaphors from science, psychology, business, sports and everyday life.* Los Angeles: Tarcher.

Lee, Martin (2000). *40 fabulous math mysteries kids can't resist.* New York: Scholastic.

MacEachern, Diane (1990). *Save our planet: 750 everyday ways you can help clean up the earth.* New York: Dell.

Masoff, Joy (2000). *Oh, yuck: The encyclopedia of everything nasty.* New York: Workman.

McLain, B. (2001). *What makes flamingos pink?* New York: HarperCollins. (A book of questions and answers about all sorts of science facts)

Murphree, Tom, & Miller, Mary (1998). *Watching weather (Accidental scientist series).* New York: Henry Holt.

Park, Robert (2000). *Voodoo science: The road from foolishness to fraud.* New York: Oxford University Press.

Paulos, John A. (1999). *Once upon a number: The hidden mathematical logic of stories.* New York: Basic Books.

Ray, C. (1997). *The New York Times science questions and answers.* New York: Anchor.

Roberts, R. (2001). *Serendipity: Accidental discoveries in science.* New York: Wiley.

Seff, Philip, & Seff, Nancy (1996). *Petrified lightning and more amazing stories from "Our Fascinating Earth."* Chicago: NTC/Contemporary.

Shermer, M. (2002). *Why people believe weird things: Pseudoscience, superstition, and other confusions of our time.* New York: Henry Holt.

Tahan, M. (1993). *The man who counted: A collection of mathematic adventures.* New York: Norton.

Waldbauer, Gilbert (2000). *Millions of monarchs, bunches of beetles: How bugs find strength in numbers.* Cambridge, MA: Harvard University Press.

Gallimaufry

Bathroom Readers' Institute (1998). *Uncle John's great big bathroom reader.* Ashland, OR: Bathroom Readers' Press.

Carroll, Robert (2003). *The skeptic's dictionary: A collection of strange beliefs, amusing deceptions, and dangerous delusions.* New York: Wiley.

Craughwell, Thomas (1999). *Alligators in the sewer and 444 other absolutely true stories that happened to a friend of a friend of a friend.* New York: Black Dog & Leventhal.

Drimmer, Frederick. (1988). *Born different: Amazing stories of very special people.* New York: Bantam.

Dunn, Jerry (Ed.). (1991). *Tricks of the trade: Over 79 experts reveal the secrets behind what they do.* Boston: Houghton Mifflin.

Goldberg, M. Hirsch (1984). *The blunder book: Colossal errors, minor mistakes and surprising slipups that have changed the course of history.* New York: Morrow.

Kohn, Alfie (1990). *You know what they say: The truth behind popular beliefs.* New York: HarperCollins.

Schott, Ben (2003). *Schott's original miscellany.* New York: Bloomsbury.

Seuling, Barbara (1991). *You can't count a billion dollars! And other little known facts about money.* New York: Ballantine.

Tuleja, Tad (1999). *Fabulous fallacies: More than 300 popular beliefs that are not true.* New York: BBS.

Dead Ends

Bass, B., & Jefferson, J. (2007). *Beyond the body farm: A legendary bone detective explores murders, mysteries and the revolution in forensic science.* New York: HarperCollins.

Donaldson, Norman, & Donaldson, Betty (1989). *How did they die?* New York: St. Martin's.

Erzinclioglu, Z. (2003). *Maggots, murder and men: Memories and reflections of a forensic entomologist.* New York: St. Martin's Press.

Johnson, M. (2006). *The dead beat.* New York: HarperCollins. (Obituaries.)

Roach, M. (2004). *Stiff: The curious lives of human cadavers.* New York: W. W. Norton.

Shushan, E. R. (1990). *Grave matters.* New York: Ballantine.

Silverman, Stephen (1991). *Where there's a will.* New York: HarperCollins.

Slee, Christopher (1990). *The Chameleon book of lasts.* Huntingdon, UK: Chameleon.

Trade Books for Science, Math, and Social Studies

Discoverers and Discoveries

Adair, Gene (1989). *George Washington Carver.* Broomall, PA: Chelsea House. (YA)

Billings, Charlene (1989). *Grace Hopper: Navy admiral and computer pioneer.* Hillsdale, NJ: Enslow. (YA)

Brooks, P. (1989). *The house of life: Rachel Carson at work.* Boston: Houghton Mifflin.

Bryson, Bill (2003). *A short history of nearly everything.* New York: Broadway Books. (Everything from the Big Bang to the rise of civilizations, including many of the scientists who made important discoveries about our world and the universe)

Feynman, Richard (1999). *Meaning of it all: Thoughts of a citizen scientist.* Boulder, CO: Perseus.

Hartman, William (2003). *A traveler's guide to Mars: The mysterious landscapes of the red planet.* New York: Workman.

Kass-Simon, G., & Farnes, P. (1993). *Women in science: Righting the record.* Bloomington: Indiana University Press.

Kidd, R., Kessler, J., Kidd, J., & Morin, K. (1995). *Distinguished African American scientists of the 20th century.* Phoenix: Oryx Press.

Smith, Jane (1990). *Patenting the sun: Polio and the Salk vaccine.* New York: Morrow.

Vare, Ethlie, & Ptacek, Greg (1989). *Mothers of invention: From the bra to the bomb, forgotten women and their unforgettable ideas.* New York: Morrow.

Disasters

Ballard, Robert (with Rick Archbold) (1987). *The discovery of the Titanic.* New York: Warner/Madison.

Gale, Robert, & Hauser, Thomas (1988). *Final warning: The legacy of Chernobyl.* New York: Warner.

Lauber, Patricia (1986). *Volcano: The eruption and healing of Mt. St. Helens.* New York: Bradbury.

Petroski, Henry (1985). *To engineer is human.* New York: St. Martin's.

Preston, Richard (1994). *The hot zone.* New York: Random House. (Outbreak of the ebola virus)

Scotti, R. A. (2003). *Sudden sea: The great hurricane of 1938.* New York: Little, Brown.

Von Drehele, David (2003). *Triangle: The fire that changed America.* New York: Atlantic Monthly Press.

Ward, Kaari (Ed.). (1989). *Great disasters.* Pleasantville, NY: Reader's Digest.

Winchester, S. (2003). *Krakatoa: The day the world exploded, August 27, 1883.* (The eruption and resultant tsunami that killed nearly 40,000 people; also describes the wave of anti-Western militancy among Muslims that followed the eruption)

Ecology and the Environment

Bash, B. (1990). *Urban roosts: Where birds nest in the city.* San Francisco: Sierra Club Books.

Buckley, B., Hopkins, E., & Whitaker, R. (2004). *Weather: A visual guide.* Richmond Hill, Ontario, Canada: Firefly Books.

Kohl, J., & Kohl, H. (2000). *The view from the oak.* New York: New Press. (How animals perceive reality differently from humans)

Krupp, F. & Horn, M. (2008). *Earth: The sequel: The race to reinvent energy and stop global warming.* New York: W. W. Norton.

LaBastille, Anne (1991). *Woodswoman.* New York: Dutton. (Autobiographical story of a woman who lived alone in the Adirondacks, showing both the beauties and stark realities of nature)

McDonough, William & Braungart, Michael (2002). *Cradle to cradle: Remaking the way we make things.* New York: North Point Press.

Paulsen, Gary (1994). *Father Water, Mother Woods: Essays on hunting and fishing in the North Woods.* New York: Delacorte.

Mathematics

Adam, J. (2008). *Guesstimation: Solving the world's problems on the back of a cocktail napkin.* New York: Princeton University Press.

Devlin, K. (2007). *Solving crime with mathematics: The numbers behind NUMB3RS.* New York: Penguin.

Kaplan, M., & Kaplan, E. (2006). *Chances are: Adventures in probability.* New York: Penguin.

Livio, Mario (2003). *The golden ratio: The story of phi, the world's most astonishing number.* New York: Broadway Books.

McKeller, D. (2007). *Math doesn't suck.* New York: Penguin. (Suitable for middle school. Real-life applications and problems using middle school math.)

Pappas, Theoni (1991). *Math talk: Mathematical ideas in poems for two voices.* San Carlos, CA: Wide World/Tetra.

Paulos, John (1990). *Innumeracy: Mathematical illiteracy and its consequences.* New York: Random House.

Ryan, M. (2002). *Everyday math for everyday life: A handbook for when it just doesn't add up.* New York: Warner Books.

Seife, Charles (2000). *Zero: The biography of a dangerous idea.* New York: Penguin.

Stein, Sherman (2001). *How the other half thinks: Adventures in mathematical reasoning.* New York: McGraw-Hill.

Weaver, J. (2002). *What are the odds? The chances of extraordinary events in everyday life.* New York: Prometheus.

Life Sciences

Fleischman, J. (2002). *Phineas Gage: A gruesome but true story about brain science.* New York: Houghton Mifflin.

Fridell, R. (2004). *Decoding life: Unraveling the mysteries of the genome.* New York: Lerner Publishing.

McClellan, M. (2003). *Organ and tissue transplants: Medical miracles and challenges.* Berkeley Heights, NJ: Enslow.

Shubin, N. (2008). *Your inner fish: A journey into the 3.5 billion year history of the human body.* New York: Knopf.

Skurzynski, G. (2004). *Are we alone? Scientists search for life in space.* Washington, DC: National Geographic Society.

Physics and Chemistry

Aschenbach, Joel (1999). *Captured by aliens: The search for life and truth in a very large universe.* New York: Simon & Schuster.

Blanding, Sharon, & Monteleone, John (2003). *The science of sports: How things in sports work.* New York: Barnes & Noble.

Cash, T. (2001). *101 physics tricks: Fun experiments with everyday materials.* New York: Sterling Publishers.

Dickinson, Terence (1998). *Nightwatch: A practical guide to viewing the universe,* 3rd ed. Toronto: Firefly Books.

Downie, N. (2001). *Vacuum bazookas, electric rainbow jelly, and 27 other Sunday science projects.* Princeton, NJ: Princeton University Press.

Grossblatt, Ben (2003). *Air hockey science.* New York: Tangerine Press. (The physics and technology of air hockey; includes plans and instructions for building an air hockey table)

Hawking, Stephen (2003). *The theory of everything: The origin and fate of the universe.* North Miami Beach, FL: New Millennium Press.

Le Couteur, P., & Burreson, J. (2003). *Napoleon's buttons: How 17 molecules changed history.* New York: Penguin Putnam. (A true account of how chemicals changed history. Clear explanations of organic chemistry principles and vocabulary.)

Moring, G. (2000). *The idiot's guide to understanding Einstein.* Indianapolis, IN: Alpha Books.

Morris, R. (2003). *The last sorcerers: The path from alchemy to the periodic table.* Washington, DC: Joseph Henry Press. (A history of the development of the periodic chart of the elements)

Paterniti, M. (2000). *Driving Mr. Einstein.* New York: Dell. (Fictional account of the famous physicist)

Sacks, Oliver (2002). *Uncle Tungsten: Memories of a chemical boyhood.* New York: Vintage Books.

Science Fiction and Fiction about Science

Adams, Douglas (1979). *Hitchhiker's guide to the galaxy.* New York: Harmony. (The first of a series; "Hitchhiker" fans are legion)

Anderson, M. T. (2002). *Feed.* Cambridge, MA: Candlewick Press. (YA fiction; a future world where television and computers are connected directly into people's brains and teens are driven by fashion and consumerism)

Asimov, Isaac (1987). *Fantastic voyage.* New York: Bantam. (Based on the screenplay; a journey inside the human body)

Cavelos, J. (2000). *The science of Star Wars.* New York: St. Martin's Griffin.

Clancy, Tom (1991). *The sum of all fears.* New York: Putnam. (Terrorists plant a nuclear bomb)

Cook, Robin (1997). *Chromosome 6.* New York: Berkley. (Scientists researching apes in Africa venture into cloning)

Crichton, M. (2002). *Prey.* New York: HarperCollins. (The dangers of carelessly used technology.)

Defelice, Cynthia (1998). *The ghost of Fossil Glen.* New York: Avon. (YA fiction; a girl is pursued by a ghost after a near-death experience while fossil hunting)

Hesse, Karen (1996). *The music of dolphins.* New York: Scholastic. (YA fiction; child is lost at sea and adopted by dolphins; after her rescue, she is sent to a center for scientific research, where she is taught human language but yearns for her dolphin family)

Klass, David (1994). *California blue.* New York: Scholastic. (YA fiction; battle between environmentalists and community dependent on a local mill)

Lawrence, Louise (1985). *Children of the dust.* New York: Harper & Row. (Mutant and nonmutant survivors of a nuclear holocaust)

Sagan, N., Frary, M., & Walker, A. (2007). *You call this the future? The greatest inventions sci-fi imagined and science promised.* Chicago: Chicago Review Times. (Theories about different technologies, their history, emergence in the media, and realities.)

Weisman, A. (2007). *The world without us.* New York: St. Martin's Press. (What the earth would be like after extinction of the human race.)

History and Current Events

Barone, M. (2005). *Out of the ordinary.* Auburndale, MA: History Compass. (Historical fiction. Italian immigrant family working in mines in Colorado in 1914; union organizers.)

Beah, I. (2007). *A long way gone: Memoirs of a boy soldier.* New York: Farrar, Straus & Giroux. (Biography of a 12-year-old boy swept up in Sierra Leone's civil war.)

Colman, P. (2002). *Where the action was: Woman war correspondents in World War II.* New York: Crown Publishers.

Herbert, J. (2001). *Marco Polo for kids: His marvelous journey to China.* Chicago: Chicago Review Press.

Peet, Mal (2007). *Tamar: A novel of espionage, passion, and betrayal.* Somerville, MA: Candlewick. (Novel about resistance fighters in WWII Netherlands.)

Raddatz, Martha (2007). *The long road home: A story of war and family.* New York: Putnam. (U.S. troops under fire in Baghdad after the invasion of Iraq in 2004, including the son of antiwar activist Cindy Sheehan.)

Raphael, Marie (2001). *Streets of gold.* New York: Persea Books. (Polish immigrant—a teenage girl—alone in Lower East side of NYC in early 20th century.)

Sis, Peter (2007). *The wall: Growing up behind the Iron Curtain.* New York: Farrar, Straus & Girous. (Middle school level.)

Slavery Times

Armstrong, J. (1992). *Steal away . . . to freedom.* New York: Scholastic. (Story of two girls, one white, one black, and the Underground Railroad)

Clark, Margaret (1980). *Freedom crossing.* New York: Scholastic. (Underground Railroad story set in Lewiston, NY)

Cosner, Sharon (1991). *The Underground Railroad.* New York: Venture.

Franklin, John & Schweninger, Loren (2000). *Runaway slaves: Rebels on the plantation.* New York: Oxford University Press.

Hamilton, V. (1993). *Many thousand gone: African-Americans from slavery to freedom.* New York: Knopf. (African American folk tales and stories, including stories of escape from slavery)

Lester, Julius (1968). *To be a slave.* New York: Scholastic. (True narratives of the lives of slaves)

Meyers, Walter D. (1998). *Amistad: Long road to freedom.* New York: Putnam.

Rappaport, D. (1991). *Escape from slavery: Five journeys to freedom.* New York: HarperCollins.

Wisler, G. Clifton (1996). *Caleb's choice.* New York: Dutton. (YA fiction; set in Texas, the story of a white youth's entanglement in the area's sharp divisions over the Fugitive Slave Law)

Civil War

Chang, Ina (1991). *A separate battle: Women and the Civil War.* New York: Scholastic.

Clapp, Patricia (1986). *Tamarack tree.* New York: Lothrop, Lee & Shepard. (YA fiction; the siege of Vicksburg)

Freedman, R. (1987). *Lincoln: A photobiography.* Boston: Houghton Mifflin.

Hunt, Irene (1964). *Across five Aprils.* New York: Berkley. (YA fiction; life on an Illinois farm during the Civil War)

Marrin, Albert (1994). *Unconditional surrender: U.S. Grant and the Civil War.* New York: Atheneum. (Biography, illustrated with photographs)

Marrin, Albert (1994). *Virginia's general: Robert E. Lee and the Civil War.* New York: Atheneum. (Biography, illustrated with photographs)

Rinaldi, Ann (1993). *In my father's house.* New York: Scholastic. (YA fiction; story of a Southern family during the Civil War)

Shaara, Michael (1974). *The killer angels.* New York: Ballantine. (Fiction; the Battle of Gettysburg)

Immigration

Ashabranner, Brent (with Melissa Ashabranner) (1987). *Into a strange land; Unaccompanied refugee youth in America.* New York: Putnam.

Bode, Janet (1989). *New kids on the block: Oral histories of immigrant teens.* New York: Watts.

Conover, Ted (1987). *Coyotes.* New York: Vintage. (The lives of Mexicans who illegally cross the U.S. border)

Denenberg, Barry (1997). *So far from home: The diary of Mary Driscoll, an Irish mill girl.* New York: Scholastic. (YA fiction)

Hest, Amy (2003). *When Jessie came across the sea.* Cambridge, MA: Candlewick Press. (Picture book about a 13-year-old girl's journey from Eastern Europe to New York's Lower East Side)

Meltzer, M. (2002). *Bound for America: The story of the European immigrants.* Tarrytown, NY: Benchmark Books.

Paulsen, Gary (1987). *The crossing.* New York: Dell. (YA fiction; an orphaned 14-year-old attempts to cross the U.S.-Mexican border)

Rolvaag, Ole (1991). *Giants in the earth.* New York: Harper. (A story of Norwegian families who settled in the Dakotas)

Wartski, Maureen (1982). *Long way from home.* New York: Dutton. (YA fiction; a young Vietnamese refugee tries to establish himself in America)

Culturally Conscious Trade Books

African American

Busby, Margaret (Ed.). (1992). *Daughters of Africa: An international anthology of words and writings by women of African descent from the ancient Egyptian to the present.* New York: Pantheon.

Campbell, Bebe Moore (1998). *Singing in the comeback choir.* New York: Putnam.

Flake, S. G. (1998). *The skin I'm in.* New York: Jump at the Sun Hyperion Paperbacks for Children. (YA fiction; an authentic portrayal of African American teenagers; winner of the 1999 Coretta Scott King Award and chosen as the American Library Association's Best Book for Young Adults in 1999, this book humorously and cleverly pulls young reluctant readers into a world rarely represented in YA fiction)

Giovanni, Nikki (1974). *Ego-tripping and other poems for young people.* Chicago: Hill. (YA)

Giovanni, Nikki (1994). *Racism 101.* New York: Quill. (Essays on race relations)

Hamilton, Virginia (Ed.). (1985). *The people could fly: American black folktales.* New York: Knopf.

Hudson, Wade (Ed.). (1993). *Pass it on: African-American poetry for children* (Floyd Cooper, Illust.). New York: Scholastic. (Illustrated collection of poetry by such African American poets as Langston Hughes, Nikki Giovanni, Eloise Greenfield, and Lucille Clifton)

Hurston, Zora Neale (1937). *Their eyes were watching God.* New York: Harper & Row. (Story of an independent African American woman in the rural South)

Johnson, Angela (2000). *Heaven.* Thorndike, ME: Thorndike Press. (YA fiction; a fourteen-year-old girl discovers that the family she has been living with her whole life are not her real parents)

Laird, R., & Laird, T. (1997). *Still I rise: A cartoon history of African-Americans.* New York: Norton. (Graphic novel)

Lester, Julius (1987). *The tales of Uncle Remus: The adventures of Brer Rabbit.* New York: Dial.

Malcolm X (with Alex Haley) (1964). *The autobiography of Malcolm X.* New York: Ballantine.

McCall, Nathan (1994). *Makes me wanna holler: A young black man in America.* New York: Random House.

Monceaux, M., & Katcher, R. (1999). *My heroes, my people: African-Americans and Native Americans in the West.* (M. Monceaux, Illus.). New York: Farrar, Straus & Giroux. (Short biographies and illustrations; relatively easy reading; especially interesting are the many multiethnic personalities who lived, worked, and pioneered in the American West—a fascinating mingling of cultures.)

Morrison, Toni (1971). *Beloved.* New York: Knopf. (Former slave and her family; life before and after Civil War)

Myers, Walter Dean (1999). *Monster.* New York: HarperCollins. (YA fiction by prolific novelist, poet, and biographer; 16-year-old boy accused of a violent crime)

Njeri, Itabari (1990). *Every good-bye ain't gone.* New York: Random House. (A series of essays about growing up in New York City during the 1950s and 1960s by a writer of African American, East Indian, Native American, English, and French descent)

Paulsen, G. (2006). *The legend of Bass Reeves: Being the true and fictional account of the most valiant marshals in the West.* New York: Wendy Lamb Books. (Story of the first African American U.S. marshal, set in the Southwest in the late 1700s–early 1800s.)

Schroeder, Alan (1989). *Ragtime Tumpie.* Boston: Little, Brown. (YA; biography of entertainer Josephine Baker)

Taylor, Mildred (1976). *Roll of thunder, hear my cry.* New York: Dial. (YA fiction; first in a series of three novels about the struggles of a black family in Mississippi in the 1930s)

Terry, Wallace (Ed.). (1985). *Bloods: An oral history of the Vietnam War by black veterans.* New York: Ballantine.

Thomas, Joyce Carol (2001). *The blacker the berry.* New York: HarperCollins. (Poems by well-known young adult author)

Wideman, John E. (1985). *Brothers and keepers.* New York: Oxford University Press. (An African American college professor explores the painful contrasts between his life and that of his brother in prison)

Asian and Asian American

Crew, Linda (1989). *Children of the river.* New York: Dell. (YA fiction; story of a Cambodian American high school student in Oregon)

Gratz, A. (2006). *Samurai shortstop.* New York: Penguin Group. (Baseball and the influence of Western culture in late-nineteenth-century Japan.)

Hamanaka, Sheila (1990). *The journey: Japanese Americans, racism, and renewal.* New York: Orchard. (A picture book suitable for third grade through high school)

Huynh, Quang Nhuong (1986). *Land I lost: Adventures of a boy in Vietnam.* New York: Harper & Row.

Kingston, Maxine Hong (1977). *Woman warrior: Memoirs of a girlhood among ghosts.* New York: Random House. (The struggle to keep a Chinese identity while assimilating into American society)

Kiyama, H. (1999). *The four immigrants manga.* (F. Schodt, trans.). Berkeley, CA: Stone Bridge Press. (Graphic novel)

Mah, Adeline Yen (1999). *Chinese Cinderella: The true story of an unwanted daughter.* New York: Delacorte.

Na, An (2003). *A step from heaven.* New York: Puffin. (YA fiction; story of a Korean immigrant family)

Sone, Monica (1979). *Nisei daughter.* Seattle: University of Washington Press. (A Japanese American tells of growing up in Seattle in the 1930s and relocation during World War II)

Tan, Amy (1989). *The joy luck club.* New York: Random House. (Fiction)

Uchida, Yoshiko (1981). *A jar of dreams.* New York: Atheneum. (YA fiction; the first in a trilogy of books about an 11-year-old Japanese American girl)

Yang, G. L. (2006). *American, born Chinese.* New York: First Second. (Graphic novel of a boy who lives with his Taiwanese parents.)

Yep, L. (1995). *Dragon's Gate (Golden Mountain chronicles, 1867).* New York: Harper Trophy. (YA fiction set during construction of the transcontinental railroad by Chinese laborers.)

Hispanic

Alvarez, J. (2002). *Before we were free.* New York: Knopf. (YA fiction; Dominican Republic)

Anaya, Rudolfo (1976). *Bless me Ultima.* Berkeley, CA: Tonatiuh. (Fiction about a Chicano boy)

Bernardo, Anilu (1996). *Jumping off to freedom.* Houston: Piñata. (YA fiction; family leaves Cuba on a raft for the United States)

Burke, David (1999). *Street Spanish: Slang dictionary and thesaurus.* New York: Wiley.

Carlson, Lori (Ed.). (1994). *Cool salsa: Bilingual poems on growing up in the United States.* New York: Henry Holt.

Cisneros, Sandra (1986). *The house on Mango Street.* Houston: Arte Publico. (A collection of Mexican American stories)

Cofer, J. Ortiz (2004). *The meaning of Consuelo.* Boston: Beacon Press. (Growing up in Puerto Rico in the 1950s.)

Cruz, Victor Hernandez (1989). *Rhythm, content & flavor.* Houston: Arte Publico Press. (Poetry; Puerto Rican)

Day, F. A. (1997). *Latino and Latina voices in literature for children and teenagers.* Portsmouth, NH: Heinemann.

Gonzales, B. D. (1995). *Sweet fifteen.* Houston: Piñata Books. (A girl's quinceaños celebration is changed by the death of her father just before her fifteenth birthday)

Jimenéz, Francisco (2002). *Breaking through.* Boston: Houghton-Mifflin. (YA; autobiographical stories of a migrant family in California)

Mohr, Nicholasa (1979). *Felita.* New York: Dial. (YA fiction; a family faces prejudice when they move from a predominantly Hispanic neighborhood)

Poniatowska, Elene, & Stellweg, Carla (1992). *Frida Kahlo: The camera seduced.* San Francisco: Chronicle. (Photos and essays about the great Mexican artist)

Quinonez, Ernesto (2000). *Bodega dreams.* New York: Vintage. (Novel set in Spanish Harlem)

Rodriquez, Luis (1993). *Always running: La vida loca: Gang days in L.A.* New York: Touchstone.

Ryan, Pam Muñoz (2000). *Esperanza Rising.* New York: Scholastic. (YA fiction; daughter of wealthy Mexican loses her father, migrates to California during the Great Depression; unions, strikes, Okies, cultural conflicts, exploration of class differences)

Santiago, E. (1994). *When I was Puerto Rican.* New York: Prentice Hall. (Autobiographical stories of a young woman's acculturation to the mainland United States)

Soto, G. (2007). *A simple plan.* New York: Chronicle. (Poetry.)

Soto, Gary (2000). *Nickel and dime.* Albuquerque: University of New Mexico Press. (Story of three Mexican American men and street life in Oakland, California)

Thomas, Piri (1967). *Down these mean streets.* New York: Vintage. (Puerto Rican)

Valdes-Rodrigues, A. (2006). *Haters.* New York: Little, Brown. (YA fiction. A girl moves to Orange County, California, and must learn to cope with a new social reality.)

Velasquez, Gloria (1994). *Juanita fights the school board.* Houston: Piñata Press. (YA fiction)

Islam

Ansary, T. (2002). *West of Kabul, East of New York: An Afghan American Story.* New York: Bantam.

Frank, M. (2005). *Understanding the Holy Land: Answering questions about the Israeli–Palestinian conflict.* New York: Viking.

Hasan, A. G. (2004.) *American Muslims: The new generation,* 2nd ed. New York: Continuum International.

Idilibi, Ulfat (1998). *Grandfather's tale.* (Peter Clark, Trans.). London: Quartet. (A young boy's pilgrimage to Mecca, growth into adulthood, and fulfillment of his family duties)

Moaveni, A. (2005). *Lipstick jihad: A memoir of growing up Iranian in America and American in Iran.* New York: Public Affairs.

Morris, Neil (2003). *The atlas of Islam: People, daily life and traditions.* Hauppauge, NY: Barron's.

Nye, N. S. (1999). *Habibi.* New York: Simon & Schuster. (YA fiction. A Palestinian–American girl moves from the United States to occupied territories.)

Nye, N. S. (2002). *Nineteen varieties of gazelle: Poems of the Middle East.* New York: HarperCollins. (Poetry.)

Sacco, J. (2001). *Palestine.* Seattle, WA: Fantagraphic Books. (Graphic novel)

Satrapi, M. (2003). *Persepolis: The story of a childhood.* Paris: L'Association. (Graphic novel)

Siddiqui, H. (2006). *Being Muslim.* Toronto, Canada: Groundwood Books. (A history of Islam and tenants of the faith, along with a critical look at issues such as the status of women, terrorism, and Muslims in Europe.)

Wormser, Richard (2002). *American Islam: Growing up Muslim in America.* New York: Walker. (Looks at the lives of two different groups, immigrants from the Middle East and African Americans)

Jewish

Brooks, Jerome (1990). *Naked in winter.* New York: Orchard. (YA fiction; a 16-year-old boy copes with moving to a new neighborhood, family troubles, and sexual awakening)

Frank, M. (2005). *Understanding the Holy Land: Answering questions about the Israeli–Palestinian conflict.* New York: Viking.

Grossman, Mendel, & Dabba, Frank (2000). *My secret camera: Life in the Lodz ghetto.* New York: Harcourt.

Klein, G. W. (1995). *All but my life.* New York: Hill & Wang. (Holocaust survivor's story; film version won documentary Oscar in 1996)

Mazer, Norma Fox (1999). *Good night Maman.* New York: Harcourt. (YA fiction)

Singer, Isaac B. (1980). *The power of light: Eight stories for Hannukah.* New York: Farrar, Straus & Giroux.

Spiegelman, A. (1986) *Maus.* New York: Pantheon Books. (Graphic novel of the Holocaust)

Native American

Alexie, S. (2007). *The absolutely true diary of a part-time Indian.* New York: Little, Brown.

Bouchard, D. (1997). *The elders are watching.* Vancouver, BC: Raincoast.

Bruchac, J. (2006). *Code talker.* New York: Scholastic. (Navajo Marines in World War II use their native language to communicate in the Pacific theater because it will not be understood if intercepted by the Japanese.)

Fleischman, Paul (1990). *Saturnalia.* New York: HarperCollins. (YA fiction; a Narrangansett boy is sold as a slave to a Boston family in the 1660s)

Hernandez, I. (1992). *Heartbeat drumbeat.* Houston: Arte Publico Press. (YA fiction; story of a girl with a Chicano father and Navajo mother)

Norman, Howard (1989). *How Glooskap outwits the ice giants and other tales of the Maritime Indians.* Boston: Little, Brown.

Rees, Celia (2003). *Sorceress.* Cambridge, MA: Candlewick Press. (YA fiction; a Native American college student begins to investigate mysteries in her past)

Smelcer, J. (2006). *The trap.* New York: Henry Holt. (YA fiction. A Native Alaskan boy sets off into the cold wilderness to find his grandfather.)

Thorn, James (1989). *Panther in the sky.* New York: Ballantine. (A fictional account of Tecumseh, leader of the Shawnee tribe in the late eighteenth century)

Diverse Cultures

Carmi, D. (2001). *Samir and Yonatan.* (Yael Lotan, Trans.). New York: Scholastic. (YA fiction; Israel and Palestine)

Lynch, Chris (1996). *Blue-eyed son: A trilogy.* New York: HarperCollins. (YA fiction; three books about Mick, the younger son in an Irish American family, and his struggles to come to terms with his heritage, his family, racism, and alcoholism)

McBride, James (1996). *The color of water: A black man's tribute to his white mother.* New York: Riverhead.

Mead, Alice (1996). *Adem's cross.* New York: Farrar, Straus & Giroux. (YA fiction; the violence and brutality of war in the former Yugoslavia, as seen in the story of a minority Albanian boy in Serb-controlled territory)

Meyer, Carolyn (1996). *Gideon's people.* San Diego: Harcourt Brace/Gulliver Books. (YA fiction; family and ethnic conflicts around the relationship of Isaac, son of immigrant Jews, and his Amish friend Gideon)

Woodson, Jacqueline (1994). *I hadn't meant to tell you this.* New York: Delacorte. (YA fiction; a friendship between two girls, one an African American from a protective and relatively well-off family, the other a white girl who is the victim of abuse)

Zusak, Markus. (2000). *Fighting Ruben Wolfe.* New York: Push, Scholastic. (YA fiction; an intense tale about boxing, brotherly solidarity, and searching for self-respect in a family down on its luck as a result of economically hard times)

Standards for the Content Areas—Web Ready/At a Glance

English/Language Arts Standards
www.reading.org/publications/bbv/books/bk889/toc.html

Foreign Language Standards
www.actfl.org/i4a/pages/index.cfm?pageid=3392

Information Literacy Standards
www.librarycareers.org/ala/aasl/aaslproftools/learningstandards/AASL_LearningStandards.pdf

Literacy Coach Standards
www.reading.org/resources/issues/reports/coaching.html

Middle Web Guide to Standards-Based Reform
www.middleweb.com/SBRGuide.html

National Council for the Social Studies Standards
www.ncss.org

National Council of Teachers of Mathematics Standards
www.nctm.org

National Educational Technology Standards
www.iste.org/Content/NavigationMenu/NETS/ForStudents/2007Standards/NETS_for_Students_2007.htm

National Science Education Standards
www.nap.edu/catalog.php?record_id=4962

National Standards for History
www.sscnet.ucla.edu/nchs/standards

National Standards for Music Education
http://menc.org/resources/view/national-standards-for-music-education

National Standards for Physical Education
www.aahperd.org/naspe/publications-nationalstandards.html

Standards for Art Education
http://artsedge.kennedy-center.org/teach/standards.cfm

Teachers of English to Speakers of Other Languages
www.tesol.org/s_tesol/sec_document.asp?CID=1186&DID=5349

references

Abrahamson, R., & Carter, B. (1991, January). Nonfiction: The missing piece in the middle. *English Journal, 79*, 52–58.

Abu el-Haj, T. (2002). Contesting the politics of culture, rewriting the boundaries of inclusion: Working for social justice with Muslim and Arab communities. *Anthropology and Education Quarterly, 33*, 308–316.

Adamson, H. D. (1993). *Academic competence: Theory and classroom practice, preparing ESL students for content courses.* New York: Longman.

Afflerbach, P. (2007). *Understanding and using reading assessment, K–12.* Newark, DE: International Reading Association.

Agee, J. (1999, November). "There it was, that one sex scene": English teachers on censorship. *English Journal, 89*, 61–69.

Akos, P. (2007). Early adolescents' aspirations and academic tracking: An exploratory investigation. *Professional School Counseling.* Retrieved June 30, 2008, from http://findarticles.com/p/articles/mi_m0KOC/is_1_11/ai_n21093612

Alexander, P. (2005). The path to competence: A lifespan developmental perspective on reading. *Journal of Literacy Research, 7*, 416–436.

Alexander, P. (2005–2006). The path to competence: A lifespan developmental perspective on reading. *Journal of Literacy Research, 37*, 413–436.

Alexander, P. A., & Jetton, T. L. (2000). Learning from text: A multidimensional and developmental perspective. In M. L. Kamil, P. B. Mosenthal, P. D. Pearson, & R. Barr (Eds.), *Handbook of reading research: Volume 3* (pp. 285–310). Mahwah, NJ: Erlbaum.

Alfassi, M. (1998). Reading for meaning: The efficacy of reciprocal teaching in fostering reading comprehension in high school students in remedial reading classes. *American Educational Research Journal, 35*, 309–332.

Allan, C. (1999). Poets of comrades: Addressing sexual orientation in the English classroom. *English Journal, 88*(6), 97–101.

Allen, J. (1995). *It's never too late: Leading adolescents to lifelong literacy.* Portsmouth, NH: Heinemann.

Allen, J., & Gonzalez, K. (1998). *There's room for me here: Literacy workshop in the middle school.* York, ME: Stenhouse.

Allington, R. (2002). Troubling times: A short historical perspective. In R. Allington, (Ed.), *Big Brother and the national reading curriculum: How ideology trumped evidence* (pp. 3–46). Portsmouth, NH: Heinemann.

Allington, R. L., & McGill-Franzen, A. (2000, Winter). Looking back, looking forward: Excerpts from a conversation about teaching reading in the 21st century. *English Update: A Newsletter from the Center on English Learning & Achievement*, 4–5.

Alsup, J. (2003). Politicizing young adult literature. Reading Anderson's *Speak* as a critical text. *Journal of Adolescent & Adult Literacy, 47*, 158–166.

Alvermann, D. E. (1992). The discussion web: A graphic aid for learning across the curriculum. *The Reading Teacher, 45*, 92–99.

Alvermann, D. E. (1995–1996). Peer-led discussions: Whose interests are served? *Journal of Adolescent & Adult Literacy, 39*, 282–289.

Alvermann, D. E. (2000). Classroom talk about texts: Is it dear, cheap, or a bargain at any price? In B. M. Taylor, M. F. Graves, & P. Van Den Broek (Eds.), *Reading for meaning* (pp. 136–151). New York: Teachers College Press.

Alvermann, D. E. (2002). Effective literacy instruction for adolescents. *Journal of Literacy Research, 34*, 189–208.

Alvermann, D. E. (2008). Commentary: Why bother theorizing adolescents' online literacies for classroom practice and research. *Journal of Adolescent & Adult Literacy, 52*, 8–19.

Alvermann, D. E., & Commeyras, M. (1998). Feminist poststructuralist perspectives on the language of reading assessment: Authenticity and performance. In C. Harrison, M. Bailey, & A. Dewar (Eds.), *New paradigms in reading assessment* (pp. 50–60). London: Routledge.

Alvermann, D. E., & Hagood, M. C. (2000). Critical media literacy: Research, theory, and practice in "new times." *Journal of Educational Research, 93,* 193–205.

Alvermann, D. E., & Moore, D. W. (1991). Secondary school reading. In R. Barr, M. L. Kamil, P. Mosenthal, & P. D. Pearson (Eds.), *Handbook of reading research: Volume 2* (pp. 951–983). New York: Longman.

Alvermann, D. E., & Nealy, A. (2004). Professional development content for reading educators at the middle and high school levels. In D. Strickland & M. Kamil (Eds.), *Improving reading achievement through professional development* (pp. 85–93). Norwood, MA: Christopher-Gordon.

Alvermann, D. E., Commeyras, M., Young, J., Hinson, D., & Randall, S. (1996). *The gendered language of texts and classrooms: Teachers and students exploring multiple perspectives and interpretations* (Instructional Resource No. 23). Athens: University of Georgia, National Reading Research Center.

Alvermann, D. E., Dillon, D. R., & O'Brien, D. G. (1987). *Using discussion to promote reading comprehension.* Newark, DE: International Reading Association.

Alvermann, D. E., Fitzgerald, J., & Simpson, M. (2006). Teaching and learning in reading. In P. Alexander & P. Winne (Eds.), *Handbook of educational psychology* (2nd ed., pp. 427–455). Mahwah, NJ: Erlbaum.

Alvermann, D. E., Fitzgerald, J., & Simpson, M. (2006). Teaching and learning in reading. In P. Alexander & P. Winne (Eds.), *Handbook of Educational Psychology* (2nd ed.). Mahwah, NJ: Erlbaum.

Alvermann, D. E., Hagood, M. C., Heron, A., Hughes, P., & Williams, K. (2000a). *Critical literacy practices in after-school media clubs.* Final report submitted to the Spencer Foundation, Chicago, September 30.

Alvermann, D. E., Hagood, M. C., Heron, A., Hughes, P., & Williams, K. (2000b). *The media club study.* Paper presented at the annual meeting of the College Reading Association, St. Petersburg Beach, FL.

Alvermann, D. E., Moon, J. S., & Hagood, M. C. (1999). *Popular culture in the classroom: Teaching and researching critical media literacy.* Newark, DE: International Reading Association and the National Reading Conference.

Alvermann, D. E., O'Brien, D. G., & Dillon, D. R. (1990). What teachers do when they say they're having discussions of content reading assignments: A qualitative analysis. *Reading Research Quarterly, 25,* 296–322.

Alvermann, D. E., Olson, J., & Umpleby, R. (1993). Learning to do research together. In S. Hudelson & J. Lindfors (Eds.), *Delicate balances: Collaborative research in language education* (pp. 112–124). Urbana, IL: National Council for Teachers of English.

Alvermann, D. E., Smith, L., & Readence, J. (1985). Prior knowledge activation and the comprehension of compatible and incompatible text. *Reading Research Quarterly, 20,* 420–436.

Alvermann, D. E., Young, J. P., Green, C., & Wisenbaker, J. M. (1999). Adolescents' perceptions and negotiations of literacy practices in after-school read and talk clubs. *American Educational Research Journal, 36,* 221–264.

Alvermann, D. E., Young, J. P., Weaver, D., Hinchman, K. A., Moore, D. W., Phelps, S. F., Thrash, E. C., & Zalewski, P. (1996b). Middle and high school students' perceptions of how they experience text-based discussions: A multicase study. *Reading Research Quarterly, 31,* 244–267.

American Association of University Women Educational Foundation (2000). *Tech-savvy: Educating girls in the new computer age.* Washington, DC: American Association of University Women Educational Foundation.

Amit-Talai, V., & Wulff, H. (Eds.). (1995). *Youth cultures: A cross-cultural perspective.* New York: Routledge.

Anders, P., & Bos, C. (1986). Semantic feature analysis: An interactive strategy for vocabulary development and text comprehension. *Journal of Reading, 29,* 610–616.

Anders, P. L., & Guzzetti, B. J. (1996). *Literacy instruction in the content areas.* New York: Harcourt Brace.

Anderson, R. C. (1984). Role of the reader's schema in comprehension, learning, and memory. In R. C. Anderson, J. Osborn, & R. J. Tierney (Eds.), *Learning to read in American schools: Basal readers and content texts* (pp. 243–258). Hillsdale, NJ: Erlbaum.

Anderson, R. C., Hiebert, E., Scott, J., & Wilkinson, I. (1985). *Becoming a nation of readers: The report of the Commission on Reading.* Washington, DC: National Institute of Education.

Anderson, R. C., Reynolds, R. E., Schallert, D. L., & Goetz, E. T. (1977). Frameworks for comprehending discourse. *American Educational Research Journal, 14,* 367–382.

Anderson, T. H., & Armbruster, B. B. (1984). Content area textbooks. In R. C. Anderson, J. Osborn, & R. Tierney (Eds.), *Learning to read in American schools: Basal readers and content texts* (pp. 193–226). Hillsdale, NJ: Erlbaum.

Anderson, T. H., & Armbruster, B. B. (1984). Studying. In P. D. Pearson, R. Barr, M. Kamil, & P. Mosenthal (Eds.), *Handbook of reading research* (pp. 657–679). New York: Longman.

Anderson, V., & Hidi, S. (1988/1989). Teaching students to summarize. *Educational Leadership, 4,* 26–29.

Anderson-Inman, L., & Horney, M. (1994). The electrotext project: Hypertext reading patterns of middle school students. *Journal of Educational Multimedia and Hypermedia, 3,* 71–91.

André, M., & Anderson, T. H. (1978/1979). The development and evaluation of a self-questioning study technique. *Reading Research Quarterly, 14,* 605–623.

Andrews, S. E. (2000). Writing to learn in content area reading class. In D. W. Moore, D. E. Alvermann, & K. A. Hinchman (Eds.), *Struggling adolescent readers: A collection of teaching strategies* (pp. 217–219). Newark, DE: International Reading Association.

Applebee, A., Langer, J., Mullis, I., Latham, A., & Gentile, C. (1994). *NAEP 1992 writing report card.* Washington, DC: U.S. Department of Education, Office of Educational Research and Improvement.

Ardizzone, P. (1992, November). The journal—A tool in the ESL classroom. *Writing Teacher, 6,* 31–33.

Armbruster, B. B., Anderson, T. H., & Ostertag, J. (1987). Does text structure/summarization instruction facilitate learning from expository text? *Reading Research Quarterly, 22,* 331–346.

Arthur, B. (1991). Working with new ESL students in a junior high school reading class. *Journal of Reading, 34,* 628–631.

Aschbacher, P. R. (1991). Humanitas: A thematic curriculum. *Educational Leadership, 49*(2), 16–19.

Athanases, S. (1998). Diverse learners, diverse texts: Exploring identity and difference through literary encounters. *Journal of Literacy Research, 30,* 273–296.

Atwell, N. (1987). *In the middle: Writing, reading, and learning with adolescents.* Portsmouth, NH: Boynton/Cook.

Atwell, N. (1998). *In the middle: New understandings about writing, reading and learning* (2nd ed.). Portsmouth, NH: Heinemann.

Au, K. (1998). Social constructivism and the school literacy learning of students of diverse backgrounds. *Journal of Literacy Research, 30,* 297–319.

Au, K. H. (1980). Participation structures in reading lessons: Analysis of a culturally appropriate instructional event. *Anthropology and Education Quarterly, 11,* 91–115.

Ausubel, D. (1968). *Educational psychology: A cognitive view.* New York: Holt, Rinehart & Winston.

Baines, L. (2000). Same facts, different audience. In L. Baines & A. Kunkel (Eds.), *Going Bohemian: Activities that engage adolescents in the art of writing well,* (pp. 78–80). Newark, DE: International Reading Association.

Baker, L., & Brown, A. L. (1980). *Metacognitive skills and reading* (Tech. Rep. No. 188). Urbana: University of Illinois, Center for the Study of Reading.

Baker, L., & Brown, A. L. (1984). Metacognitive skills and reading. In P. D. Pearson, R. Barr, M. Kamil, & P. Mosenthal (Eds.), *Handbook of reading research* (pp. 353–394). New York: Longman.

Balajthy, E. (1990). Hypertext, hypermedia, and metacognition: Research and instructional implications for disabled readers. *Reading, Writing and Learning Disabilities, 6,* 183–190.

Bank, S. (1986). Assessing reading interests of adolescent students. *Educational Research Quarterly, 10*(3), 8–13.

Barnes, J. (1999). Creative writing in trigonometry. *Mathematics Teacher, 92,* 498–503.

Barron, R. (1969). The use of vocabulary as an advance organizer. In H. Herber & P. Sanders (Eds.), *Research in reading in the content areas: First year report* (pp. 29–39). Syracuse, NY: Syracuse University Reading and Language Arts Center.

Barry, A. (1998). Hispanic representation in literature for children and young adults. *Journal of Adolescent & Adult Literacy, 41,* 630–637.

Barton, M. L., Heidema, C., & Jordan, D. (2002). Teaching reading in mathematics and science. *Educational Leadership, 60,* 24–28.

Barwell, R. (2005). Critical issues for language and content in mainstream classrooms: Introduction. *Linguistics and Education, 16,* 143–150.

Bauer, E. (1999). The promise of alternative literacy assessments in the classroom: A review of empirical studies. *Reading Research & Instruction, 38,* 153–168.

Bauer, E., & Garcia, G. (1997). Blurring the lines between reading assessment and instruction: A case study of a low-income student in the lowest reading group. In C. Kinzer, K. Hinchman, & D. Leu (Eds.), *Inquiries in literacy theory and practice* (pp. 166–176). 46th Yearbook of the National Reading Conference. Chicago, IL: National Reading Conference.

Baumann, F. J., Kame'enui, E. J., & Ash, G. W. (2003). Research on vocabulary instruction: Voltaire Redux. In J. Flood, D. Lapp, J. Squire, & J. Jensen (Eds.), *Handbook of research on teaching the English language arts* (2nd ed., pp. 752–785). Mahwah, NJ: Erlbaum.

Baumann, J. (1984). The effectiveness of a direct instruction paradigm for teaching main idea comprehension. *Reading Research Quarterly, 20,* 93–115.

Beach, R. (1997). Stances of resistance and engagement in responding to multicultural literature. In T. Rogers & A. Soter (Eds.), *Reading across cultures: Teaching literature in a diverse society* (pp. 69–94). New York: Teachers College Press.

Bean, T. (1992). Combining writing fluency and vocabulary development through writing roulette. In E. Dishner, T. Bean, J. Readence, & D. Moore (Eds.), *Reading in the content areas: Improving classroom instruction* (3rd ed., pp. 247–254). Dubuque, IA: Kendall/Hunt.

Bean, T., & Bishop, A. (1992). Polar opposites: A strategy for guiding students' critical reading and discussion. In E. Dishner, T. Bean, J. Readence, & D. Moore (Eds.), *Reading in the content areas: Improving classroom instruction* (3rd ed., pp. 247–254). Dubuque, IA: Kendall/Hunt.

Bean, T., Bean, S., & Bean, K. (1999). Intergenerational conversations and two adolescents' multiple literacies: Implications for redefining content area literacy. *Journal of Adolescent & Adult Literacy, 42,* 438–448.

Bean, T., Kile, R., & Readence, J. (1996). Using trade books to encourage critical thinking about citizenship in high school social studies. *Social Education, 60,* 227–230.

Bean, T. W. (1997). Preservice teachers' selection and use of content area literacy strategies. *Journal of Educational Research, 90,* 154–163.

Beane, J. A. (1990). *A middle school curriculum from rhetoric to reality.* Columbus, OH: National Middle School Association.

Beck, I., & McKeown, M. (1991). Social studies texts are hard to understand: Mediating some of the difficulties. *Language Arts, 68,* 482–490.

Beck, I., McKeown, M., Hamilton, R., & Kucan, L. (1997). *Questioning the author: An approach for enhancing student engagement with text.* Newark, DE: International Reading Association.

Beers, K. (1996). No time, no interest, no way! The three voices of aliteracy. *School Library Journal, 42,* 110–113.

Beers, K. (2003). *When kids can't read: What teachers can do. A guide for teachers 6–12.* Portsmouth, NH: Heinemann.

Berenson, S., & Carter, G. (1995). Changing assessment practices in science and mathematics. *School Science & Mathematics, 95,* 182–186.

Bergeron, B., & Rudenga, E. (1996). Seeking authenticity: What is "real" about thematic literacy instruction? *The Reading Teacher, 49,* 544–551.

Berliner, D., & Biddle, B. (1995). *The manufactured crisis: Myths, frauds, and the attack on America's public schools.* Reading, MA: Addison-Wesley.

Bernhardt, E. B. (2000). Second-language reading as a case study of reading scholarship in the 20th century. In M. L. Kamil, P. B. Mosenthal, P. D. Pearson, & R. Barr (Eds.), *Handbook of reading research: Volume 3* (pp. 791–811). Mahwah, NJ: Erlbaum.

Bernhardt, E. B. (2003). Challenges to reading research from a multilingual world. *Reading Research Quarterly, 38,* 112–117.

Biancarosa, G., & Snow, C. E. (2004). *Reading Next—A Vision for Action and Research in Middle and High School Literacy: A Report to Carnegie Corporation of New York.* Washington, DC: Alliance for Excellent Education. Also available online at www.all4ed.org/publications/ReadingNext/index.html

Biloff, E. (1996). *The Killer Angels:* A case study of historical fiction in the social studies curriculum. *Social Studies, 87,* 19–23.

Bintz, W. P. (1993). Resistant readers in secondary education: Some insights and implications. *Journal of Reading, 36,* 604–615.

Bishop, J. H. (1989). Why the apathy in American high schools? *Educational Researcher, 18*(1), 6–10, 42.

Bishop, R. (1990). Walk tall in the world: African American literature for today's children. *Journal of Negro Education, 59,* 556–565.

Blachowicz, C. (1986). Making connections: Alternatives to the vocabulary notebook. *Journal of Reading, 29,* 543–549.

Blachowicz, C. (1991). Vocabulary instruction in content classes for special needs learners: Why and how? *Reading, Writing, and Learning Disabilities, 7,* 297–308.

Blachowicz, C., & Fisher, P. (2000). Vocabulary instruction. In M. Kamil, P. Mosenthal, P. D. Pearson, & R. Barr (Eds.), *Handbook of reading research* (Vol. 3, pp. 503–523). Mahwah, NJ: Erlbaum.

Blachowicz, C., & Zabroske, B. (1990). Context instruction: A metacognitive approach for at-risk readers. *Journal of Reading, 33,* 504–508.

Black, R. W. (2007). Fanfiction writing and the construction of space, *E-Learning, 4*(4), 384–397. Retrieved June 27, 2008, from http://dx.doi.org/10.2304/elea.2007.4.4.384

Black, R. W. (2008). *Adolescents and online fan fiction.* New York: Peter Lang.

Blackman, J. A. (1992). Confronting Thomas Jefferson, slave owner. *Phi Delta Kappan, 74,* 220–222.

Blake, M., & Majors, P. (1995). Recycled words: Holistic instruction for LEP students. *Journal of Adolescent & Adult Literacy, 39,* 132–137.

Blanco, J. (2003). *Please stop laughing at me.* Toronto, Canada: Adams Media Corporation.

Bloom, H. (1994). *The western canon: The books and school of the ages.* New York: Harcourt Brace.

Bloome, D. (1992, April). Researching language: Languaging research. *Newsletter of the Reading & Writing Program.* Amherst: University of Massachusetts, School of Education.

Bloome, D., & Green, J. L. (1992). Educational contexts of literacy. *Annual Review of Applied Linguistics, 12,* 49–70.

Bolter, D. J. (1992). Literature in the electronic writing space. In M. Tuman (Ed.), *Literacy online: The promise (and peril) of reading and writing with computers.* Pittsburgh, PA: University of Pittsburgh Press.

Bond, L., & Roeber, E. (1995). *The status of state student assessment programs in the United States.* Washington, DC: Council of Chief State School Officers/North Central Regional Educational Laboratory.

Boorstin, D., & Kelley, B. (2005). *A history of the United States.* Needham, MA: Prentice Hall.

Bormuth, J. (1968). Cloze test readability: Criterion referenced scores. *Journal of Educational Measurement, 5,* 189–196.

Boyd, D. (1996). Dominance concealed through diversity: Implications of inadequate perspectives on cultural pluralism. *Harvard Educational Review, 66,* 609–630.

Bragstad, B. J. (1983). Mapping: Using both sides of the brain. *Reading '83.* Newark, DE: International Reading Association.

Bransford, J. D. (1979). *Human cognition: Learning, understanding, and remembering.* Belmont, CA: Wadsworth.

Bransford, J. D., & McCarrell, N. S. (1974). A sketch of a cognitive approach to comprehension. In W. B. Weimer & D. S. Palermo (Eds.), *Cognition and the symbolic processes.* Hillsdale, NJ: Erlbaum.

Brautigan, R. (1971). *Revenge of the lawn.* New York: Simon & Schuster.

Britzman, D. P. (1987). Cultural myths in the making of a teacher: Biography and social structure in teacher education. In M. Okazawa-Rey, J. Anderson, & R. Traver (Eds.), *Teachers, teaching, and teacher education* (pp. 220–233). Cambridge, MA: Harvard University Press.

Brock, C. H., & Gavelek, J. R. (1998). Fostering children's engagement with texts: A sociocultural perspective. In T. E. Raphael & K. H. Au (Eds.), *Literature-based instruction: Reshaping the curriculum* (pp. 71–94). Norwood, MA: Christopher-Gordon.

Brodkey, L., (1989). On the subjects of class and gender in "The Literacy Letters." *College English, 51,* 125–141.

Bromley, K. (1993). *Journaling: Engagements in reading, writing, and thinking.* New York: Scholastic.

Brown, A. L., & Campione, J. C. (1994). Guided discovery in a community of learners. In K. McGilly (Ed.), *Classroom lessons: Integrating cognitive theory and classroom practice* (pp. 229–270). Cambridge, MA: MIT Press.

Brown, A. L., & Palincsar, A. S. (1989). Guided, cooperative learning and individual knowledge acquisition. In L. B. Resnick (Ed.), *Knowing, learning, and instruction: Essays in honor of Robert Glaser* (pp. 393–451). Hillsdale, NJ: Erlbaum.

Brown, G. T. L. (2003, September/October). Searching informational texts: Text and task characteristics that affect performance. *Reading Online, 7*(2). Available online at www.readingonline.org/articles/art_index.asp?HREF=brown/index.html

Brown, J. S., & Duguid, P. (1996). Stolen knowledge. In H. McLellan (Ed.), *Situated learning perspectives* (pp. 47–56). Englewood Cliffs, NJ: Educational Technology Publications.

Brown, J. S., Collins, A., & Duguid, P. (1989). Situated cognition and the culture of learning. *Educational Researcher, 18*(1), 32–42.

Brown, R. (2002). Straddling two worlds: Self-directed comprehension instruction for middle schoolers. In C. Block & M. Pressley (Eds.), *Comprehension instruction: Research-based best practice* (pp. 337–350). New York: Guilford.

Brownlie, F., Feniak, C., & Schnellert, L. (2006). *Student diversity*, 2nd ed. Portland, ME: Stenhouse.

Brozo, W. (2000). Hiding out in secondary classrooms: Coping strategies of unsuccessful readers. In D. Moore, D. Alvermann, & K. Hinchman (Eds.), *Struggling adolescent readers: A collection of teaching strategies* (pp. 51–56). Newark, DE: International Reading Association.

Brozo, W. (2002). *To be a boy, to be a reader: Engaging teen and preteen boys in active literacy.* Newark, DE: International Reading Association.

Brozo, W. G. (2003). Writing to learn with SPAWN prompts. *Thinking Classroom, 4*(3), 44–45.

Brozo, W., & Simpson, M. (1995). *Readers, teachers, learners: Expanding literacy in secondary schools* (2nd ed.). Columbus, OH: Merrill.

Bruce, C. (1997). *The Einstein paradox.* Reading, MA: Perseus Books.

Bruner, J. S. (1986). *Actual minds, possible worlds.* Cambridge, MA: Harvard University Press.

Bucher, K., & Manning, M. L. (2007, Fall). Intellectual freedom for young adolescents. *Childhood Education, 84*, 8–14.

Buckingham, D. (1993). Just playing games. *The English & Media Magazine, 28*, 21–25.

Buckingham, D., & Sefton-Green, J. (1994). *Cultural studies goes to school: Reading and teaching popular media.* London: Taylor & Francis.

Buehl, D. (2001). *Classroom strategies for interactive learning* (2nd ed.). Newark, DE: International Reading Association.

Bulgren, J., Deshler, D., & Lenz, K. (2007). Engaging adolescents with LD in higher order thinking about history concepts using integrated content enhancement routines. *Journal of Learning Disabilities, 40*, 121–133.

Bunting, E. (1990). *The Wall.* (R. Himler, Illust.). New York: Clarion.

Burns, B. (1998). Changing the classroom climate with literature circles. *Journal of Adolescent and Adult Literacy, 42*, 110–113.

Bussert-Webb, K. (1999). To test or teach: Reflections from a holistic teacher-researcher in south Texas. *Journal of Adolescent & Adult Literacy, 42*, 582–585.

Bussert-Webb, K. (2000). Did my holistic teaching help students' standardized test scores? *Journal of Adolescent & Adult Literacy, 43*, 572–573.

Byars, B. (1976). *The TV kid.* New York: Viking.

Cadenhead, K. (1987). Reading level: A metaphor that shapes practice. *Phi Delta Kappan, 68*, 436–441.

Cairney, T. H. (2000). Developing parent partnerships in secondary literacy learning. In D. W. Moore, D. E. Alvermann, & K. A. Hinchman (Eds.), *Struggling adolescent readers: A collection of teaching strategies* (pp. 58–65). Newark, DE: International Reading Association.

Calkins, L. (1994). *The art of teaching and writing.* Portsmouth, NH: Heinemann.

Callahan, R. M. (2005). Tracking and high school English learners: Limiting opportunity to learn. *American Educational Research Journal, 42*, 305–328.

Carlo, M. S., August, D., McLaughlin, B., Snow, C. E., Dressler, C., Lippman, D. N., Lively, T. J., & White, C. E. (2004). Closing the gap: addressing the vocabulary needs of English-language learners in bilingual and mainstream classrooms. *Reading Research Quarterly, 39*, 188–215.

Carnegie Council on Adolescent Development. (1989). *Turning points: Preparing American youth for the 21st century.* New York: Carnegie.

Carnegie Council on Adolescent Development. (1996). *Great transitions: Preparing adolescents for a new century* (Abridged Version). New York: Carnegie.

Carr, E., & Ogle, D. (1987). K-W-L Plus: A strategy for comprehension and summarization. *Journal of Reading, 30,* 626–631.

Carroll, P. S. (2000). Journal to the third power. In L. Baines & A. Kunkel (Eds.), *Going Bohemian: Activities that engage adolescents in the art of writing well* (pp. 5–9). Newark, DE: International Reading Association.

Carroll, P. S., Blake, F., Camalo, R. A., & Messer, S. (1996). When acceptance isn't enough: Helping ESL students become successful writers. *English Journal, 85,* 25–33.

Carver, C. (1991). *A history of English in its own words.* New York: HarperCollins.

Cavelos, J. (2000). *The science of Star Wars.* New York: St. Martin's Griffin.

Cazden, C. (1988). *Classroom discourse: The language of teaching and learning.* Portsmouth, NH: Heinemann.

Cazden, C. B. (2000). Taking cultural differences into account. In B. C. Cope & M. Kalantzis (Eds.), *Multiliteracies: Literacy learning and the design of social futures* (pp. 249–266). New York: Routledge.

Cena, M., & Mitchell, J. (1998). Anchored instruction: A model for integrating the language arts through content area study. *Journal of Adolescent & Adult Literacy, 41,* 559–561.

Center for Research on Education, Diversity and Excellence. (2003a). *A national study of school effectiveness for language minority students' long-term academic achievement.* Available online at www.cal.org/crede/pubs/ResBrief10.htm

Center for Research on Education, Diversity and Excellence. (2003b). *Research evidence: Five standards for effective pedagogy and student outcomes.* (Technical Report No. G1). University of California, Santa Cruz: CREDE.

Chandler-Olcott, K., & Mahar, D. (2003). Adolescents' *anime*-inspired "fanfictions": An exploration of multiliteracies. *Journal of Adolescent & Adult Literacy, 46,* 556–566.

Christian, D. (1994). *Two-way bilingual education: Students learning through two languages* (Educational Practice Report No. 12). Santa Cruz: University of California, The National Center for Research on Cultural Diversity and Second Language Learning.

Ciardiello, A. (1998). Did you ask a good question today? Alternative cognitive and metacognitive strategies. *Journal of Adolescent & Adult Literacy, 42,* 210–219.

Cisneros, S. (1989). *The house on Mango Street.* New York: Vintage/Random House.

Civil, M., Andrade, R., & Gonzalez, N. (2002). *Linking home and school: A bridge to the many faces of mathematics* (Final Report). University of California, Santa Cruz: CREDE.

Clancy, T. (1984). *The hunt for Red October.* Annapolis, MD: Naval Institute Press.

Clark, C., Chow-Hoy, T., Herter, R., & Moss, P. (2001). Portfolios as sites of learning: Reconceptualizing the connections to motivation and engagement. *Reading Research Quarterly, 33,* 211–241.

Coble, C., Rice, D., Walla, K., & Murray, E. (1993). *Earth science.* Englewood Cliffs, NJ: Prentice Hall.

Coiro, J., & Dobler, E. (2007). Exploring the online reading comprehension strategies used by sixth-grade skilled readers to search for and locate information on the Internet. *Reading Research Quarterly, 42,* 214–257.

Collier, J., & Collier, C. (1974). *My brother Sam is dead.* New York: Four Winds.

Collier, J., & Collier, C. (1985). *The bloody country.* New York: Four Winds.

Commeyras, M., & Alvermann, D. E. (1996). Reading about women in world history textbooks from one feminist perspective. *Gender and Education, 8*(1), 31–48.

Conley, M. W. (2008a). Cognitive strategy instruction for adolescents: What we know about the promise, what we don't know about the potential. *Harvard Educational Review, 78,* 84–106.

Conley, M. W. (2008b). Improving adolescent comprehension: Developing comprehension strategies in the content areas. In S. Israel & G. Duffy (Eds.), *Handbook of research on reading comprehension.* New York: Erlbaum.

Cook-Gumperz, J. (Ed.) (1986). *The social construction of literacy.* Cambridge, UK: Cambridge University Press.

Cooper, C. R., & Petrosky, A. R. (1976). A psycho-linguistic view of the fluent reading process. *Journal of Reading, 20,* 184–207.

Cooper, J. D. (1997). *Literacy: Helping children construct meaning* (3rd ed.). Boston: Houghton Mifflin.

Cope, B., & Kalantzis, M. (Eds.) (2000). *Multiliteracies: Literacy learning and the design of social futures.* London: Routledge.

Cormier, R. (1974). *The chocolate war.* New York: Dell.

Corno, L., & Snow, R. E. (1986). Adapting teaching to individual differences among learners. In M. C. Wittrock (Ed.), *Handbook of research on teaching* (3rd ed., pp. 605–629). New York: Macmillan.

Crafton, L. (1983). Learning from reading: What happens when students generate their own background information? *Journal of Reading, 26,* 586–593.

Crane, S. (1964). *The red badge of courage.* New York: Bantam. (Original work published 1895)

Creech, J., & Hale, G. (2006, February). Literacy in science: A natural fit. *Science Teacher, 73,* 22–27.

Crichton, M. (1991). *Jurassic Park.* New York: Ballantine.

Crocco, M. S. (2005). Teaching *Shabanu:* The challenges of using world literature in the U.S. social studies curriculum. *Journal of Curriculum Studies, 37,* 561–582.

Cullinan, B., & Fitzgerald, S. (1985, January). IRA, NCTE take stand on readability formula. *Reading Today, 2,* 1.

Cummins, J. (1994a). The acquisition of English as a second language. In K. Spangenberg-Urbschat & R. Pritchard (Eds.), *Kids come in all languages: Reading instruction for ESL students.* (pp. 36–62) Newark, DE: International Reading Association.

Cummins, J. (1994b). Knowledge, power and identity in teaching English as a second language. In E. Genesee (Ed.), *Educating second language children* (pp. 33–58). Cambridge, UK: Cambridge University Press.

Cummins, J. (1999). Alternative paradigms in bilingual education research: Does theory have a place? *Educational Researcher, 28*(7), 26–32, 41.

Cunningham, J. (1982). Generating interactions between schemata and text. In J. Niles & L. Harris (Eds.), *New inquiries in reading research and instruction, Thirty-first Yearbook of the National Reading Conference* (pp. 42–47). Washington, DC: National Reading Conference.

Cunningham, J. (2002). The National Reading Panel report (A review). In R. Allington, (Ed.), *Big Brother and the national reading curriculum: How ideology trumped evidence* (pp. 49–74). Portsmouth, NH: Heinemann.

Curtis, C. (1995). *The Watsons go to Birmingham—1963.* New York: Delacorte.

Cushman, K. (1994). *Catherine, called Birdy.* New York: HarperCollins.

Dalji, H., & Miner, B. (1998). "Listen to your students": An interview with Oakland high school English teacher Hafeezah AdamaDavia Dalji. In T. Perry & L. Delpit (Eds.), *The real Ebonics debate: Power, language, and the education of African-American children* (pp. 105–115.) Boston: Beacon.

Dalton, S. S. (1998). *Pedagogy matters: Standards for effective teaching practice.* (Research Report No. 4). Santa Cruz, CA: Center for Research on Education, Diversity, and Excellence.

Daniels, C., Madden, N., & Slavin, R. (in press). The success for all middle school: Adding content to middle grades reform. *Middle School Journal.*

Daniels, H. (1994). *Literature circles: Voice and choice in the student-centered classroom.* York, ME: Stenhouse.

Davis, B., Sumara, D., & Luce-Kapler, R. (2000). *Engaging minds: Learning and teaching in a complex world.* Mahwah, NJ: Erlbaum.

De La Paz, S. (2005). Effects of historical reasoning instruction and writing strategy mastery in culturally and academically diverse middle school classrooms. *Journal of Educational Psychology, 97,* 139–156.

Deal, D. (1999, December). *Writing in the lab: Five research scientists talk about their use of writing in pursuit of scientific inquiry.* Paper presented at the National Reading Conference, Orlando, FL.

DeLorenzo, R. (1999). When hell freezes over: An approach to develop student interest and communication skills. *Journal of Chemical Education, 76,* 503.

Delpit, L. (1995). *Other people's children: Cultural conflict in the classroom.* New York: New Press.

Delpit, L. (1997, Fall). Ebonics and culturally responsive instruction. *Rethinking Schools Online, 12*(1), n.p. Available online at www.rethinkingschools.org/archive/12_01/ebdelpit.shtml.

Delpit, L. (1998). What should teachers do? Ebonics and culturally responsive instruction. In T. Perry & L. Delpit (Eds.), *The real Ebonics debate: Power, language, and the education of African-American children* (pp. 17–26). Boston: Beacon.

Delpit, L., & Dowdy, J. K. (Eds.). (2002). *The skin that we speak: Thoughts on language and culture in the classroom.* New York: New Press.

Denig, S. (2004). Multiple intelligences and learning styles: Two complementary dimensions. *Teachers College Record, 106*(1), 96–111.

Deshler, D. D., Schumaker, J. B., Lenz, B. K., Bulgren, J. A., Hock, M. F., Knight, J., & Ehren, B. J. (2001). Ensuring content-area learning by secondary students with learning disabilities. *Learning Disabilities Research & Practice, 16*, 96–109.

Devine, T. G., & Kania, J. S. (2003). Studying: Skills, strategies, and systems. J. Flood, D. Lapp, J. Squire, & J. Jensen (Eds.), *Handbook of research on teaching the English language arts* (2nd ed., pp. 942–954). Mahwah, NJ: Erlbaum.

Dewey, J. (1998). School and society. In M. Dworkin, (Ed.), *Dewey on education.* New York: Teachers College Press. (Original work published 1899)

Dillon, D. R., & Moje, E. B. (1998). Listening to the talk of adolescent girls: Lessons about literacy, school, and life. In D. E. Alvermann, K. A. Hinchman, D. W. Moore, S. F. Phelps, & D. R. Waff (Eds.), *Reconceptualizing the literacies in adolescents' lives* (pp. 193–223). Mahwah, NJ: Erlbaum.

Dirnberger, J. M., McCullagh, S., & Howick, T. (2005). Writing and drawing in the naturalist's journal. *Science Teacher, 72*(1), 38–42.

Dolan, T., Dolan, E., Taylor, V., Shoreland, J., & Harrison, C. (1979). Improving reading through group discussion activities. In E. Lunzer & K. Gardner (Eds.), *The effective use of reading.* London: Heinemann Educational Books.

Dole, J. A., Duffy, G. G., Roehler, L. R., & Pearson, P. D. (1991). Moving from the old to new: Research on reading comprehension instruction. *Review of Educational Research, 61*, 239–264.

Dolly, M. (1990). Integrating ESL reading and writing through authentic discourse. *Journal of Reading, 35*, 360–365.

Drake, S. (1998). One teacher's experiences with student portfolios. *Teaching History, 23*, 60–76.

Duff, P. A. (2004). Intertextuality and hybrid discourses: The infusion of pop culture in educational discourse. *Linguistics and Education, 14*, 231–276.

Duffelmeyer, F. (1994). Effective anticipation guide statements for learning from expository prose. *Journal of Reading, 37*, 452–457.

Duffelmeyer, F., & Baum, D. (1992). The extended anticipation guide revisited. *Journal of Reading, 35*, 654–656.

Duffelmeyer, F., Baum, D., & Merkley, D. (1987). Maximizing reader-text confrontation with an extended anticipation guide. *Journal of Reading, 31*, 146–151.

Duffy, G. (2002). The case for direct explanation of strategies. In C. Block & M. Pressley (Eds.), *Comprehension instruction: Research-based best practice* (pp. 28–41). New York: Guilford.

Duncan, B. (1996). *Mass media and popular culture* (2nd ed.). Toronto, Canada: Harcourt Brace.

Durkin, D. (1978/1979). What classroom observations reveal about reading comprehension instruction. *Reading Research Quarterly, 14*, 481–533.

Eanet, M., & Manzo, A. (1976). R.E.A.P.—A strategy for improving reading/writing study skills. *Journal of Reading, 19*, 647–652.

Echevarria, J., Vogt, M., & Short, D. (2000). *Making content comprehensible for English language learners. The SIOP model.* Boston: Allyn & Bacon.

Ehlinger, J., & Pritchard, R. (1994). Using Think Alongs in secondary content areas. *Reading Research & Instruction, 33*, 187–206.

Eisenhart, M., Finkel, E., & Marion, S. F. (1996). Creating the conditions for scientific literacy: A re-examination. *American Educational Research Journal, 33*, 261–295.

Eisner, W. (1986). *New York: The Big City.* Princeton, WI: Kitchen Sink Press.

El Dinary, P. (2002). Challenges of implementing transactional strategies instruction for reading comprehension. In C. Block & M. Pressley (Eds.), *Comprehension instruction: Research-based best practice* (pp. 351–364). New York: Guilford.

Elbow, P. (1973). *Writing without teachers.* New York: Oxford University Press.

Escamilla, K. (2007, October 8). Considerations for literacy coaches in classrooms with English language learners. *Literacy Coach Clearinghouse.* Retrieved June 1, 2008, from http://www.literacy coachingonline.org/briefs/Escamilla_BRIEF.pdf

Evans, E., & Engelberg, R. (1985). *A developmental study of student perceptions of school grading.* Paper presented at the biennial meeting of the Society for Research in Child Development, Toronto, Ontario, April. (ERIC No. ED 256 482)

Ezell, H., Hunsicker, S., Quinque, M., & Randolph, E. (1996). Maintenance and generalization of QAR reading comprehension strategies. *Reading Research & Instruction, 36*, 64–81.

Fagella-Luby, M., & Deshler, D. (2008). Reading comprehension in adolescents with LD: What we know; what we need to learn. *Learning Disabilities Research & Practice, 23*, 70–78.

Fahey, K., Lawrence, J., & Paratore, J. (2007). Using electronic portfolios to make learning public. *Journal of Adolescent & Adult Literacy, 50*, 460–471.

Fecho, B. (1998). Crossing boundaries of race in a critical literacy classroom. In D. Alvermann, K. Hinchman, D. Moore, S. Phelps, & D. Waff (Eds.), *Reconceptualizing the literacies in adolescents' lives* (pp. 75–101). Mahwah, NJ: Erlbaum.

Fecho, B. (2000). Critical inquiries into language in an urban classroom. *Research in the Teaching of English, 34*, 368–395.

Feldhusen, J. (1989). Issue: The sorting of students into ability groups has come under increasing fire recently. Should schools end the practice of grouping students by ability? *ASCD Update*, 31(1), 1–8.

Feldman, A., Alibrandi, M., & Kropf, A. (1998). Grading with points: The determination of report card grades by high school science teachers. *School Science & Mathematics, 98*, 140–148.

Felton, M. K. (2005). Approaches to argument in critical thinking instruction. *Thinking Classroom, 6*(4), 6–13.

Fernsten, L. A. (2007). A writing workshop in mathematics: Community practice of content discourse. *Mathematics Teacher, 101*, 273–278.

Fetterly, J. (1978). *The resisting reader.* Bloomington: Indiana University Press.

Finn, P. J. (1999). *Literacy with an attitude: Educating working-class children in their own self-interest.* Albany; State University of New York Press.

Fisher, D. (2004). Setting the "opportunity to read" standard: Resuscitating the SSR program in an urban high school. *Journal of Adolescent & Adult Literacy, 48*, 138–150.

Fisher, D., & Frey, N. (2003). Writing instruction for struggling adolescent readers: A gradual release model. *Journal of Adolescent & Adult Literacy, 46*, 396–405.

Fisher, J., Schumaker, J., & Deshler, D. (2002). Improving reading comprehension of at-risk adolescents. In C. Block & M. Pressley (Eds.), *Comprehension instruction: Research-based best practice* (pp. 351–364). New York: Guilford.

Fisher, P. J., & Blachowicz, C. L. Z. (2005). Vocabulary instruction in a remedial setting. *Reading & Writing Quarterly, 21*, 281–300.

Fitzgerald, J., (1995). English-as-a-second-language learners' cognitive reading processes: A review of research in the United States. *Review of Educational Research, 65*, 145–190.

Fitzgerald, J., & Cummins, J. (1999). Bridging disciplines to critique a national research agenda for language-minority children's schooling. *Reading Research Quarterly, 34*, 378–390.

Flood, J., & Lapp, D. (2000). Reading comprehension instruction for at-risk students: Research-based practices that can make a difference. In D. W. Moore, D. E. Alvermann, & K. A. Hinchman (Eds.), *Struggling adolescent readers: A collection of strategies* (pp. 138–147). Newark, DE: International Reading Association.

Floriani, A. (1993). Negotiating what counts: Roles and relationships, texts and contexts, content and meaning. *Linguistics and Education, 5*, 241–273.

Focused Reporting Project. (1999, Fall). *Changing schools in Long Beach: Independent reporting on the growth and achievement of young adolescents.* Atlanta: Edna McConnell Clark Foundation.

Fogarty, R. (1994, March.) Thinking about themes: Hundreds of themes. *Middle School Journal, 25*, 30–31.

Forbes, E. (1945). *Johnny Tremaine.* Boston: Houghton Mifflin.

Foster, S., & Padgett, C. (1999). Authentic historical inquiry in the social studies classroom. *The Clearing House, 72*, 357–363.

Fournier, D. N. E., & Graves, M. F. (2002). Scaffolding adolescents' comprehension of short stories. *Journal of Adolescent & Adult Literacy, 48*, 30–39.

Fradd, S. H., & Lee, O. (1999). Teacher's roles in promoting science inquiry with students from diverse language backgrounds. *Educational Researcher, 28*(6), 14–20, 42.

Frager, A., & Thompson, L. (1985). Conflict: The key to critical reading instruction. *Journal of Reading, 28*, 676–683.

Frayer, D. A., Frederick, W. C., & Klausmeier, H. J. (1969). A schema for testing the level of concept mastery. *Working Paper no. 16.* Madison, WI: Wisconsin R&D Center for Cognitive Learning.

Freire, P., & Macedo, D. (1987). *Literacy: Reading the word and the world.* Hedley, MA: Bergin & Garvey.

French, D. (2003, September). A new vision of authentic assessment to overcome the flaws in high stakes testing. *Middle School Journal, 35,* 14–23.

Fretzin, L. (1992, November). Double-entry journals. *Writing Teacher, 6,* 36–37.

Frey, N., & Fisher, D. (2004, January). Using graphic novels, anime, and the Internet in an urban high school *English Journal, 93*(3), 19–25.

Friedman, A. (2000, September). Writing and evaluating assessments in the content areas. *English Journal, 90,* 107–116.

Fritschmann, N., Deshler, D., & Schumaker, J. (2007). The effects of instruction in an inference strategy on the reading comprehension skills of adolescents with disabilities. *Learning Disability Quarterly, 30,* 245–262.

Fry, E. (1977). Fry's readability graph: Clarifications, validity, and extension to level 17. *Journal of Reading, 21,* 242–252.

Fry, E. (1989). Reading formulas—maligned but valid. *Journal of Reading, 32,* 292–297.

Fuchs, D. & Fuchs, L. (2006). Introduction to response to intervention. What, why, and how valid is it? *Reading Research Quarterly, 41,* 93–99.

Gabay, J. (1991). Issue: Motivation. ASCD *Update, 33, 7.*

Gadsden, V. (2000). Intergenerational literacy within families. In M. L. Kamil, P. Mosenthal, P. D. Pearson, & R. Barr (Eds.), *Handbook of reading research* (Vol. 3, pp. 871–887). Mahwah, NJ: Erlbaum.

Galbraith, M., Hennelly, J., & Purves, A. (1994). *Using portfolios to negotiate a rhetorical community.* Albany, NY: National Research Center on Literature Teaching & Learning.

Gamow, G. (1993). *Mr. Tompkins in paperback.* Cambridge, UK: Cambridge University Press.

Garcia, E., Rasmussen, B., Stobbe, C., & Garcia, E. (1990). Portfolios: An assessment tool in support of instruction. *International Journal of Education, 14,* 431–436.

Garcia, G. (1991). Factors influencing the English reading test performance of Spanish-speaking Hispanic children. *Reading Research Quarterly, 26,* 371–392.

Garcia, G., & Pearson, P. D. (1994). Assessment and diversity. *Review of Research in Education, 20,* 339–391.

Garcia, G. E. (2000). Bilingual children's reading. In M. L. Kamil, P. B. Mosenthal, P. D. Pearson, & R. Barr (Eds.), *Handbook of reading research* (Vol. 3, pp. 813–834). Mahwah, NJ: Erlbaum.

Gardner, H. (1999). *Intelligence reframed: Multiple intelligences for the 21st century.* New York: Basic Books.

Gardner, J. E., & Wissick, C. A. (2002). Enhancing thematic units using the World Wide Web: Tools and strategies for students with mild disabilities. *JSET e-journal, 17*(1). Retrieved October 21, 2003, from http://jset.unlv.edu/17.1/gardner/first.html

Gardner, S., Benham, H., & Newell, B. (1999, September). Oh, what a tangled web we've woven! Helping students evaluate sources. *English Journal, 89,* 39–44.

Garner, R., & Alexander, P. (1989). Metacognition: Answered and unanswered questions. *Educational Psychologist, 24,* 143–158.

Garner, R., & Gillingham, M. (1987). Students' knowledge of text structure. *Journal of Reading Behavior, 29,* 247–259.

Gavelek, J. R., & Raphael, T. E. (1996). Changing talk about text: New roles for teachers and students. *Language Arts, 73,* 182–192.

Gay, S., & Keith, C. J. (2002). Reasoning with linear equations. *Mathematics Teaching in the Middle School, 8,* 146–148.

Gearhart, M., & Herman, J. (1995, Winter). Portfolio assessment: Whose work is it? In *Evaluation Comment.* Los Angeles: UCLA Center for the Study of Evaluation & The National Center for Research on Evaluation, Standards, and Student Testing.

Gee, J. P. (1988). Legacies of literacy: From Plato to Freire through Harvey Graff. *Harvard Educational Review, 58,* 195–212.

Gee, J. P. (1996). *Social linguistics and literacies: Ideology in discourses* (2nd ed.). London: Taylor & Francis.

Gee, J. P. (1999). Reading and the new literacy studies: Reframing the National Academy of Sciences report on reading. *Journal of Literacy Research, 31,* 355–374.

Gee, J. P. (2000). Teenagers in new times: A new literacy studies perspective. *Journal of Adolescent & Adult Literacy, 43,* 412–420.

Genesee, E. (1994). *Integrating language and content: Lessons from immersion* (Educational Practice Report No. 11). Santa Cruz: University of California,

National Center for Research on Cultural Diversity and Second Language Learning.

Gergen, K. (1999). *An invitation to social construction.* Thousand Oaks, CA: Sage.

Gernsacher, M. A., & Kaschak, M. P. (2003). Neuroimaging studies of language production and comprehension. *Annual Review of Psychology, 54*, 91–114.

Gersten, R., Fuchs, L., Williams, J., & Baker, S. (2001). Teaching reading comprehension strategies to students with learning disabilities: A review of research. *Review of Educational Research, 71*, 279–320.

Ghatala, E. S. (1986). Strategy-monitoring training enables young learners to select effective strategies. *Educational Psychologist*, 21, 43–54.

Gill, B. P. & Schlossman, S. L. (2004). Villain or savior? The American discourse on homework, 1850–2003. [Electronic version] *Theory into Practice, 43*(3), 174(8).

Gilles, C., Bixby, M., Crowley, P., Crenshaw, S., Henrichs, M., Reynolds, E., & Pyle, D. (Eds.) (1988). *Whole language strategies for secondary students.* New York: Richard C. Owen.

Gillespie, C. (1990). Questions about student-generated questions. *Journal of Reading, 34*, 250–257.

Glatthorn, A. (1991). Secondary English classroom environments. In J. Flood, J. M. Jensen, D. Lapp, & J. R. Squire (Eds.), *Handbook of research on teaching the English language arts* (pp. 438–456). New York: Macmillan.

Glazier, J., & Seo, J. (2005). Multicultural literature and discussion as mirror and window? *Journal of Adolescent & Adult Literacy, 48*, 686–700.

Goatley, V. J., Brock, C. H., & Raphael, T. E. (1995). Diverse learners participating in regular education book clubs. *Reading Research Quarterly, 30*, 352–380.

Godina, H. (1996). The canonical debate—Implementing multicultural literature and perspectives. *Journal of Adolescent & Adult Literacy, 39*, 544–549.

Goerss, B. (1996). Interdisciplinary planning within cooperative groups. *Journal of Adolescent & Adult Learning, 40*, 110–116.

Goldman, S., & Rakestraw, J. (2000). Structural aspects of constructing meaning from text. In M. Kamil, P. Mosenthal, P. D. Pearson, & R. Barr (Eds.), *Handbook of reading research* (Vol. 3, pp. 311–335). Mahwah, NJ: Erlbaum.

Gonzalez, O. (1999). Building vocabulary: Dictionary consultation and the ESL student. *Journal of Adolescent & Adult Literacy, 43*, 264–270.

Goodson, T. (2004). Teaching in the time of dogs. *The Quarterly, 26*(3). Retrieved September 3, 2005, from www.writingproject.org/cs/nwpp/print/nwpr/1979

Gordon, C. (1990, Winter). Contexts for expository text structure use. *Reading Research & Instruction, 29*, 55–72.

Grady, M. (1998). *Qualitative and action research: A practioner handbook.* Bloomington, IN: Phi Delta Kappa.

Graham, S., & Perin, D. (2007). *Writing next: Effective strategies to improve writing of adolescents in middle and high schools—A report to Carnegie Corporation of New York.* Washington, DC: Alliance for Excellent Education.

Graves, D. (1983). *Writing: Teachers and children at work.* Portsmouth, NH: Heinemann.

Graves, M. (1986). Vocabulary learning and instruction. *Review of Research in Education, 13*, 49–89.

Graves, M., & Prenn, M. (1986). Costs and benefits of various methods of teaching vocabulary. *Journal of Reading 29*, 596–602.

Graves, M., & Slater, W. (1996). Vocabulary instruction in content areas. In D. Lapp, J. Flood, & N. Farnan (Eds.), *Content area reading and learning: Instructional strategies.* Boston: Allyn & Bacon.

Graves, M. F., Cooke, C. L., & LaBerge, M. J. (1983). Effects of previewing difficult short stories on low ability junior high school students' comprehension, recall, and attitudes. *Reading Research Quarterly, 18*, 262–276.

Green, B. (1991). Reading "readings": Towards a postmodernist reading pedagogy. In C. D. Baker & A. Luke (Eds.), *Towards a critical sociology of reading pedagogy.* Philadelphia: Benjamins.

Greene, M. (1991). The literacy debate and the public school: Going beyond the functional. *Educational Horizons, 69*, 129–134, 164–168.

Greenlaw, M. J. (1987). Science fiction as moral literature. *Educational Horizons, 65*, 165–166.

Greenleaf, C., Jiménez, R., & Roller, C. (2002). Conversations: Reclaiming secondary reading interventions: From limited to rich conceptions, from narrow to broad conversations. *Reading Research Quarterly, 37*, 484–496.

Greenleaf, C. L., Schoenbach, R., Cziko, C., & Mueller, F. L. (2001). Apprenticing adolescent readers to academic literacy. *Harvard Educational Review, 71*, 79–129.

Gronna, S., Chin-Chance, S., & Abedi, J. (2000, April). Differences between the performance of limited English proficient students and students who are labeled proficient in English on different content areas: Reading and mathematics. Paper presented at the meeting of the American Educational Research Association, New Orleans.

Grossman, P. L., & Stodolsky, S. S. (1995, November). Content as context: The role of school subjects in secondary school teaching. *Educational Researcher, 24,* 5–23.

Gumperz, J., Cook-Gumperz, J., & Szymanski, M. (1999). Collaborative practices in bilingual cooperative learning classrooms. (Research Report No. 7). Santa Cruz, CA & Washington, DC: Center for Research on Education, Diversity & Excellence.

Gunderson, L. (2000). Voices of the teen-aged diasporas. *Journal of Adolescent & Adult Literacy, 43,* 692–706.

Gunel, M., Hand, B., & Gunduz, S. (2006). Comparing student understanding of quantum physics when embedding multimodal representation into two different writing formats: Presentation format versus summary report format. *Science Education, 90,* 1092–1112.

Guthrie, J., & Ozgungor, S. (2002). Instructional contexts for reading engagement. In C. Block & M. Pressley (Eds.), *Comprehension instruction: Research-based best practice* (pp. 275–288). New York: Guilford.

Guzzetti, B., & Hynd, C. (Eds.). (1998). *Perspectives on conceptual change: Multiple ways to understand knowing and learning in a complex world.* Mahwah, NJ: Erlbaum.

Guzzetti, B., & Hynd, C. (Eds.). (1998). *Theoretical perspectives on conceptual change.* Mahwah, NJ: Erlbaum.

Guzzetti, B., & Williams, W. (1996). Gender, text, and discussion: Examining intellectual safety in the science classroom. *Journal of Research in Science Teaching, 33,* 5–20.

Guzzetti, B., Snyder, T., Glass, G. V., & Gamas, W. S. (1993). Promoting conceptual change in science: A comparative meta-analysis of instructional interventions from reading education and science education. *Reading Research Quarterly, 28,* 116–159.

Guzzetti, B. J., & Williams, W. D. (1996). Changing the pattern of gendered discussion: Lessons from science classrooms. *Journal of Adolescent & Adult Literacy, 40,* 38–47.

Hadaway, N., & Mundy, J. (2000). Children's informational picture books visit a secondary ESL classroom. In D. Moore, D. Alvermann, & K. Hinchman (Eds.), *Struggling adolescent readers: A collection of teaching strategies* (pp. 83–95). Newark, DE: International Reading Association.

Haggard, M. (1982). The vocabulary self-collection strategy: An active approach to word learning. *Journal of Reading, 26,* 203–207.

Haggard, M. (1986). The vocabulary self-collection strategy: Using student interest and world knowledge to enhance vocabulary growth. *Journal of Reading, 29,* 634–642.

Hagood, M. C. (2002). Critical literacy for whom? *Reading Research & Instruction, 41,* 247–266.

Hall, S., & Whannel, P. (1998). The young audience. In J. Storey (Ed.), *Cultural theory and popular culture; A Reader* (2nd ed., pp. 61–67). Athens: University of Georgia Press.

Hamilton, L. (2003). Assessment as a policy tool. *Review of Research in Education, 27,* 25–68.

Haney, G., & Thistlethwaite, L. (1991). A model critical reading lesson for secondary high-risk students. *Reading, Writing and Learning Disabilities, 7,* 337–354.

Hansen-Krening, N., & Mizokawa, D. (2000). Exploring ethnic-specific literature: A unity of parents, families, and educators. In D. Moore, D. Alvermann, & K. Hinchman (Eds.), *Struggling adolescent readers: A collection of teaching strategies* (pp. 96–106). Newark, DE: International Reading Association.

Hardin, L. F. (1999, Fall/Winter). Netting the past: Putting our town's history on the web. *Bread Loaf Rural Teacher Network Magazine,* 7–9.

Hare, V., & Borchardt, K. (1984). Direct instruction of summarization skills. *Reading Research Quarterly, 20,* 62–78.

Hare, V., Rabinowitz, M., & Schieble, K. (1989). Text effects on main idea comprehension. *Reading Research Quarterly, 24,* 72–88.

Hargreaves, A. (1989). *Curriculum assessment and reform.* Philadelphia: Open University Press.

Hargreaves, D. H. (1967). *Social relations in a secondary school.* London: Routledge & Kegan Paul.

Harklau, L. (2002). The role of writing in classroom second language acquisition. *Journal of Second Language Writing, 11,* 329–350.

Harmon, J. M. (2000). Vocabulary teaching and learning in a seventh-grade literature-based classroom. In D. W. Moore, D. E. Alvermann, & K. A. Hinchman (Eds.), *Struggling adolescent readers: A collection of teaching strategies* (pp. 174–188). Newark, DE: International Reading Association.

Harmon, J. M., Hedrick, W. B., & Wood, K. D. (2005). Research on vocabulary instruction in the content areas: Implications for struggling readers. *Reading and Writing Quarterly, 21,* 261–280.

Harper, C., & de Jong, E. (2004). Misconceptions about English-language learners. *Journal of Adolescent & Adult Literacy, 48,* 152–162.

Harris, V. (1991). "Have you heard about an African Cinderella story?": The hunt for multiethnic literature. *Publishing Research Quarterly, 7* (3), 23–36.

Harris, V. (Ed.). (1997). *Using multicultural literature in the K–8 classroom.* Norwood, MA: Christopher Gordon.

Harste, J., Short, K. G., & Burke, C. (1988). *Creating classrooms for authors.* Portsmouth, NH: Heinemann.

Harvey, K., & Povletich, K. (1999, November). *From prose to poetry.* Presentation at the National Council of Social Studies Annual Conference, Orlando, FL.

Hayes, J. R. (1989). *The complete problem solver.* Hillsdale, NJ: Erlbaum.

Heath, S. B. (1983). *Ways with words: Language, life, and work in communities and classrooms.* Cambridge, UK: Cambridge University Press.

Heath, S. B. (1986b). The functions and uses of literacy. In S. DeCastell, A. Luke, & K. Egan (Eds.), *Literacy, society, and schooling: A reader* (pp. 15–26). London: Cambridge University Press.

Heath, S. B. (1991). The sense of being literate; Historical and cross-cultural features. In R. Barr, M. L. Kamil, P. Mosenthal, & P. D. Pearson (Eds.), *Handbook of reading research* (Vol. 2, pp. 3–25). New York: Longman.

Helfeldt, J., & Henk, W. (1990). Reciprocal question-answer relationships: An instructional technique for at-risk readers. *Journal of Reading, 33,* 509–514.

Heller, R., & Greenleaf, C. (2007). *Literacy instruction in the content areas: Getting to the core of middle and high school improvement.* Washington, DC: Alliance for Excellent Education.

Helms, J. (1992). Why is there no study of cultural equivalence in standardized cognitive ability testing? *American Psychologist, 47,* 1083–1101.

Hemphill, L. (1999). Narrative style, social class, and response to poetry. *Research in the Teaching of English, 33,* 275–302.

Henze, R. C., & Hauser, M. E. (1999). *Personalizing culture through anthropological and educational perspectives* (Educational Practice Report No. 4). Santa Cruz, CA: Center for Research on Education, Diversity and Excellence.

Herber, H. (1978). *Teaching reading in content areas* (2nd ed.). Englewood Cliffs, NJ: Prentice Hall.

Herber, H. L. (1970). *Teaching reading in content areas.* Englewood Cliffs, NJ: Prentice Hall.

Herber, H. L., & Nelson-Herber, J. (1987). Developing independent learners. *Journal of Reading, 30,* 584–588.

Hicks, D., & Dolan, T. K. (2003). Haunted landscapes and girlhood imaginations: The power of horror fictions for marginalised readers. *Changing English, 10*(1), 45–57.

Hidi, S., & Anderson, V. (1986). Producing written summaries: Task demands, cognitive operations, and implications for instruction. *Review of Educational Research, 56,* 473–494.

Hill, H. (1989). *Effective strategies for teaching minority students.* Bloomington, IN: National Educational Service.

Hill, M. (1991). Writing summaries promotes thinking and learning across the curriculum—But why are they so difficult to write? *Journal of Reading, 34,* 536–539.

Hinchey, P. H. (1998). *Finding freedom in the classroom: A practical introduction to critical theory.* New York: Peter Lang.

Hinchman, K., & Zalewski, P. (1996). Reading for success in a tenth-grade global-studies class: A qualitative study. *Journal of Literacy Research, 28,* 91–106.

Hirsch, E. D. (1987). *Cultural literacy.* Boston: Houghton Mifflin.

Hodgkinson, H. L. (1992). *A demographic look at tomorrow.* Washington, DC: Center of Demographic Policy.

Hoffman, J. (1992). Critical reading/thinking across the curriculum: Using I-charts to support learning. *Language Arts, 68,* 121–127.

Hoffman, J. V. (1979). The intra-act procedure for critical reading. *Journal of Reading, 22,* 605–608.

Hoffman, J. V., Paris, S. G., Salas, R., Patterson, E., & Assaf, L. (2003). High-stakes assessment in the language arts: The piper plays, the players dance, but who pays the price? In J. Flood, D. Lapp, J. Squire, & J. Jensen (Eds.), *Handbook of research on teaching the English language arts* (2nd ed., pp. 619–630). Mahwah, NJ: Erlbaum.

Hoffman, L. (1999). Key statistics on public elementary and secondary schools and agencies. *Education Statistics Quarterly, 1*(4), 67–70.

Hofstadter, R. (1970). *Anti-intellectualism in American life.* New York: Knopf.

Hopkins, G., & Bean, T. (2000). Vocabulary learning with the verbal-visual word association strategy in a Native American community. In D. Moore, D. Alvermann, & K. Hinchman (Eds.), *Struggling adolescent readers: A collection of teaching strategies* (pp. 107–115). Newark, DE: International Reading Association.

Howes, E. V., Hamilton, G. W., Zaskoda, D. (2003). Linking science and literature through technology: Thinking about interdisciplinary inquiry in middle school. *Journal of Adolescent & Adult Literacy, 46,* 494–504.

Hruby, G. G. (2001). Sociological, postmodern, and new realism perspectives in social constructionism: Implications for literacy research. *Reading Research Quarterly, 36,* 48–62.

Hruby, G. G. (in press). Grounding reading comprehension in the neurosciences. In G. Duffy & S. Israel (Eds.), *Handbook of research on reading comprehension.* New York: Erlbaum/Taylor and Francis.

Hudelson, S. (1999, May/June). ESL writing: Principles for teaching young writers. *ESL Magazine, 2,* 8–10, 12.

Hughes, R. (1993). *Culture of complaint.* New York: Oxford University Press.

Hughes-Hassell, S., & Rodge, P. (2007). The leisure reading habits of urban adolescents. *Journal of Adolescent and Adult Literacy, 51,* 22–33.

Hull, G., & Schultz, K. (Eds.). (2002). *School's out! Bridging out-of-school literacies with classroom practice.* New York: Teachers College Press.

Hynd, C., McNish, M., Lay, K., & Fowler, P. (1995). *High school physics: The role of text in learning counterintuitive information* (Technical Report No. 46). Athens, GA: National Reading Research Center.

Indrisano, R., & Paratore, J. R. (1991). Classroom contexts for literacy learning. In J. Flood, J. M. Jensen, D. Lapp, & J. R. Squire (Eds.), *Handbook of research*

on teaching the English language arts (pp. 477–488). New York: Macmillan.

Innocenti, R. (1985). *Rose Blanche.* London: Jonas Cape.

Inos, R. H., & Quigley, M. A. (1995). *Research review for inclusive practices.* November Newsletter (pp. 1–6). Honolulu, HI: Pacific Region Educational Laboratory.

International Reading Association. (1982). Misuse of grade equivalents. *The Reading Teacher, 35,* 464.

International Society for Technology in Education. (2007). *National educational technology standards for students: Connecting curriculum & technology* (2nd ed.). Eugene, OR: International Society for Technology in Education. Available online at http://cnets.iste.org/currstands

Irvine, J. (1990). Transforming teaching for the 21st century. *Educational Horizons, 69*(1), 16–21.

Ivey, G. (1999). A multicase study in the middle school: Complexities among young adolescent readers. *Reading Research Quarterly, 34,* 172–192.

Ivey, G. (2000). Reflections on teaching struggling middle school readers. In D. W. Moore, D. E. Alvermann, & K. A. Hinchman (Eds.), *Struggling adolescent readers: A collection of teaching strategies* (pp. 27–38). Newark, DE: International Reading Association.

Ivey, G., & Broaddus, K. (2001). "Just plain reading": A survey of what makes students want to read in middle school classrooms. *Reading Research Quarterly, 36,* 350–377.

Jacobs, H. (1987). The perils of a slave woman's life. In M. E. Washington (Ed.), *Invented lives: Narratives of black women, 1860–1960* (pp. 16–69). New York: Anchor.

Jacobs, V. A. (2008). Adolescent literacy: Putting the crisis in context. *Harvard Educational Review, 78,* 7–39.

Jenkins, J. R., Johnson, E., & Hileman, J. (2004). When is reading also writing: Sources of individual differences on the new reading performance assessments. *Scientific Studies of Reading, 8,* 125–151.

Jiménez, R., Garcia, G., & Pearson, P. D. (1996). The reading strategies of bilingual Latina/o students who are successful English readers: Opportunities and obstacles. *Reading Research Quarterly, 31,* 90–112.

Jiménez, R. T., & Gámez, A. (2000). Literature-based cognitive strategy instruction for middle school Latina/o students. In D. W. Moore, D. E. Alvermann, & K. A. Hinchman (Eds.), *Struggling adolescent readers: A collection of teaching strategies* (pp. 74–82). Newark, DE: International Reading Association.

Jiménez, R. T., Moll, L. C., Rodriguez-Brown, F. V., & Barrera, R. B. (1999). Latina and Latino researchers interact on issues related to literacy learning. *Reading Research Quarterly, 34,* 217–230.

Johnson, D., & Pearson, P. D. (1984). *Teaching reading vocabulary* (2nd ed.). New York: Holt, Rinehart and Winston.

Johnston, P. H., & Winograd, P. N. (1985). Passive failure in reading. *Journal of Reading Behavior, 17,* 279–301.

Jones, B. F., Pierce, J., & Hunter, B. (1988/1989). Teaching students to construct graphic representations. *Educational Leadership, 46*(4), 20–25.

Jordan, S., & Purves, A. (1993). *Issues in the responses of students to culturally diverse texts: A preliminary study.* Albany, NY: National Research Center on Literature Teaching and Learning.

Jurdak, M., & Abu Zein, R. (1998). The effect of journal writing on achievement in and attitudes toward mathematics. *School Science & Mathematics, 98,* 412–419.

Just, M., & Carpenter, P. (1987). *The psychology of reading and language comprehension.* Boston: Allyn & Bacon.

Kaiser Family Foundation. (2003). *Key facts: Media literacy* (Publication Number: 3383). Retrieved October 9, 2005, from www.kff.org/entmedia/Media-Literacy.cfm

Kamler, B. (1999, November). *The politics of teaching writing and the changing nature of teachers' work.* Paper presented at the annual meeting of the National Council of Teachers of English, Denver.

Kamler, B., & Comber, B. (1996). Critical literacy: Not generic—not developmental—not another orthodoxy. *Changing Education, 3*(1), 1–9.

Katz, C. A., Boran, K., Braun, T. J., Massie, M. J., & Kuby, S. A. (2003). The importance of being with Sir Ernest Shackleton at the bottom of the world. *Journal of Adolescent & Adult Literacy, 47,* 38–49.

Kennedy, M., Fisher, M., & Ennis, R. (1991). Critical thinking: Literature review and needed research. In L. Idol & B. F. Jones (Eds.), *Educational values and cognitive instruction: Implications for reform* (pp. 11–40). Hillsdale, NJ: Erlbaum.

Kenney, J. M., Hancewicz, E., Heuer, L., Metsisto, D., & Tuttle, C. L. (2005). *Literacy strategies for improving mathematics instruction.* Alexandra, VA: Association for Supervision and Curriculum Development.

Keys, C. (1999). Revitalizing instruction in scientific genres: Connecting knowledge production with writing to learn in science. *Science Education, 83,* 115–130.

Keys, C. W., Hand, B., Prain, V., & Collins, S. (1999). Using the Science Writing Heuristic as a tool for learning from laboratory investigations in secondary science. *Journal of Research in Science Teaching, 3,* 1065–1084.

Kibby, M. (1995). The organization and teaching of things and the words that signify them. *Journal of Adolescent & Adult Literacy, 39,* 208–223.

Kinzer, C. K. (2005). The intersection of schools, communities, and technology: Recognizing children's use of new literacies. In R. A. Karchmer, M. H. Mallette, J. Kara-Soteriou, & D. J. Leu, Jr. (Eds.), *Innovative approaches to literacy education: Using the Internet to support new literacies* (pp. 65–82). Newark, DE: International Reading Association.

Kist, W. (2005). *New literacies in action: Teaching and learning in multiple media.* New York: Teachers College Press.

Klare, G. (1984). Readability. In P. D. Pearson (Ed.), *Handbook of reading research* (pp. 681–744). New York: Longman.

Klenk, L., & Kibby, M. (2000). Re-mediating reading difficulties: Appraising the past, reconciling the present, constructing the future. In M. L. Kamil, P. B. Mosenthal, R. Barr, & P. D. Pearson (Eds.), *Handbook of reading research* (Vol. 3, pp. 667–690). Mahwah, NJ: Erlbaum.

Klingner, J. K., & Vaughan, S. (1996). Reciprocal teaching of reading comprehension strategies for students with learning disabilities who use English as a second language. *Elementary School Journal, 96,* 275–293.

Knoblauch, C. H. (1990). Literacy and the politics of education. In A. A. Lunsford, H. Moglen, & J. Slevin (Eds.), *The right to literacy* (pp. 74–80). New York: Modern Language Association of America.

Knowles, J. (1960). *A separate peace.* New York: Macmillan.

Koki, S. (2000, February). Bullying in Pacific schools— Should we be concerned? *Pacific Education Updates*, 1–12.

Kolich, E. M. (1991). Effects of computer-assisted vocabulary training on word knowledge. *Journal of Educational Research, 84*, 177–182.

Konopak, B., Martin, S., & Martin, M. (1990). Using a writing strategy to enhance sixth-grade students' comprehension of content material. *Journal of Reading Behavior, 22*, 19–38.

Konopak, B., Sheard, C., Longman, D., Lyman, B., Slaton, E., Atkinson, R., & Thames, D. (1987). Incidental versus intentional word learning from context. *Reading Psychology, 8*, 7–21.

Krashen, S. (1985). *The input hypothesis: Issues and implications.* New York: Longman.

Krashen, S. (1989). *Language acquisition and language education.* New York: Prentice Hall.

Krashen, S. (2002). More smoke and mirrors: A critique of the National Reading Panel report on fluency. In R. Allington, (Ed.), *Big Brother and the national reading curriculum: How ideology trumped evidence* (pp. 112–124). Portsmouth, NH: Heinemann.

Krashen, S. D. (1988). Do we learn to read by reading? The relationship between free reading and reading ability. In D. Tannen (Ed.), *Linguistics in context: Connecting observation and understanding* (pp. 269–298). Norwood, NJ: Ablex.

Krasny, K. A., Sadoski, M., & Paivio, A. (2007). Unwarranted return: A response to McVee, Dunsmore, and Gavelek's (2005) "Schema theory revisited." *Review of Educational Research, 77*, 239–244.

Kreidler, W. J. (1984). *Creative conflict resolution.* Glenview, IL: Scott, Foresman.

Kuykendal, C. (1992). *From rage to hope: Strategies for reclaiming Black and Hispanic students.* Bloomington, IN: National Educational Service.

LaBerge, D., & Samuels, S. J. (1974). Toward a theory of automatic information processing in reading. In H. Singer & R. Ruddell (Eds.), *Theoretical models and processes of reading* (3rd ed., pp. 689–718). Newark, DE: International Reading Association.

LaConte, R. T. (1981). *Homework as a learning experience: What research says to the teacher.* Arlington, VA: ERIC Document Reproduction Service. (ED 217 022)

Ladson-Billings, G. (1994). *The dreamkeepers.* San Francisco: Jossey-Bass.

Lam, W. S. E. (2006). Re-envisioning language, literacy, and the immigrant subject in new mediascapes. *Pedagogies: An International Journal, 1*, 171–195.

Lambros, A. (2004). *Problem-based learning in middle and high school classrooms: A teacher's guide to implementation.* Thousand Oaks, CA: Corwin Press.

Langer, J. (1986). Learning through writing: Study skills in the content areas. *Journal of Reading, 29*, 400–406.

Langer, J. (1989). Literate thinking and schooling. *Literacy Research Newsletter, 5*(1), 1–2.

Langer, J. (2000). *Beating the odds: Teaching middle and high school students to read and write well.* Albany, NY: National Center on English Learning and Achievement.

Langer, J. A. (2001). Beating the odds: Teaching middle and high school students to read and write well. *American Educational Research Journal, 38*, 837–880.

Lankshear, C., & Knobel, M. (2003). *New literacies: Changing knowledge and classroom learning.* Philadelphia: Open University Press.

Lankshear, C., & Knobel, M. (2006). *New literacies: Everyday practices and classroom learning*, 2nd ed. New York: Open University Press.

Lankshear, C., & Knobel, M. (2007). Sampling "the new" in new literacies. In M. Knobel & C. Lankshear (Eds.), *A new literacies sampler* (pp. 1–24), New York: Peter Lang.

Lankshear, C., & McLaren, P. (Eds.). (1993). *Critical literacy: Politics, praxis, and the postmodern.* Albany, NY: State University of New York Press.

Laursen, B., Hartup, W. W., & Koplas, A. L. (1996). Towards understanding peer conflict. *Merrill-Palmer Quarterly, 42*(1), 76–102.

Lave, J., & Wenger, E. (1991). *Situated learning.* Cambridge, UK: Cambridge University Press.

Lebauer, R. (1985). Nonnative English speaker problems in content and English classes: Are they thinking or reading problems? *Journal of Reading, 29*, 136–142.

Lee, J., Grigg, W., & Donahue, P. (2007). *The nation's report card: Reading 2007* (NCES no. 2007-496). Washington, DC: U.S. Department of Education, Institute of Education Sciences, National Center for Education Statistics.

Lehr, F. (1984). ERIC/RCS: Cooperative learning. *Journal of Reading, 27*, 458–461.

Lehr, F. (1984). ERIC/RCS: Cooperative learning. *Journal of Reading, 27*, 458–461.

Leinhardt, G. (1983, April). *Routines in expert math teachers' thoughts and actions.* Paper presented at the annual meeting of the American Educational Research Association, Montreal.

Lemke, J. L. (1995). *Textual politics: Discourse and social dynamics.* London: Taylor & Francis.

Lenhart, A., Madden, M., Macgill, A. R., & Smith, A. (2007, December). Teens and social media. *PEW Internet & American Life Project.* Washington, DC: Pew Charitable Trusts. Retrieved June 29, 2008, from http://www.pewinternet.org/PPF/r/230/report_display.asp

Lensmire, T. (1994). *When children write: Critical revisions of the writing workshop.* New York: Teachers College Press.

Lesley, M. (2008). Access and resistance to dominant forms of discourse: Critical literacy and "at risk" high school students. *Literacy Research and Instruction, 47*, 174–194.

Leu, D., Coiro, J., Castek, J., Hartman, D., Henry, L., & Reinking, D. (2008). Research on instruction and assessment in the new literacies of online reading comprehension. In C. Block & S. Parris (Eds.), *Comprehension instruction: Research-based best practices.* New York: Guilford Press.

Leu, D. J. (1997). Caity's question: Literacy as deixis on the Internet. *The Reading Teacher, 51*, 62–67.

Leu, D. J., & Kinzer, C. K. (2003). *Effective literacy instruction K-8: Implementing best practice* (5th ed.). Upper Saddle River, NJ: Merrill Prentice Hall.

Leu, D. J., & Leu, D. D. (1999). *Teaching with the Internet: Lessons from the classroom.* Norwood, MA: Gordon.

Leu, D. J., Jr., Ataya, R., & Coiro, J. L. (2002, December). *Assessing assessment strategies among the 50 states: Evaluating the literacies of our past or the literacies of our future?* Paper presented at the National Reading Conference, Miami, FL.

Leu, D. J., Jr., Mallette, M. H., Karchmer, R. A., & Kara-Soteriou, J. (2005). Contextualizing the new literacies of information and communication technologies in theory, research, and practice. In R. A. Karchmer, M. H. Mallette, J. Kara-Soteriou, & D. J. Leu, Jr. (Eds.), *Innovative approaches to literacy education: Using the Internet to support new literacies*

(pp. 1–12). Newark, DE: International Reading Association.

Lewis, C. (1998). Rock 'n' roll and horror stories: Students, teachers, and popular culture. *Journal of Adolescent & Adult Literacy, 42*, 116–120.

Lewis, C. (2000). Limits of identification: The personal, pleasurable, and critical in reader response. *Journal of Literacy Research, 32*, 253–266.

Lewis, C., Ketter, J., & Fabos, B. (2001). Reading race in a rural context. *International Journal of Qualitative Studies in Education, 14*, 317–350.

Linder, R., & Falk-Ross, F. (2004). Reading between the lines: Middle school readers uncover messages in magazine advertisements. In J. R. Dugan, P. E. Linder, M. B. Sampson, B. A. Brancato, & L. Elish-Piper (Eds.), *Celebrating the power of literacy: The twenty-sixth yearbook of the College Reading Association* (pp. 376–393). Commerce, TX: Texas A&M University.

Long, A. (2004). *Cyber schools.* Denver, CO: Education Commission of the States.

Luke, A. (1988). *Literacy, textbooks, and ideology.* London: Falmer.

Luke, A., Freebody, P., & Land, R. (2000). *Literate futures: Report of the literacy review for Queensland state schools.* Brisbane, Australia: Education Queensland. Retrieved March 28, 2008, from http://education.qld.gov.au/curriculum/learning/literate-futures/pdfs/lf-review.pdf

Luke, C. (2000). Cyber-schooling and technological change: Multiliteracies for new times. In B. Cope & M. Kalantzis (Eds.), *Multiliteracies: Literacy learning and the design of social futures* (pp. 69–91). London: Routledge.

Macaulay, D. (1973). *Cathedral.* New York: Houghton Mifflin.

Macaulay, D. (1974). *City: A story of Roman planning and construction.* Boston: Houghton Mifflin.

Macaulay, D. (2003). *Mosque.* Boston: Houghton/Walter Lorraine.

Madaus, G., & O'Dwyer, L. (1999). A short history of performance assessment: Lessons learned. *Phi Delta Kappan, 80*, 688–695.

Malcolm X (with A. Haley) (1965). *The autobiography of Malcolm X.* New York: Ballantine.

Mandler, J., & Johnson, N. (1979). Remembrance of things parsed: Story structure and recall. *Cognitive Psychology, 9*, 111–151.

Manzo, A. (1969). The ReQuest procedure. *Journal of Reading, 13*, 23–26.

Manzo, A., Manzo, U., & Albee, J. J. (2002). iREAP: Improving reading, writing, and thinking in the wired classroom. *Journal of Adolescent & Adult Literacy, 46*, 42–47.

Manzo, A., Manzo, U., & Estes, T. (2001). *Content area literacy: Interactive teaching for interacive learning*, 2nd ed. New York: Wiley.

Marsh, J. P., & Stolle, E. (2006). Re/constructing identities: A tale of two adolescents. In D. E. Alvermann, K. A. Hinchman, D. W. Moore, S. F. Phelps, & D. R. Waff (Eds.), *Reconceptualizing the literacies in adolescents' lives* (2nd ed., pp. 47–63). Mahwah, NJ: Erlbaum.

Marshall, N. (1996). The students: Who are they and how do I reach them? In D. Lapp, J. Flood, & N. Farnan (Eds.), *Content area reading and learning* (2nd ed., pp. 79–93). Boston: Allyn & Bacon.

Martin, C., Martin, M., & O'Brien, D. (1984). Spawning ideas for writing in the content areas. *Reading World, 11*, 11–15.

Martin, J. R. (1993). Life as a noun: Arresting the university in science and humanities. In M. A. K. Halliday & J. R. Martin (Eds.), *Writing science: Literacy and discursive power* (pp. 221–267). Pittsburgh, PA: University of Pittsburgh Press.

Martin, M., & Konopak, B. (1987). An instructional investigation of students' ideas generated during content area writing. In J. Readence & R. S. Baldwin (Eds.), *Research in literacy: Merging perspectives* (pp. 265–271). Rochester, NY: National Reading Conference.

Martin, S. (2000). Tabloid exposé. In L. Baines & A. Kunkel (Eds.), *Going Bohemian: Activities that engage adolescents in the art of writing well* (pp. 123–124). Newark, DE: International Reading Association.

Marzano, R., & Kendall, J. (1996). *The fall and rise of standards-based education* (National Association of State Boards of Education *Issues in Brief*). Aurora, CO: Mid-Continent Regional Educational Laboratory.

Mason, J. M., Kniseley, E., & Kendall, J. (1979). Effects of polysemous words on sentence comprehension. *Reading Research Quarterly, 15*, 49–65.

Mason, R. T., & McFeetors, P. J. (2002). Interactive writing in mathematics class: Getting started. *Mathematics Teacher, 95*, 532–536.

Mastropieri, M., Scruggs, T., & Graetz, J. (2003). Reading comprehension instruction for secondary students: Challenges for struggling students and teachers. *Learning Disability Quarterly, 26*, 103–116.

Mayher, J. S., Lester, N., & Pradl, G. M. (1983). *Learning to write: Writing to learn.* Portsmouth, NH: Heinemann.

McCain, T. (2005). *Teaching for tomorrow: Teaching content and problem solving skills.* Thousand Oaks, CA: Corwin Press.

McCarthy, C. (1998). Multicultural education, minority identities, and the challenge of curriculum reform. In A. Willis (Ed.), *Teaching and using multicultural literature in grades 9–12: Moving beyond the canon* (pp. 1–16). Norwood, MA: Christopher Gordon.

McCombs, B. L. (1995). Understanding the keys to motivation to learn. In *What's noteworthy on learners, learning, schooling* (pp. 5–12). Aurora, CO: Mid-Continent Regional Educational Laboratory.

Mchan, H. (1991). *Sociological foundations supporting the study of cultural diversity* (Research Report No. 1). Santa Cruz: University of California, National Center for Research on Cultural Diversity and Second Language Learning.

McIntosh, M., & Draper, R. (1995). Applying the question–answer relationship strategy in mathematics. *Journal of Reading, 39*, 120–131.

McIntosh, M. E., & Draper, R. J. (2001). Using learning logs in mathematics: Writing to learn. *Mathematics Teacher, 94*, 554–557.

McKenna, M. C., & Robinson, R. D. (1990). Content literacy: A definition and implications. *Journal of Reading, 34*, 184–186.

McKinney, D., & Michalovic, M. (2004, November). Teaching the stories of scientists and their discoveries. *The Science Teacher, 71*, 46–51.

McMahon, S. I., & Raphael, T. E. (Eds.). (1997). *The book club connection.* New York: Teachers College Press.

McTighe, J., & Brown, J. (2005). Differentiated instruction and educational standards: Is détente possible? *Theory Into Practice, 44*, 234–244.

McVee, M. B., Dunsmore, K., & Gavelek, J. R. (2005). Schema theory revisited. *Review of Educational Research, 75*, 531–566.

Mehan, H. (1991). Sociological foundations supporting the study of cultural diversity. (Research Report No. 1). Santa Cruz, CA: Center for Research on Educaiton, Diversity & Excellence.

Meier, T. (1998a). Kitchen poets and classroom books: Literature from children's roots. In T. Perry & L. Delpit (Eds.), *The real Ebonics debate: Power, language, and the education of African-American children* (pp. 94–104). Boston: Beacon.

Meier, T. (1998b). Teaching teachers about black communications. In T. Perry & L. Delpit (Eds.), *The real Ebonics debate: Power, language, and the education of African-American children* (pp. 117–125.) Boston: Beacon.

Mellom, P. (2008, June 30). *New portraits of competence: Uses of L1/L2 resources and peer scaffolding in the classroom.* Paper presented at College of Education, University of Georgia, Athens, GA.

Met, M. (1994). Teaching content through a second language. In F. Genesee (Ed.), *Educating second language children* (pp. 159–182). Cambridge, UK: Cambridge University Press.

Middleton, J. (1991). Student-generated analogies in biology. *The American Biology Teacher, 53,* 42–46.

Mike, D., & Rabinowitz, J. (1998). Collaborative projects on the Internet. *Language & Literacy Spectrum, 8,* 48–60.

Miller, C. M. (2005). Student-researched problem-solving strategies. *Mathematics Teacher, 93,* 136–138.

Miller, G., & Gildea, P. (1987). How children learn words. *Scientific American, 257,* 94–99.

Miller, K., & George, J. (1992). Expository Passage Organizers: Models for reading and writing. *Journal of Reading, 35,* 372–377.

Miller, T. (1998). The place of picture books in middle-level classrooms. *Journal of Adolescent & Adult Literacy, 41,* 376–381.

Minami, M., & Ovando, C. J. (1995). Language issues in multicultural contexts. In J. A. Banks & C. A. McGee Banks (Eds.), *Handbook of research on multicultural education* (pp. 427–444). New York: Macmillan.

Moffit, M., & Wartella, E. (1992). Youth and reading: A survey of leisure reading pursuits of female and male adolescents. *Reading Research and Instruction, 31,* 1–17.

Moje, E. (1996). "I teach students, not subjects": Teacher-student relationships as contexts for secondary literacy. *Reading Research Quarterly, 31,* 172–195.

Moje, E. (2007). Developing socially just subject-matter instruction: A review of the literature on disciplinary literacy teaching. *Review of Research in Education, 31,* 1–44.

Moje, E., Brozo, W., & Haas, J. (1994). Portfolios in a high school classroom: Challenges to change. *Reading Research and Instruction, 33,* 275–292.

Moje, E., Collazo, T., Carillo, R., & Marx, R. (2001). "Maestro, what is 'quality'?" Language, literacy, and discourse in project-based science. *Journal of Research in Science Teaching, 38,* 469–496.

Moje, E. B., Willes, D. J., & Fassio, K. (2001). Constructing and negotiating literacy in a seventh-grade writer's workshop. In E. B. Moje & D. G. O'Brien (Eds.), *Constructions of literacy: Studies of teaching and learning in secondary classrooms and schools.* Mahwah, NJ: Erlbaum.

Moll, L. (1991). Literacy research in community and classrooms: A sociocultural approach. In C. Baker & A. Luke (Eds.), *Towards a critical sociology of reading pedagogy* (pp. 211–245). Philadelphia: Benjamins.

Momaday, S. (1996). *The Way to Rainy Mountain.* Albuquerque, NM: University of New Mexico Press.

Moore, D., & Moore, S. (1992). Possible sentences: An update. In E. Dishner, T. Bean, J. Readence, & D. Moore (Eds.), *Reading in content areas: Improving classroom instruction* (3rd ed., pp. 196–201). Dubuque, IA: Kendall/Hunt.

Moore, D. W. (1996). Contexts for literacy in secondary schools. In D. J. Leu, C. K. Kinzer, & K. A. Hinchman (Eds.), *Literacies for the twenty-first century: Research and practice* (pp. 15–46). Chicago: National Reading Conference.

Moore, D. W., Alvermann, D. E., & Hinchman, K. A. (Eds.). (2000). *Struggling adolescent readers: A collection of teaching strategies.* Newark, DE: International Reading Association.

Moore, D. W., Bean, T. W., Birdyshaw, D., & Rycik, J. R. (1999). Adolescent literacy: A position statement. *Journal of Adolescent & Adult Literacy, 43,* 97–112.

Mora, J. K., Wink, J., & Wink, D. (2001). Dueling models of dual language instruction: A critical review of the literature and program implementation guide. *Bilingual Research Journal, 25,* 435–460.

Morgan, W., & Beaumont, G. (2003). A dialogic approach to argumentation: Using a chat room to develop early adolescent students' argumentative writing. *Journal of Adolescent & Adult Literacy, 47*, 146–157.

Morrison, T. (1994). *The bluest eye.* New York: Plume/Penguin.

Moulton, M. (1999). The multigenre paper: Increasing interest, motivation, and functionality in research. *Journal of Adolescent & Adult Literacy, 42*, 528–539.

Mountain, L. (2002). Flip-a-chip to build vocabulary. *Journal of Adolescent & Adult Literacy, 46*, 62–28.

Murray, D. (1984). *Writing to learn.* New York: Holt, Rinehart and Winston.

Nagy, W., & Herman, P. (1987). Breadth and depth of vocabulary knowledge: Implications for acquisition and instruction. In M. McKeown & M. Curtis (Eds.), *The nature of vocabulary acquisition* (pp. 19–35). Hillsdale, NJ: Erlbaum.

Nagy, W., & Scott, J. (2000). Vocabulary processes. In M. Kamil, P. Mosenthal, P. D. Pearson, & R. Barr (Eds.), *Handbook of Reading Research* (Vol. 3, pp. 269–284). Mahwah, NJ: Erlbaum.

Nagy, W., Herman, P., & Anderson, R. C. (1985). Learning words from context. *Reading Research Quarterly, 20*, 233–253.

Naipaul, V. S. (1984). *A house for Mr. Biswas.* New York: Vintage.

National Assessment of Educational Progress (NAEP). (2007). *Nation's report card in reading.* Retrieved October 15, 2008 from http://nationsreportcard.gov/reading_2007/r0001.asp

National Center for Education Statistics (NCES). (2007). *The nation's report card: Writing 2007.* Retrieved July 18, 2008, from http://nationsreportcard.gov

National Commission on Writing. (2008). *Writing, technology and teens.* Retrieved July 18, 2008, from http://www.writingcommission.org

National Council of Teachers of Mathematics. (2000). *Principles and standards for school mathematics.* Reston, VA: National Council of Teachers of Mathematics.

National Endowment for the Arts. (2007). *To read or not to read: A question of national consequence* (Research Report no. 47). Washington, DC: Author.

National Reading Panel. (2000). *Report of the National Reading Panel: Teaching children to read.* (NIH Publication No. 00-4769). Washington, DC: National Institute of Child Health and Human Development.

National Research Council. (1996). *National science education standards.* Washington DC: National Academy Press.

Neal, J., & Moore, K. (1991/1992). *The Very Hungry Caterpillar* meets *Beowulf* in secondary classrooms. *Journal of Reading, 35*, 290–296.

Neilsen, A. (1991). Examining the forces against change Fulfilling the promise of professional development. *Reflections on Canadian Literacy, 9*(2), 66–69.

Neilsen, J. (1990). *Hypertext and hypermedia.* Boston: Academic Press.

Neilsen, L. (1991). Of parachutes, mockingbirds, and bat-poets: A new paradigm for professional growth. *The Reading Teacher, 45*, 64–66.

Neilsen, L. (1998). Playing for real: Performative texts and adolescent identities. In D. Alvermann, K. Hinchman, D. Moore, S. Phelps, & D. Waff (Eds.), *Reconceptualizing the literacies in adolescents' lives* (pp. 3–26). Mahwah, NJ: Erlbaum.

Nelson, B. (1996). *Learning English: How school reform fosters language acquisition and development for limited English proficient elementary school students.* Santa Cruz, CA: National Center for Research on Cultural Diversity and Second Language Learning.

Neufeld, B., & Roper, D. (2003). *Coaching: A strategy for developing instructional capacity.* Washington, DC and Providence, RI: The Aspen Institute Program on Education and the Annenberg Institute for School Reform.

New London Group. (1997). A pedagogy of multiliteracies: Designing social futures. *Harvard Educational Review, 66*, 60–92.

Newmann, F. M. (1988). Can depth replace coverage in the high school curriculum? *Phi Delta Kappan, 69*, 345–348.

Nieto, S. (1994). Lessons from students on creating a chance to dream. *Harvard Educational Review, 64*, 392–426.

Nilsen, A. P., & Nilsen, D. L. F. (2000). Language play in Y2K: Morphology brought to you by Pokémon. *Voices from the Middle, 7*(4), 32–37.

Nippold, M., Duthie, J., & Larsen, J. (2005). Literacy as a leisure activity: Free-time preferences of older children and young adolescents. *Language, Speech, and Hearing Services in Schools, 36*, 93–102.

No Child Left Behind Act of 2001, Pub. L. No. 107-110, 115 Stat. 1452. Retrieved July 8, 2005, from www.ed.gov/policy/elsec/leg/esea02/index.html

Nolan, T. (1991). Self-questioning and prediction: Combining metacognitive strategies. *Journal of Reading, 35,* 132–138.

Nolen, S. B., & Haladyna, T. M. (1989, March). *Psyching out the science teacher: Student motivation, perceived teacher goals and study strategies.* Paper presented at the annual meeting of the American Educational Research Association, San Francisco.

Northern Illinois University's Office of Public Affairs. (2005, August 31). NIU literacy professor works to close reading achievement gap for African American adolescent males. Retrieved September 28, 2005, from www.niu.edu/PubAffairs/RELEASES/2005/aug/tatum.shtml.

Norton, D. (1990). Teaching multicultural literature in the reading curriculum. *The Reading Teacher, 44,* 28–40.

Nystrand, M., Gamoran, A., & Heck, M. J. (1992, April). *Using small groups for response to and thinking about literature.* Paper presented at the annual meeting of the American Educational Research Association, San Francisco.

Oakes, J. (1985). *Keeping track: How schools structure inequality.* New Haven, CT: Yale University Press.

Oakes, J. (1986). Keeping track, Part I: The policy and practice of curricular inequality. *Phi Delta Kappan, 68,* 12–17.

Obidah, J. E. (1998). Black-mystory: Literate currency in everyday schooling. In D. E. Alvermann, K. A. Hinchman, D. W. Moore, S. F. Phelps, & D. R. Waff (Eds.), *Reconceptualizing the literacies in adolescents' lives* (pp. 51–71). Mahwah, NJ: Erlbaum.

O'Brien, D. (1998). Multiple literacies in a high-school program for "at-risk" adolescents. In D. E. Alvermann, K. A. Hinchman, D. W. Moore, S. F. Phelps, & D. R. Waff (Eds.), *Reconceptualizing the literacies in adolescents' lives* (pp. 27–49). Mahwah, NJ: Erlbaum.

O'Brien, D. (2001, June). "At-risk" adolescents: Redefining competence through the multiliteracies of intermediality, visual arts, and representation. *Reading Online, 4.* Retrieved October 18, 2003, from http://readingonline.org/newliteracies/lit_index.asp?HREF=/newliteracies/obrien/index.html

O'Brien, D. G., Stewart, R., & Moje, E. B. (1995). Why content literacy is difficult to infuse into the secondary school: Complexities of curriculum, pedagogy, and school culture. *Reading Research Quarterly, 30,* 442–463.

O'Brien, D. G., Stewart, R., & Moje, E. B. (1995). Why content literacy is difficult to infuse into the secondary school: Complexities of curriculum, pedagogy, and school culture. *Reading Research Quarterly, 30,* 442–463.

O'Dell, S. (1980). *Sarah Bishop.* Boston: Houghton Mifflin.

Offner, S. (1992). Teaching biology around themes: Teach proteins & DNA together. *The American Biology Teacher, 54,* 93–101.

Ogle, D. (1986). K-W-L: A teaching model that develops active reading of expository text. *The Reading Teacher, 39,* 563–570.

Ogle, D. & Blachowicz, C. (2002). Children searching and using informational text: A critical part of comprehension. In C. Block & M. Pressley (Eds.), *Comprehension instruction: Research-based best practice* (pp. 259–274). New York: Guilford.

O'Neil, W. (1998). If Ebonics isn't a language, then tell me, what is? (pace James Baldwin, 1979). In T. Perry & L. Delpit (Eds.), *The real Ebonics debate: Power, language, and the education of African-American children* (pp. 38–47). Boston: Beacon.

Organisation for Economic Cooperation and Development (OECD). (2003). *The PISA 2003 assessment framework—Mathematics, reading, science, and problem solving knowledge and skills.* Paris, France: Author. Retrieved July 30, 2008, from http://www.oecd.org/dataoecd/38/52/33707212.pdf

Orner, M. (1992). Interrupting the calls for student voice in "liberatory" education: A feminist post-structuralist perspective. In C. Luke & J. Gore (Eds.), *Feminisms and critical pedagogy* (pp. 74–89). New York: Routledge. Otto, W. (1990). Getting smart. *Journal of Reading, 33,* 368–370.

Otto, W. (1990). Getting smart. *Journal of Reading, 33,* 368–370.

Ovando, C. J. (2003). Bilingual education in the United States: Historical development and current issues. *Bilingual Research Journal, 27*(1).

Pahl, K., & Rowsell, J. (Eds.). (2005). *Travel notes from the new literacy studies: Instances of practice.* Buffalo, NY: Multilingual Matters.

Palincsar, A. S. (1986). The role of dialogue in providing scaffolded instruction. *Educational Psychologist, 21*, 73–98.

Palincsar, A. S., & Brown, A. L. (1984) Reciprocal teaching of comprehension-fostering and comprehension-monitoring activities. *Cognition and Instruction, 1*, 117–175.

Palmatier, R. A. (1973). A notetaking system for learning. *Journal of Reading, 17*, 36–39.

Palmer, R. G., & Stewart, R. A. (1997). Nonfiction trade books in content area instruction: Realities and potential. *Journal of Adolescent & Adult Literacy, 40*, 630–641.

Palumbo, A., & Sanacore, J. (2007). Classroom management: Help for the beginning secondary school teacher. *Clearing House, 81*(2), 67–70.

Pang, V., Colvin, C., Tran, M., & Barba, R. (1992). Beyond chopsticks and dragons: Selecting Asian-American literature for children. *The Reading Teacher, 46*, 216–224.

Paris, S., Wasik, B., & Turner, J. (1991). The development of strategic readers. In R. Barr, M. Kamil, P. Mosenthal, & P. D. Pearson (Eds.), *Handbook of reading research* (Vol. 2, pp. 609–640). New York: Longman.

Paris, S. G., Lipson, M. Y., & Wixson, K. K. (1983). Becoming a strategic reader. *Contemporary Educational Psychology, 8*, 293–316.

Patterson, A., Mellor, B., & O'Neill, M. (1994). Beyond comprehension: Poststructuralist readings in the English classroom. In B. Corcoran, M. Hayhoe, & G. M. Pradl (Eds.), *Knowledge in the making* (pp. 61–72). Portsmouth, NH: Boynton/Cook.

Patterson, N. (1999, September). Making connections: Hypertext and research in a middle school classroom. *English Journal, 89*, 69–73.

Paulu, N. (1995). *Helping your child with homework.* Washington, DC: U.S. Department of Education, Office of Educational Research and Improvement.

Pearson, P. D. (1998). Standards and assessment: Tools for crafting effective instruction? In J. Osborn and F. Lehr (Eds.), *Literacy for all: Issues in teaching and learning* (pp. 264–288). New York: Guilford.

Pearson, P. D., & Fielding, L. (1991). Comprehension instruction. In R. Barr, M. Kamil, P. Mosenthal, & P. D. Pearson (Eds.), *Handbook of reading research* (Vol. 2, pp. 815–860). New York: Longman.

Pearson, P. D., & Gallagher, M. C. (1983). The instruction of reading comprehension. *Contemporary Educational Psychology, 8*, 317–344.

Pearson, P. D., & Johnson, D. (1978). *Teaching reading comprehension.* New York: Holt, Rinehart & Winston.

Peltz, C., Powers, M., & Wycoff, B. (1994, March). Teaching world economics: An interdisciplinary approach for the middle-level classroom. *Middle School Journal, 25*, 23–25.

Peralta-Nash, C., & Dutch, J. A. (2000). Literature circles: Creating environment for choice. *Primary Voices K-6, 8*(4), 29–37.

Perry, T., & Delpit, L. (Eds.) (1998). *The real Ebonics debate: Power, language, and the education of African-American children.* Boston: Beacon.

Phelps, S. (1984). A first step in content area reading instruction. *Reading World, 23*, 265–269.

Phelps, S. (2007). *Resources for critical literacy teaching about Islam in middle and high school.* Paper presented at the National Reading Conference, Austin, TX.

Phelps, S. F., & Weaver, D. (1999). Public and personal voices in adolescents' classroom talk. *Journal of Literacy Research, 31*, 321–354.

Phelps, T. (1992). Research or three-search? *English Journal, 81*(2), 76–78.

Phillips, D. C. (Ed.). (2000). *Constructivism in education: Opinions and second opinions on controversial issues.* Chicago: University of Chicago Press.

Pierce, L. (1988). *Facilitating transition to the mainstream: Sheltered English vocabulary development* (Program Information Guide Series No. 6). Wheaton, MD: National Clearinghouse for Bilingual Education.

Pilgreen, J. (2000). *The SSR handbook: How to organize and manage a sustained silent reading program.* Portsmouth, NH: Boynton/Cook.

Pitcher, S., Albright, L., DeLaney, C., Walker, N., Seunarinesingh, K., Mogge, S., et al. (2007). Assessing adolescents' motivation to read. *Journal of Adolescent & Adult Literacy, 50*, 378–396.

Pressley, M. (1998). Comprehension strategies instruction. In J. Osborn & F. Lehr (Eds.), *Literacy for all: Issues in teaching and learning* (pp. 113–133). New York: Guilford.

Pressley, M. (2002). Comprehension strategy instruction: A turn-of-the-century status report. In C. Block & M. Pressley (Eds.), *Comprehension instruction: Research-based best practice* (pp. 11–27). New York: Guilford.

Pressley, M., El-Dinary, P. B., & Brown, R. (1992). Skilled and not-so-skilled reading: Good information processing and not-so-good information processing. In M. Pressley, K. R. Harris, & J. T. Guthrie (Eds.), *Promoting academic competence and literacy in school* (pp. 91–127). San Diego: Academic Press.

Pressley, M., Hogan, K., Wharton-MacDonald, R., Mistretta, J., & Ettenberger, S. (1996). The challenges of instructional scaffolding: The challenges of instruction that supports student thinking. *Learning Disabilities Research & Practice, 11*, 138–146.

Pugh, S., & Garcia, J. (1990). Portraits in black: Establishing African American identity through nonfication books. *Journal of Reading, 34*, 20–25.

Quatroche, D. J., Bean, R. M., & Hamilton, R. L. (2001). The role of the reading specialist: A review of research. *The Reading Teacher, 55*, 282–294.

Quellmalz, E. D., & Haertel, G. D. (2008). Assessing new literacies in science and mathematics. In J. Coiro, M. Knobel, C. Lankshear, & D. J. Leu (Eds.), *Handbook of research on new literacies* (pp. 941–972). New York: Erlbaum/Taylor & Francis.

Rakow, S., & Gee, T. (1987, February). Test science, not reading. *The Science Teacher, 54*, 28–31.

Randall, S. N. (2000). Information charts: A strategy for organizing student research. In D. Moore, D. Alvermann, & K. Hinchman (Eds.), *Struggling adolescent readers: A collection of strategies* (pp. 198–205). Newark, DE: International Reading Association.

Raphael, T. (1982). Question-answering strategies for children. *The Reading Teacher, 36*, 186–191.

Raphael, T. (1984). Teaching learners about sources of information for answering comprehension questions. *Journal of Reading, 27*, 303–311.

Raphael, T. (1986). Teaching question-answer relationships, revisited. *The Reading Teacher, 39*, 516–522.

Raphael, T., & Au, K. (2005). QAR: Enhancing comprehension and test taking across grades and content areas. *Reading Teacher, 59*, 206–221.

Raphael, T., & Gavelek, J. (1984). Question-related activities and their relationship to reading comprehension: Some instructional implications. In G. Duffy, L. Roehler, & J. Mason (Eds.), *Comprehension instruction: Perspectives and suggestions* (pp. 234–250). New York: Longman.

Raphael, T., & Pearson, P. D. (1982). *The effect of metacognitive awareness training on children's question answering behavior,* Technical report #238. Urbana, IL: Center for the Study of Reading.

Rasinski, T., Padak, N., McKeon, C., Wilfong, L., Friedauer, J., & Heim, P. (2005). Is reading fluency a key for successful high school reading? *Journal of Adolescent & Adult Literacy, 49*, 22–27.

Ratekin, J., Simpson, M., Alvermann, D., & Dishner, E. (1985). Why teachers resist content reading instruction. *Journal of Reading, 28*, 432–437.

Ratekin, N., Simpson, M. L., Alvermann, D. E., & Dishner, E. K. (1985). Why teachers resist content reading instruction. *Journal of Reading, 28*, 432–437.

Rawls, J., & Weeks, P. (1985). *Land of liberty.* New York: Holt, Rinehart and Winston.

Readence, J. E., Moore, D. W., & Rickelman, R. J. (2000). *Prereading activities for content area reading and learning* (3rd ed.). Newark, DE: International Reading Association.

Reehm, S. P., & Long, S. A. (1996). Reading in the mathematics classroom. *Middle School Journal, 27*(5), 35–41.

Reif, L. (1990). Finding the value in evaluation: Self-assessment in a middle school classroom. *Educational Leadership, 47*, 24–29.

Reimer, K. M. (1992). Multiethnic literature: Holding fast to dreams. *Language Arts, 69*, 14–21.

Rekrut, M. (1997). Collaborative research. *Journal of Adolescent & Adult Literacy, 41*, 26–34.

Rekrut, M. (1999). Using the Internet in classroom instruction: A primer for teachers. *Journal of Adolescent & Adult Literacy, 42*, 546–557.

Rekrut, M. D. (1994). Peer and cross-age tutoring: The lessons of research. *Journal of Reading, 37*, 356–362.

Reppen, R. (1994/1995, Winter). A genre-based approach to content writing instruction. *TESOL Journal, 4*, 32–35.

Resnick, D. P., & Goodman, M. (1994). American culture and the gifted. In P. O. Ross (Ed.), *National excellence: A case for developing America's talent: An anthology of readings* (pp. 109–121). Washington, DC:

U.S. Department of Education, Office of Educational Research and Improvement.

Reyes, M. L., & Molner, L. A. (1991). Instructional strategies for second-language learners in the content areas. *Journal of Reading, 35*, 96–103.

Reynolds, R., Taylor, M., Steffensen, M., Shirey, L., & Anderson, R. (1982). Cultural schemata and reading comprehension. *Reading Research Quarterly, 17*, 353–366.

Rhodes, L. K., & Shanklin, N. L. (1993). *Windows into literacy.* Portsmouth, NH: Heinemann.

Richardson, J. (2000). *Read it aloud! Using literature in the secondary content classroom.* Newark, DE: International Reading Association.

Richardson, J. S., & Morgan, R. F. (2000). *Reading to learn in the content areas* (4th ed.). Belmont, CA: Wadsworth/Thompson Learning.

Richgels, D., McGee, L., Lomax, R., & Sheard, C. (1987). Awareness of four text structures: Effects on recall of expository text. *Reading Research Quarterly, 22*, 177–196.

Ridgeway, V. G. (1997, December). *The use of e-mail to foster pedagogical dialogue within a content area reading discourse community.* Paper presented at the 47th Annual Meeting of the National Reading Conference, Scottsdale, AZ.

Rinaldi, A. (1993). *The fifth of March.* New York: Harcourt Brace.

Rinaldi, A. (1995). *A ride into morning.* New York: Harcourt Brace.

Robinson, F. P. (1961). *Effective study I* (Rev. ed.). New York: Harper & Row.

Rosenblatt, L. (1978). *The reader, the text, the poem: The transactional theory of the literary work.* Carbondale, IL: Southern Illinois University Press.

Rosenblatt, L. (1982). The literary transaction: Evocation and response. *Theory into Practice, 21*, 268–277.

Rosenblatt, L. (1985). Transaction versus interaction–A terminological rescue operation. *Research in the Teaching of English, 19*, 96–107.

Rosenshine, B., & Meister, C. (1992). The use of scaffolds for teaching higher-level cognitive strategies. *Educational Leadership, 49*(7), 26–33.

Rosenshine, B., & Meister, C. (1994). Reciprocal teaching: A review of the research. *Review of Educational Research, 64*, 479–530.

Rosenshine, B., Meister, C., & Chapman, S. (1996). Teaching students to generate questions: A review of the intervention studies. *Review of Educational Research, 66*, 181–221.

Rothenberg, S. S., & Watts, S. M. (2000). Students with learning difficulties meet Shakespeare: Using a scaffolded reading experience. In D. W. Moore, D. E. Alvermann, & K. A. Hinchman (Eds.), *Struggling adolescent readers: A collection of teaching strategies* (pp. 148–156). Newark, DE: International Reading Association.

Rozycki, E. G. (2005). Can we trust "best practices"? *Educational Horizons, 83*, 226–230.

Rubenstein, R. N., & Thompson, D. R. (2001). Learning mathematical symbolism: Challenges and instructional strategies. *Mathematics Teacher, 94*, 265–271.

Rubenstein-Avila, E. (2003). Facing reality: English language learners in middle school classes. *English Education, 35*, 122–136.

Ruddell, M. (1996). Engaging students' interest and willing participation in subject area learning. In D. Lapp, J. Flood, & N. Farnan (Eds.), *Content area reading and learning: Instructional strategies* (2nd ed., pp. 95–110). Boston: Allyn & Bacon.

Ruddell, M., & Shearer, B. (2002). "Extraordinary . . . magnificent": Middle school at-risk students become avid word learners with Vocabulary Self-Collection Strategy. *Journal of Adolescent & Adult Literacy, 45*, 352–363.

Ruddell, M. R. (1997). *Teaching content reading and writing* (2nd ed.). Boston: Allyn & Bacon.

Rudge, D., & Howe, E. (2004, November). Incorporating history into the science classroom. *The Science Teacher, 71*, 52–57.

Russell, M., & Plati, T. (2000). *Mode of administration effects on MCAS composition performance for grades four, eight, and ten.* Retrieved October 8, 2005 from www.bc.edu/research/nbetpp/statements/WE052200.pdf.

Sáenz, L., & Fuchs, L. (2002). Examining the reading difficulty of secondary students with learning disabilities: Expository versus narrative text. *Remedial and Special Education, 23*, 31–41.

Salahu-Din, D., Persky, H., & Miller, J. (2008). *The nation's report card: Writing 2007* (NCES no. 2008-468). Washington, DC: U.S. Department of

Education, Institute of Education Sciences, National Center for Education Statistics.

Samuels, B. (1989). Young adults' choices: Why do students "really like" particular books? *Journal of Reading, 32*, 714–719.

Sanacore, J. (2000). Promoting the lifetime reading habit in middle school students. *The Clearinghouse, 73*, 157–161.

Santa, C., Havens, L., & Harrison, S. (1996). Teaching secondary science through reading, writing, studying, and problem-solving. In D. Lapp, J. Flood, & N. Farnan (Eds.), *Content area reading and learning: Instructional strategies* (2nd ed., pp. 165–180). Boston: Allyn & Bacon.

Santa, C. M. (1988). *Content reading including study systems.* Dubuque, IA: Kendall/Hunt.

Sarroub, L., Pearson, P. D., Dykema, C., & Lloyd, R. (1997). When portfolios become part of the grading process: A case study in a junior high setting. In C. Kinzer, K. Hinchman, & D. Leu (Eds.), *Inquiries in literacy theory and practice* (pp. 101–113). Chicago: National Reading Conference.

Saunders, W. M., & Goldenberg, C. (1999). *The effects of instructional conversations and literature logs on the story comprehension and thematic understanding of English proficient and limited English proficient students.* Santa Cruz, CA: Center for Research on Education, Diversity and Excellence.

Scanlon, D., Deshler, D. D., & Schumaker, J. B. (1996). Can a strategy be taught and learned in secondary inclusive classrooms? *Learning Disabilities Research & Practice, 11*, 41–57.

Schatz, E., & Baldwin, S. (1986). Context clues are unreliable predictors of word meanings. *Reading Research Quarterly, 21*, 439–453.

Schell, L. (1988). Dilemmas in assessing reading comprehension. *The Reading Teacher, 42*, 12–16.

Schimberg, A., & Grant, H. (1998, Fall). Who-dun-it? A mystery thematic unit. *Science Activities, 35*, 29–35.

Schmidt, H. G. (1993). Foundations of problem-based learning: Some explanatory notes. *Medical Education 27*, 422–432.

Schoenbach, R., Braunger, J., Greenleaf, C., & Litman, C. (2003, October). Apprenticing adolescents to reading in subject-area classrooms. *Phi Delta Kappan, 85*, 133–138.

Schoenbach, R., Greenleaf, C., Cziko, C., & Hurwitz, L. (1999). *Reading for understanding: A guide to improving reading in middle and high school classrooms.* San Francisco: Jossey-Bass.

Schraer, W., & Stoltze, H. (1993). *Biology: The study of life* (5th ed.). Englewood Cliffs, NJ: Prentice Hall.

Schrock, K. (2002). *The ABCs of web site evaluation.* Retrieved July 30, 2008, from http://school.discoveryeducation.com/schrockguide.eval.html

Schultz, K., & Fecho, B. (2000). Society's child: Social context and writing development. *Educational Psychologist, 35*, 51–62.

Schwartz, R. (1988). Learning to learn vocabulary in content area textbooks. *Journal of Reading, 32*, 108–118.

Schwartz, R., & Raphael, T. (1985). Concept of definition: A key to improving students' vocabulary. *The Reading Teacher, 39*, 198–205.

Schwarz, G. (2004, October). Graphic novels: Multiple cultures and multiple literacies. *Thinking Classroom, 5*, 17–24.

Schwarz, G. E. (2002). Graphic novels for multiple literacies. *Journal of Adolescent & Adult Literacy, 46*, 262–265.

Scott, J. C. (1990). *Domination and the arts of resistance.* New Haven, CT: Yale University Press.

Scott, T. (2005). Consensus through accountability? The benefits and drawbacks of building community with accountability. *Journal of Adolescent & Adult Literacy, 49*, 48–59.

Sefton-Green, J. (1999). Young people, creativity and new technologies: The challenge of digital arts. London: Routledge and the Arts Council of England.

Sefton-Green, J. (2003). Informal learning: Substance or style? *Teaching Education, 12*, 37–52.

Sewall, G. (1988). American history textbooks: Where do we go from here? *Phi Delta Kappan, 69*, 553–558.

Shaara, M. (1974). *The killer angels.* New York: Ballantine.

Shanahan, T. (1995). Avoiding some of the pitfalls of thematic units. *The Reading Teacher, 48*, 718–719.

Shanahan, T., & Shanahan, C. (2008). Teaching disciplinary literacy to adolescents: Rethinking content-area literacy. *Harvard Educational Review, 78*, 40–59.

Shealy, A. (2000, Spring/Summer). On becoming a teacher and writer. *Bread Loaf Rural Teacher Network Magazine*, 10–11.

Sheehan, A. D., & Sheehan, C. M. (2000). Lost in a sea of ink: How I survived the storm. *Journal of Adolescent & Adult Literacy, 44*, 20–32.

Shefelbine, J. (1990). Student factors related to variability in learning word meanings from context. *Journal of Reading Behavior, 22,* 71–97.

Short, D. J., & Fitzsimmons, S. (2007). *Double the work: Challenges and solutions to acquiring language and academic literacy for adolescent English language learners.* Washington, DC: Alliance for Excellent Education. Retrieved July 18, 2008, from http://www.all4ed.org/files/DoubleWork.pdf

Simmons, J. (1990, March). Adapting portfolios for large-scale use. *Educational Leadership, 47,* 28.

Sinatra, G., Brown, K. & Reynolds, R. (2002). Implications of cognitive resource allocation for comprehension strategies instruction. In C. Block & M. Pressley (Eds.), *Comprehension instruction: Research-based best practice* (pp. 62–76). New York: Guilford.

Singer, H., & Donlan, D. (1982). Active comprehension: Problem-solving schema with question generation for comprehension of complex short stories. *Reading Research Quarterly, 17,* 166–186.

Singer, H., & Donlan, D. (1989). *Reading and learning from text.* Hillsdale, NJ: Erlbaum. Skilton-Sylvester, E. (2002). Literate at home but not at school. In G. Hull & K. Schultz (Eds.), *School's out! Bridging out-of-school literacies with classroom practice* (pp. 61–90). New York: Teachers College Press.

Skilton-Sylvester, E. (2002). Literate at home but not at school. In G. Hull & K. Schultz (Eds.), *School's out! Bridging out-of-school literacies with classroom practice* (pp. 61–90). New York: Teachers College Press.

Slavin, R. E. (1984a). Students motivating students to excel: Cooperative incentives, cooperative tasks, and student achievement. *Elementary School Journal, 85,* 53–63.

Slavin, R. E. (1984b). Team assisted individuation: Cooperative learning and individualized instruction in the mainstreamed classroom. *Remedial and Special Education, 5*(6), 33–42.

Smith, C., & Bean, T. (1980). The guided writing procedure: Integrating content reading and writing improvement. *Reading World, 19,* 290–298.

Smith, F. R., & Feathers, K. M. (1983a). Teacher and student perceptions of content area reading. *Journal of Reading, 26,* 348–354.

Smith, F. R., & Feathers, K. M. (1983b). The role of reading in content classrooms: Assumption vs. reality. *Journal of Reading, 27,* 262–267.

Smith, M., & Wilhelm, J. (2002). *Reading don't fix no Chevys: Literacy in the lives of young men.* Portsmouth, NH: Heinemann.

Smolen, L., Newman, C., Wathen, T., & Lee, D. (1995). Developing student self-assessment strategies. *TESOL Journal, 5,* 22–27.

Spears-Bunton, L. (1990). Welcome to my house: African American and European American students' responses to Virginia Hamilton's *House of Dies Drear. Journal of Negro Education, 59,* 566–576.

Spears-Bunton, L. (1991, December). *Literature, literacy and resistance to cultural domination.* Paper presented at the meeting of the National Reading Conference, Palm Springs, CA.

Spears-Bunton, L. (1998). All the colors of the land: A literacy montage. In A. Willis (Ed.), *Teaching and using multicultural literature in grades 9–12: Moving beyond the canon* (pp. 17–36). Norwood, MA: Christopher Gordon.

Spiegelman, A. (1986) *Maus.* New York: Pantheon Books.

Spires, H. A., & Stone, P. D. (1989). The directed note-taking activity: A self-questioning approach. *Journal of Reading, 33,* 36–39.

Sprague, M., & Cotturone, J. (2003, March). Motivating students to read physics content. *The Science Teacher, 70,* 24–29.

Stahl, S., & Clark, C. (1987). The effects of participatory expectations in classroom discussion on the learning of science vocabulary. *American Educational Research Journal, 24,* 541–556.

Stahl, S., & Kapinus, B. (1991). Possible sentences: Predicting word meanings to teach content area vocabulary. *The Reading Teacher, 45,* 36–43.

Stahl, S. A. (1983). Differential word knowledge and reading comprehension: *Journal of Reading Behavior, 15*(4), 33–50.

Stahl, S. A., & Fairbanks, M. M. (1986). The effects of vocabulary instruction: A model-based meta-analysis. *Review of Educational Research, 56,* 72–110.

Stallworth, B. J., Gibbons, L., & Fauber, L. (2006). It's not on the list: An exploration of teachers' perspectives on using multicultural literature. *Journal of Adolescent & Adult Literacy, 49,* 478–489.

Stanovich, K. E. (1980). Toward an interactive-compensatory model of individual differences in the development of reading fluency. *Reading Research Quarterly, 16,* 32–71.

Staples, S. F. (1989). *Shabanu: Daughter of the wind.* New York: Random House.

Stauffer, R. (1969). *Directing reading maturity as a cognitive process.* New York: Harper & Row.

Stauffer, R. (1976). *Teaching reading as a thinking process.* New York: Harper & Row.

Steffensen, M., Joag-Dev, C., & Anderson, R. (1979). A cross-cultural perspective on reading comprehension. *Reading Research Quarterly, 15,* 10–29.

Stein, N., & Glenn, C. (1979). An analysis of story comprehension in elementary school children. In R. O. Freedle (Ed.), *New directions in discourse processing.* Norwood, NJ: Ablex.

Steinbeck, J. (1989). *The pearl.* In R. Anderson, J. Brinnin, J. Leggett, & D. Leeming (Eds.), *Elements of literature* (pp. 674–712). Austin, TX: Holt, Rinehart & Winston.

Sternberg, R. J. (1987). Teaching critical thinking: Eight easy ways to fail before you begin. *Phi Delta Kappan, 68,* 456–459.

Sternberg, R. J., & Grigorenko, E. L. (2000). *Teaching for successful intelligence.* Arlington Heights, IL: Skylight.

Sternberg, R. J., Grigorenko, E. L., Jarvin, L., Clinkenbeard, P., Ferrari, M., & Torff, B. (2000, Spring). The effectiveness of triarchic teaching and assessment. *The National Center on the Gifted and Talented Newsletter,* pp. 3–8.

Stewart, R. A., & O'Brien, D. G. (1989). Resistance to content area reading: A focus on preservice teachers. *Journal of Reading, 32,* 396–401.

Stiggins, R., Frisbie, D., & Griswold, P. (1989). Inside high school grading practices: Building a research agenda. *Journal of Educational Measurement, 8,* 5–14.

Stiggins, R. J. (2002). Assessment crisis: The absence of assessment *FOR* learning. *Phi Delta Kappan, 83,* 758–765. Retrieved June 17, 2008, from www.pdkintl.org/kappan/k0206sti.htm

Stodolsky, S. S. (1988). *The subject matters.* Chicago: University of Chicago Press.

Strategic Literacy Initiative. (2004a). *Increasing student achievement through schoolwide reading apprenticeship, 2001–2004.* Retrieved September 22, 2005, from www.wested.org/cs/sli/print/docs/sli/widereading.htm

Strategic Literacy Initiative. (2004b). *Reading apprenticeship classroom study: Linking professional develop-ment for teachers to outcomes for students in diverse subject-area classrooms, 2001–2004.* Retrieved September 22, 2005, from www.wested.org/cs/sli/print/docs/sli/classroomstudy.htm

Strategic Literacy Initiative. (2004c). *Studies of student reading growth in diverse professional development networks, 1999–2002.* Retrieved September 22, 2005, from www.wested.org/cs/sli/print/docs/sli/readinggrowth.htm

Street, B. (2003). What's "new" in New Literacy Studies? Critical approaches to literacy in theory and practice. *Current Issues in Comparative Education, 5,* 1–14. Available online at www.tc.columbia.edu/cice/articles/bs152.pdf

Street, B. V. (1995). *Social literacies: Critical approaches to literacy in development, ethnography, and education.* New York: Longman.

Strother, D. B. (1985). Adapting instruction to individual needs: An eclectic approach. *Phi Delta Kappan, 67,* 308–311.

Sturtevant, E. G. (1996). Lifetime influences on the literacy-related instructional beliefs of experienced high school history teachers: Two comparative case studies. *Journal of Literacy Research, 28,* 227–257.

Survey finds students, teachers show bias. (2000, May). *The Council Chronicle,* p. 13.

Sutherland, L. (2005). Black adolescent girls' use of literacy practices to negotiate boundaries of ascribed identity. *Journal of Literacy Research, 3,* 365–406.

Sutherland-Smith, W. (2002). Weaving the literacy Web: Changes in reading from page to screen. *The Reading Teacher, 55,* 662–669.

Swafford, J. (1988, December). *The use of study strategy instruction with secondary school students: Is there a research base?* Paper presented at the annual meeting of the National Reading Conference, Tucson, AZ.

Swan, K. (2000). Nonprint media and technology literacy standards for assessing technology integration. *Journal of Educational Computing Research, 23*(1), 85–100.

Swanson, P., & de la Paz, S. (1998). Teaching effective comprehension strategies to students with learning and reading disabilities. *Intervention in School and Clinic, 33,* 209–218.

Taba, H. (1967). *Teacher's handbook for elementary social studies.* Reading, MA: Addison-Wesley.

Tatum, A. W. (2000). Breaking down barriers that disenfranchise African American adolescent readers in low-level tracks. *Journal of Adolescent & Adult Literacy, 44*, 52–64.

Tatum, A. W. (2005). *Teaching reading to black adolescent males: Closing the achievement gap.* Portland, ME: Stenhouse.

Taylor, B., & Beach, R. (1984). The effects of text structure instruction on middle-grade students' comprehension and production of expository text. *Reading Research Quarterly, 19*, 134–146.

Taylor, D., & Dorsey-Gaines, C. (1988). *Growing up literate: Learning from inner-city families.* Portsmouth, NH: Heinemann.

Taylor, M. (1976). *Roll of thunder, hear my cry.* New York: Dial.

Taylor, T. (1984). *The hostage.* New York: Bantam.

Taylor, W. (1953). Cloze procedure: A new tool for measuring readability. *Journalism Quarterly, 30*, 415–433.

Teemant, A., Pinnegar, S., Tharp, R., & Harris, C. (2001). The Mara Mills case: A video ethnography of biological science in a sheltered English class room. Center for Research on Education, Diversity & Excellence. Available online at www.crede.ucsc.edu/products/multimedia/cdroms.html.

Temple, C. (2005). Critical thinking and critical literacy. *Thinking Classroom: A Journal of the International Reading Association, 6*(2), 15–20.

Temple, F. (1993). *Grab hands and run.* New York: Orchard.

Tharp, R., & Gallimore, R. (1988). *Rousing minds to life: Teaching, learning, and schooling in social context.* Cambridge, UK: Cambridge University Press.

Tharp, R., Dalton, S. S., & Yamauchi, L. (1994). Principles for culturally compatible Native American education. *Journal of Navajo Education, 11*(3), 33–39.

Thomas, J. W., & Rohwer, W. D. (1986). Academic studying: The role of learning strategies. *Educational Psychologist, 21*, 19–41.

Thomas, W. (1986, February). Grading—Why are school policies necessary? What are the issues? *NASSP Bulletin, 70*, 22–26.

Thomas, W., & Collier, V. (2002). *A national study of school effectiveness for language minority students' long-term academic achievement.* Santa Cruz, CA and Washington, DC: Center for Research on Education, Diversity and Excellence.

Tierney, R., Clark, C., Fenner, L., Herter, R., Simpson, C., & Wiser, B. (1998). Portfolios: Assumptions, tensions and possibilities. *Reading Research Quarterly, 33*, 474–486.

Tierney, R., Readence, J., & Dishner, E. (2000). *Reading strategies and practices: A compendium* (5th ed.). Boston: Allyn & Bacon.

Tierney, R., Soter, A., O'Flahavan, J., & McGinley, W. (1989). The effects of reading and writing upon thinking critically. *Reading Research Quarterly, 24*, 134–173.

Toll, C. (2005). *The literacy coach's survival guide: Essential questions and practical answers.* Newark, DE: International Reading Association.

Tovani, C. (2000). *I read it, but I don't get it: Comprehension strategies for adolescent readers.* Portland, ME: Stenhouse.

Trelease, J. (2006). *The new read-aloud handbook.* (6th ed.). New York: Penguin.

Trujillo, L. (2000, March 12). Latino or Hispanic? *The Arizona Republic*, pp. A1, A22.

Twain, M. (1961). *Life on the Mississippi.* New York: New American Library.

U.S. Department of Education (1998). *Pocket projections: Projections of education statistics to 2008* (NCES Report No. 98-017). Washington, DC: National Center for Education Statistics.

Unsworth, L. (1999). Developing critical understanding of the specialized language of school science and history texts: A functional grammatical perspective. *Journal of Adolescent & Adult Literacy, 42*, 508–521.

Valdez, P. (2001, November). Alternative assessment. *Science Teacher, 68*, 41–43.

Valencia, S., & Wixson, K. (2000). Policy-oriented research on literacy standards and assessment. In M. Kamil, P. Mosenthal, P. D. Pearson, & R. Barr (Eds.), *Handbook of reading research* (Vol. 3, pp. 909–935). Mahwah, NJ: Erlbaum.

Van Slyck, M., & Stern, M. (1999). A developmental approach to the use of conflict resolution interventions with adolescents. In L. R. Forcey & I. M. Harris (Eds.), *Peacebuilding for adolescents: Strategies for educators and community leaders* (pp. 177–193). New York: Lang.

Van Voorhis, F. L. (2003). Interactive homework in middle school: Effects on family involvement and science achievement. *Journal of Educational Research, 96*, 323–340.

Vande Steeg, M. (1991). A new challenge for teachers. *The American Biology Teacher, 53*, 20–21.

Vaughn, J. L., & Estes, T. H. (1986). *Reading and reasoning beyond the primary grades.* Boston: Allyn & Bacon.

Vaughn, T. H., & Vaughn, J. L. Jr. (1985). *Reading and learning in the content classroom: Diagnostic and instructional strategies.* Boston: Allyn & Bacon.

Vogt, M., & Shearer, B. A. (2003). *Reading specialists in the real world: A sociocultural view.* Boston: Pearson Education.

Vygotsky, L. (1986). *Thought and language.* Cambridge, MA: MIT Press.

Vygotsky, L. S. (1978). *Mind in society: The development of higher psychological processes.* Cambridge, MA: Harvard University Press.

Wade, S. E., & Moje, E. B. (2000). The role of text in classroom learning. In M. L. Kamil, P. B. Mosenthal, P. D. Pearson, & R. Barr (Eds.), *Handbook of reading research* (Vol. 3, pp. 609–627). Mahwah, NJ: Erlbaum.

Wade, S. E., & Reynolds, R. E. (1989). Developing metacognitive awareness. *Journal of Reading, 33,* 6–14.

Walker, B. (2007). *Diagnostic teaching of reading: Techniques for instruction and assessment* (6th ed.). New York: Prentice-Hall.

Wandersee, J. H. (1987). Drawing concept circles: A new way to teach and test students. *Science Activities, 24*(4), 9–20.

Warger, C. L., & Rutherford, R. B., Jr. (1997). Teaching respect and responsibility in inclusive classrooms: An instructional approach. *Reclaiming Children and Youth, 6*(3), 171–175.

Warschauer, M., Grant, D., Del Real, G., & Rousseau, M. (2004). Promoting academic literacy with technology: Successful laptop programs in K–12 schools. *System, 32,* 525–537.

Watson, B., & Konicek, R. (1990). Teaching for conceptual change: Confronting children's experience. *Phi Delta Kappan, 71,* 680–685.

Weber, A. (2000). Playful writing for critical thinking: Four approaches to writing. *Journal of Adolescent & Adult Literacy, 43,* 562–568.

Webster's New World Dictionary of American English (Third College Edition). (1991). New York: Prentice Hall.

Weiner, B. (1986). *An attributional theory of motivation and emotion.* New York: Springer-Verlag.

Welner, K. G., & Oakes, J. (1996). (Li)ability grouping: The new susceptibility of school tracking systems to legal challenges. *Harvard Educational Review, 66,* 451–470.

Wenger, E. (1998). *Communities of practice: Learning, meaning, and identity.* Cambridge, UK: Cambridge University Press.

Wertsch, J. V. (1985). *Vygotsky and the social formation of mind.* Cambridge, MA: Harvard University Press.

Wertsch, J. V. (1991). *Voices of the mind.* Cambridge, MA: Harvard University Press.

Westera, J., & Moore, D. W. (1995). Reciprocal teaching of reading comprehension in a New Zealand high school. *Psychology in the Schools, 32,* 225–232.

White, R. M. (1995). How thematic teaching can transform history instruction. *The Clearinghouse, 68,* 160–162.

White, T., Graves, M., & Slater, W. (1990). Growth of reading vocabulary in diverse elementary schools: Decoding and word meaning. *Journal of Educational Psychology, 82,* 281–289.

Wigfield, A., Wilde, K., Baker, L., Fernandez-Fein, S., & Scher, D. (1996). *The nature of children's motivations for reading, and their relations to reading frequency and reading performance.* (Research Report No. 63). Athens: University of Georgia, National Reading Research Center.

Wiggins, G. (1993, Fall). Assessment to improve performance, not just monitor it: Assessment reform in the social sciences. *Social Science Record, 30,* 5–12.

Wiggins, G. (1998). *Educative assessment: Designing assessments to inform and improve student performance.* San Francisco: Jossey-Bass.

Wiggins, G., & McTighe, J. (1998). *Understanding by design.* Alexandria, VA: Association for Supervision and Curriculum Development.

Wigginton, E. (1985). *Sometimes a shining moment: The Foxfire experience.* New York: Doubleday.

Wilber, D. J. (2008). iLife: Understanding and connecting to the digital literacies of adolescents. In K. A. Hinchman & H. K. Sheridan (Eds.), *Best practices in adolescent literacy instruction* (pp. 57–77). New York: Guilford.

Williams, N. B., & Wynne, B. D. (2000). Journal writing in the mathematics classroom: A beginner's approach. *Mathematics Teacher, 93,* 132–135.

Willinsky, J. (1990). *The new literacy: Redefining reading and writing in the schools.* New York: Routledge.

Willis, A. (Ed.). (1998). *Teaching and using multicultural literature in grades 9–12: Moving beyond the canon.* Norwood, MA: Christopher Gordon.

Willis, A., & Palmer, M. (1998). Negotiating the classroom: Learning and teaching multicultural literature. In A. Willis (Ed.), *Teaching and using multicultural literature in grades 9–12: Moving beyond the canon* (pp. 215–250). Norwood, MA: Christopher Gordon.

Willis, S. (1993). Are letter grades obsolete? *ASCD Update, 35*, 1, 4, 8.

Wineburg, S. (1991). On the reading of historical texts: Notes on the breach between school and academy. *American Educational Research Journal, 28*, 495–519.

Winograd, P. N. (1984). Strategic difficulties in summarizing texts. *Reading Research Quarterly, 19*, 404–425.

Wolf, D., King, J. (Producers), & Van Sant, G. (Director). (2000). *Finding Forrester* [Motion picture]. United States: Columbia Pictures.

Wolf, K., & Siu-Runyan, Y. (1996). Portfolio purposes and possibilities. *Journal of Adolescent & Adult Literacy, 40*, 30–37.

Wolf, S., Edmiston, B., & Encisco, P. (1997). Drama worlds. In J. Flood, D. Lapp, & S. B. Heath (Eds.), *Handbook of research on teaching literacy through the communicative and visual arts* (pp. 492–505). New York: Macmillan.

Wolfe, R. R. (2000). Protein supplements and exercise. *The American Journal of Clinical Nutrition, 72*, 551–557.

Wong, B. (1997). Research on genre-specific strategies for enhancing writing in adolescents with learning disabilities. *Learning Disability Quarterly, 20*, 140–159.

Wong, B., Butler, D., Ficzere, S., & Kuperis, S. (1997). Teaching adolescents with learning disabilities and low achievers to plan, write, and revise compare-and-contrast essays. *Learning Disabilities Research & Practice, 12*, 2–15.

Wood, D., Bruner, J. S., & Ross, G. (1976). The role of tutoring in problem solving. *Journal of Child Psychology and Psychiatry, 17*, 89–100.

Wood, K. (1986). The effect of interspersing questions in text: Evidence for "slicing the task." *Reading Research & Instruction, 25*, 295–307.

Wood, K. (1988). Guiding students through informational text. *The Reading Teacher, 41*, 912–920.

Woods 100 helps to restore self-respect. (1978, December 30). *The Australian* (No. 4497).

Woodward, A., & Elliott, D. L. (1990). Textbook use and teacher professionalism. In D. L. Elliott & A. Woodward (Eds.), *Textbooks and schooling in the United States* (Eighty-ninth Yearbook of the National Society for the Study of Education, Part I, pp. 179–193). Chicago: University of Chicago Press.

Worthy, J., Moorman, M., & Turner, M. (1999). What Johnny likes to read is hard to find in school. *Reading Research Quarterly, 34*, 12–27.

Wu, S., & Rubin, D. (2000). Evaluating the impact of collectivism and individualism on argumentative writing by Chinese and North American college students. *Research in the Teaching of English, 35*, 148–178.

Wysocki, K., & Jenkins, J. (1987). Deriving word meanings through morphological generalization. *Reading Research Quarterly, 22*, 66–81.

Yatvin, J. (2002). Babes in the woods: The wanderings of the National Reading Panel. In R. Allington, (Ed.), *Big Brother and the national reading curriculum: How ideology trumped evidence* (pp. 125–136). Portsmouth, NH: Heinemann.

Young, A. J., Arbreton, A. J., & Midgley, C. (1992, April). *All content areas may not be created equal: Motivational orientation and cognitive strategy use in four academic domains.* Paper presented at the annual meeting of the American Educational Research Association, San Francisco.

Young, J. P. (2000). Critical literacy: Young adolescent boys talk about masculinities within a home-school context. *Reading Research Quarterly, 35*, 312–337.

Young, J. P., Mathews, S. R., Kietzmann, A. M., & Westerfield, T. (2000). Getting disenchanted adolescents to participate in school literacy activities: Portfolio conferences. In D. W. Moore, D. E. Alvermann, & K. A. Hinchman (Eds.), *Struggling adolescent readers: A collection of teaching strategies* (pp. 302–316). Newark, DE: International Reading Association.

Zimmerman, B. J. (1994). Dimensions of academic self-regulation: A conceptual framework for education. In D. H. Schunk & B. J. Zimmerman (Eds.), *Self-regulation of learning and performance* (pp. 3–21). Hillsdale, NJ: Erlbaum.

Zinsser, W. (1988). *Writing to Learn.* New York: Harper & Row.

name index

subject index